# NowHere

# NowHere
# Space, Time and
# Modernity

■ ■ ■

EDITED BY
## Roger Friedland and Deirdre Boden

FOREWORD BY
## Anthony Giddens

UNIVERSITY OF CALIFORNIA PRESS
*Berkeley   Los Angeles   London*

University of California Press
Berkeley and Los Angeles, California
University of California Press, Ltd.
London, England
© 1994 by
The Regents of the University of California


**Library of Congress Cataloging-in-Publication Data**
NowHere : space, time and modernity / edited by Roger Friedland and
Deirdre Boden.
    p.    cm.
    Includes bibliographical references and index.
    ISBN 0-520-08017-3 (alk. paper).—ISBN 0-520-08018-1 (pbk. :
alk. paper)
    1. Civilization, Modern—20th century.  2. Space and time—Social
aspects.  I. Friedland, Roger.  II. Boden, Deirdre.  III. Title:
Now here.
CB430.N68   1994
909.82—dc20                                  93-1444
                                          CIP
Printed in the United States of America
9 8 7 6 5 4 3 2 1
The paper used in this publication meets the minimum requirements
of American National Standard for Information Sciences—Permanence of Paper for Printed Library Materials, ANSI Z39.48-1984. ⊚

*For Harry Friedland and Michael Kevin Boden, whom we miss so very much, and for Hannah Rose Friedland and Sarah Margaret Friedland, whose explorations of space, time, and modernity will take us into the next millennium.*

*We shall not cease from exploration*
*And the end of our exploring*
*Will be to arrive where we started*
*And to know the place for the first time.*
T. S. ELIOT, *Little Gidding*

# CONTENTS

# FOREWORD

Space, time and modernity—words which encompass the modern era and its transformations. Modernity, one could argue, *is* precisely the transmutation of time and space—or, at least, such a transmutation is at the core of the institutional dynamism which has torn apart traditional orders and lodged all of us aboard a careering juggernaut whose track and destination we only partially control.

Of course, reorderings of time and space provide key clues to human history well before the advent of modern institutions. Indeed, "history" in a basic sense did not exist before the arrival of literate civilizations. The invention of writing was much more than a means of giving permanence to speech; in its origins, in fact, writing had nothing particularly to do with speech. It was first of all a means of coding information—and a way of reconstructing time and space. Because writing "records," it permits a reappropriation of past time and a novel "cutting into" the future; and it allows for the control of space, making possible the coordination of objects, events, and human actions well beyond what could be achieved in oral cultures. "History" begins when space as well as time are subjected to novel modes of social control.

Time and space thus became organizationally conjoined in traditional civilizations, but this process did not reach deeply into the lives of the majority of the population. A "cosmopolitan" order was produced, located largely in the cities and dominated by religious cosmologies. Yet the lives of those in the local, rural communities—which after all formed 90 percent or more of the members of such societies—remained relatively untouched by these phenomena. Moreover, conceptions of time and space, by virtue of their cosmological connections, remained saturated with moral, aesthetic, and sacred symbols.

Only with the coming of modernity, and as an absolutely integral element of that development, did time and space become both universalized and integrated with the day-to-day activities of everyone. As I would express this phenomenon, space and time became "empty" categories, specifically separated from one another as distinct dimensions of existence. The emptying of time and space was signaled philosophically by the Kantian categories; but much more important, it became an organizing medium of modernity's institutional dynamism.

So far as social life goes, the universal global map and the intervals on the face of the mechanical clock are the most cogent expressions of the emptying of time and space. Yet they are just this: "expressions" of much deeper transitions. "Empty space" only comes into existence on an institutional level once the world has been thoroughly "explored" and universal degrees of latitude and longitude established. The mechanical clock is a largely irrelevant device before the establishing of agreed-upon time zones—which themselves eventually become global with the construction of "world standard time." Once time and space have become emptied and disentangled, they can be systematically reappropriated: most significantly, in the shape of disembedded social relations of indefinite time-space extension. "Who says modernity says organization," it has been remarked; but the decontextualized organizations of modernity are possible only once the abstract and empty dimensions of space-time have become thoroughly incorporated into the constitution of everyday life.

The globalizing tendencies of modernity, so apparent in the present day, should be understood in these terms. Modernity globalizes insofar as space is separated from place and reintegrated with the empty dimension of time. Globalization represents the formation of social ties of indefinite space-time spans, whose transforming properties are evident on an intensional as well as extensional basis. In other words, one of the most distinctive features of the contemporary period is the burgeoning of complex ties between the global and the local, where "the local" includes not just the regional locality but intimate aspects of our personal lives.

The global and local are today linked in dialectical fashion. Although what happens at one "pole" directly influences the other, the connections involved are frequently oppositional. Thus, a process of global economic development which generates prosperity in one region of the world may bring impoverishment to another. On a more subtle level, our personal experiences and needs may exist in contradictory relation to the global impact of our actions. For instance, the pursuit of a particular type of life-style, designed to provide material and psychic security for the individual, might actually accentuate global risks, thus producing increasing uncertainty on a collective plane.

Analyzing the conjunctions of time, space, and modernity requires conceptual as well as substantive reorientation in social thought and research. As the preceding remarks indicate, such a rethinking cannot be limited to the interpretation of time and space alone; it has to be directly related to the conceptualizing of modernity as such. Modern institutions are opening up terrains of social existence which have never been trodden before. No one in previous civilizations lived "in the world"—a world simultaneously both fragmenting and unifying—in the way in which we do now. We have global markers—such as "the year 2000"—which shape our collective identity in a more integrated way than ever before; yet modernity consistently "falls apart" as a disjointed series of contextual and material divisions.

It is hardly surprising that, in the social sciences, we are as yet groping toward a satisfactory means of conceptually encompassing this new universe of social activity. To achieve this aim, we will need a rich diversity of resources, to which this book makes a brilliant and fundamental contribution. The issues portrayed above connect scholars in many different fields and point to new forms of debate and dialogue. The reader who turns the pages of this book will find a compelling series of contributions to this emerging framework of discussion.

*Anthony Giddens*

# ONE

# NowHere:
# An Introduction to Space, Time and Modernity

*Roger Friedland and Deirdre Boden*

There is a way in which ideas take on a life all their own not only because they are separate from their authors but also because they move freely in space and time. Separated by enormous intellectual and physical distances, scholars suddenly develop shared fields of vision. This book reflects that simultaneity and essential community of thought. Across the rapidly changing landscape of modernity, social thinkers are reconsidering the fundamental relationship between ground and moment; they are rethinking the delicate and dynamic balance between space and time. In the last decade, throughout the humanities and social sciences, there has been a theoretical return to these two elemental constituents of social life. Space and time have thus become a medium through which to rethink the organization and meaning of modernity.

The authors represented in *NowHere* have returned to the seen but unnoticed existential center of social life in radically different ways. The anthropologists and art historians, religionists and geographers, sociologists and historians whose work is collected here present a vivid range of ways in which human societies organize and are organized by space and time. In the pages that follow, we explore the considerable intellectual and practical problem posed by the changing conditions and challenging consequences of space, time, and modernity. In our discussion we will propose that *thinking* with space and time results both in deeper theoretical insight in and broader practical application of the contemporary critique of modernity. At the same time, we hope to draw the reader into what we take to be one of the most exciting new zones of interdisciplinary writing and research whose genuine engagement and exploration is likely to reshape the ways in which we understand social life.

Each of the chapters that follow examines quite detailed aspects of these topics, usually with particular emphasis on either space or time. This introduction seeks to provide an analytic map of the frontiers of our topic, so that the reader will be able to readily locate the work of our authors within this challenging and highly plastic discourse.

Modernity will be the constant backdrop of our discussion. Although it is tempting to say that people in all periods regard theirs as "modern,"[1] we share the view that the transformations of the past two hundred years have etched out this era as a distinct and discontinuous period of human history.[2] Rather than entering directly into the lively debate over modernity and postmodernity,[3] we treat modernity simply as the intertwined emergence of capitalism, the bureaucratic nation-states, and industrialism, which, initiating in the West but now operating on a global scale, has also entailed extraordinary transformations of space and time.[4] It will be our goal to sketch some of the consequences of those transformations. In our discussion we will consider a number of "large" institutional themes such as nationalism, progress, and emancipation and argue that their practical realization entails reflexive "human-size" actions and reactions.[5]

Modernity changed the representation of space and time and hence the way we experience and understand them.[6] Specifically, it entailed a rise and fall of fixed-point perspective in the visual arts and the linear narrative in fiction. In the early Renaissance, painting began to develop linear perspective,[7] coinciding with a rediscovery of Euclidean geometry, the camera obscura, and the emergence of new techniques of spatial representation such as the mapmaking of the age of discovery and, later, the development of the ordinance survey.[8]

In the past hundred years artists first fragmented light (and thus time) with impressionism. Within a few years postimpressionists such as Cézanne forged "a new language, abandoning linear and aerial perspective and making the spatial dispositions arise from the modulations of color."[9] The cubists fractured the space-time barrier itself, providing simultaneous images of the same moment from different points in space and multiple views of a single scene at various points in time (see Kern's essay in this volume), anticipating, as artists so often do, the mood of modernity.

There were parallel developments in narrative form. The novel was emblematic and constitutive of modern individuality, the particularity of characters established by the particularity of their trajectory through specific spaces and times.[10] Novelists such as James Joyce and Thomas Mann and poets such as T. S. Eliot and Ezra Pound transformed the twentieth century, ringing changes in the space-time equation. In *Finnegans Wake* Joyce explodes the conventions of language and the novel;

moreover, the resonating text itself is circular, starting in the middle of a sentence whose beginning ends the work, while the author explores multiple levels of experience in which "the boundaries of the personality become fluid."[11]

Recent work by the British painter David Hockney is a contemporary advance on these movements away from what he calls "one-eyed art," dominated by the camera as a perspectival mode of seeing.[12] Fixed-point perspective, Hockney argues, freezes space and time, and thus it was not accidental that Renaissance painters were visually obsessed with cruci-fixion, a slow death at a perpendicular intersection which did not de-mand the representation of time.[13]

In *Red Bridge,* our cover illustration, Hockney represents the tension between somewhere and everywhere, hence nowhere, and *also* now/ here—present and absent.[14] Unlike an image painted with fixed-point perspective, which assumes a static spectator outside the painting, Hock-ney's work assumes a painter/observer who is an embodied subject in motion, involved in a temporal relationship with the objects depicted and the depiction itself. Like the medieval artists and mapmakers and the Chinese scroll painters who represented space as they moved through it, Hockney's painting thus slides, just as we do, between space and place, between now and just a moment ago, and between being "out there" in the objective world and inside the inner horizon of subjective perception. It is simultaneously external and internal, extending the point made by his earlier photocollages and his studies in reverse per-spective that the eye composes—in both senses—in the phenomenal mo-ment and also in the extended historicity and spatiality through which *now* connects to *then, here* to *there.*[15] We humans, not the object world, are the locus of human truth.[16]

As the work of modern physics demonstrates, time and space coexist and are mutually elaborative through action, generating new dimen-sions both of physical and mental life.[17] Indeed, they are so indicative and indexical of each other that it is theoretically problematic to think of them separately. Yet most social research does exactly that. This analytic division, however, reflects modernity's distinct spatiotemporal organiza-tion. Modern systems of transportation, communication, and, above all, information have achieved a *separation* of time and space from the cen-tral, premodern preeminence of place. Giddens refers to this transfor-mation as the "emptying" of space and time: "The severance of time from space . . . provides the very basis for their recombination in ways that coordinate social activities without necessary reference to the partic-ularities of place."[18] People, events, organizations, and whole societies are no longer simply tied to single places or particular times. Instead, the essence of modernity is its ability, indeed necessity, to connect local times, spaces, and people with global agendas, standardized time horizons and constantly shifting spatial arrangements.

This introductory essay is organized in four main sections: first, we examine the absence of both theoretical and empirical consideration of space and time in most of the short history of the social sciences; second, we trace out the main features of the terrain of modernity, its rough edges and smooth connections; third, we discuss the most important contemporary writers who have begun to wrestle theoretically with the essential conjunction of space and time; and, fourth, we present a brief overview of the diverse authors and perspectives gathered in the following chapters. We conclude our own contribution to this interdisciplinary collection with a number of speculations about the trajectory of modernity along its quite distinctive and, at times, dangerous space-time parabola.

## THEORETICAL ABSENCE

Until recently, social theorists tended to view space and time as abstract containers, irrelevant except as sites or settings for the analysis of central social phenomena. Beyond passing reference, they have been treated as taken-for-granted metrics and markers in the social world, unanalyzed and unacknowledged in any basic sense. The division of labor was simple: space was assumed to be the domain of geography, and time, or sequences of events, was left to historians, and neither played any focal part in social theory.

The search for universals in an objective social world drove social theorists to situate themselves and their object out of space and time, divorced from the particularities of place and period. Social science literally presumed a view from nowhere.[19] Anthropologists and economists, for instance, both constructed worlds out of time—the first in a timeless past and the second in a timeless present. In neoclassical economics, by contrast, the marketplace was celebrated for having no place at all, for being an abstract universe of traders. Economic Man was also endowed with preferences assumed to be invariant through time, lest the entire theoretical corpus be made nonfalsifiable, a rhetorical castle in hyperspace.[20] Basing its theory around a multitude of atomic moments, economics has been incapable of theorizing the history or geography of production or reproduction.[21] Space and time were all but banished in a friction-free, history-less world.

Anthropology, for its part, generally represented the many worlds it interpreted as though they were out of time, and particularly *our* Western time, altogether. In the "natural" temporality of anthropology, different cultures were understood as more or less distant from the civilizational present.[22] And, while cultural anthropology constructed peoples without history,[23] historians constructed histories without people, state-centered narratives controlled by elite actions and events.[24] Historical narratives assumed a temporal order; they did not study it. And although Fernand Braudel made geography a central organizing principle of the *longue durée*, the spatiality of this temporal order remained largely hidden from view even in the works of the students in his school.[25]

In sociology, society also tended to be theorized out of historical time, reconstructed as a cybernetic system, an abstract structure developing according to its own laws of motion. Quantitative studies by sociologists and historians alike have used time and discrete time intervals as variables or units of observation to add precision, to better approximate social process or infer causality. The social organization of time has not, however, been a subject in its own right until recently. Thus, although time has recently moved into analytic focus,[26] it was more typically treated as a technical resource to be budgeted or a neutral environment for social life.[27] Most important for the analysis that follows, neither the sequential nor situated quality of human action has typically figured in sociological theory. Temporality as a consequential moment-to-moment social constituent, and history as a resource for present action, have only recently become problems for social analysis.[28]

The social construction of space and the theoretical consequences of the spatial environment of action and structure have been still more invisible in research and theory. Until recently the work of human geography was largely cut off from the main currents of social theory.[29] Even as a growing number of critics noted the lack of temporality in much social theory, the absence of spatiality was rarely stressed. This perhaps reflects the fact that space is more concrete than time. In all languages everyday temporal expressions tend to derive historically from those which designate spatial relations.[30] Space's naturalness, its existential "thereness," may have made it more difficult to understand its consequentiality for social life. Beyond the examples already cited, organizational theorists, as Friedland and Palmer argue (in their essay in this volume), completely disregarded organizational location as well as the geographical dimensions of organizational structure and strategy.

More generally, Anthony Giddens has argued that sociology failed to theorize the spatial boundedness of its central object—society, which looked suspiciously like the nation-state.[31] Giddens locates this antispatiality of social theory in the historic aversion to environmentalism, while geographer Edward Soja attributes it also to the anti-Hegelianism of the Marxists who derided Hegel's notion of the territorial state as "perfected reason."[32] In critical social theory Soja (in his essay in this volume) argues that an obsession with the making of history has resulted in a blindness to the making of geography as the central stake to be contested in any project of human liberation. Certainly modernity has had an obsessive temporality about it, so that space was dead and time alive.[33]

Recently, however, there has been a remarkable convergence of interest, research, and theorizing in space and time, as well as interesting and, we think, important blending of approaches and strategies (see "Contemporary Theories of Space and Time," below).[34] Space and time are no longer the privileged and hence impoverished preserve of geographers and historians, philosophers and physicists. Scholars in an impressive number of fields have turned to how humans organize and understand the spatiotemporal dimensions of their lives, as well as the ways in which all forms of social organization are shaped by their particular forms of spatiality and temporality. The social organization of space and time, and the spatial and temporal organization of society, have suddenly everywhere become central concerns.

## THE COLLAGE OF MODERNITY

What are the reasons for this new excitement? In one sense, time and space are so central to human existence as to be obvious. That, of course, is part of the problem. Social actors and social actions are *embodied*, which means that they *always* entail genuine engagement of concrete moments in time and particular points in space; people are always somewhere, things have to happen in particular places, objects exist in a spatiotemporal relation to each other, and so on. The twenty-four-hour clock or seven-day week are social conventions, to be sure,[35] yet the basic features of physical existence are intractable problems for social life.[36] Modernity has, however, brought enormous and increasing changes in the tensions between the immediacy of here and now, our physical location in space and time, and the sorts of experiences, actions, events, and whole worlds in which we can partake at a distance. Our experience of here and now has increasingly lost its immediate spatiotemporal referents and has become tied to and contingent on actors and actions at a distance. The experiential here and now of modernity is thus in a real sense nowhere yet everywhere.

Presence and absence are therefore a fundamental tension of modernity. Virtually every writer who has tackled the topics of time or space, and the few who have attempted to theorize their conjunction, have done so on the basis of puzzles posed by this intersection. Just how and with what consequences the modern era has transformed relations of space and time, and thus relationships between people and their history, has been a central question for a growing range of authors (see "Contemporary Theories of Space and Time," below). The actual, potential, eventual, and even counterfactual links between space and time in modernity underline, we believe, both the excitement and the puzzle.

Transformations in time and space can be traced far back into human history; they mark the most abstract yet highly practical organizing phenomena of social life. Language was the first of many human inventions designed to manage space and time, and on the basis of recent archeological evidence, it also became a remarkable resource for defining and spanning space.[37] Across the centuries of prehistory, oral societies transmitted whole cultures from generation to generation through spoken discourse, the patterns of poetry, and the rituals of religions. The myths of old were conservative mechanisms of social control, necessarily rigid in formulation and deeply rooted in the past.[38]

With the introduction of writing, language traced not only history but the capacity of emerging civilizations to centralize power by coordinating information through accounting: counting and recording crops, people, and territories became an important form of social control and thus power.[39] Writing, with its decontextualization of communication and its fixity across time and space, emerges out of administrative notation. Written notation allowed the emergence of a sense of linear time and hence the development of chronological—both narrative and historical—forms.[40] The symbolic force of language and its ability to define and contain knowledge, as well as transcend space and time, formed the basis of whole civilizations from the heart of the Chinese Middle Kingdom to the high Andes culture of the Incas. Control of both information and its symbolic content, coupled with the capacity to transmit it along designated channels of communication, shaped the Roman Empire, for example, making both Roman law and the Roman roads a practical reality in the ancient world.[41] The ideology of *pax romana* was based on the organization and control of space; both the ability to define boundaries of territories and control those confines constituted the empire itself. Similarly, time was defined and subsumed under Roman control through *consecutio temporum,* the linear and irreversible logic, direction, and ordering of official time.[42]

After Gutenberg and the invention of printing, the link between empires and communication, and between discourse and surveillance, became ever more defined.[43] Yet it also opened up the genuine possibility of emancipation and democracy, exposing one of the first contradictions of the early modern era. Even by the time of the French Revolution, however, the two rather invisible elements of transportation and information were fairly undeveloped by contrast with the last hundred years. For example, whereas the many instant newssheets of the revolution fueled social change locally in Paris, it took several weeks for news of the fall of the Bastille to reach Marseilles.[44] Revolution, however tumultuous, was a generally local affair. Even the "Springtime of Europe" half a century later had little of the deep transformatory effect of more recent upheavals.

The rise of capitalism also assumed a cultural transformation in the meaning and measurement of time, which had intimately involved religion. It was the monastic orders who, seeking to develop new disciplinary mechanisms, had first developed precise, abstract time measurement.[45] But for capital markets to evolve, the bourgeoisie had to replace the cosmology of the Latin church, which held that time belonged to God, not man, and thus prevented a good Christian from selling it.[46] Max Weber pointed to the way in which Protestantism formed a new relationship between biographical and cosmological narratives, creating the first capitalists whose methodical self-control and high valuation of a predetermined future made efficiency and capital accumulation so natural. The Western origins of individual rationality lay in the secularized Calvinist ethic of election, a state which was determined for the future but which could only be indicated in the present by ascetic, rational self-control.[47]

By the early nineteenth century the joint energies of capitalism, industrialization, nationalism, science, and technology were developing enormous momentum. The railroads, exploding in every direction across the Old and New Worlds, simultaneously increased access to raw materials and markets.[48] With the railroads, space was conquered and time standardized.[49] In the American West, for example, demand for land and beef closed the once open ranges and transformed the freedom-loving American cowboy into a wage laborer in the pay of distant cattle barons who could now manage huge stretches of territory at a distance.[50] The railroad, with its gargantuan demands for capital and its need to precisely coordinate flows across enormous distances and to define clear time zones, created the essential entrepreneurial conditions of the modern industrial firm.[51] Across the Western world, space, time, and labor were also being converted into commodities.[52] The discovery of electricity further transformed not only industry but the daily lives of entrepreneurs and laborers alike, turning night into a new frontier.[53] With the telegraph, information was permanently separated from constraints of space and time, the notion of "news" took on utterly transformed meaning, and modernity was racing toward distant horizons of both hope and despair.[54]

The development of the factory as the bureaucratic, industrial, and capitalist workplace made possible new forms of solidarity based on social class. And the new urban agglomerations in which factories were concentrated extended the division of social space and time into a private sphere of family and a public one of work and politics (see Robertson's essay in this volume).[55] This social division of time and space gave rise to our particularly modern conceptions of the private and gendered person. In the modern art of Manet and Toulouse-Lautrec, women were rarely represented in public spaces, only on its margins, in balconies and gardens.[56] Even the physical reorientation of space in private homes meant that space became defined as either intimate and private or public and formal. The gendered division of time and space, initially defined in the nineteenth century, is with us today in women's continued segregation in work and the public spheres of social life (see Gardner's essay in this volume).[57]

In the process, modern social actors developed a heightened sense of time as an arrow, moving in a straight line from past to future through the lived experience of the present. This linear sense arose within the project of modernity, and transformations of space-time brought with them dramatic changes in the ways humans saw themselves and their history. Individuals were now assumed to be active participants in their own biographies and in history itself. Moreover, the rise in life expectancy made *certain* lifetimes out of once uncertain life spans, making it possible (and necessary) to *plan* for the future on both an individual and collective level.[58] The ability to shape the future thus made what Marlis Buchmann calls "lifescripts" a necessary component of modernity.[59] Across the span of the twentieth century, each of these components of modernity has gathered speed.

### Why Now, Why Here?

As both a material order and a cosmology, modernity has been constructed around the controlling center and the reasoning subject, around city, state, and firm and the active participation of residents, citizens, and capitalists. The manipulation of apparently abstract, homogeneous space and time has been critical to both poles of the system. The proliferation of bureaucratic forms, together with ever-developing mechanisms of production, transmission, storage, and transportation of both signs and objects, allows elites in those centers to project themselves over ever greater zones of space and time. Interesting, for instance, is the fact that the development of major new technologies for bounding space and time were directly associated with new organizational forms: writing (bureaucracy), the railroad (the staff-line firm), the computer (the multidivisional and ultimately the multinational firm).[60] As the centers reached out to control the periphery and the future, their subjects also achieved increasing control over the space and time of their lives as distinctions between work time and family time grew.[61] Bureaucracies enabled as they constrained, and the controlling centers were to assume that expanding and rather singular rationality that characterizes modernity.[62]

The project of modernity has always pointed toward tomorrow, although for many writers it is an unfinished and contradictory enterprise.[63] The modern world has been one which could always be improved, a perpetual movement between the dark weight of necessity and the bright light of freedom. In this sense, there has been little difference between capitalism and socialism. It is a world characterized by profound personal and collective historicity, where the present marks frequent breaks with the past. As moderns we believe that we can consciously make history, and we make it "forward" into the future.[64] Whereas peoples of previous epochs lived a present suffused with the past, moderns inhabit one bursting with the future and with the assumed rational ability to create that future. We write and live personal and collective narratives that go somewhere. We move forward in linear time. Collective historicity and individual subjectivity are reflexively tied one to the other.[65] The modern child, a recent invention like the nation-state, wants "to be something" when she grows up.

One of the first orders of business in a social revolution is the writing of a new national history and the fashioning of a new cartography, to create a story and a map in terms of which the future world can be projected.[66] Thus, the professional historian emerged in the nineteenth century at the same time that states were struggling to create a unified nation in the territories over which they claimed sovereignty.[67] These historians were funded by the state, which saw the creation of a "national" history as a way to bolster its power and integrate linguistically and culturally diverse populations under its control. The historians in their turn also wrote a state-centered history, rooted in official documents of the state, which assumed that the state and its leaders were the dominant source of social change and cohesion in the society. Historians hired by the state wrote the history that they believed that state made using documents produced by the same state. Nationalism is predicated on the territorial "historicity" of the Western nation-state and its "controlled use of reflection upon history as a means of changing history."[68] That territorial historicity is the core of the nation-state's legitimacy and an element in the narrative of modernity.

Yet in these late moments of the twentieth century, modernity has also become something of a mirage, a shimmering oasis that is shifting and losing shape, disintegrating and reforming on the distant horizon of both individual experience and institutional endeavor. The social particularity of space and time is never so clear as when it ceases to work, when the spatialities and temporalities that undergird social life markedly change. We live in a world where the territorial maps and temporal schedules that constitute modernity make less and less sense.

Progress and nationalism, as two central constructions of space and time in the constitution of modernity, have proved their poverty at the same time that they have become more powerful. Each is premised on a spatiotemporal myth. Integral to each is an image of the reasonable human agent who becomes the myth's subject and object.[69] It is assumed that instrumental interaction with nature facilitates and even forces human beings to expand their reason, leading to an ever more perfect world.[70] The nation—and, by implication, the nation-state—assumes an identity between a parcel of land, the people who inhabit it, and the history they have shared there, as well as a government which claims sovereignty over that territory. Like progress, nationalism is predicated on the notion of the reasoning and reasonable subject, the citizen. The cultural formation of a nation and its mobilization through nationalism were the precondition and harbinger of democratic revolutions in which territorial states were assumed to somehow "represent" masses of equally rational citizens.[71]

As cultural coordinates of spatiotemporal existence, progress and national sovereignty have, over the course of the twentieth century, revealed their limits. The poverty of progress is there for all to see in the growing incapacity of human beings to reproduce their natural habitat. In capitalist and, even more, socialist societies,[72] the organization of the material world according to the linear time of industrial production has, perhaps irrevocably, perturbed the cyclical time of nature. Indeed, even the possibility of a separate and independent Nature, as exterior to us in space and time, no longer exists.[73] The progressive degradation of the earth has proceeded to such an extent that the reproducibility of a whole host of species, including our own, is now at issue.[74]

Nationalism too, as a major spatial coordinate, has become problematic even as it remains a powerful force. In the nineteenth century the rise of military power together with nationalism irrevocably transformed the organization of war. The call to fight for *la patrie* turned citizens into soldiers and proved a remarkably effective device for first defining and then defending the boundaries of the new nation-states. Masses of citizens were now willing to give their lives for the flag, and military might shifted from subduing domestic populations to supporting the external relations of the state.[75] In the twentieth century, though, many nationalisms have given rise to barbarous racisms, and the nation-state has proved a violent and *un*reasonable force, capable of mass destruction of entire civilian populations. The industrialization of violence and the marketplace for deadly weapons has also led to transnational diffusion of instruments of mass death. Most recently, the Gulf War was a dramatic example of space-time dynamics, with satellites for the first time playing a critical, if invisible, role in everything from weather forecasts to real-time CNN coverage of the opening air attack on Baghdad, as the global village looked on.[76]

### Sovereign Spaces and Market Places

We write as the predominant form of socialism collapses over vast areas of the globe's surface. The limits of socialism are currently a popular theme, yet such limits also point to those of capitalism. One central mechanism of socialist states—whether Russia or China—has been the ability to fix people in space and time. Without knowing where people are and being able to keep them there, one-party rule disintegrates. And once goods, information, and people move freely, the system of centralized control must erode.

By contrast, the free movement of goods and people in space and time is the hallmark of the capitalist marketplace. As the marketplace goes "global," firms must be increasingly flexible, able to respond quickly to unpredictable shifts in both product and labor. Not only is the global market always of potential local relevance, but the local firm always has a potential global marketplace. The technologies that enable and compel this flexibility have dramatically shifted modern time sensibilities so that less and less of economic life can be confidently scripted. Just like material goods, ever larger segments of the entire labor market are being transformed to follow "just-in-time" models used for the supply of material components.[77]

For most of the period of industrial capitalism, industries went through a typical product cycle characterized by progressive routinization, with the subsequent search for cheaper, unskilled labor pushing production ever further into the periphery. Today, the post-Fordists argue, the temporal rhythms of industrial innovation look markedly different because programmable, multiuse machines can efficiently produce specialized, tailor-made products almost immediately for small market niches. Computer programming has also erased many of the comparative advantages of bureaucratic forms which formerly required large concentrations of resources. The largest corporations' employment in the United States has shrunk over the last decade, which in turn has required labor to move further in search of work producing the restlessness of many work forces and shortening work careers.

In a competitive market economy, cities used to connect firms. Market geographies were so powerful that what was produced was determined by where it was produced. Today, firms span regions and nation-states, and corporate geographies increasingly determine what is produced where. Thus, firms now connect cities.[78] A firm's ability to redeploy assets across space, its capacity to cross countries and continents, has become an increasingly important basis of competitive advantage. Because of their newfound capacity to instantaneously coordinate production and distribution around the globe, to downsize and subcontract, factories and firms have lost their dependence on particular cities or regions.[79] Geographic redeployment is a corollary both of strategies to minimize costs and to reallocate across sectors. Some argue that in an increasingly interconnected world, location and regionalization have become less and less important to economic productivity.[80] Indeed, with the rise of a truly global marketplace, there is a growing debate as to whether the material conditions of the corporation's "home" territory and by implication the territorial authority of the nation-state are impediments or necessary conditions for the future productivity and profitability of the multinational corporation.[81]

There is a hierarchy of spatial elasticities in the modern marketplace—which factors move fastest and farthest in response to spatial differentials in returns: liquid capital moves fastest and farthest, fixed capital investment less so, and wage workers slowest and least of all. Capital has progressively separated in time and space from labor. Economic restructuring thus brings in its wake radical geographical restructuring and the disruption of communities and mass migration. Nation-states have been relatively powerless to prevent, shape, and sometimes even adequately respond to these geographical transformations. As corporations become global, they increasingly become like states whose workers have material benefits (pensions, child care, health insurance, job security, seniority systems) and procedural citizenship rights, while states become increasingly like firms that compete among themselves to provide private industry with the best possible mix of minimum tax obligation and maximum expenditure benefit in order to secure their investment within their boundaries.

While capital has conquered space and time, capitalists have not. Roger Friedland and Donald Palmer (in their essay in this volume) point to the continued geographic concentration of corporate headquarters and financial intermediaries in the dominant cities of the world's most powerful capitalist nations, while also pointing to the consequentiality of its variation. These cross-national variations in spatial concentration of corporate elites matter both to strategy and structure, thus underlining the continued competitive relevance of variability itself.

The division of labor is therefore not just social but spatial and temporal. Edward W. Soja (in this volume) suggests that capital accumulation depends on interregional transfers of profit which both require and generate uneven development at ever-changing scales. Such transfers occur first between city and countryside, then metropole and periphery within the same state, between developed and undeveloped pieces of the globe, and most recently—in Los Angeles par excellence—between neighborhoods and nation-states.[82] The geographical search for profits sets capital and labor in motions which are ever faster, ever farther, and ever more discriminating. Value transfers are obscured from view through the spatiality of uneven development, workers' demands constrained by the ever greater ease of capital flight, and their capacity for organization muted by the spatial fragmentation of production and producers both within the metropole and across the globe.

Capitalism, Soja argues, transfers surplus from place to place behind the backs of resident workers living here or there, and, one might add, now and then. Most critically, it moves virtually instantly through the global markets of modernity, whereas particular workers take time to move across space. American car workers, for example, are becoming a whole new category of migrant workers in an attempt to hold onto once solid intergenerational employment. Struggles to control the organization of daily life necessarily become urban social movements or forms of regionalism that reflect the varying scales of uneven development generated by capitalism.[83]

## The Medium of Modernity

Modernity is not, however, simply a marketplace. Indeed, as the former communist world tries to make the "market" a kind of catchall solution for extraordinarily complex problems, there is a quite serious danger that the other modalities of modernity will be missed (and misunderstood). In this section we want to slow the pace of our own presentation and examine a number of the most fluid and least visible features of the modern age: money, information, and telecommunication.

The spatiality and temporality of modernity are, we believe, changing quite radically today; that change is due in part to the invisible connections of the electronic era in which the "mode of information" may well demand the kind of attention and analysis that classic modes of production once received.[84] The timing and spacing of social interaction and institutional actions are being subtly but rapidly changed by this latest spin of the globe (see Boden and Molotch's essay in this volume). It is not just that the modern institutional ordering of space and time is filled with new tensions and contradictions. The significance of highly local and immediate actions and events has instead taken on a distinctly dialectical relationship with distant, global moments and structures. Rather than a continued penetration and strategic control from spatially fixed centers, we suspect that the dialectic of local and global is far more complex, simultaneously involving global and planetary configurations while contrastively creating the conditions for reorganization into quite distinctly local and regional groupings.

Modernity is now marked by instantiation as well as distantiation. The development of satellite technology, facsimile machines, ever smaller, ever more powerful computers hard-wired or linked through microwave networks, answering machines with remote call-in features, satellite pagers, pocket telephones, and car phones now means that people are potentially available to each other everywhere and continuously. And they are available in real time. For the first time in human history, there is a global present.[85] Now and here work differently. Cities, states, and firms no longer function as before. The centers do not hold; the former Union of Soviet Socialist Republics provides an almost unimaginable example of this tendency, and the recent "Second Russian Revolution" was one achieved at a global as well as local level.

As Foucault's Panopticon goes electronic, many activities are no longer contained and bounded by localized physical settings. Place evaporates in the reorganization of space and time, and the dialectic of presence and absence becomes a central organizing principle of the age. The ability to instantly link people to people, individuals to organizations, and organizations to networks of organizations is at the heart of late modernity. Telecommuting, teleshopping, computer dating, electronic job markets, automatic tellers, desktop publishing, electronic parole—all presage a delocalized, potentially nomadic future.[86] In 1990, for example, Miss Italy was chosen in real time on television by telephone, Orthodox Jews around the United States constituted themselves into a continental yeshiva and were studying the Gemara by phone, and in 1991, bowing to inevitability, the Vatican opened international telephone lines so that the world's 875 million Roman Catholics can dial in to hear the pope's latest message.[87] More urgently, during the recent Gulf War, French war photographers bypassed the "pool" censorship imposed by the Pentagon by beaming their photos to their London office via portable Hasselblad satellite transmitters.[88] More recently, both the Russian revolution of 1991 and the tragic Yugoslavian civil war have seen extensive use of electronic mail networks and cellular telephones both to get news to the West and to provide limited news internally.[89]

Presence and absence, mediated by multiple channels of communication and thus control, link local to global, and vice versa, in potentially terrible ways as well. For example, high unemployment and desperate poverty in the Third World have resulted in data banks for organ transplants, especially in India and Egypt. The market for organs is, moreover, growing, in a tragic unidirectional flow from South to North.[90]

States are also connected to their citizens and each other in radically new ways. Twenty years ago, advances in film processing and jet travel made America's war in Vietnam a war at home which quickly became relevant at the front. Today, not only does satellite technology guide so-called smart bombs to selected targets, but the recent Gulf War was fought in real time and prime time, greatly altering the dynamic of modern warfare. Information once available only to elites on both sides of a struggle was now being beamed directly to dinner and coffee tables around the world. While this new realm of information produced new dimensions of censorship, it also resulted in an intensity and instantaneity never before experienced. Indeed, the speed resulted in a strange inversion of news. For instance, in the autumn months leading up to war, American soldiers sitting in the Saudi Arabian desert complained first about the heat but also, and as loudly, about the fact that they were cut off from the world media network and thus from the global significance of their own actions.[91] Yet the soldiers' many free phone calls home throughout the conflict (again via satellite) allowed them to track their own war at a distance, in ways which critically boosted morale. Local and global thus reflexively shape each other—often instantly.

Since the mid 1980s and the extensive use of satellites for the commercial transmission of voices, images, and texts, world politics have increasingly been played out in real time. Even newspapers have gone global by cloning themselves via fax, sending page by page around the world. Both newspapers and news weeklies, moreover, have abandoned the attempt to compete directly with radio and television by shifting to an emphasis on depth coverage in contrast with the momentary immediacy and shallowness of the electronic media. Moreover, while academics continue to work almost exclusively with the printed word, the offices of politicians, government bureaucrats, stockbrokers, and business executives more generally are increasingly tracking local and global events live on television and by computer news services: the immediate consequences of actions which are publicly available are different than before. For centuries bureaucratic elites could privately negotiate positions with each other which would *then* be transmitted to relevant publics who would react to them. Now elite decision making is publicly available. This interaction creates a new dynamic between "public" and "private," one which is simultaneously more intensive and extensive. Each domain depends on the ability to trust and reflexively monitor the other, yet with a tension built into the modes and media of information and social transformation.

Libraries, for example, were until very recently instruments of state power, closed except to a regulated group of elites. Records, including the historical record, were the stuff of state control.[92] It is of course true that now, as the mechanisms of observation, recording, and transmittal become ever more powerful and ever more widespread, bureaucracies can better monitor and control their workers, clients, and publics, as noted above.[93] But ordinary people are also far more—and more constantly—informed than ever before, and they are much more able to communicate with each other about these same events. This, then, is the dialectic of local and global we wish to underline.

The explosion in communications technology that has transformed the world into an increasingly unified marketplace also allows the same signs and symbols to transcend sovereign states. As markets globalize electronically and as the world economy becomes increasingly an exchange of signs rather than material goods, governments are less and less able to seal their borders. The development of the photograph, the telephone, the mimeograph, the photocopying machine, the tape recorder, and the fax, all essential tools of economic development, has simultaneously vitiated the attempt of states to control communication and hence to construct reality in centralized ways. Censorship is difficult to maintain—whether in Shi'ite Iran or socialist Poland—when ordinary people have unregulated access to videocassettes, audiotapes, fax machines, and copiers. Rock music, Hollywood movies, and revolutionary critique also disseminate invisibly and extensively. For instance, the transmission of audiotapes helped the Ayatollah Khomeini push the shah from power in the late 1970s, yet today the educated middle classes in Teheran continue to watch Jane Fonda movies at home on private videocassettes while their women wear the chador on the street. Ten years ago in Poland, the outlawed workers' movement was known as the "VCR proletariat,"[94] and, more recently, Mikhail Gorbachev tracked his own imprisonment in the Crimea on the BBC World Service.[95]

National governments similarly used to be able to influence monetary flows inside and outside their borders. As a result, national banks could operate as government-regulated cartels in which the interest rates they paid were set by law. In exchange for high and stable profits, the bankers underwrote government deficits and helped enforce governmental tax collection and exchange controls.[96] But computer programming has undercut the comparative advantage of large bank bureaucracies and thus of the largest financial centers around the world. Increasingly placeless money markets, mutual funds, and capital markets all connected by computer terminals have undercut the profitability of savings and loan institutions, commercial banks, and the largest brokerages. Cashless consumption and investment can be done anywhere, anytime.[97] Similarly, a single individual can destabilize entire national currencies and supranational exchange mechanisms without leaving the comfort of an air-conditioned office in Manhattan, as has been demonstrated several times during the recent European monetary crises.

It was Georg Simmel who first noted the time- and space-defying properties of money. The recent reorganization of capital and credit as electronic traces has further transformed the form and flow of what we think of as "money."[98] Market cycles have sped up considerably. Measures of monetary aggregates, by which governments try to regulate economic activity, multiply. In previous periods of global economic uncertainty, investors turned to precious metals and the dominant currency, once the pound sterling, then the dollar, and now perhaps the German mark or the Japanese yen. Because of the growing double deficits of the United States and the ability to transfer assets instantaneously around the globe, both gold and the reserve currency have lost their utility as safe stores of value. With the explosion of the Eurodollar markets—that is, of dollars circulating outside the United States—and the sheer size of global currency markets, governments, including that of the United States, have effectively lost control of the value of their currencies. Nation-states are steadily losing their authority to control the representation of value.

Computer networks have given rise to new kinds of computer-controlled exchanges which parallel and occasionally paralyze the world's equity markets. We are, of course, referring to the rise of futures contracts, a computerized market in which people largely speculate and hedge on the various futures of equity, bond, and commodity markets. These markets, too, offer instruments which allow investors to hedge their holdings against inflation or deflation without having to turn to precious metals, real estate, or the reserve currency. Unlike normal markets, with market makers who are supposed to create liquidity, these are markets which clear instantaneously. And unlike equity markets, where all information about every future is contained in the current price, futures markets have much more information because investors take price positions on particular dates, thereby creating collective valuations of time and risk.[99] These markets are, moreover, huge—global both in fact and fancy. In the American stock market crash of 1987, all attention was on Wall Street, where approximately a quarter of the market capitalization was wiped out. But the value of highly leveraged futures trading that day was *many times* the value of the equity drop! And unlike the equity market, where everybody lost, futures markets clear so that the trillions of dollars lost by some are won by others. Futures markets are linked to equity, bond, and currency markets through program trading. These new computer-controlled exchanges and their derivative products valuate assets which shape inflationary expectations which affect real inflation. In these and other ways, analysts argue, those who bet on the future increasingly make that future.

The significance of this proposed global connectivity was also evident in the unfolding of the revolutions of 1989, the global management of the Gulf War in 1991, and the Russian Revolution of August 1991. The brevity and irreversibility of these events are also a feature of the instant world.[100] Surely the Chinese students' choice of Beijing, the timing of their mass demonstration in mid May 1989, and their brave if unsuccessful capacity to resist the central state in China was conditioned by the fact that Mikhail Gorbachev, the architect of perestroika, was due to visit China's capital then, and with him came the journalists and satellite dishes of modern news making. The students capitalized on the fact that the world would be watching and they spoke to that world in signs and symbols such as democracy placards in English and the statue of the French image of Liberty. As Deirdre Boden remarks: "they changed history just because the whole world was able to observe those enthusiastic and pure messages in real time. The whole world was, indeed, watching and—reflexively—they were watching us watching them." [101] Most centrally, perhaps, Gorbachev as both man and maker of history learned the lesson of that global event, a lesson which was soon to shape his reaction to events in Eastern Europe though, rather poignantly, not enough to guide his handling of more local rebellions in the Soviet Union.[102] Nonetheless, the blaze of real-time, global publicity in which world leaders are now forced to make decisions is a dramatic feature of modernity.

When the Nazi regime, run by the world's first media dictator, conducted its genocide, the world could claim it did not know. No longer. Despite strict censorship, the United States and its "coalition" allies were forced to conduct the Gulf War as a relentless real-time event, and key actors were visibly conscious of their ability to converse with each other via global television. Earlier in the crisis, when Larry King, for example, interviewed Jean Kirpatrick, America's former ambassador to the United Nations, on CNN about the situation in the Gulf, she remarked that Saddam Hussein's regime watched CNN on a continuous basis. For an instant, she seemed to turn self-consciously to the camera, as if to look him in the eye. And months later, twenty-four hours after the first allied bombing of Baghdad, Larry King anchored participants in Washington, New York, Baghdad, and Tel Aviv, asking Israeli Deputy Defense Minister Benjamin Netanyahu for his assessment of the effects of television on the war. His response was especially instructive: "What we are facing now is political communication. As we speak it may be that in a bunker in Baghdad they listen to us. In fact, I'll delete the 'maybe,' I'm sure they are. They are listening to us in Moscow, in Washington, and everywhere else. So the impact of what is *seen* and *said* on television is an integral *part* of the war effort on *both* sides . . . : television is no longer a spectator." [103] This "interactive" awareness persisted throughout the war, with Hussein and Bush communicating with each other via CNN even though their embassies had suspended diplomatic relations. Political elites also often first learned of each other's actions and maneuvers through television broadcasts. In contrast with past wars, there was no steady flow of diplomats, statesmen, and generals to the White House. With everyone glued to their television sets, the centrality of the "Situation Room" in the White House basement was considerably diminished.[104]

And despite an awareness on the part of both elites and their populace of this new instant world, a sense of the *consequences* was notably lacking. In the first days of the war, again as CNN broadcast live from Baghdad, Bernard Shaw announced he was hiding under a table to evade detection as an Iraqi official knocked at the door. It did not occur to him that Iraqis were listening to him watch them. It took a day before the Israelis restricted broadcasts about the location of Iraqi Scud missile strikes in order not to provide their enemies with information for subsequent targeting. The instantaneity of the war was a central feature of it, yet the consequences have yet to be fully assessed.[105] In a thoroughly modern manner, the world viewer—whether a banker in Tokyo or a naval bride in San Diego—was closer and more intimately involved, yet curiously more distant.

There is also a global unity of discourse shaping events around the globe. During the Gulf crisis, for instance, both the *Wall Street Journal* and Saddam Hussein made use of an international media image— Rambo—to denigrate their respective enemies. We are closer to the conqueror Alexander the Great's dream of a "cosmopolis," the world as a city in which each nation would be a self-governing neighborhood, than he ever dreamed possible. Yet as Foucault has insisted, that same global language is so reflexive as to create a kind of existential emptiness: it "always seems to be inhabited by the other, elsewhere, distant, far away; it is hollowed by absence."[106] Individuality, the reasoning subject whose identity lies at the core of modernity, must be fashioned anew, over and over.

These, then, are the contours of modernity as we would like to characterize them. The transformations in time and space that began with the emergence of human language and its ability to transcend symbolically the immediate moment have accelerated up to our moment in history. We have traced, briefly, the development of oral traditions, the establishment of writing, of early and late modes of transportation, and of increasing diversity in media of communication and the transmission of capital. With these invisible transformations came the far more visible changes in the space-time organization of labor and production which has produced the large industries and vast bureaucracies of both capitalism and socialism. The latter, with their distinct approaches to nationalism and progress, have etched human history with a mixed legacy of technological advance and ecological disaster. At the same time, the rationality and historicity that have also become a central feature of modernity offer hope of a possible corrective and of a much more tentative brave new world. In the next section we turn to the ways contemporary social thinkers in both the humanities and social sciences are attempting to rethink the basic human "bargain with modernity." [107]

## CONTEMPORARY THEORIES OF SPACE AND TIME

As we approach the millennium, modernity is at a crossroads. For some the future remains an open project, optimistic and somewhat upbeat. For others at various points in this most violent of centuries, the picture has been bleak indeed, fraught with danger and getting darker daily. Our postindustrial and now post-Marxist world is also overshadowed by the Holocaust and by Hiroshima. Against this contradictory social landscape a variety of social analysts are attempting to rethink the consequences of modernity with new understandings of space and time. In this section we provide a flavor of the theoretical issues in general and, in more detail, the central ideas of several key writers whose work has taken them furthest in actually articulating time with space (and vice versa), namely, Pierre Bourdieu, Michel Foucault, Anthony Giddens, and David Harvey.

Pierre Bourdieu was among the first analysts to make the social organization of space and time into a central problematic. Building on earlier anthropological research on temporal and spatial aspects of premodern cultures,[108] Bourdieu began by studying a traditional Algerian society, the Kabyle. Durkheim and his followers, for example, Marcel Mauss, had been interested in the ways in which reciprocity and the normative rhythms of collective life were organized.[109] For Mauss, the exchange of gifts engendered such cyclical rhythms.[110] Pierre Bourdieu also saw gift giving as a critical means of generating symbolic capital—honor—necessary to assure labor supply at the critical junctures of planting and harvest.[111] But whereas Mauss viewed gift exchange as obligatory reciprocity, Bourdieu argued that it is not only profligate use of time in the production of a gift but a *gap in time* in its exchange that makes reciprocity delicately contingent rather than strictly normative. Both are essential to the appearance of generosity to giver and recipient, yet an apparent indifference, not economization of time, generates the underlying "misrecognition" essential to the meaning and self-interested effect of the gift.[112]

Bourdieu's work thus develops the *dual* roles of space and time in *all* social organization. He initially studied a traditional Algerian society resisting modernity and later went on to apply his analysis to the very modern cultural patterns of contemporary French society in *Distinction*.[113] Bourdieu developed a theoretical framework whose core concepts involve a spatiotemporal matrix which locates actors and structures through the notions of *habitus* and *field*. *Habitus* is an analytic device which both identifies and articulates individuals in time and space, sedimenting the social distinctions that separate them yet embodying those very divisions in their actions. Habitus, dispositions appropriate to one's position in these divisions, are literally embodied, learned through early bodily experiences in space and time, experiences filtered through systems of classification and enacted in a social world whose spatiotemporality objectifies that same system of classification.[114] Foreshadowing Foucault's microphysics, the routines and rhythms of one's body are a "second nature," an unreflexive representation of the external social world of objects. One's subjectivity is structured according to the same principles as the objective world in which one learns them both.[115] Bourdieu insists that early bodily experiences in space and time become the central filtering device through which individuals recognize themselves and others in a system of social classification.[116] Through their habitus, actors' improvised strategies are rendered compatible with the structural requisites of the fields or institutionalized social spaces—economic, political, familial, cultural—in which they participate.[117]

Bourdieu argues that spatiotemporal processes such as location, concentration, synchronization and pace provide both a material and logical integration of action. Through these processes the social divisions of all societies are given their distinctive representation and differentiation, and through them the improvisation of social life is also achieved: "The reason why submission to the collective rhythms is so rigorously demanded is that the temporal forms or the spatial structures structure not only the groups' representation of the world but the group itself, which orders itself in accordance with this representation."[118] By identifying social divisions in space and time, and by specifying their pace and duration, societies naturalize their arbitrariness. The choreography materializes the system of classification in such a way that the arbitrariness of the social structure is "misrecognized," a misrecognition which, as noted above, is essential to its operation.[119] Class relations are transformed into classifications, materialized in space-time, which conceal the structures that organize them.

Bourdieu's analysis began and continues with an interest in what he calls "reflexive anthropology," in which he is centrally concerned with the "co-incidence" of objective structures and embodied structures in time and space. His departure point is a phenomenological one in which he shares with Husserl, Schutz, and Garfinkel an attention to lived experience, but he also takes a more structural position on political significance and, ultimately, power.[120]

The role of phenomenology and hermeneutics in the emerging interest in spatiotemporal matters has been critical for many of the theorists discussed here. Earlier writers such as Dilthey and Husserl initially influenced a number of strains of twentieth-century European philosophy and social theory in the writings of Bergson, Heidegger, and Merleau-Ponty. The emerging development of spatial and temporal ideas in phenomenology particularly stressed the contingent nature of action and meaning, which entered the Anglo-American community as the "linguistic" or "interpretive" turn. For Heidegger, for example, Aristotle's metaphysical question on the nature of Being was combined with Husserl's phenomenology. The result was a massive examination, in *Sein und Zeit*,[121] of what he termed *Dasein,* or being-in-the-world. Being, space, time, language, and thus meaning are so intertwined as to have intrigued philosophers and theologians since the dawn of Western philosophy, yet Heidegger managed to mount a quite new analysis.[122] Put most simply, for Heidegger, Being *is* time and being-in-the-world *defines* space. Noting that "relativity theory in physics grew out of the tendency to expose nature's own coherence as it is 'in itself,' "[123] he suggests that Being is made visible in its temporal and spatial character. Thus, the "elemental historicity of *Dasein,*" its inherent and unfolding discovery of itself, locates it in a phenomenological present.[124] The concept of *Dasein* also grounds Being in a spatial context. Moreover, the immediacy of *presence* is extended by humans, first through language, now through technology, back into the past and forward toward a never-to-be-arrived-at future. For Heidegger, as Fred Dallmayr notes, "the future was in a sense privileged over the past owing to its 'impending' character."[125]

For phenomenologists, including Maurice Merleau-Ponty and Alfred Schutz, the irreducible problem of human existence is the conjunction of time, space, and bodies, and the equally unavoidable fact that individual praxis and relations between individuals create and are mediated by space and time.[126] The sedimentation of actions and the durability of objects across time and space give to the social world its structured and "already there" quality.[127] Phenomenologists drew attention, in the process, to the *lived* quality of experience and to an inner *durée* of action, stressed by Bergson. In particular, Heidegger's elaborate analysis of *Dasein* exposes the way we "lean" on the taken-for-granted or tacit dimensions of time and space while exposing the tensions between inner temporal duration, lived bodily experience, actions in space, and the multiple realities of social life.[128] Thus, Schutz, Heidegger, and

Merleau-Ponty all emphasize the problem of being and becoming and the phenomenal ways in which body, action, and space merge across a time horizon.

Writers such as Ricoeur and Gadamer have taken up these themes in a hermeneutical manner and transformed them into abstract yet informative explorations of meaning and human narrative. Paul Ricoeur, in particular, has developed a major set of writings on time and narrative which incorporates trends in both hermeneutics and linguistic philosophy.[129] Working first with historical narrative and then with fiction, he has traced a thoughtful philosophical analysis that seeks to capture the configuration of time as a phenomenal yet permanent element in human affairs. His writings elaborate the notion that time is created in the lived experience of human beings *and* in the reflexive recollections of humans as they trace the narrative of their lives and of history. Ricoeur draws on a range of work to establish a transhistorical yet not atemporal sense of the narrative form.[130] In the spirit of the cultural geographer's notion of place, as a fusion of space and experience and a context for action, Ricouer demonstrates the ubiquity of narrative understanding in social life.[131] Narratives shape the logic of relations of contiguity in space and time and, in so doing, pattern the organization and meaning of our lives.

In the writing of Michel Foucault, time, space, narrative, and power/knowledge come together in an elaborate discourse on modernity. Indeed, the organizing motif of Foucault's oeuvre was his focus on a range of what he termed "disciplinary discourses," and his energy was concentrated on conducting "archaeologies" of these discourses. In the process he highlighted what he considered to be essential discontinuities of epistemological positions in Western history—the similitude between sign and signified in the Renaissance, a spatial order of representation in the Classical Age, and, finally, the temporal, causal sequences and historicity of interpretation and analogy in modernity. In each age, these *epistemes* order the production of truth across a range of social elements, from nature to wealth.[132] Foucault did not lay out causal lines connecting present to past but insisted on the unbridgeable differences between them. The past is a foreign country; "history," for Foucault, is the history of the present.

Modernity's truth is disciplinary. It simultaneously involves new material sites and mechanisms of social control, as well as new human scientific discourses, new ways of controlling human bodies, and new bodies of knowledge. Power and discourse are integral, not exterior, to one another.[133] Modernity, Foucault argues, is characterized by the adoption of new disciplinary mechanisms that reorder or form new spaces in the military, prisons, hospitals, factories, and clinics, as well as new disciplines that constitute new discursive spaces within which subjects are classified.[134] Thus, for example, the physical segregation of the "mad" into asylums was integral to the emergence of human sciences that claimed competence over the new category "mental illness." The body of the modern subject is periodically fixed in bounded, observable spaces, objectified and compared through the means of different "bodies" of knowledge according to examinations and the accumulation of records, and there fixed as individuals.[135] These physical and conceptual spaces make possible a normalization and reconstitution of the human subject. Subject and subjection proceed in concert.

The power/knowledge couplet has a distinctive spatiotemporal base. Foucault's most spatiotemporal treatment of modern disciplinarity is *Discipline and Punish*.[136] Here Foucault analyzes power by developing a historical " 'political economy' of the body."[137] In the century before 1840 there was a transformation in punishment from visible to invisible, from a focus on punishment to conviction, from the infliction of pain on the individual body leaving marks of monarchical power to a set of signs, an "economy of suspended rights."

Foucault links this change in which the surplus power of the king becomes the discretionary power of the penal institution to a generalized rise of disciplinary techniques designed to normalize life, to make power more productive. These disciplinary techniques all involve increased pacing and positioning of the body, teaching it disciplined moves, enclosing it, defining the temporal order of its gestures, and generally developing what he calls *corps dociles* or "docile bodies"—first in the military, asylums, and prisons and eventually in the factories of capitalism. By defining moves, partitioning people and activities, and creating mechanisms of supervision, the body is "rearranged" in a manner that achieves what Foucault calls "a political anatomy of detail."[138] Power is achieved automatically; reduced to its ideal form, frictionless and polyvalent, managed through "a type of location of bodies in space, of distribution of individuals in relation to one another, of hierarchical organization, of disposition of centres and channels of power, of definition of the instruments and modes of intervention of power."[139] The useful human body is the subjected human body.

The rise of disciplinarity involves a fundamental rearrangement of the architecture of power. Disciplinary methods move from an architecture designed to make the powerful few spectacularly visible by the many—public executions and monumental palaces—to making the many routinely visible by the few—punishment in hidden prisons managed by anonymous bureaucratic offices.[140] Foucault finds a paradigmatic expression of this change in Bentham's concept of the Panopticon. In the Panopticon the prisoner is observed constantly from centralized watchtowers but cannot see the observer, and in the process the permanent visibility enters the consciousness of the observed.

Although Foucault locates the first forms of modern disciplinarity in segments of the state apparatus, he does not believe the space of society is built from a central nation-state.[141] Rather, it is composed locally through mechanisms colonized and assembled in a plurality of sites. Government is just another form of disciplinary discourse and technique aimed at the regulation of populations with the objective of increased collective productivity. Its science is political economy, and its dominant technical means are the security apparatuses of the state.[142] Foucault's power-centered analysis of modern society unhinges "governmentality" from any particular institutional configuration, and particularly the central state.[143]

Foucault, like Bourdieu, uses the language of capital to conceptualize power. He is not, however, an economic determinist. Foucault recognizes that discipline allowed societies in the West to adjust the demographic explosion to the enormous burst in productive forces. Nonetheless, he refuses to reduce the origins of discipline to a particular institutional locus.[144] *Discipline,* in Foucault's sense, "may be identified neither with an institution nor with an apparatus; it is a type of power, a modality for its exercise, comprising a whole set of instruments, techniques, procedures, levels of application, targets; it is a 'physics' or 'anatomy' of power, a technology."[145] These disciplinary technologies, wherever they arise, break free of their original institutional moorings and diffuse throughout the "whole social body."[146] As a result, all modern institutions tend to have a homologous structure. The invisible surveillance of the Panopticon becomes a global capacity.

Although Foucault spatializes power, he delocalizes discourse. Indeed, it has no author, no determinative social origin or institutional locus. Although he rejects the premise of a totality, its site is in fact a particular epoch, within which it diffuses across institutional fields. As a result, Foucault's analysis is curiously consensual, the history of the subject without any subjects.[147] The result is a history of the present oddly frozen in time. Part of the problem is methodological, for Foucault is neither a social historian who constructs a causal narrative nor a historian of ideas. Rather, he describes discourses. Foucault does not, however, analyze the actual consequences of these discourses; he merely illustrates them. But by insisting on the truth/power couplet and the materiality of discourse, by believing that he understands "how truth-effects are produced inside discourses which are not in themselves either true or false,"[148] an assumption of statistical coherence, indeed of causality, is necessarily embedded in his interpretive descriptions.

Foucault has partly obviated the problem of specifying the historical

causes of modern disciplinarity because he fuses the modern bureaucratic state and capitalist property based on discipline as a "unitary technique." "The accumulation of men and the accumulation of capital," he
writes, "cannot be separated."[149] Foucault economizes power, making it
into a technology of control. The power relation of the prison, he contends, is "an empty economic form."[150] These two institutional spheres
have homologous forms, the temporal quantification of the prison sentence paralleling the hourly wage.[151] Without institutional tension between state and economy, without a public sphere, Foucault can easily
economize power, but he must depoliticize politics. As a result, Foucault
is unable to specify the conditions of discipline's efficacy.[152]

Part of the problem is that Foucault, like his friend Bourdieu, is interested in bodies rather than human agents. This is related to his belief
that the self-interpreting subject is a modern object created by confes-
sional and therapeutic practices. The problem of bodies in space-time,
for Foucault, is analytically distant from the concepts of the French phenomenologists sketched above, just because his *corps dociles* are so constrained and his discourses so independent of concrete action. Reflexive
monitoring, as Giddens calls it, is entirely absent from Foucault's
scheme. For Foucault, institutionally disembodied discourse and its associated power mechanisms manage the invisible individual's movement in
space and time. This microphysical choreography and its investment
with new meanings and motives are the material preconditions of new
subjectivities he develops.[153] For example, psychoanalysis, an ostensibly
liberatory theory, is offered instead as a discourse of domination that
constitutes our sexuality as modernity's obsessive preoccupation.
Through this bodily economics we give form to our "human nature,"
and through the disciplinary discourses we discover the world:[154] "The
circuits of communication are the supports of an accumulation and centralization of knowledge; the play of signs defines the anchorages of
power; it is not that the beautiful totality of the individual is amputated,
repressed, altered by our social order, it is rather that the individual is
carefully fabricated in it, according to a whole technique of forces and
bodies."[155] Thus, Foucault stresses the disciplinary reach of modernity
and the specific and at times devastating ways in which power and
knowledge combine.

Across his remarkable range of writings Foucault has influenced
many researchers, perhaps ironically at times, in the very human sciences he sought so eloquently to critique. Among them are a number of
human geographers and anthropologists, such as Allan Pred and Paul
Rabinow, who take up Foucault's themes of discourse and practice in an
empirical vein (see Rabinow's essay in this volume). Pred, for example,
draws creatively on the work of the Swedish geographer Torsten Häger-

strand and from Foucault to insist on a theory of space-time. His theory, which has developed over a number of key writings in the past ten years, locates real people with more success than Foucault along what he calls "life-paths."[156] Pred's interest is in analyzing the "lived biographies" of actual people whose lives and actions are mediated through historical and geographical conjunctions and contingencies. These contingencies involve the essential dialectic between presence and absence noted above, as in the work of Goffman and Giddens, as well as the much more abstract and often rhetorical writings of Derrida:[157] "The situations of human activity and social interaction in time and space makes them dependent upon the now-here, upon the historically and geographically particular context of presences and absences."[158] "Situated" human activities under conditions of advanced modernity especially mean both the immediacy of face-to-face copresence and the ability to coordinate what Giddens calls "action at a distance" (see also Boden and Molotch's essay in this volume).[159]

Anthony Giddens, more than any other social theorist, has developed a social theory based on the active articulation of time and space *together*. Giddens regards the period of modernity as distinct and discontinuous with previous epochs of human history, one distinguished by its ability to coordinate social systems in a dialectical relation between presence and absence. He draws on Heidegger, Hägerstrand, Foucault, Goffman, and Garfinkel to produce a flexible space-time grid for human action. Through modernity's unique capacity for what he calls "time-space distanciation," or the ability of social systems to "stretch" their influence and control across vast reaches of space and time, social institutions are able to act "at a distance." And through their ability to affect events that are distant in space or time, modern actors are able to produce and reproduce their uniquely complex social order.

Power, in Giddens's thinking, is inherent in all social relations, but, echoing Foucault, he argues that the ability to control the timing and spacing of human activities and thus the "locales" of action is central to modernity. Across a range of writings, Giddens has elaborated a theory of power which is built into his theory of structuration, drawing on Foucault's notion of surveillance but building in the ethnomethodological insistence on members' knowledge of action and on actors' ability to monitor reflexively their stream of activities.[160] At the same time, Giddens is preoccupied with institutional reflexivity, which, he claims, gives to modernity its unique sense of its own history. This is a version of Marx's dictum of people using history to make history, to which has been added an institutional level. The rising administrative power of the state derives both from its capacities to code information and to supervise activity and, thus, from its ability to control its timing and spacing.

The diffusion of technologies that allow distantiation—road and rail networks, telegraph, aviation, and finally computers—are all driven by the requisites of state power, particularly warfare.[161] Unlike Soja, who derives the territorial organization of contemporary state power from class power, Giddens argues that historically the capitalist labor market was contingent on the prior surveillance of the state. It was that strong, administrative state which made industrial capitalism possible, not the reverse.

Giddens's analyses clearly show both territorial sovereignty and national historicity to be constructed discursively. Giddens argues that the state is an organization which, like others in its genus, reflexively uses knowledge about the conditions of its reproduction in order to modify them. The formation of a modern state is not simply a matter of coordination of the movements of its population. Expansion of state surveillance is impossible without mass knowledge of the conceptual apparatus of the sovereign state, a symbolic order which is integral to its existence.

Moreover, the same processes that operate within nation-states also operate between them. As Giddens has noted, the formation of the state is shaped by a body of discursive knowledge which states then use to regulate relations between them. The sovereignty of the nation-state, its universal equivalence and unit character, is derived from the progressively widening interaction of several states around this discourse.

Contrary to those who argue that interstate interdependencies regulated through diplomacy, modern warfare, spheres of influence, and international organizations erode state sovereignty, Giddens contends that it is through these cross-national ties that national sovereignty is in fact achieved and universalized. It is that discourse of sovereignty which paves the way for another discourse—that of citizenship. The ruling ideas are not those of the ruling class; they are the ideas of rule.

The role of these discourses in the particular organization of space and time—in the making of political geography and history—is clear. Giddens's own analysis suggests that space and time are not just material constraints to be overcome or resources to be used; rather, they have different qualities depending on the historically specific discourse through which they are understood. Thus, new interpretive frames by which space and time are understood are integral to the creation of institutions which achieve new forms of control over the spacing and timing of human activity.

In his most recent work, Giddens has extended his examination of modernity by considering how the distantiating capacities of institutions and individuals alike involve heightened dependence on trust and a remarkable transformation of intimacy and self-identity.[162] Individual and institution are thus constituted through a dialectic of local and global which, through modernity's distinctive reorganization of time and space, transforms the connections between presence and absence.

In contrast to Giddens's continuing critique of historical materialism, the geographer David Harvey uses the master logic of geographic materialism to derive modernity's changing spatiotemporalities from the logic of capital accumulation and class struggle. Harvey's latest writings appropriate the discourse of postmodernism to restate this equation.

For Giddens, money is a symbolic token whose most important function is its ability to "bracket" time and space, "coupling instantaneity and deferral," a device for distantiation; money is capitalist property's condition of possibility. For Marx, in contrast, production had primacy in determining the forms of distantiation. Marx argued that through capitalism, time annihilates space, as capital and commodity increasingly circulate impervious to the frictions and particularities of place. However, capitalism's expansive temporality originates in the logic of exploitation, not in the bounding capacities of business or state bureaucracies, the delocalization of money and text.

Harvey draws on the theory of capitalism's inherent tendency toward *overaccumulation,* where there is more capital than can be profitably invested as a result of capitalist dependency on unpaid labor time as the basis of profitability. There are, he argues, periodic efforts at temporal displacement (e.g., investment for future consumption, accelerated turnover time) and spatial displacement (territorial expansion and the production of new, more efficient spaces). Capital, however, can conquer space only through the medium of space, by the creation of physical centers for production and circulation. Because money is both a measure of contemporary value as specie and a claim to and about future values as credit, this spatiotemporal displacement is possible. When displacement does not suffice, there are economic crises, money fails to represent value, and paroxysms of devaluation, including the centers of production and circulation, ensue.[163] Unlike Giddens's structuration theory, in which distantiation is integral to social reproduction, the capitalist landscape is systemically unstable.

Each of these discontinuous periods of space-time compression, Harvey contends, is associated with a crisis of representation, a retreat from a temporal moral project toward a spatial aesthetic project, from the time of a universal but transitory *becoming* toward a particular yet timeless *being.*[164]

In Harvey's reading, money, as both measure and mask of social labor, becomes the mother of representation. By the early twentieth century, he argues, money was palpably insufficient to play its global role. This insufficiency was reflected in transnational depression, attempted revolution, and the first global war. The failure, the crisis of the value of value, was reflected in almost every other form of representation: language unhinges from the objective world in linguistics, the realist narrative line is abandoned in literature, homogeneous, perspectivist space is replaced by relative and heterogeneous spaces in art (cubism and collage) and science (relativity).

Some continued to fight for the universally progressive through "heroic" modernism of space subjugated by a progressive temporality. But as global space became more abstract, others turned toward the particularities of place, accentuated through the rituals and relics of a national culture, the aestheticized geopolitics of a spatialized state over the moral politics of a universal, progressive class.

The post–World War II, Fordist world—based on massive fixed capital investments in mass production, agglomeration in industrial regions, strong labor unions and state management of national business cycles, and the American dollar as the global reserve currency—provided the material basis for "high" modernity in which form appeared to follow function in every constructed space from factory and office to home and city. Steady expansion of long-term investment, continuous productivity gains, often associated with economies of scale, translated into expanding private and social wages.

Over three decades declining corporate productivity and profitability pushed the system into crisis. Capitalism bumped into the limits of spatiotemporal displacement, leading to devaluation of assets and erosion of the global role of the dollar. Since 1973 the fixity of Fordism has been increasingly replaced by a new form of "flexible" accumulation based on smaller units of productions spread out in space, capable of small-batch, specialized production. Through increasingly rapid technological change, automation, and just-in-time inventory flows, as well as the reformation of tastes and the formation of desire, there have been speed-ups in the turnover of capital, increasingly rapid obsolescence of goods and skills, as well as ever more extensive and volatile geographical restructuring. Against the fixity of corporate forms within which bureaucratic careers and union-negotiated labor contracts unfold, "flexible" accumulation is characterized by production which is fragmented and in flight both from unions and state obligations, as well as the proliferation of subcontracting and part-time, temporary work. Real wages and working conditions deteriorate for an increasingly large proportion of the work force. The rise of an increasingly autonomous global financial system, Harvey maintains, has enabled capital and capitalism to turn on a dime.

It is to this spatiotemporal experience that Harvey attributes the rise of the postmodern.[165] With the collapse of Bretton Woods, money, the master signifier and major medium of spatiotemporal displacement, was unhinged from gold. Because money and the commodification it makes possible are "the primary bearers of cultural codes," other systems of representation are naturally thrown into crisis.[166]

Thus, in the rhetoric of postmodernism, Harvey claims that aesthetics triumphs over morality, flat, ephemeral images over deep, enduring realist narratives, fragmented "language games" over a unified subjectivity. Rather than grapple with the conditions of its own possibility, postmodernism rejects the materiality of social relations as source of explanation and object of politics, turning rather toward an autonomous cultural realm fragmented into a seemingly limitless number of "language games." It embraces, rather than critiques, the new sensibilities generated by more extensive commodification and increasingly volatile and uncontrollable circulation of signs and symbols generated by ever-accelerating global capital flows.[167] In Harvey's hands the postmodern becomes a retreat from "the modernist faith in becoming" towards the "reactionary politics of an aestheticized spatiality."[168] Its ever more evanescent cultural productions—local vernacular architecture, symbols and commercialized spectacles to hold the decaying urban center, the contrived subjectivity of Cindy Sherman's photos—reflect, refract, and reproduce the objective spatiotemporalities of post-Fordist capitalism.[169] Both post-Fordism and postmodernism, Harvey maintains, predominate to the extent that they are profitable.[170] Harvey thus uses the language games of the Marxist community to appropriate postmodernism, but he remains the master materialist, turning capital into culture and thereby extending the reach of its determinations.[171]

Space and time provide privileged vehicles for reconfiguring the relationship between the material world and its representation. The authors we have reviewed all show how the meanings of space and time are integral, not exterior, to the organization of modernity. They all variously demonstrate that a careful consideration of spatiotemporality allows us to reexamine the reifications that clutter social theory, whether society, institution, state, or subject.

These theorists, with the exception of Giddens, all have a tendency to make modernity's space-time unitary and hegemonic, not multiple and contradictory. They people the world with human bodies subjected to the routines of societal space-time, not with subjects living in the historical world. In their writings the theoretical possibilities of historical change tend to coincide with the possibilities of independent consciousness, namely societal crisis when these space-time routines break down.

There are many tasks ahead. The authors all challenge us to see the ways in which spatiotemporal and cognitive structures are co-constitutive of modernity. But to do so we must better understand the historical, political, and daily practical relationships between representation and materiality, the still ambiguous duality of meaning and matter of time and space. We must array and articulate the multiple institutitional, ethnic, gendered, and civilizational space-times whose relationship contains both the seeds of crisis and a better here and now.[172]

Here we leave this selective consideration of recent writings on space and time to turn to a brief introduction to the essays in this collection. In our own conclusion we then offer a few speculations on what, when, and where all these insights into transformations in space and time may be leading us, as we tentatively cross the temporal threshold into the yet uncharted space of the next millennium.

## STUDIES IN SPACE AND TIME

Throughout the chapters of this book, issues of time and space inform new explorations of art history, urban studies, sociology, and history, as well as geography, religious studies, linguistics, anthropology, and so forth. The essays that make up this collection are insistently empirical, in contrast to the primarily theoretical and admittedly speculative tenor of our introductory discussion. Each of the authors works within a particular disciplinary domain with an acute awareness of the sorts of issues, challenges, and emerging trends we have raised but with the goal of exposing the temporal or spatial strata of particular empirical veins of social life. Their work ranges from heaven to earth, from hand to mouth: from sacred sites in Japan and Jerusalem to the profane factories and offices of Los Angeles and Lancashire, from the spaces and times of production and reproduction to those of art, language, and representation. In the process the essays move through the times and spaces that have shaped modernity, from the Meiji period in Japan, through the Industrial Revolution, the Gilded Age in America, to Paris between the wars, to the intense pace of modern Los Angeles.

Individuals, organizations, and societies construct space and time in the way they do *because* of the meanings they impart to them. In art, spatiotemporal representation is therefore more than "visual ideology"; it is integral to particular forms of spatiotemporal practice.[173] Ann Bermingham (in her essay in this volume) shows the ways in which visual representation of space and time has an ideological function of masking the powers and interests served by its material organization.[174] Rustic landscape painting and the enclosure of the English countryside happened together. Bermingham deconstructs the perceptual naturalism of the English landscape painter John Constable (1776–1837), whose paintings, she maintains, "inscribe and obscure the naturalization of political economy and its power to reorder the experience of space and historical time." This issue may also be raised for linear perspective in general, in that the very genre of landscape painting itself is linked to the emergence of land as individual property and state territory.[175]

Bermingham shows how Constable's images of the countryside "naturalized" its capitalist transformation, visually referring to the marks of capitalist property and production while masking their meaning, subordinating them to and merging them into nature. She also points out how Constable's mode of representation paralleled the emerging bourgeoisie's legitimation of its power under the sign of "nature." Subject and object are thus joined by ways of seeing, by culturally particular subjectivities on the one hand and by particular patterns of spatiotemporal organization on the other.[176]

Through language, as the primary human mode of representation, space and time are organized in still more fundamental ways. The very structure of language, its syntax, is temporal. However individual languages may vary in terms of word order, that order then shapes the unfolding dialogue of its speakers in a quite structured manner. As the study of language grew, the Swiss philologist Ferdinand de Saussure developed a unique approach to language, distinguishing between *langue*, the formal structure of a language, and *parole*, the spoken form.[177] All languages, he proposed, change across time, *diachronically*, and across space at the same time, *synchronically*.

The most pervasive form of language is, oddly enough, the form Saussure (and many modern linguists) exclude from their analysis, namely *parole*, spoken language, or, most simply, talk. In their contribution to this volume, Deirdre Boden and Harvey Molotch argue that despite the many telecommunication advances discussed earlier, people everywhere show a remarkable compulsion to get together and talk—face-to-face or, more accurately, in situations of copresence. These authors acknowledge and build on the general position proposed by Foucault, Giddens, Goffman, and others that modernity is organized in a tense dance between presence and absence. They insist, however, that the flood of clues and cues available only in physical copresence, together with the subtle, sequential flow of meaning and intention that is revealed in turn-by-turn talk, drives people to seek out each other's company. This compulsion for proximity also seems to have a nested or hierarchical organization in that the more complex or important the topic or task, the more people "upgrade" the level, speed, and ultimate intimacy of interaction, from letters to electronic mail to telephone to copresence, from large meeting to small committee, from public setting to the privacy of the VIP lounge, dinner table, or bedroom. Their discussion further underlines the importance of trust in that as modernity collapses time and space, apparently obviating the need for copresence through technology, people—whether presidents and premiers or sales managers and their staffs—persist in reaffirming bonds of basic trust through copresence.

Friedland and Palmer (in their essay in this volume) likewise argue that the copresence of corporate elites shapes the possibilities of trust between them. And in consequence it affects the extent to which corporations develop structures and strategies to cope with market uncertainty. Yet, as they show, space has been almost completely neglected in organizational and class theory. Amplifying Boden and Molotch's argument about the importance of copresence, they argue that the proximity of a corporation's headquarters to the centers of industrial and financial power affects corporate behavior. Furthermore, cross-national differences in the spatial structure of the capitalist class in the United States, Germany, France, and Britain may help explain variations in corporate strategy and structure. Thus, as noted earlier, capital may be able to escape the constraints of space, but capitalists cannot.

Copresence and the use of space and time to organize daily life can also be deeply problematic for some categories of people.[178] Carol Brooks Gardner, working in an essentially Goffmanian tradition, has conducted a number of studies that examine women's use and, more centrally, access to public spaces. Erving Goffman, across a considerable range of empirical work but especially in his more discursive and theoretical writings, has revealed the subtle operation of human contact in public settings, treating these as regions of potential interaction that have to be negotiated. In particular, he stressed the organization of "focused" or deliberate encounters and the "boundedness" of all social situations.[179] Central to this idea is the "accessibility" and "communicability" of both the setting and its participants to ratified others and to bystanders. Bystanders are expected to "extend a type of civil inattention" through which they visibly signal that their attention is explicitly focused away from others and that they are maintaining a position of noninvolvement, thereby giving to public settings that disinterested civility so typical of modern street life.[180]

Gardner has used this framework to examine the multiple ways in which women feel out of place in public settings. Drawing on interviews with agoraphobic women,[181] she examines the complex social-psychological perceptions of public space that force some women to live in their bedrooms behind locked windows or to crawl along the edges of public pavements pretending to have lost their keys when, in fact, they are too terrified to stand up and confront the open space around them. Gardner's analysis takes her beyond the particulars of this debilitating neurotic condition to the considerable risk that open public spaces pose to all women in modern society.

Working from a much more abstract and historical perspective, Stephen Kern reads the composition of modern space in the images of World War I society.[182] Through a phenomenological metaphor, he lays out an "interpretive association" between camouflage and cubism, the organization of World War I and democratization, searching for an essential human consciousness.[183] Kern acknowledges diverse motives and technological preconditions (machine guns and electric lights, for example) for these developments. But beneath these multiple phenomena he discerns a common essential experiential structure: the constitutive use of negative space. In art, poetry, architecture, and music, the new modern artists compose with space (or silence in the case of music), breaking the division between subject and background and equalizing the picture's surface. This move was paralleled in social organization by making soldiers blend into their surroundings, eroding the visibility of military rank, and bringing a previously invisible and potentially rebellious mass of commoners into prominence as a politically productive public. "If you shuck democracy of its accidental political connotation," Kern writes, "the result is the affirmation of 'positive negative space' as the foundation for the distribution of power over others." Through an interplay of cubism and military camouflage, a playful yet thoughtful analysis is provided of a critical historical period of this century's transformation of space and time.

Historians are also breaking with the conventions of social history, revealing stories once invisible and generally exploring the fine edges between narrative and history and between history and collective memory. One of the terrible memories of this century will always be that of the Holocaust, the willed ignorance of a whole people, the shame of those who survived, and the "nebula of explanations" offered by a shocked world.[184] Saul Friedlander and Adam Seligman explore how the State of Israel formulated a collective memory of the Holocaust by identifying the establishment of the new state as a "redemptive moment in history." To do this, they draw on the old Jewish theme of Catastrophe and Redemption.

After Jerusalem, the Jews' sacred and sovereign center, was destroyed by the Romans in 70 C.E., the Jews adapted to their exile by holding tightly to their map of history, to the repeated and promised cycle of exile and redemption. The Jews survived as a people, Eli Wiesel is fond of saying, because they remembered. As Friedlander and Seligman show, the Israelis placed the Shoah, the Nazi destruction of European Jewry, into this classic narrative form, the singular evilness of exile followed by national redemption. This sequence had a double reading of its necessity: both as a "secular" statement of historical cause and reason for nationhood, and as a "religious" statement of God's direction of history. This collective memory was progressively brought to Israel's sacred center: as a memorial in Jerusalem and as its legitimating mandate. But as Friedlander and Seligman point out, the tension between nationalist history and religious theodicy provided an opening for forces on the religious nationalist Right to seize the Shoah and reconstruct its meaning so that the singularities of the destruction, of Jerusalem, and of the Jewish people are of a piece, undercutting the universalist vision of the Zionist founders who sought to transform the Jews at last into a normal nation like any other.

Many contemporary theorists of modernity marginalize the role of religion generally, confining its potential relevance to preindustrial societies. But there is no question that religious cosmographies and cosmologies were integral to the emergence of modernity and remain relevant today. Within Europe, for example, there is a historical correlation between Protestantism and successful early nation-state formation.[185] Protestantism transformed not only the symbolic geography of the world but the cosmos as well. As a result of the Reformation, national elites were able to sacralize their own territorial identity, to monopolize symbolic power within their territorial borders through a national vernacular that was a language of statecraft and of worship in "national" churches not subject to the transnational symbolic claims of Rome. Protestantism not only rejected the centrality of Rome but refused the importance of the material site of the Church of the Holy Sepulcher—where Jesus was believed to have been crucified—and of the panoply of holy shrines that littered the Occidental world. In Protestantism God was neither immanent in the natural world nor in history, thereby providing a cleaner ground on which the state could resacralize its territory in terms of its own historicity. The imagining of an undifferentiated space, where no location was ontologically privileged, may have opened the way for the world to be divided up into putatively equal sovereign pieces, thereby destroying the cosmographical nature of local territory in the process but making it possible to imagine a world of beings just like us.

Similarly, it is impossible to understand almost any aspect of the geopolitics of the Near East—from the Israeli-Arab struggle, the Iranian revolution, the dissolution and dismembering of Lebanon, and the apparently illogical defiance of Iraq's Saddam Hussein—without returning to the meanings of territorial conquest in Islam. Unlike Christianity, Islam was from its foundation a conquering faith whose veracity was proven by the territorial conquests of the faithful. The coherence and inviolability of the original lands—the *umma*, including Jerusalem, taken by the Prophet's first armies in the seventh century—provide a permanent template for Arab unity and a mandate for revolt against the infidel.[186] One literally defends the foundations of the faith by defending the land. As war approached, Saddam Hussein donned an Islamic mantle and cloaked his defiance in the language of *jihad*. It was not merely political rhetoric that, as American, Saudi, Kuwaiti, British, and Italian airplanes rained destruction on his strategic sites in 1991, Saddam Hussein vowed to liberate Palestine. By taking back the land, he declared, the Arab would feel "whole" again.

The links between religion, space, and time thus seem critically important in this interdisciplinary collection and are represented with essays by Richard D. Hecht and Allan Grapard. In the two millennia since Christ's death, the Christian world has fragmented into dozens of churches, each of which reads the sacred texts differently. Hecht identifies the intense, political struggles they have waged over their respective rights to space and time at the site where they all believe Jesus was crucified. Just like property rights in any market, their ritual rights at the sacred center, codified in a system known as the *Status Quo,* must be defended by state authority. Jerusalem as ritual center has repeatedly been both stake and instrument in geopolitical conflict. As Hecht shows, these geopolitics sometimes lead to discontinuous and dramatic reversals. The implication of Hecht's analysis is that, contrary to Mircea Eliade, sacred space and time are not ontologically unique, substantive categories but social constructions tied to and dependent on political power.[187]

Grapard's interest, by contrast, is focused on how multiple forms of spatial representation and behavior can operate on the same landscape. His essay offers a sweeping analysis of Japanese Buddhist culture and landscape and a rather ingenious if complex spatiotemporal typology. In *geosophia*, practiced by rulers and ruled, the landscape was read as revealing the relationship between nature and society. Spatial behavior—geomancy, divination—was oriented toward practical knowledge about, justification for, and instrumental control over both. *Geognosis,* practiced by ascetics and aristocrats, was based on sacred landscapes as representations of the mind-body of Buddha. Spatial behaviors—movements and positionings within these sacred landscapes—were oriented toward salvation, the acquisition of a timeless truth. Through positioning and control of the body in sacred space, the esoteric ascetic conquered historical time. *Geopiety,* which began much later during the Edo period (seventeenth through nineteenth centuries), was based on the landscape as representation of historical narrative. Spatial behavior, particularly pilgrimage and later the "tourism" practiced by less educated commoners, was oriented toward memorial. Grapard argues that the Japanese treatment of landscape as text was premised on a Foucauldian episteme of resemblance, in which the world is assumed to be composed of an infinite number of similitudes, in which language mirrors reality, and in which, therefore, nature can also be understood as text.[188]

The anthropologist Paul Rabinow also takes up a Foucauldian theme of discourse and difference with a modern topic, namely, the social constitution of the French city between the wars. Drawing on a larger study,[189] Rabinow tackles the operation of Foucault's notion of biopower in an "open" space, identifying a historical sequence of agents and agencies through which power/discourse operate. In France, not surprisingly, the discourse—shared by socialist, Catholic, and fascist alike—finds its coherence in the highly centralized French state and its historical possibility in the experience of war and colonial pacification. In his archaeology of French planning, Rabinow offers two moments of modernism, distinct discourses through which new state officials of the French capital sought to normalize social life through the conscious, scientific reordering of urban space. The first, *technocosmopolitanism*, attempted to repair the historical-natural place by reshaping it. This discourse was built into a succession of urban forms: the *cité industrielle*, zoned into functions and held together by the symbols and architectural motifs, and the *agglomerations urbaines*, supplied with new public spaces of sociality to compensate for the "desocialization" and social segregation of the capitalist division of labor. The second discourse, *middling modernism*, attempted to fashion an abstract, empty space into new forms by reshaping the norms of a sociotechnical milieu. This discourse was organized through emerging techniques of social measurement (social statistics in particular) in which norms were created as they were operationalized; these norms then became operative criteria for access to housing and other services.

Cities and the urban system rather naturally draw scholars interested in space.[190] Henri Lefebvre was the first major Marxist theorist to spatialize the capitalist social order, to indicate the ways in which capitalism produced a particular space, a spatiality increasingly necessary to its material and political reproduction.[191] Space, he argued, had increasingly become a productive force as well as a commodity whose production was necessary to sustain the profitability of the system. Lefebvre distinguished between abstract spaces produced for domination and absolute spaces constructed for the sensual use of human beings.[192] He argued that any social movement that wanted to challenge the capitalist state must necessarily confront its particular spatiality.

Working in the Lefebvrian tradition, Edward Soja conjoins historical and geographic materialist perspectives to argue that the peculiar temporalities and spatialities of modernity derive from the requisites of reproducing capitalism. The urban derives its form and specificity from the political contradictions of capitalism. "The urban is specified not by production or consumption or exchange in themselves," he writes, "but rather by *their* collective surveillance, supervision, and anticipated control within the power-filled context of nodality" (our italics). Soja, unlike Giddens, rejects the autonomous generative role of industrial technology, state surveillance, and military power.

Soja presents Los Angeles, one of America's central storehouses of "superprofits," as a polycentric, amoebic mass at the center of a new Pacific capitalism, an open-shop metropole quickly filling with Third World workers (and capital), and, as such, a prototypical case of the sort of local and global mix we have been suggesting. He then takes us on a voyage around and through his Californian citadel, Los Angeles, an industrial metropole ringed by military installations whose explosive growth was propelled by the American war machine. Contrary to the conventional image of Los Angeles as a decentered mass of superhighways and suburbs, Soja shows us that the center is "there" surveilling the scene, keeping the citizens in place.

Time, space, and labor connect in complex ways. Benjamin Franklin first proposed the link between time and money, but it took, as we noted earlier, a more critical analysis, by the historian E. P. Thompson, to establish the commodification of time.[193] Indeed, for the society at large, time became an abstract, scarce, and fungible resource only with the rise of a wage-labor market. Although merchants knew the price of time, it was measured on a mass scale only when labor productivity became a temporal problem.[194] A number of analysts have shown that a uniform clock time emerged and diffused according to the diffusion of capitalist wage-labor market and later factory production. Watches and clocks began to show themselves in private homes and on the bodies of private persons only during the Industrial Revolution.[195] The need to precisely control and coordinate an ever larger, more complexly differentiated labor force, it is argued, generated a functional need for an abstract, uniform time which could be specified independently of events.[196]

Richard Biernacki suggests that given the inaccuracy of most clocks and the ability to coordinate equally well through a variable temporal metric, the initial importance of the new temporal reckoning was its contribution not to coordination but to accounting. And although it is true that industrial capitalism converts time into money and back again, Biernacki also points out that the new temporality was part of the general revaluation of time in religion, ethics, and education which *predated* the rise of the factory. Perhaps the new temporality, with its many noneconomic sources, was itself a necessary condition for industrial capitalism to emerge?

For industrial capitalism, time and work became intertwined. In a careful comparison between technically and economically similar British and German late nineteenth century textile mills, Biernacki shows there were major national differences in the way in which working time was understood. In Germany working time itself was bought and sold through the labor contract; in England, by contrast, working time was simply a means to produce a product which workers exchanged for wages. Although both German and English workers were paid by piece rates, these differences in what Biernacki calls "time sense" had major implications for the ways in which labor contracts were understood and that shaped the nature of legitimate workers' demands, employers' strategies to control them, and the kinds of political ideologies around which class struggle was most likely to be organized. For example, Biernacki surmises that because of their view of labor as a temporal "commitment of labor capacity," German workers were more receptive to Marxist economic discourse, with its emphasis on exploitation as the extraction of "surplus" labor time, than were British workers, who long believed that the inadequacies of their wages derived from the superior power of the middleman employer in the marketplace.

The social organization of the labor market is located within wider relationships to other institutions with structures and meanings of their own, whether state, family, or community. Each has its own spatial and temporal frames and forms.[197] A. F. Robertson, for example, shows how the long cycles of reproduction and the shorter cycles of exchange for production interpenetrate in historically changing ways. Contrary to conventional wisdom, Robertson shows how a particular family form— the compact two-generation household—creates particular temporal patterns of uncertainty across the reproductive cycle. The uncertainties of this form, which dates back to before the sixteenth century, provided a motive force for material accumulation and were the engine of protoindustrialization. This discussion links the social organization of reproduction to history in a useful new way and lays out an important set of considerations for a reexamination of space and time under conditions of modernity as well.

## CONCLUSION: SPACE, TIME AND THE MILLENNIUM

We live in risky times.[198] The transformations of space and time we have attempted to trace in this essay are accelerating. Information is now instantly and simultaneously available, operating laterally, collapsing time and dissolving space. At the same time, however, different institutional orders organize and understand space and time differently, and the forces of communication that we have stressed are also forces of domination that contain their own contradictions. In their attempt to create bonds that hold across borders, for instance, states now face new sets of contradictory demands—for protectionism and internal economic policies from their electorates on the one hand, and on the other, for free trade and stable monetary policies from the multinational corporations on whom they depend but on whose local loyalty they cannot.

*Thinking* with space and time requires *re*thinking central concepts of social theory, most particularly the notion of the territorially and temporally bounded and bonded society. Through participation in the global community, our sense of who and where we are, as well as the range and relevance of our actions, is constantly shifting. Thus, everyday actors engage just those elements that intellectual theorizing has often missed of late. The internal logic of modernity is transforming the tacit dimensions of social life, yet our ability, as it were, *to produce* the features and consequences of modernity from within is also fundamental to social order. As the local goes global (and vice versa), we need to understand this new dialectic. Identities and narratives have historically been grounded in place, revolving around powerful and sacred centers. Now the cultural calculus of self, time, and space—that collective "structure of feeling" that Raymond Williams has stressed as linking social groups to a particular place and time—is changing.[199] We may know more about what is happening in Moscow than to our neighbors, but we must operate both in local and global arenas whose multidimensional complexity has become part of the seen-but-unnoticed features of our lives. The circulation of populations and symbols is progressively undercutting the essential relation between territory and culture, the link between place and identity.[200] Simultaneously, the struggle to find a place in the new globality has produced a profusion of separatist movements and politicized racisms.

Individual lives are interconnected as never before, and the result will surely mean that collective narratives will involve global themes. The timing and spacing of individual actions are now constantly in concert with distant others. Those far-off collaborators are, moreover, no longer merely members of the human race in some vague and largely symbolic sense but are active participants in local actions—whether economic, political, religious, or social. When, for instance, students in Srinigar watched Nelson Mandela in real time give his first speech in freedom, in Cape Town in December 1989, they went out into the streets *immediately* to demonstrate for their own freedom.[201] The Russians who dared the Moscow streets during the 1991 revolution will never forget the experience, but for millions of television viewers around the globe, those events have also entered quite personal yet collective memories through the *virtual experience* of the global village.

Some may be tempted to argue that the Kennedy assassination thirty years ago produced the same effect, and this is true. But that was a singular event, an isolated moment of global focus. The difference now, and in the future, is that satellite saturation means *constant* updating of events and even pseudoevents around the globe, in real time and without restrictions of distance. The effect of constant updating, in contrast to occasional world-shattering news flashes devoid of detail—Chamberlain's announcement of war with Germany to the British people, the bombing of Pearl Harbor, the Kennedy assassination—is that it is the fine and continuous detail of distant events, available via fax and cellular phone as well as by radio and television, that integrates them with our own minute-to-minute actions so that the local and the global are articulated as one.

Once isolated or isolationist systems or states can no longer maintain institutional boundaries or borders. The collapse of the current systems in Cuba and China is as inevitable as was the collapse in Albania; satellites are indifferent to dictators or gerontocracies, and with so many channels of communication, their messages can now be only slowed, not blocked, jammed in limited ways, not controlled. States now have enormous capacities to control and intrude on the momentary lives of citizens, yet those same individuals act out and react to local conditions in ways that change the global context of both society and citizen. Democracy, for all its faults and critics, with its many definitions, has taken on new life.[202]

Moreover, with the collapse of state socialism, capitalism has acquired a most unlikely halo, that of liberator as well as marketeer to the global community. However, the gap between the velocity of money and the particularity of people has grown huge. Profits move instantaneously; people do not. Further, the interplay of local and global is tense, more complex than market factors, with individuals and institutions caught in a reflexive relationship. Thus, the tensions between global forces and local action can be as contradictory as they are convulsive. The dialectic of modernity is such that each transformation contains the seeds of unpredictable and potentially cataclysmic change. For all its sophistication, modernity totters on the brink.

These risky times are not, however, "postmodern"; rather, they take modernity to its limits. Nor do we believe that the deconstructionist nihilism of postmodern theorizing can solve the quite concrete conditions and consequences of modernity. Baudrillard's recent and patently ridiculous prediction that the Gulf War was somehow a simulacrum and therefore need not really be fought is a case in point, albeit an extreme one.[203] The continuing (often circular) critique of rationality is also going nowhere, not because modern actors are "irrational" but because there are many rationalities, at both individual and institutional levels.[204]

Throughout this essay we have been recommending an alternative: by thinking with space and time, we become aware of the "essential revolution" that is occurring.[205] We see, perhaps for the first time, that global culture depends on local structures of action. Yet we can also see that the logic of institutions and the constraints of power structures have taken on new energy and an increased ability to bind social actors across space and time. Similarly, the interpenetration of local and global reveals that once-simple causal explanations of revolution, religious revival, or environmental upheaval—whether the recent Russian revolution, the rise of militant Islam, or the long-term consequences of Chernobyl—are indeed simplistic.

Indeed, to understand the new millennium, we need to take today's revolutionaries seriously not as bearers of a history brought forward from the past but as *creators* of a history of the present. It is a present projected into the future from the past, to be sure, but essentially and insistently predicated on the immediate contingencies of the present and on an evolving and eclectic set of possible worlds, some luminous with potential, others quite terrible. Late modernity is, more than any other era, fundamentally shaped from within, its speed and trajectory made possible by the intensified logic of local and global conditions which will increasingly both extend and limit human endeavor.

In the words of Václav Havel, the autonomy of individuals, which includes local decision and discipline of action, takes us beyond classic parliamentary democracy and beyond conventional notions of state control and authority into a *postdemocratic* era. Traditional democracies, he reminds us, have been incapable of genuinely opposing totalitarianism and the violence that characterizes this age, nor have they been able to guarantee each individual genuine dignity and independence. Havel recommends instead community structures that are "open, dynamic, and small" and organizations that are born and die in response to local contingencies, inspired by concrete goals, based on trust and solidarity, and operating "from below" and in continuing dialogue; such organizations would base their existence and significance on actual needs and the active involvement of their constituent members and would avoid the accumulation of normative power. Above all, these small structures would permit and even encourage "parallel polities" whose goals and objectives are part of the aggregation that creates the society, a society with the conscious goal of "living in truth," a posttotalitarian, postdemocratic world.[206] Havel wrote these lines under house arrest in 1978, wondering when they would be read. He ended rhetorically: "For the real question is whether the 'brighter future' is really always so distant. What if it has been right here for a long time now, and only our blindness and weakness has prevented us from seeing it around us and within us?"[207] These lines are part of an essay called "The Power of the Powerless." Havel has now, as president of the Czech republic, crossed to the other side of the power equation, discovering for himself more of the contra-

dictions of the age. Nonetheless, it is hardly surprising that recent beneficiaries of modernity's space-time transformations should be among its
most acute observers.

We all hope to recognize, comprehend, and live in this emerging
global society. Yet the spatiotemporal coordinates of modernity pose a
powerful problematic for the new millennium, at once *NowHere,* simultaneously nowhere and everywhere. We invite you to explore an exciting
range of essays that explore these changing space-time configurations
of modernity.

## NOTES

We are grateful to Nick Entrikin, Anthony Giddens, Harvey Molotch, Paul Rabinow, Sandy Robertson, Edward Soja, and Benno Werlen, for reading this essay
with involvement and insight, as well as for a number of stimulating comments
from the Editorial Committee of the University of California Press. We wish to
thank David Hockney for his generous contributions to the volume, both his
provision of the cover and his discussions of the topic. Without the kind connection of Joan Genser, these contributions would never have taken place. And
thanks to Debra Friedland for the title concept.

We have been fortunate to have Naomi Schneider as our editor, both for her
challenging guidance at critical stages and her considerable support of the book
throughout. As non-copresent coauthors, our own complex intersections in time
and space have shaped the sequential unfolding of this joint work. We have had
a great deal of fun along the way, as well as a stimulating exchange of ideas and
rather diverse disciplinary perspectives. The success of these pathways traced in
space-time is for others to judge.

1. See Terry Eagleton, *Ideology: An Introduction* (London: Verso, 1991); see
also Jürgen Habermas, *The Philosophical Discourses of Modernity* (Cambridge: Polity, 1987).

2. See, e.g., Habermas, *Philosophical Discourses;* Anthony Giddens, *The Consti-
tution of Society: Outline of the Theory of Structuration* (Berkeley and Los Angeles:
University of California Press, 1984); Allan Pred, *Lost Words and Lost Worlds:
Modernity and the Language of Everyday Life in Late Nineteenth-Century Stockholm*
(Cambridge: Cambridge University Press, 1990); for a deeply negative yet per-
ceptive appraisal of the break with tradition and loss of continuity inherent in
modernity, see Walter Benjamin, *Illuminations: Essays and Reflections,* ed. Hannah
Arendt (1955; rpt. London: Jonathan Cape, 1968).

3. We take "modernism" to be the movement in art and literature that characterized the early part of this century, and "postmodernism" to be its response.
Where social scientists have appropriated the latter term to provide post-Marxist
and post-poststructuralist critiques of modernity, the debate becomes quite
blurred and the issues often polemic. It is this rhetoric we seek to sidestep in our
own discussion. A number of thinkers have challenged the historical coherence
of the postmodern. See, for instance, Craig Calhoun, "Postmodernism as Pseu-
dohistory," paper presented at the World Congress of Sociology, July 1990, Ma-

drid. See also Hubert L. Dreyfus and Paul Rabinow, "What Is Maturity? Habermas and Foucault on 'What Is Enlightenment?' " in David Couzens Hoy, ed., *Foucault: A Critical Reader* (New York: Basil Blackwell, 1986), 109–21. "Modernity," they write, "is not a specific historical event, but a historical conjuncture which has happened several times in our history" (117).

4. For a number of very interesting recent discussions and debates on modernity, see, e.g., Marshall Berman, *All That Is Solid Melts into Air: The Experience of Modernity* (New York: Simon and Schuster, 1982); Zygmunt Baumann, *Modernity and Ambivalence* (Cambridge: Polity, 1990); Anthony Giddens, *The Consequences of Modernity* (Stanford: Stanford University Press, 1990); David Harvey, *The Condition of Postmodernity* (Oxford: Basil Blackwell, 1989); Edward Soja, *Postmodern Geographies: The Reassertion of Space in Critical Theory* (London: Verso, 1989); Paul Rabinow, *French Modern: Norms and Forms of the Social Environment* (Cambridge: MIT Press, 1989); Scott Lash and John Urry, *The End of Organized Capitalism* (Cambridge: Polity, 1987); and Jean-François Lyotard, *The Postmodern Condition: A Report on Knowledge* (Minneapolis: University of Minnesota Press, 1984).

5. We borrow these interlocking ideas from a number of contemporary theorists. Randall Collins has recently expressed his approach to the "micro-macro" distinction as one in which "human-size" events are linked together through the macro medium; see, e.g., *Theoretical Sociology* (San Diego: Harcourt Brace Jovanovich, 1988), 397–407. Anthony Giddens, by contrast, dismisses this distinction throughout his writings, especially since the publication of *New Rules of Sociological Method* (London: Hutchinson, 1976); for an interesting recent discussion, see Richard Hilbert, "Ethnomethodology and the Micro-Macro Order," *American Sociological Review* 55 (1990): 794–808.

6. Martin Jay argues that Western civilization privileges the visual, the rational subject seeing with the mind's eye. See his "In the Empire of the Gaze: Foucault and the Denigration of Vision in Twentieth-Century French Thought," in Hoy, *Foucault*, 175–204.

7. Linear perspective in painting developed in the early Renaissance in Italy and was, in its own time and space, a symbolic form of expression of *that* age; see, e.g., Peter Burke, *The Italian Renaissance: Culture and Society in Italy* (1972; rpt. Cambridge: Polity, 1986), 22–26.

8. See Denis Cosgrove, "Prospect, Perspective, and the Evolution of the Landscape Idea," *Transcripts of the Institute of British Geographers* 10 (1985): 45–62; for an interesting discussion of the maps of early discoverers, see Vitorino Magalhàes Godinho, "Entre mythe et utopie: Les grands découvertes, la construction de l'espace et l'invention de l'humanité au XV et XVI siècles," *European Journal of Sociology* 32 (1991): 3–52.

9. Charles Taylor, *Sources of the Self: The Making of the Modern Identity* (Cambridge: Cambridge University Press, 1989), 468; see also Maurice Merleau-Ponty, "Cézanne's Doubt," in his *Sense and Nonsense* (Evanston: Northwestern University Press, 1964), 17–18.

10. Jack Goody, "The Time of Telling and the Telling of Time in Written and Oral Cultures," in John Bender and David E. Wellbergy, eds., *Chronotypes: The Construction of Time* (Stanford: Stanford University Press, 1991), 77–96.

11. Taylor, *Sources of the Self,* 463.

12. Paul Joyce, *Hockney on Photography: Conservations with Paul Joyce* (New York: Jonathan Cape, 1988), 22–23, 34–35.

13. Ibid., 123–24.

14. See also *David Hockney: Some New Pictures* (Los Angeles and Honolulu: L. A. Louver and the Museum of Contemporary Art, 1989).

15. David Hockney, "Vogue Par David Hockney," *Vogue*, December–January 1985–86, 219–59. "My joke was that all ordinary photographs are taken by a one-eyed frozen man" (Joyce, *Hockney on Photography*, 25). Hockney argues, in fact, that perspective sacrificed time for depth and thereby made the representation of narrative much more difficult (39). See also David Hockney, *Cameraworks* (New York: Knopf, 1984).

16. "The idea of infinity was the God that died at the end of the nineteenth century. My idea of the God that's here now means we are part of him. . . . You see then that the Renaissance was part of the movement of bringing the human being to God. But now, we have to get rid of that distance by seeing another way" (Joyce, *Hockney on Photography*, 124).

17. See especially Stephen Hawking's lucid (and best-selling!) exposition of contemporary physics, *A Brief History of Time* (London: Penguin, 1987), and his colleague Roger Penrose's remarkable explorations of mathematics, physics, and their consequences for the study of the human mind, *The Emperor's New Mind: Concerning Computers, Minds, and the Laws of Physics* (Oxford: Oxford University Press, 1988).

18. Giddens, *Consequences of Modernity*, 18; see also his foreword to this volume.

19. Thomas Nagel, *The View from Nowhere* (New York: Oxford University Press, 1986).

20. For the importance of stable preferences for falsifiability, see Anthony Oberschall and Eric M. Leifer, "Efficiency and Social Institutions: Uses and Misuses of Economic Reasoning in Sociology," *Annual Review of Sociology* 13 (1987): 233–53.

21. See also Roger Friedland and A. F. Robertson, "Beyond the Marketplace," in Roger Friedland and A. F. Robertson, eds., *Beyond the Marketplace: Rethinking Economy and Society* (New York: Aldine de Gruyter, 1990), 3–52.

22. See Johannes Fabian, *Time and the Other: How Anthropology Makes Its Object* (New York: Columbia University Press, 1983). Fabian speaks of the way in which the technique of the ethnographic present denies coevality. Anthropology, in this view, is understood not as a science of the "other" but as an integral part of an effort to construct our own position in the world. See also George Marcus, "Past, Present, and Emergent Identities: Requirements for Ethnographies of Late Twentieth-century Modernity Worldwide," in Scott Lash and Jonathon Friedman, eds., *Modernity and Identity* (Oxford: Basil Blackwell, 1992), 309–30.

The other was also out "there," as though it had no relation to other peoples in other places, and its "thereness" had not been materially and ideally constructed by here. Akhil Gupta and James Ferguson, "Beyond 'Culture': Space, Identity, and the Politics of Difference," *Cultural Anthropology* 7, no. 1 (February 1992): 6–25.

23. This earlier, generally structural-functional tendency within anthropol-

ogy has, however, given rise to an important corrective; see, e.g., Eric Wolf, *Europe and the People Without History* (Berkeley and Los Angeles: University of California Press, 1982); Marshall Sahlins, *Islands of History* (Chicago: University of Chicago Press, 1985).

24. *Male* elites, we add, since women were mere ornaments to the moments recorded by such history; see, e.g., Sheila Rowbotham, *Hidden from History: Three Hundred Years of Women's Oppression and the Fight Against It* (London: Pluto Press, 1974).

25. On the Annales school, see Lynn Hunt, "French History in the Last Twenty Years: The Rise and Fall of the *Annales* Paradigm," *Journal of Contemporary History* 21 (1987): 209–24.

26. Pitirim Sorokin, *Social and Cultural Dynamics*, vol. 4 (New York: Bedminster, 1941); Sorokin, *Sociocultural Causality, Space, Time* (Durham: Duke University Press, 1943); Barry Schwartz, "Waiting, Exchange, and Power: The Distribution of Time in Social Circles," *American Journal of Sociology* 79 (1974): 841–71. See also the penetrating work of Eviatar Zerubavel: "The French Republican Calendar: A Case Study in the Sociology of Time," *American Sociological Review* 42 (1976): 868–77; "Private Time and Public Time: The Temporal Structure of Social Accessibility and Professional Commitments," *Social Forces* 58 (1979): 38–58; see also note 35 below.

27. See, for example, Talcott Parsons, *The Social System* (New York: Free, 1951), in which time is primarily understood as a resource; compare the theoretical approach of Giddens, *Constitution of Society;* Barbara Adam, *Time and Social Theory* (Cambridge: Polity, 1990).

28. See Deirdre Boden, "People Are Talking: Conversation Analysis and Symbolic Interaction," in Howard S. Becker and Michal M. McCall, eds., *Symbolic Interaction and Cultural Studies* (Chicago: University of Chicago Press, 1990), 244–74.

29. See, for example, Nigel J. Thrift, "On the Determination of Social Action in Time and Space," *Society and Space* 1, no. 1 (1983): 23–57.

30. See Charles Li, "Ancestor-Descendent and Cultural-Linguistic Relativity," in Sandra Thompson and M. Shibutani, eds., *A Tribute to Charles Fillmore* (Amsterdam: John Benjamin's Publishing, forthcoming).

31. Giddens, *Consequences of Modernity*, 12–13.

32. Anthony Giddens, *Central Problems in Social Theory* (Berkeley and Los Angeles: University of California Press, 1979), and Soja, *Postmodern Geographies.*

33. See Habermas, "Modernity's Consciousness of Time and Its Need for Self-reassurance," in his *Philosophical Discourses,* 1–22.

34. In history, see, for example, the work of Hayden White, *The Content of Form: Narrative Discourse and Historical Representation* (Baltimore: Johns Hopkins University Press, 1987). In geography, see, for example, Denis Cosgrove and Stephen Daniels, eds., *The Iconography of Landscape* (Cambridge: Cambridge University Press, 1988).

35. See especially the work of Eviatar Zerubavel: "Timetables and Scheduling: On the Social Organization of Time," *Sociological Inquiry* 46 (1976): 48–90; *Hidden Rhythms: Schedules and Calendars in Social Life* (Berkeley and Los Angeles: University of California Press, 1981); earlier writings include W. E. Moore, *Man,*

*Time, and Society* (New York: Wiley, 1963), and F. H. Colson, *The Week* (Cambridge: Cambridge University Press, 1926).

36. Social theory thus has the problem of contending with real, live bodies "bumping about" in time and space; the problem is unavoidable, yet most writers finesse it into abstract theorizing. We are indebted to Harold Garfinkel for underlining this point for us.

37. Colin Renfrew, *Archaeology and Language: The Puzzle of Indo-European Origins* (London: Jonathan Cape, 1988).

38. Walter J. Ong, *Interfaces of the Word* (Ithaca: Cornell University Press, 1977); Harold A. Innes, *Empire and Communication* (Toronto: University of Toronto Press, 1950).

39. For a most illuminating discussion of the role of writing, see Jack Goody, *The Logic of Writing and the Organization of Society* (Cambridge: Cambridge University Press, 1986).

40. Goody, "Time of Telling"; Goody also challenges the prevalence of narrative in nonliterate cultures, arguing they tend to be confined to authoritative contexts and reflect the ethnographer's desire for texts.

41. For a discussion of the importance of Roman roads see, e.g., Victor W. von Hagen, *Le grande strade di Roma nel mondo* (London: Newton Compton, 1978). Murray Edelman's examination of the symbolic force of language remains one of the best: *The Symbolic Uses of Politics* (Urbana: University of Illinois Press, 1964).

42. Umberto Eco, *I limiti dell'interpretazione* (Milan: Bompiani, 1990), 42.

43. Innes, *Empire and Communication;* see also Harold A. Innes, *The Bias of Communication* (Toronto: University of Toronto Press, 1951).

44. We are indebted to Bernard Conein for illuminating this point for us.

45. See Jacques LeGoff, *Time, Work and Culture in the Middle Ages* (Chicago: University of Chicago Press, 1980).

46. Ibid.

47. Max Weber, *The Protestant Ethic and The Spirit of Capitalism* (New York: Scribners, 1958). Not a few people have argued that it is the failure to imagine the future, to value it, to see it as a condition which can be manipulated, predicted, or prepared for that marked off "underdeveloped" peoples—whether they be Africans who fail to maximize the output of their fields, Mexican Americans who did not encourage their children to study, or black Americans who fail to save. See, for example, David C. McClelland, *The Achieving Society* (New York: Irvington, 1975). While some might argue that these temporal orientations are rational adaptations to a structure of limited opportunities, a stratagem to minimize maximum losses, they raise the question of how views of time shape the organization of the economy. Pierre Bourdieu, for example, has taken a materialist approach to temporal orientation in what he called the "causality of the probable," in which the probabilities which attach to movements within the social structure are internalized as dispositions and expectations which serve to reproduce the past in the present. Giddens, by contrast, has recently emphasized the notion of "colonizing of the future" (*Modernity and Self-Identity: Self and Identity in the Late Modern Age* [Cambridge: Polity, 1992], 114), and it would certainly seem that the sweep of democracy we are observing has the counterfactual qual-

ity that builds possible worlds out into the future, rather than tradition-bound encampments of the past in the present.

48. See, e.g., Frank Dobbin, "The Institutionalization of the State: Industrial Policy in Britain, France, and the United States," Ph.D. diss., Stanford University, 1987.

49. Zerubavel, "Timetables and Scheduling." See also Zerubavel, *Hidden Rhythms.*

50. See Janet Gouldner Ver Plank, "Between Myth and Moment: The American Cowboy, 1865–1885," Ph.D. diss., Washington University, St. Louis, 1988.

51. Alfred D. Chandler, Jr., *Scale and Scope: The Dynamics of Industrial Capitalism* (Cambridge: Harvard University Press, 1990).

52. E. P. Thompson, "Time, Work-Discipline, and Industrial Capitalism," *Past and Present* 38 (1967): 56–97.

53. Murray Melbin, "Night as Frontier," *American Sociological Review* 43 (1978): 3–22; see also Henri Lefebvre, *La vie quotidienne dans le monde moderne* (Paris: Editions Gallimard, 1968).

54. See, for example, the changing meaning of news and locale in Susan R. Brooker-Gross, "The Changing Concept of Place in the News," in Jacqueline Burgess and John R. Gold, eds., *Geography, the Media, and Popular Culture* (London: Croom Helm, 1985); for earlier classics, see also Harold A. Innes, *Bias of Communication;* Marshall McLuhan, *The Gutenberg Galaxy: The Making of Typographic Man* (Toronto: University of Toronto Press, 1964); Michael Schudson, *Discovering the News: A Social History of Newspapers* (New York: Basic, 1978); and for provocative recent treatments of the whole issue of information and speed of communication, see John B. Thompson, *Ideology and Modern Culture: Critical Social Theory in the Era of Mass Communication* (Cambridge: Polity, 1990), and Mark Poster, *The Mode of Information: Poststructuralism and Social Context* (Cambridge: Cambridge University Press, 1990).

55. See T. K. Hareven, *Family Time and Industrial Time* (Cambridge: Cambridge University Press, 1982).

56. We are indebted to Janet Wolff for pointing this out to us.

57. William T. Bielby and James N. Baron, "A Woman's Place Is with Other Women: Sex Segregation Within Organizations," in Barbara F. Reskin, ed., *Sex Segregation in the Workplace: Trends, Explanations, Remedies* (Washington, D.C.: National Academy Press, 1984), 27–55.

58. See Hanns-Georg Brose, "Coping with Instability: The Emergence of New Biographical Patterns," *Life Stories/Récits de vie* 5 (1989): 3; for a more general and highly informative discussion of these interlocking themes of modernity, see Berman, *All That Is Solid Melts into Air.* Giddens has also recently exposed a number of these themes in terms of personal identity in *Modernity and Self-Identity* (Cambridge: Polity, 1991).

59. See also her more expanded discussion in chapter 1 of *The Script of Life in Modern Society: Entry into Adulthood in a Changing World* (Chicago: University of Chicago Press, 1989).

60. Michael Storper and Richard Walker, *Capitalist Imperative: Territory, Technology, and Capitalist Growth* (Oxford: Basil Blackwell, 1989); Neil Fligstein, *Transformation of Corporate Control* (Cambridge: Harvard University Press, 1990); Ar-

thur Stinchcombe, *Information and Organization* (Berkeley and Los Angeles: University of California Press, 1990).

61. Hareven, *Family Time and Industrial Time.*

62. See Deirdre Boden, *The Business of Talk: Organizations in Action* (Cambridge: Polity, in press), ch. 7.

63. See, e.g., Habermas, *Philosophical Discourses;* Bauman, *Modernity and Ambivalence.*

64. This is what Giddens terms "colonizing the future" in, e.g., *Consequences of Modernity.* See also note 47 above.

65. Michel Foucault, *The Archaeology of Knowledge and the Discourse on Language* (New York: Harper, 1969).

66. "No ruling group and no society . . . can function without possessing some form of historical consciousness satisfactory to itself"; in Isaac Deutscher, *The Unfinished Revolution: Russia 1917–1967* (London: Oxford University Press, 1967), 103.

After the French Revolution, the new elites fashioned a new calendar and a new rational and egalitarian geographic partitioning of France. See Eviatar Zerubavel, "Timetables and Scheduling"; *Hidden Rhythms;* and William H. Sewell, "Ideologies and Social Revolutions: Reflections on the French Case," *Journal of Modern History* 57, no. 1 (1985): 57–85.

67. Burke, 1980.

68. Anthony Giddens, *The Nation State and Violence* (Berkeley and Los Angeles: University of California Press, 1985), 212.

69. Not surprisingly, the critique of the notion of progress has been associated with, as Adam Seligman puts it, the "destructuring of the Cartesian ego"; "Towards a Reinterpretation of Modernity in an Age of Postmodernity," in Bryan Turner, ed., *Theories of Modernity and Postmodernity* (London: Sage, 1992), 119. Seligman argues that it was the future image of a perfect human that made possible the development of the notion of the individual in the first place.

70. This belief in progress as the perfectibility of man is an Enlightenment secularization of the millennial belief that heaven on earth is possible; see Jeffrey C. Alexander, "Between Progress and Apocalypse: Social Theory and the Dream of Reason in the Twentieth Century," in Jeffrey C. Alexander and Piotr Sztompka, eds., *Rethinking Progress* (London: Unwin Hyman, 1990), 15–38; cf. Norman Cohn, *The Pursuit of the Millennium* (New York: Secker and Warburg, 1957).

71. See the state-centered analysis of Stein Rokkan, "Dimensions of State Formation and Nation-Building: A Possible Paradigm for Research on Variations Within Europe," in Charles Tilly, ed., *The Formation of National States in Western Europe* (Princeton: Princeton University Press, 1975), 562–600.

72. Clearly, we mean here the until recently "Soviet" socialist countries, as well as China and other Soviet-style socialist societies.

73. See especially Bill McKibben, *The End of Nature* (London: Penguin, 1989).

74. For an interesting "postmodern" discussion of the collapse of faith in progress, see Lyotard, *Postmodern Condition.*

75. See, e.g., Christopher Dandeker, *Surveillance, Power and Modernity* (Cambridge: Polity, 1990).

76.  See Deirdre Boden, "The Global Village Grows Up: The Media, the Gulf War, and the Consequences of Instant Information," typescript, Department of Sociology, University of Lancaster, 1993.

77.  Harvey, *Condition of Postmodernity.*

78.  Donald Palmer and Roger Friedland, "Corporation, Class and the City System," in Mark S. Mizruchi and Michael Schwartz, eds., *Structural Analysis of Business* (New York: Cambridge University Press, 1987), 145–87.

79.  See Scott Lash and John Urry, *The End of Organized Capitalism* (Cambridge: Polity, 1987), 306–7. See also the work of Manuel Castells, "High Technology, Economic Restructuring, and the Urban-Regional Process in the United States," in Castells, ed., *High Technology, Space, and Society* (Beverly Hills: Sage, 1985).

80.  Scott and Lash, *End of Organized Capitalism.*

81.  For the continuing importance of industrially specific "home" conditions, see Michael Porter, *The Competitive Advantage of Nations* (New York: Free, 1990). For the rise of a stateless world firm, see Kenichi Ohmae, *The Borderless World* (New York: Harper Business, 1990). For a macabre vision of the "justice" of the future multicorporate globe, see the movie *Rollerball.*

82.  ₁ndeed, it appears that intraregional inequalities in wages and working conditions have been increasing in a number of nations at the same time that interregional differentials decline.

83.  See also Manuel Castells, *The City and the Grass Roots* (Berkeley and Los Angeles: University of California Press, 1983), and Michael Hechter, *Internal Colonialism: The Celtic Fringe in British National Development, 1536–1966* (Berkeley and Los Angeles: University of California Press, 1975).

84.  Poster, *Mode of Information.*

85.  Stephen Kern, *The Culture of Time and Space, 1880–1918* (London: Weidenfeld and Nicolson, 1983); David Harvey, *Condition of Postmodernity.*

86.  See, for example, Joshua Meyrowitz, *No Sense of Place: The Impact of Electronic Media on Social Behavior* (New York: Oxford University Press, 1985); see also Shosana Zuboff, *In the Age of the Smart Machine* (New York: Basic, 1988).

87.  Now, in the words of Associated Press, "there's a service that lets your fingers do the walking all the way to St. Peter's," with the Vatican collecting half the charge on the call and thus creating "the world's first electronic collection plate" (*International Herald Tribune,* 27 September 1991, 1).

88.  The war photographer Derek Hudson set up his own desert processing lab and "with a Hasselblad transmitter, sent pictures by satellite direct to his London office" of the French agency Sygma (according to John G. Morris, "War as a Photo Opportunity," *International Herald Tribune,* 27 September 1991, 12); for a fuller discussion of the media and war propaganda during the Gulf crisis, see Philip M. Taylor, *War and the Media: Propaganda and Persuasion in the Gulf War* (Manchester: Manchester University Press, 1992).

89.  During the Russian coup, for example, eyewitness accounts of the dramatic events at Moscow's "White House" were flashed via electronic mail networks from "the Baltic republics to the Ukraine to the Far-Eastern city of Khabarovsk" (John C. Ausland, "Tales of Electronic Resistance," *International Herald Tribune,* 25 September 1991, 5).

90. A number of European newspapers have been reporting regularly on this "burning issue" of the World Health Organization, in contrast to notable silence in the United States, where organs from Third World children have brought medical technology to an especially sad advance; see, e.g., Chris Hedges, "Cairo's Poor Offer Their Own Kidneys for Cash," *International Herald Tribune*, 24 September 1991, 1.

91. Michael R. Gordon, "GIs Ill-Suited for Boredom," *International Herald Tribune*, 4 September 1990.

92. See, e.g., Goody, *Logic of Writing*.

93. This is surely Foucault's central point in *Discipline and Punish*.

94. Steward Brand, *The Media Lab: Inventing the Future at M.I.T.* (New York: Penguin, 1987).

95. Within a month, the media world was saluting the BBC World Service by awarding it the coveted President's Prize in the "Prix d'Italia" series (1991).

96. Norman Macrae, "Banks in Trouble: Sweaty Brows, Slippery Fingers," *The Economist*, 8 September 1990, 21–24.

97. For example, a colleague in the Netherlands reports that one of the most successful investors in that small country is a retired physician living in a small Dutch town who does his own analysis and trades from his home computer. This is but one example of the decentralization and distantiation of information and action in late modernity. We thank Gerhard Meerthens for pinpointing this one for us.

98. Georg Simmel, *The Philosophy of Money* (London: Routledge and Kegan Paul, 1978); see also Jürgen Habermas, "The Normative Content of Modernity," in *Philosophical Discourses*, 336–67.

99. We are indebted to Reza Zafari and Daniel Gabay, who explained computer-controlled exchanges to us.

100. Deirdre Boden, "Reinventing the Global Village: Communication and the Revolutions of 1989," typescript, European University Institute, Florence, 1991.

101. Ibid., 16.

102. We are indebted here to discussions with Harvey Molotch in Santa Barbara and, in the same vein but another time zone, exchanges with Michael MccGwire at Cambridge; see also MccGwire, *Perestroika and Soviet National Security* (Washington, D.C.: Brookings Institution, 1990).

103. For a more extended discussion of the media and globalization, see Boden, "Global Village Grows Up."

104. Maureen Dowd, "Washington Goes to War, Besieging the TV Set," *New York Times*, 29 January 1991.

105. Taylor, *War and the Media*, 275–77.

106. Foucault, 154 (our translation).

107. A passing phrase borrowed from Giddens, *Consequences of Modernity*, 90.

108. See, e.g., E. E. Evans-Pritchard, *The Nuer* (London: Chatto and Windus, 1961); Claude Levi-Strauss, *Anthropologie structurale* (1958; rpt. Paris: Librarie Plon, 1974).

109. See Eviatar Zerbavel's discussion in *Hidden Rhythms*, 8–12; for an elegant discussion of time across time, see also Murray Wax, "Ancient Judaism and the Protestant Ethic," *American Journal of Sociology* 65 (1960): 449–55.

110. Marcel Mauss, *The Gift: The Form and Reason for Exchange in Archaic Societies* (1926; rpt. London: Routledge, 1990).

111. For an interesting discussion, see Merleau-Ponty, "De Mauss à Claude Lévi-Strauss," in his *Signes* (Paris: Gallimard, 1960), 141–57. Merleau-Ponty offers a rather similar interpretation of the "gift": namely, that rather than exchange being dictated *by* society, it is instead society in action ("en acte" [145–46]). As with Bourdieu, the obligatory quality of gift exchange described by Mauss is understood instead as symbolic and as part of a system of social differentiation.

112. Pierre Bourdieu, *Outline of a Theory of Practice* (Cambridge: Cambridge University Press, 1977), 171, 180, and Bourdieu, *Le sens pratique* (Paris: Editions de Minuit, 1980). The same "misrecognition" derived from this temporal gap would seem to apply to the opprobrium heaped on *speculation* in contemporary markets.

In his studies of the Balinese, Clifford Geertz provides a contrasting example that makes the same kind of point. Geertz identifies the multiplicity of nonsynchronized calendrical cycles which not only display but *generate* particular sensibilities, in this case an atomized and nondirectional time. This view of time, he argues, is integral to the highly ascriptive social structure of traditional Bali in which persons are subordinated to roles regulated according to highly formalized, routinized temporal cycles. See Geertz, "Person, Time, and Conduct in Bali," in his *The Interpretation of Cultures* (New York: Basic, 1973), 360–411.

113. Pierre Bourdieu, *Distinction: A Social Critique of the Judgment of Taste* (Cambridge: Harvard University Press, 1984).

114. Pierre Bourdieu, *The Logic of Practice* (Stanford: Stanford University Press, 1990), 68–79.

115. For an extended review of Bourdieu, see Roger Friedland, "Mapping the Space of Pierre Bourdieu," typescript, Department of Sociology, University of California, Santa Barbara, 1991.

116. Ibid.

117. Bourdieu, *Outline*, 141–43.

118. Ibid., 163.

119. Ibid., 164.

120. This position is presented most recently in Pierre Bourdieu, *Réponses: Pour une anthropologie réflexive*, with Loïc J. D. Wacquant (Paris: Editions du Seuil, 1992), 52–54.

121. Martin Heidegger, *Being and Time* (1927; New York: Harper and Row, 1962); see also *On Time and Being*.

122. See also Hans-Georg Gadamer's discussion of *Dasein* in "Heidegger's Later Philosophy," in his *Philosophical Hermeneutics*, trans. and ed. by David E. Linge (Berkeley and Los Angeles: University of California Press, 1976), 213–28.

123. Heidegger, *Being and Time*, 51.

124. Ibid., 64–73.

125. Fred Dallmayr, *Life-World, Modernity and Critique: Paths Between Heidegger and the Frankfurt School* (Cambridge: Polity, 1991), 51.

126. See, e.g., Maurice Merleau-Ponty, "Temps historique, espace historique," in his *Le visible et l'invisible* (Paris: Editions Gallimard, 1964), 312.

127. Merleau-Ponty, *Le visible et l'invisible*, 51; see also extensive discussions

of what Merleau-Ponty calls the "retrospective illusion" of the "thereness" of the world in *Phénoménologie de la perception* (Paris: Editions Gallimard, 1945).

128. Martin Heidegger's work remains the classic here; see also Henri Bergson, *Essai sur les données immediates de la conscience* (Paris: Presses Universitaires de France, 1927); Michael Polanyi, *The Tacit Dimension* (New York: Doubleday, 1966); and, in a more sociological vein, the work of Harold Garfinkel, *Studies in Ethnomethodology* (Englewood Cliffs, N.J.: Prentice Hall, 1967), and Anthony Giddens, *Constitution of Society*. For a recent ethnomethodological discussion of these issues, see Melvin Pollner, *Mundane Reason* (Cambridge: Cambridge University Press, 1987); also Melvin Pollner, "Left of Ethnomethodology," *American Sociological Review* 56 (1991): 370–80.

129. Paul Ricouer, *Temps et récit*, 3 vols. (Paris: Editions Seuil, 1983–1985); published in English as *Time and Narrative*, 3 vols. (Chicago: University of Chicago Press, 1984–1986).

130. Ricoeur, *Time and Narrative*, vol. 2.

131. On epistemology of place, see also J. Nicholas Entrikin, *The Betweenness of Place: Towards a Geography of Modernity* (Baltimore: Johns Hopkins University Press, 1991); see also Ricoeur, *Time and Narrative*, vol. 2.

132. Michel Foucault, *The Order of Things: An Archaeology of the Human Sciences* (New York: Random House, Vintage, 1973).

133. The "double hermeneutic" begins here: Giddens's proposition that the work of the social sciences uniquely involves a dual engagement with the social world, both as detached observer and as a producer of the discourses that shape the ongoing actions observed.

134. There is a sense in which Foucault's iron cage of discipline resembles Weber's. It is important to remember that Weber, too, argued that bureaucratic domination was both a material social relation and a claim to legitimacy based on rationality, a claim integral to the efficacy of the social relation. For a fascinating analysis of the ways in which categorical structures of accounting create "calculable spaces" necessary to modern organizations and the "calculable selves" they demand, see Peter Miller, "Calculating Selves and Calculable Spaces," paper presented at Workshop on Controlling Social Life, European University Institute, Florence, May 1989.

135. We might argue, then, that the bureaucratic file is a spatializing technology of power (Foucault, *Discipline and Punish*, 190–93).

136. It should be noted that the French title *Surveiller et punir* (1975) captures his larger argument better in that *surveiller* incorporates the concept of surveillance and thus constant monitoring as well as discipline.

137. Foucault, *Discipline and Punish*, 25.

138. Ibid., 138–39.

139. Ibid., 205.

140. Ibid., 177, 216.

141. Unlike structuration theory, as noted below; see, e.g., Giddens, *Constitution of Society* and *The Nation-State and Violence*.

142. Michel Foucault, "Governmentality," *Ideology and Consciousness* 6 (1979): 5–21, and Foucault, "The Subject and Power," in H. Dreyfus and P. Rabinow, eds., *Michel Foucault: Beyond Structuralism and Hermeneutics* (Chicago: University of Chicago Press, 1983), 208–23.

143. Michel Foucault, *The History of Sexuality*, vol. 1, *An Introduction*, trans. Robert Hurley (New York: Random House, 1978), 93.

144. Discipline, he writes, made "it possible to adjust the multiplicity of men and the multiplication of the apparatuses of production" (ibid., 218–19).

145. Ibid., 215.

146. Ibid., 207, 209, 211.

147. Hubert L. Dreyfus and Paul Rabinow thus argue that "Foucault has singled out the practices . . . of confession and self-mastery which made us into self-interpreting, autonomous, meaning-giving subjects. These . . . practices . . . converged after the enlightenment to form a *coherent form of life which we call modernity*" ("What Is Maturity?" 116).

148. Mark Poster, "Foucault and History," *Social Research* 49 (1982): 128.

149. Foucault, *History of Sexuality*, 220–21.

150. Ibid., 243.

151. Ibid., 244.

152. Indeed, he even makes its failure—recidivism—into a functional component of disciplinarity.

153. For a discussion of the relationship between power mechanisms and motives, see Dario Melossi, *The State of Social Control* (New York: St. Martin's, 1990). See also Dreyfus and Rabinow, *Michel Foucault*.

154. Foucault, *History of Sexuality*.

155. Foucault, *Discipline and Punish*, 24.

156. Giddens's notion of "time-space paths" is similarly derived from the work of Hägerstrand; see *Constitution of Society*, 112–13.

157. Erving Goffman, *The Presentation of Self in Everyday Life* (New York: Doubleday, 1959); see also Goffman, *Behavior in Public Places: Notes on the Social Organization of Gatherings* (London: Greenwood, 1969).

158. Allan Pred, "Context and Bodies in Flux: Some Comments on Space and Time in the Writings of Anthony Giddens," in Jon Clark, Celia Modgil, and Sohan Modgil, eds. *Anthony Giddens: Consensus and Controversy* (London: Falmer, 1990), 119; see also: "Place as Historically Contingent Process: Structuration and the Time-Geography of Becoming Places," *Annals of the Association of American Geographers* 74 (1984): 279–97.

159. Giddens, *Consequences of Modernity*.

160. For an overview of Giddens's theory of structuration, see Ira J. Cohen, *Structuration Theory* (New York: St. Martin's, 1989); for emerging debates over his work, see, e.g., Clark et al., *Anthony Giddens;* David Held and John B. Thompson, eds., *Social Theory of Modern Societies: Anthony Giddens and His Critics* (Cambridge: Cambridge University Press, 1990).

161. Giddens argues that innovations in military technology drove civilian technological change much more than the reverse (*Nation-State and Violence*, 237).

162. Giddens, *Modernity and Self-Identity*, 21–22.

163. David Harvey, *The Limits to Capital* (Oxford: Basil Blackwell, 1982); Harvey, *The Urbanization of Capital* (Oxford: Basil Blackwell, 1985).

164. This is a rather postmodernist take on Heidegger's approach, as described above.

165. "We can link the schizophrenic dimension to postmodernity which Jameson emphasizes . . . with acceleration in turnover times in production, exchange, and consumption that produce, as it were, the loss of a sense of the future except and insofar as the future can be discounted into the present" (Harvey, *Condition of Postmodernity,* 291).

166. "Since money and commodities are entirely bound up with the circulation of capital, it follows that cultural forms are firmly rooted in the daily circulation process of capital. It is, therefore, with the daily experience of money and the commodity that we should begin" (ibid., 299).

167. Ibid., 117.

168. Ibid., 305.

169. In David Lynch's *Twin Peaks,* the characters are literally in search of a narrative, and nothing is quite true. The hero is a psychic who sees the future and dreams up the past. It is arguable that film, from the very beginning, broke up the narrative quality of time and space. In Orson Welles's classic 1948 movie *Lady from Shanghai,* right to the end—which takes place in a hall of mirrors—we never know who the heroine really is.

Regarding the "image production industry," Harvey notes: "This whole industry specializes in the acceleration of turnover time through the production and marketing of images. . . . It is the organizer of fads and fashions and, as such, it actively produces the very empherality that has always been fundamental to the experience of modernity. It becomes a social means to produce that sense of collapsing time horizons which it in turn so avidly feeds upon" (*Condition of Postmodernity,* 290–91). Postmodern fiction, he argues, mimics the conditions of flexible accumulation.

170. Harvey, *Condition of Postmodernity,* 344.

171. Harvey thus dismisses Lefebvre's more open-ended argument that there is a dialectical relationship among experienced material spatial practices, perceived representations of space, and imagined spaces of representation as "much too vague," preferring instead the more deterministic links drawn by Bourdieu (ibid., 218–19).

172. See, for example, the postcolonial critique of Hegelian time in Gayatri Chakravorty Spivak, "Time and Timing: Law and History," in Bender and Wellerby, *Chronotypes,* 99–117.

173. "It is not surprising," Denis Cosgrove writes, "that landscape representation has always achieved its greatest expression in periods and places of rapid development in agrarian capitalism (sixteenth-century Venice, seventeenth-century Holland and eighteenth-century England). Landscape then is the visual inscription of new meanings being attached to land as a factor of social production." See Cosgrove, "The Geographical Study of Environmental Symbolism: Review and Prospect," paper presented at the Twenty-fourth Congresso Italiano, Torino, 26–31 May 1986. See also Cosgrove, *Social Formation and Symbolic Landscape* (London: Croom Helm, 1983).

174. This essay derives from her larger study, *Landscape and Ideology: The English Rustic Tradition, 1740–1860* (Berkeley and Los Angeles: University of California Press, 1986).

175. Thus, Denis Cosgrove writes: "In painting and garden design landscape

achieved visually and ideologically what survey, map making and ordnance charting achieved practically: the control and domination over space as an absolute, objective entity, its transformation into the property of individual and state. And landscape achieved these ends by use of the same techniques as the practical sciences, principally by applying Euclidian geometry as the guarantor of certainty in spatial conception" ("Prospect, Perspective, and the Evolution of the Landscape Idea," *Transactions of the Institute of British Geographers,* n.s., 10 [1985]: 46).

176. Regarding "the search for accurate visual techniques of land survey," Cosgrove writes, "the significance accorded to it indicates the importance attached to the power of vision linked to intellect through geometry, and how the principles which underlay perspective theory were the everyday skills of the urban merchant" (ibid., 50). Leonardo da Vinci, Cosgrove reports, believed that perspective transformed the painter into a "divine mind" (ibid., 52). Cosgrove points out that transformations in geometry, technologies of spatial representation (surveyors' charts, optics, photography), and genres of art have tended to coincide.

177. Ferdinand de Saussure, *Cours de linguistique générale* (1916; rpt. Paris: Payot, 1983).

178. See, for example, Carol Brooks Gardner, "Passing By: Street Remarks, Address Rights, and the Urban Female," *Sociological Inquiry* 50, nos. 3–4 (1980): 328–56.

179. Goffman, *Behavior in Public Places,* 151–78.

180. Ibid., 156.

181. The vast majority of agoraphobics *are* women, as Gardner notes in her essay in this volume.

182. Here Kern extends the argument in his book *The Culture of Time and Space, 1880–1918* (Cambridge: Harvard University Press, 1983).

183. Husserl, Eric Charles White has written, tried "to reconcile the idea that the world is in consciousness with its contrary, that consciousness is in the world" (*Kaironomia: On the Will-to-Invent* [Ithaca: Cornell University Press, 1987], 76–77).

184. Primo Levi, *The Drowned and the Saved,* trans . Raymond Rosenthal (New York: Summit, 1988).

185. Rokkan, "Dimensions of State Formation."

186. See Roger Friedland and Richard D. Hecht, *Jerusalem: The Profane Politics of a Sacred Place* (Cambridge: Cambridge University Press, forthcoming); Friedland and Hecht, *To Rule Jerusalem* (Cambridge: Cambridge University Press, forthcoming).

187. Eliade spent his life looking for universal symbolic structures or metaphors—such as center, *axis mundi,* sacred mountain—which he believed were manifested in the construction of all sacred cities and temples. Sacred space and time become unique sites connecting this world to the next, whose organization can be read in parallel with canonical texts. See Eliade, *The Sacred and the Profane* (New York: Harcourt Brace, 1959); Eliade, "Sacred Architecture and Symbolism" and "Barabudur, the Symbolic Temple," in his *Symbolism, the Sacred and the Arts,* ed. and trans. Diane Apostolos-Cappadona (New York: Crossroads, 1985).

188. This sort of treatment also contains strong echoes of some of Jean Bau-

drillard's work, see, e.g., *Jean Baudrillard: Selected Writings,* edited by Mark Poster (Cambridge: Polity, 1988).

189. For a more extensive treatment, see Paul Rabinow, *French Modern: Norms and Forms of the Social Environment* (Cambridge: MIT Press, 1989).

190. Architects too, such as Kevin Lynch, have also been active in analyzing space-time aspects of the ways people use urban areas; see Lynch, *What Time Is This Place?* (Cambridge: MIT Press, 1972).

191. Henri Lefebvre, *The Production of Space,* trans. Donald Nicholoson-Smith (Oxford: Basil Blackwell, 1991); Lefebvre, *The Survival of Capitalism* (London: Allison and Busby, 1976). See also Harvey Molotch, "The Space of Lefebvre," *Theory and Society,* forthcoming.

192. Sharon Zukin has recently developed this theme in her analysis of the contradictions between market and place (*Landscapes of Power: From Detroit to Disney World* [Berkeley and Los Angeles: University of California Press, 1991]).

193. Edward P. Thompson's classic statement on this relationship is announced in "Time, Work-Discipline, and Industrial Capitalism."

194. This is also Foucault's point when he underlines the control of bodies in time and space, but, as indicated, he identifies *discipline* and *surveillance* also as arising prior to industrialism in the disciplinary development of the military, hospitals, and prisons; see *Discipline and Punish,* 135–69.

195. David S. Landes, *Revolution in Time: Clocks and the Making of the Modern World* (Cambridge: Harvard University Press, 1983).

196. Thompson, "Time, Work-Discipline, and Industrial Capitalism."

197. See also Michael Mann, *The Sources of Social Power: A History of Power from the Beginning to A.D. 1760* (Cambridge: Cambridge University Press, 1986).

198. The concept of the "risk society" is developed especially by Ulrich Beck in *Risikogesellschaft, Auf dem Weg in eine andere Moderne* (Frankfurt: Suhrkamp, 1986); Giddens, in his more optimistic essay on modernity, proposes instead a dialectical relation between trust and risk, as discussed above; see *Consequences of Modernity.*

199. See, for example, Raymond Williams, *The Long Revolution* (London: Chatto and Windus, 1961); Williams, *The Country and the City* (Oxford: Oxford University Press, 1977); see also Allan Pred, *Place, Practice, and Structure: Social and Spatial Transformation in Southern Sweden, 1750–1850* (Cambridge: Polity, 1986).

200. James Clifford, *The Predicament of Culture* (Cambridge: Harvard University Press, 1988).

201. We thank Richard Appelbaum for pointing out this moment of modernity to us.

202. Robert A. Dahl, *Democracy and Its Critics* (New Haven: Yale University Press, 1989); see also David Held, *Models of Democracy* (Stanford: Stanford University Press, 1987).

203. Jean Baudrillard, *La querre de Golfe n'a pas eu lieu* (Paris: Editions Galilée, 1991).

204. Deirdre Boden, *The Business of Talk: Organizations in Action* (Cambridge: Polity, in press), esp. ch. 8. On the matter of multiple organizational rationalities, it is striking to find Stinchcombe and Garfinkel in such close agreement; see Arthur Stinchcombe, *Information and Organizations* (Berkeley and Los Angeles:

University of California Press, 1990); Harold Garfinkel, *Studies in Ethnomethodology;* for a discussion of multiple institutional rationalities, see Roger Friedland and Robert Alford, "Bringing Society Back In: Symbols, Practices, and Institutional Contradictions," in Walter W. Powell and Paul DiMaggio, eds., *The New Institutionalism in Organizational Analysis* (Chicago: University of Chicago Press, 1991), 232–63.

205.  We borrow the term *essential revolution* from Václav Havel, who used it more thoughtfully to describe what he called the operation of "parallel polities" that laid down the "structuring" foundation of Charter 77 and, ultimately, the Czechoslovakian "velvet revolution" of 1989; see Havel, *The Power of the Powerless,* ed. John Keane (London: Hutchinson, 1985), esp. 89–92.

206.  By "living in truth," Havel argues that every human being needs an area of personal privacy in which he or she can be authentic; otherwise, we are forced to "live with a lie." It is a lie that reduces "human action—and therefore history itself—to false pretense," and it is this central lie which Havel had sought to defeat, with notable success in very recent years; see Paul Wilson, Introduction to *Disturbing the Peace: A Conversation with Václav Havel* (London: Faber and Faber, 1990), xi–xvii; see also Havel, *Power of the Powerless,* 89–94.

207.  Havel, *Power of the Powerless.* This is our own translation from the Italian version (101); see also the English language version (96).

# TWO

# Time Cents:
# The Monetization of the Workday in Comparative Perspective

*Richard Biernacki*

Historical investigators who study the apprehension of daily time have asked how the cultural framework for perceiving time changed with the development of commercial and capitalist society in the West. Their inquiries have led to a discovery of fundamental interest for social theory: at the close of the Middle Ages the townspeople of Europe pioneered the adoption of a strikingly new set of concepts to measure the passage of everyday time. Urban merchants, scholars, and workers adopted a time metric, novel for the age, by which they could in principle parse the day into hours of uniform duration. The task of identifying the reasons for the advent of this revolutionary framework is representative of the challenges taken on by cultural historians and historical sociologists of time. Their approaches to it illustrate both the original insights and the methodological shortcomings of an emerging family of studies into the history of everyday time's measurement and perception.[1]

The shift to hours of uniform duration near the end of the Middle Ages is of interest for social theory because the institutional setting may not only lend everyday time its significance but even constitute the structure of daily time itself. Until the late fourteenth century Europeans punctuated their day with "hours" whose length varied across the seasons. They divided the interval between sunrise and sunset into twelve parts, analogous to hours. On any single day the length of each part was, to be sure, equal. Yet the duration of each of these fractions of time depended on the length of daylight at a given term of the year. The bell ringers in charge of tolling the community bell prolonged or abridged each "hour" they announced so that both sunrise and sunset fell at the beginning of the same "hour" year-round.[2] The measurement of time, however precise, was bound tò the visible diurnal cycle. Time as such did not pass; the day's round did.[3]

The introduction of the modern method of calibrating hours in a metric independent of tangible occurrences, with units that are interchangeable and uniform across the seasons, coincided with the expansion of urban wage labor during the fourteenth century.[4] In the process of change that led to the adoption of an abstract metric for gauging daily time, what roles were played by the capitalist institutions of work, by the advent of the mechanical clock, and, perhaps, by the cultural beliefs that lent time its human significance? Was there an essential and unavoidable relation between the development of wage labor and the advent of the new means for measuring and interpreting daily time? Investigators' responses—one hesitates to say "answers"—to these questions suggest the need for a comparative method that will illuminate more clearly the causes or effects of time's social fabrication.

At least one part of the cultural historians' research into the time revolution of late medieval Europe has led to a sure conclusion: the technology at hand for timekeeping contributed to the adoption of the modern time metric, but it did so indirectly. As the landmark studies of Gustav Bilfinger showed, the mechanical clock was not a requisite for the adoption of invariable units of time. The sundial, one of the simplest and oldest means of timekeeping, could be constructed without much ado for tracking either uniform or seasonally flexible hours. Indeed, Europeans refitted their sundials after the shift to constant hours to stay in march with the new mode of reckoning.[5] A framework with uniform segments of daily time could have been adopted in Europe at an earlier historical juncture if the setting had made such reckoning socially meaningful or useful.

If the mechanical clock was not required for the constitution of abstract time, neither was it sufficient. The modern clock, an uncanny invention whose originators have never been identified, first appears in the historical record of the West during the thirteenth century.[6] Some early models of this appliance were designed with movable weights or adjustable faces that could be changed according to the length of sunlight to mark variable "hours."[7] Europeans had used similar expedients to extend or shorten "hours" across the seasons on their ancient water clocks, whose core mechanism, like that of the modern clock, ran in principle at a uniform rate.[8] The recurrent adjustment of the mechanical clock to mark seasonally flexible "hours" seems bothersome at first blush. Given the state of horological technique in late medieval and early Renaissance Europe, however, even mechanical clocks designed to announce constant hours had tempos so erratic they needed frequent resetting.[9] Since the historical record shows that timekeeping inventions are adapted to suit the prevailing categories of daily time, several socio-logical theorists, including Moishe Postone and Rudolf Wendorff, have emphasized that a change in the social context must have encouraged the adoption of constant hours apart from the new clock technology.[10]

If both the design and deployment of the clocks are taken for granted, it can seem as if the townspeople had no choice but to accept the new time metric. Municipal authorities in the early fourteenth cen-tury began to mount the mechanical clocks in public towers and added bell trains to the basic mechanism to trigger a chime on the hour.[11] As David Landes underscored in *Revolution in Time*, these automatic chimes presupposed the adoption of the new time metric, because for large clocks with a single escapement it was not technically feasible to adjust the bell train to mark variable hours.[12] Use of this kind of bell train for announcing the passage of day and night was not inevitable, however. Bilfinger, the pioneer investigator on this as on other issues, found that cities which could afford mechanical clocks but not the expense of the automatic chime instructed a toller to follow the clock and strike a bell on the hour.[13] This practice lasted more than two centuries. In princi-ple, the bell ringer could just have easily adjusted his readings by season to ring out correct variable hours.[14] If it was not imperative to introduce an automated bell train, and so the new time metric, the change must have brought other benefits.

*Cui bono?* Urban employers who paid their wage laborers by the day wanted not only to mark the start and end of work shifts in a public, official fashion but also to establish a standard work shift regardless of the season.[15] Where employers hired workers in number to cope with an expanding market and paid them by the day, there the mechanical clocks and the observance of uniform hours often followed. The cultural historian Jacques Le Goff, who to date has provided perhaps the best evidence on this issue, hypothesized that cities which led in the growth of the textile trade, the first branch of capitalist manufacture for export to a dynamic market, also led in the installation of clock towers with bell trains.[16] The clocks proliferated in older employments, too, such as blacksmithing and mining, where entrepreneurs not always in the fore-front of economic change purchased and valued labor time all the same.[17] But the adoption of uniform hours did not offer employers an immediate pecuniary advantage. They already had a network of bells in place based on the old time system that enforced the punctual start of work.[18] In addition, by departing from the principle that work lasted from dawn to nightfall, the new time metric could reduce the duration of summer labor. (In rural districts of Germany, for example, some fac-tory owners struggled until the nineteenth century against the principle that work started at a fixed time rather than at sunrise.)[19] The adoption of constant hours reflected considerations broader than that of directly augmenting employers' profits.

What other gains might the automatic chimes and system of uniform hours have brought? Not greater precision in timekeeping. During the era of transition to hours that were in principle uniform, the mechanical clocks could stray from the expected beat by more than sixty minutes a day.[20] The public clocks proved so inaccurate that cities reset them by reference to a sundial several times a week.[21] Instruments which demanded unceasing adjustment could not ease conflict between employers and wage laborers by providing an impartial means of gauging the duration of work. Nor could they offer an essential advantage in synchronizing urban residents' busy schedules. As the sociologist Eviatar Zerubavel demonstrated in his case study of Benedictine monks, people who sanctified punctuality and adhered to rigid schedules could coordinate their activities with the old system of variable hours.[22] The advantage of uniform hours lay not in synchronization at a single point *in* time, but in accounting *over* it.[23]

The system of constant hours suited time's calculated, systematic use. It permitted an assessment of commitments as if time were not just a resource but an object that could be spent or invested in a standard denomination. Several historians of the late medieval and early Renaissance worldviews, including Ricardo Quinones and Aaron Gurjewitsch, have traced this novel handling of time to educated persons' development of self-consciousness about their individuality.[24] At the close of the Middle Ages people could view themselves as having a unique character whose potential they were pressed to develop within a limited interval of time. The Italian humanists of the thirteenth and fourteenth centuries, the most articulate of the early exponents of this life outlook, extolled the calculation of time expenditures. Indeed, a Venetian thinker of the second half of the fourteenth century advised that scholars equip their studies with a clock.[25] The development of popular iconography also discloses a growing sense that the use of time imposed an ethical challenge on the individual: as the art historian Erwin Panofsky showed in his exemplary essay "Father Time," by the early fourteenth century engravings had begun portraying "time" as a deadly spirit against which people fought to render an accounting of themselves.[26] The alterations in the perception and division of time near the close of the Middle Ages indicate not that people had necessarily become more diligent or energetic but only that they experienced an intensified concern with time's calculated manipulation.[27] With the new metric in place, one could conceive of time "reduced to a standard, the bullion of the day minted out into hours."[28]

If the system of invariable hours did not enable urban employers to increase straightaway the amount of labor they appropriated, it was still of economic value for them. Textile merchants represented the first significant group of entrepreneurs to serve extralocal markets in which demand could rapidly outstrip production capacity. These business people had an interest in measuring not only the cost of labor but improvements in their ability to supply cloth promptly. Workdays of uniform duration gave textile employers a yardstick by which they could accurately gauge changes in the productivity of labor.[29] The new framework of daily time also served as an important symbol of capitalist employers' preeminence. Religious authorities had rejected the notion that time represented an earthly property of people, as the church leaders' condemnation of usury illustrated.[30] The church supported the old system of variable hours. The new, uniform hours marked by the mechanical clocks signaled the employers' autonomy from the church.[31] Indeed, the earliest mechanical clocks installed in municipal towers broke so frequently that it is no exaggeration to say commercial leaders looked up to them as if they were icons of the age rather than simple keepers of the hour.[32]

In a word, the shift to a uniform time metric in the centers of commerce coincided with the expansion of wage labor for a dynamic market, but it also followed broad changes in the cultural valuation of time, even among persons unconcerned about the exchange of labor. If the metric introduced a standard currency for accounting, the reckoning was both moral and economic. Attention to the complexities of the historical record makes it increasingly implausible to attribute the advent of the new time framework to changes in economic institutions or to humanist ideas alone. Nor is it feasible to assess their respective contributions in this instance. To be sure, one could attempt a comparison between, say, Chinese and Western development in the early modern period for the sake of isolating the contribution of commercial labor for an extended market to the development of European time sense. But China and Europe differed from each other on innumerable dimensions that bear on the apprehension of time, including religion, the autonomy of cities, and even the distribution of craftsmen available for learning or practicing clock making.[33] Studies that compare the apprehension of daily time between China and the West, including the well-informed contributions of Carlo Cipolla and David Landes, can show that time sense is enmeshed in social structure.[34] Whether ideas about time not only express and reinforce but also give rise to forms of social practice—this issue the emerging family of time studies has not explicitly addressed.

The question has nonetheless bedeviled the most instructive enquiries into the apprehension of daily time. In his celebrated "Time, Work-Discipline, and Industrial Capitalism," E. P. Thompson associated the inculcation of a more stringent time ethic among the English common people with the transition from self-paced manufacture in the home to supervised labor in the factory. Did Thompson mean to imply that the perception and valuation of everyday time simply mirrors the functional demands of the workplace? Surely not, for he presented evidence that Puritan moralists such as Richard Baxter had successfully enjoined a stricter husbandry of time on the common people a century before the rise of the factory.[35] Centralized manufacture under the factory roof may have created a greater need for time discipline, but its adoption, Thompson suggested, depended on the ethical reach of those behind the pulpit and the schoolmaster's desk to revalue time in the culture at large. Once more, the question arises whether the cultural framework for interpreting daily time can vary independently of economic institutions and make a contribution of its own to the course of historical development.

To address this issue, investigators can juxtapose work settings in which the significance of time differed but in which the economic environments remained alike. If producers maintained differing interpretations of time in the same organizational settings, and if their interpretations led them to different courses of action, then time sense made an independent contribution to social practice. This logic requires investigators to ponder contrasts in the perception of time that are significant but less prominent in the historical record than, say, the epochal shift from medieval to modern hours. Otherwise, they will not be able to pair cases that are structurally similar enough to highlight the autonomy of time sense from the institutional environment (or, alternatively, that permit the identification of the specific institutional differences responsible for the adoption of contrasting outlooks on time). Researchers such as Carlo Cipolla and David Landes have compared Asia with the West to dramatize the contrasts in the apprehension of time between eras and civilizations. Choosing closely related cases on more narrow methodological grounds offers the chance of establishing time sense not just as a window on history but as one of its creators.

## AN ILLUSTRATION: TIME REGIMES IN GERMAN AND BRITISH TEXTILE MILLS

For an extended illustration of the opportunities for comparative research, let us move from the nascent textile trade of the medieval cities to the mechanized textile factories of industrial Europe. Inspired by the example of Thompson's pioneering work on time discipline, historians have accumulated an imposing body of evidence about the development of time consciousness in early industrial societies.[36] Their inquiries have focused on the historical processes by which individuals came to value time's methodical expenditure. Certainly by the nineteenth century most workers in Western Europe had sensitized themselves to this time economy.[37] Yet within this new regime distinctive variations developed between countries in time's cultural significance for production. Can we identify cases that enable us to identify with rigor the independent effect of time sense on the construction of industrial practice?

A comparison of time apprehension in selected German and British textile mills from the second half of the nineteenth century meets the criteria for comparing cases that display compelling structural similarities. In many branches of the trade these factories developed contemporaneously under similar economic conditions. Britain's reputation as a textile pioneer rests on intense, perhaps excessive attention devoted to the mechanization of cotton production in Lancashire at the end of the eighteenth century. In Yorkshire, however, home of the wool trade, power looms did not prevail until after the middle of the nineteenth century—by which time the wool and cotton mills in Germany had also begun to mechanize.[38] A comparison of textile factories which draws on the cases of Yorkshire in Britain and includes regions in Germany such as the Wupper Valley and the Rhineland, whose companies mechanized at an early date, lets one contrast factories that developed within a decade or so of each other.[39] A focus on such concentrations of factories also allows one to compare firms which employed the same technology in the two countries, usually were of comparable size, and as a rule were family owned.[40] To demonstrate that contrasts in the apprehension of labor time prevailed at the national level, evidence from other regions' textile enterprises is included.

Germany and Britain were both world leaders in the textile trade. With the maturing of technology for weaving and spinning in the nineteenth century, these two nations occupied positions as the leading exporters of textile products and machinery.[41] Each viewed the other as its chief competitor in international markets. At the end of the nineteenth century the textile industry still employed an important part—by some measures the single largest part—of the factory labor forces in Germany and England.[42] When Europeans viewed the spiry chimneys of the textile mills as an emblem for the age, their senses had not misled them.

### Contrasting Forms of Industrial Time Sense at Work

Despite similarities in the machinery, economic environment, and organization of German and British textile mills, the producers in each country adopted different views of the significance of time in the exchange of labor for a wage. German factory managers and workers viewed employment as a service relation in which workers committed their labor capacity to the firm. Workers sold the disposition over their labor activity and over their labor time (*Arbeitskraft*).[43] British managers and workers, by contrast, saw factory employment as the appropriation of workers' labor as objectified in its product.[44] The Germans treated living labor time itself as part of the commodity of labor, whereas the British treated time as a means for delivering labor in the form of a product. Both viewpoints were compatible with the capitalist organization of industry, both treated time as a scarce resource, yet they coincided with different practices and perceptions in the workplace. In particular, they organized the employment contract, disciplinary rules, and workers' choice of temporal frameworks for gauging their earnings.

The terms of labor for weaving, by far the largest occupation in the textile industry, illustrate the difference between the German and British outlooks on time. Economic necessity dictated that weavers in Germany and Britain receive their wages in the form of piece rates. Managers in both countries found that they could minimize production costs by paying weavers according to their individual output.[45] Despite this similarity in the mode of payment, however, the British and the Germans arrived at different interpretations of the employment contract for weavers. In Britain, the employment relation for weavers followed the rules that applied to the sale of products from independent contractors. Weavers had to deliver products at a regular pace to their employers, but they did not necessarily have to deliver their own labor time. In Yorkshire, for example, weavers who wanted to attend to domestic chores during the workday or who wanted to avoid overtime could send substitutes of their choosing to operate their looms.[46] In Germany, by contrast, weavers were not only obligated to show up but, having committed their time, had to work on any kind of machine or in any department the factory owner chose. German workers had not contracted for the delivery of particular products but had sold the disposition over their time.

Although the German view of labor may have suited some of the employers' interests, German workers turned it against employers to articulate far-reaching demands. Unlike British weavers, the Germans insisted that when technical problems disrupted production, workers deserved compensation for the commitment of their labor time per se. This difference in the textile workers' arguments arose although workers in both countries faced similar problems on the shop floor.

Weaving mills in both nations suffered from frequent interruptions in production. The factories usually waited for a merchant house to submit orders for a particular run of fabric before they began its manufacture.[47] If the stream of orders became sporadic, weavers found themselves waiting for the overseers to install warps in their looms. Even if a mill had a full line of orders, another kind of delay could stop weavers' activity. On receiving an order, a weaving mill undertook the sizing and winding of the warps and began securing the necessary weft yarn. Since these procurement measures began after receipt of the order, weavers sometimes encountered a delay after they began working on a portion of a warp installed in their loom: they found, to their frustration, that the mill did not have sufficient weft yarn wound and ready for them to complete their piece.

The days that textile workers lost waiting on materials amounted to a significant portion of work time in both Britain and Germany. In Germany the Union of Christian Textile Workers kept statistics on the matter, and its reports show that days lost waiting accounted for most of the time which its members spent "unemployed." The union calculated that from 1910 to 1912, for example, 64 percent of the work days which members lost resulted from waiting on materials. During these years the union received more than nine thousand reports of unemployment due to this cause.[48] In Britain overseers' estimates and the report of the secretary of the weavers' union in Yorkshire indicate that Yorkshire weavers normally lost about one-quarter of their work time for lack of warps or weft.[49]

Drawing on their view of employment as the commitment of a labor capacity, German weavers argued that they had a right to payment for the time they spent waiting without working (*Wartegeld*). "During the period of the labor contract we must place all our labor power (*Arbeitskraft*) at disposal," the workers in Lörrach complained in 1906. "In return the firm is contractually obligated to take care of the prompt delivery of work tools and materials."[50] In Forst the textile workers issued a statement in 1899 which called the worker's time a kind of capital for which workers had to be paid even while waiting on materials.[51] In comparative perspective, not the lodging of the demand but only its design and rationale are significant: German workers demanded indemnification not to ensure minimum take-home pay but to receive compensation for the timed disposal over labor power. The degree to which weavers were ready to contest the loss of time is illustrated by a weaver who went to court in Neugersdorf in 1909. He demanded compensation for having waited a mere two hours when a company official had to double-check the fabric pattern.[52] German workers attached a value to the commitment of time with such precision that when they formulated strike demands for waiting money, they often requested that managers graduate the pay not only for lost days but for lost hours.[53]

Strike demands for reimbursement of waiting time originated in each of Germany's major textile regions, including the Wupper Valley, the lower Rhine, the Münsterland, Saxony, and Silesia.[54] The workers enjoyed a measure of success: reports from the textile workers' newspapers and factory rule books show that the custom of paying "waiting money" was geographically widespread.[55] In the Wupper Valley a survey of thirty-nine ribbon-weaving firms near Barmen conducted on the eve of World War I found that almost half paid weavers for waiting on materials, including sixteen companies which offered restitution calculated to the hour.[56] An inquiry in Bocholt, taken in 1901 during a severe business downturn which idled more than a quarter of the town's looms, showed that the practice of paying "waiting money" could persist during periods when employers enjoyed an abundance of labor. During this extreme slump in the textile business nine of forty-two weaving mills in Bocholt paid workers for lost time.[57]

By contrast with German practice, British factory owners did not offer their piece-rate workers waiting money. Nor did British workers ask for it. In fact, the textile workers' press suggests that British workers did not even conceive this possibility. The *Yorkshire Factory Times,* whose first issue appeared in 1889, published more than a dozen grievances each week from textile factories in a feature called "Echoes from Mills and Workshops." This newspaper had the largest circulation of any weekly in the province. From 1890 to 1893 it published more than twenty complaints from weavers about reductions in earnings caused by waiting on materials.[58] Not one mentioned that the employer ought to compensate employees for the loss of time. Nor did the complaints up to 1914 voice such a demand.

In Germany the textile workers' grievances made their way into print through two channels. Both the "free" or Social Democratic textile union as well as the Christian union issued weekly newspapers in which they published the complaints workers submitted to union officials or voiced at meetings. Thirty-nine complaints about waiting appeared from 1899 to 1902, the earliest years for which issues of these two German newspapers survive. Eight of these complaints included the demand that the owner offer reimbursement for lost time.

The response of British workers to waiting certainly cannot be attributed to a lack of "time thrift" or to the discounting of time as a resource. Even in Elland, a sleepy, isolated village near Bradford, the weavers complained in 1889 that their employer forced them to wait on weft at their shop rather than giving them the chance of "profitably utilising" their time at home.[59] The textile workers' union in Yorkshire reported that some of its members were under the false impression that they qualified for out-of-work benefits from the union if they were waiting on a warp.[60] In Lancashire workers even proposed that the unions ought to undertake the task of supporting members who had not been formally laid off but who were waiting on materials. In the end the unions rejected such proposals because of the projected expense.[61] British textile workers sought remedies for the loss of time but did not articulate a demand for compensation from the employer.[62]

In view of the added expense which the payment of "waiting money" imposed on factory owners, why did the German employers, but not the British, provide it? From a comparative perspective the economic environment does not offer a promising place to look for the source of this variation. A market analyst would be apt to assume that owners paid "waiting money" to discourage the idled workers from seeking employment at another firm. German managers might have had a greater incentive for holding on to their workers under two circumstances: if labor resources were scarcer in Germany than in Britain, or if the skills the owners required were so specialized that they could not easily be purchased in the general labor market. The evidence undermines both varieties of explanation. Factories in Britain which suffered from severe labor shortages never paid waiting money;[63] nor did companies who relied on unique skills from their workers, such as the isolated silk firms in Bradford and Halifax.[64] In Germany the incidence of compensation for lost time also contradicts conventional economic logic. Although the high-paid weaving branch offered "waiting money" more often than other textile departments, it was the branch least likely to suffer from labor shortages. Workers in spinning occupations, which had lower status and wages, transferred to weaving when they had the opportunity.[65]

The terms by which German firms dispensed waiting money also indicate that the practice was not well designed for the purpose of retaining labor. Companies began crediting the money to workers before the workers had lost enough time to consider changing employers. The payments were triggered as quickly as after two hours of waiting and almost always within one workday after the commencement of idleness. If companies wanted to retain labor, they had other means at their disposal. They could offer bonuses to workers who stayed in their employ for a long period, a plan which several German textile firms implemented.[66]

If the German owners did not benefit by paying for waiting time, then the pressure which workers exercised from below probably constituted the critical force in the introduction of the practice. For an analysis of workers' view of the significance of time, it is important to consider the origin of these demands. Could these national differences in the treatment of time have reflected nothing more than the strategies and demands which the textile union elite chose to propagate among workers? Or, alternatively, did they arise as an expression of the everyday assumptions which workers drew on to enact the labor process? An examination of the origin and distribution of the demands for "waiting money" can adjudicate between these possibilities.

Weavers in Germany raised demands for waiting money prior to their incorporation into the factory system. In the Wupper Valley, for instance, hand weavers as early as the mid 1840s won some partial successes in their effort to receive money for the time lost between contracts or for the time they spent setting up the warps for their next job.[67] In 1848 the weavers who worked under putting-out systems in the Wuppertal and on the left side of the Rhine, in the Mönchengladbach district, advanced claims for guaranteed compensation when waiting for materials.[68] They put this claim forward in the initial stage of the revolution that year. The weavers' articulation of this demand prior to the development of a coherent leadership for workers or of formal trade union ideologies suggests that it reflected a popularly based conviction about the nature of the employment relation. Further, the early appearance of the demand indicates that the German definition of "labor" as the commitment of a labor capacity *preceded* the incorporation of weavers into the mechanized textile factories. It arose not from the structural features of the German mill system but from an older tradition.[69]

The demands of the British hand-loom weavers reveal a different view of the exchange of labor as a commodity. The hand-loom weavers in Britain proposed all manner of remedies during the early nineteenth century to arrest the decline of their earnings, including a legislated minimum wage. Yet they never arrived at the notion that the employer owed them compensation simply for the commitment of time.[70] Their proposals set forth minimum piece rates for cloth actually delivered. In keeping with the principles of the exchange of labor via its products, they thought that they ought to earn enough for products delivered during the good weeks to tide them over the bad.[71] Their successors in the mechanized factories retained the same view of the matter. At the turn of the century Yorkshire weavers argued that prices for fabrics delivered ought to take into consideration time lost waiting.[72]

If the genesis of the demand for waiting money in Germany demonstrates that it represented a popular conviction about the employment relation, so does the incidence of the demand after the development of the mature factory system. A strike in a rural area of the Münsterland offers a telling emblem of German textile workers' belief that they ought to be compensated for the loss of their time. When workers in the village of Neuenkirchen left work to counter a proposed wage reduction in May 1891, they succeeded not only in maintaining the previous piece rates but also in drawing compensation (*Entschädigung*) from the company for the *time* out of work because of the strike![73] The demand for this compensation could hardly have been recommended by union leaders, for organizers did not reach this rural area until almost a decade later.[74] German textile workers raised the demand for waiting money in other backwater areas where union representatives had not set foot.[75] The weavers' claims about time were not formulated by union elites but arose from popular beliefs.

### Rhythms of Payment and Production

Unlike their British counterparts, German weavers calculated their earnings in a temporal framework based on the delivery of abstract work time. In both Germany and Britain the piece-rate earnings of the weavers fluctuated severely from week to week even when business remained steady. Employers generally paid workers at the end of each week, but the workers received credit for the cloth on which they worked only on completion of the whole piece. It required at least several days' labor to come to a piece's end. If a weaver had almost finished a piece at the end of a pay period, but a small patch remained, he or she would take home nothing for it that week. By contrast, the following week the weaver might succeed in turning in twice as much as normal. Although the procedure for paying wages was the same in both countries, German and British weavers arrived at different interpretations of the relation between remuneration and the passage of time.

Weavers could cite their earnings in two basic ways: they could quote the wage they received per piece of cloth handed in, or they could convert their pay to a wage received over an interval of time. The reports about wages and working conditions submitted to the textile workers' newspapers in Germany and Britain provide an index of workers' choice of expression. I analyzed weavers' descriptions of their wages from the earliest surviving issues of the textile union newspapers, those from 1890 in Britain and from 1899 to 1902 in Germany. In both countries the reports, which often quoted verbatim the negotiations over piece rates and the scales for remuneration, were apt to cite wages in terms of earnings per piece without reference to time (see table 1). This is hardly surprising since the choice depended on the purpose for which the pay was cited. For example, comparing past and future earnings per piece, without reference to the time required for completion, sufficed to convey the magnitude of a pay hike or decline. The real question of interest, however, is how weavers converted the bare amounts for cloth into a temporal framework to judge their well-being or the returns to their effort.

Sharp differences emerge if one considers the specific intervals selected by British and German weavers when they did allude to time. When British weavers put their earnings into a temporal framework, in virtually all cases they chose the week (table 2). They simply followed the cycle of paydays. German weavers were less likely to choose the period of a week, but when they did so, they had a specific purpose in mind.

TABLE 1. Citations of Earnings, British Versus German Weavers

|  | British Weavers % (n) | German Weavers % (n) |
|---|---|---|
| Cite rate per piece | 44.7 (47) | 28.8 (45) |
| Cite both rate per piece and earnings received over interval of time | 8.6 (9) | 15.4 (24) |
| Cite earnings received over interval of time | 46.7 (49) | 55.8 (87) |
| *Total* | 100 (105) | 100 (156) |

SOURCES: References to specific earnings in correspondents' reports to textile workers' newspapers. For Britain: *Yorkshire Factory Times*, 1890. For Germany: *Der Textilarbeiter*, 1899–1902, and *Der christliche Textilarbeiter*, 1899–1902. The German sample drew two-thirds of its cases from the Social Democratic union's newspaper and one-third from the Christian union's newspaper, corresponding approximately to the proportion of textile workers who belonged to each union. There were no statistically significant differences between the results for the Social Democratic and Christian newspapers.

TABLE 2. Time Intervals Used in Citations, British Versus German Weavers

| Interval Used in Converting Pay Per Piece to Earnings over Time | British Weavers % (n) | German Weavers % (n) |
|---|---|---|
| Hour | 5.2 (3) | 11.7 (13) |
| Day | 0 | 26.1 (29) |
| Week | 93.1 (54) | 49.5 (55) |
| Month | 1.7 (1) | 0 |
| Year | 0 | 12.6 (14) |
| *Total* | 100 (58) | 99.9 (111) |

NOTE: British weavers citing hourly rates were pattern weavers paid for fabric samples.

They chose the week when they also said that the pay was inadequate for the survival of their household (see table 3). The week was the most meaningful unit for making a comparison between the famiy's receipts and expenditures.[76] Workers cited this fraction of time when they wanted to complain that their earnings led to a beggarly existence or, as they often put it, amounted to "starvation wages."

TABLE 3.    Effect of Referring to Inadequate Standard of Living
on German Weavers' Choice of Time Intervals

| Interval Used in Converting Piece-rate Earnings to Wage over Time | No Reference to Standard of Living % (n) | Complaint About Standard of Living % (n) |
|---|---|---|
| Hour | 14.5 (12) | 3.6   (1) |
| Day | 32.5 (27) | 7.1   (2) |
| Week | 39.8 (33) | 78.6 (22) |
| Year | 13.2 (11) | 10.7   (3) |
| Total | 100    (83) | 100    (28) |

In contrast to British practice, German weavers who converted their piece-rate earnings to a time equivalent expressed this conversion in the majority of instances with periods other than the week. In more than a quarter of cases they chose the interval of a day, whereas the British weavers never did so. When German workers used the unit of a day to express their piece-rate earnings, they were oriented to the daily expenditure of labor power in the production process. If German weavers referred to specific daily earnings, they related the pay to the disposition over their activity during this time interval in the production process.[77] For example, in the textile town of Schildesche the weavers who threatened a strike in 1905 informed the owner that "a middling worker should earn with normal exertion at least two-and-a-half marks a day."[78] In only two of twenty-nine instances in which German weavers converted their piece-rate earnings to a daily average did they also refer to the adequacy of this wage for supporting themselves or their families. This lack of correlation indicates that the Germans did not use the period of a day to measure the consumption cycle.

By adopting quotidian or even hourly intervals for measuring their earnings, German weavers applied an abstract time frame to their employment relation, removed from both the tangible cycle of paydays and from the rhythm of finishing a piece of cloth. The vagaries of the weaving process, with unpredictable changes in the speed at which difficult warps could be turned into cloth and fluctuations in earnings over time, did not suggest the day or hour as a convenient measure of earnings. No piece of fabric could be completed in such short order. German weavers distanced themselves from the delivery of cloth credited per week and from the weekly disbursal of wages to analyze the wage they received in return for the disposition over hypothetical intervals of time in the production process. For instance, weavers in Gera who required many days to complete a piece of fabric converted the piece-rate earning to a wage based on what they called the "daily expenditure of time" (*Zeitaufwand*).[79] For the British weavers time was a quantifiable resource, but time per se was not what they sold their employer. As would be expected, therefore, when British weavers looked at their earnings over time, they did so only with regard to the concrete cycle of paydays. They did not invent an independent framework based on the delivery of abstract labor time.

### Time and Disciplinary Techniques

If German workers treated time itself as a kind of property transferred in the employment contract, so did their employers. Their handling of the monies withheld from workers for tardiness makes this clear. After 1891 German law prohibited factory owners from putting into their general till the monies they collected from disciplinary punishments. The law allowed owners to pocket the fines collected from workers for property damage, however. They could keep as "compensation" the deductions they made for broken windows or for the misuse of equipment, for example. Therefore, employers were supposed to separate these two basic types of fines in their bookkeeping. Factory inspectors who conducted audits found that some German textile owners believed that the fines they levied on workers arriving late to work belonged to the category of compensation for property losses.[80]

It would be easy to dismiss the employers' conduct in this instance as underhanded, ad hoc attempts to appropriate funds. But the evidence conflicts with this interpretation. The books in which employers recorded their fines, the very records which the factory inspectors and the courts used to arraign the avaricious employers, did not group other disciplinary fines, such as those inflicted for horseplay or inattentiveness, into the category of "damage compensation." The employers whom the factory inspectors accused of misappropriating fines for tardiness presented their reasoning to the courts. Rather than avoiding the publicity of a trial—a matter about which employers generally showed great sensitivity[81]—they defended their withholdings in public.

The scales by which German employers determined the amount of the fine they would assess for lateness offers another indicator that they treated time itself as a form of property. German textile firms graduated the amount of the fine according to the minutes the workers absented themselves.[82] Many adopted a sliding scale of fines for tardiness which adjusted the penalty per minute to the workers' average earnings.[83] British textile mill owners attempted to discipline workers for lateness but usually did not take in "damages" graduated for the loss of minutes.[84] They typically bolted latecomers out of the mill and prevented them from entering and earning piece rates until the midmorning break or until lunch. By locking workers out, the British owners did not treat the workers' time itself as a form of property for whose loss they claimed restitution, but they enforced their expectation that anyone working for them deliver products quickly.

### FROM TIME IN THE FACTORY TO TIME IN POLITICS

Time sense is not a simple correlate of social institutions, as this comparison of differing assumptions about time under similar factory conditions makes clear. The concepts of labor time that prevailed in Britain and Germany led workers to articulate different sets of demands and their employers to adopt correspondingly different disciplinary techniques. Since the practices, demands, and ideas of workers and employers formed a consistent whole in each country based on different notions of time in employment, and since the immediate economic environments in Yorkshire and in leading textile regions of Germany such as the Wupper Valley were similar, the comparison offers presumptive evidence for the independent contribution of time sense to the development of labor practices and perceptions. The concept used to apprehend labor time not only coordinated practices on the shopfloor but also constructed them.

The German and British workers' views of the sale of labor time in the factory had important implications for workers' reception of economic ideology in their union movements. During the last decade of the nineteenth century workers and employers in Britain and Germany, the two countries with the strongest trade unions, believed they were witnessing a revolution in the labor movement.[85] In Germany the decade was marked by a surge in union membership and by the widespread adoption of Marxist discourse by organized workers.[86] In Britain, too, many trade unions during the same period adopted for the first time the goal of developing a socialist society.[87] Up to World War I, however, most unionized workers in Britain, even those with radical aspirations, turned a deaf ear to Marxist economic ideas. There are compelling parallels between workers' reception of formal ideologies in each country and their views of labor time.

Karl Marx's argument that workers did not receive pay for all their labor time rested on a comparison between the time placed at the disposal of employers versus the labor time embodied in the products workers purchased with their wages. Marx did not assume that the worker was simply "underpaid." He contended that a certain quantity of *time* per day remained unpaid.[88] British workers conceived of the transfer of labor to employees not in terms of the work time they put at the disposal of employers but in terms of the labor embodied in their products. British workers could envision that employers took advantage of them, but they could not imagine that this exploitation was regularly accomplished at the point of production as a result of the employers' disposition over unpaid labor time.

In the early nineteenth century spokesmen for the radical movements among British workers formulated the notion that employers could take advantage of labor because their control of capital allowed them to control the marketing of products. William Thompson became perhaps the best known of the early socialist theorists who wrote on economic theory. Like other radical contemporaries, he contended that labor did not acquire "the whole produce of its exertions" because of the employers' ability to force wages down through competition and because of the employers' control over the disposal of the product in the market.[89] Historians of economic theory have called these authors "Ricardian socialists,"[90] and some have supposed that they influenced Marx.[91] But they reasoned about exploitation in a different manner than Marx. These British authors argued that, on the level of the economy as a whole, employers who received an income without working must be living off the labor of others. In their formulation the owners' ability to profit unjustly from labor derived from their function as middlemen: they exploited workers by controlling the marketing of labor's products.[92] Profit originated in the sphere of exchange rather than through the control of time at the point of production.

The development of the socialist movement in Yorkshire at the close of the nineteenth century illustrates the survival of this marketing theory of profit among British weavers. The textile communities in Yorkshire served as the home base of the Independent Labour party in its early years. The delegates who founded the party in the worsted textile city of Bradford in 1893 counted "socialism" and the communal ownership of property among their goals.[93] Although the leaders of the Labour party and the correspondents for the *Yorkshire Factory Times* criticized textile workers' exploitation under capitalism, they viewed socialism as little more than a means to assure workers of an adequate standard of living.[94] They did not focus on the need to remove unequal exchanges in the employment relation based on the control of time. Until the 1920s the British socialist movement did not advance beyond the "market" theory of profit articulated in the early nineteenth century. The *Bradford Labour Echo,* the organ of the Bradford Independent Labour party, told workers in 1898 that they were exploited because "all sorts of middle-men" cut workers out of the full value of their products.[95] Workers supposed that owners made a profit through "buying cheap and selling dear."[96]

In Germany, by contrast, at least in the "free" or Social Democratic textile unions, the Marxist theory prevailed—that is, that employers secured a profit by extracting surplus labor time at the point of production.[97] The journal of the "free" German textile union, *The Textile Worker*, used the general term *labor* to describe the factors necessary for production. But its reporters used the more precise term *labor power*— the disposition over time in the workplace—when they referred to the employment relation.[98] The unionists in the Social Democratic textile union assumed that workers ought to support the shortening of the workday and withholding of labor time because "under the present system" the exchange of labor time for a wage was inevitably exploitative.[99] The analysis of everyday practices on the shop floor in Germany suggests that the newly introduced Marxist economic discourse could rest on long-established factory customs that treated employment as the sale of the disposition over labor time.[100] A substantial body of British intellectuals tried to disseminate Marxist ideas about time, but even workers who sought revolutionary change in the ownership of production did not absorb this thought.[101]

## THE GENESIS OF INDUSTRIAL TIME INTERPRETATIONS

The pairing of German and late-developing British textile mills was suited for a synchronic comparison that would identify the independent *effect* of time sense. The riddle of beginnings remains: how did the contrasting British and German interpretations of time in the workplace originate? Formulating a response to this question requires a shift away from the local industrial setting. Looking at the whole spectrum of textile factories within each country, the distinctive British and German assumptions about time prevailed in mills that developed under extremely different circumstances. For example, they governed practices in Lancashire as in Yorkshire, in Silesia as in the Wupper Valley. This regional similarity suggests that the adoption of ideas about time within each country depended on the national, not the local, context.

Although the immediate circumstances of production in many textile factories closely paralleled each other in the two countries, the course of economic development in Germany and Britain as wholes were fundamentally different. The differences are too extensive for the same comparative framework to provide a definitive explanation for the origins of the ideas about labor time. Within the limits of an Anglo-German comparison, a tentative hypothesis can be proposed.

The carryover of feudal traditions into modern industrial society has dominated analyses of intellectual life and politics for Germany as for no other country.[102] Could not the feudal legacy have also shaped the cultural construction of labor as a commodity? The compressed transition from feudal to capitalist industrial relations of production in Germany may have allowed producers to move directly from the feudal assumption that labor was transferred in the form of a personal service capacity to the later view that industrial workers sold not a product but their labor capacity or labor time.[103] Guild restrictions on the marketing of labor survived in Germany up to the moment of industrialization. Britain, by contrast, went through an extended period before the rise of the factory in which labor was sold as a commodity in an extensive market free of significant restrictions on its mobility or employment.[104] During the era of artisanal production in the eighteenth century, workers and employers imagined that labor was exchanged in the form of a product between free and independent commodity producers.[105] This view enabled British employers and workers to carry into the factory age the assumption that labor is delivered in the form of a product rather than as a service capacity.

This hypothesis about the origins of the British and German views of time in the employment relation can be tested and refined by looking for two parallels: first, between the outlook on labor time in Germany and in other countries with a feudal legacy, such as France; and, second, between the outlook on labor time in Britain and countries such as Italy, which in some regions shared the absence of a strong feudal tradition.[106] How does the timing of the breakdown of guild restrictions influence the cultural process of defining labor as a commodity? Will these comparative investigations uncover alternative cultural constructions of labor as a ware? Investigation can proceed by considering variation and similarities in commercial or capitalist time sense across closely related societies at similar periods of change. With this modest logic, inquiries into the perception of daily time can hold on to a humanistic perspective of the historical process while they gain the analytic power needed to place them in the mainstream of comparative-historical analysis.

## CONCLUSION: THE HISTORICAL CIRCUMSCRIPTION OF THEORY

Sociological theories about the penetration of capitalist logic into everyday life, such as those of Georg Lukács and, more recently, Anthony Giddens, have portrayed the commodification of time as a generic feature of capitalist society that follows a uniform process.[107] This study's comparison of the cultural construction of labor as a commodity in Germany and Britain uncovered multiple ways of commodifying time, which may have resulted from the tradition of interpretation created in response to each country's historical route to a free market in labor.[108]

A focus on textile mills in regions of Germany and Britain that developed under locally similar economic conditions reveals that the commodification of labor time does not simply mirror the exigencies of the capitalist labor process. It also depends on cultural assumptions that can vary independently of the immediate institutional environment. In each country the terms of employment, disciplinary techniques, and workers' strike demands formed a consistent constellation based on assumptions about the significance of time.

The contrasting interpretations of labor time laid the ground for the development of correspondingly different political ideas among German and British textile workers, as their reception of economic ideologies before World War I reveals. If ideas about time in the workplace depend on a tradition of interpretation and not merely on the immediate circumstances of production, what forces guide the continuing evolution of time sense in the factory? Are ideas about labor time eroded by political change outside the workplace, or do they direct that change? Do concepts of labor time sustained in the workplace provide the essential backround for the reception of formal political ideology in contemporary society as well? The transformations of the varieties of capitalist time sense remain to be explored—and so do the political repercussions.

## NOTES

For support of the research on which portions of this article are based, I would like to acknowledge my debt to the German Academic Exchange Service, the Social Science Research Council, the Allan Sharlin Memorial Program at the University of California, Berkeley, the International Research and Exchanges Board, the Mabelle McLeod Lewis Memorial Fund, the Fulbright Fellowship Program in Western European Comparative Studies, and the National Endowment for the Humanities Fellowship Program for University Teachers. I am indebted to Joanna Bornat for permission to cite from her oral history collection. I would also like to thank Matias Valenzuela for assistance in coding.

1. Representative studies of economic change and the apprehension of daily time that have appeared in English during the last decade include Gerard T. Moran, "Conceptions of Time in Early Modern France: An Approach to the History of Collective Mentalities," *Sixteenth Century Journal* 12, no. 4 (Winter 1981): 3–19; David Landes, *Revolution in Time* (Cambridge: Harvard University Press, 1983); Mark Harrison, "The Ordering of the Urban Environment: Time, Work, and the Occurrence of Crowds," *Past and Present*, no. 110 (1986): 134–68. The debate which followed the publication of Harrison's article reveals fundamental issues in the interpretation of evidence about time sense: David Landes and Mark Harrison, comment and response on "The Ordering of the Urban Environment," *Past and Present*, no. 116 (1987): 192–205. See also Thomas Smith, "Peasant Time and Factory Time in Japan," *Past and Present*, no. 111

(1986): 165–97; Gary Cross, *A Quest for Time: The Reduction of Work in Britain and France, 1840–1940* (Berkeley and Los Angeles: University of California Press, 1989); Michael O'Malley, *Keeping Watch: A History of American Time* (New York: Viking, 1990); Tamara K. Harevan, "Synchronizing Individual Time, Family Time, and Historical Time," in *Chronotypes: The Construction of Time,* ed. John Bender and David Wellbery (Stanford: Stanford University Press, 1991). Paul Blyton and his coauthors offer a bibliography in *Time, Work, and Organization* (London: Routledge, 1989) that incorporates historical research into the labor process and time management.

2. Eviatar Zerubavel, "The Benedictine Ethic and the Modern Spirit of Scheduling: On Schedules and Social Organization," *Sociological Inquiry* 50, no. 2 (1980): 158. The exceptions to the use of variable "hours" are discussed in G. J. Whitrow, *The Nature of Time* (New York: Holt, Rinehart, and Winston, 1972), 69, and G. Bilfinger, "Antike Stundenzählung," in *Programm des Eberhard-Ludwigs-Gymnasiums in Stuttgart zum Schlusse des Schuljahrs 1882–1883* (Stuttgart: G. Lemppenau, 1883), 3.

3. W. Rothwell, "The Hours of the Day in Medieval French," *French Studies* 13 (July 1959): 240–51. For a philosophical commentary on the abstraction of time from its context, see J. Gibson, "Events Are Perceivable But Time Is Not," in *The Study of Time II,* ed. J. Fraser (Berlin: Springer-Verlag, 1975), 295–301.

4. Moishe Postone has developed by far the most sophisticated exposition of the relation between the treatment of labor as a commodity and the adoption of uniform hours in *Time, Labor, and Social Domination: A Reinterpretation of Marx's Critical Theory* (Cambridge: Cambridge University Press, 1993), ch. 5. Other social theorists who have emphasized the relation between the commodification of labor and the adoption of an abstract time metric include Anthony Giddens, *A Contemporary Critique of Historical Materialism* (Berkeley and Los Angeles: University of California Press, 1981), 130–35; Günter Dux, *Die Zeit in der Geschichte* (Frankfurt am Main: Suhrkamp, 1989), 335–36; and Georg Lukács, *History and Class Consciousness* (Cambridge: MIT Press, 1971), 90. Hans-Willy Hohn has highlighted the role of merchant capital rather than of wage labor in the genesis of isochronic reckoning in *Die Zerstörung der Zeit: wie aus einem göttlichen Gut eine Handelsware wurde* (Frankfurt am Main: Fischer, 1984), ch. 4.

5. Gustav Bilfinger, *Die mittelalterlichen Horen und die modernen Stunden* (Stuttgart: W. Kohlhammer, 1892), 144. The Chinese were already constructing their sundials to measure invariable units of time when European visitors intruded in the sixteenth century; see David Landes, *Revolution in Time* (Cambridge: Harvard University Press, 1983), 28. For documentation about the prevalence of sundials in Europe through the eighteenth century, see Rachel Doggett, ed., *Time: The Greatest Innovator* (Washington, D.C.: Folger Shakespeare Library, 1986), 11–12.

6. Landes soberly reviews the evidence in *Revolution in Time,* 53–58.

7. For Italy, see Rudolf Wendorff, *Zeit und Kultur* (Opladen: Westdeutscher, 1980), 146–47; Doggett, *Time,* 61. J. D. North discusses a mechanism which might have permitted the striking of variable hours on public clocks in "Monasticism and the First Mechanical Clocks," in Fraser, *Study of Time II,* 392. See also Antonio Simoni, "Striking Evolution in Early Clocks," *La Clessidra,* January 1955. Craftsmen in seventeenth-century Japan redesigned the mechanical clock so

that it accorded with the Japanese system of variable hours. They introduced two controllers so that the clock ran at different rates for day and night hours. They also simplified the method of adjusting the clock every fortnight to stay abreast of the seasonal interval of daylight; J. Drummond Robertson, *The Evolution of Clockwork, with a Special Section on the Clocks of Japan* (London: Cassell and Company, 1931), 240–45.

8. Bilfinger, *Die mittelalterlichen Horen*, 146.

9. Carlo M. Cipolla, *Clocks and Culture 1300–1700* (London: Collins, 1967), 43. Even after the shift to constant hours established a metric that was independent of tangible occurrences, the start and end points of that metric might still depend on the season. For example, Italian cities that implemented constant hours adjusted the start of the cycle of twenty-four hours to coincide with sunset each day. Thus, recurrent setting of the clock was required even with uniform hours; Ernst Zinner, *Die ältesten Räderuhren und modernen Sonnenuhren*, Naturforschende Gesellschaft, Report 28 (Bamberg, 1939), 61.

10. Rudolf Wendorff, *Zeit und Kultur* (Opladen: Westdeutscher Verlag, 1980), 147–48. Postone provides convincing examples of the priority of the social context in the molding of isochronic reckoning (*Time, Labor, and Social Domination*, 202–16).

11. The evidence cited by Zinner, *Die ältesten Räderuhren*, 60–61, suggests that the automatic chimes were not part of the public clocks' mechanism from the start. C. F. C. Beeson contends that for church clocks, at least, the striking systems appeared with the very earliest models; Beeson, *English Church Clocks 1280–1850* (London: Antiquarian Horological Society, 1971), 33. See also H. Alan Lloyd, "Mechanical Timekeepers," in *A History of Technology*, ed. Charles Singer, E. J. Holmyard, A. R. Hall, and Trevor I. Williams (Oxford: Clarendon, 1957), 3:650–51.

12. Landes, *Revolution in Time*, 77; Bilfinger, *Die mittelalterlichen Horen*, 163.

13. Bilfinger, *Die mittelalterlichen Horen*, 170; on the high expense of installing public clocks, see Cipolla, *Clocks and Culture*, 41.

14. On the hiring of bell tollers, see D. M. Palliser, "Civic Mentality and the Environment in Tudor York," *Northern History* 18 (1982): 86, and E. P. Thompson, "Time, Work-Discipline, and Industrial Capitalism," *Past and Present*, no. 38 (1967): 63.

15. Jacques Le Goff, "Merchant's Time and Church's Time in the Middle Ages," in his *Time, Work, and Culture in the Middle Ages* (Chicago: University of Chicago Press, 1980), 36.

16. Jacques Le Goff, "Labor Time in the 'Crisis' of the Fourteenth Century: From Medieval Time to Modern Time," in *Time, Work, and Culture*, 46. Bronislaw Geremek cites supporting evidence in *Le salariat dans l'artisant Parisien aux XIIIe–XVe siècles* (Paris: Mouton, 1962), 65. For a discussion of the evidence concerning the spread of the public mechanical clocks, consult Philippe Wolff, "Le temps et sa mesure au moyen âge," *Annales E.S.C.* 17 (1962): 1144, and Beeson, *English Church Clocks*, ch. 2.

Dux suggests that growth of the putting-out system beyond the city walls magnified interest in abstract, constant hours in the countryside (*Die Zeit in der Geschichte*, 335–36).

17. G. J. Whitrow, *Time in History* (Oxford: Oxford University Press, 1988),

113; Karl-Heinz Ludwig, "Arbeit, Technik und Arbeitszeit im Geschichtsverlauf: Eine Einführung," *Technikgeschichte* 47, no. 3 (1980): 184–85; Bilfinger, *Die mittelalterlichen Horen*, 164.

18. Le Goff, "Labor Time," 44ff.

19. Stadtarchiv Borken A 539, 1894.

20. Jacques Attali, *Histoires du temps* (Paris: Fayard, 1982), 103.

21. Cipolla, *Clocks and Culture*, 43. The widespread introduction of mechanical clocks did not supplant but instead stimulated the manufacture of sundials. Because of the need to correct the time kept by the clocks, production of the sundials grew from the sixteenth to the eighteenth centuries; Edoardo Proverbio and Giulian Bertuccioli, "On a Singular Chinese Portable Sundial," *Nuncias* 1, no. 1 (1986): 48.

22. Zerubavel, "Benedictine Ethic," 158–59.

23. Jürgen Rinderspracher makes a similar point when he distinguishes between time systems that coordinate activities versus those that constitute time as a calculable resource; see his *Gesellschaft ohne Zeit. Individuelle Zeitverwendung und soziale Organisation der Arbeit* (Frankfurt am Main: Campus, 1985), 55.

24. Ricardo J. Quinones, *The Renaissance Discovery of Time* (Cambridge: Harvard University Press, 1972), 25–27; Aaron J. Gurjewitsch, *Das Weltbild des mittelalterlichen Menschen* (Munich: C. H. Beck, 1980), 178–79. See also Jacques Le Goff, "The Time of Purgatory," in his *The Medieval Imagination* (Chicago: University of Chicago Press, 1988), 77.

25. Le Goff, "Labor Time," 51.

26. Erwin Panofsky, "Father Time," in his *Studies in Iconology* (New York: Oxford University Press, 1939), 69–93.

27. The historian Michael O'Malley prudently cautions against supposing that time diligence requires time's measured exploitation (*Keeping Watch: A History of American Time* [New York: Viking, 1990], 11–12).

28. *Poor Richard's Almanac*, January 1751, in *The Papers of Benjamin Franklin*, ed. L. W. Labaree and W. J. Bell (New Haven: Yale University Press, 1961), 4:86, cited by E. P. Thompson in "Time, Work-Discipline, and Industrial Capitalism," 89.

29. Postone, *Time, Labor, and Social Domination*, ch. 5. As W. Rothwell remarks, medieval entrepreneurs who lived with variable hours had every reason to be interested in the profitable use of time but could not subject time to rational manipulation ("Hours of the Day," 247). For a reference to contrivances adopted in China to arrive at approximate measures of production over work days of irregular length, see Lien-Sheng Yang, "Schedules of Work and Rest in Imperial China," *Harvard Journal of Asiatic Studies* 18 (1955): 316–17.

30. Le Goff, *Time, Work, and Culture*, 29, 48.

31. Jacques Le Goff, "Temps du travail, temps du loisir au moyen âge," *Temps Libre* 1 (1980): 56.

32. See Cipolla, *Clocks and Culture*, 103, for discussion of the public clock's prestige value.

33. On the role of religion in the adoption of time frameworks, see Giddens's comments in *Contemporary Critique of Historical Materialism*, 132–33. Cipolla, *Clocks and Culture*, 99, discusses the shortage of skilled artisans in China.

34. Cipolla, "Chinese Mandarins and the Self-Ringing Bell," in his *Clocks and Culture;* Landes, *Revolution in Time,* chs. 1–2. For other studies that compare time sense between China and the West, consult J. T. Fraser, N. Lawrence, and F. C. Haber, *Time, Science, and Society in China and the West* (Amherst: University of Massachusetts Press, 1986), ch. 3; Joseph Needham, *Science and Civilisation in China,* vol. 4, *Physics and Physical Technology* (Cambridge: Cambridge University Press, 1965), part 2; 532–46.

35. Thompson, "Time, Work-Discipline, and Industrial Capitalism," 87.

36. Ibid.; Christoph Deutschmann, *Der Weg zum Normalarbeitstag* (Frankfurt: Campus, 1985). See also the references cited in note 1 of this essay.

37. David Sabean, "Intensivierung der Arbeit und Alltagserfahrung auf dem Lande—ein Beispiel aus Württemberg," *Sozial-wissenschaftliche Informationen für Unterricht und Studium* 6, no. 4 (1977): 149–51.

38. Frederick James Glover, "The Rise of the Heavy Woollen Trade of the West Riding of Yorkshire in the Nineteenth Century," *Business History* 4 (1961): 9–15. One-quarter of the looms in Huddersfield in 1868 were still worked by hand; J. H. Clapham, "The Decline of the Handloom in England and Germany," *Bradford Textile Journal,* 1905, 45. In Germany in 1875, 34 percent of all looms in the woolen branches were mechanized; Horst Blumberg, *Die deutsche Textilindustrie in der industriellen Revolution* (Berlin: Akademie, 1965), 89–90.

39. The mechanization of looms for wool was essentially complete in Elberfeld by 1875; Wolfgang Hoth, *Die Industrialisierung einer rheinischen Gewerbestadt, dargestellt am Beispiel Wuppertal* (Cologne: Rheinisch-Westfälisches Wirtschaftsarchiv, 1975), 200; Alphons Thun, *Die Industrie am Niederrhein und ihre Arbeiter,* part 2, *Staats- und socialwissenschaftliche Forschungen* 2, no. 3 (1879): 197. For the Rhineland, see, for example, Horst Matzerath, "Industrialisierung, Mobilität und sozialer Wandel am Beispiel der Städte Rheydt und Rheindahlen," in Hartmut Kaelble et al., eds., *Probleme der Modernisierung in Deutschland* (Opladen: Westdeutscher Verlag, 1979), 23.

40. On patterns of ownership, see Gerhart von Schulze-Gävernitz, *Der Großbetrieb* (Leipzig: Duncker & Humblot, 1892), 69, 91; Karl Emsbach, *Die soziale Betriebsverfassung der rheinischen Baumwollindustrie im 19. Jahrhundert* (Bonn: Röhrscheid, 1982), 407–11. For German and British industry at large, consult David Landes, "The Structure of Enterprise in the Nineteenth Century: The Cases of Britain and Germany," *Comité International des Sciences Historiques* 5 (1960).

The size of textile firms in Germany and Britain varied greatly by town and market specialty. Yet in both countries the weaving departments of woolen mills at the close of the century might typically employ sixty looms. See J. H. Clapham, *The Woollen and Worsted Industries* (London: Methuen, 1907), 133; *Textile Mercury,* 8 April 1911, 271; *Statistik des deutschen Reichs* 214 (1910): 303.

The technical literature shows that in the decades before World War I, German and British looms from the woolen branches typically ran at similar speeds, as measured by the number of crossings which the looms' shuttles could finish each minute. See *Parliamentary Papers* (hereafter *PP*), 1892, XXXV, p. 207, and Hauptstaatsarchiv Düsseldorf Regierung Aachen 1634, report of 4 February 1899.

41. As early as the 1880s the textile magazines in Britain focused on Germany rather than France as the country's most important challenger (*Textile Manufacturer*, 1883, 272). After the outbreak of World War I, the business journal *Textile Mercury* said, "We have been lamenting or resenting 'foreign competition'—meaning by that term almost exclusively German competition in the outside markets of the world" (22 August 1914).

42. For Germany, see Germany, Statistisches Reichsamt, *Die Deutsche Volkswirthschaft am Schlusse des 19. Jahrhunderts* (Berlin: Puttkammer & Mühlbrecht, 1900), 103, 25 (industrial figures excluding self-employed). For Britain, see *Census of England and Wales 1891* (London: HMSO, 1893) 3:ixff.

43. For a discussion by employers of how labor should be conceived as a commodity, see "Arbeit'geber' und Arbeit'nehmer,' " *Sächsische Industrie*, 10 August 1907, 337–38.

44. See, for example, the discussion and principles employed in 1895 to draw up a piece-rate scale for weavers in Bradford; Bradford Chamber of Commerce, *Annual Report*, 1896, 57ff., and *Bradford*, 9 November 1895. For the iron and steel business, see Sidney and Beatrice Webb, *The History of Trade Unionism* (London: Longmans, Green, 1894), 484, and Iron and Steel Trades Confederation, *Men of Steel by One of Them* (London: Iron and Steel Trades Confederation, 1951), 160–61. For the early nineteenth century, see Clive Behagg, "Controlling the Product: Work, Time, and the Early Industrial Workforce in Britain, 1800–1850," in Gary Cross, ed., *Worktime and Industrialization: An International History* (Philadelphia: Temple University Press, 1988), 41–58.

45. For examples of managers converting from flat day wages to piece rates for weavers, see *Der christliche Textilarbeiter*, 9 December 1899; Ludwig Bernhard, *Die Akkordarbeit in Deutschland* (Leipzig: Duncker & Humblot, 1903), 125; Sydney J. Chapman, *The Lancashire Cotton Industry: A Study in Economic Development* (Manchester: University of Manchester Press, 1904), 262.

46. *Yorkshire Factory Times*, 7 October 1892 (Marsden); 14 July 1893; 1 December 1893; 26 October 1894 (Buttershaw area); *PP*, 1890–91, LXXVIII, p. 220.

An incident from a mill in Yeadon illustrates the treatment of spinners as independent contractors. The manager at a department which paid by output required that the spinners increase their production by hiring workers to operate their own machines during an evening shift. The daytime spinners received piece rates for the entire output of their machine and decided on their own how to pay the night workers. When the night workers went on strike in 1908, the Conciliation Board defined the day spinners, not the factory owner, as the "employers" of the striking workers (*Yorkshire Factory Times*, 3 April 1908, 1).

47. *Jahresberichte der mit Beaufsichtigung der Fabriken betrauten Beamten*, 1888, 26; Hauptstaatsarchiv Düsseldorf Regierung Düsseldorf, Jahresbericht des Fabrikinspektors, Mönchengladbach, 1902.

48. The workers who waited on materials lost on average more than ten days of work; Zentralverband Christlicher Textilarbeiter Deutschlands, *Geschäftsbericht*, July 1910–July 1912, 112 (b).

49. *Yorkshire Factory Times*, 5 August 1892, 8. Allen Gee, secretary of the union, testified to the Royal Commission on Labour that "a man never expects to be fully employed as a weaver" (*PP*, 1892, XXXV, transcript of 11 November 1891, 200). In its wage census of 1885–1886, the British Board of Trade esti-

mated that "broken time" might reduce the estimated annual earnings of weavers by 13 percent in woolens and by 10 percent in the worsted trade (cited by K. Laybourn, "Attitude of Yorkshire Trade Unions to the Economic and Social Problems of the Great Depression 1873–1896," Ph.D. diss., Lancaster, 1973, 315).

50. Wirtschaftsarchiv Baden-Württemberg B-25-319, 11 May 1906.

51. Stadtarchiv Forst, Kommission der Forster Textilarbeiterschaft, 8 August 1899.

52. *Der Textilarbeiter,* 12 February 1909 (Neugersdorf).

53. For examples of strike demands for hourly compensation for waiting, see Stadtarchiv Mönchengladbach 1c 913, 26 March 1912; Staatsarchiv Detmold IU 429, 21 March 1905, Schildesche; Hauptstaatsarchiv Düsseldorf Regierung Düsseldorf 24701, 23 February 1906, p. 223; Hauptstaatsarchiv Düsseldorf Landratsamt Mönchengadlbach 70, 22 February 1906, p. 103; Hauptstaatsarchiv Düsseldorf Regierung Düsseldorf 24699, 1 May 1905, p. 286; Staatsarchiv Münster, Kreis Steinfurt 1311, 25 July 1906; *Der Textilarbeiter,* 17 January 1902 (Sonthofen); 12 February 1909, "Aus der Bewegung in der Textilindustrie" (Mönchengladbach); *Westdeutsche Landeszeitung,* 7 March 1906 (Rheydt); *Die Textilarbeiter-Zeitung,* 27 June 1908. Another complaint indicates the precision with which German weavers gauged their time: weavers objected that at some mills the waiting time for which they were compensated extended only to the moment when the warp was delivered to the loom, not to the point at which the installers had actually completed putting in the warp (*Der Textilarbeiter,* 4 January 1907).

54. See the preceding two notes and Hauptstaatsarchiv Düsseldorf Landratsamt Euskirchen, 27 February 1905, p. 355; Hauptstaatsarchiv Düsseldorf Regierung Aachen, Birkesdorf, January 1900; Hauptstaatsarchiv Düsseldorf Regierung Düsseldorf 24690, 3 December 1898, p. 148; Hauptstaatsarchiv Düsseldorf Regierung Düsseldorf 24692, 3 August 1899; Hauptstaatsarchiv Düsseldorf Regierung Düsseldorf 24692, 16 August 1899; Staatsarchiv Detmold Regierung Minden I.U. no. 431, Buntweberei von Knemeyer & Co.; Zentrales Staatsarchiv Merseburg, 77 2524, no. 3, vol. 1, p. 13; *Der christliche Textilarbeiter,* 6 April 1901 (Viersen); *Die Textilarbeiter Zeitung,* 6 March 1909 (Münstertal), and 13 March 1909 (Mülhausen, i. Els). For other complaints about waiting on warps, see *Der Textilarbeiter,* 28 December 1906 (Sommerfeld and Mönchengladbach), and 12 August 1910. The weavers, who constituted the largest textile occupation, were not alone in articulating demands for "waiting money." German spinners also included it among their strike demands: see *Der Textilarbeiter,* 31 March 1905 (Mönchengladbach), and 29 May 1914 (Gronau). For spinners' informal requests for "waiting money," see *Der Textilarbeiter,* 19 May 1905 (Zwötzen). For examples of spinners who received "waiting money," see *Der christliche Textilarbeiter,* 3 February 1900 (Düren); *Der Textilarbeiter,* 21 May 1909 (Zwickau), and 12 June 1909 (Mülhausen i. Els). For spoolers and beamers requesting "waiting money," see *Der Textilarbeiter,* 13 October 1905.

55. Stadtarchiv Velbert VI e 7 Bestand Langenburg, 15 December 1893; Hauptstaatsarchiv Düsseldorf Regierung Düsseldorf 24692, 16 August 1899; *Jahrbuch des deutschen Textilarbeiter-Verbandes, 1913* (Berlin: Karl Hübsch, 1914), 134 (Bocholt); Zentralvorstand der christlicher Textilarbeiter Deutschlands, *Geschäftsbericht,* 1906–1908, 72 (Gronau district, Firma Gaidoel); *Bocholter Volks-*

*blatt*, 1 October 1901. In *Der Textilarbeiter*, see 13 September 1901 (Penig); 23 May 1902 (Kettwig); 24 January 1902 (Sonthofen [Algau]); 2 March 1906 (Rheydt); 14 May 1909 (Neustadt a.d. Orla); 6 August 1909 (Viersen); 29 October 1909 (Bergisches Land); 10 December 1909 (Wuppertal); 27 January 1911 (Kunzendorf i. Schl.); 19 May 1911 (Hof); 4 August 1911 (Unterurbach [Württemburg]); 22 May 1914, Osnabrück. In *Der christliche Textilarbeiter*, see 9 December 1899 (Süchteln); 1 February 1902; *Die Textilarbeiter Zeitung*, 16 May 1908 (Gronau); 2 July 1910 (Großschönau); 10 September 1910 (Bocholt); 20 May 1911 (Coesfeld). See also Hauptstaatsarchiv Düsseldorf Gewerbegericht Elberfeld, 80/50, 1891, case 225 and cases on p. 2; *Textil-Zeitung*, 11 September 1899, 734; Hermann Hölters, *Die Arbeiterverhältnisse in der niederrheinischen Baumwollindustrie mit besonderer Berücksichtigung der männlichen Arbeiter*, Ph.D. diss., Heidelberg, 1911, 25.

56. *Der Textilarbeiter*, 3 July 1914 (Barmen).

57. *Der christliche Textilarbeiter*, 10 August 1901.

58. I sampled only every third issue of the *Yorkshire Factory Times* from this era, so a full count of the number of complaints appearing about lost time would surely yield a larger number.

59. *Yorkshire Factory Times*, 1 November 1889, 5.

60. *Yorkshire Factory Times*, 23 January 1891. In some instances, however, the union did grant out-of-work pay to weavers who were discriminated against in the distribution of materials (Wakefield Archives, C 99/585, 27 January 1903).

61. *Cotton Factory Times*, 28 May 1897 (Rochdale).

62. True, the powerful unions for mule spinners in Lancashire saw to it that owners might pay workers something when the machines were stopped for repairs, but the employers owed the money only if they needed the spinners' assistance in carrying out the repair (British Association for the Advancement of Science, *On the Regulation of Wages by Means of Lists in the Cotton Industry* [Manchester: John Heywood, n.d.], 7: Spinning, Manchester Meeting, 1887). The same provision governed the Nottinghamshire lace trade; see W. A. Graham Clark, House of Representatives Committee on Interstate and Foreign Commerce, *Lace Industry in England and France* (Washington, D.C.: Government Printing Office, 1909), 27.

63. For reports of textile labor shortages in Britain, see *Yorkshire Factory Times*, 11 August 1905 (Bradford); *Journal of the British Association of Managers of Textile Works*, 1912–1913, 93. In 1906 the *Textile Manufacturer* reported that "more or less through the whole wollen area of Yorkshire the shortage of labour is becoming a serious trouble" (161).

64. *PP*, 1892, XXXV: Royal Commission on Labour, 11 November 1891 hearing, p. 222, and 13 November 1891, p. 282.

65. Hauptstaatsarchiv Düsseldorf Grevenbroich 319, 28 October 1899; *Jahresberichte*, Handelskammer Mönchengladbach, 1896, 5–6; *Jahresberichte*, 1897, 5; Hölters, "Die Arbeiterverhältnisse," 21.

66. Hauptstaatsarchiv Düsseldorf Regierung Düsseldorf 25015, p. 43, for 1893, and Regierung Düsseldorf 25022, p. 42, for 1900; Hölters, "Die Arbeiterverhältnisse," 23; Franz Decker, *Die betriebliche Sozialordnung der Dürener Industrie im 19. Jahrhundert* (Cologne: Rheinisch-Westfälisches Wirtschaftarchiv, 1965), 87.

67. Karl Emsbach, *Die soziale Betriebsverfassung der rheinischen Baumwollindustrie im 19. Jahrhundert* (Bonn: Röhrscheid, 1982), 179.

68. Ibid., 648–50.

69. The local business courts' recognition of the weavers' right to compensation for "waiting time" as early as the 1840s undermines arguments which would explain the owners' payment strategies as a response to labor scarcity. In this era the employers enjoyed the benefit of a healthy supply of labor (Emsbach, *Die soziale Betriebsverfassung*, 322; Willy Brendgens, *Die wirtschaftliche, soziale, und communale Entwicklung von Viersen* [Viersen: Gesellschaft für Druck & Verlag, 1929], 109).

70. Kenneth Carpenter, ed., *The Framework Knitters and Handloom Weavers: Their Attempts to Keep Up Wages* (New York: Arno, 1972), pamphlets from 1820 to 1845; Duncan Bythell, *The Handloom Weavers* (Cambridge: Cambridge University Press, 1969), 175.

71. Bythell, *Handloom Weavers*, 149.

72. As an example, see *PP*, 1892, XXXV, Royal Commission on Labour, 11 November 1891, pp. 208–10.

73. Staatsarchiv Münster, Kreis Steinfurt 1311, 2 May 1891, and Neuenkirchen and Regierung Münster 718, 14 May 1891, p. 146.

74. Karl Hüser, *Mit Gott für unser Recht: Ein Beitrag zur Geschichte der Gewerkschaftsbewegung im Münsterland* (Paderborn: Gewerkschaft Textil-Bekleidung, 1978), 28–29; Heinrich Camps, *Geschichte und Entwicklung des Bezirks Westfalen des Zentralverbands christlicher Textilarbeiter Deutschlands* (Münster, 1924). Indeed, the initial promoter of textile unions in this region, the Christian textile workers' association, had not been established in Germany yet (Michael Schneider, *Die christlichen Gewerkschaften 1894–1933* [Bonn: Neue Gesellschaft, 1982], 74–77).

75. In Eschendorff, a town in the Münsterland, weavers went on strike without notice in 1899 and by all accounts spontaneously demanded an end to waiting without pay for materials or equipment (Staatsarchiv Münster, Kreis Steinfurt 1311, Eschendorff, 29 March 1899; Zentrales Staatsarchiv Merseburg 77/2524, no. 3, vol. 1, p. 13, 1 April 1899, Amt Rheine).

76. For examples of German workers paying for their lodging and budgeting other household expenses by the week, see "Ein Jammerleben . . . ," *Der Textilarbeiter*, 1 October 1909, and *Der christliche Textilarbeiter*, 27 January 1900 (Düren). For British parallels, see *PP*, 1892, XXXV, Royal Commission on Labour, 11 November 1891 hearing, pp. 210, 229, 235.

77. *Der Textilarbeiter*, 20 September 1901 (Gera); Hauptstaatsarchiv Düsseldorf Regierung Aachen 1634, February 1900, Düren. See also the discussion of the effort needed to earn an adequate "daily wage" in home weaving (*Der rheinische Weber*, 1 September 1899). German weavers who complained about the hard effort that defective warps caused them could convert their piece rates to earnings per day (*Der christliche Textilarbeiter*, 27 January 1900 [Düren]).

78. Staatsarchiv Detmold IU 429, 21 March 1905. In February 1900, when weavers in Düren issued an exhortation for strike support, their leaflets averaged out their piece-rate earnings and expressed them as wages per day (*Die westdeutsche Arbeiter Zeitung*, 17 September 1904 [Krefeld]). For a parallel example, see Staatsarchiv Münster Kreis Steinfurt 1116, 11 December 1910, Neunkirchen; see also Hauptstaatsarchiv Düsseldorf Regierung Aachen 1634, Düren.

Similarly, the dispute at the town of Emsdetten in 1906 turned on the question of whether weavers' earnings averaged 3.2 marks per day (Stadtarchiv Emsdetten, "Industrialisierung am Beispiel Emsdettens: Ein Rückblick aus dem Jahre 1924"). For an example where employers and weavers on piece rates negotiated over wage increases in terms of daily averages, see *Jahrbuch des deutschen Textilarbeiterverbandes, 1913* (Berlin: Karl Hübsch, 1914), 118 (Balingen).

79. *Der Textilarbeiter,* 14 March 1902 (Gera).

80. Hauptstaatsarchiv Düsseldorf Regierung Düsseldorf 25027, printed story on employer from Neersen at *Oberlandesgericht Köln,* published 22 December 1904; Hauptstaatsarchiv Düsseldorf Regierung Düsseldorf 24684, 26 May 1894; Staatsarchiv Weimar, Landesregierung Greiz, n Rep A Kap XII, no. 206, p. 163.

81. One owner specified in the factory's employment rules that workers had to notify the owner before going public with their complaints in the courts; Hauptstaatsarchiv Düsseldorf Landratsamt Grevenbroich 271, p. 184, circa 1910.

82. The *Leipziger Monatschrift für Textil-Industrie* considered one pfennig per minute appropriate (1909, no. 3, p. 80). The model factory code which the employers' association for the left bank of the Rhine issued in 1890 imposed a fine of only ten pfennig for the first half-hour of lateness (Hauptstaatsarchiv Düsseldorf Regierung Düsseldorf 24658). For actual codes, see Stadtarchiv Mönchengladbach, 25c, no. 1754, for the firms Ax, Daniels, etc., in Rheydt; firm Bertelsmann & Niemann, 1892, Staatsarchiv Detmold M2 Bielefeld no. 760, p. 60; Hauptstaatsarchiv Düsseldorf, Landratsamt Geilenkirchen 88, pp. 1898ff.; the large collection in Hauptstaatsarchiv Düsseldorf, Regierung Düsseldorf BR 1015 169, is especially valuable for examples of factory ordinances issued before they became obligatory and somewhat standardized. See also *Die Fabrikordnung der Firma F. Brandts zu Mönchengladbach, Ausgabe von 1885* (Mönchengladbach: Stadtarchiv Mönchengladbach, 1974).

83. See a model ordinance from the Wupper Valley, 1838, in Emsbach, *Die soziale Betreibsverfassung,* 674. For the Rhineland's woolen industry, see Decker, *Die betriebliche Sozialordnung,* 216.

84. Kirklees Library Oral History Collection, heavy woolen district: Maria Shaw, born 1893, on a mill in Batley; Mrs. Dransfield, born 1896, on Taylor's Cheapside Mill; Mr. Robinson, report from year 1916 on a mill in Birkenshaw; Mrs. Hanley, reporting on mother's experience at Mark Oldroyd's mill. Interview transcripts of Joanna Bornat from Colne Valley: Mrs. T., born 1896, about first job; Mr. B., born 1901, on John Edward's mill, Marsden; Miss A., born 1897, on "Bruce's Mill," Marsden; Mrs. W., born 1900, on Crowther's Mill, Marsden; Mrs. B., born 1900, on Robinson's mill, Marsden; Mrs. O., born 1888, on Dewhirst's mill, Elland. My interview with Mrs. E. Brook, weaver at Newsome Mills, Almondbury; my interview with A. Murgatroyd, born 1902, half-timer at Crossley's Mill, Halifax. A woman weaver from a village near Halifax recalled as one of the highlights of her working life the day she climbed a wall and clambered through a mill window to get into the mill after starting time (my interview with May Broadbent, born 1896, Midgley). Dr. A. H. Clegg, a former half-time worker in Halifax, wrote down his memories of getting locked out in a manuscript at Calderdale Archives (MISC 482). For the account of a dialect poet, see

James Burnley, *Phases of Bradford Life* (London: Simpkin, Marshall, 1889), 45. Newspaper reports include *Yorkshire Factory Times*, 18 February 1898 (Bradford); 13 January 1905 (Batley); 21 July 1905 (Shipley and Saltaire); 25 April 1890 (Slaithwaite); 28 August 1903 (Dewsbury); 28 July 1893 (Batley). For Lancashire, see *Cotton Factory Times*, 5 February 1897 (Darwen); 19 March 1897, 1; Lancashire Record Office, DDX 1089, 4 November 1904, 194. The minutes of the Halifax Overlookers' Society indicate that an overlooker was locked out from a mill for arriving one minute late (Calderdale Archives TU 102/2/1, Mssrs. Martin and Son, 13 February 1897). Some British mills combined fines with locking out; workers who arrived, say, less than a quarter-hour late could pay a penny, although the fining period could last a mere three or five minutes after the starting time before all were locked out for good; see *Yorkshire Factory Times*, 21 July 1905 (Shipley and Saltaire), and 28 July 1905 (Manningham Mills). For an autobiographical account of experience with the practice of combining locking out with fining, see Maggie Newberry, *Reminiscences of a Bradford Mill Girl*, Bradford Local Studies Department Publication no. 3 (1980), 50. The tally of employees locked out could represent a significant part of the work force. In Burnley, Lancashire, when the porter at one mill in 1897 allegedly shut the gate two minutes early, sixty-seven weavers who found themselves outside could not work until breakfast (*Cotton Factory Times*, 19 March 1897 [Burnley]).

In *Das Kapital* Marx delights in citing a set of British factory rules that specify excessive fines for late arrival. His anecdotes suited his rhetorical purpose by illustrating the monetarization of human relations, yet his example of fining does not correspond to the most widespread form of entry control in Britain (*Das Kapital. Kritik der politischen Ökonomie* [Berlin: Dietz Verlag, 1980] 1:447–48).

85. In keeping with the sense of change, a Lancashire journal for factory owners, the *Textile Mercury*, commented in 1890 on the shift in workers' visions of the future: "The introduction of socialistic principles into English trades-unionism has completely transformed the latter" (30 August 1890. See also 27 September 1890).

86. See, for example, Mary Nolan, "Economic Crisis, State Policy, and Working-Class Formation in Germany," in *Working-Class Formation*, ed. I. Katznelson and A. Zolberg (Princeton: Princeton University Press, 1986), 388–89; Klaus Schönhoven, *Expansion und Konzentration: Studien zur Entwicklung der freien Gewerkschaften im Wilhelminischen Deutschland 1890 bis 1914* (Stuttgart: Ernst Klett, 1980).

87. Robert Perks, *"The New Liberalism and the Challenge of Labour in the West Riding of Yorkshire 1885–1914,"* Ph.D. diss., Huddersfield Polytechnic, 1985; Henry Pelling, ed., *The Challenge of Socialism* (London: Adam & Charles Black, 1968).

88. Marx, *Das Kapital*, vol. 1, sec. 3, "The Production of Absolute Surplus Value," 192–213.

89. William Thompson, *Labour Rewarded. The Claims of Labour and Capital Conciliated; or, How to Secure to Labour the Whole Product of Its Exertion* (London: Hunt & Clarke, 1827), 17, 115. Thomas Hodgskin and J. F. Bray adopted a similar view of the matter: Thomas Hodgskin, *Labour Defended Against the Claims of Capital* (1825; rpt. London: Labour Publishing Company, 1922), 108; J. F.

Bray, *Labour's Wrongs and Labour's Remedy; or, The Age of Might and the Age of Right* (Leeds: David Green, 1839), 48–49.

90. Joseph Schumpeter, *History of Economic Analysis* (New York: Oxford University Press, 1954), 583.

91. Ernest Mandel, *The Formation of the Economic Thought of Karl Marx* (New York: Monthly Review Press, 1971), 45.

92. *The Poor Man's Advocate,* a journal which gave particular attention to factory conditions, said that entrepreneurs, "being able to conceal the real state of the transaction," made their profit by "trickery" when they bought cheap and sold dear (21 January 1832, 8).

93. See the transcript of the debate at the founding meeting of the Independent Labour party reprinted in Pelling, *Challenge of Socialism,* 187–89. Bradford's significance in the rise of this party can be gauged from its share of national membership dues. In 1895 Bradford provided one-sixth of the party's affiliation fees (J. Reynold and K. Laybourn, "The Emergence of the Independent Labour Party in Bradford," *International Review of Social History* 20 [1975]: 315). E. P. Thompson makes a strong case for the dynamic of local factors and for the contribution of Yorkshire to the development of the Independent Labour party in "Homage to Tom Maguire," in *Essays in Labour History,* ed. Asa Briggs and John Saville (London: Macmillan, 1960), 277.

94. A speech given at the outdoor May Day celebration in Bradford in 1898 sums up the reasoning which British socialists usually applied to justify the communal ownership of factories. The chief speaker reasoned that "the true object of industry being the production of the requirements of life, the responsibility should rest with the community collectively, therefore . . . the capital necessary for industrial production should be declared and treated as public property." Here workers focused on ensuring distribution of sufficient goods, not on the mechanism of exchange between workers and employers (*Yorkshire Factory Times,* 6 May 1898, 6; see also *Yorkshire Factory Times,* 13 May 1892, 7 [Oakworth]).

95. *Bradford Labour Echo,* 6 April 1898.

96. Stuart Macintyre, *A Proletarian Science* (Cambridge: Cambridge University Press, 1980), 166.

97. *Der Textilarbeiter,* 8 October 1909 (Bautzen).

98. "Produktion," *Der Textilarbeiter,* 4 November 1904.

99. They said that socialists should always support the idea that it is better "not to deliver so much 'labor power' to the capitalists" (*Der Textilarbeiter,* 24 March 1905; see also 26 February 1909 [Gründberg]).

100. The workers' experience of factory practices on the shop floor may have ruled out certain possibilities of development, but it did not directly select the political vision of the labor movement. The German treatment of employment as the sale of labor time represented a necessary but not sufficient condition for the adoption of the belief that the owner's extraction of unpaid labor time was intrinsic to the capitalist employment relation. German textile workers who were encapsulated in the Catholic subculture and joined the Christian unions were not apt to encounter the Marxist theory of profit before World War I.

Despite the self-proclaimed conservatism of the Christian movement, the Christian textile unions adopted the German notion of the sale of "labor power" to elaborate their economic philosophy. The Christians referred to the owner's exploitation "of the [labor] power of the worker" (*Der christliche Textilarbeiter,* 28 July 1900 [Borken]). When the Christian unionists in Germany addressed economic issues, they reasoned in terms of abstract labor time, as did the German socialists. "Money is the representation of human labor," the Christian textile newspaper concluded in an editorial on economic principles (*Der christliche Textilarbeiter,* 24 February 1900). Most important, one finds the same pattern of worker concepts of time on the Catholic left bank of the Rhine as in textile regions where Protestants and socialists dominated: the same emphasis on the payment of waiting time and on the calculation of piece-rate earnings in terms of daily averages.

101. In 1895 the Social Democratic Federation, one of the chief organizations which attempted to propagate Marx's economic ideas in Britain, counted 10,500 members. For Tom Mann's conversion to Marxism and preaching of Marxism in 1895 in Yorkshire, see *Tom Mann's Memoirs* (London: Labour Publishing Company, 1923), 39ff., 129; for the appearance of another Marxist ideologue in Yorkshire, see Bernard Barker, "Anatomy of Reformism: The Social and Political Ideas of the Labour Leadership in Yorkshire," *International Review of Social History* 18, no. 1 (1973): 8. For the availability of Marxist ideas in Britain generally, see Eric Hobsbawm, ed., *Labour's Turning Point 1880–1900* (London: Lawrence & Wishart, 1948), 23, 41; E. P. Thompson, *William Morris: Romantic to Revolutionary* (New York: Pantheon, 1976), 332–33; E. J. Hobsbawm, "Karl Marx and the British Labour Movement," in his *Revolutionaries: Contemporary Essays* (London: Weidenfeld and Nicolson, 1973); Stanley Pierson, *Marxism and the Origins of British Socialism* (Ithaca: Cornell University Press, 1973).

102. David Blackbourn and Geoff Eley provide a useful overview of studies that emphasize the Germans' failure to break with the legacies of feudalism, although these scholars take exception to some of the theoretical assumptions in this literature; see Blackbourn and Eley, *The Peculiarities of German History: Bourgeois Society and Politics in Nineteenth-Century Germany* (Oxford: Oxford University Press, 1984), 6–8, 209–10, 228.

103. For an example of workers making analogies between feudal labor services and wage labor, see *Die Verbrüderung,* 14 September 1849, 399. For an example of an economist working out a concept of wage labor by drawing on feudal relations, see Johann Georg Busch, *Abhandlung von dem Geldsumlauf in anhaltender Rücksicht auf die Staatswirtschaft und Handlung* (Hamburg: C. E. Bohn, 1780), book 1, sec. 1.

104. Christiane Eisenberg, *Deutsche und englische Gewerkschaften* (Göttingen: Vandenhoeck & Ruprecht, 1986), 25–26.

105. Adam Smith represents this view of the conveyance of labor in *The Wealth of Nations* (Chicago: University of Chicago Press, 1976), 15. M. Beer discusses the origins of the assumption that labor is traded in the form of a finished product in *A History of British Socialism* (New York: Humanities Press, 1940) 1:190–92.

106. A comparative analysis of the commodification of labor in Western Europe appears in Richard Biernacki, *The Fabrication of Labor* (Berkeley and Los Angeles: University of California Press, forthcoming).

107. Giddens, *Contemporary Critique of Historical Materialism*, 130–35; Anthony Giddens, *The Constitution of Society* (Berkeley and Los Angeles: University of California Press, 1984), 144; Lukács, *History and Class Consciousness*, 90.

108. Several recent historical studies highlight national differences in workers' and employers' concepts of time, although they have not used a comparative framework to identify the causes of these differences. Marianne Debouzy suggests that religious traditions contributed to the development of a distinctive culture of time among nineteenth-century textile workers in New England; see "Aspects du temps industriel aux Etats-Unis au début du XIXe siècle," *Cahiers Internationaux de Sociologie* 67 (1979): 197–220.

# THREE

# Time and the Modern Family: Reproduction in the Making of History

*A. F. Robertson*

If we were immortal, as some have craved, we would probably live in a world (like heaven or hell) without sex and without history. Real life, however hectic it may be, is at least more interesting. The best we can hope for is a painless passage from the extreme dependence of infancy, to reproductive maturity, and then to senescence and death. This life course takes us through a sequence of engagements with society in which our personalities are developed, changed, and ultimately extinguished. In these transactions we rely on many different social institutions more durable than ourselves. Yet, however much we may depend on a stable social order, that too is inconstant. It has a history, essentially because it is built on the shifting sands of our many lives.

I see this book as an effort to transcend old dogmas, dichotomies, and disciplines by returning to a scrutiny of the spatial and temporal coordinates of social existence. My own concern is with a troublesome fracture in our comprehension of time in social structure, and with the ways in which it might be healed. I shall explain how, in modern thinking, the organization of human reproduction has fallen victim to a narrow and conservative definition of social process, which has prevented us from understanding its cardinal importance within progressive, *historical* meanings of time.

Organizing reproduction is more than a domestic chore. It has made and remade human societies, and it continues to shape the world in which we live. This statement may seem entirely obvious, but within the rubric of modern social science it has proved very elusive. At one level the problem of understanding can be posed quite simply: we assume that reproduction is strictly and properly a family affair, but at the same time we believe that families are being squeezed out of business by the proliferation of more efficient institutions in industrial society. Embedded within our emotionally charged understanding of the modern family, reproduction has been lost to sight as an active force in society and history.

Although the problem of how to construe the influence of biological processes on social activities has always been contentious, most social scientists take the facts of individual reproduction and the premise of reproductive instability for granted. Human regeneration is "natural"; it is autonomic and nonrational, a private rather than a public affair. It makes a significant impact on the organization of societies only by weight of numbers: over- or underpopulation, imbalanced sex ratios, and so on. It is accordingly adduced to the study of history through the mediation of demography or biology. We can accept it as a simple biological fact that reproduction is the instrument of human *evolution,* but to argue that reproduction is an instrument of human *history*—something closer to our own life span—evokes a peculiar skepticism.

We may acknowledge readily enough that the relations of reproduction (extended to "lineages," "clans," etc.) are fundamental to the social organization of the "traditional" societies studied by anthropologists. But why should they be deemed to lose their broader social significance with the process of modernization? It seems that our conception of history has robbed reproduction of its social meaning: in the homely image, reproduction is deemed to make the world go *round,* while essentially economic forces make it go *forward.* We must blame this misconception on the historical trauma of industrialization, which not only changed the world but also altered our understanding of that world.[1] Our explanations of modernity have been fundamentally economic, and our interpretations of time have likewise been economistic.[2] The materialist juggernaut has reduced other social processes (language, culture, power, reproduction) to dependent variables in explanations of the making of history. Only as we try to make some objective sense of modernity and the emerging postindustrial world are these "lost" processes being rediscovered.[3]

Few social scientists would take issue with the assertion that "biological reproduction always takes place within a determinate structure of relations of production, distribution, and consumption and occurs simultaneously with economic activity."[4] Here I want to explore why such widely held assumptions should be so misleading. The intergenerational span of reproduction transcends the duration of most economic activities. To reduce the concurrence of these two sorts of process to "simultaneity" not only obscures the influence of each on the other but presumes that the immediacies of economic activity explain the more protracted life processes, not vice versa. We are simply not accustomed to reversing the causal flow and asking what part reproduction plays in the organization of banks, or schools, or governments. Yet it is surely apparent that how we organize savings, education, or the quest for political security is profoundly affected by the cycle of birth, maturation, procreation, and death.

Seeking to rehabilitate the organization of reproduction as a force in social structure and history,[5] I have encountered a very basic difficulty in the way we have come to think about time in social structure. We have exaggerated the distinctions between processes which *sustain* social organization and processes which *change* it. Here I shall try to explain why, in modern social science, reproductive processes have been interpreted within the *substantive* rather than the *historical* meaning of time— and how, accordingly, they have been lost to modern perceptions of social change.

I shall begin by characterizing human reproduction as perpetually disruptive and destabilizing, insisting that it poses a persistent and pervasive challenge to human ingenuity. The organization of reproduction is not confined to the narrow entity we call "The Family" but pervades all social institutions. This influence has extended to the organization of industrialization itself. I conclude with the reflection that all social institutions are ideologized as a victory over instability and uncertainty: intellectual institutions are no exception, and explanations of social change are in constant tension with this passion for continuity.

## THE DYNAMISM OF REPRODUCTIVE RELATIONS

Very intermittently in the history of social science, "The Family" has been recognized for what it is: the victory of human ingenuity over biological necessity and material constraint, a relentless process rather than a state, a ubiquitous instigator of social change.[6] What is intriguing is the evident failure of this discovery to find a durable niche in modern social theory. One problem is our tendency to equate "reproduction" with childbirth. Maturation and death are no less essential to the process (if individuals were born but did not die, we presumably would not speak of *re*production). Reproduction transcends an individual life course, for individuals are produced and replaced by other individuals: hence the *relations* of reproduction, conventionally treated in various branches of social science under such headings as "the family" or "kinship and marriage." In stark, functional terms the importance of these relations is determined by the degree of physical dependence of individuals on one another at different stages in their lives. The cardinal and most enduring bond is between mother and child—the means by which an individual makes the transition from the extreme dependence of embryo and infant toward independent, sexually mature adult. Society is based on this dynamic group, not on "the individual" construed as some immutable morphological unit. This is why an economistic view of reproduction as the outcome of innumerable autonomous decisions makes little sense.

The way in which the reproductive core secures its survival is not "natural" but *social*, a long-term engagement with other people in pursuit of the material and emotional necessities of life. This is how societies persist, and without social organization, without the moral fabric we call culture, the reproductive core itself could not survive. If individual lives destabilize, it is the business of social institutions to stabilize ("The King is dead: Long live the King!"). In this contest the group which we call the family has been perpetually in the front line. It must strive to contain the stresses of birth, mating, and death and to win for its members a materially secure and socially respectable place in the community. The family is a writhing knot of individual interests, the nexus of relationships which we love to hate, reviled in our radical youth and revered in our conservative age.[7] As a matter of routine we pursue our own freedom by breaking up our parents' household; yet, vulnerable and mortal, we need to believe that the family is secure, stable, and enduring, a rigid building block for the fabric of society. Even when we are seeking to escape its toils, we often lament the decline of the family as our "haven in a heartless world."[8]

The earliest notable exploration of this predicament, and its remedy in moral retrenchment and good management, may be traced to the nineteenth-century polymath Frédéric Le Play. He observed that families in industrializing Europe were pared down to the basic reproductive nucleus of parents and children. He identified this form of family organization by its most characteristic trait, *instability:* "It establishes itself by the union of two free adults, grows with the birth of children, shrinks with the successive departure of the members of the new generation, and dissolves finally, without leaving a trace, with the early death of the abandoned parents."[9] Le Play contrasted this pattern with that of the extended *patriarchal* family, originating in pastoral society and fast disappearing at the time of his studies.[10] The larger domestic corporation was more secure and autonomous in socioeconomic space, and more persistent in time: the cooperative bonds of family extension, retaining family members as a ramifying economic unit through three or four generations, allow the differential development of the component nuclei to counteract the effects of instability.[11] According to Le Play, these economies of scale were achieved by the conservative force of custom, the patriarch authorizing the "hiving off" of a subsidiary family corporation when internal ramification became too unwieldy. By contrast, when the household contracts to a single reproductive nucleus, the brevity of its life span, the fluctuations in its needs and capacities, and its dependence on external support become more pronounced.[12]

Le Play's view was robustly deterministic: "The family regime," he declared, "imparts a distinctive character to populations and thus creates their destiny."[13] If the patriarchal family "maintained the spirit of tradition and community," the "instable family" which had all but replaced it in nineteenth-century Europe "develops the spirit of innovation and individualism."[14] Le Play recognized, with mixed feelings, that for modern households neither nature nor culture was an adequate substitute for shrewd calculation and strategy:

> The precocious use of reason, encouraged by teaching in the schools, parental advice, or the example of the upper classes, leads the new generation to do good or evil according to its moral predisposition. This reliance on reasoning often results in an excessive propensity for innovation rather than a spirit of tradition. In this system, a single or married individual is no longer responsible for the needs of his relatives and rapidly rises to a higher situation if he possesses outstanding aptitudes. But in contrast, if he is unskilled or morally delinquent, he falls even faster to a wretched condition, unable to claim any assistance.[15]

The effects of this volatility could be seen all too clearly in the class-differentiated societies of nineteenth century Europe.[16] As a solution to the pathology of emerging capitalism, Le Play favoured a third alternative, the "stem" family pattern. In this prudent blend of tradition and rationality the family was sustained by impartible inheritance and deferred marriage within the limits afforded by scarce material resources, while members surplus to domestic capacity found socially constructive places in expanding armies and colonies. However, while this "vigorous and admirable" pattern has rarely if ever found a niche in industrial society, the "frail shrub" of the nuclear family has flourished prodigiously.[17] It has done so not by retreating frugally within its own resources but by placing demands on, and stimulating the growth of, economic and political institutions far beyond the range of the household.

Not long after Le Play drew attention to domestic instability among the industrial working classes, Seebohm Rowntree published the results of his pioneering surveys of the English industrial city of York. With intuitive brilliance he went beyond the synchronic evidence of his statistical data to observe that the population was not permanently distributed around the baseline which he had meticulously constructed to define poverty in the city. Rather, as their needs and capacities waxed and waned with the reproductive process, individual households rose above or fell below it. A young couple were pulled down into poverty after the birth of their children, whose maturity eventually relieved the pressures of dependency and brought relative prosperity to the family again. The departure of the children to start their own families left their parents increasingly dependent on their own dwindling capacities.[18]

Rowntree's investigations made it evident that the "natural" variations of the reproductive process must be continually balanced against the opportunities and constraints of the productive process. Just as accumulation of wealth alleviates domestic stress and permits family expansion, so poverty can reduce the household beyond the nuclear core to the elemental—and very vulnerable—mother-child dyad.[19] In extracting labor from the masses, expanding capitalism did not discriminate according to variable need and capacity in individual households. The reformist thrust of Rowntree's work is that public remedies for poverty must deal with both the "absolute" distribution of wealth in industrial society and the "relative" inequalities generated by the reproductive cycle.[20]

Although Rowntree's particular concern was to draw attention to the social crises of industrialization and the responsibilities of the modern welfare state, we must recognize that social organization has *always* been under pressure to accommodate the demands of the reproductive cycle. Instead of our morbid fixation on the modern family as "frail shrub," or tactical failure, or victim of the industrial juggernaut, let us turn the coin and marvel at the extent to which it has managed to transfer the costs of reproductive organization out to a mass of modern social institutions—including the apparatus of the state. If this seems too great a leap of the imagination, it is essentially because it is denied by our conventional understanding of the forces which make history.

## THE SOCIAL EXIGENCIES OF REPRODUCTION

For all its emotive force, the idea of "The Family" is analytically very weak, being little more than an egocentric view of the ramification of reproductive relations. It is what family members *do*, the life-supporting activities they share, which bring them together into objectively identifiable groups. The most important and most evident of these is the *household*, a residential group in which the organization of reproduction and economic processes converge in the first instance.[21] If the household was ever, at some historically or ethnographically distant point, the *only* social institution constituted by reproductive and economic processes, this is no longer so in the kinds of society in which we now live. It is abundantly evident that material production and exchange now transcend the household, but the notion that reproduction is exclusively and properly a domestic affair is peculiarly tenacious.

In studies of kinship in nonindustrial societies, anthropologists have made much of the ramifications of reproductive relationships. Family growth and subdivision build, over time, the lineages and clans which characterize "tribal" society. The interests of biological and social reproduction converge in a pattern of competition and cooperation, to secure mates and progeny as well as access to material resources. Good breeding is ambiguously a private and public affair: it involves transactions among the individual lives which constitute a household, between the households of parents and offspring engendered over time, and among families in the wider community which exchange mates. If its disruptions are to be minimized, reproduction must be moderated and constrained by normative ideas about how households should properly, as well as advantageously, develop through time.

The most notable proponent of this view of family dynamism was the British anthropologist Meyer Fortes. Fortes was fascinated by the ways in which intimate family relationships were writ large in social structure. For example, a sequence of generations would transform two brothers into the eponymous ancestors of two distinct lineages or clans, large-scale political units related by the fraternal metaphor. In the empirical context of Ghana, Fortes evoked the interdependence of the "internal" domestic and the "external" social (or, as he called it, *jural*) domains to explain how the cyclical development of households both contributed to and was regulated by more comprehensive levels of political organization. Unlike most other characterizations of the typical stages of family development as the process of growth and decline within a single household, Fortes stressed the internal-external link through the consecutive phases of expansion, fission, and *replacement,* this last comprising the demise of one generation and the domestic establishment of another. This paradigm of social reproduction could, he asserted, be applied *"mutatis mutandis . . . to all social systems."*[22]

Central to Fortes's understanding of reproductive dynamism is the notion that a single normative program of family development can have socially extensive consequences, generating at any moment a range of residential, economic, or political groupings. In his pathbreaking essay "Time and Social Structure,"[23] he resolved an empirical puzzle posed by the results of an extensive socioeconomic survey in Ashanti: two apparently different *types* of household, one organized around the conjugal pair, the other around an extended matrifamily segment, were simply the spatial expression of an earlier and a later stage of the same growth process. Fortes's account of the relationship between reproductive strategy and social morality presents us with a notional hierarchy in time and social space. Individual lives are formed and defined socially within the context of the household, and the development of individual households is transcended by social institutions and collective ideals of much greater historical duration. Architecture and nomenclature, political status and land laws, rules of inheritance and funeral rituals—all are parts of the social fabric within which individual families transact the reproductive process. In effect, family and society re-create each other over time.

"The Family" in a particular locality is thus a portmanteau idea, a network of reproductive relationships which meshes with many others in a complex of activities distributed over social space and lengthy periods of time. The interplay of reproductive organization with such categories of activity as "religion" is evident not only in the primitive veneration of ancestors but also in the institutions of the major modern churches. Jack Goody has explored the intricate relationships between family, church, and state in early Europe: the expansion of church power depended on controlling the deposition of family property, and this control in turn involved intricate manipulation of the customs of birth, marriage and death, including such details as wet-nursing, concubinage, and surrogate parenthood.[24] The institutionalization of chastity and celibacy has influenced the aggregate fertility of entire populations to the present century.

In preindustrial societies the relations of reproduction are extended through space, time, and metaphor into the political communities of lineage, clan, and tribe. In modern society the relations of reproduction remain fundamental to our conception of ethnic identity and *nationality,* expressive of the bond between individual and state. Official monitoring of parental and conjugal relations in claims of citizenship reminds us that modern governments can take as close an interest in the organization of reproduction as did the medieval church. They continue to police incest and license marriage, legislate for or against abortion, and tacitly build whole fiscal programs from child allowances to death duties on the domestic cycle. China's "one-child" policy is probably the most obvious example, but of much greater significance are the multifarious social welfare institutions which sustain the reproductive process throughout the modern world: clinics, schools, insurance policies, mortgages, geriatric communities, and, only a little less obviously, the farms and factories, banks and municipalities, classes and political parties on which our material survival has come to depend.

## THE SUBSTANTIVE INTERPRETATION OF REPRODUCTION

Anthropological recognition of the pervasive significance of the relations of reproduction has become rather too firmly associated with an ahistorical understanding of nonindustrial, precapitalist societies. It seems, for example, that Fortes's structural-functional account leaves us trapped in an explanatory loop: over time the various social institutions concerned with organizing reproduction reinforce each other; but where do these institutions come from, and how and why do they *change*? If the organization of reproduction is so broadly diffused, where can we pick up a causal thread that will tell us which institution influences which?

At the heart of the matter is a persistent ineptitude in dealing with issues of time in social structure. Our understanding of temporality is divided into those *substantive* processes which are thought of as sustaining society, the routines which keep it functioning, and the *historical* processes which transform social structure.[25] Legal procedures in courts or electoral processes in councils are typically thought of as substantive, carrying out and reinforcing the social routine without directly originating that routine. The two sorts of process are often discriminated structurally by the levels at which they operate: the substantive processes concern individuals and "primary" groups, while history connotes the more comprehensive "macro" levels of society. A particular trial, election, or individual birth must be socially momentous to make history. Otherwise, it is the long-term accumulation of legal precedent, the cumulative actions of legislatures, or the birth of individuals en masse—the demographic phenomenon of the birth *rate*—which are of historical interest. What is missing is some coherent means of explaining precisely how and when substantive processes "make" history.

The problem rests both in the nature of the evidence and in our analytical tools. Together they have placed constraints on our understanding which have reinforced a narrowly substantive interpretation of reproductive dynamics. A basic problem is that the process of reproduction is simply *too long* for the conventional modes of analysis in social science. The mother discipline of economics has not only made us scientific materialists but has also dictated the periodicities in which behavior is to be explained. Exchange is construed as an almost instantaneous transaction which, as analyses are elaborated and refined, becomes burdened with unimaginable detail. Production is monitored from one crop season to the next or through a manufacturing cycle of a few months or years. However, economics has been afflicted by a conceptual gap between the essentially synchronic analysis of individual agents and firms (the domain of microeconomics) and the more diachronic concerns of macroeconomics and of economic history. The sporadic efforts of economists to come to terms with the reproductive process have revealed the difficulties of extending an essentially synchronic analytical framework to a series of activities which transcend whole lifetimes, and interests which are transferred forward from one generation to the next. "As we proceed beyond the stationary economic state, we enter an uncharted frontier," one economist interested in reproduction has acknowledged. "Our analytical maps do not tell us how to proceed. . . . The families we observe are seldom if ever in a state of equilibrium. This uncharted frontier is beset with all manner of disequilibria."[26]

Time undermines our efforts to come to terms analytically with the reproductive process. Families and households are empirically elusive: forming, merging, dissolving, and constantly changing the configuration of individuals who live, work, eat, and sleep together.[27] However, "deconstruction" of the family to the lives of its component members does not always leave us better informed about the dynamics of the household unit.[28] A "proper" study of the reproductive process must involve protracted longitudinal observation which would in itself take time, exceeding the life of the observer as well as the particular historical context which interests him or her.[29] Instead, efforts to abstract family development patterns from a mass of differentially timed individual lives have depended on cross-sectional analyses of survey data,[30] the results of which have been shown to diverge markedly from longitudinal evidence.[31] Synchronic, statistical treatment reduces family ties to demographic ciphers of age, sex, and number, revealing little of the economic and political meaning which attaches to the intergenerational relations of father, son, daughter-in-law, stepson, or cousin.[32]

Fortes's work was remarkable in that he was able to apply ethnographic insight to deduce the moral dimension and the social construction of family life from his survey data. However, the ethnographic abstraction itself has serious limitations, not the least of which is the tacit assumption that norms apply without discrimination to everyone in "the society," regardless of differences of status or wealth. Furthermore, although Fortes did so much to illuminate the *substantive* meaning of time in social structure, its historical meaning was lost in his structural-functional conspectus. Thus, although he acknowledges that "Ashanti today is not a stable and homogeneous society," his argument precludes rather than challenges an alternative historical hypothesis that at least some of the smaller conjugal households he observed in his Ashanti survey were in fact a product of the economic changes wrought by the expansion of cocoa farming and the modern breakdown of matrilineal extended family traditions.[33] Fortes offers no means of discriminating which families might be conforming to the "traditional" and which to a "modern" paradigm of domestic development.[34]

Fortes was concerned with the vital question of how reproduction was constituted in the matrilineal principles which gave Ashanti society its most fundamental political characteristics. What he did not and could not explain was why Ashanti should be characterized by these principles rather than some other. In other words, to understand the influence of reproduction in social structure we must proceed beyond the substantive processes, the routines which sustain social institutions, to the historical processes which tell us why these particular institutions have come to characterize particular societies at particular times.

## THE HISTORICAL INTERPRETATION OF REPRODUCTION

These substantive and historical understandings of time have acquired qualitative distinctions which have obstructed our comprehension of their interrelationship. While history has come to signify time in a linear, progressive sense, substantive processes connote conservatism, passivity, even stasis. Dividing up the continua of social time and social space in this way has *not* enhanced our ability to explain what social structure is and how and why it changes. Instead, the dichotomy has become ideologically entrenched in the factions of modern social science. While liberal evolutionary functionalism has retained its preoccupation with social continuity, with how social institutions constrain individual actions and form the interlocking mosaic of society and culture, historical materialism has urged the necessity of social transformation, by collective rather than individual action. In functionalism spatial metaphors predominate: the mapping of relationships and institutions within the confines of "a society" or "a culture." Substantive processes explain the persistence of this mosaic,[35] and transformation is dealt with awkwardly as adjustment to exogenous disturbance.

For its part, historical materialism is a narrative of grand social events rather than the gyrations of daily life. Change is derived from the interaction of people and nature in the development of the forces of production, not from the exigencies of physical reproduction. Insofar as they are interested in reproduction or the family, most Marxists would conclude that because the relations of reproduction have shown little susceptibility to technical development ("the development of the reproductive means") they have in themselves no historical dynamism.[36] Viewed on the grand scale, human breeding is therefore taken for granted as the provision of the raw material of social formations and of economic transformations.

The relationship between reproductive process and the historical forms of society became the subject of intense debate among Russian intellectuals in the early decades of this century. In an influential study in 1925 summarizing the views of the populist "Organization and Production" school, the agronomist A. V. Chayanov explained how the reproductive process in farming families accounted for the structure and persistence of the Russian peasantry.[37] Chayanov characterized the farming household as dependent on its own resources of labor and argued that this dependence disposed its members to be much less concerned with the pursuit of profit than the drudgery of work and with balancing variable inputs (in this case including land) according to internal cyclical changes in consumption needs. The peasantry was not, as an orthodox Marxist would see it, economically and socially inert: it was continually reconstituted as households responded tactically to the changing balance of their own needs and capacities. This perpetual motion was disguised in aggregate statistics of the distribution of wealth, which revealed only the marginal changes.

It was change at the margins which claimed the attention of contemporary Marxist scholars interested in the historical transformation of the peasantry with advancing capitalism. Lenin had used much the same synchronic survey data as Chayanov but to very different effect, explaining how the differential response of households to economic opportunities resulted in the resolution of the peasantry into strata distinguished by the hiring of labor and the accumulation of capital.[38] The "Chayanov-Lenin debate" has become the classic doctrinal clash of the substantive and historical modes of explanation.[39] Chayanov's argument that the peasant family farm was inaccessible to modes of economic analysis designed to explain the modern development of capital has been subjected to wide-ranging empirical and theoretical criticism.[40] The strength of his argument rests in his insistence that the organization of reproduction was at the heart of rural social structure in Russia. It explained the active *persistence* of the peasantry, the lower productivity of its labor when compared to capitalist enterprise, and its resistance to intrusive economic forces.[41] The main deficiency of Chayanov's argument was that it became doctrinally detached from the explanation of history. Frequently accused of reducing the peasant economy to stasis, he could point to no inherent process of change other than piecemeal response to external markets.[42]

His failure to connect the "internal" dynamics of the family to the transformation of society rests in large measure in his characterization of the reproductive process as "demographic variation." Deprived of social and ideological meaning, the family cycle was reduced to little more than a statistical effect, a cipher in an argument about marginal utilities. Chayanov's peasant household was autonomous and economically isolated, balancing its own needs and capacities—an unreal image of any peasant economy, in which factor and commodity exchanges are pervasive.[43] His analytical model is a drastic demographic abstraction of family *growth* between two generations, presuming that a child is born to a couple every three years over a twenty-seven-year period.[44] This tells us little about fission and replacement, the very significant process by which the parental household declines and divests itself of productive resources. Comparative studies make it clear that such decumulation is vital to an explanation of "suboptimal" levels of productivity in farming communities.[45] To understand the process, we must know how consolidation of the ideal expanded patriarchal family in Russia was balanced against pressures to devolve capital promptly to the rising generation.[46] It is this reproductive strategy, rather than some demographic formula predicated on a rate of breeding, which explains the relationship between rural conservatism and emerging capitalism and thus the true historical constitution of the Russian peasantry.[47]

If Chayanov lost sight of the historical definition of substantive processes, the converse is no less true of his theoretical adversaries. For the orthodox Marxist, history is linear and progressive; it subsumes repetitive processes but is not subordinate to them. Cyclical interpretations of history are regarded with particular skepticism. Nevertheless, reconciling teleology with the persistence of social forms has greatly exercised recent generations of Marxists, evoking such substantive locutions as "the articulation of modes of production."[48] While Marxists have expressed little interest in physical reproduction, the word has become a complex metaphor for social continuity, recurring in such phrases as the "reproduction of labor power" or the "reproduction of the means of production."[49] Reproduction thus connotes various substantive processes which it is the business of history to alter. The vector for historical change must be sought in technical development and in the social relations of *production*.[50]

Although these ideas have illuminated the expansion of industrial capitalism, their applicability to the kinds of society patronized by anthropologists (which did not greatly interest Marx himself) has proved troublesome. Claude Meillassoux has written extensively and persuasively about the importance of reproduction in the organization of pre-capitalist societies. He argues that in such societies control of the reproductive power of women is (for males) a material imperative, the means of producing labor and subsistence through the regeneration of productive units—households. This enterprise, influenced fundamentally by available technology (hunting and gathering, forest agriculture, grain production, etc.) is sustained in broader political structures of kinship and locality. The reproduction of these social structures is therefore dependent on the organization of human reproduction. The successful outcome is the assurance of self-adjusting social *stability*.[51]

In his efforts to place such systems authoritatively within the materialist developmental scheme, Meillassoux has encountered fundamental problems in accounting for the *historical* significance of reproduction. He charts an evolutionary progression in the material organization of society in which human reproduction is superseded by the reproduction of capital: "The relations of production revolve now around the means of material production and not any more on the means of human reproduction. . . . The structural reproduction of the productive enterprise is not related any more to human reproduction but to the reproduction of capital, as a means of perpetuating and enlarging the relations of production."[52] In this formulation reproduction in primitive societies has thus become a *metaphor* for the regeneration and expansion of capital. By little more than semantic sleight the "reproduction of life as a precondition to production" is robbed prematurely of its historical significance.[53] The confusion is compounded when the Marxist apparatus developed for the analysis of capitalism, now incorporating the metaphoric use of "reproduction," is carried back into interpretation of the primitive world.

The awkward consequences of these efforts to explain both the *continuity* of precapitalist societies and their *historical transformation* are very evident in Meillassoux's work. Dealing with historical evolution, Meillassoux gives orthodox priority to development of the productive means. "Natural reproduction" is recast as a problem of demographic growth and regarded as subordinate to the exigencies of "social reproduction."[54] This formulation is not easy to reconcile with his earlier emphasis on the structural interplay of human reproduction and production, nor does it square with his recognition of the enduring importance of human reproduction in the advanced capitalist societies. Meillassoux insists that "all modern modes of production, all classes of societies depend, for the supply of labor power, on the domestic community."[55] His explanation of this dependence reveals very clearly the discontinuity between the substantive and the historical meanings of time. What he calls variously the domestic "society," "community," "economy," or "mode of production,"[56] characterized by its reproductive processes, persists as a *historical anachronism* in modern industrial society: "up to now and for the indefinite future, the domestic relations of production have been organically integrated into the development of each and all the subsequent modes of production."[57] Encapsulated within the substantive definition of time, the "archaism" of family process and the "relic" of the domestic relations of reproduction are allowed to transcend history.[58] "The agricultural domestic community, through its organized capacity for production and reproduction, represents an integrated form of social organisation which has existed since the neolithic period and upon which still depends an important part of the reproduction of the labor power necessary to the development of capitalism."[59] Fossilized within the substantive meaning of time, detached from history by a metaphoric transformation of the meaning of reproduction, and confined within the bounds of the household, the past is allowed an explanatory role in the present. An elaborate homage to Marxist orthodoxy, such an explanation only makes the influence of human reproduction on the organization of modern society more deeply mysterious.

Reviewing the Chayanov-Lenin debate, Jairus Banaji concludes: "We must not ask which of these tempos or tendencies adequately describes the dynamics of peasant farm-composition, but rather, *how they are related.*"[60] In a recent exploration of the relationships between reproductive processes and economic institutions, I have argued that the development of capitalism and the social organization of reproduction can each be regarded as a process within *both* the substantive and the historical meanings of time.[61] "Capitalistic" relations are episodic in that their importance can be seen to advance and recede within the context of an enduring relationship of two individuals. For many, this observation will appear to be a bizarre confusion of two distinct sorts of process. The progress of capitalism, it may be argued, can be construed only on the grand scale, in the interaction of competing social classes; the drift of individuals in and out of wage labor or independent smallholding acquires significance only in aggregate terms and in the long term. However, like Chayanov I do not believe that scrutiny of the *margins* of expanding capitalism is sufficient. Without an understanding of its substantive dynamism in the main body of rural society, pronouncements about the formation and consolidation of classes depend on faith rather than empirical validation.

For this examination of family dynamics and history, I chose the multifarious and theoretically vexatious arrangement of sharecropping, pursuing it in the relatively unexplored empirical context of Africa. I sought to show how, in each of four regions, share contracts have been instituted in a manner which accommodates both cyclical shifts in family needs and capacities, and erratic developments in the world economy. I accordingly distinguished the substantive life of the individual share contract as it develops over a number of years, responding to the changing reproductive interests of the contracting parties, from its historical development as a regional institution over many decades.[62] My purpose was to show that without an understanding of the interdependence of these two orders of time, conflicting assertions about the efficiency, equity, and historical persistence of share contracting, which have dogged its theoretical history since the days of Adam Smith, have little meaning. Viewed over time, the malleability and thus the social and economic utility of the institution become evident: at one phase in its life span an individual share contract has all the appearances of capitalistic labor hire; a little later it closely resembles peasant proprietorship. These maneuvers provide a repertory of arrangements by which farmers respond to good times and bad: when factor or commodity markets are bullish, share contracts may take on a decidedly capitalist demeanor of fixed rents and wages; in periods of slump they may retreat into a peasantlike pattern of non-cash exchanges in which the hazards of loss rather than of profit are shared.

Such social institutions in rural Africa embody the fact—well known to the people themselves—that both family life and economic opportunities are instable. Over more than a century capitalism has grown into the social life of African communities in ways which Westerners might not always recognize.[63] Reciprocally, African family life is now instituted in arrangements, like these share contracts, which transcend the "traditional village" and connect each hearth and farm to the financial institutions of the Western metropolises. It is no longer intellectually fashionable to regard the Ghanaian family and Wall Street as discontinuous in social and economic space. Here I am arguing that the temporal processes which animate each must also be regarded as integral.

## REPRODUCTION AND THE ORGANIZATION
## OF INDUSTRIAL SOCIETY

Our attention to reproduction as a historical force has been distracted by its designation as a substantive process, its subjection to theories of material progress, and its association with the fate of an encapsulated "modern family." Social scientists have made much of the fact that industrialization has driven a wedge between the household and the workplace. The family in America and Europe, it has generally been assumed, has become thoroughly subordinated to the institutions of industrial society—even in matters of time. Family life, from daily routine to the organization of childbearing and retirement, is now scheduled by the factory clock and by bureaucratic process.[64] More than this, the institutions of advanced industrial society are reckoned to be putting the family out of business, supplanting its economic, educational, recreational, and other functions, and reducing it to chronically instable fragments.[65] In recent years a new historiography of the family has been challenging these assumptions. "The long-recognized effect of the economy on the family has too often obscured the converse—that the family may have important consequences for the economic system. To understand the complicated relationship between the economy and the family, we cannot simply view the family as the dependent variable in the relationship."[66] The fundamental difficulty in these historical revisions has been defining the instrumentality of an institution as mutable and multifarious as "The Family." I am arguing here that this causal force rests in the processes and relations of reproduction which basically define "The Family"—*among many other* social institutions.

However diminished the family in industrial society may appear, the persistence of human reproduction cannot be in doubt. Like any other economic system, industrial capitalism depends on the regeneration of labor power and thus ultimately on some variant of the parent-child nexus. The family may indeed seem a vestige of its former self, but with the consolidation of industrial capitalism the organization of reproduction is not *displaced* so much as *dispersed* outward from the reproductive core. Parturition, child care and socialization, physical welfare, geriatric care, and disposal of the dead are all managed by institutions far beyond the compass of the family.

Hypotheses about the relationship between family structure and industrialization have been changing in recent years. Talcott Parsons's view that industrial pressures reduced the form and function of families yielded to William J. Goode's more equivocal notion of an interactive "fit" between the small, mobile "conjugal family type" and the demands of industrialization.[67] More recently, historical research has subverted the assumption that industrialization in Europe and North America brought a shift from the agrarian extended family to the "nuclear" pattern. Small households based on the relationship of husband and wife, with the children leaving home early in adulthood, were evidently common in England since the fourteenth century and were probably typical of the earlier feudal and ecclesiastical domains.[68] If industrial development reshaped family organization, it was neither in the ways nor to the extent hitherto supposed.

The fine-grained empirical work of social historians has "revealed that the role of the family was in fact that of an active agent, fostering social change and facilitating the adaptation of its members to new social and economic conditions."[69] A reversal of the "Nuclear Family" argument now seems in order: the industrial revolution in Europe was made possible by a preexisting pattern of reproductive relationships which encouraged rapid transformation of the means and relations of production. With their rapid cycle of expansion and contraction, the two-generation households of preindustrial Europe were in effect little engines of economic growth. Married couples had only a few fleeting years to overcome the consumer demands of their (numerous) children and to insulate themselves from the impoverishment of their own physical decline after their children left home. This urgency was the making of the merchant class, which became the pioneer of surrogate institutions for the extended family and the bonds of agrarian community: guilds, mutual security associations, the embryonic apparatus of local government and the state.[70] This class made its fortune by putting the rural households to work, mainly in the production of cloth. Laboring as a "semiproletariat" in the twilight world of "proto-industrialization," these artisans in turn initiated the most momentous epoch in human history. With little more than the resources of the village carpenter and black-smith, they finally broke the labor squeeze by making new machines instead of babies.[71] It is striking that while the capital-enhancing innovations of motive power and organizational scale were supplied by the town-based middle class, the major labor-substituting inventions which set in motion the industrial epoch—the spinning jennies and weaving shuttles—emanated from these humble but intensely active artisan households.

There is nothing to suggest that the creative interaction between the relations of reproduction and the emerging relations of industrial production was harmonious or autonomic. Indeed, the early phases of industrial expansion were marked by a heightened sense of opposition between household and society. While new relations of production were in the making, domestic relations bore much of the stress.[72] Hareven points out that the various rhythms of the individual's life, the family, and the factory were *more* hectic and variable than today: "Households functioned like accordions, expanding and contracting in accordance with changing family needs and external conditions."[73] These memories undoubtedly linger in our emotional commitment to "The Family" as the custodian of our own ephemeral lives and our bastion against an insecure and threatening world. But they also disguise the extent to which the burdens of reproductive stress and insecurity have been passed out into the institutions of modern society.

Industrialization brought a revolutionary expansion in political scale, and with it a transformation in the social organization of reproduction. In the modern world, relations between generations were no longer confined within family and community but were transacted between entire classes of strangers. Through the medium of state pensioning, younger people worked to support a whole category of elders which might, or might not, include their own parents. Strategies to secure the reproductive process, which had hitherto pitched fathers into conflict with sons, now became factionalized within the emerging class structure. But institutions were constructed as much from below as from above: while the privileged were making direct use of the powers of government to secure their private lives, the relentlessly expanding proletariat was at work on the foundations of the modern welfare state. To raise their children and protect themselves from sickness and old age, they struggled to construct mutual assurance societies, penny banks, pension funds, retail cooperatives, and ultimately political parties. Their efforts were very often challenged and subverted by the owners of capital; but the sheer momentum of public need forced the hand of government, which saw to it that these proletarian innovations were co-opted, regulated, and incorporated within the rubric of the nation state.

In their twentieth-century towers of stone and steel, modern banks or life insurance corporations have very pointedly shed visible references to the turmoil of human lives and the struggle of social classes on which they were built. We must take a studiously "timeful" view of these institutions if we are to perceive either their humble origins or the reproductive functions behind their decorous facades. For example, a history of banking must give an adequate account not only of the development of trade and the rise of merchant classes but also of the temporal logic of personal savings, which derives from pressures to accumulate and decumulate during the course of the family life cycle. In aggregate, these microscopic fluctuations have a profound effect on the structure of banking institutions and on the economy at large.[74]

To illustrate how economic history and reproductive process have conspired in the making of modern institutions, let us consider the distinction between the *salary*—the system by which the managerial and professional class is rewarded—and its proletarian counterpart, the *wage*. Although we might think of the salary as a "purely economic" arrangement, its most notable characteristic is a *career*-related incremental structure which guarantees that the professional will be lifted *at the right time* above the episodes of reproductive stress. Salary curves have a distinctive convexity, rising steeply during the period in family development of most acute demand, the "homemaking" phase when children are young.[75] Pensioning and other salary-related privileges sustain high levels of income after retirement (another modern innovation). The stark contrast with the principle of the wage can be construed most effectively in a framework of social time.[76] John Rex has pointed out that while proletarians sell their labor by the hour or week, middle-class bureaucrats sell theirs *by the life*.[77] Wages bear little relation to the age of the worker and, as Rowntree discovered long ago in York, offer no relief in periods of stress in the reproductive cycle. Thrust on their own resources, household members must intensify their own efforts, women and children going out to scavenge in the lower reaches of the labor market, to beg and borrow in neighborhood and family networks, or to seek supplementary benefits from the state or public charities.[78]

Economists seeking to explain the peculiar temporal structure of the salary have had recourse to the notion of *human capital:* as people get older, "investments occur that augment the productive capacity of the human agent."[79] Hence the typically convex incremental pattern of the salary: the income of skilled people rises more steeply and peaks later in life because this is when returns to investment in human capital, essentially the cost of an education, are reaped.[80] This approach raises more questions than it can plausibly answer: what exactly is "human capital," and how are the costs and returns of investment, or its depreciation, to be measured? In precisely what sense are the services of a sixty-year-old professional "worth" four or five times those of one who is young and freshly trained? It is evident that we are looking not at the effects of an evenhanded market but at boundaries of political privilege. Quite simply, the terms of trade are set so that laborers cannot and do not bargain for salaries; they are constrained to bargain for something institutionally different—a wage. The young professional can be secure in the knowledge that if he bides his time and is respectful toward the senior generation, the momentum of his own career will quadruple his income.

However, conventional economics can tell us very little about how the costs (education) and incremental benefits of a salary are distributed across whole lifetimes. While the imagery of rational actors in free markets effectively disguises a system of entitlement in which social scientists are themselves conspicuous beneficiaries, it gives a relatively clear account of wages: these are more explicitly negotiated by collective bargaining either within enterprises or across whole industries, are concerned with immediate rather than deferred benefits, and are more obviously susceptible to short-term shifts in factor markets.[81] Something more potent and reliable than a market for skills determines the high rewards of salaries, the peculiar timing of increments, and the capacity of some occupations to accumulate more "human capital" ("political credit"?) than others. Middle-class investment in the education of their offspring is not simply a matter of faith in future demand for that kind of labor. It depends on the power to assert who is entitled to cash in a particular qualification for a secure and privileged form of employment.

If a Marxist perspective may help to explain the political history of wages, the grand materialist teleology can say very little about the essentially substantive patterns of lifetime earnings or why privileged servants of capital all over the industrial world should have secured this distinctively incremental, career-based system of rewards. The temporal logic of a salary occupies that awkward middle ground between, as it were, the neoclassical moment and the materialist epoch. The mediating process is human reproduction; but, alas, in social science this process has been reduced conceptually to synchronic inertia and consigned to the intellectual purdah of "The Family." It is no accident that measures to release it have coincided with the development of radical feminist thought, which is similarly torn between a commitment to modern materialism and to "postmodern" inventiveness, and between metaphors of class war and the brute reality of reproductive dimorphism.[82]

## THE SOCIAL CONSTRUCTION OF STATICS AND DYNAMICS

Our understanding of reproduction has been closeted within "The Family," and "The Family" in its modern "nuclear" form has in turn become embedded in the ideologies of modernity. Its compactness, integrity, sexual privacy, and "independence" are pieties which we—the middle classes—have propagated and which only we can afford. As Hareven notes, "native middle class American families" were the first to make a virtue of the necessarily compact household, marrying younger, controlling fertility, spacing their children more closely, and seeking an "orderly progression along the life course."[83] As one of many consequences, "children have subtly but rapidly developed into a labor-intensive, capital-intensive product."[84] We like to think of our families as bastions against the ravages of material change emanating from the wider world. There is certainly no place in our mythology for the notion that the Family has helped to make the wicked world we now inhabit; rather, it is the demon of industrial society which breaks up our marriages and renders our children unmanageable. But our cozy and costly domestic domains could never have survived if the middle class had not also devised and controlled that vast fabric of *other* institutions—ranging from salaries and mortgages to prenatal clinics and retirement communities—in which our reproductive interests are more truly secured.

The historical thrust of current events is notoriously hard to perceive, but if a "postindustrial" and "postmodern" age is indeed upon us, there is no sign that it is restoring to the Family anything resembling its old preeminence in social organization. On the contrary, it is being further reduced to the most elemental relations of reproduction, to fragile parent-child dyads. Development of the technical means of reproduction is already obviating the need for sexual partnerships and may one day render even the womb redundant. But as the demand for more extensive public services in child rearing, and the strenuous debates about surrogate parenthood or in vitro fertilization make plain, the pressure on broader social institutions to organize reproduction continues to increase rather than diminish.

If in the modern world social scientists purport to have a privileged understanding of what families are all about, there is still room for self-doubt: how well can social science itself perceive and evaluate its own understandings? Viewed from the Left, the liberal functionalist tradition has certainly overspecified the Family in ways which have distracted attention from its constitution in competing social classes and from questions of its ultimate necessity. The reproductive cycle is a "noisy" mutable fragment in the mosaic of social institutions which supposedly incline to equilibrium and which are certainly not *characterized* by instability. But while dismissing the family as a bourgeois fixation, historical materialism has failed to offer a clearer understanding of, or prognosis for, the social relations of reproduction. Both theoretical traditions have failed to liberate family dynamics from its substantive bounds. The historical significance of reproduction remains lost between arguments about the grand transformative conflict of classes on the one hand, and the culturally conservative interaction of individuals on the other.

I suspect the ultimate reason for the inhospitability of social theory to the significance of reproductive dynamics lies deeply embedded in the sociology and philosophy of knowledge and concerns our predilection for analytical images which are static and typological rather than processual. Our keenest emotional interests are expressed in a social ideology which asserts the continuity and stability of family life. We idealize the family in its heyday of growth, a snapshot of domestic bliss, but do not care to dwell on the wider reality of the reproductive process: the fission and decline of the household, the inevitability of death, and the replacement of our own generation by another. The pervasive ideology of family stability admits the notion of time only with reluctance, and in that restricted and repetitive sense which I have called "substantive."[85]

On a more fundamental level, beyond the emotional gratification, moral propriety, and strategic utility of static representations of the family, we are in a deeper intellectual bind. As Roger Friedland and Donald Palmer remark in their contribution to this volume, it seems that statics have a logical, perhaps physiological priority over dynamics in human perception: we can comprehend the sequence of how things happen only by freezing time. Processes, whether reiterative or linear, are understood and explained essentially by metaphors of stasis, which put us at a peculiar disadvantage in dealing with causation—the essentially temporal question of *why* things happen as they do. There are those who, like the linguist Ferdinand de Saussure, can only despair of reconciling the synchronic and the diachronic frames of reference.[86] Here I have suggested that one way of resolving this difficulty is to recognize that although we have invested time with distinct meanings, all social processes mediate between continuity and change. Finding ways of explaining this mediation is not an intellectual luxury: it is a necessity.[87] If we continue to relegate our view of reproduction to the substantive meaning of time, our understanding of both the fate of the beloved family and the course of human history will remain impoverished.

## NOTES

For their painstaking advice and comments, I would like to thank John Barnes, Bill Bielby, Francesca Bray, Roger Friedland, Jack Goody, Tamara Hareven,

Elvin Hatch, Don Symons, and members of the Economy and Society seminar at the University of California, Santa Barbara.

1. See Ernest Gellner, *Thought and Change* (New York: Weidenfeld and Nicolson, 1964).

2. These issues are discussed more fully in Roger Friedland and A. F. Robertson, eds., *Beyond the Marketplace: Rethinking Economy and Society* (New York: Aldine de Gruyter, 1990), 3–49.

3. I have in mind, for example, Michel Foucault's reconfiguration of the meanings of power (*Discipline and Punish: The Birth of the Prison* [New York: Random, Vintage, 1979]); Jack Goody's investigations of the force of literacy (*The Logic of Writing and the Organization of Society* [Cambridge: Cambridge University Press, 1986]); and the rising tide of "postmodernist" challenges to the meaning of meaning itself.

4. Eric J. Arnould, "Marketing and social reproduction in Zinder, Niger Republic," in R. McC. Netting, R. R. Wilk, and E. J. Arnould, eds., *Households* (Berkeley and Los Angeles: University of California Press, 1984), 130.

5. I have explored this matter at length in A. F. Robertson, *Beyond the Family: The Social Organization of Human Reproduction* (Berkeley and Los Angeles: University of California Press, 1991).

6. An early example can be found in Ibn Khaldun's discussion in the fourteenth century of the dynamics of dynasties: *The Muqaddimah: An Introduction to History* (London: Routledge and Kegan Paul, 1967).

7. This remark about the life cycle and political taste should not be taken lightly: as an institution, the family is widely revered as the foundation of liberal society but was excoriated by Marx and Engels in the *Communist Manifesto*. And as Eric Hobsbawm notes, radicalism is a decidedly youthful tendency, a luxury incompatible with more mature domestic liabilities (*Primitive Rebels* [Manchester: Manchester University Press, 1959], 18).

8. See Christopher Lasch, *Haven in a Heartless World: The Family Besieged* (New York: Basic, 1977).

9. Frédéric Le Play, *La réforme sociale* (Tours: Alfred Mame et Fils, 1872), quoted in translation by Catherine B. Silver, *Frédéric Le Play: On Family, Work, and Social Change* (Chicago: University of Chicago Press, 1982), 80.

10. In making this distinction, Le Play did not have in mind a simple evolutionary progression. The instable family was characteristic of both hunting-foraging societies and industrial societies.

11. This point is made, from a very different perspective, by David Newbery, "Agricultural Institutions for Insurance and Stabilization," in P. Bardhan, ed., *The Economic Theory of Agrarian Institutions* (Oxford: Clarendon Press, 1989), 267–98. A solution to "the problem of moral hazard in credit markets," especially where alternative social institutions are lacking, "is the *vertically extended household*, which is composed of nuclear units of successive generations. Older members of the household have had time to accumulate assets which are either directly available for consumption smoothing, or can be used as collateral. Members will leave the extended household once they have accumulated enough to ensure adequate self-insurance." See also S. P. Reyna, "The Extending Strategy: Regulation of the Household Dependency Ratio," *Journal of Anthropological Research* 32, no. 2 (1976): 182–98.

12. The pattern of changing needs and capacities is typically measured as a *dependency ratio*—the proportion of producers (able-bodied adults) to consumers (children, the aged). See, for example, Wanda Minge-Kalman, "On the Theory and Measurement of Domestic Labor Intensity," *American Ethnologist* 4, no. 2 (1977): 273–84.

13. Frédéric Le Play, *L'organisation de la famille selon le vrai modele signale par l'histoire de toutes les races et de tous les temps,* 4th ed. (Tours: Alfred Mame et Fils, 1895), 11 (my translation). The idea that the family may be the cause rather than an institutional consequence of reproductive instability has proved tenacious. In the 1930s the Russian émigré sociologist Pitirim Sorokin was still lamenting the "unstable" urban family, comparing it unfavorably with the "stable," "integrated," and morally robust rural family; see Pitirim Sorokin, Carle C. Zimmerman, and Charles J. Galpin, *A Systematic Source Book in Rural Sociology* (New York: Russell and Russell, 1931), 27–33. A recent example of "family determinism" may be found in the work of Emmanuel Todd; see, for example, *The Explanation of Ideology: Family Structures and Social Systems* (Oxford: Basil Blackwell, 1985).

14. Le Play, *L'organisation de la famille,* 11.

15. Le Play, *La reforme sociale* quoted in Silver, *Frédéric Le Play,* 260–61.

16. Le Play, *L'organisation de la famille,* 18.

17. Silver, *Frédéric Le Play,* 80.

18. B. Seebohm Rowntree, *Poverty: A Study of Town Life* (1922; rpt. New York: Howard Fertig, 1971), 169–71.

19. For accounts of this process in diverse cultures, see, for example, Maurice Freedman, *Chinese Lineage and Society: Fukien and Kwangtung,* 2d ed. (London: Athlone Press, University of London, 1971), 45; William Davenport, "The Family System of Jamaica," *Social and Economic Studies* 10 (1961): 420–54; and Thomas Espenshade, "The Recent Decline of American Marriage: Blacks and Whites in Comparative Perspective," in Kingsley Davis, ed., *Contemporary Marriage: Comparative Perspectives on a Changing Institution* (New York: Russell Sage Foundation, 1985), 53–90.

20. Unfortunately, a one-sided interest in Rowntree's "Cycle of Poverty" has fostered the complacent assumption that poverty is "only temporary," thus distracting attention from its bases in class inequality. For a critical commentary, see Margaret Wynn, *Family Policy* (London: Michael Joseph, 1970).

21. Sylvia J. Yanagisako provides a useful survey of the often problematic definition of "household"; see Yanagisako, "Family and Household: The Analysis of Domestic Groups," *Annual Review of Anthropology* 8 (1979): 161–205. See also Ira R. Buchler and Henry A. Selby, *Kinship and Social Organization: An Introduction to Theory and Method* (New York: Macmillan, 1968); and R. McC. Netting, R. R. Wilk, and E. J. Arnould, eds., *Households* (Berkeley and Los Angeles: University of California Press, 1984).

22. Meyer Fortes, Introduction to Jack Goody, ed., *The Developmental Cycle in Domestic Groups* (Cambridge: Cambridge University Press, 1958), 4–5.

23. Meyer Fortes, "Time and Social Structure," in Fortes, ed., *Social Structure: Essays Presented to A. R. Radcliffe-Brown* (Oxford: Clarendon, 1949), 54–84.

24. Jack Goody, *The Development of the Family and Marriage in Europe* (Cambridge: Cambridge University Press, 1983).

25. Teodor Shanin uses the word "substantive" in a very similar context, to distinguish cyclical changes in peasant households from aggregate changes in peasant social structure; see Shanin, *The Awkward Class: Political Sociology of Peasantry in a Developing Society, Russia 1910–1925* (Oxford: Clarendon, 1972), 81–95. "Substantive" is his translation of the Russian Populist term *organicheskie izmeneniya*, which plainly owes much to earlier organic images of social organization, of functionally complex processes which serve to sustain the body of society. I am arguing here that the enthusiasm for evolution and social transformation generated by the industrial revolution has made *history* the more urgent interest. "Substantive" has also gained currency through the work of Karl Polanyi and others as a means of distinguishing the "social embeddedness" of economic transactions from the individualistic utilitarian transactions of the market place; see Polanyi, "The Economy as Instituted Process," in Polanyi and C. Arensberg, ed., *Trade and Markets in Early Empires* (Glencoe, Ill.: Free, 1957), 243–70; and Polanyi, "Our Obsolete Market Mentality," in G. Dalton, ed., *Primitive, Archaic, and Modern Economies* (New York: Doubleday, Anchor, 1968), 59–77. Fredrik Barth (*Models of Social Organization*, Royal Anthropological Institute, Occasional Paper 23 [London: RAI, 1966]) explores the generative processes underlying social structure, and John Barnes ("Time Flies Like an Arrow," *Man*, n.s. 6, no. 4 [1971]: 537–52) examines their relationship to interpretations of history.

26. Theodore W. Schultz, "The Value of Children: An Economic Perspective," *Journal of Political Economy* 81, no. 2, part 2 (1973): S12.

27. For this reason, long-range panel studies are usually obliged to relinquish the "family" or "household" as a unit of observation in favor of component individuals. See Glen H. Elder, "Families and Lives: Some Developments in Life-Course Studies," *Journal of Family History* 12 (1987): 186–90. However, the limited explanatory power of the individual life cycle has been demonstrated by simple comparisons with family-cycle models. See John B. Lansing and Leslie Kish, "Family Life Cycle as an Independent Variable," *American Sociological Review* 22 (1957): 512–19; and A. F. Robertson and G. H. Hughes, "The Family Farm in Buganda," *Development and Change* 9, no. 3 (1978): 432.

28. Recently historians have sought to reduce the family to its assemblage of individual life courses. See especially Tamara K. Hareven, "Family Time and Historical Time," in A. S. Rossi, J. Kagan, and T. K. Hareven, eds., *The Family* (New York: Norton, 1978), 57–70; Hareven, *Family Time and Industrial Time: The Relationship Between Family and Work in a New England Industrial Community* (Cambridge: Cambridge University Press, 1982). See also Michael Anderson, "The Emergence of the Modern Life Cycle in Britain," *Social History* 10, no. 1 (1985): 69–87; and Glen H. Elder, ed., *Life Course Dynamics: Trajectories and Transitions, 1968–1980* (Ithaca: Cornell University Press, 1985). While this approach helps to tease out the underlying significance of the relations of reproduction, the family or household tends to be regarded as an epiphenomenon of the life of one person—typically the adult male "head," sometimes the wife or mother. For critical comments, see, for example, E. A. Hammel, "The Family Cycle in a Coastal Peruvian Slum and Village," *American Anthropologist* 63, no. 5, part 1 (1961): 989–1005; and Paul C. Glick and Robert Parke, "New Approaches in Studying the Life Cycle of the Family," *Demography* 2 (1965): 187–202.

29. Commenting on this problem, John Barnes tells me: "I always like to think of forestry as the discipline where this difficulty is most wide-spread. A forester often has to start an experiment merely in the hope that long after he is dead some successor will be sufficiently interested in the results to publish them" (personal communication).

30. In various ways this has been the procedure of all the main contributors to the discussion of family dynamics: e.g., Le Play in his worker surveys, Rowntree in his York studies, Fortes in Ashanti, Chayanov in his scrutiny of Russian statistics, and Glick in his work on U.S. census data. See Rowntree, *Poverty;* Fortes, "Time and Social Structure"; A. V. Chayanov, "Peasant Farm Organization," in D. Thorner, B. Kerblay, and R. F. Smith, eds., *On the Theory of Peasant Economy* (Homewood, Ill: Richard Irwin, 1966), 29–269; and Paul C. Glick, *American Families* (New York: John Wiley, 1957).

31. See Charles P. Loomis and C. Horace Hamilton, "Family Life Cycle Analysis," *Social Forces* 15, no. 2 (1936): 225–31.

Browning makes the interesting observation that time-series data (unless they extend over several decades) are more likely to reveal short-run cyclical changes, while cross-sectional data are more likely to express "variations which are long-standing in nature." The problem is that we have no means of knowing for sure which kind of change is which, and no means of explaining how durable differences detected by cross-sectional analysis should be adduced to that grand "time series" of history. See Mark Browning, "Time-Series, Cross-Sections, and Pooling," in Ghazi M. Farooq and George B. Simmons, eds., *Fertility in Developing Countries* (New York: St. Martin's, 1985), 150.

32. For such reasons it is not surprising that even the most sophisticated demographic models of family development have lost much of their explanatory power. For example, Paul C. Glick's scrutiny of U.S. census data (see his *American Families*) indicated very significant correlations with income distribution and other macroeconomic indicators, but his efforts to deploy the family cycle as a major "independent variable" in the analysis of industrial society were vitiated by the fact that for him it remained essentially a demographic *effect*. Specification of the stages of family development was largely intuitive and their varying degree of "normality" among different classes and social categories tacitly assumed.

33. Meyer Fortes, *Kinship and the Social Order: The Legacy of Lewis Henry Morgan* (London: Routledge and Kegan Paul, 1970), 61.

34. See Colin Murray, "Class, Gender, and the Household: The Developmental Cycle in Southern Africa," *Development and Change* 18 (1987): 236.

35. For example, "Society must *reproduce* itself in and through individual behavior and relies on institutions for this purpose" (Anthony Oberschall and Eric M. Leifer, "Efficiency and Social Institutions: Uses and Misuses of Economic Reasoning in Sociology," *Annual Review of Sociology* 12 [1986]: 235–36).

36. See C. C. Harris, *The Family in Industrial Society* (London: George Allen and Unwin, 1983), 181.

37. Few observers have shown a more acute interest in the significance of time in social and economic organization than Chayanov. For example, he devised an elaborate twenty-one-step model of the process of agricultural intensification. It appears that his interest in family dynamism was already well established in the Russian populist tradition to which he belonged, for example, in the

economic writings of Prince Vasiltchikoff. Chayanov's populism found literary expression in his novel *Journey of My Brother Alexei to the Land of Peasant Utopia*, published in 1920. See Basile Kerblay, "A. V. Chayanov: Life, Career, Works," in D. Thorner, B. Kerblay, and R. F. Smith, eds., *On the Theory of Peasant Economy* (Homewood, Ill: Richard Irwin, 1966), xxv–lxxv.

38. See especially V. I. Lenin, *The Development of Capitalism in Russia*, 2d ed. (Moscow: Progress Publishers, 1964), 175–90.

39. Lenin's teleology prevailed, and in the era of Stalin, Chayanov was discredited. Historicism, it seems, was effectively purged of the influence of substantive "demographic" process. Following publication of an English translation of Chayanov's work in 1966, there was an efflorescence of interest in the West. Teodor Shanin, for example, reaffirmed the importance of "cyclical mobility" in the constitution of the Russian peasantry, in a book which dwelt on the need to temper an enthusiasm for historical transformation with recognition of "*processes reinforcing the stability* of the social system" (see Shanin, *Awkward Class*, 3). Positive tests of Chayanov's hypotheses have followed, in regions as diverse as Taiwan (Susan Greenhalgh, "Is Inequality Demographically Induced? The Family Cycle and the Distribution of Income in Taiwan, 1954–1978," *American Anthropologist* 87 [1985]: 571–94), Switzerland (Wanda Minge-Kalman, "On the Theory and Measurement of Domestic Labor Intensity," *American Ethnologist* 4, no. 2 [1977]: 273–84), Peru (Carmen D. Deere and Alain de Janvry, "Demographic and Social Differentiation among Northern Peruvian Peasants," *Journal of Peasant Studies* 8, no. 3 [April 1981]: 335–66), and North Carolina (Charles P. Loomis, "The Study of the Life Cycle of Families," *Rural Sociology* 1 [1936]: 180–99). See also Terry Cox, "Awkward Class or Awkward Classes? Class Relations in the Russian Peasantry Before Collectivisation," *Journal of Peasant Studies* 7, no. 1 (October 1979): 70–85; and E. Paul Durrenberger, ed., *Chayanov, Peasants, and Economic Anthropology* (Orlando: Academic Press, 1984).

40. See, for example, Utsa Patnaik, "Neo-populism and Marxism: The Chayanovian View of the Agrarian Question and Its Fundamental Fallacy," *Journal of Peasant Studies* 6, no. 4 (1979): 375–420; Mark Harrison, "The Peasant Mode of Production in the Work of A. V. Chayanov," *Journal of Peasant Studies* 4, no. 4 (1977): 323–36; and Mark Harrison, "Chayanov and the Marxists," *Journal of Peasant Studies* 7, no. 1 (1979): 86–100.

41. Chayanov's argument about the inherent *underproductivity* of the peasantry and its resistance to capitalist transformation has been adduced to the study of the contemporary "Third World." For example, Marshall Sahlins has generalized Chayanov's model to a "domestic mode of production" which constitutes "an impediment to development of the productive means" (see Sahlins, *Stone Age economics* (London: Tavistock, 1974), 101.

42. See Chayanov, "Peasant Farm Organization," 242–69.

43. See Donald L. Donham, *Work and Power in Maale, Ethiopia* (Ann Arbor: University Microfilms International Research Press, 1985).

44. Chayanov describes his model as a *"rough scheme"* ("Peasant Farm Organization," 57–60).

45. See Loomis, "Study of the Life Cycle"; and Robertson and Hughes, "Family Farm in Buganda," 425.

46. See Shanin, *Awkward Class*, 28–41.

47. Shanin (*Awkward Class*, 101) goes so far as to characterize Chayanov's approach as "biological determinism."

48. See, for example, Harold Wolpe, ed., *The Articulation of Modes of Production* (London: Routledge and Kegan Paul, 1980).

49. See, for example, Louis Althusser, "Ideology and Ideological State Apparatuses," in Ben Brewster, ed., *Lenin and Philosophy* (London: New Left Books, 1971), 123–73. Confusion about these meanings of reproduction has become a notable issue in feminist critiques; see Maureen Mackintosh, "Gender and Economics: The Sexual Division of Labour and the Subordination of Women," in K. Young, C. Wolkowitz, and R. McCullagh, eds., *Of Marriage and the Market: Women's Subordination Internationally and Its Lessons*, 2d ed. (London: Routledge and Kegan Paul, 1984), 11–13.

50. Marxist views of the family and reproduction in the industrial context are discussed helpfully by C. C. Harris (*Family in Industrial Society*, 179–80). Harris recognizes that the Marxist tradition "provides us with an elaborate theory of capitalist society, but tells us very little about the family." Harris asserts that "economic production and human reproduction are the two activities without which any society cannot persist, and both activities are, each in its own way, equally fundamental." He concludes, however, that "while in economic production the means of production are highly variable and have varied enormously, the means of biological reproduction appear, in contrast, relatively fixed. The transformation of family life would appear to be always the resultant of the transformation of economic life, not because of any universal power of the latter to determine the former, but because of the absence of any dynamic process within the sphere of biological reproduction which could transform the *relations* of reproduction" (ibid., 180). Implicit is the assumption that any "development of the means of reproduction" must be homologous with the technical expansion of the productive means. If we were to accept this logic, the current spate of reproductive innovations in all areas from fertilization to geriatrics might dispose us to expect immanent revolution (see Suzanne Keller, "Does the Family Have a Future?" in A. Skolnick and J. Skolnick, eds., *Family in Transition*, 3d ed. [Boston: Little, Brown, 1980], 74–79; Mary O'Brien, *Reproducing the World: Essays in Feminist Theory* [Boulder: Westview Press, 1989]). But it is plain that techniques of conception and contraception, for example, are a very ancient human preoccupation (see Angus McLaren, *Reproductive Rituals: The Perception of Fertility in England from the Sixteenth to the Nineteenth Century* [Oxford: Basil Blackwell, 1984]; and Jean-Louis Flandrin, *Families in Former Times: Kinship, Household and Sexuality* [Cambridge: Cambridge University Press, 1976]).

51. Claude Meillassoux, *Maidens, Meal, and Money: Capitalism and the Domestic Community* (Cambridge: Cambridge University Press, 1981), 33.

52. Ibid., 168.

53. Ibid., 101.

54. Claude Meillassoux, "The Economic Bases of Demographic Reproduction: From the Domestic Mode of Production to Wage-Earning," *Journal of Peasant Studies* 11, no. 1 (1983): 52–53.

55. Meillassoux, *Maidens, Meal, and Money*, xii.

56. Ibid.; Meillassoux, "Economic Bases," 50.

57. Meillassoux, *Maidens, Meal, and Money*, xiv.

58. Ibid.

59. Ibid., 3.

60. Jairus Banaji, "Chayanov, Kautsky, Lenin: Considerations Towards a Synthesis," *Economic and Political Weekly* [Bombay], 2 October 1976, 1606.

61. A. F. Robertson, *The Dynamics of Productive Relationships: African Share Contracts in Comparative Perspective* (Cambridge: Cambridge University Press, 1987).

62. Using a biological analogy, I distinguished these respectively as the *ontogenetic* and *phylogenetic* life of the contract.

63. See John Iliffe, *The Emergence of African Capitalism* (London: Macmillan, 1983).

64. See E. P. Thompson, "Time, Work-Discipline, and Industrial Capitalism," *Past and Present* 38 (1967): 56–97; and Lotte Bailyn, "Accommodation of Work to Family," in Skolnick and Skolnick, *Family in Transition*, 566–79.

65. See Talcott Parsons, "The Social Structure of the Family," in R. N. Anshen, ed., *The Family: Its Function and Destiny* (New York: Harper, 1949), 173–201. See also Keller, "Does the Family Have a Future?" 66–79; Espenshade, "Recent Decline"; and David Popenoe, *Disturbing the Nest: Family Change and Decline in Modern Societies* (New York: Aldine de Gruyter, 1988).

66. Frank F. Furstenberg, "Industrialization and the American Family: A Look Backward," *American Sociological Review* 31, no. 3 (1966): 327.

67. See Talcott Parsons, "Social Structure of the Family"; and William J. Goode, *World Revolution and Family Patterns* (New York: Free Press, 1963).

68. See especially Peter Laslett, "Size and Structure of the Household in England over Three Centuries," *Population Studies* 23, no. 2 (1969): 199–223; and Peter Laslett, "Introduction: The History of the Family," in P. Laslett and R. Wall, eds., *Household and Family in Past Time* (Cambridge: Cambridge University Press, 1972), 1–89; Alan Macfarlane, *Marriage and Love in England 1300–1840* (Oxford: Basil Blackwell, 1986); J. Hajnal, "Two Kinds of Pre-industrial Household Formation Systems," in R. Wall, J. Robin, and P. Laslett, eds., *Family Forms in Historic Europe* (Cambridge: Cambridge University Press, 1983) 65–104; and Richard Wall, "The Household: Demographic and Economic Change in England, 1650–1970," in Wall, Robin, and Laslett, *Family Forms in Historic Europe*, 493–512.

69. Hareven, "Family Time and Historical Time," 58. See also Frank F. Furstenberg, "Industrialization and the American Family," 326–37; and Natalie Z. Davis, "Ghosts, Kin, and Progeny: Some Features of Family Life in Early Modern France," in Rossi, Kagan, and Hareven, *The Family*, 87–114.

70. A revealing example is the Monte delle Doti of medieval Florence, which was originally concerned with mustering funds for dowry; Donald E. Brown observes that this prototypical bank "went beyond material interests in the usual sense to link the very reproductive interests of Florentines with their city" (Brown, *Hierarchy, History, and Human Nature: The Origins of Historical Consciousness* [Tucson: University of Arizona Press, 1988], 269); see also Julius Kirshner, "Pursuing Honor While Avoiding Sin: The *Monte delle doti* of Florence," *Studi Senesi* 87 (1977): 177–258.

71. See, for example, Esther N. Goody, ed., *From Craft to Industry: The Ethnography of Proto-industrial Cloth Production* (Cambridge: Cambridge University Press, 1982); Medick, "Proto-industrial Family Economy"; Franklin F. Mendels, "Proto-industrialization: The First Phase of the Industrialization Process," *Journal of Economic History* 32, no. 1 (1972): 241–61; Eric R. Wolf, *Europe and the People Without History* (Berkeley and Los Angeles: University of California Press, 1982); and David Levine, ed., *Proletarianization and Family History* (Orlando: Academic Press, 1984).

72. This is described graphically by David Levine in his *Family Formation in an Age of Nascent Capitalism* (Orlando: Academic Press, 1977); see also Levine, *Proletarianization*.

73. Hareven, "Family Time and Historical Time," 165. Valuable accounts of this turbulence may be found in Michael Anderson, *Family Structure in Nineteenth Century Lancashire* (Cambridge: Cambridge University Press, 1971), and Elizabeth A. Kusnesof, "Household Composition and Headship as Related to Changes in Mode of Production: Sao Paulo 1765 to 1836," *Comparative Studies in Society and History* 22, no. 1 (1980): 78–108. See also Hans Medick, "The Proto-industrial Family Economy: The Structural Function of Household and Family During the Transition from Peasant Society to Industrial Capitalism," *Social History* 3 (1976): 291–315.

74. See Harold Lydall, "The Life Cycle in Income, Saving, and Asset Ownership," *Econometrica* 23, no. 2 (1955): 133–50; A. Ando and F. Modigliani, "The Life Cycle Hypothesis of Saving: Aggregate Implications and Tests," *American Economic Review* 53 (1963): 55–84; J. E. Meade, "Life-cycle Savings, Inheritance, and Economic Growth," *Review of Economic Studies* 33, part 1 (1966): 61–78; and Walter Gove, James W. Grimm, Susan C. Motz, and James D. Thompson, "The Family Life Cycle: Internal Dynamics and Social Consequences," *Sociology and Social Research* 57, no. 2 (1973): 182–95.

75. "Men in occupations with peak median earnings of $7,000 or more in 1959 are much more likely to have experienced earnings increases over time that roughly parallel increases in the cost of maintaining a family," says Valerie Oppenheimer ("The Life Cycle Squeeze: The Interaction of Men's Occupational and Family Life Cycles," *Demography* 11, no. 2 [1974]: 227). "1960 census data on earnings patterns by age indicate that in only relatively high-level professional, managerial and sales occupations do average earnings peak at the same time family needs are peaking" (ibid., 241). See also Lydall, "Life Cycle," 141–42.

76. An early but very clear statistical account of this appears in Harold F. Clark, *Life Earnings in Selected Occupations in the United States* (New York: Harper and Brothers, 1937). He concludes, for example, that "in unskilled and semi-skilled labor the pay is determined by the kind of work done and not by the length of service" (p. 138). By comparison, the salary of an architect increased incrementally over forty years of service by 500 percent (8). Analyzing gross rates of remuneration rather than occupational categories, Oppenheimer produces a very similar pattern of income–life cycle variance for more recent times: the lower-paid "are truly occupations with 'early ceilings,'" while "in the case of the higher-income groups, although average earnings are low for the young, they rise rapidly from age group to age group, finally peaking at a rather late age" (240, 237). See also Glick and Robert, "New Approaches," 199–200; Alvin

L. Schorr, "The Family Cycle and Income Development," *Social Security Bulletin* 29, no. 2 (1966): 14–25; and Sherwin Rosen, "A Theory of Life Earnings," *Journal of Political Economy* 84, no. 4, part 2 (1976): S45–S67.

77. John Rex, *Key Problems in Sociological Theory* (London: Routledge and Kegan Paul, 1961), 142.

78. See Michael R. Haines, "Industrial Work and the Family Life Cycle, 1889–1890," in Paul Uselding, ed., *Research in Economic History* (Greenwich, Conn.: JAI Press, (1979), 4: 301. It is plain that working-class and middle-class women go out to work for quite different reasons and at quite different stages of the family life cycle (see Glick and Robert, "New Approaches," 201; Oppenheimer, "Life Cycle Squeeze," 244).

79. T. Paul Schultz, "Comments on 'Estimates of a Human Capital Production Function Embedded in a Life-cycle Model of Labor Supply' [by James J. Heckman]," in Nestor E. Terleckyj, ed., *Household Production and Consumption* (New York: National Bureau of Economic Research, 1975), 259. See also Gary Becker, *Human Capital* (New York: Columbia University Press, 1964); Becker, *A Treatise on the Family* (Cambridge: Harvard University Press, 1981); Yoram Ben-porath, "The Production of Human Capital and the Life Cycle of Earnings," *Journal of Political Economy* 75, no. 4, part 1 (August 1967): 352–65; and James J. Heckman, "Estimates of a Human Capital Production Function Embedded in a Life-cycle Model of Labor Supply," in Terleckyj, *Household Production and Consumption*, 227–64.

80. James P. Smith, "Family Labor Supply over the Life Cycle," *Explorations in Economic Research* 4, no. 2 (1977): 220.

81. See Andrew Thomson, "The Structure of Collective Bargaining in Britain," in Angela M. Bowey, ed., *Handbook of Salary and Wage Systems*, 2d ed. (Aldershott: Gower, 1975), 37–53. Dore remarks that in Britain, "although some other factors may be taken into account in practice, the notion that there *is* a market which operates to standardize the price of various skills is the starting point for all discussions of wage determination" (Dore, *British Factory–Japanese Factory: The Origins of National Diversity in Industrial Relations* [London: George Allen and Unwin, 1973], 74).

82. See, for example, Heidi Hartmann, "The Family as the Locus of Gender, Class, and Political Struggle: The Example of Housework," *Signs: Journal of Women in Culture and Society* 6, no. 3 (1981): 366–94; and Mary O'Brien, *Reproducing the World: Essays in Feminist Theory* (Boulder: Westview, 1989).

83. Hareven, "Family Time and Historical Time," 67.

84. Wanda Minge-Kalman, "The Industrial Revolution and the European Family: The Institutionalization of 'Childhood' as a Market for Family Labor," *Comparative Studies in Society and History* 20, no. 3 (1978): 466.

85. The elusiveness of the idea of family dynamism is very striking. It has failed to find a durable niche in conventional social theory, and with each rediscovery the "neglect" of the subject is lamented. The name of Chayanov provides some tenuous continuity, but the reader needs sharp eyes: in French he is "Cajanov," Sorokin cites "Tschaianov," Loomis "Tschajanow," and Wolf "Chaianov"; Thorner et al. finally gave currency to "Chayanov." The convolutions of this last rediscovery are very telling: Thorner, the radical expatriate American scholar working in Paris, was encouraged by a Russian-educated Indian scholar who had

worked with the German text to collaborate with French and British colleagues on an English translation of Chayanov's *Theory of Peasant Economy* (1966). See Sorokin, et al., *Systematic Source Book*, 12, 144–46; Loomis, "Study of the Life Cycle"; Eric Wolf, *Peasants* (Englewood Cliffs, N.J.: Prentice Hall, 1966); and Thorner, Kerblay, and Smith, *On the Theory of Peasant Economy*. The main pioneers of family dynamics are widely dispersed in time and space and are notable interdisciplinarians: Le Play the engineer-historian-philosopher, Chayanov the agronomist-political economist, Fortes the psychologist-anthropologist. They were not intimidated by the disciplinary thresholds which tended to preclude their wide-ranging quest for *temporal* explanations of social phenomena. Fortes, for example, was greatly inspired by the biologist D'Arcy Thompson's classic *Growth and Form* (Cambridge: Cambridge University Press, 1942).

86. Ferdinand de Saussure, *Course in General Linguistics* (New York: Philosophical Library, 1959), 83.

87. In recent years there have been some significant efforts to close the analytical gap between synchrony and diachrony and to place the coordinates of space and time in social theory. In *A Contemporary Critique of Historical Materialism* (Berkeley and Los Angeles: University of California Press, 1981), Anthony Giddens remarks that "we can identify three 'layers' of temporality involved in the analysis of the structuration of social systems; each is also an aspect of the contingent character of social interaction. Temporality enters into: (a) the immediate nexus of interaction as contingently 'brought off' by social actors, the most elemental form of social reproduction, (b) the existence of *Dasein,* as the living organism, the contingency of life in the face of death, and of biological reproduction, and (c) the long-term reproduction of *institutions* across the generations, the contingency of the transformation/mediation relations implicated in the structural principles of system organisation" (28). Giddens's interest in *the duality of structure* (as the medium and the outcome of the conduct it recursively organizes) fixes his attention on the first and third of these temporalities, the second ("the life-cycle of the organism" [19–20]) serving very occasionally as a medium for relating human consciousness to the immediacies of action. The *Dasein* is certainly not presented as a transgenerational notion of the sort I am proposing here. See also Anthony Giddens, *The Constitution of Society* (Berkeley and Los Angeles: University of California Press, 1984).

# FOUR

# Postmodern Geographies: Taking Los Angeles Apart

*Edward W. Soja*

Did it start with Bergson or before? Space was treated as the dead, the fixed, the undialectical, the immobile. Time, on the contrary, was richness, fecundity, life, dialectic.[1]

The great obsession of the nineteenth century was, as we know, history: with its themes of development and of suspension, of crisis and cycle, themes of the ever-accumulating past, with its great preponderance of dead men and the menacing glaciation of the world. . . . The present epoch will perhaps be above all the epoch of space. We are in the epoch of simultaneity: we are in the epoch of juxtaposition, the epoch of the near and far, of the side-by-side, of the dispersed. We are at a moment, I believe, when our experience of the world is less that of a long life developing through time than that of a network that connects points and intersects with its own skein. One could perhaps say that certain ideological conflicts animating present-day polemics oppose the pious descendants of time and the determined inhabitants of space.[2]

The nineteenth-century obsession with history, as Foucault described it, did not die in the fin de siècle. Nor has it been fully replaced by an affective spatialization of thought and experience. An essentially historical epistemology continues to pervade the *critical* consciousness of modern social theory and philosophy, reproducing the "great obsession" in an emancipatory rationality that seeks practical understanding of the world primarily through the dynamics of *durée,* the sequential unfolding of events, the emplacement of social being and becoming in the interpretive contexts of time: in what Kant called *nacheinander* and Marx defined so transfiguratively as the contingently constrained "making of history." This enduring epistemological presence has preserved a privileged place for the "historical imagination" in defining the very nature of critical insight and interpretation.

The persistence of this historicism of theoretical consciousness has blocked the development of an equivalent critical sensibility to the *spatiality* of social life, a practical theoretical consciousness that sees the life world of being creatively located not only in the making of history but also in the construction of human geographies, the social production of space, the restless formation and reformation of geographical landscapes: social being actively emplaced in time *and* space, in an explicitly historical *and* geographical contextualization, in a balanced fusion of *nacheinander* and *nebeneinander*, the inKantation of spatiality. Although others joined Foucault to urge a rebalancing of this prioritization of time over space, no hegemonic shift has yet occurred to allow the critical eye—or the critical I—to see spatiality with the same acute depth of vision that comes with a focus on historicity. The critical hermeneutic is still powerfully enveloped in a temporal master narrative, in a historical but not yet comparably geographical imagination. Foucault's revealing glance back over the past hundred years thus continues to apply today, at least in the mainstreams of critical thought in the human sciences. Space still tends to be treated as fixed, dead, undialectical; time as richness, life, dialectic, the revealing context for critical social theorization.

As we move closer to the end of the twentieth century, however, Foucault's premonitory observations on the emergence of an "epoch of space" are beginning to take on a more reasonable cast. There has been a rather startling rise of what might best be described as a distinctively *postmodern* and *critical* human geography, brashly reasserting the interpretive significance of space in contemporary critical thought. In the 1980s the hoary traditions of a space-blinkered historicism have been challenged with unprecedented explicitness by convergent calls for a far-reaching *spatialization* of the critical imagination. Geography has not yet displaced history at the hegemonic heart of contemporary theory and criticism, but there is a new animating polemic on the theoretical and political agenda, one which rings with significantly different ways of seeing time and space together, the interplay of history and geography, the "vertical" and "horizontal" dimensions of being-in-the-world freed from the imposition of inherent categorical privilege.

These shifts and turns have produced new possibilities for a simultaneously historical and geographical materialism; a more encompassing and revealing "trialectics" of space, time, and social being; and a transformative retheorization of the relations between history, geography, and modernity. The interpretation of what I call *postmodern geographies,* in the double sense of significant changes in the material landscape of the contemporary world and in the interpretive terrain of critical thought and theory, defines the compelling core of these new possibilities. I will explore both of these realms of postmodern geographies here, first in a brief overview of the developing interpretive terrain and then in a more empirical journey through the restructured spaces of postmodern Los Angeles.

## LOCATING THE ORIGINS OF POSTMODERN GEOGRAPHIES

The first insistent voices of a postmodern critical human geography appeared in the late 1960s, but they were barely heard against the prevailing temporal din. For more than a decade the spatializing project remained strangely muted by an untroubled reaffirmation of the primacy of history over geography that enveloped both Western Marxism and liberal social science in a virtually sanctified vision of the ever-accumulating past. One of the most comprehensive and convincing pictures of this continuously historical contextualization of critical social theory was drawn by C. Wright Mills in his paradigmatic portrayal of *The Sociological Imagination* (1959). Mills's work provides a useful point of departure for spatializing the historical narrative and reinterpreting the course of critical social theory.

### The Silenced Spatiality of Historicism

Mills maps out a sociological imagination that is deeply rooted in a historical rationality—what Martin Jay would call a "longitudinal totalization"—that applies equally well to critical social science and to the critical traditions of Marxism.[3]

> [The sociological imagination] is a quality of mind that will help [individuals] to use information and to develop reason in order to achieve lucid summations of what is going on in the world and of what may be happening within themselves.
>
> The first fruit of this imagination—and the first lessons of the social science that embodies it—is the idea that the individual can understand his own experience and gauge his own fate only by locating himself within his period, that he can know his own chances in life only by becoming aware of those of all individuals in his circumstances. . . . We have come to know that every individual lives, from one generation to the next, in some society; that he lives out a biography, and that he lives it out within some historical sequence. By the fact of his living he contributes, however minutely, to the shaping of this society and to the course of history, even as he is made by society and by its historical push and shove.

He goes further:

> The sociological imagination enables us to grasp history and biography and the relations of the two within society. This is its task and its promise.

> To recognize this task and this promise is the mark of the classic social analyst. . . . *No social study that does not come back to the problems of biography, of history, and of their intersections within society, has completed its intellectual journey.*

I draw on Mills's depiction of what is essentially a historical imagination to illustrate the alluring logic of historicism, the rational reduction of meaning and action, being and becoming, to the temporal constitution and experience of social life. This connection between the historical imagination and historicism needs further elaboration, for it is at once a daring leap and a springboard for all that will follow. First, there is the easier question of why "sociological" has been changed to "historical." As Mills himself notes, "Every cobbler thinks leather is the only thing," and as a trained sociologist Mills names his leather after his own disciplinary specialization and socialization. The nominal choice personally specifies what is a much more widely shared "quality of mind" that Mills claims should pervade, indeed embody, all social theory and analysis, an emancipatory rationality that is grounded in the intersections of history, biography, and society.

To be sure, these "life stories" have a geography too; they have milieux, immediate locales, provocative emplacements which affect thought and action. The historical imagination is never completely spaceless, and critical social historians have written, and continue to write, some of the best geographies of the past. But time and history always provide the primary "variable containers" in these geographies, the most revealing discourses, the most affecting story lines. This would be just as clear whether the imaginative glance is described as sociological or political or anthropological—or for that matter phenomenological, existential, hermeneutic, or historical materialist. The particular emphases may differ, but the encompassing perspective is shared. An already made geography sets the stage, and the willful making of history dictates the action and defines the story line.

It is important to stress that this historical imagination has been particularly central to *critical* social theory, to the search for practical understanding of the world as a means of emancipation versus maintenance of the status quo. Social theories which merely rationalize existing conditions and thereby serve to promote repetitive behavior, the continuous reproduction of established social practices, do not fit the definition of critical theory. They may be no less accurate with respect to what they are describing, but their rationality (or irrationality, for that matter) is likely to be mechanical, normative, scientific, or instrumental rather than critical. It is precisely the critical and potentially emancipatory value of the historical imagination, of people "making history" rather than taking it for granted, that has made it so compulsively appealing.

The constant reaffirmation that the world can be changed by human action, by *praxis*, has always been the centerpiece of critical social theory whatever its particularized source and emphasis.

The development of critical social theory has revolved around the assertion of a mutable history against perspectives and practices that mystify and obscure the changeability of the world. The critical historical discourse thus sets itself against abstract and transhistorical universalizations (including notions of a general "human nature" which explain everything and nothing at the same time); against naturalisms, empiricisms, and positivisms which proclaim physical determinations of history apart from social origins; against religious and ideological fatalisms which project spiritual determinations and teleologies (even when carried forward in the guises of human consciousness); against any and all conceptualizations of the world which freeze the frangibility of time, the possibility of "breaking" and remaking history.

Both the attractive critical insight of the historical imagination and its continuing need to be forcefully defended against distracting mystifications have contributed to its exaggerated assertion as historicism. Historicism has been conventionally defined in several different ways. Raymond Williams, for example, presents three contemporary choices, which he describes as (1) "neutral," a method of study using facts from the past to trace the precedents of current events; (2) "deliberate," an emphasis on variable historical conditions and contexts as a privileged framework for interpreting all specific events; and (3) "hostile," an attack on all interpretation and prediction which is based on notions of historical necessity or general laws of historical development.[4] I wish to give an additional twist to these options by defining historicism as *an overdeveloped historical contextualization of social life and social theory that actively submerges and peripheralizes the geographical or spatial imagination.* This definition does not deny the extraordinary power and importance of historiography as a mode of emancipatory insight; rather, it identifies historicism with the creation of a critical silence, an implicit subordination of space to time that obscures geographical interpretations of the changeability of the social world and intrudes on every level of theoretical discourse, from the most abstract ontological concepts of being to the most detailed explanations of empirical events.

This definition may appear rather odd when set against the long tradition of debate over historicism that has flourished for centuries. But the failure of this debate to recognize the peculiar theoretical and interpretive peripheralization of space that accompanied even the most neutral forms of historicism is, however, precisely what began to be discovered in the late 1960s. The most persistent and powerful spatializing voice came from the French Marxist philosopher Henri Lefebvre, whose critical theorization of the social production of space not only infused the explosion of Paris in 1968 but also inspired the reassertion of space in critical social thought over the next two decades. But Lefebvre rarely attacked historicism directly, preferring instead to create a rigorous historical and geographical materialism by positive demonstration rather than exegetic deconstruction. Finding the roots of a more explicit critique of the epistemological priority of time over space, history over geography, takes us to the works of Michel Foucault and John Berger, whose active spatializing projects have been largely hidden from view by their more comforting and familiar identification as historians.

### The Ambivalent Spatiality of Michel Foucault

The contributions of Foucault to the development of critical human geography must be drawn out archaeologically, for he buried his precursory spatial turn in brilliant whirls of historical insight. He would no doubt have resisted being called a postmodern geographer, but he was one, *malgré lui,* from his early *Madness and Civilization* to his last works in *The History of Sexuality.* His most explicit and revealing observations on the relative significance of space and time, however, appear not in his major published works but almost innocuously in his lectures and, after some coaxing interrogation, in two revealing interviews: "Questions on Geography" and "Space, Knowledge, and Power."[5]

The epochal observations which head this chapter, for example, were first made in a 1967 lecture entitled "Des espaces autres." They remained virtually unseen and unheard for nearly twenty years, until their publication in the French journal *Architecture-Mouvement-Continuité* in 1984 and, translated by Jay Miskowiec as "Of Other Spaces," in *Diacritics* (1986). In these lecture notes Foucault outlined his notion of "heterotopias" as the characteristic spaces of the modern world, superseding the hierarchic "ensemble of places" of the Middle Ages and the enveloping "space of emplacement" opened up by Galileo into an early modern, infinitely unfolding "space of extension" and measurement. Moving away from both the "internal space" of Bachelard's brilliant poetics and the intentional regional descriptions of the phenomenologists, Foucault focused our attention on another spatiality of social life, an "external space," the actually lived (and socially produced) space of *sites* and the relations between them.

> The space in which we live, which draws us out of ourselves, in which the erosion of our lives, our time and our history occurs, the space that claws and gnaws at us, is also, in itself, a heterogeneous space. In other words, we do not live in a kind of void, inside of which we could place individuals and things. We do not live inside a void that could be colored with diverse

shades of light, we live inside a set of relations that delineates sites which are irreducible to one another and absolutely not superimposable on one another. ("Of Other Spaces," 23)

These heterogeneous spaces of sites and relations—Foucault's hetero-topias—are constituted in every society but take quite varied forms and change over time, as "history unfolds" in its adherent spatiality. He iden-tifies many such sites: the cemetery and the church, the theater and the garden, the museum and the library, the fairground and the "vacation village," the barracks and the prison, the Moslem hamman and the Scan-dinavian sauna, the brothel and the colony. Foucault contrasts these "real places" with the "fundamentally unreal spaces" of utopias, which present society in either "a perfected form" or else "turned upside down."

> The heterotopia is capable of juxtaposing in a single real place several spaces, several sites that are in themselves incompatible. . . . They have a function in relation to all the space that remains. This function unfolds between two extreme poles. Either their role is to create a space of illusion that exposes every real space, all the sites inside of which human life is partitioned, as still more illusory. . . . Or else, on the contrary, their role is to create a space that is other, another real space, as perfect, as meticulous, as well arranged as ours is messy, ill constructed, and jumbled. The latter type would be the heterotopia, not of illusion, but of compensation, and I wonder if certain colonies have not functioned somewhat in this manner. ("Of Other Spaces," 25, 27)

With these remarks Foucault exposed many of the compelling direc-tions he would take in his lifework and indirectly raised a powerful argu-ment against historicism—and against the prevailing treatments of space in the human sciences. Foucault's heterogeneous and relational space of heterotopias is neither a substanceless void to be filled by cognitive intu-ition nor a repository of physical forms to be phenomenologically de-scribed in all its resplendent variability. It is another space, what Lefeb-vre would describe as *l'espace vécu,* actually lived and socially created spatiality, concrete and abstract at the same time, the habitus of social practices. It is a space rarely seen, for it has been obscured by a binary vision that persistently views space as either purely "ideational" (a men-tal construct) or purely "empirical" (a physical form). This deceptive du-alism, the source of what Lefebvre described as alternative illusions of transparency and opaqueness, has dominated philosophical and scien-tific debate on the theory of space for centuries.

To illustrate his innovative interpretation of space and time and to clarify some of the often confusing polemics which were arising around it, Foucault turned to the current debates on structuralism, one of the twentieth century's most important avenues for the reassertion of space in critical social theory. Foucault vigorously insisted that he himself was not (just?) a structuralist, but he recognized in the development of structuralism a different and compelling vision of history and geography, a critical reorientation that was connecting space and time in new and revealing ways.

> Structuralism, or at least that which is grouped under this slightly too general name, is the effort to establish, between elements that could have been connected on a temporal axis, an ensemble of relations that makes them appear as juxtaposed, set off against one another, in short, as a sort of configuration. Actually structuralism does not entail a denial of time; it does involve a certain manner of dealing with what we call time and what we call history. ("Of Other Spaces," 22)

This synchronic "configuration" is the spatialization of history, the making of history entwined with the social production of space, the structuring of a historical geography.[6]

Foucault refused to project his spatialization as an antihistory, but his history was provocatively spatialized from the very start. This was not just a shift in metaphorical preference, as it frequently seemed to be for Althusser and others more comfortable with the structuralist label than Foucault. It was the opening up of history to an interpretive geography. To emphasize the centrality of space to the critical eye, especially regarding the contemporary moment, Foucault becomes most explicit: "In any case I believe that the anxiety of our era has to do fundamentally with space, no doubt a great deal more than with time. Time probably appears to us only as one of the various distributive operations that are possible for the elements that are spread out in space" ("Of Other Spaces," 23). He would never be quite so explicit again. Foucault's spatialization took on a more demonstrative rather than declarative stance, confident perhaps that at least the French would understand the intent and significance of his strikingly spatialized historiography.

In an interview conducted shortly before his death, Foucault reminisced on his exploration "Of Other Spaces" and the enraged reactions it engendered from those he once identified as the "pious descendants of time." Asked whether space was central to the analysis of power, he answered:

> Yes. Space is fundamental in any form of communal life; space is fundamental in any exercise of power. To make a parenthetical remark, I recall having been invited, in 1966, by a group of architects to do a study of space, of something that I called at that time "heterotopias," those singular spaces to be found in some given social spaces whose functions are different or even the opposite of others. The architects worked on this, and at

the end of the study someone spoke up—a Sartrean psychologist—who firebombed me, saying that *space* is reactionary and capitalist, but *history* and *becoming* are revolutionary. This absurd discourse was not at all unusual at the time. Today everyone would be convulsed with laughter at such a pronouncement, but not then.[7]

Amidst today's laughter—which is still not as widespread and convulsive as Foucault assumed it would be—one can look back and see that Foucault persistently explored what he called the "fatal intersection of time with space" from the first to the last of his writings. And he did so, we are only now beginning to realize, infused with the emerging perspective of a posthistoricist and postmodern critical human geography.

Few could see Foucault's geography, however, for he never ceased to be a historian, never broke his allegiance to the master identity of modern critical thought. To be labeled a geographer was an intellectual curse, a demeaning association with an academic discipline so far removed from the grand houses of modern social theory and philosophy as to appear beyond the pale of critical relevance. Foucault had to be coaxed into recognizing his formative attachment to the geographer's spatial perspective, to admit that geography was always at the heart of his concerns. This retrospective admission appeared in an interview with the editors of the French journal of radical geography, *Herodote*, subsequently published in English as "Questions on Geography." In this interview Foucault expanded on the observations he made in 1967, but only after being pushed to do so by the interviewers.

At first Foucault was surprised—and annoyed—at being asked by his interviewers why he has been so silent about the importance of geography and spatiality in his works despite their profuse geographical and spatial metaphors. The interviewers suggest to him: "If geography is invisible or ungrasped in the area of your explorations and excavations, this may be due to the deliberately historical or archeological approach which privileges the factor of time. Thus one finds in your work a rigorous concern with periodization that contrasts with the vagueness of your spatial demarcations." Foucault responds immediately by diversion and inversion, throwing back the responsibility for geography to his interviewers (while remembering the critics who reproached him for his "metaphorical obsession" with space). After further questioning, however, he admits (again?) that space has been devalued for generations by philosophers and social critics, reasserts the inherent spatiality of power/knowledge, and ends with a volte-face.

I have enjoyed this discussion with you because I've changed my mind since we started. I must admit that I thought you were demanding a place for geography like those teachers who protest when an education reform is proposed because the number of hours of natural sciences or music is being cut. . . . Now I can see that the problems you put to me about geography are crucial ones for me. Geography acted as the support, the condition of possibility for the passage between a series of factors I tried to relate. Where geography itself was concerned, I either left the question hanging or established a series of arbitrary connections. . . . Geography must indeed lie at the heart of my concerns. ("Questions on Geography," 77)

Foucault's argument here takes a new turn, from simply looking at "other spaces" to questioning the origins of "this devaluation of space that has prevailed for generations." It is at this point that he makes the comment cited earlier on the post-Bergsonian treatment of space as passive and lifeless, time as rich, fecund, dialectical.

Here, then, are the inquisitive ingredients for a direct attack on historicism as the source of the devaluation of space, but Foucault had other things in mind. In a revealing aside he takes an integrative rather than deconstructive path, holding on to his history but adding to it the crucial nexus that would flow through all his work: the linkage between space, knowledge, and power.

For all those who confuse history with the old schemas of evolution, living continuity, organic development, the progress of consciousness or the project of existence, the use of spatial terms seems to have an air of an anti-history. If one started to talk in terms of space that meant one was hostile to time. It meant, as the fools say, that one "denied history," that one was a "technocrat." They didn't understand that to trace the forms of implantation, delimitation and demarcation of objects, the modes of tabulation, the organisation of domains meant the throwing into relief of processes—historical ones, needless to say—of power. The spatialising description of discursive realities gives on to the the analysis of related effects of power. ("Questions on Geography," 77)

Elsewhere Foucault restates his ecumenical project: "A whole history remains to be written of *spaces*—which would at the same time be the history of *powers* (both of these terms in the plural)—from the great strategies of geopolitics to the little tactics of the habitat."[8] Foucault thus diverts his critique of historicism through an acute lateral glance, at once maintaining his spatializing project but preserving his historical stance. "History will protect us from historicism," he optimistically concludes.[9]

### Envisioning Space Through the Eyes of John Berger

Like Foucault, John Berger dwells on the intersection of time and space in virtually all of his writings. Among his most recent works is a play entitled *A Question of Geography* and a personalized volume of poetry and prose that conceives visually of love, *And our faces, my heart, brief as photos.*[10] Symbolizing his insistent balancing of history and geography, lineage and landscape, period and region, Berger opens this slim volume by stating, "Part One is About Time. Part Two is About Space." The embracing themes follow accordingly: the first part labeled *Once,* the second *Here:* neither one inherently privileged, both necessarily faceted together. But Berger does make an explicit choice in at least one of his earlier writings, and it is this assertive choice that I wish to focus attention upon.

In what still stands as perhaps the most direct declaration of the end of historicism, this most spatially visionary of art historians—dare one call him an art geographer?—calls openly for a spatialization of critical thought. In the following passage Berger condenses the essence of postmodern geographies in a spatially politicized aesthetic.

> We hear a lot about the crisis of the modern novel. What this involves, fundamentally, is a change in the *mode of narration.* It is scarcely any longer possible to tell a straight story sequentially unfolding in time. And this is because we are too aware of what is continually traversing the story-line *laterally.* That is to say, instead of being aware of a point as an infinitely small part of a straight line, we are aware of it as an infinitely small part of an infinite number of lines, as the centre of a star of lines. Such awareness is the result of our constantly having to take into account the *simultaneity and extension* of events and possibilities.
>
> There are so many reasons why this should be so: the range of modern means of communication: the scale of modern power: the degree of personal political responsibility that must be accepted for events all over the world: the fact that the world has become indivisible: the unevenness of economic development within that world: the scale of the exploitation. All these play a part. *Prophesy now involves a geographical rather than historical projection: it is space not time that hides consequences from us.* To prophesy today it is only necessary to know men [and women] as they are throughout the whole world in all their inequality. Any contemporary narrative which ignores the urgency of this dimension is incomplete and acquires the oversimplified character of a fable.[11]

This pointed passage pops out of an essay on modern portrait painting in which Berger tries to explain why the historical significance of portraiture, so often in the past the visual personification of authoritative lineage and social (class) position, has changed so dramatically in the twentieth century. To make his point, he turns to an analogous change in the modern novel, a shift in the context of meaning and interpretation which hinges on the impress of simultaneity versus sequence, spatiality versus historicity, geography versus biography. In so doing, he begins to set into place a train of arguments that define the postmodern turn against historical determinations and vividly announce the need for an explicitly spatialized narrative.

The first of these assertively postmodern geographical arguments rests in the recognition of a profound and crisis-induced *restructuring* of contemporary life, resulting in significant changes in "the look of things" and, if I may continue to draw on Berger's captivating book titles, in our "ways of seeing." This restructuring, for Berger, involves a fundamental recomposition of the "mode of narration" arising from a new awareness that we must take into account "the simultaneity and extension of events and possibilities" to make sense of what we see. We can no longer depend on a story line unfolding sequentially, an ever-accumulating history marching straight forward in plot and denouement, for too much is happening against the grain of time, too much is continually traversing the story line laterally. A contemporary portrait no longer directs our eye to an authoritative lineage, to evocations of heritage and tradition alone. Simultaneities intervene, extending our point of view outward in an infinite number of lines connecting the subject to a whole world of comparable instances, complicating the temporal flow of meaning, short-circuiting the fabulous stringing out of one damned thing after the other. The new, the novel, now must involve an explicitly geographical as well as historical configuration and projection.

To explain why this is so, Berger astutely situates the restructured narrative in a pervasive context and consciousness of *geographically uneven development,* into a constellation of lines and photography of surfaces connecting every (hi)story to an attention-shaping horizontality that stretches everywhere in its power, indivisibility, exploitation, and inequality. Our urgent awareness of geographically uneven development and the revived sense of our personal political responsibility for it as a product that we have collectively created spatializes the contemporary moment and reveals the insights to be derived from a deeper understanding of contemporary crisis and restructuring in art and literature, in science and philosophy, in our daily lives and in the conditions of men and women "as they are throughout the whole world in all their inequality." I emphasize again Berger's provocative conclusion: *"Prophesy now involves a geographical rather than historical projection; it is space not time that hides consequences from us."*

What a shattering assertion for those who see only through the spectacles of time! Arising from the recognition of a profound restructuring of contemporary life and an explicit consciousness of geographically (and not just historically) uneven development is an extraordinary call for a new critical perspective, a different way of looking at and seeing the world in which human geography not only "matters" but provides the primary interpretive viewpoint, the most revealing critical glance.

Before jumping to other conclusions, however, let us not forget that this spatialization of critical thought does not have to project a simplistic antihistory. As with Foucault, the reassertion of space in critical social theory does not demand an antagonistic subordination of time and history, a facile substitution and replacement. It is instead a call for an appropriate interpretive balance between space, time, and social being, or what may now more explicitly be termed the creation of human geographies, the making of history, and the constitution of society. To claim that, in the contemporary context, it is space, not time, that hides consequences from us is thus both an implied recognition that history has hitherto been accepted as the primary variable container, the privileged mode of critical disclosure and discourse, and an argument that this privileged position, *insofar as it has blocked from view the critical significance of the spatiality of social life,* is no longer apt. It is the dominance of a *historicism* of critical thought that is being challenged, not the importance of history. Almost as if he were turning Mills's sociological imagination upside down, Berger notes that any contemporary narrative which ignores the urgency of the spatial dimension "is incomplete and acquires the oversimplified character of a fable."

Berger thus joins Foucault in pushing us toward a significant and necessary restructuring of critical social thought, a recomposition which enables us to see more clearly the long-hidden instrumentality of human geographies, in particular the encompassing and encaging spatializations of social life that have been associated with the historical development of capitalism. Foucault's path took him primarily into the microspaces of power, discipline, and surveillance, into the carceral city, the asylum, the human body. Berger's path continues to open up new ways of seeing art and aesthetics, portraits and landscapes, painters and peasants, in the past (once) and in the present (now). To expand these spatial fields of insight and to attach postmodern critical human geography even more forcefully to the instrumental spatiality of the contemporary world, the present narrative can now/here be shifted significantly.

## TAKING LOS ANGELES APART: THE DECONSTRUCTION AND RECONSTITUTION OF MODERNITY

"The Aleph?" I repeated.

"Yes, the only place on earth where all places are—seen from every angle, each standing clear, without any confusion or blending." . . .

. . . Then I saw the Aleph. . . . And here begins my despair as a writer. All language is a set of symbols whose use among its speakers assumes a shared past. How, then, can I translate into words the limitless Aleph, which my floundering mind can scarcely encompass? [12]

Los Angeles, like Jorge Luis Borges's Aleph, is exceedingly tough to track, peculiarly resistant to conventional description. It is difficult to grasp persuasively in a temporal narrative, for it generates too many conflicting images, confounding historicization, always seeming to stretch *laterally* instead of unfolding *sequentially*. At the same time, its spatiality challenges orthodox analysis and interpretation, for it too seems limitless and constantly in motion, never still enough to encompass, too filled with "other spaces" to be informatively described. Looking at Los Angeles from the inside, introspectively, one tends to see only fragments and immediacies, fixed sites of myopic understanding impulsively generalized to represent the whole. To the more farsighted outsider, the visible aggregate of the whole of Los Angeles churns so confusingly that it induces little more than illusionary stereotypes or self-serving caricatures—if its reality is ever seen at all.

What is this place? Even knowing where to focus, to find a starting point, is not easy, for perhaps more than any other place Los Angeles here and now is *everywhere*. It is global in the fullest senses of the word. Nowhere is this more evident than in its cultural projection and ideological reach, its almost ubiquitous screening of itself as a rectangular Dream Machine for the world. Los Angeles broadcasts its self-imagery so widely that probably more people have seen this place—or at least fragments of it—than any other on the planet. As a result, the seers of Los Angeles have become countless, even more so as the progressive globalization of its urban political economy flows along similar channels, making Los Angeles perhaps the epitomizing World City, *une ville dévenue monde*.

Everywhere seems also to be *in* Los Angeles. To it flows the bulk of the transpacific trade of the United States, a cargo which currently surpasses that of the smaller ocean to the east. Global currents of people, information, and ideas accompany the trade. It was once dubbed Iowa's seaport, but today Los Angeles has become an entrepôt to the world, a true pivot of the four quarters, a congeries of East and West, North and South. And from every quarter's teeming shores have poured pools of cultures so diverse that contemporary Los Angeles represents the world in connected urban microcosms, reproducing in situ the customary colors and confrontations of a hundred different homelands. Extraordinary heterogeneity can be exemplified endlessly in this fulsome urban landscape. The only place on earth where all places are? Again I appeal to Borges and the Aleph for appropriate insight.

> Really, what I want to do is impossible, for any listing of an endless series is doomed to be infinitesimal. In that single gigantic instant I saw millions of acts both delightful and awful; not one of them amazed me more than the fact that all of them occupied the same point in space, without overlapping or transparency. What my eyes beheld was simultaneous, but what I

shall now write down will be successive, because language is successive. Nonetheless, I will try to recollect what I can. (*Aleph*, 13)

I too will try to recollect what I can, knowing well that any totalizing description of the L.Aleph is impossible. What follows is a succession of fragmentary glimpses, a freed association of reflective and interpretive field notes which aim toward constructing a postmodern critical human geography of the Los Angeles urban region. My observations are necessarily and contingently incomplete and ambiguous, but the target, I hope, will remain clear: to appreciate the specificity and uniqueness of a particularly restless geographical landscape while simultaneously seeking to extract insights at higher levels of abstraction, to explore *through* Los Angeles glimmers of the fundamental spatiality of social life, the adhesive relations between society and space, history and geography, the splendidly idiographic and the enticingly generalizable features of contemporary spatializations of modernity.

## A ROUND AROUND LOS ANGELES

I saw a small iridescent sphere of almost unbearable brilliance. At first I thought it was revolving; then I realized that this movement was an illusion created by the dizzying world it bounded. (*Aleph*, 13)

We must have a place to start, to begin reading the context. However much the formative space of Los Angeles may be global (or perhaps Mandelbrotian, constructed in zigzagging nests of fractals), it must be reduced to a more familiar and localized geometry to be seen. Appropriately enough, just such a reductionist mapping has popularly presented itself. It is defined by an embracing circle drawn sixty miles (about a hundred kilometers) out from a central point located in the downtown core of the City of Los Angeles. Whether the precise central point is City Hall or perhaps one of the more recently erected corporate towers, I do not know. But I prefer the monumental twenty-eight-story City Hall, up to the 1950s the only erection in the entire region allowed to surpass the allegedly earthquake-proofing 150-foot height limitation. It is an impressive punctuation point, capped by a 1920s interpretation of the Mausoleum of Halicarnassus, wrapped around a Byzantine rotunda, and etched with this infatuating inscription: "THE CITY CAME INTO BEING TO PRESERVE LIFE, IT EXISTS FOR THE GOOD LIFE." Significantly, City Hall sits at the corner of Temple and Spring Streets.

The Sixty-Mile Circle so inscribed covers the thinly sprawling "built-up" area of five counties, a population of more than 14 million individuals, at least 134 incorporated cities, and, it is claimed, the greatest concentration of technocratic expertise and militaristic imagination in the

United States. Its workers produce, when last estimated, a gross annual output worth nearly $250 billion, more than the 800 million people of India produce each year. This is certainly Greater Los Angeles, a dizzying world.

The determination of the Sixty-Mile Circle is the product of the largest bank headquartered within its bounds, a bank potently named by connecting together two definitive pillars of the circumscribed economy: "Security" and "Pacific." [13] How ironic, indeed oxymoronic, is the combination of these two words, security and pacific. The first is redolent of the lethal arsenal emanating from the Sixty-Mile Circle's technicians and scientists, surely today the most powerful assemblage of weapon-making expertise ever grounded into one place. In contrast, the second signals peacefulness, tranquility, moderation, amity, concord. Holocaust attached to halcyon, another of the many simultaneous contraries, interposed opposites, which epitomize Los Angeles and help to explain why conventional categorical logic can never hope to capture its historical and geographic signification. One must return again and again to these simultaneous contraries to depict Los Angeles.

### Circumspection

Securing the Pacific rim has been the manifest destiny of Los Angeles, a theme which defines its sprawling urbanization perhaps more than any other analytical construct. Efforts to secure the Pacific emblazon the history of Los Angeles from its smoky inception as El Pueblo de Nuestra Señora la Reina de Los Angeles de Porciuncula in 1781, through its heated competition for commercial and financial hegemony with San Francisco, to the unfolding sequence of Pacific wars that has marked the last half of the American century. It is not always easy to see the imprint of this imperial history on the material landscape, but an imaginative cruise directly above the contemporary circumference of the Sixty-Mile Circle can be unusually revealing.

The circle cuts the south coast at the border between Orange and San Diego Counties, near one of the key checkpoints regularly set up to intercept the northward flow of undocumented migrants and not far from the San Clemente "White House" of Richard Nixon and the fitful SONGS of the San Onofre Nuclear Generating Station. The first rampart to watch, however, is Camp Pendleton Marine Corps Base, the largest military base in California in terms of personnel, whose freed spouses have helped to build a growing high-technology complex in northern San Diego County. After cruising over the moors of Camp Pendleton, the Cleveland National Forest, and the vital Colorado River Aqueduct draining in from the east, we can land directly in Rampart 2, March Air Force Base, adjacent to the city of Riverside. The insides of

March have been a ready outpost for the roaming Strategic Air Command.

Another quick hop over Sunnymead, the Box Spring Mountains, and Redlands takes us to Rampart 3, Norton Air Force Base, next to the city of San Bernardino and just south of the almost empty San Manuel Indian Reservation. The guidebooks tell us that the primary mission of Norton has been military airlifts, just in case. To move on we must rise still higher to pass over the ski-sloped peaks of the San Bernardino Mountains and National Forest, through Cajon Pass and passing the old Santa Fe Trail, into the picturesque Mojave Desert. Near Victorville is Rampart 4, George Air Force Base, specializing in air defense and interception. Almost the same distance away—our stops seem remarkably evenly spaced thus far—takes us by dry Mirage Lake to the giant Edwards Air Force Base, Rampart 5, site of NASA and USAF research and development activities and a primary landing field for the space shuttle. Stretching off to the south is an important aerospace corridor through Lancaster, to Palmdale Airport and Air Force Plant 42, which serves Edwards's key historical function as testing ground for advanced fighters and Stealth bombers. People who live around here call it Canyon Country, and many want it broken off from the County of Los Angeles down below.

The next leg is longer and more serene: over the Antelope Valley and the Los Angeles Aqueduct (tapping the Los Angeles–owned segments of the life-giving but rapidly dying Owens River Valley two hundred miles farther away); across Interstate 5 (the main freeway corridor to the north), a long stretch of Los Padres National Forest and the now condorless Wild Condor Refuge, to the idyll-ized town of Ojai (site for the filming of *Lost Horizon*), and then to the Pacific again at the Mission of San Buenaventura, in Ventura County. A few miles away (the Sixty-Mile Circle actually cut right through the others) is Rampart 6, a complex consisting of a now inactive Air Force base at Oxnard, the Naval Construction Battalion Center of Port Hueneme, and, far above all, the longsighted Naval Air Missile Center at Point Mugu. If we wished, we could complete the full circle of coincidence over the Pacific, picking up almost directly below us the U.S. Naval Facilities on San Nicolas and San Clemente Islands. It is startling how much of the perimeter is owned and preserved by the federal government in one way or another. Premeditation may be impossible to ascribe, but postmeditation on the circumscriptive federal presence is certainly in order.

## *Enclosures*

What in the world lies behind this Herculean wall? What appears to need such formidable protection? In essence, we return to the same question with which we began: What is this place? There is, of course, the far-reaching Dream Machine and its launching pads, transmitting visual images and evocative sounds of that "good life" announced on the façade of City Hall. But the "entertainment" industry is itself a façade, and significant though it may be, much more than show business is being screened behind it, much more that has developed within the Sixty-Mile Circle demands to be protected and preserved.

If a compelling focus has emerged in the recent academic literature on Los Angeles, it is the discovery of extraordinary industrial production, a revelation so contrary to popular perceptions of Los Angeles that its explorers are often compelled to exaggerate to keep their lines of vision sufficiently open and clear of external obfuscations. Yet it is no exaggeration to claim that the Sixty-Mile Circle contains the premier industrial growth pole of the twentieth century, at least within the advanced capitalist countries. Oil, orange groves, films, and flying set the scene at the beginning of the century and tend to remain fixed in many contemporary images of industrious, but not industrial, Los Angeles. Since 1930, however, Los Angeles has probably led all other major metropolitan areas in the United States, decade by decade, in the accumulation of new manufacturing employment.

For many, industrial Los Angeles nevertheless remains a contradiction in terms. When a colleague at UCLA began his explorations of the industrial geography of Los Angeles, his appeal to a prominent national scientific funding agency brought back a report by a confidential referee (an economist, it appeared) proclaiming the absurdity of studying such a fanciful subject, something akin to examining wheat farming in Long Island. Fortunately, sounder minds prevailed and the research progressed in exemplary fashion. Further evidence of the apparent invisibility of industrial production in Los Angeles came at about the same time from *Forbes* magazine, that self-proclaimed sourcebook for knowing capitalists (who should know better). In 1984 *Forbes* published a map identifying the major centers of high-technology development in the United States. Cartographic attention was properly drawn to the Silicon Valley and the Route 128 axis around Boston, but all of Southern California was left conspicuously blank! Apparently invisible, hidden from view, was not only one of the historical source-regions for advanced technology in aerospace and electronics but also what may well be the largest concentration of high-technology industry and employment in the country if not the world, the foremost Silicon Landscape, a region that has *added* over the past fifteen years a high-technology employment pool roughly equivalent to that of the whole image-fixing Silicon Valley of Santa Clara County to the north.

Still partially hidden behind this revelation are the primary generative agencies and the intricate processes producing this preeminent production complex. One key link, however, is abundantly clear. In the past half century no other area has been so pumped with federal money as Los Angeles, via the Department of Defense to be sure, but also through numerous federal programs subsidizing suburban consumption (suburbsidizing?) and the development of housing, transportation, and water delivery systems. From the last Great Depression to the present, Los Angeles has been the prototypical Keynesian state-city, a federalized metro-sea of State-rescued capitalism enjoying its place in the sunbelt, demonstrating through the decades its redoubtable ability to go first and multiply the public seed money invested in its promising economic landscape. No wonder it remains so protected. In it are embedded many of the crown jewels of advanced industrial capitalism.

If anything, the federal flow accelerated through the 1980s, under the aegis of the military Keynesianism of the Reagan administration and the permanent arms economy of the Warfare State. At Hughes Aircraft Company in El Segundo, engineers used millions of dollars in prime Star Wars contracts to mock up a giant infrared sensor so acute that it can pick up the warmth of a human body at a distance of a thousand miles in space, part of their experimentation with "kinetic" weapons systems. Nearby, TRW and Rockwell International's Rocketdyne division competitively developed powerful space lasers—capable, it would appear, of incinerating whole cities if necessary—under such project code names as Miracl, Alpha, and Rachel. Research houses such as the Rand Corporation, just to the north in Santa Monica, still jockey for more strategic positions, eager to claim part of what seemed likely to reach a total of $1.5 trillion if not stopped in time.[14] Today it is not only the space of the Pacific that is being secured and watched over from inside the Sixty-Mile Circle.

*Outer Spaces*

The effulgent Star Wars colony that bloomed around Los Angeles International Airport (LAX) is part of a much larger Outer City which has taken shape along the Pacific slope of Los Angeles County. In the context of this landscape, through the story line of the aerospace industry, can be read the explosive history and geography of the National Security State and what Mike Davis once called the "Californianization" of Late-Imperial America.[15]

If there is a single birthplace for this Californianization, it can be found at old Douglas Field in Santa Monica, today close by a once important transit point for former President Reagan's frequent West Coast trips. From this spot fifty years ago the first DC-3 took off to begin a career of military accomplishment in war after war after war. Spinning off in its tracks has been an intricate tracery of links, from defense and space-related expenditures on research and development and the associated formation of the aerospace industry on the base of civilian aircraft manufacturing; to the piggybacked instigation of computerized electronics and modern information-processing technology, meshing with an ancillary network of suppliers and demanders of goods and services that stretches out to virtually every sector of the contemporary economy and society. Some claim that nearly half the manufacturing jobs in Los Angeles County are related in one away or another to the aerospace industry, with half of these aerospace workers employed on military projects. Over half a million people now live in this "Aerospace Alley," as it has come to be called. During working hours perhaps 800,000 are present to sustain its global preeminence. Millions more lie within its extended orbit.

Attached around the axes of production are the representative locales of the industrialized Outer City: the busy international airport; corridors filled with new office buildings, hotels, and global shopping malls; neatly packaged playgrounds and leisure villages; specialized and master-planned residential communities for the high technocracy; armed and guarded housing estates for top professionals and executives; residual communities of low-pay service workers living in overpriced homes; and the accessible enclaves and ghettoes which provide dependable flows of the cheapest labor power to the bottom bulge of the bimodal local labor market. The LAX-City compage reproduces the segmentation and segregation of the Inner City based on race, class, and ethnicity but manages to break it down still further to fragment residential communities according to specific occupational categories, household composition, and a broad range of individual attributes, affinities, desired lifestyles, and moods.

This extraordinary differentiation, fragmention, and social control over specialized pools of labor is expensive. Housing prices and rental costs in the Outer City are easily among the highest in the country, and the provision of appropriate housing increasingly absorbs the energy not only of the army of real estate agents but of local corporate and community planners as well, often at the expense of long-time residents fighting to maintain their foothold in "preferred" locations. From the give-and-take of this competition have emerged peculiarly intensified urban landscapes. Along the shores of the South Bay, for example, part of what Reyner Banham once called "Surfurbia," there has developed the largest and most homogeneous residential enclave of scientists and engineers in the world.[16] Coincidentally, this beachhead of the high technocracy is also one of the most formidable racial redoubts in the region. Although just a few miles away, across the fortifying boundary of the San Diego Freeway, is the edge of the largest and most tightly segregated concentration of blacks west of Chicago, the sunbelted beach communities stretching south from the airport have remained almost 100 percent white.

The Sixty-Mile Circle is ringed with a series of these Outer Cities at varying stages of development, each a laboratory for exploring the contemporaneity of capitalist urbanization. At least two are combined in Orange County, seamlessly webbed together into the largest and probably fastest growing Outer City complex in the country (world?). The key nucleus here is the industrial complex embedded in the land empire of the Irvine Company, which owns one-sixth of the entire county. Arrayed around it is a remarkable accretion of master-planned New Towns which paradigmatically evince the global cultural aspirations of the Outer City imposed atop local visions of the experimental community of tomorrow.

Illustratively, the New Town of Mission Viejo (never mind the bilingual pun) is partially blocked out to re-create the places and people of Cervantes's Spain and other quixotic intimations of the Mediterranean. Simultaneously, its ordered environment specifically appeals to Olympian dreams. Stacked with the most modern facilities and trainers, Mission Viejo has attracted an elite of sports-minded parents and accommodating children. The prowess of determined local athletes was sufficient for Mission Viejo to have finished ahead of 133 of the 140 countries competing in the 1984 Olympic Games in the number of gold medals received. Advertised as "The California Promise" by its developer, currently the Philip Morris Company, Mission Viejo coughs up enticing portions of the American Dream to the chosen few. As one compromising resident described it, "You must be happy, you must be well rounded and you must have children who do a lot of things. If you don't jog or walk or bike, people wonder if you have diabetes or some other disabling disease."[17]

The Orange County complex has also been the focus for detailed research into the high-technology industrial agglomerations that have been recentralizing the urban fabric of the Los Angeles region and inducing the florescence of master-planned New Towns. This pioneering work has helped us see more clearly the transactional web of industrial linkages that draws out and geographically clusters specialized networks of firms, feeds off the flow of federal contracts, and spills over to precipitate a supportive local space economy.[18] What has been provided is a revealing glimpse into the generative processes behind the urbanization of Orange County and, through this window, into the deeper historical interplay between industrialization and urbanization that has defined the development of the capitalist city wherever it is found.

Other Outer Cities fringe the older urban core. One has taken shape in the Ventura Corridor through the west San Fernando Valley into Ventura County (sometimes called the "Peripheral Valley"). Another is being promoted (although not yet in place) in the "Inland Empire" stretching eastward from Pomona (General Dynamics is there) through Ontario (with Lockheed and a growing international airport and free trade zone) to the county seats of San Bernardino and Riverside, hard by their military ramparts. The Inland Empire, however, is still more of an anticipatory Outer City, cruelly packed with new housing estates that automaniacally lure families ever farther away from their places of work in Los Angeles and Orange Counties, a truly transitory landscape.

Inland empirics aside, these new territorial complexes seem to be turning the industrial city inside out, recentering the urban to transform the metropolitan periphery into the core region of advanced industrial production. Decentralization from the Inner City has been taking place selectively for at least a century all over the world, but only recently has the peripheral condensation become sufficiently dense to challenge the older urban cores as centers of industrial production, employment nodality, and urbanism. This restructuring process is far from complete, but it is beginning to have some profound repercussions on the way we think about the city, on the words we use to describe urban forms and functions, and on the language of urban theory and analysis.

## BACK TO THE CENTER

I saw the teeming sea; I saw daybreak and nightfall; I saw the multitudes of America; I saw a silvery cobweb in the center of a black pyramid; I saw a splintered labyrinth ... I saw, close up, unending eyes watching themselves in me as in a mirror. (*Aleph*, 13)

To see more of Los Angeles, it is necessary to move away from the riveting periphery and return, literally and figuratively, to the center of things, to the still adhesive core of the urbanized landscape. In Los Angeles as in every city, the nodality of the center defines and gives substance to the specificity of the urban, its distinctive social and spatial meaning. Urbanization and the spatial divisions of labor associated with it revolve around a socially constructed pattern of nodality and the power of the occupied centers both to cluster and disperse, to centralize and decentralize, to structure spatially all that is social and socially produced. Nodality *situates* and *contextualizes* urban society by giving material form to essential social relations. Only with a persistent centrality can there be Outer Cities and peripheral urbanization. Otherwise, there is no urban at all.

It is easy to overlook the tendential processes of urban structuration that emanate from the center, especially in the postmodern capitalist landscape. Indeed, in contemporary societies the authoritative and allocative power of the urban center is purposefully obscured or, alternatively, detached from place, ripped out of context, and given the stretched-out appearance of democratic ubiquity. In addition, as we have seen, the historical development of urbanization over the past century has been marked by a selective dispersal and decentralization, emptying the center of many of the activities and populations which once aggregated densely around it. For some, this dispersal has signaled a negation of nodality, a submergence of the power of central places, perhaps even a Derridean deconstruction of all differences between the "central" and the "marginal."

Yet the centers *hold*. Even as some things fall apart, dissipate, new nodalities form and old ones are reinforced. The specifying centrifuge is always spinning, but the centripetal force of nodality never disappears. And it is the persistent residual of *political power* which continues to precipitate, specify, and contextualize the urban, making it all stick together. The first cities appeared with the simultaneous concentration of commanding symbolic forms, *civic* centers designed to announce, ceremonialize, administer, acculturate, discipline, and control. In and around the institutionalized locale of the *citadel* adhered people and their node-ordered social relations, creating a *civil* society and an accordingly built environment which were urbanized and regionalized through the interplay between two interactive processes, *surveillance* and *adherence*, looking out from and in toward a center through the panoptic eye of power. To be urbanized still means to adhere, to be made an adherent, a believer in a specified collective ideology rooted in extensions of *polis* (politics, policy, polity, police) and *civitas* (civil, civic, citizen, civilian, civilization). In contrast, the population beyond the reach of the urban is comprised of *idiotes*, from the Greek root *idios*, meaning "one's own, a private person," unlearned in the ways of the *polis* (a root akin to the Latin *sui*, "of its own kind"; with *generis*, "constituting a class alone"). Thus, to speak of the "idiocy" of rural life or the urbanity of its opposition is primarily a statement of relative political socialization and spatialization, of the degree of adherence/separation in the collective social order, a social order hinging on urban nodality.

To maintain adhesiveness, the civic center has always served as a key surveillant node of the state, supervising locales of production, consumption, and exchange. It still continues to do so, even after centuries of urban recomposition and restructuring, after waves of reagglomerative industrialization. The urban is specified not by production or consumption or exchange in themselves, but rather by their collective surveillance, supervision, and anticipated control within the power-filled context of nodality. In Foucauldian terms, cities are the convergent sites of (social) space, knowledge, and power, the headquarters of societal modes of *regulation* (from *regula* and *regere*, "to rule," the root of our key word, *region*).

This does not mean that a mechanical determinism is assigned to nodality in the specification of the urban. Adherence is a sticky notion and is not automatically enacted by location in an urbanized landscape; nor is it always expressed in practical consciousness. Surveillance, too, is problematic, for it can exist without being embracingly effective—and can be embracingly effective without appearing to exist! There is thus always room for resistance, rejection, and redirection in the nonetheless structured field of urban locales, creating an active politics of spatiality, struggles for place, space, and position within the regionalized and nodal urban landscape. As a result, adherence and surveillance are unevenly developed in their geographical manifestation, their regionalization, their reactive regionalisms. Simultaneously, this patterned differentiation, this immediate superstructure of the urban spatial division of labor, becomes a critical arena in which the human geography of the city is shaped, in which *spatialization* takes place. It maps out an urban cartography of power and political *praxis* that is often hidden in idiographic (from *idios* again) histories and geographies.

### Signifying Downtown

The Downtown core of the City of Los Angeles, which the signs call "Central City," is the agglomerative and symbolic nucleus of the Sixty-Mile Circle, certainly the oldest but also the newest major node in the region. Given what is contained within the circle, the physical size and appearance of Downtown Los Angeles seem almost modest, even today after a period of enormous expansion. As usual, however, appearances can be deceptive.

Perhaps more than ever before, Downtown serves in ways no other place can as a strategic vantage point, an urban panopticon counterposed to the encirclement of watchful military ramparts and defensive Outer Cities. Like the central well in Bentham's eminently utilitarian design for a circular prison, the original Panopticon, Downtown can be seen (when visibility permits) by each separate individual, from each territorial cell, within its orbit. Only from the advantageous outlook of the center, however, can the surveillant eye see everyone collectively, disembedded but interconnected. Not surprisingly, from its origin the Central City has been an aggregation of overseers, a primary locale for social control, political administration, cultural codification, ideological surveillance, and the incumbent regionalization of its adherent hinterland.

Seen down and out from atop City Hall, the site is especially impressive to the overviewing observer. Immediately below and around is the largest concentration of government offices and bureaucracy in the country outside the federal capital district. To the east, over a pedestrian skyway, are City Hall East and City Hall South, relatively new civic additions enclosing a shopping mall, some murals, a children's museum, and the Triforium, a splashy sixty-foot fountain of water, light, and music entertaining the lunchtime masses. Just beyond is the imposing police administration building, Parker Center, hallowing the name of a former police chief of note. Looking farther, outside the central well of Downtown but within its eastern salient, one can see an area which houses 25 percent of California's prison population, at least twelve thousand inmates held in four jails designed to hold half that number. Included within this carceral wedge are the largest women's prison in the country (Sybil Brand), the seventh largest men's prison (Men's Central), and the brand-new and in-close Federal Detention Center, bunkered next to the Federal Building. More enclosures are being insistently planned by the State to meet the rising demand.

On the south along First Street are the State Department of Transportation (CALTRANS) with its electronic wall maps monitoring the arterial freeways of the region, the California State Office Building, and the headquarters of the fourth estate, the monumental Times-Mirror building complex, which many have claimed houses the unofficial governing power of Los Angeles, the source of many stories that mirror the times and spaces of the city. Near the spatial sanctum of the *Los Angeles Times* is also St. Vibiana's Cathedral, mother church to one of the largest Catholic archdioceses in the world (nearly four million strong) and controller of another estate of significant proportions. The pope slept here, across the street from Skid Row missions temporarily closed so that he could not see all his adherents.

Looking westward now, toward the Pacific and the smog-hued sunsets which brilliantly paint the nightfalls of Los Angeles, is first the Criminal Courts Building, then the Hall of Records and Law Library, and next the huge Los Angeles County Courthouse and Hall of Administration, major seats of power for what is by far the country's largest county in total population (now over eight million strong). Standing across Grand Avenue is the most prominent cultural center of Los Angeles, described by Unique Media Incorporated in their pictorial booster maps of Downtown as "the cultural crown of Southern California, reigning over orchestral music, vocal performance, opera, theatre and dance." They add that the Music Center "tops Bunker Hill like a contemporary Acropolis, one which has dominated civic cultural life since it was inaugurated in 1964." Just beyond this cultural crown is the Department of Water and

Power (surrounded by usually waterless fountains) and a multilevel extravaganza of freeway interchanges connecting with every corner of the Sixty-Mile Circle, a peak point of accessibility within the regional transportation network.

Along the northern flank is the Hall of Justice, the U.S. Federal Courthouse, and the Federal Building, completing the ring of local, city, state, and federal government authority comprised in the potent civic Center. Sitting more tranquilly just beyond, cut off by a swath of freeway, are the preserved remains of the old civic center, now part of El Pueblo de Los Angeles State Historical Park, additional testimony to the lasting power of the central place. Since the origins of Los Angeles the sites described have served as the political citadel, designed with other citadels to command, protect, socialize, and dominate the surrounding urban population.

Still another segment of the citadel-panopticon cannot be overlooked. Its form and function may be more specific to the contemporary capitalist city, but its mercantile roots entwine historically with the citadels of all urbanized societies. Today it has become the acknowledged symbol of the urbanity of Los Angeles, the visual evidence of the successful "search for a city" by the surrounding sea of suburbs. This skylined sight contains the bunched castles and cathedrals of corporate power, the gleaming new Central Business District of the Central City, pinned next to its aging predecessor just to the east. Here too the L.Aleph's unending eyes are kept open and reflective, reaching out to and mirroring global spheres of influence, localizing the world that is within its reach.

Nearly all the landmarks of the new LA CBD have been built over the past fifteen years and flashily signify the consolidation of Los Angeles as a World City. Now more than half the major properties are in part or wholly foreign owned, although much of this landed presence is shielded from view. The most visible wardens are the banks which light up their logos atop the highest towers: Security Pacific, First Interstate, Bank of America (co-owner of the sleak, black Arco Towers before their recent purchase by the Japanese), Wells Fargo, Citicorp (billing itself as "the newest city in town"). Reading the skyline, one sees the usual corporate panorama: large insurance companies (Manulife, Transamerica, Prudential), IBM and major oil companies, the real estate giant Coldwell Banker, the new offices of the Pacific Stock Exchange, all serving as attachment points for silvery webs of financial and commercial transactions extending practically everywhere on earth.

The two poles of the citadel, political and economic, connect physically through the condominium towers of renewed Bunker Hill but "interface" less overtly in the planning apparatus of the local state. Contrary to popular opinion, Los Angeles is a tightly planned and plotted urban environment, especially with regard to the social and spatial divisions of labor necessary to sustain its preeminent industrialization and consumerism. Planning choreographs Los Angeles through the fungible movements of the zoning game and the flexible staging of supportive community participation (when there are communities to be found), a dance filled with honorable intent, dedicated expertise, and selective beneficence. It has excelled, however, as an ambivalent but nonetheless enriching pipeline and placemaker to the domestic and foreign developers of Los Angeles, using its influential reach to prepare the groundwork and facilitate the selling of specialized locations and populations to suit the needs of the most powerful organizers of the urban space-economy.

Although conspiracy and corruption can be easily found in this hyperactive public-private interface, the planned and packaged selling of Los Angeles usually follows a more mundane rhythm played to the legitimizing beat of dull and thumping market forces. In the created spaces which surround the twin citadels of Los Angeles, the beat has drummed with a particularly insistent and mesmerizing effect. Through a historic act of preservation and renewal, there now exists around Downtown a deceptively harmonized showcase of ethni-cities and specialized economic enclaves which play key roles, albeit somewhat noisily at times, in the contemporary redevelopment and internationalization of Los Angeles. Primarily responsible for this packaged and planned production of the Inner City is the state-legislated but locally supervised Community Redevelopment Agency, probably the leading public entrepreneur of the Sixty-Mile Circle.

There is a dazzling array of sites in this compartmentalized corona of the Inner City: the Vietnamese shops and Hong Kong housing of a redeveloping Chinatown; the Big Tokyo—financed modernization of old Little Tokyo's still resisting remains; the induced pseudo-SoHo of artists' lofts and galleries hovering near the exhibitions of the "Temporary Contemporary" art warehouse; the protected remains of El Pueblo along Calmexified Olvera Street and in the renewed Old Plaza; the strangely anachronistic wholesaling markets for produce and flowers and jewelry growing bigger while other downtowns displace their equivalents; the fetid sweatshops and bustling merchandise marts of the booming Garment District; the Latino retail festival along pedestrian-packed Broadway (another preserved zone and inch-for-inch probably the most profitable shopping street in the region); the capital site of urban homelessness in the CRA-gilded Skid Row district; the enormous muraled barrio stretching eastward to the still unincorporated East Los Angeles; the deindustrializing and virtually residentless wholesaling City of Vernon to the south, filled with chickens and pigs awaiting their slaughter; the Central American and Mexican communities of Pico-Union and Alvarado abutting the high rises on the west; the obtrusive oil wells and aggressive graffiti in the backyards of predominantly immigrant Temple-Beaudry progressively being eaten away by the spread of Central City West (now being called "The Left Bank" of Downtown); the intentionally yuppifying South Park redevelopment zone hard by the slightly seedy Convention Center; the revenue-milked towers and fortresses of Bunker Hill; the resplendently gentrified pocket of "Victorian" homes in old Angelino Heights overlooking the citadel; the massive new Koreatown pushing out west and south against the edge of Black Los Angeles; the Filipino pockets to the northwest, still uncoalesced into a "town" of their own; and so much more: a constellation of Foucauldian heterotopias "capable of juxtaposing in a single real place several spaces, several sites that are in themselves incompatible" but "function in relation to all the space that remains."

What stands out from a hard look at the Inner City seems almost like an obverse (and perverse) reflection of the Outer City, an agglomerative complex of dilapidated and overcrowded housing, low-technology workshops, relics and residuals of an older urbanization, a sprinkling of niches for recentered professionals and supervisors, and above all the largest concentration of cheap, culturally splintered, occupationally manipulable Third World immigrant labor to be found so tangibly available in any First World urban region. Here in this colonial corona is another of the crown jewels of Los Angeles, carefully watched over, artfully maintained, and reproduced to service the continued development of the manufactured region.

The extent and persistence of agglomerated power and ever-watchful eyes in Downtown Los Angeles cannot be ignored by either captive participants or outside observers. The industrialization of the urban periphery may be turning the space economy of the region inside out, but the old center is more than holding its own as the preeminent political and economic citadel. Peripheral visions are thus not enough when looking at Los Angeles. To conclude this spiraling tour around the power-filled Central City, it is useful to recall Anthony Giddens's observations on the structured and structuring landscapes of modern capitalism.

> The distinctive structural principle of the class societies of modern capitalism is to be found in the disembedding, yet interconnecting, of state and economic institutions. The tremendous economic power generated by the harnessing of allocative resources to a generic tendency towards technical improvement is matched by an enormous expansion in the administrative "reach" of the state. Surveillance—the coding of information relevant to the administration of subject populations, plus the direct supervision by officials and administrators of all sorts—becomes a key mechanism fur-

thering a breaking away of system from social integration. Traditional practices are dispersed (without, of course, disappearing altogether) under the impact of the penetration of day-to-day life by codified administrative procedures. The locales which provide the settings for interaction in situations of co-presence [the basis for social integration] undergo a major set of transmutations. The old city-countryside relation is replaced by a sprawling expansion of a manufactured or "created environment."[19]

Here we have another definition of spatial planning, another indication of the instrumentality of space and power, another example of spatialization.

### Lateral Extensions

Radiating from the specifying nodality of the Central City are the hypothesized pathways of traditional urban theory, the transects of eagerly anticipated symmetries and salience which have absorbed so much of the attention of older generations of urban theoreticians and empiricists. Formal models of urban morphology have conventionally begun with the assumption of a structuring central place organizing an adherent landscape into discoverable patterns of hinterland development and regionalization. The deeper sources of this structuring process are usually glossed over and its problematic historical geography is almost universally simplified, but the resultant surfaces of social geometry continue to be visible as geographical expressions of the crude orderliness induced by the effects of nodality. They, too, are part of the spatialization of social life, the extended specificity of the urban.

The most primitive urban geometry arises from the radial attenuation of land-use "intensity" around the center to an outer edge, a reflection of the Thunian landscape that has become codified most figuratively in the irrepressible Two-Parameter Negative Exponential Population Density Gradient. The TPNEPDG, in part because of its nearly universal and monotonous exemplification, has obsessed urban theorists with its projectable objectivity and apparent explanatory powers. From the Urban Ecologists of the Old Chicago School to the New Urban Economists, and including all those who are convinced that geographical analysis naturally begins with the primal explanation of variegated population densities (the most bourgeois of analytical assumptions, Marx claimed), the TPNEPDG has been the lodestar for a monocentric understanding of urbanism. And within its own limited bands of confidence, it works efficiently.

Population densities do mound up around the centers of cities, even in the polycentric archipelago of Los Angeles (where there may be several dozen such mounds, although the most pronounced still falls off from the Central City). There is also an accompanying concentric residential rhythm associated with the family life cycle and the relative premiums placed on access to the dense peaks versus the availability of living space in the sparseness of the valleys (at least for those who can afford such freedoms of choice). Land values (when they can be accurately calculated) and some job densities also tend to follow in diminishing peaks outward from the center, bringing back to mind those tented webs of the urban geography textbooks.

Adding direction to the decadence of distance reduces the Euclidian elegance of concentric gradations, and many of the most mathematical of urban geometricians have accordingly refused to follow this slightly unsettling path. But direction does indeed induce another fit by pointing out the emanation of fortuitous wedges or sectors starting from the center. The sectoral wedges of Los Angeles are especially pronounced once you leave the inner circle around Downtown.

The Wilshire Corridor, for example, extends the citadels of the Central City almost twenty miles westward to the Pacific, picking up several other prominent but smaller downtowns en route (the Miracle Mile that initiated this extension, Beverly Hills, Century City, Westwood, Brentwood, Santa Monica). Watching above it is an even lengthier wedge of the wealthiest residences, running with almost staggering homogeneities to the Pacific Palisades and the privatized beaches of Malibu, sprinkled with announcements of armed responsiveness and signs warning that "trespassers will be shot." Here are the hearths of the most vocal homeowners' movements, arms raised to slow growth and preserve their putative neighborhoods in the face of the encroaching, view-blocking, street-clogging, and déclassé downtowns.

As if in counterbalance, on the other side of the tracks east of Downtown is the salient containing the largest Latino barrio in Anglo-America, where many of those who might be shot are carefully barricaded in poverty. And there is at least one more prominent wedge, stretching southward from Downtown to the twin ports of Los Angeles—Long Beach, still reputed to be one of the largest consistently industrial urban sectors in the world. This is the primary axis of Ruhral Los Angeles.

A third ecological order perturbs the geometrical neatness still further, punching wholes into the monocentric gradients and wedges as a result of the territorial segregation of races and ethnicities. Segregation is so noisy that it overloads the conventional statistical methods of urban factorial ecology with scores of tiny but "significant" ecocomponents. In Los Angeles, arguably the most segregated city in the country, these components are so numerous that they operate statistically to obscure the spatiality of social class relations deeply embedded in the zones and wedges of the urban landscape, as if they needed to be obscured any further.

These broad social geometries provide an attractive model of the urban geography of Los Angeles, but like most of the inherited overviews of formal urban theory they are seriously diverting and illusory. They mislead not because there is disagreement over their degree of fit: such regular empiricist arguments merely induce a temporary insensibility by forcing debate on to the usually sterile grounds of technical discourse. Instead, they deceive by involuting explanation, by the legerdemain of making the nodality of the urban explain itself through its mere existence, one outcome explaining another. Geographical covariance in the form of empirico-statistical regularity is elevated to causation and frozen into place without a history—and without a human geography which recognizes that the organization of space is a social product filled with politics and ideology, contradiction and struggle, comparable to the making of history. Empirical regularities are there to be found in the surface geometry of any city, including Los Angeles, but they are not explained in the discovery, as is so often assumed. Different routes and different roots must be explored to achieve a practical understanding and critical reading of urban landscapes. The illusions of empirical opaqueness that blinker and distort most modern geographical analysis must be shattered to reveal the spatiality of postmodern geographies.

### Deconstruction

Back in the center, shining from its circular turrets of bronzed glass, stands the Bonaventure Hotel, an amazingly storied architectural symbol of the splintered labyrinth that stretches sixty miles around it.[20] Like many other Portman-teaus which dot the eyes of urban citadels in New York and San Francisco, Atlanta and Detroit, the Bonaventure has become a concentrated representation of the restructured spatiality of the contemporary capitalist city: fragmented and fragmenting, homogeneous and homogenizing, divertingly packaged yet curiously incomprehensible, seemingly open in presenting itself to view but constantly pressing to enclose, to compartmentalize, to circumscribe, to incarcerate. Everything imaginable appears to be available in this micro-urb but real places are difficult to find: its spaces confuse an effective cognitive mapping; its pastiche of superficial reflections bewilder coordination and encourage submission instead. Entry by land is forbidding to those who carelessly walk, but entrance is nevertheless encouraged at many different levels, from the truly pedestrian skyways above to the bunkered inlets below. Once the visitor is inside, however, it becomes daunting to get out again without bureaucratic assistance. In so many ways, the Bonaventure's architecture recapitulates and reflects the sprawling manufactured spaces of Los Angeles.

There has been no conspiracy of design behind the building of the Bonaventure or the socially constructed spatiality of the New World Cities. Both designs have been conjunctural, reflecting the specifications and exigencies of time and place, of *period and region*. The Bonaventure both simulates the restructured landscape of Los Angeles and is simultaneously simulated by it. From this interpretive interplay of micro- and macrosimulations there emerges an alternative way of looking critically at the human geography of contemporary Los Angeles, of seeing it as a mesocosm of postmodernity.

From the center to the periphery, in both Inner and Outer Cities, the Sixty-Mile Circle today encloses a shattered metro-sea of fragmented yet homogenized communities, cultures, and economies confusingly arranged into a contingently ordered spatial division of labor and power. As is true for so much of the patterning of twentieth-century urbanization, Los Angeles both set the historical pace and most vividly epitomizes the extremes of contemporary expression. Municipal boundary making and territorial incorporation, to take one example, has produced the most extraordinary crazy quilt of opportunism to be found in any metropolitan area. Tiny enclaves of county land and whole cities such as Beverly Hills, West Hollywood, Culver City, and Santa Monica pockmark the "Westside" bulk of the incorporated City of Los Angeles, while thin slivers of City land reach out like tentacles to grab on to the key seaside outlets of the port at San Pedro and Los Angeles International Airport.[21] Nearly half the population of the City, however, lives in the quintessentially suburban San Fernando Valley, one and a half million people who statistically are counted as a part of the Central City of the Los Angeles–Long Beach SMSA. Few other places make such a definitive mockery of the standard classifications of urban, suburban, and exurban.

More than 130 other municipalities and scores of county-administered areas adhere loosely around the irregular City of Los Angeles in a dazzling patchwork mosaic. Some have names which are startlingly self-explanatory. Where else can there be a City of Industry and a City of Commerce, so flagrantly commemorating the fractions of capital which guaranteed their incorporation? In other places, names casually try to recapture a romanticized history (as in the many new communities called Rancho Something-or-Other) or to ensconce the memory of alternative geographies (as in Venice, Naples, Hawaiian Gardens, Ontario, Manhattan Beach, Westminster). And then there are the evocations of the Dream Machine, from the many Hollywoods to Studio City, Century City, Paramount, Tarzana (home to Edgar Rice Burroughs), and that champion of spatial aggrandizement, Universal City. In naming, as in so many other contemporary urban processes, time and space, the "once" and the "here," are being increasingly played with and packaged to serve the needs of the there and the now, making the lived experience of the urban increasingly vicarious, screened through simulacra, those exact copies for which the real originals have been lost.

For at least fifty years Los Angeles has been defying conventional categorical description of the urban, of what is city and what is suburb, of what can be identified as community or neighborhood, of what copresence means in the elastic urban context. It has in effect been deconstructing the urban into a confusing collage of signs which advertise what are often little more than imaginary communities and outlandish representations of urban locality. I do not mean to say that no genuine neighborhoods can be found in Los Angeles. Indeed, finding them through car voyages of exploration has become a popular local pastime, especially for those who have become isolated from propinquitous community in the repetitive sprawl of truly ordinary-looking landscapes that make up most of the region. But again the urban experience becomes increasingly vicarious, adding more layers of opaqueness to *l'espace vécu.*

Underneath this semiotic blanket there remains an economic order, an instrumental nodal structure, an essentially exploitive spatial division of labor, and this spatially organized urban system has for the past half century been more continuously productive than almost any other in the world.[22] But it has also been increasingly obscured from view, imaginatively mystified in an environment more specialized in the production of encompassing mystifications than practically any other you can name. As has so often been the case in the United States, this conservative deconstruction is accompanied by a numbing depoliticization of fundamental class, race, and gender relations and conflicts. When all that is seen is so fragmented and filled with whimsy and pastiche, the hard edges of the capitalist, racist, and patriarchal landscape seem to disappear, melt into air.

With exquisite irony, contemporary Los Angeles has come to resemble more than ever before a gigantic agglomeration of theme parks, a life space of Disneyworlds. It is a realm divided into showcases of global village cultures and mimetic American landscapes, all-embracing shopping malls and crafty Main Streets, corporation-sponsored magic kingdoms, high-technology-based Experimental Prototype Communities of Tomorrow, attractively packaged places for rest and recreation all cleverly hiding the buzzing workstations and labor processes which help to keep it together. Like the original "Happiest Place on Earth," the enclosed spaces are subtly but tightly controlled by invisible overseers despite the open appearance of fantastic freedoms of choice. The experience of living here can be extremely diverting and exceptionally enjoyable, especially for those who can afford to remain inside long enough to establish their own modes of transit and places to rest. And, of course, the enterprise has been enormously profitable over the years. After all, it was built on what began as relatively cheap land, has been sustained by a constantly replenishing army of even cheaper imported labor, is filled with the most modern technological gadgetry, enjoys extraordinary levels of protection and surveillance, and runs under the smooth aggression of the most efficient management systems, almost always capable of delivering what is promised just in time to be useful.

O God! I could be bounded in a nutshell, and count myself a King of infinite space. *Hamlet* 2.2; first epigraph to *The Aleph*

But they will teach us that Eternity is the Standing still of the Present Time, a *Nunc-stans* (as the Schools call it); which neither they, nor any else understand, no more than they would a *Hic-stans* for an infinite greatness of Place. *Leviathan* 4.46; second epigraph to *The Adeph*

## NOTES

This essay combines parts of chapter 1 ("History: Geography: Modernity") and chapter 9 ("Taking Los Angeles Apart: Toward a Postmodern Geography") from E. W. Soja, *Postmodern Geographies: The Reassertion of Space in Critical Social Theory* (London and New York: Verso, 1989).

1. Michel Foucault, "Questions on Geography," in C. Gordon, ed., *Power/Knowledge: Selected Interviews and Other Writings 1972–1977* (New York: Pantheon, 1980), 70; hereafter cited in text as "Questions on Geography."

2. Michel Foucault, "Of Other Spaces," *Diacritics* 16 (1986): 22; hereafter cited in text as "Of Other Spaces."

3. C. Wright Mills, *The Sociological Imagination* (New York: Oxford University Press, 1959), 11–12 (my emphasis). See also Martin Jay, *Marxism and Totality* (Berkeley and Los Angeles: University of California Press, 1984).

4. Raymond Williams, *Keywords: A Vocabulary of Culture and Society* (London: Fontana, 1983).

5. Foucault, "Space, Knowledge, and Power," can be found in Paul Rabinow, ed., *The Foucault Reader* (New York: Pantheon, 1984), 239–56. See also Gwendolen Wright and Paul Rabinow, "Spatialization of Power: A Discussion of the Work of Michel Foucault" and "Interview: Space, Knowledge and Power," *Skyline*, 1982, 14–20.

6. Structuralism's presumed "denial" of history has triggered an almost maniacal attack on its major proponents by those imbued most rigidly with an

emancipatory historicism. What Foucault is suggesting, however, is that structuralism is not an antihistory but an attempt to deal with history in a different way, as a spatiotemporal configuration, simultaneously and interactively synchronic and diachronic (to use the conventional categorical opposition).

7. Rabinow, *Foucault Reader*, 252–53.

8. Foucault, "The Eye of Power," in Gordon, *Power/Knowledge*, 149.

9. Rabinow, *Foucault Reader*, 250.

10. John Berger, *And our faces, my heart, brief as photos* (New York: Pantheon, 1984).

11. John Berger, *The Look of Things* (New York: Viking, 1974).

12. Jorge Luis Borges, *The Aleph and Other Stories: 1933–1969* (New York: Bantam, 1971), 12–13; hereafter cited in text as *Aleph*.

13. Security Pacific National Bank published at least eight editions of its pamphlet on "the Sixty-Mile Circle," each pumping up the region to its fullest proportions. Most recently, Security Pacific was swallowed whole by the Bank of America, but its symbolic orbit lingers on.

14. For the details of the now slowed-down Star Wars campaign, see D. Sanger, "Star Wars Industry Rises," *New York Times,* 19 November 1985.

15. Mike Davis, "The Political Economy of Late Imperial America," *New Left Review* 143 (1984): 6–38.

16. Reyner Banham, *Los Angeles: The Architecture of the Four Ecologies* (New York: Harper and Row, 1971).

17. M. Landsbaum and H. Evans, "Mission Viejo: Winning Is the Only Game in Town," *Los Angeles Times,* 22 August 1984.

18. Allen J. Scott, "High Technology Industry and Territorial Development: The Rise of the Orange County Complex 1955–1984," *Urban Geography* 7 (1986): 3–45. See also Scott's *Metropolis: From the Division of Labor to Urban Form* (Berkeley and Los Angeles: University of California Press, 1988).

19. Anthony Giddens, *The Constitution of Society: Outline of the Theory of Structuration* (Berkeley and Los Angeles: University of California Press, 1984), 183–84.

20. The Westin Bonaventure, financed and part-owned by the Japanese, figured prominently in the early debates on postmodernism and continues to be a focus of controversy even as it today edges into bankruptcy and foreclosure. See Fredric Jameson, "Postmodernism, or the Cultural Logic of Late Capitalism," *New Left Review* 146 (1984): 53–92; Mike Davis, "Urban Renaissance and the Spirit of Postmodernism," *New Left Review* 151 (1985): 106–13; and Edward Soja, "Heterotopologies: A Remembrance of Other Spaces in the Citadel-LA," *Strategies: A Journal of Theory, Culture, and Politics* 3 (1990): 6–39.

21. Another outlet reached near LAX is the Hyperion Sewage Treatment Plant, excreting from the City of Los Angeles a volume of waste equivalent to the fifth or sixth largest river to reach the ocean in California, and creating an increasingly poisoned food chain reaching back into the population of its drainage basin. Over the past several years there have been claims that Santa Monica Bay may have the highest levels of toxic chemicals along the West Coast. Signs were posted to warn of the hazards of locally caught fish (especially the so aptly named croaker), and doctors warned many of their patients not to swim off

certain beaches. The fault lines in the garbage chains of the region may ultimately prove more threatening than those better-known cracks in the earth's surface.

22. The root of *semiotic* and *semiology* is the Greek *semeion,* which means "sign," "mark," "spot," or *"point in space."* You arrange to meet someone at a *semeion,* a particular place. The significance of this connection between semiotics and spatiality is too often forgotten.

FIVE

# Cubism, Camouflage, Silence, and Democracy: A Phenomenological Approach

*Stephen Kern*

To identify something as historical, one must be able to sort out of it what is *trans*historical, and to do that requires a theory of the essentials of human experience. One rich source of such theory is phenomenology.

Around 1900 Edmund Hesserl began to consider how the world is actually experienced in acts of consciousness. His goal was to make philosophy into a "rigorous science" by using a method of description that would yield indubitable knowledge. To achieve these high standards he at first limited his focus to the simplest perceptual experiences—a sheet of paper, a melody of seven notes—but eventually broadened his subject matter to embrace more complex experiences of judgment, desire, intersubjectivity, and finally history. There remains much controversy about whether he ever achieved the certainty that he aspired to, even for the simple perceptual phenomena with which he began. But his standards for precision and thoroughness have continued to inspire philosophers and social scientists. A number of psychiatrists have also been drawn to phenomenology, in particular to its identification of essential aspects of experience, a procedure that Husserl called the *Wesenschau*, or "intuiting essences."

Historians tend to be suspicious of essences, since they betoken *a*historicism; but it is important to understand precisely what does *not* change to help clarify what does. Husserl believed that he was describing the consciousness of a melody in a way that would necessarily be true for all human beings, not just twentieth-century philosophers. His detailed account of perception and apperception, of retention, recollection, and protention, is about the essential components of *any* temporal experience.[1] In this essay I identify the *constituency of space* as one essential. It is not possible to be a human being and not experience the constituency of space. Individuals may not have a word for that experience; they may not realize that they experience it; or they may describe it with confusion; and they will conceive of and experience modes of it differently—but they must experience it.

In 1983 I published a study of historical modes of time and space between 1880 and 1918.[2] I was led to focus on these fundamental categories by reading phenomenologically oriented psychiatrists, especially Eugène Minkowski, who, largely under the influence of Henri Bergson, interpreted his patients' symptoms according to the way they experienced "lived time."[3] In expanding my focus to include modes of "lived space," I uncovered some intriguing associations between various cultural affirmations of what I called "positive negative space" and the rise of democracy. These associations occurred to me late in the writing of the book, however, and so the evidence for them was less than I would have liked. The arguments were also scattered throughout the book, because my basic expository commitment was to philosophical categories and not to documenting connections between democracy and the new sense of space. In this essay I have collected those pieces of evidence, supplemented them with some new material, and critically evaluated how I came to make such an argument.

Among the various methods of phenomenology, one proved especially helpful: the use of "presuppositionless" terms.[4] The word is unfortunate, for it suggests that phenomenologists can entirely eliminate all presuppositions, even those arising from language, which, of course, is naive, and it suggests an arrogance—that phenomenologists alone comprehend the presuppositions that contaminate all other philosophies and keep them from being pure. In practice the term merely indicates the continuing effort to clarify presuppositions and eliminate what remains unclarified; I use it to describe terminology that avoids, as much as possible, accidental associations such as the connection between democracy and values associated with politics of the Left or Right, or connecting cubism with the so-called breakdown of values in modern art. In describing democracy as access to power over others, I attempt to minimize such accidental or nonessential associations. What is left is an essential structure of experience at the core, for example, of the depiction of prostitutes in Picasso's *Les demoiselles d'Avignon* or the electoral system of Wilhelmine Germany. And it is only by theoretically dissociating such accidental associations with, and unclarified presuppositions about, the nature of cubism, camouflage, silence, and democracy that their essential nature may be discerned and their common historical significance may be interpreted.

What in the world, one might well wonder, do those four things have to do with one another? "Cubism" refers to a movement in art that started with a painting by Picasso in 1907; military camouflage was invented by a French soldier in 1914; "democracy" is a political system conceived by the ancient Greeks; and silence is a universal. To clarify why I attempted to link them, I must address one problem that cultural historians have making any generalization about an age—the range of sources. If I were to characterize this period as the age of cubism, and present as evidence the comments of ten cubist painters, one would naturally object that such a concept might hold for painting, but what about other areas of experience? To respond to such an objection, historians scan the historical record to find sources widely ranging in point of view. In my work I have taken "widely" seriously and have introduced the term *conceptual distance* to formalize its spatial sense. Thus, I assume that there is greater conceptual distance between the thinking of a painter and that of an artillery officer on a given subject then there is between the thinking of two painters, and I assume further that any generalization about an age is the more persuasive, the greater the conceptual distance between the sources on which it is based. That is why I have undertaken to explicate how the thinking of an artist and an artillery officer might be linked to the absence of sound and a political philosophy. The conceptual distance between these historical sources must not be too great, however, or the juxtaposition becomes forced. Mindful of that problem, I was particularly gratified to discover a direct connection between Cubism and the "composition" of World War I.

In 1938 Gertrude Stein looked back on World War I and made the following interpretation: "Really the composition of this war . . . was not the composition of all previous wars, in which there was one man in the center surrounded by a lot of other men, but *a composition in which one corner was as important as another corner,* in fact [it was] the composition of Cubism." This metaphor was intriguing. But one of Stein's unforgettable anecdotes suggested more explicitly the suitability of her cubist metaphor. "I very well remember at the beginning of the war, being with Picasso on the Boulevard Raspail when the first camouflaged truck passed. It was night, we had heard of camouflage but had not yet seen it, and Picasso, amazed, looked at it, and then cried out, *yes* it is we who made it, that is Cubism."[5]

The armies of the nineteenth century were outfitted in bright colors to display the wealth, polish, and discipline of the advancing army and intimidate the enemy. But with the extension of the range of accuracy from the one hundred yards of the older musket to the two thousand yards of the breech-loading rifle, and with the increased firepower of sweeping lines of bullets from a machine-gun blast, colorful uniforms and tight formations were suicidal. The British switched to khaki during the Boer War, and by the outbreak of World War I the Germans were suited in field gray. But in 1914 the French soldier still wore the red cap and pantaloons of the Second Empire. General Messimy tried to change the uniform, but the army at first refused to dress its soldiers in some drab, earthy color. "Eliminate the red trousers?" The outraged former war minister Etienne protested, "Never! Le pantalon rouge, c'est la France!"[6] After the August and September slaughters, however, the proud, hierarchical-minded, and aristocratic officer corps, which at first protested against making French soldiers blend into the surroundings, now desperately looked for some way to make them invisible.

When I first came on Picasso's remark that the cubists had invented camouflage, since neither he nor Stein documented any direct connection, I assumed that he was just pointing out similarities, much as I had done with other developments throughout my book. The functions of both were strikingly analogous. The cubists tried to blend the fruit into the backgrounds of their still lifes, just as camouflage attempted to blend soldiers into the terrain. But was there any direct, intended connection? I was never able to discover whether Picasso knew about the man who invented camouflage, but I did discover that he knew about Picasso.

In September 1914 the French painter Guirand de Scevola was working as a telephone operator for an artillery unit at the Battle of the Marne. Just after transmitting an order from telephone headquarters to his frontline unit, it was hit by enemy fire, and he realized that they had been spotted. As he later wrote: "At this instant, vaguely at first, then ever more precisely, the idea of camouflage was born. There must be, I thought, a practical way to dissimulate not only our gun but also the men who operated it. . . . My first thought was to render the form and color of the material less visible if not invisible." His idea was to conceal an artillery gun under a net splashed with earth colors. He interested Marshall Joffre, who sanctioned the first camouflage section in the French Army to develop techniques for concealing equipment. The bright red cap and pantaloons were also abandoned for new uniforms of horizon blue. Scevola also reflected on the connection between cubism and his discovery. "In order to deform objects, I employed the means Cubists used to represent them—later this permitted me to hire for my camouflage section some painters, who, because of their very special vision, had an aptitude for decomposing any kind of form whatsoever."[7] By the end of the war, camouflage sections employed three thousand *camoufleurs* (including such prominent artists as Claude Forain and Franz Marc) to dissimulate the big guns. Their insignia was a chameleon.

There is thus evidence that camouflage was conceived by an artist who reported having been in part influenced by cubist techniques; however, we must not overemphasize that factor. First of all, cubists were interested in far more than just making fruit blend into the backgrounds of their still lifes. Picasso and Braque were undertaking a revolution in the nature and purpose of art. Where their Realist predecessors were devoted to depicting the external world more or less as it appeared to the eye, modern artists began to depict colored forms on canvases for largely aesthetic reasons, independent of the dictates of empirical reality. Cubists reduced depth, introduced multiple perspectives and multiple light sources, simplified and geometrized forms, diminished the number and intensity of colors, and broke up objects and reconstructed them in a purely artistic space. Picasso and Braque gave space the same colors, textures, and substantiality as material objects and made objects and space interpenetrate so as to be almost indistinguishable. As a result, fruit seemed to blend into the surrounding space. And, of course, the invention of camouflage was "caused" by far more than the cubist influence on Scevola. He survived the Battle of the Marne and witnessed the deaths of tens of thousands of men for a number of reasons, in addition to the insanity of dressing soldiers in brightly colored uniforms. These other influences must be kept in mind in linking cubism and camouflage.

Having assessed that link, we may now try to understand the connection between them and democracy. The precise political meaning of *democracy* is "government by the people." Between 1880 and 1920 democracy became a palpable reality for tens of millions of people who had never before participated in choosing their rulers. In addition to this exclusively political sense, "democratization" also refers to the erosion of the aristocracy's social, and what remained of its legal, privileges. These two phenomena have independent histories, but for present purposes, I am combining them under the single rubric of "democratization," because the essential element of a *leveling* of a former hierarchical distinction applies to both. Although they are not necessarily linked in theory, these developments in fact occurred throughout the Western world at around the same time and were in many ways interdependent. And one implication of my interpretation of this period will be that they are linked thematically as part of a broad process of leveling of older hierarchies in many areas of human experience beyond the social and political.

To connect cubism and democracy, or camouflage and democracy, the nature of my argument must change at this point, because the remaining connections will be juxtapositions of functionally similar parallel historical developments, for which I have found no evidence of direct causal connection. Before explicating these parallels, a brief discussion of the phenomenological view of causation is in order.

To enhance the rigor of phenomenological descriptions, Husserl systematically suspended from consideration aspects of human experience which he believed could not be known for certain, including causal relations. This method of suspension or "bracketing," known as the phenomenological reduction, involved holding in abeyance belief in these aspects of experience because they were not directly and immediately perceived and hence could not be admitted into philosophical descriptions that measured up to his standard for certainty. Husserl did *not* deny that there are causes, but he believed that they cannot be known with as high a degree of certainty as direct and immediate "acts of consciousness." By bracketing causality one can focus more clearly what is perceived, unconfused by quasi- or pseudocausal notions. And by identifying the essentials of an experience, it may then be possible to understand more clearly its significance or even its causes.

Instead of trying to explain how cubism might have "caused" democracy or how democracy "caused" cubism, I have devised a method of exposition grounded in select aspects of the method of phenomenological description. I have identified one essential structure (the constituency of space); elaborated how diverse aspects of culture affirmed its positive nature; suggested a fundamental coherence among them; and interpreted its historical significance. Aside from the one exception of the connection between cubism and camouflage, causal connections remain bracketed, and my essay remains interpretive.

To identify this fundamental coherence, we must now look at one distinctive feature of cubism—its constitutive use of the space that traditionally was a negativity framing the prominent subject. In Braque's *Still Life with Violin and Pitcher* (1910), the neck of the violin retains its discreteness, but the body is fractured into sections that open into a space rendered as substantially as the splinters of wood. It is impossible to distinguish clearly between subject and background as plaster, glass, wood, paper, and space are rendered in a pattern of similar forms. Braque explained: "The fragmentation enabled me to establish the space and the movement within space, and I was unable to introduce the object until I had created the space."[8] The pitcher and violin are just different kinds of space occupied by solid objects that can be simplified, geometrized, fragmented, and reformed. In Braque's painting all spaces are equal. That equality is the basis for my claim that the cubists democratized the picture surface.

In traditional portraits, the subject (often referred to as "positive space") was more important than the background (referred to as "negative space"). The cubists obliterated that distinction and filled their canvases with nothing but what I call "positive negative space." The term implies that the space itself is a positive element of equal importance with the subject. The term is somewhat unwieldy, but it accurately suggests the historical shift, since it implies that what was formerly regarded as negative (or at least less positively) now has a positive, constitutive function. An illustration of that change comes from a comparison with procedures in the studio of Sir Joshua Reynolds, the eighteenth-century portraitist, who depicted the British upper classes. The critical parts of his portraits (and of virtually all other portrait painters of this period)— the pose and the face—were executed by Sir Joshua himself, while the subjects' clothing and the background were done by an assistant—the drapery painter. That hierarchical arrangement in his studio mirrored the hierarchical aristocratic world of the eighteenth century. The cubists wiped out that hierarchy in their paintings and thus "democratized" the picture surface.

Most pre-cubist artists were devoted to the depiction of external reality and to the conviction that certain parts of their paintings were more important than others. Modern artists in general, and cubists in particular, rejected that hierarchy. Cubist paintings were a declaration of independence from the tradition that imposed on artists the necessity of rendering the forms and the space of visual reality. There is no negative space in the cubist canvas. Cubists democratized the picture surface and, in so doing, emancipated art from its conventional obedience to the dominant hierarchical conception of the painting's structure.[9]

Three distinct levelings in all this must be clarified. There is a leveling of the social hierarchy in Reynolds's studio, a leveling of the artistic hierarchy implied in the notion that the artist was subordinated to the dictates of empirical reality, and a leveling of the traditional artistic conventions that certain parts of paintings were of greater value than others. In this context I am using "democracy" metaphorically, as I do throughout this essay. Metaphors link things in unconventional ways and thus impart new meaning by suggesting new contexts. But there must be some fundamental similarity to make the metaphor intelligible. My method of juxtaposition uses metaphors to bridge the conceptual distance between different aspects of experience and to build a generalization about the "spirit of the age" on that fundamental similarity. In order to relate artistic technique to a political process, we must dissociate both terms from some of their conventional associations. This maneuver is a kind of "shucking," a removing of a hard casing and an exposing of the essential core.

The assertion "Cubism was democratic" can be used as the starting point for constructing a broader argument about an essential, though variously manifested, pattern of experience. If you shuck cubism of its exclusively artistic connotation, the result is, in part, an affirmation of "positive negative space" in the depiction on a flat surface of objects in space. Similarly, if you shuck democracy of its accidental political connotation, the result is, in part, the affirmation of "positive negative space" as the foundation for the distribution of power over others. Thus, the affirmation of positive negative space is found to be an essential core and hence conjunctive basis of the link between cubism and democracy. This specific constitution of space is now available for juxtaposition with other historical phenomena, which can be similarly analyzed.

To what extent, then, does camouflage involve an affirmation of a former negativity, and how is it related to democracy? Camouflage wiped out the hierarchical social implications of rank associated with differently coded uniforms and hence had a democratizing function. At this point we see a similar function between cubism, camouflage, and democracy. Camouflage, like cubism, diminished the traditional priority of the subject in contrast to the background in a visual phenomenon. Together they implied that traditional ways are not necessarily the best ways of ordering objects in pictorial space or men and guns on a battlefield or, with a bit of interpretive stretching, classes or the electorate in society. The abandonment of the old military uniform, so intimately associated with aristocratic society, compromised the convention of deference to rank in the army and in the civilized world. Henceforth troops and artillery guns, like pictorial objects, would be given prominence only if the situation required, not because of outmoded conventions. Cubism and camouflage leveled older hierarchies in order to rehierarchize the world in ways that suited the urgent demands of the current situation.

I have theoretically shucked camouflage of its accidental military connotation to reveal another affirmation of positive negative space as the foundation for the deployment of men. By stripping all these phenomena of conventional presuppositions of art, politics, and warfare, I have clarified an essential feature common to each. If this feature is indeed fundamental, it might be possible to find other modes of it scattered across the cultural record of this period.

The history of architecture is the history of the shaping of space for a variety of personal, political, social, and religious reasons. Greek temples and theaters, Roman basilicas and baths, Gothic cathedrals, baroque palaces—each style embodied a distinctive sense of space. Around the turn of the century, however, architects began to modify the way they conceived of space in relation to their constructions. Whereas formerly they tended to think of space more as a negative element between the positive elements of floors, ceilings, and walls, in this period they began to think more in terms of composing with "space" itself as a positive element rather than with differently shaped "rooms." This change in *terminology* and in thinking was facilitated by three inventions from this period (electric light, reinforced concrete, and air-conditioning) that liberated architects from many structural requirements for illumination, load bearing, and ventilation and made it possible to sculpt more freely with interior space.

This conceptual shift was presented forcefully in the writings and buildings of Frank Lloyd Wright. His Larkin Soap Company building (Buffalo, 1904) was essentially a single room closed to the outside. Wright himself identified its role in the history of architecture. It was "the original affirmative negation" that showed "the new sense of 'the space within' as reality." Interior spaces designed to conform to human needs were the rationale for the structure. Space was the basic element in his Unity Temple (Oak Park, Illinois, 1906), which had a plain cubical interior constructed with simple blocks of cement. He explained that his initial conception was "to keep a noble ROOM in mind, and let the room shape the whole edifice." Although this account used the more traditional architectural terminology that conceived of space in terms of rooms, the sense of it was modern, as Wright went on to make clear in a bold historical claim about his conception of the positive function of space: "The first conscious expression of which I know in modern architecture of the new reality—the 'space within to be lived in'—was Unity Temple in Oak Park. . . . In every part of the building freedom is active. Space [is] the basic element in architectural design."[10]

This reference to a sense of freedom evoked by space echoed the aesthetic theory of the German philosopher Theodor Lipps and its application to architecture by the British architect Geoffrey Scott. In 1903 Lipps argued that our bodies unconsciously empathize with architectural forms. We feel free when there are no external constraints on our bodily movements, and buildings with large open spaces offer that freedom.[11] In 1914 Scott elaborated an "architecture of humanism" based on this theory. Architects project human feelings into a building, and it in turn impresses viewers with an immediate physical response. We feel uncomfortable in a room fifty feet square and seven feet high because it constricts our sense of freedom. Heretofore architects had neglected the importance of space in their art. "The habits of our mind are fixed on matter. We talk of what occupies our tools and arrests our eyes. Matter is fashioned; space comes. Space is 'nothing'—a mere negation of the solid. And thus we come to overlook it." In emphasizing that architecture is the one art form that creates with space directly, Scott summarized the thoughts of a generation of architects striving to acknowledge the constituent function of space.[12]

Another development was the elimination of ornament, which had traditionally been added onto buildings, especially palaces, where status was visibly on display with coats of arms as well as a lexicon of architectural symbols of aristocracy, linking the current nobility with its ancestry. Such ornamental excess and slavish historicism inspired Louis Sullivan, negatively, to envision a new "democratic architecture," as he called it, that would create new structures appropriate to the antimonarchical modern ethos. Although Sullivan identified numerous structures as monarchical, he unfortunately did not say precisely what kinds of structures were democratic. But we may conclude that the elimination of ornamentation and façade; construction with simple materials of wood, stone, glass, and concrete; and the functional use of space were all part of a new democratic spirit in architecture.

The American historian Frederick Jackson Turner argued that the empty spaces of the frontier in America "promoted democracy." In 1903 Turner concluded: "Whenever social conditions tended to crystallize in the East, whenever capital tended to press upon labor, there was this gate of escape to the free conditions of the frontier. There lands promoted individualism, economic equality, freedom to rise, and democracy."[13] The creation of national parks in America was a new affirmation of a former wasteland. The first was Yellowstone Park in 1872, and many followed in the 1880s and 1890s. Such parks were open to the public, in contrast to the older private estates of kings, noblemen, and the wealthy.[14]

In literature, works appeared in which voids form the subject, as in Conrad's *Heart of Darkness,* where negativities abound: the silence of the jungle, omnipresent images of death, and especially the darkness, which is at the heart of Africa, the story, its main character, and, by implication, humankind itself. The darkness is a leveling force that negates European class distinctions: in the wilderness those distinctions become absurd. Cannibalism and head-hunting rather palpably obliterate conventional marks of status. Marlow notices the sharp contrast between the hierarchical society at home and the more egalitarian Congo when he returns to London and is at last able to understand the creative potential of the wilderness. In the face of danger, in darkness, all people are pretty much alike.

Although it would misrepresent *Heart of Darkness* to classify it as democratic, there can be little question that it assailed the hierarchical structure of fin de siècle society. It would be even more absurd to characterize Marcel Proust as a democrat. However, some of the themes of *Remembrance of Things Past* include the futility of Marcel's social aspirations, the vacuity of the aristocratic society of the Princess de Guermantes, and the new forces of social change that made it impossible for the old aristocracy to maintain its status. "Enfeebled or broken," Proust wrote, "the springs of the machine could no longer perform their task of keeping

out the crowd; a thousand alien elements made their way in, and all
. . . consistency of form and color was lost." [15] In place of the old social
hierarchy, Proust establishes a new hierarchy of the artist, who alone can
create worthy values in his work.

One subject of Proust's novel was the silence of a generation that came
home after four years of killing and discovered that nobody spoke the
same language or felt the old feelings anymore. Forgetting, silence, and
time lost are variations on the theme of negation. The novels of the
nineteenth century were as vivid as Jean Valjean's flight through the
sewers of Paris, as palpable as the Count of Monte Cristo's treasure.
They revolved around great, noisy events—war and revolution, crime
and punishment, passion and betrayal. Even Flaubert—who claimed he
wanted "to write a book about nothing, a book without any exterior support, which would sustain itself by the inner force of its style . . . a book
which would be almost devoid of subject, or at least in which the subject
would be almost invisible"—even he structured *Madame Bovary* around
the passionate outbursts of seduction and adultery, the agonized cries of
the victim of a botched surgical operation, and the sounds of a grotesque
suicide. But Proust centered his novel on the forgetting and remembering of tea and cakes and the lost time that that recollection enabled him
to understand. He was a great architect of silence. The ting of a spoon
striking a cup was one of the most significant sounds of his novel. Silences cast lovers into despair as forcefully as the whisperings of betrayal
or the shouting of insults.

Some poets also aimed to give substance to traditional voids. In poetry
there was a formal shift in the conception of the poem from merely an
arrangement of words to a composition of words *and* the blank spaces
between them. Already in the 1880s French symbolists began to experiment with "free verse" stretched across intentionally shaped white
spaces on the page. This technique was developed by Mallarmé, who
believed that poetry should be evocative, and he urged, in an often-
quoted instruction, "Paint not the thing, but the effect it produces."
Once again the subject—*the thing*—lost its former prominence. As
Braque toppled its pictorial authority by rendering the space around it
with equal substance, Mallarmé diminished its literary authority by leaving it out of poems and creating verbal compositions out of its shadows
and effects. The new poetry, he wrote, dispenses with precise description and employs rather evocation, allusion, suggestion. It makes "sudden jumps and noble hesitations" that hint at things and allow the reader
to respond with his own associations.

What can we make of Mallarmé's other instruction: "We must forget
the *title,* for it is too resounding"? I cannot resist the temptation to read
into this a subtle democratic thrust, playing on the double meaning of

"title." His use of first lines for titles of many of his poems was an attempt to diminish the resounding authority of the title and let the work unfold, in sequence, image by image, with each word contributing its proper share to the overall artistic impression along with the blank spaces in between. Indeed, Mallarmé further explained that he used the blanks between words for a visual pause to establish a rhythmic movement of words and images like notes in a musical composition.[16]

Rilke's narrator, Malte Laurids Brigge, observed the Paris cityscape of the early 1900s in similar egalitarian terms, linking what he saw with the simplified and unified picture surface of modern art, which he interpreted as beginning with Manet.

> The foreground takes on the colors of distance. . . . And everything related to expanse . . . has taken that expanse behind it. . . . Everything is simplified, brought onto a few correct planes, like the face in a Manet portrait. And nothing is trivial or superfluous. The booksellers on the quai open their stalls, and the fresh or worn yellow of the books, the violet brown of the bindings, the larger green of an album: everything is in harmony, has value, everything takes part and forms a plenitude in which there is nothing lacking.[17]

Although the language of politics and of democracy does not suit Rilke's aestheticism, his vision is unmistakably eqalitarian.

In *The Principles of Psychology* (1890) William James illustrated the power of negativities in a discussion of the stream of consciousness of sound: "What we hear when the thunder crashes is not thunder pure, but thunder-breaking-upon-silence-and-contrasting-with-it." The interdependence of sound and its absence is one example of the many mutual interactions of positives and negatives that make up our mental life. Although the "radical" in his *Essays in Radical Empiricism* (1909) was not primarily political, his philosophy had political implications, as Horace Kallen, a philosopher at the University of Wisconsin, noted in 1914, in connection with the leveling effect of positive negative space in James's thought. "Pure experience has no favorites. It admits into reality . . . evil as well as good, discontinuities as well as continuities. . . . [James] is the first democrat of metaphysics." James refused to detest the material world as did the idealists: nothing was more or less real to him than anything else. He recognized the "democratic consubstantiality of every entity in experience with every other."[18] This characterization of the "democratic" nature of James's metaphysics, which would include his argument about the mutual interdependence of sound and silence, leads to my final topic.

Creative uses of silence are scattered all across nineteenth-century culture. Among the Romantics, silence meant melancholy, separation, and loneliness; it was a reminder of the futility of verbal communication. Among Symbolist poets, silence suggested mystery, the forgotten, the infinite, the unknown.

In music, silence is as essential to the recognition of sound as the white of paper is to the identification of print. Throughout the history of music there had been significant silences, but they generally occurred at the end of movements and had a separating function. In some new music of this period, pauses occurred in the middle of sections and took on a more constitutive function. The music of Von Webern is full of negativities: his extremely brief compositions (whole movements less than a minute long) echo with all that is left out, and what can be heard is laced with breathtaking silences.

In France the most striking composer of silences was Debussy, who attempted to suggest the silent communication of lovers in *La demoiselle élue* and again in *Pelléas et Mélisande*. In a letter of 1893 Debussy explained his intentions: "Quite spontaneously, I used a method which seemed rather *exceptional*. I refer to silence (don't laugh) used like a mode of expression and perhaps the only way of getting the most emotion out of a phrase."[19] Debussy's claim that his creative use of silence was "exceptional" accords with the claims to historical specificity of a number of literary and music critics of this period and justifies the periodizing of this development with other examples of positive negativities, including cubism and camouflage. They all affirmed the primacy and more positive function of what had formerly been thought of as secondary and background.

But what might the constitutive use of silence in music have to do with democracy? Debussy's statement makes no reference to politics or social structure, and it would be absurd to argue that it was so intended. But perhaps I can suggest some ways to view the new function of silence in the music of this period as part of a broad assault on the monarchical tradition and, by implication, social hierarchy.

Debussy's music was a reaction against the lush Romantic orchestration that had mushroomed into the massive sound of Wagner, culminating the connection between grand opera and ceremony that had been intimately associated with aristocratic tradition. For centuries monarchies had celebrated births, marriages, coronations, royal entries, victories, and dedications with spectacles of sound and martial airs. Monarchs were announced by loud trumpet fanfares. As one historian of music concluded, "These swaggering processions were necessary to perpetuate the mystique of glory, affluence, and power of royal absolutism."[20] Debussy's use of creative silences, suggests something political in its bold use of a creative negativity to counter the blatant noisiness of the monarchical tradition.

A more explicit source for the link between silence and democracy is the work of the Belgian mystic Maurice Maeterlinck, who drew from the Symbolist tradition and wrote an influential essay on silence as well as *Pelléas et Mélisande,* which Debussy scored into an opera. Maeterlinck explored the mysterious intuitions, the inexpressible feelings and unconscious thoughts that course beneath the surface. In his essay on silence, he argued that we fear the absence of sound because it betokens death; we therefore spend a lot of time making senseless chatter. But there is a positive silence, a "real silence," which he related to a political leveling: "It is a thing that knows no limit, and before it, all men are equal; and the silence of king or slave in the presence of death or love reveals the same features."

Maeterlinck further claimed that he was identifying a new foundation for human relations in the modern age: "Men are nearer to their brothers; in the look of their eyes there is deeper earnestness and tender fellowship." These new patterns relate to a recognition of the positive function of silence. "A transformation of silence—strange and inexplicable—is upon us." This change may be seen in literature, which is beginning to turn away from the great, noisy events of the past for its subject and toward quiet events of the lives of "insignificant" individuals. "In the work-a-day lives of the very humblest of men are manifested spiritual phenomena that bring soul nearer to soul; and of all this we can find no record in former times." Modern music and painting, he insisted, have seen that persons and events overladen with "superficial ornament" are no more important than the feelings and activities of the simplest peasant. "The true artist," he wrote, "no longer chooses Marius triumphing over the Cimbrians, or the assassination of the Duke de Guise as fit subjects for his art." And in the most frequently quoted of all his writings, Maeterlinck suggested the kind of everyday event that ought to constitute the subject of art:

> I have grown to believe that an old man, seated in his armchair, waiting patiently, with his lamp beside him; giving unconscious ear to all the eternal laws that reign about his house, interpreting, without comprehending, the silence of doors and windows and the quivering voice of the light, submitting with bent head to the presence of his soul and his destiny . . . motionless as he is, does yet live in reality a deeper, more human and more universal life than the lover who strangles his mistress, the captain who conquers in battle, or "the husband who avenges his honor."[21]

This speculation is quintessentially democratic in spirit and provides an image with which to link my several themes. The old man sitting alone, hearing no audible sounds, is a kind of new hero for Western literature, art, or music. This shift constitutes a radical rehierarchization of traditional subject matter away from rich, powerful, aristocratic indi- viduals toward poor, politically powerless ones. And quiet and under- stated music, punctuated with evocative silences, is the score of this mod- ern, democratic sensibility. If painters no longer have to depict assassinations or military victories to get viewers' attention, then music does not have to evoke such moments of high passion. Although Mal- larmé's poem and hence Debussy's *Prélude à l'après-midi d'un faune* tell the story of a seduction of two nymphs by a faun, neither the audience nor the faun is really certain if the whole thing was dream or reality. In these two works seduction has been tamed and quieted. The old man sitting alone is the new positive negative space of democracy. He is the ground against which noisy and youthful heroes were contrasted and highlighted in traditional literature. Formerly he was generally the con- fidant, the sidekick, the consoler; now he is as significant as Marius tri- umphing over the Cimbrians. His *waiting* is as engaging as traditional heroic activity; he is indeed *camouflaged* with all the *ordinary* objects in his *modest* room, all bathed *equally* in the lamplight, all listening to the *silence* of the doors and the subdued "voice of the light." Thus do form and content align themselves: cubism, camouflage, silence, and democracy can be conjoined thematically with an interpretation of Maeterlinck's justly famous icon.

I began with data about the way space was conceived and experienced between 1880 and 1918. Among those data I discovered a new sense of the positive function of space, which many observers from this period believed was new in their time. From reading in phenomenology I knew that the concept of space and various subconcepts—form, distance, and direction as well as the constituency of space (as either empty or full)— had been identified as essential structures of experience. I had no a pri- ori master list of essentials crucial to understanding this or any other period (there is no such list) but merely a working list of essentials, in- cluding those about spatial subconcepts, from which I selected the best documented and the most informative about this period. These latter judgments were just that: intuitive decisions based on a reading of phe- nomenology and a consideration of the data of history. Phenomenolo- gists need history to break out of their self-reflective hermeticism as much as historians need phenomenology to clarify their unexamined presuppositions and sleight-of-hand causal explanations.

Once the focal topic was established and its distinctive historical mode provisionally determined, I was then able to begin to consider how other aspects of the culture "lined up with," "conjoined," or "paralleled" the basic function of positive negative space. My use of such a variety of verbs to express these connections reveals the centrality of this expository technique and its vulnerability, for it is a variant of the suspect method of arguing by analogy. I have indeed used metaphor and analogy to link material from especially "distant" sources and extend my interpretation beyond the limitations of strict academic disciplines and their exacting requirements for evidence and argumentation. But I am convinced that such connections are made in reality, particularly by leading artists and intellectuals. And if the surviving documentation cannot support such connections with direct causal influences, we must force them a bit, right up to the edges of plausibility, because human consciousness ranges over vast and often untraceable stretches of experience, taking in all sorts of hints. These borrowings and influences are sometimes conscious and explicit, sometimes unconscious and hidden, and sometimes even emphatically denied.[22] The identification of these connections—largely by metaphor and analogy—constitutes the open end of my thinking. Even though I do not expect them all to pan out as conscious, causal connections, they make possible the discovery of such a connection, as I did find between cubism and camouflage; but more important, they point to fundamental changes that cut across the conventional dividers of human experience.

This basic change in one aspect of the sense of space, I then reasoned, must be manifest in the important social and political developments of the period: the leveling of aristocratic society and the rise of political democracy. Although I had no evidence for a direct causal connection, I nevertheless became convinced that the essential nature of both sets of developments was grounded in the same new sense of the constitutive function of what had formerly been seen as a negativity. The final argument was thus based on (1) a single piece of evidence about direct causal connection between cubism and camouflage, neither of which was directly linked with social or political change in the documentation of the time; (2) a few metaphorical connections between politics and culture, such as Sullivan's concept of a new "democratic architecture" and Kallen's assessment of James as the "first democrat of metaphysics"; and (3) a series of juxtapositions of diverse and conceptually "distant" cultural phenomena with a common foundation in the new sense of the constituency of space.

The debt to phenomenology may now be made explicit. The *Wesenschau* identified essential structures of experience; the concept of "presuppositionlessness" indicated the kind of terminology that must be used for descriptions of transhistorical structures as well as their distinctive historical modes; and the bracketing of "causality" liberated me from having to provide explanatory arguments (which the lack of evidence of direct causal connection made impossible) and supplied theoretical justification for my basic expository mode as interpretive.

Reconstructions of such essential historical developments cannot be limited to temporally synchronous, spatially proximate, and causally related phenomena. If they were, these reconstructions would be fragmentary and lack coherence. One major methodological problem for the cultural historian is how to go beyond causally related phenomena, which are often the most obvious and the best known. I have suggested a way of going beyond, while adhering to rigorous philosophical methods. Although these methods were originally devised to describe the simplest human perceptual experiences, they may be adapted to undertake historical generalizations.

## NOTES

1. See Edmund Husserl, *The Phenomenology of Internal Time-Consciousness* (Bloomington: Indiana University Press, 1964), for the basic phenomenological text.

2. Stephen Kern, *The Culture of Time and Space 1880–1918* (Cambridge: Harvard University Press, 1983).

3. Eugène Minkowski, *Lived Time: Phenomenological and Psychopathological Studies* (Evanston: Northwestern University Press, 1970).

4. Marvin Farber, "The Ideal of a Presuppositionless Philosophy," in *Philosophical Essays in Memory of Edmund Husserl* (Cambridge: Harvard University Press, 1948), 44–64.

5. Gertrude Stein, *Picasso* (1938; rpt. New York: Beacon, 1959), 11, 41.

6. Cited in Barbara Tuchman, *The Guns of August* (New York: Dell, 1971), 55.

7. Guirand de Scevola, "Souvenirs du camouflage (1914–1918)," *La revue,* Christmas 1950, 719–20. This source and a vast amount of additional information on the subject can be found in Elizabeth Kahn Baldewicz, "Les Camoufleurs: The Mobilization of Art and the Artist in Wartime France, 1914–1918," Ph.D. diss., University of California, Los Angeles, 1980.

8. Dora Vallier, "Braque, la peinture et nous: Propos de l'artiste recueillis," *Cahiers d'art* 29 (October 1954): 15–16.

9. The cubist introduction of multiple perspectives in a single painting also had egalitarian implications. Although this feature is not aligned thematically with my particular emphasis here—the cubists' constitutive use of space—the connection is compelling and was drawn around that time by José Ortega y Gasset, whose philosophy of "perspectivism" affirmed the value of multiple perspectives over a rigid objectivism. Ortega believed that the voices of the many, however untrained or chaotic, are a desirable check on the judgment of a single class, culture, or political interest group. Although many of the defenses of multiple perspectives and subjectivism in this period did not address themselves to the issues of social equality versus social privilege or of democracy versus monarchy,

they formed part of a general cultural reorientation in this period that was essentially pluralistic and democratic.

10. Frank Lloyd Wright, "A Testament" and "An Autobiography," in Edgar Kaufmann and Ben Raeburn, eds., *Frank Lloyd Wright: Writings and Buildings* (New York: World, 1960), 314, 76, 313.

11. Theodor Lipps, *Grundlegung der Aesthetik* (Hamburg, 1903), ch. 3, "Raum-aesthetik."

12. Geoffrey Scott, *The Architecture of Humanism* (1914; rpt. London, 1924), 226–28.

13. Frederick Jackson Turner, "Contributions of the West to American Democracy," in his *The Frontier in American History* (New York: Holt, 1921), 259.

14. Roderick Nash, "The American Invention of National Parks," *American Quarterly* 22 (Fall 1970): 726–35.

15. Marcel Proust, *The Past Recaptured* (1927; rpt. New York: Random, 1970).

16. Stéphane Mallarmé, "La musique et les lettres," in his *Oeuvres complètes* (Paris: Pléiade, 1965), 635–57.

17. Rainer Maria Rilke, *The Notebooks of Malte Laurids Brigge* (1910; rpt. New York: Vintage Books, Random, 1986), 18, 24. Rilke began working on the notebooks in Rome in 1903 and completed them in Paris in 1910.

18. William James, *The Principles of Psychology*, 2 vols. (New York: Dover, 1950), 1:240; Horace Meyer Kallen, *William James and Henri Bergson: A Study in Contrasting Theories of Life* (Chicago: University of Chicago Press, 1914), 11, 30, 105.

19. Letter to Ernest Chausson, 2 October 1893, quoted in Richard Langham Smith, "Debussy and the Pre-Raphaelites," *Nineteenth-Century Music* 5 (Fall 1981): 105.

20. Robert Isherwood, *Music in the Service of the King: France in the Seventeenth Century* (Ithaca: Cornell University Press, 1973), 281.

21. Maurice Maeterlinck, "Silence," in his *The Treasure of the Humble* (New York, 1897), 12, 26, 32, 33, 101, 105–6.

22. In 1923, for example, Picasso explicitly denied that cubism was related to anything else outside of art: "Mathematics, chemistry, psychoanalysis, music and whatnot, have been related to Cubism to give it an easier interpretation. All this has been pure literature, not to say nonsense" (statement to Marius de Zayas, quoted in Edward Fry, *Cubism* [New York: McGraw-Hill, 1966], 168).

# SIX

# The Construction and Management of Sacred Time and Space: *Sabta Nur* in the Church of the Holy Sepulcher

*Richard D. Hecht*

From the gallery [inside the Church of the Holy Sepulcher], I had the pleasure of watching the congregation for some time without being disturbed. The Greeks took their place on one side of the Sepulchre, . . . where they conduct their service, while the Armenians gathered on the other side of the Tomb. These latter were composed, while the Greeks behaved in a most indecent manner and were so noisy that my ears rang. The constantly growing crowd consisted of men of all ages. . . . It was a carnival, and instead of a Christian celebration one seemed to be attending a Bacchanalian feast. . . . The Descent of the Holy Fire is a triumph for the Greeks, by which the Armenians, Copts, etc., should also be convinced. They pride themselves a great deal on this, and in order to humiliate their chief enemy, the Armenians, they tell the following story. Once, it seems, the Armenian clergy paid a large sum of money to the governor of the city in order to obtain permission to be the recipients of the Holy Fire. The Armenian bishop had already entered the Tomb and everyone was in a ferment of expectation. Then, after a long period of waiting, the Armenian clergy came out again, ashamed and afraid, and explained that they could not obtain the Holy Fire through their prayers. Then the Greek bishop entered the Tomb and in a few minutes the Holy Fire appeared. Angry with the audacity of the Armenians, the governor had them seized and forced them to eat something which politeness does not permit me to name.[1] Every educated Greek knows it [the Holy Fire ritual] to be a shameful imposition; but the ignorant Syrians and the fanatical Russian peasants still believe the fire to descend from heaven. The clergy dare not enlighten them, and that crafty diplomacy which encourages pilgrimage to Jerusalem by government aid, fosters the superstition which is the main inducement for the Russian pilgrims to visit the Holy City.[2]

Ulrich Jasper Seetzen and Claude Conder were among the most famous nineteenth-century European travelers to the Middle East. Seetzen, a German physician, had studied Arabic and the cultures of Islam for many years before arriving in the Middle East. His knowledge of Arabic and the customs of Muslim peasants was so extensive that on many occasions he disguised himself as a wandering Bedouin or a merchant physician going by the name of Sheik Mussa. He reached Jerusalem in 1806, moving on to Cairo and then Mecca in 1809. His death in Yemen in 1811 was rumored to be the result of poison administered by order of a Muslim cleric. Conder was commissioned to survey Palestine for the British Palestine Exploration Fund and arrived in Jerusalem in the early 1870s. He freely admitted in his letters to his mother that mapping Palestine was only a secondary interest. He was there to make a name for himself in the newly fashionable field of archaeology. However, he concluded prematurely that all the archaeological remains of Palestine had been reused and completely destroyed. He threw himself into the survey and wrote extensive accounts of the cultures of Palestine. For a time he was joined by Horatio Herbert Kitchener, then only a royal engineer of the age of twenty-four. Kitchener's early interest in Palestine would be eclipsed by his fame as "Kitchener of Khartoum" and later the British minister of war during World War I.[3]

Seetzen and Conder, like almost every other visitor to Jerusalem, were fascinated by the city's curious inhabitants and especially the variety of rituals in Christendom's most sacred place, the Church of the Holy Sepulcher. And among all of its rituals none seemed more bizarre, more fantastic, or more fabricated than the Holy Fire ritual of Jerusalem's Orthodox churches. Visitors like Seetzen and Conder saw the Holy Fire ritual of Great Saturday preceding Easter Sunday in the Orthodox calendar as a barbaric practice of the Christianity of the Orient. It was a living fossil for the theological veracity of Western European Christianity, Catholicism, the Anglican Church, and the Protestant traditions. This was a ritual degraded by political rivalries over who would control the Holy Places between Jerusalem's Greek Orthodox and the Armenian Orthodox. Even the Latins, as the Catholics are historically known in Jerusalem, were not immune to the "petty" rivalries over the Holy Places. The Holy Fire ritual, which seemingly linked the Passion of Christ on Good Friday with the Easter Sunday mystery of the Resurrection, was nothing but a cruel hoax or a magnificent fraud, cleverly manipulated to exploit the superstitious Eastern European and Russian pilgrims.

In reality, these conflicts over the Holy Places of Jerusalem concerned much more than the quarrels among the Greeks, the Armenians, and the Latins.[4] The smaller Christian communities of the Holy Land—the Copts, the Ethiopians, and the Syrian Jacobites—all asserted their own claims to the Holy Places. Smaller Christian communities, such as the

Maronites, the Syrian Catholics, the Armenian Catholics, and the Greek Melkites, also got involved.

Communal conflicts in Jerusalem over its sacred sites were used as a rationale for warfare fought over the heads of those in the Holy Places themselves. The Crimean War broke out in 1854 after a Latin star and inscription were stolen from their places in Bethlehem's Church of the Nativity. By the 1870s Russia was seeking to represent the more than twenty million Greek Orthodox subjects in the vast Ottoman Empire, a policy intended to drive a wedge between them and the Greek Orthodox church hierarchy on the one hand, and the Ottomans on the other. Even while the savage battles of World War I raged, the issue of who would control the Holy Places was never far from the front. England, France, and Russia were each quick to advance reasons why they should be entrusted with the Holy Places once the guns fell silent. Even the German emperor and Austria were willing to suggest to their Turkish ally that the Sultan should make a gift to them of the Church of the Holy Sepulcher so they could return it to its "rightful" custodian, the Vatican.

These conflicts between Christians were complicated by the rise of Jewish and Arab nationalism in Palestine. With the Balfour Declaration of November 1917, the Jewish national movement had won qualified British support for a Jewish homeland in Palestine. Speaking to the College of Cardinals in March 1919, Pope Benedict XV reacted to the Balfour Declaration and shared his apprehension of what might happen to the Holy Places. He reiterated the sacrifices made by Christians to secure them from "the dominion of the infidel." He concluded that "our anxiety is most keen as to the decisions which the Peace Congress in Paris is soon to take concerning them. For surely it would be a terrible grief for us and for all the Christian faithful if the infidels were placed in a privileged and prominent position, much more if those most holy sanctuaries of the Christian religion were given to the charge of the non-Christians."[5] In his *Causa nobis* of June 1921 he spelled out who he meant by "infidels" and "non-Christians." Trusteeship of the Holy Places, he proclaimed, was in the hands of "alien non-Catholic Christians" [i.e., British Anglicans]. A Jewish national home in the Holy Land would "deprive Christendom of the position which it had always occupied in the Holy Places."[6]

Whereas the Jews, Protestants, and to a lesser degree even the Greek Orthodox held that the Holy Places were limited to specific buildings and their immediate grounds, the Vatican's view was that the Holy Places involved extensive areas of Jerusalem, Bethlehem, Nazareth, Tiberias, Jericho, and Mount Carmel in Haifa. By the beginning of the 1920s the Vatican policy wanted to freeze the development of Palestine, maintaining it only as a museum. Thus, the Vatican objected to the plan to build a cable car up Mount Carmel and to the British City Plan for Jerusalem, which would provide a promenade on the city's wall; it even accused the British of introducing cinemas and prostitutes into the city. Sir Ronald Storrs, the first governor of Jerusalem under the British, responded to these last charges by saying that the city had cinemas before the British arrived and that they had eliminated the throng of prostitutes.[7]

In the history of religions, sacred space and time have largely been understood as substantive and consensual categories. This has been the dominant paradigm since Durkheim formulated the dichotomy between sacred and profane and Rudolf Otto's later attempt to ground these categories in the epistemology and ontology of the sacred. Indeed, the Durkheimian collective representations which lie at the heart of religious and social phenomena tend to minimize conflictual meanings. The history of religions, then, has come to understand that the sacred manifests itself at specific places and moments, making them, for all purposes, sacred for all time. It has then created an "aesthetics" of sacred space and time which it conveys through a rich, metaphorical language. Its analyses of sacred space and time are largely devoid of conflicts over their organization and meaning. Very little attention has been given to cases in which more than one community lays claim to a particular place or how the meanings of time and space are collectively reproduced, constructed, and managed.

The conflicts over the Holy Places of Christendom, especially how those conflicts manifested themselves in the Church of the Holy Sepulcher, are thus very instructive for the history of religions. This architectural complex houses rival geographies of sacred space and time. Conflicts over custody, over which community should be where and when in the church, are bound up with conflicts over the meaning of the places themselves. This essay will take up the case of the Church of the Holy Sepulcher and the system—called the *Status Quo*—by which its sacred space and time are constructed and managed. No inch of the Church of the Holy Sepulcher is outside the control of the Status Quo, and no moment in the church's yearly calendar there is without its sanction.

The Status Quo can best be seen working on the one day in which all the communities of the Church of the Holy Sepulcher must share its space and time, Holy or Great Saturday, between Good Friday and Easter Sunday of the Passion Week in the Orthodox calendar. In the predominantly Arabic-speaking Greek Orthodox and Eastern Orthodox communities of the eastern Mediterranean world, Holy Saturday has historically been referred to as *Sabta Nur,* "the Saturday of Fire" or "the Saturday of Light," because of the most characteristic ritual of the Church of the Holy Sepulcher, the descent of the Holy Fire on Great

Saturday. Much of the research for this paper arises from my fieldwork in the Church of the Holy Sepulcher between 1983 and 1986 when I was able to observe the Sabta Nur and many of the ritual "events" of Holy Week in the Latin and Greek Orthodox calendars. On 21 April 1984, Easter in the Catholic and Orthodox calendars coincided, as they do every four or five years, providing an opportunity to observe the workings of the Status Quo when the Catholic liturgy of Holy Saturday and the Orthodox Sabta Nur both took place in the Church of the Holy Sepulcher.[8]

## THE POLITICAL MANAGEMENT OF THE SACRED

As their mandate over Palestine began at the close of World War I, the British were confronted by enormous problems. Much of Palestine had been pauperized by centuries of Ottoman rule, both Jewish and Palestinian nationalisms were pressing their claims for self-rule, and the infrastructure of Palestine's major cities was woefully inadequate, with little systematic planning. Many of these problems had their sharpest expression in Jerusalem, but none was more acute than the conflict over the Holy Places which had been reignited at Versailles. The British sought to respond to these issues in Jerusalem by establishing the Pro-Jerusalem Society, whose members reflected the diverse religious, social, and political forces in the city.[9] The Pro-Jerusalem Society was given the task of developing the first modern town plan for Jerusalem and maintaining the "traditional custodies" within the Holy Places of the city. H. C. Luke was given the responsibility of defining these for both the Pro-Jerusalem Society and the Mandatory government. However, his report, based on predominantly Western European accounts of the Status Quo and published as part of the official record of the society, did little more than trace the history of the Christian communities in the Church of the Holy Sepulcher and locate their claims to custody within the architectural space of the church. He concluded:

> It will not, of course, be forgotten that it was an aspect of the question concerning the Holy Places which, by exacerbating the general Eastern Question, brought about the Crimean War. A settlement was reached in 1878 at the Congress of Berlin; and Article LXII of the Treaty of Berlin reads as follows: "It is well understood that no alterations can be made in the *status quo* of the Holy Places." Thus it will readily be realized how the words *status quo* have assumed so tremendous a significance in matters affecting the Holy Sepulchre, for it is to them that appeal is made in all questions which still arise within those sacred and much contested walls.[10]

The term *status quo*, first used in the Berlin treaty, defined the de facto situation in the Holy Places. The Mandatory Laws of Palestine reconfirmed the earlier position of the Treaty of Berlin that there should be no change in the Status Quo.[11] Luke's work gave no overarching context in which conflicts might be resolved or how the issue of custody might be played out in the liturgical life of the church.

Between 1922 and 1929 British attention was drawn away from Christian Holy Places to the Western Wall of the Temple Mount, or *al-haram al-sharif*. Here a series of clashes took place between Muslims and Jews over the issue of custody as set out in the Status Quo. The struggle over this site was a critical event in the early reciprocal mobilization of Jewish and Palestinian nationalisms. The Grand Mufti of Jerusalem, al-Hajj Amin al-Husayni, who headed the Supreme Muslim Council, chose this battlefield to intensify his struggle against the Jews.[12] According to Yehoshua Porath, Hajj Amin al-Husayni and the Supreme Muslim Council successfully used the conflict over the Western Wall to intensify the Arab struggle against the Jews, giving it a religious dimension and allowing them to enlist the support of the urban and rural masses, who until then had not been attracted by the secular nationalist slogans. This also made it a contest over the Status Quo, and one of the central motifs was the claim that the Jews aimed at taking over *al-Buraq* (as the Muslims called the Western Wall), which was holy to the Muslims as an inseparable part of *al-Masjid al-Aqsa*. The Muslims would never agree to any change in the Status Quo, which had existed from Ottoman times and had been explicitly defined in the decision of Jerusalem's district court in 1911.[13]

This almost decade-long conflict ended in August 1929 with massive communal rioting and violence between Palestinians and Jews that spread from Jerusalem to Hebron and Safed. These events gave further impetus to British attempts to determine in greater detail what the Christians, Jews, and Muslims were claiming within the Status Quo. In July 1929, just before the rioting, L. G. A. Cust, a former district officer of Jerusalem under the Mandate, completed a definitive account of the Status Quo, published the following year. Cust sought to offer more than a history of the Christian communities in their Holy Places as Luke had done almost a decade before and to present the actual workings of the Status Quo.

Cust pointed out that the *firman*, or sultanic decision of the Ottoman Sultan Abdul Mejid in 1852, had effectively frozen the distribution of custody between the communities in the Holy Places. "This firman," Cust wrote, "constitutes the official Declaration of the Status Quo in the Holy Places" and was reaffirmed in several international treaties in the 1860s and 1870s. Cust set out the places incorporated within the Status Quo: (1) the Holy Sepulcher with all its dependencies; (2) the Deir al-Sultan on the western roof of the Church of the Holy Sepulcher; (3) the Sanctuary of the Ascension; (4) the Tomb of the Virgin; and (5) the

Church of the Nativity. He also added the Milk Grotto and the Shepherd's Field in Bethlehem among the Christian sites under the jurisdiction of the Status Quo. He also added that "the Wailing Wall [the Western Wall of the Temple Mount] and Rachel's Tomb, of which ownership is in dispute between the Moslems and the Jews, are similarly subject to the Status Quo." [14]

He pointed out that "certain fixed principles" are followed in the administration of the Status Quo. Thus, he wrote, "Authority to repair a roof or floor implies the right to an exclusive possession on the part of the restorers. Again, the right to hang a lamp or picture or to change a lamp or picture is a recognition of exclusive possession of a pillar or wall. The right of other communities to cense at a chapel implies that the proprietorship is not absolute." [15] Cust delineated two principles active in all matters of the Status Quo. First, repair, restoration, or changing any of the accoutrements in any place within the Holy Places was a declaration of possession, ownership, or, in the technical Latin terminology, of *praedominium,* privileged habitation in a specific location. Second, access to a certain location for religious purposes—for example, to cense a section of the Church of the Holy Sepulcher—implies that the proprietorship is not absolute.

Cust then defined the types of sacred space as they were distributed among the three major "rites" of the Holy Places, the Greek Orthodox, the Latins, and the Armenian Orthodox. First were spaces accepted to be the common and equal property by all three communities. Second were spaces which were claimed by one community as under its exclusive jurisdiction but in which others claimed joint proprietorship. Third were spaces whose ownership was contested between two communities. Fourth were spaces where one community's exclusive use was qualified by the right of others to operate ritually within them. Last were spaces which were in the exclusive jurisdiction of one community but were compromised by the claims of others to use those spaces ritually. [16] The application of the Status Quo varies in strictness. In those parts in dispute, he wrote, no party may carry on any innovation or repair. Where the matter is urgent, the work has to be carried out by the government with the question of payment left in suspense. The government is also bound by the Status Quo. In some cases of conflict, groups actually engaged in reciprocal trades of rights of renovation.

Repair and restoration of ancient buildings such as the Church of the Holy Sepulcher or the Church of the Nativity were then very complicated issues. When fire damaged the Church of the Holy Sepulcher in 1808, the Greek Orthodox, with the support of Russia, seized the opportunity to rebuild the church and in the process effaced the Tombs of the Latin Kings near Golgotha and erected the square structure that now constitutes the Edicule or burial chamber under the building's rotunda. The Latins countered and received a *firman* which stipulated that this restoration did not have any influence on the rights and privileges of other communities within the Church of the Holy Sepulcher.[17] It took almost fifty years for the restoration to be completed. Another example of the difficulties posed by repairs is the project to rebuild and strengthen the supporting structure of the dome over the rotunda. This work was begun in the mid-1960s, but since the rotunda is held in common by the Latins, the Greek Orthodox, the Copts, and the Armenians, the work has progressed very slowly despite Jordanian and then Israeli funding to complete the project. The visitor to the church today will still see the temporary scaffolding supporting the dome, which is intended to minimize danger to those below.

The resolution of a disagreement over the cleaning of a wall and a minor repair in the Church of the Nativity in 1964 provides an illustration of the way in which the communities use the principles of the Status Quo to adjudicate complex compromises between them. Here the contending parties were Greek Orthodox and the Armenians. The agreement was signed by the Greek Orthodox patriarch, the Armenian patriarch, and the Jordanian governor of Jerusalem. The agreement began by indicating that both communities and the Jordanians have entered into the agreement in order to promote peace and foster better understanding between the Greek Orthodox community and the Armenian community. The cleaning did not constitute any breach in the Status Quo and did not prejudice existing rights, privileges, practices or claims that both communities might have. Nor did it establish any new rights or claims in favor of one community or the other. It then stipulated that the Armenians will allow the Greek Orthodox Choir passage through the Armenian section of the church and will allow them to stand on the semicircular outer steps of the northern door of the Grotto of the Nativity leading to the Armenian church during Christmas processions. In return, the Greek Orthodox patriarch agreed to allow the southern wall of the Armenian Altar of the Circumcision in the Basilica of the Nativity, which belonged to the Greek Orthodox church, to be cleaned by the Armenians during the general cleaning of the building and on other occasions when the need arose. The communities further agreed to allow the door held in common by the two communities to be painted from the Armenian church's side by the Greeks. The color on both sides of the door would be the same. A fallen Armenian chain previously affixed to the Greek wall would be repaired by a person jointly chosen by the two communities and the cost of repairs shared equally between the two.[18]

In some cases no resolution of conflicting claims has been possible;

hence, repairs on some segments of the Church of the Holy Sepulcher, for example, have remained unattended to or incomplete. For example, the Seven Arches of the Virgin on the northern side of the Katholikon is claimed by both the Latins and the Greek Orthodox.[19] Neither party has agreed to allow the other to do any repair work or to divide the costs of such work. At present two of the pillars holding up the arches have been temporarily buttressed with steel stanchions, and around the base of each pillar are heaped collections of stone slabs to be used in any restoration efforts. Sometimes the conflicts lead to violence. During Christmas 1983–84 an Armenian monk who attempted to refill a small oil lamp in the Church of the Nativity was stabbed in the arm by a Greek Orthodox monk who believed that the task was reserved only for the Greek Orthodox community. Passions over this incident continued to boil, and there was real danger that violence would erupt between these communities during the Easter week.

There is literally no space outside the regulation of the Status Quo, but some groups either have comparatively little claim to it, such as the Latins, or are entirely outside it, such as the Protestants. There is a difference in the descriptive language used by those communities *outside* the Church of the Holy Sepulcher and its Status Quo and those *within* it.[20] Those outside saw the communities within as exercising only guardianship, stewardship, or custodianship of the holy places for all of Christianity. For example, Daniel Rossing, director of Christian Relations within the Israeli Ministry of Religious Affairs, said that "there is a very real problem of terminology here. . . . My use of [the term] 'ownership' would be a very questionable usage in this respect. Perhaps more proper [is] 'rights.' . . . Ownership is a very dangerous term." Similarly, Father Nicolaus Egender, abbot of the Dormition Abbey and a Dominican outside the Latin community, which is represented in the Status Quo only by the Franciscans, said "the Holy Places do not belong to the sects." But those inside saw things very differently. Diane Herbert summarizes her interviews with many of those people directly involved with the administration of the Status Quo by suggesting that

> within the communities themselves, there are no such qualifications to the degree of proprietorship. Bishop Kapikian of the Armenian Orthodox Church asserts that the three major sects "are the owners of the Holy Places, and when I say 'owners,' it is their property." Father Basileos, Metropolitan of Caesarea for the Greek Orthodox Church, corroborates this statement. He claims rights of "possession, ownership and usage" of the Holy Places as their "private property." Archbishop Yacoub of the Syrian Orthodox Church concurred that Christian groups "own" the Holy Places and were not simply inhabiting them. Asked if it were possible to own sacred as well as secular space, Bishop Kapikian replied, "Of course."

However, it is universally agreed among the major sects that the other communities, the Syrians and the Ethiopians, do not have rights of ownership, only those of usage.[21]

The three major communities within the Church of the Holy Sepulcher—the Greek Orthodox, the Latin Franciscans, and the Armenian Orthodox—all claim exclusive *praedominium* to the places they believe they own.

Nikos Kazantzakis visited the Church of the Holy Sepulcher during his trip to the Middle East in 1926 and 1927. "This entire church," he was told by a Greek Orthodox monk, "belongs to us, the Orthodox. All the sacred shrines are ours. The heretics, whom God has damned, want to take them from us; but we're fencing off the disputed areas with iron bars and won't let anyone set foot inside! . . . Come what may, we're not giving them another inch. Now we're going to throw the Armenians out; they've overstepped their boundaries and are standing on our ground. Whatever the Latins tell you is a lie. All their shrines are fakes. I hope to God the day comes when we can throw them out!"[22] At best the three major groups are willing to grant rights of usage only to the other communities, the Syrians, the Ethiopians, and the Copts, and nothing to those outside the Church of the Holy Sepulcher. Thus, the meaning, the very ontology, of sacred time and space is conditioned by whether one is within the Status Quo or outside it. At Christianity's ritual center, neither sacred time nor sacred space is substantive or consensual.

## PATROLLING THE BOUNDARIES OF SACRED PROPERTY

Cust presented the contemporary distribution of custody and ownership in the Church of the Holy Sepulcher. These were the Parvis (or courtyard) and Entrance, the Rotunda, the Katholikon, and the commemorative shrines and chapels which surround them. Each of these structures was either laid claim to by one or more of the communities or was understood to be held in common.

1.  The Entrance Doorway and the Facade, the Stone of Unction, the Parvis of the Rotunda, the great Dome and the Edicule are common property. The three rites consent to the partition of the costs of any work of repair between them in equal proportion. The Entrance Courtyard is in common use, but the Orthodox alone have the right to clean it.
2.  The Dome of the Katholikon is claimed by the Orthodox as being under their exclusive jurisdiction. The other communities do not recognize this, maintaining that it is part of the general fabric of the Church, and demand a share in any cost of repair. The Ortho-

dox, however, refuse to share payment with any other community. The same conditions apply *mutatis mutandis* to the Helena Chapel, claimed by the Armenians, and the Chapel of the Invention of the Cross claimed by the Latins.

3. The ownership of the Seven Arches of the Virgin is in dispute between the Latins and the Orthodox, of the Chapel of St. Nicodemus between the Armenians and the Syrian Jacobites, and of the Deir al-Sultan between the Copts and Abyssinians. In these cases neither party will agree to the other doing any work of repair or to divide the costs.

4. The Chapel of the Apparition, the Calvary Chapels, and the Commemorative shrines are in the sole possession of the one or other of the rites, but the others enjoy certain rights of office therein. Any projected innovation or work of repair is to be notified to the other rites.

5. The Katholikon, the Galleries and the Chapels in the Courtyard (other than the Orthodox Chapels on the West) are in the exclusive jurisdiction of one or other of the rites, but subject to the main principles of the Status Quo as being within the ensemble of the Holy Sepulcher.[23]

Small alterations to these basic claims to custody and ownership according to the Status Quo arose in some cases as the result of external pressure. For example, it was the custom for the Muslims at the doorway of the church to force visitors and pilgrims to pay an entrance fee (*khafar*) and a gratuity (*bakshish*). To facilitate this custom, half of the door leading into the church was closed. When a shocked Russian officer reported this situation to Mehemet Ali Pasha in Egypt in 1834, the pasha immediately ordered the practice halted. Both sides of the door leading into the church were then opened to the public.[24]

Cust's volume examines each of these areas in turn. This relatively small area is packed with an enormous number of separate but frequently contested parcels of sacred property. For example, in a description of the entrance to the Parvis or courtyard of the church, Cust notes that the pavement of the Parvis and the external doors leading on the eastern and western sides to the chapels are the common property of the three patriarchates, who bear jointly the expenses for repairs in these areas. The Greek Orthodox have the responsibility of cleaning the Parvis and also hold the keys to the external doors leading to it. However, the actual key to the church's door is not held by any Christian community. Indeed, the conflict between the rival Christian communities was so intense at the end of the Latin Kingdom that the Muslims had to take the key so that one community could not lock out another.

The key was entrusted to one of Jerusalem's most prominent Muslim families, the Nusseibehs, in 1289. Even today one of the Nusseibehs comes to the church every morning to open it and returns in the evening to lock it.

The Parvis is surrounded by a number of chapels belonging to the different communities. On the southern side is the Greek Orthodox Convent of Gethsemane, which is situated next to the Mosque of Umar, rebuilt in 1193 by Saladin after he took the city from the Crusaders.[25] On the western side are the Chapels of St. James, St. Mary Magdalene, and, at the base of the church's belfry, the Chapel of the Forty Martyrs. These chapels are separated by a doorway and staircase leading to the roof and the Greek Orthodox Patriarchate. These belong to the Greek Orthodox, and the Chapel of St. James is used exclusively by the Arabic-speaking Greek Orthodox community of Jerusalem. Although Greek Orthodox pilgrims use the passageway and the staircase to reach the Patriarchate above, they do not attend the liturgy in this chapel during the Passion Week. On the northern side of the Parvis is the Latin Chapel of St. Mary's Agony, which can be reached by a staircase on the outside of the church's façade. Below it is the Greek Orthodox Chapel of St. Mary of Egypt. On the eastern side of the Parvis is the Chapel of St. Michael, which is situated directly under the Chapel of the Four Living Creatures. When Cust wrote his study in 1929–30, these chapels belonged to the Copts. Next to the Chapel of St. Michael are the Armenian Chapel of St. James and the Greek Orthodox Convent of Abraham.

According to Cust, the stairs leading up to the Latin Chapel of St. Mary's Agony are the property of the Latins. The lowest step, which is three inches above the level of the stone-slab pavement of the Parvis, has often been a point of conflict between the Greeks and the Latins. In 1901 Greek Orthodox monks attempted to sweep it as part of their responsibilities involving the general cleaning of the Parvis. A fight ensued and as Cust notes, "Several Spanish and Italian monks were injured, and their respective Consuls took measures to obtain satisfaction on their behalf. This was objected to by the French representatives, who maintained that this was their prerogative in view of the protectorate exercised by France over all Roman Catholics in the Ottoman Empire. They were not, however, successful in their pretensions."[26] This conflict was resolved by having the Latins sweep the step daily at dawn, and the Greek Orthodox would sweep it at the times when they cleaned the Parvis.

Last, Cust points out that bands and the unfurling of flags in the Parvis are strictly forbidden by the Status Quo. In 1983 I observed an interesting challenge to this point. On Good Friday in the Latin calendar I followed a group of twenty-five charismatic Catholics from San Diego,

California, up the Via Dolorosa, beginning in the vicinity of Al-Omariya school and ending in the Church of the Holy Sepulcher. For more than a year they had been preparing to reenact the drama of the Crucifixion. They had assigned themselves parts, designed and made clothing in the fashion of a Hollywood movie, and written music and lyrics as the sound track for their ritual ascent of the Via Dolorosa. One individual played the part of Jesus, complete with a crown of thorns and make-up for his bruises and welts; others played Roman soldiers and centurions, the three Marys, Joseph of Aramithea, and the populace of first-century Jerusalem. One group member carried a portable cassette player or "boom box" which contained the tape of their music recorded in San Diego. At each station these pilgrims, accompanied by their music and songs, paused and reenacted the relevant event. When they reached the entrance of the Parvis, they were stopped by the city police. The police were dumbfounded not only by this unusual enactment of the Way of the Cross but also by the challenge of the boom box to the Status Quo. If it was indeed a "band," the Status Quo prohibited it. Several policemen were consulted before the group was allowed entry. For a long period there was a heated discussion among the police in which the pros and cons of this issue were argued: some took the position that the cassette player was a band and therefore could not be allowed into the Parvis; others believed that it was not a band and the group could use it in the Parvis. The group from San Diego surrounded the police as they debated this issue. One policeman, who had not seen the cassette player as a band, instinctually turned to the pilgrim in the role of Jesus. With whom better to discuss the sanctity of the church? The policeman urged Jesus to consider the feelings of others in the Parvis. In the end the cassette player was taken by the police, and the group sang their lyrics in the Parvis without musical accompaniment.

## THE CHAPEL OF NICODEMUS AND THE DEIR ES-SULTAN

The two most difficult problems within the Status Quo at the present involve a conflict between the Armenians and the Syrian Jacobites over the small chapel of Nicodemus on the western side of the rotunda of the church and a major conflict between the Copts and the Ethiopians over possession of the Deir es-Sultan on the roof of the church, directly over the Chapel of St. Helena. The conflict between the Armenians and the Jacobites over the ownership of the Chapel of Nicodemus flared in 1927 when the Armenians asserted their exclusive right to possession of this chapel.[27] They argued that they owned the doors, kept the keys to the chapel, and did the cleaning in that area of the church. Further, the Status Quo gave them the right to officiate in the Chapel of Nicodemus whenever they liked. The altar, the picture on it, the twelve lamps above it, and the pictures on the outer wall of the chapel were theirs as well. The Jacobites claimed their right to the chapel by virtue of the Status Quo, which allowed them to hang three pictures on the walls at various times throughout the year, to keep their liturgical vestments in two closets allotted them by the Armenians in the chapel, and to officiate at the chapel every Sunday. During Holy Week they were also allowed the use of a room above the chapel by the Armenians, the key of which must be returned on Monday morning following Easter Sunday. They also claimed that the Chapel of Nicodemus was theirs because a monk from their community lived in the chapel during the fifteenth century. Later they claimed that the Armenians took possession of the chapel unlawfully and without their consent. However, Cust noted that the "Syrian-Jacobites have never been able to produce convincing evidence in support of their claim to the proprietorship of this chapel" and that the picture situated over the altar "clearly bears an Armenian inscription." [28] This conflict remains unresolved to this day. The chapel remains in disrepair, and whenever the Armenians or the Jacobites attempt to make repairs, the other community immediately removes the renovated work. In 1985 and again in 1986, for example, the Armenians attempted to repair stonework at the chapel's entrance; just as soon as it had been completed, it was removed by the Syrians.

Daniel Rossing, the director of Christian Relations within the Israeli Ministry of Religious Affairs, is often called in to mediate these conflicts. For example, he described the conflict between the Syrians and the Armenians in the Chapel of Nicodemus in this way:

> But there arose most recently about a year ago a dispute about the entryway [to the Chapel of Nicodemus] between two columns. Is this part of the dispute or is it not part of the dispute? The Armenians put down new paving stones in this area, and the Jacobites claimed that this is part of the dispute and they should not be doing anything there. So on one Sunday morning when they have rights to pray there, they brought a large congregation from Bethlehem, Beit Jalah, and Beit Sahur to fill up the area. As they were praying, they picked up the paving stones and the Armenians heard of this and I was called to come immediately before there were physical blows. I have authority there, but I would rather use my good relations with both sides to resolve the situation. First of all I said, "Let's go away from the scene because it is very heated and emotional here." The Greek Orthodox archbishop was there and he invited us to their monastery. "Let's go sit down and talk," I said to them. So I was able to arrive at a solution with them somewhat by order and somewhat by agreement with them that nothing more will be done, either to pick up or put down paving stones, until we have a chance to try to work this out. And over the course of the months and until this day, I am meeting with the sides, and they

present maps and documents all of which are contradictory coming from
five, six, or even eight centuries ago and even earlier. It's a mess and you
can't really straighten it out.[29]

Rossing's solution followed the principles set forth by Cust's formulation
of the Status Quo; in those areas where the *praedominium* is contested
between two communities, neither will allow the other to make repairs.
In this case the Armenians understood the entrance to the Chapel of
Nicodemus to be outside the contested area while the Syrians understood the entrance to be part of it.

Just like war between states in which smaller nations make alliances
with the larger for self-defense, both the Syrian and Coptic communities
often side with the larger communities in disputes. This is especially the
case when their claimed rights depend on the goodwill of one of those
communities whose power is projected by the number of members in
the community and its financial or political power under a specific regime. For example, in the case of the conflict between the Armenians
and Greek Orthodox over the refilling of an oil lamp and the cleaning
of the walls of the Altar of Circumcision in the Church of the Nativity
during 1983–84, the Syrians aligned themselves with the Armenians
and the Copts with the Greek Orthodox. During the Sabta Nur of 1984
the police were forced at various points in the ritual to separate physically the contending groups, one made up of Armenians and Jacobites
and the other of Greek Orthodox and Copts.

The conflict between the Copts and Ethiopians over the Deir es-
Sultan is even more complex and demonstrates how geopolitical factors
become intertwined in the politics of the Church of the Holy Sepulcher.
The Deir es-Sultan comprises a monastery compound, the Chapel of the
Four Living Creatures, which is on the roof level of the church, and the
Chapel of St. Michael, which is level with the Parvis. The two chapels
are connected by a stairway; entrance to the Chapel of the Four Living
Creatures is through a doorway at the southwestern corner of the monastery, and a doorway leads directly from the Chapel of St. Michael to
the Parvis. Ownership and possession of this complex is contested between the Copts and Ethiopians. When Cust compiled his summary, it
was in the hands of the Copts. This issue is complicated by the historical
origins of the Ethiopian Orthodox church as the "daughter church" of
the Coptic Egyptian Patriarchate and the independence of the Ethiopian
patriarch in 1951 from the Coptic church. The Ethiopians have long
argued that this complex is theirs and that the Copts illegally occupied
it in 1838 when a plague decimated the Ethiopian community of Jerusalem. The Ethiopians pursued this issue first with the Ottomans and then
later the British. Both did nothing and left the Copts in control of the

Deir es-Sultan.[30] The Ethiopians continued to press their case under the Jordanians. In 1961 a Jordanian ministerial committee finally found in their favor and ordered the Copts to vacate the Deir es-Sultan. The Jerusalem Copts complied with the Jordanian order and left the Deir es-Sultan. However, the Copts in Egypt, through their patriarch in Alexandria, pressured Nasser's government to intervene. The Jordanians had no reason to quarrel with the Egyptians over the Ethiopians. After only forty days the Jordanians reversed the decision, and the Ethiopians were evacuated from the Deir es-Sultan.

This is how the situation remained through the late 1960s. During Easter 1969 there was a serious clash between the two communities in which stones were thrown and the Ethiopian ceremonies, which begin at 9:00 P.M. on Saturday evening, had to be halted. A year later, on Easter eve, the Ethiopians took matters into their own hands and changed the locks on the doors leading to the two chapels. This action effectively altered the Status Quo, locking the Copts out of what they believed was theirs. When they asked the police for help, they were refused it. The Coptic archbishop, Anba Basilios, pursued the issue to the Israeli Supreme Court. In 1971 the court declared it was not enpowered to intervene in this dispute and to decide the issue of *praedominium* but criticized the police for not helping the Copts to restore the situation to the Status Quo. The court made its injunction against the police absolute and ordered them to take the keys from the Ethiopians and to give them to the Copts, but it gave the government a year's grace to deal with the conflict. At the end of this year the government decided "to appoint a special ministerial committee to deal with the dispute, declaring that, in the meantime, 'the present *status quo* would remain.' "[31]

To the present, this ministerial committee has not ruled on how the matter should be resolved, thereby leaving the Ethiopians in control. Rossing drew a distinction between the mediation of these conflicts under the Israeli administration of the Status Quo and former regimes. He pointed out that both the Ottomans and the Jordanians resolved conflicts within the Status Quo through bribes. "One day," he said, "it was such and such and the next it would be something entirely different. One day it would belong to this community and a month later they would reverse themselves and give it to another community. A lot of money in gold changed hands." This handling would not be acceptable to the government of Israel. Rossing believed that the Israelis are able only to mediate and in some cases have had limited success. Rossing put it this way: "We try to mediate, we try to encourage some reconciliation, but we cannot use the tactics of the Ottomans. This is not a possibility for us!"[32]

Although money was not at issue for the Israelis in resolving the conflict at the Deir es-Sultan, geopolitics help explain why the committee froze the situation through inaction during much of the 1970s. Until the overthrow of Haile Selassie in 1974, the Israel government maintained good relations with Ethiopia. Yisrael Lippel, who was then the director of the Ministry of Religious Affairs, gave some insight into the government's position. First, the Jordanian committee had ruled in favor of the Ethiopians in 1961, and the Israeli committee could simply defer to the earlier position. Second, the Israeli government was interested in gaining the support of the Ethiopian government for emigration of the Falasha Jews. Third, the Israeli government wanted access to Ethiopian airspace for its commercial airline routes to sub-Saharan Africa. Fourth, diplomatic recognition of Israel by the Ethiopian government would further Israel's foreign policy toward the African nations.[33]

All of this changed with Anwar Sadat's diplomatic initiative in the late 1970s. The Ethiopian lockout had had dramatic effects on the Coptic community of Jerusalem, whose offices are situated next door to the Deir es-Sultan. Anba Basilios, as the archbishop of the Coptic church in Jerusalem, was required by the Status Quo to enter the Church of the Holy Sepulcher for ritual occasions by walking across the Deir es-Sultan, entering the Chapel of the Four Living Creatures, descending the staircase to the Chapel of St. Michael, and then entering the Parvis through its exit. The Ethiopian action made him a ritual prisoner in his own office. From 1970 until his death in 1991 he was not able to officiate at any of the formal rituals in the Church of the Holy Sepulcher. To have taken an alternative route to the Church of the Holy Sepulcher would have legitimated the Ethiopian takeover.

The Coptic archbishop saw the events in a very different light. The Ethiopians were not the ones who had changed the locks to the doors of the chapels. It had been done by the Israeli army. "The authorities here," he told me, "asked the Ethiopians to announce that they did this thing, while in reality a contingent of Israel Defence Forces perpetrated the deed, witnessed by Coptic monks. The government asked the Ethiopians to admit to it because it is a very big scandal for the authorities here or for the government to do such a thing."[34] In recalling Sadat's dramatic trip to Jerusalem, he told me that when Sadat came to visit him, he encouraged him to make the Coptic position on the Deir es-Sultan part of any negotiations with Menahem Begin and other officials of the Israeli government. By the late 1970s the press regularly reported that the Israeli government's position was shifting toward the Copts and that the small Ethiopian community would soon be removed from the Deir es-Sultan.[35] Restoration of the Coptic rights to the Deir es-Sultan became an issue in the Taba border dispute between Israel and Eygpt in 1986, with the Israeli side arguing that the matter should be submitted to international arbitration. The Egyptians argued that the issue should remain a condition for the normalization of diplomatic relations between Jerusalem and Cairo, which had been severed with Israel's invasion of Lebanon in 1982. Until the matter was resolved in favor of the Coptic church, Coptic tourists and pilgrims would not go to Israel.[36]

Despite the open borders between Israel and Egypt resulting from the Camp David Accords, the Coptic patriarch, Pope Shenouda, has forbidden Copts from Egypt to go to Jerusalem as long as the Deir es-Sultan remains in the hands of the Ethiopians. This interdiction does not mean, however, that one will not find Coptic pilgrims in the Church on Sabta Nur. In 1985 and 1986 there were large contingents of Copts from their diaspora in the Church of the Holy Sepulcher for Easter celebrations. Many of these came from North America and Australia and in a reversal of the traditional Coptic pilgrimage planned to visit their homes and relatives in Egypt *after* spending Holy Week in Jerusalem. More recently Pope Shenouda has called on the Arabs to unite and to persuade Israel to relinquish control of Jerusalem. However, this controversy took a most interesting twist with the influx of Falasha Jews brought to Israel from Ethiopia in 1985 and 1986 through "Operation Moses." Rahamim Elazar, the secretary of the National Council for Ethiopian Jews in Israel, issued an official press release in spring 1986 in which he supported the just claims of the Ethiopian community in the Church of the Holy Sepulcher. He urged the Israeli government to resist Egyptian pressure and to reexamine the implications of removing the Ethiopians from the Deir es-Sultan for Israeli-Ethiopian relations and for the Ethiopian Jewish community. "We must remember," he said, "the Jews still living in Ethiopia. We don't believe anything will happen to them, but still, if we want to do anything for them, we must do it through the Ethiopian government."[37]

## THE DESCENT OF THE HOLY FIRE

The operations of the Status Quo can best be seen in the ritual celebrations of Easter week in the Orthodox calendar, when all the communities with the exception of the Latins must use the space and time of the Church of the Holy Sepulcher. While the liturgical calendar of Roman Catholics and the Protestant denominations builds toward the reenactment of the resurrection on Easter Sunday, the culmination of the Orthodox Easter week in Jerusalem is the descent of the Holy Fire on Great Saturday. The miraculous appearance of fire on Great Saturday or Sabta Nur remains one of the most characteristic rituals of the Church of the Holy Sepulcher.[38] Indeed, the Holy Fire was understood in the Middle Ages as a miraculous sign of the unique character of Jerusalem in the Christian topography, an *inennarabile misterium*.[39] It was the very core of the liturgical cycle that reenacted the most central event in the history of salvation. Its appeal was so strong that a twelfth-century monk argued that Pope Urban had used it in his call for the Crusade at Clermont a hundred years before.[40] Julian Morgenstern interpreted the meaning of the ritual as the most dramatic presentation of the transformation of Christ into a divine light after his death on the Cross. He wrote, "The bursting forth of the light from the Tomb means that the Christ, the Son of God, has prevailed over the powers of darkness, has risen from the netherworld, from death and has returned to this world of light and life and to his Church, there to give forth new light, to protect, to guide and to bless."[41]

This ritual of the Holy Fire evolved from a series of rituals in the Church of the Holy Sepulcher centered on the use of fire and the lighting of candles and lamps. Fire in the early church's ritual is first attested in the travel itinerary of Egeria, who visited Jerusalem between 381 and 384 C.E. She described a daily ritual which began at four o'clock in the afternoon called the *Lychnicon* by the Greek speakers in the Church and the *Lucernare* by the Latin speakers. The Bishop of Jerusalem would enter the Edicule, which she described as a cave, and light a small candle from the flame burning in the *taphos* or burial chamber. The bishop would later light other ceremonial lamps from the candle kindled in the taphos. On Holy Saturday, during the Easter Vigil, the daily Lucernare was performed without alteration.[42]

Egeria's account of the Lucernare does not give a miraculous origin to the fire: the bishop simply went into the Anastasis and kindled his candle from the fire burning in the taphos. However, as early as the close of the fourth century Christian pilgrims to the Holy Land had begun to report miraculous events at the biblical sites they visited on their pilgrimages: the fountain of Gerasa flowed with wine on the feast of the Epiphany; at Diospolis a column in the nave of the Church of St. George ran with blood for three hours on the saint's feast day; the River Jordan provided the sick, crippled, and barren with miraculous cures; and miraculous cures were also available in the Church of Nativity.[43] All of these are common topoi in the descriptions of sacred sites in late antiquity and the early Middle Ages and are of course not limited to pilgrimage narratives from the Holy Land or Jerusalem.[44] The Easter Vigil's Lucernare, likewise, was given a miraculous interpretation.

The first reference to a miraculous fire in the Church of the Holy Sepulcher appears in the *Life of Theodore the Sabaite* from the eighth century. There is no suggestion prior to this text that the fire in the taphos had some divine origin. Almost a century later we have the first descriptive account of a miraculous fire given by a monk named Bernard, who

may have come from St. Michel in France. In his description of Jerusalem he included a brief remark about the ritual of Holy Saturday and
the Easter Vigil. He wrote that during the morning liturgy the congregation sang *Kyrie eleison* until an angel came and kindled fire in the lamps
which hang above the sepulcher.[45]

By the late tenth and early eleventh centuries, the miraculous origin
of the fire had been embellished by eastern Christians. So an Arab Christian by the name of Abu Sahl al-Masihi related that every year, "in the
night when God Jesus ascended into heaven, . . . a fire descends, clearly
beheld by the people assembled in the Church, and kindles all the lights
within the Church. This it does despite the fact that there is no window
in the building nor any opening in its roof. Rather, the fire forces its way
through the roof without the wood thereof catching fire."[46] The most
detailed account of the miracle of the Holy Fire is preserved in the Russian Abbot Daniel's description of Jerusalem. He visited the city in 1106
shortly after the Crusaders had taken it from the Muslims. His account
began with a catalogue of the "tales" of how the fire descends into the
church. "Many pilgrims," he wrote, "relate incorrectly the details about
the Holy Light. Some say that the Holy Spirit descends upon the Holy
Sepulchre in the form of a dove; others that it is lightning from heaven
that kindles the lamps above the Sepulchre of the Lord. This is all un-
true for neither dove nor lightning is to be seen at that moment; but the
divine grace comes down unseen from heaven and lights the lamps in
the Sepulchre of our Lord." He then went on to describe the ritual as he
had seen it with his own eyes. Prince Baldwin went to the church shortly
before the arrival of the religious officials to inspect the tomb and to
ensure that no combustible material had been secreted within. When
the prayers of the clergy and laity reached a crescendo with the faithful
weeping torrents of tears, a small cloud appeared from the east and
came to rest directly over the open dome of the Church of the Holy
Sepulcher. A light rain began to fall and then suddenly the light, "stun-
ningly bright and splendid," appeared in the sepulcher. At that moment, "the bishop, followed by four deacons, then opened the doors of
the Holy Sepulchre and went in with the candle he had taken from
Prince Baldwin, the first to be lit from this holy fire." Daniel stressed that
this fire is not like ordinary fire but burned with almost indescribable
brightness and with a red color much like cinnamon.[47]

The Orthodox liturgy of the Holy Fire was fixed in its present form
by the middle of the thirteenth century. The sealing of the patriarch
into the tomb was added to the ritual between the thirteenth and the
seventeenth centuries. Kevork Hintlian, the secretary of the Armenian
Orthodox patriarchate, indicated in an interview that already by the
High Middle Ages Armenian pilgrims who had participated in the Holy

Fire ritual were addressed as "Fire Brother" or "Fire Sister."[48] This usage suggests that the pilgrims formed an elite group within Armenian society as their identities were altered by the ritual. It is also clear that the ritual of the Holy Fire extended back to the pilgrims' homes and villages. Both Greek and Armenian pilgrims took the fire back with them, carefully guarded in lanterns to protect it from the wind. Whole villages and towns went without fire and light from Good Friday until the pilgrims returned from the Church of the Holy Sepulcher. They were met by their neighbors and clergy as "messengers" bearing the miraculous fire and were immediately taken to the churches of their villages, where the candles of the altar were kindled from the Holy Fire. Villagers would take candles lit from the pilgrims' laterns and light their own hearths and candles (figures 1 and 2). Center and periphery were then connected by the pilgrims. In some cases male and female pilgrims were buried with the candles they had kindled from the miraculous fire in the Church of the Holy Sepulcher.[49]

Both Muslim and Catholic writers maintained that the entire ritual was a carefully orchestrated deception on the part of the Orthodox. Some contended that a fine wire or string, coated with a highly combustible oil or naphtha, was stretched between the tomb and the dome. At the proper moment, when the emotions of the crowd below were at their highest, the upper end of the string was ignited like a fuse; the flame ran down as a beam of light and kindled the sacred fire in the tomb.[50] According to Maundrell, writing at the beginning of the seventeenth century, the Greeks released a pigeon in the upper levels of the dome to deceive the people into believing that it was the visible descent of the Holy Spirit. He described the Greek and Armenian patriarchs as "two miracle mongers" who exploited the ritual to encourage pilgrimage. He believed that there was nothing miraculous about the fire. Those who handled the fire, rubbing it into their faces, beards, and bodies, did so quickly and with such dexterity that they were unharmed. There was nothing pure or unearthly about it. Only the Latins took pains to expose the shameful behavior of the Greeks, but only because they were envious of how profitable such miracles can be.[51] The Comte de Volney, who observed the ritual in 1784, had much the same to say, indicating that while the Orthodox believe that the fire is brought down by an angel, "the Franks [i.e., the Latin Catholics] have recognized that it is the priests, concealed in the sacristy, who bring it about by the most natural of means."[52] Other observers were content simply to describe the Holy Fire as an example of the "mock-miracles still played off on human credulity."[53]

Almost all the modern commentators on the ritual were incredulous and sought to find some "natural" explanation for the ritual they had

Figure 1. A Greek Orthodox woman from Greece proudly displays her lantern containing the holy fire in the courtyard of the Church of the Holy Sepulcher. Author's photograph.

Figure 2. Greek Orthodox women from Cyprus in the courtyard of the Church of the Holy Sepulcher with their bundled thirty-three candles representing the years of Jesus' life. Author's photograph.

observed. Charles Warren, who spent considerable time in Jerusalem in the latter half of the nineteenth century, was most curious about this ritual. He tells us that he had heard from the Bishop of Petra that the Greek Orthodox believe they have the handkerchief of Saint Veronica. This relic is carried into the tomb by the patriarch and placed on top of the tomb. The fire collects on this handkerchief, and then, he continues, "by picking up the four corners, the fire was in a bag, and could be ladled or poured into the goblet." He was seemingly astounded by this description; when he had an opportunity to visit the Greek Orthodox patriarch, with whom he had been friendly, he asked about what he had been told. The patriarch described what really happened. Once in the taphos, the elderly patriarch told him, "He kneels down in front of the stony couch, facing north, and as he prays that the fire be manifest, it gradually appears. It does not descend from heaven, but appears on and emanates from the stone itself. As he prays more fervently the fire becomes stronger, springing up in a soft flame about an inch high; this he collects together with both hands and carefully places it in a goblet, which fills itself up to the brim with the flame." The patriarch told him flatly that there was no truth to the rumor about the handkerchief of Saint Veronica. One miraculous interpretation was substituted for another, and Warren was left perplexed.[54]

While the Holy Fire ritual developed among Orthodox Christians in the eastern Mediterranean, Catholic Christians developed a very different ritual and liturgy for Holy Saturday.[55] The western Christian "New Fire" ritual developed in its place and centered on the Paschal Candle and the baptism of catechumens, both of which harkened back to the early ritual in the Church of the Holy Sepulcher as it was observed by Egeria.[56] The first recorded account of the Latin version of the Lucernare is from the third century in Rome. The candle used in the ritual was hidden behind an altar at the end of the Good Friday evening liturgy which marked the death of Jesus. On Saturday evening two torches were lit from this candle. In the fourth and fifth centuries elaborate hymns of praise were composed for the candle, and the tradition of fashioning it from beeswax is first attested. A number of traditions quickly developed which were intended to signify that the candle was indeed the resurrected Christ: its wax was the flesh of Christ, the wick his soul, and the flame the divine element which dominated and united body and soul. The candle usually rested next to the lectern in the church from Easter Sunday to Ascension Sunday. During this period the body or wax of the candle melted away and was transformed into the light that illuminated the Gospel placed on the lectern. In Spain during the early Middle Ages, the practice of inscribing the candle with the cross, the current year, and the Greek letters *alpha* and *omega* were added to the ritual of the "New Fire." By the fourteenth century the ritual had developed to include the use of five pieces of incense embedded in red wax "nails" placed on the candle's inscribed cross. Some elements of the Jerusalem ritual had parallels in the Latin version of the New Fire. The lighting of the bishops' tapers from the candle burning in the taphos had its parallel in the Spanish practice of striking a new fire from a consecrated flint and brazier situated in the vestibule or at the door of the local church.[57] But in the Latin West, the New Fire did not have any of the miraculous connotations given to it in the Church of the Holy Sepulcher. O. B. Hardison underscores this by pointing out that in the ninth-century liturgy the fire must "be created by 'natural' means, by the rubbing of flint on stone or by using a burning glass."[58] The domestication of the fire's origin then radically changed the meaning of the ritual. Certainly the Latin liturgy maintains a relationship between the Resurrection experience and the fire, but the fire is now only a metaphor for the triumphant Christ and not the symbolization of the Resurrection.

The Easter Vigil in the Western Church was traditionally viewed as the goal of Lenten rituals. Both Lenten observances and the more rigorous fasts of Passion Week officially ended at noon on Holy Saturday. Until the fourteenth century the Easter Vigil began with the Holy Saturday Vespers ritual or with the appearance of the evening star. After the fourteenth century the night ritual was moved to Holy Saturday morning. In 1955 Pope Pius VII restored the Easter Vigil to its original nocturnal schedule. However, the Latin Easter Vigil in the Church of the Holy Sepulcher continues to be enacted in the post-fourteenth-century manner in the morning beginning at 6:30 A.M.[59] Pius VII gave the Latins of the Holy Land a special dispensation to continue the older ritual schedule since the Status Quo gave them no time after 9:30 A.M., especially when Holy Week falls on the same dates every fourth year in the Latin and Orthodox calendars. This block of time compresses the liturgy so severely that the actual baptism of new converts to the Catholic church, normally a part of the blessing of the baptismal waters, must take place outside of the Church of the Holy Sepulcher. But even this compromise does not completely eliminate the potential for conflicts. In 1983 the Latin Easter fell several weeks before the Orthodox Easter. Nevertheless, as prescribed by the Status Quo, the ritual must begin at its appointed time in the early morning. The church was darkened in accord with ritual requirements symbolizing the death of Jesus. At approximately 7:45 A.M. the Armenian monks assembled for their morning liturgy, and one of the monks noticed that the building was dark. He simply went to the light switch which controls the few electrical lights in the rotunda and turned them on. A Catholic monk near the Paschal

Candle at the altar immediately went to the very same switch and turned
them off. This sequence was repeated a number of times until the Catholic gave up at the suggestion of one of his colleagues. I approached the
Armenian monk who had initiated this curious set of actions and whom
I had gotten to know. I knew that he spoke some English and a little less
Hebrew. I asked him why he had turned the lights on. He told me quite
bluntly that it was dark and the Catholics were not really celebrating
Easter, so it did not matter to him. The Latin ritual of the New Fire in
the Church of the Holy Sepulcher then represents a liturgical compromise forced on the Catholic church by the dictates of the Status Quo's
management of sacred time.

### THE CONSTRUCTION AND MANAGEMENT OF SACRED TIME AND SPACE ON SABTA NUR

The operations of the Status Quo in the Church of the Holy Sepulcher
are twofold. First, it organizes the conflicting claims of the church's communities to sacred time and sacred space. It then could be understood
to construct and determine the meaning of their very sacrality. Sacred
time and space do not exist apart from the Status Quo's ability to organize the often conflicting assertions of ownership and custody to the holy
places within the walls of the Church of the Holy Sepulcher. Second, it
situates each community's claims within both time and space so that it
manages the structure and claims to sacred time and space. This twofold
nature of the Status Quo, of construction and management of sacred
time and space, is best seen on Sabta Nur, which begins the Friday evening preceding Holy Saturday. Throughout the year the doors of the
Church of the Holy Sepulcher and the two entrances to the Parvis at the
Muristan gate on the east (at Suq ed-Dabbagha Street) and at St. Helene
Street on the west are closed at sunset. However, on Friday night during
the Orthodox Holy Week the gates leading into the Parvis are left open
so that pilgrims can assemble throughout the night in preparation for
the opening of the church on Holy Saturday at 6:30 A.M. By sunset the
Parvis is filled to capacity with pilgrims. Almost all of the pilgrims carry
small folding stools, food, and drink.

There is a twofold grammar of place in the Parvis. Obviously, those
closest to the doors will have the first opportunity to find the best space
in the church the next morning. But many of the pilgrims want to be
situated near the columns on the eastern side of the doorway into the
church. The door is flanked by two sets of triple columns which are part
of the Crusader façade of the building.[60] Both sets of columns have been
heavily incised with graffiti and crosses by pilgrims. The middle column
of those on the western side has a fissure running from approximately

its midpoint to its base. Greek Orthodox pilgrims press to be as close as possible to this column throughout their night vigil in the Parvis. According to the Greek Orthodox, the column was split in the tenth century as fire issued from both the Edicule and the column during the Sabta Nur ritual. Indeed, throughout Holy Week, Greek Orthodox pilgrims stop at the column and kiss the fissure before entering the church. Many push notes and petitions as informal *ex votos* into the crevice, and each day the pile of notes at the foot of the column grows larger. Some pilgrims will take a penknife or pencil and dig out petitions deposited earlier so that they can push their own notes into the fissure. Many of these petitions appeal for health and well-being; others mention the names of family and friends left behind in town or village.[61] Such petitions are regularly submitted to priests during the liturgy either for the healing of those who are ill or for the salvation of the souls of the dead.

The deposit of notes or other material representations of the pilgrim is a well-attested component of pilgrimage rituals.[62] As with the ritual use of the fire of the Sabta Nur, these notes are an element in the pilgrim's strategy to overcome the spatial distance between center and periphery. The notes connect those left behind with those who have completed the pilgrimage to the center of the world; they allow those at the periphery to participate in the normative ritual at the center. Throughout Holy Week (indeed, throughout the year) pilgrims from the Catholic, Orthodox, and Eastern churches bring bags of objects from home to be laid on the Stone of Unction in the foyer of the Church of the Holy Sepulcher. This is the thirteenth Station of the Cross, where Jesus' body was prepared for burial. It is very common for both men and women to pause at the stone and to empty the contents of paper and plastic bags onto it. Crucifixes, rosaries, pictures of sick or deceased relatives, and burial shrouds are brought into contact with the stone, transferring the power of Jesus and the Resurrection to these items. Throughout the year there is a constant flow of these "bag people" around the stone. During Holy Week and especially on Good Friday, the ritual at the stone is transformed by women who cleanse the stone with oils and rosewater as a reenactment of the preparation of Jesus' body for burial (figure 3).

When the Latin and Orthodox Easters fall together, the church is opened for the Latin ritual at 6:30 AM. But this opening also allows the Orthodox pilgrims to flood into the Church. Orthodox pilgrims outnumber the Latins, and estimates of the number of people in the Church of the Holy Sepulcher for Holy Saturday during the years 1983–1986 ranged from five thousand to six thousand. These estimates are considerably less than the number of pilgrims who attended the ritual during the nineteenth century.[63] However, the places taken up by the pilgrims usually do not correspond to the places reserved according

Figure 3. A Greek Orthodox pilgrim at the Stone of Unction on Good Friday. The pilgrim places a plastic bag with her burial shroud on the stone. Author's photograph.

to the Status Quo for the various communities of the Church of the Holy Sepulcher. Cust indicated that during the ritual "each rite must be confined to its allotted floor space, within which the area may be divided by towns."[64] Further, he wrote that the Orthodox area is on the northern side of the tomb. Moving counterclockwise through the space under the rotunda, the Jacobites are next to them, and the dividing line between them is contested. The Coptic area is next to the Jacobites, and the Armenians are next to them. The patriarchs or archbishops of each community are located above each of the communities in the second-floor gallery which runs around the rotunda. Each community also has space for guests, and Cust indicated that the "spaces immediately below these balconies [in the gallery] are reserved for guests of the Patriarchates, Orthodox to the north, and Armenian to the south, and should not be filled except with the consent of the Dragoman. Tiers of seats may not be constructed in these spaces, but benches may be placed for the convenience of those present."[65]

Cust noted that disputes were almost inevitable when the Dragomans or police began to move the pilgrims to the areas assigned to their communities or attempted to maintain the separation of the communities throughout the ritual.[66] The difficulties in maintaining the spatial divisions between the communities remained constant until the Easter celebrations of 1968, which was the first year that the Israelis encountered the complexities of the Status Quo. In the first Sabta Nur ritual after the Six Day War of June 1967, they mobilized four hundred policemen to maintain order, and with the cooperation of the different Christian communities, a detailed, almost military, timetable was prepared. The Jerusalem chief of police announced in a news conference before Holy Saturday that the communities within the Church of the Holy Sepulcher had agreed on a slight alteration in the Status Quo. In contrast to previous years, mobile police barriers would be used to separate the worshippers and their guests within the church during the descent of the Holy Fire. Under the Ottomans, the British, and the Jordanians, the spatial allocations had been enforced by policemen and military personnel.[67] Two hundred policemen were stationed within the church to maintain order, and for the first time they used asbestos gloves to extinguish the candles lit by the fire.[68] By the early 1980s the number of policemen had decreased to less than one hundred, and Egged bus drivers, who could not drive their buses because of Sabbath regulations in the city, were enlisted specifically to serve as "fire marshals." In addition to asbestos gloves, each carried a small fire extinguisher with a directional nozzle allowing them to put out candles several yards away.

In 1984, the second year that I observed the ritual, the police began to move the mobile barriers into the church at approximately 8:30 AM, even while the Latin Holy Saturday ritual was still going on. When the Easters do not coincide, the barriers are set up before the doors of the church are opened. With these barriers the police construct enclosures for the various communities, beginning with the Armenian sections on the southern side of the Edicule and moving clockwise to the Coptic, Jacobite, and Greek Orthodox sections. Once these sections are established, everyone within them is asked to leave. In some cases pilgrims who believe that they have the best vantage points for the fire ritual are exceedingly reluctant to move; they usually have to be carried from the enclosures by the police. After the enclosures have been cleared, the various communities bring their visitors and guests into the church in official processions, which in the case of the Armenian community begins at the Patriarchate and the Cathedral of St. James. These barriers are the materialization of the Status Quo, and their placement is supervised by a high-ranking police officer and representatives of the Greek Orthodox, the Armenians, the Copts, and the Jacobites. This group uses a detailed blueprint of the church's floor, color coded for each community to ensure that each barrier will be placed exactly.

The ritual begins with the entrance of the Armenian patriarch and his procession at exactly 10:30 AM. The patriarch and his procession pass in front of the entrance to the Edicule and then make their way around the Edicule in the passageway that has been created by the barriers, proceeding to the Armenian vestry. The Armenian patriarch receives distinguished visitors in the vestry until the entrance of the Orthodox patriarch later in the ritual. When the Greek Orthodox patriarch enters the church with his retinue, the Armenian patriarch will proceed to the Armenian section of the gallery to await the fire. At 11:00 the tomb is sealed after being thoroughly searched by two Greek Orthodox and Armenian Archimandrites for any instrument which might be used to ignite a fire during the ritual. When both are satisfied that no candle or lamp is burning in the tomb and no lighter or book of matches is concealed anywhere within, the door is closed and sealed. The Archimandrites stretch two white ribbons from the door's interior hinges to its exterior handles, crisscrossing the door. A large block of wax is then placed over the crisscrossed ribbons. The ends of the ribbons are held by the two Archimandrites, who take up positions on each side of the door. A member of the Nusseibeh family, who holds the key to the doors of the Church of the Holy Sepulcher, is then called to inspect the sealing and impresses the wax with the family's signet ring (figure 4).

The Greek Orthodox patriarch enters the Church of the Holy Sepulcher at 12:00 noon, making his way with his procession to the Katholikon. Here he assumes his throne, and representatives from the other communities then request formal approval to participate in the ritual. First come the Jacobites, who enter the church through the main entrance and also proceed to the Katholikon. Ten or twelve young men are carried on the shoulders of men in the procession as they enter the Katholikon and march to the entrance of the Edicule. The Jacobites are the first to enter because in order to reach the Chapel of Nicodemus they must pass through the area reserved by the Status Quo for the Copts. The Copts enter the church officially only after the Jacobites have reached the Chapel of Nicodemus. They shout a number of traditional cheers, which are accompanied by men playing the *darabukkeh* or drum. At this point the emotional temper of the people assembled for the ritual changes markedly. The cheers of the Jacobites are taken up by the other communities of the church. First the Copts respond by hoisting young men onto their shoulders and a wild dance begins, accompanied by drums and cheers (figure 5). Waves and counterwaves of cheers reverberate off the walls of the rotunda and throughout the church as one community responds to another. The people crushed together in the rotunda now appear to be fans supporting their favorite teams in a sporting match.

The cheering and seemingly wild dancing in the ritual have often

Figure 4. Armenian *(left)* and Greek Orthodox *(right)* Archimandrites in front of the sealed tomb. Note the impression of the Nusseibeh family ring in the wax. Author's photograph.

been criticized by Western observers. Robert Curzon, who visited the church in 1834 as part of his tour of Levantine monasteries, described the scene with characteristic scorn: "At one time, before the church was full, they made a racecourse round the sepulcher; and some, almost in a state of nudity, danced about with frantic gestures, yelling and screaming as if they were possessed. Altogether it was a scene of disorder and profanation, which it is impossible to describe."[69] The seeming chaos that most observers have seen in the ritual at this point is not disorder. It is completely choreographed by the Status Quo. For example, seemingly wild dancing is done within the spatial confines created by the Status Quo; the Syrians and the Copts remain within their areas, for to intrude on the others would transform the managed ritual into unchecked violence. Also, the shouts which go back and forth are by no means random and are repeated each and every year. Conder recorded the most complete version of the cycle of cheers used in the ritual in 1873 and 1875.[70]

Figure 5. The Copts respond to the cheers of the Jacobites. Author's photograph.

Some of the cheers recorded by Conder (e.g., *Allah anser es-sultan*, "God help the Sultan!") no longer have relevance. More problematic, however, are the anti-Semitic cheers, such as "O Jews, O Jews! Your feast is a feast of apes." The feast referred to here is of course Passover, which occurs at the same period as the Orthodox and Latin Easters. These anti-Semitic cheers were never prohibited by the Israeli government. During the early years of Israeli rule over the Old City, they were suppressed by the communities themselves, perhaps from fear of what they might provoke from the Jewish police authorities in the newly unified city. Meron Benvenisti, then a deputy mayor of the city, recalls that during the first Holy Fire ritual in the united city in 1968, "few of the Jewish policemen could appreciate the historic moment they were experiencing. Some of the traditional songs sung at the fire festival had, in previous years, insulted the Jews."[71] An ecumenical effort was made in the 1970s and early 1980s to remove the anti-Semitism not only of these cheers but also of sermons given in the Orthodox communities during Easter.[72] A series of new cheers were introduced in the late 1970s (e.g.,

"We will have the fire!"), but the most popular cheer remains *Hadha kubir said-na,* "This is the tomb of our Lord!"

Almost simultaneously with this dramatic change in the crowd's mood heralded by the Orthodox patriarch's entrance into the church, the Holy Lamp, in which the Holy Fire will burn from this Holy Saturday until the next Good Friday, is carried from the Katholikon to the Edicule by a Greek Orthodox Archimandrite. The door is now unsealed and the lamp is deposited in the vestibule of the Edicule. The two Archimandrites holding the ends of the white ribbons are now replaced by two bishops from the Greek Orthodox and Armenian communities. These bishops, who stand on both sides of the doorway leading into the Edicule, are later joined by two sextons, one Armenian and the other Greek Orthodox, two Dragomans, again one Armenian and the other Greek Orthodox, representatives from the Jacobite and Coptic communities, and finally, as an ecumenical gesture, a representative of the Franciscan community (figure 6). As the ritual begins, the entire Christian community of the Church of the Holy Sepulcher is represented by the individuals flanking both sides of the doorway.

The drama of the ritual continues to intensify, the crowd becomes ever more anxious, and the cheers and dancing continue until exactly 12:30. At that moment the Greek Orthodox patriarch leaves the Katholikon with his procession and enters the rotunda. The Orthodox patriarch's entrance into the Rotunda is the signal for the Armenian patriarch to leave the Armenian vestry and climb the steps immediately outside it to the Armenian section of the gallery above. Here a throne has been placed in the first opening of the gallery, where the patriarch will be able to see the entire ritual below. Thirteen banners precede the patriarch, carried by members of the notable Greek Orthodox families in Jerusalem. The banners depict the events of the Passion and the Resurrection of Jesus. Representatives of the Romanian Orthodox church and the Red Russian Orthodox church participate in the procession as groups within the Greek Orthodox patriarch's immediate party. As formal members of the patriarch's party, they are allowed to wear their church vestments. However, the head or chief representative of the White Russian Orthodox church follows the patriarch's party and is not allowed to wear any official vestments; he is treated instead as an ordinary pilgrim in the ritual.[73] The official Greek Orthodox torches which will be used with the Holy Fire are also carried in the procession. The procession circles the Edicule counterclockwise three times. At the conclusion of the third, the procession arrives at the entrance of the Edicule.

The Armenian bishop who has been selected to accompany the Greek Orthodox patriarch into the tomb, but who will await him in the vesti-

Figure 6. All the communities of the Church of the Holy Sepulcher are represented at the sealed entrance of the Edicule as the ritual progresses toward the
descent of the fire. Author's photograph.

bule and not accompany him into the sealed inner burial chamber, now
joins him in front of the Edicule. The Greek Orthodox patriarch is now
disrobed and ritually searched for any implement which might be used
to strike fire within the tomb. His mitre and vestments are carried to the
altar in the Katholikon. The door to the Edicule is now opened and the
Greek Orthodox patriarch and the Armenian bishop enter the tomb.
The door is closed and will not be opened again until the patriarch
knocks from within. This takes place just a few minutes before one
o'clock and marks another dramatic mood swing in the ritual. Just a few
moments before, the Rotunda was filled with shouts and cheers, but
once the door has been closed with the two men inside, the assembled
crowd becomes almost totally silent. On both the northern and southern
sides of the Edicule are doubled portholes which reach to the vestibule
of the tomb. These are attended by single representatives of the Greek
Orthodox on the northern side and the Armenians on the southern side.

Figure 7. The Armenians on the southern side of the Edicule await the fire. The man holding up the white handkerchief is watched intensely by those further away. He will drop his arm to signal that the fire has appeared. Author's photograph.

Each man has the responsibility of peering into the darkened tomb and receiving the fire. The fire will then be passed to younger men who stand with them and carry torches. On the northern side are torchbearers representing the Greek Orthodox and the Jacobites; on the southern side, those who represent the Armenians and Copts.

While the fire has always appeared with the certainty of clockwork, the assembled pilgrims are never certain that it will appear again. The portholes in the Edicule remain dark. The fire receivers and torchbearers peer into darkness. The faces of the pilgrims reflect their anxiety about the fire. Women cry and men pound their chests as they look up into the rotunda for some indication that the presence of God has entered the church. On the southern (Armenian) side of the Edicule, the fire receiver or *lucihan* holds a white handkerchief in his upraised hand as a signal (figure 7). He looks into the darkness of the tomb; when he drops his hand, the fire has emerged with the Greek Orthodox patriarch from the inner burial chamber. But in the minutes which have crept by with agonizing slowness since the patriarch and bishop were sealed into the tomb, people have actually climbed the walls of the Edicule to be

Figure 8. The fire is transferred to those outside the Edicule. Author's photograph.

closer to those fire portholes. Everyone in the church leans toward the
fire holes and awaits the moment of its appearance (figure 8).

Suddenly the Armenian lucihan drops his hand and the orange of
fire can be seen in the portholes. In a matter of seconds the lucihan
has reached in through the portholes and has the fire in his hands. He
immediately transfers it to the torches of the young men who await him.
Cust notes that the Status Quo stipulates that the fire must first be given
to the Greek Orthodox torchbearer on the northern side of the Edicule.[74] The Greek Orthodox torchbearer them immediately runs with
the blazing torch to the Greek Katholikon, where the Greek pilgrims
await the fire. Next the Jacobite lights his torch and carries the fire to
his community in the Chapel of Nicodemus. On the southern side the
Armenian torchbearer is the first to receive the fire, and he immediately
turns and runs to the staircase leading to the Armenian gallery and the
Armenian patriarch. The Copt next lights his torch and runs to his community at the western side of the Edicule (figure 9). While the Greeks
get the fire first, it is the Armenian patriarch who receives the fire first.

Figure 9. The Copts prepare their torch for the ritual earlier in the morning. Author's photograph.

It appears that each torchbearer is running as fast as he can to his destination, but in reality the Status Quo guarantees that the Armenian community will officially receive the fire first. The Armenian patriarch leans out of his opening in the gallery with the torch in his hands, showing the fire to those below.

In a matter of seconds the fire has spread to the assembled crowd. Almost all of them carry bunches of thirty-three candles representing the years of Jesus' life. The Holy Fire spreads from one to the next until the church is filled with burning candles (figures 9 and 10). The bells of the church begin to ring, and pandemonium transforms the silence which only minutes before hung through the church. Within seconds of the fire's passing through the portholes to the awaiting crowd, the Greek Orthodox patriarch and the Armenian bishop emerge from the Edicule. First comes the patriarch, carrying two huge bunches of lighted candles. As the door opens and he emerges, the crowd on both sides of the door strains toward him to light their candles from his. He is immediately escorted to the Katholikon entrance, where his attendants help him put on his Easter vestments. Now a series of processions around the Edicule begins; the banners reappear, and all of the communities of the Church of the Holy Sepulcher march around the Edicule with their fire. Mean-

Figure 10. The fire spreads to the candles of all assembled in the rotunda. Author's photograph.

while, the pandemonium increases. Men and women demonstrate that this is not a dangerous fire, a fire which can burn. They rub the fire into their faces and pass it under their arms, seemingly oblivious to any pain from it. This contemporary phenomenon is well documented in the historical descriptions of the Holy Fire. For example, A. P. Stanley, dean of Westminster, who observed the ritual in in 1853, wrote that "for a short time the pilgrims run to and fro—rubbing their faces and breasts against the fire to attest its supposed harmlessness."[75]

The pandemonium associated with the descent of the Holy Fire has long been recorded by the many visitors to the Church of the Holy Sepulcher. Seetzen's comment that this was some kind of Bacchanalian feast is by no means an isolated judgment. But on many occasions the spread of the fire among the ritual participants, the frenzy associated with it, and the numbers of people in the church have combined to make the ritual deadly. The Greek Orthodox monk Neophitos of Cyprus recorded such a deadly combination in 1834, when the Church of the Holy Sepulcher was filled with more than fifteen thousand pilgrims and spectators. According to his account, as soon as the Holy Fire appeared, the people inside and outside the church rushed to light their candles from it. Many who tripped and fell to the ground were trampled to death.

Almost 150 people were killed and 300 were injured in the melee.[76] Robert Curzon was in the church at the same time, and his *Visits to Monasteries in the Levant,* published in 1850, contains a more detailed account of the panic and death which accompanied the Holy Fire in that year. Once the panic set in, Curzon and his friends tried to escape the church with the aid of a group of Ottoman soldiers who pushed their way through the crowd. As he reached the place where the three Marys had stood during the Crucifixion, he scrambled over bodies which he believed were merely people who, exhausted by the ritual or overcome by heat, had paused to rest; but looking down, he realized that they were dead. Those around him were covered with blood from those who had already been killed in the panic. The mass of frightened pilgrims pushed toward the doors of the church, where the Ottoman guards thought that they intended to attack them. The guards bayonetted many as they emerged from the church. Others fell to the ground after being hit by the stocks of the guards' rifles and were trampled to death.[77]

The descriptions of the chaos associated with the appearance of the Holy Fire have often masked the conflicts between the various communities within the Status Quo. James Finn, the British consul in Jerusalem from 1845 to 1863, reported such a conflict between the Greek Orthodox and the Armenians in 1855. Both sides had prepared for the conflict and provided their pilgrims "with stones and cudgels, which had been previously concealed (it was believed by the Armenians) behind columns and in dark corners." Some of these materials were secreted in the Armenian gallery; when the fighting broke out, they were thrown down to the Armenians below. Once the fighting began, the pasha, according to Finn, rushed to direct his men in their effort to suppress the conflict. The pasha himself was hit several times and cut by a knife. Some twenty-five Greeks and Armenians were severely wounded in the fighting, and many others received serious injuries. The next day Finn returned to the Church of the Holy Sepulcher to survey the damage. The Parvis was filled with Ottoman soldiers with fixed bayonets. The damage was extensive: "The pavement all around the Sepulchre Chapel, especially between it and the Greek church, was strewn with broken lamps, fragments of glass and pictures, oil swimming over the floor. Many valuable pictures had been torn; vases, lamps, candlesticks, and other church ornaments thrown down and destroyed." Many silver oil lamps and silver chains disappeared in the fighting and were never seen again.[78] In this case the ritual chaos and violence were triggered by conflict between the Greek Orthodox and Armenians, perhaps over their contradictory claims to sacred space and time in the church.

Yet this ritual disorder, which has consistently attracted the comment of Western observers, needs interpretation beyond the conflict between rival religious communities. Elias Canetti has used Curzon's account of the pandemonium in the Holy Fire ritual as an example of the process by which social groups or "packs" are transformed. According to Canetti, during the ritual the "lamenting pack" which is formed to reexperience the death of Jesus is transformed into a "triumphant pack" which reexperiences his victory over death. The actual mechanism of the Holy Fire's production is irrelevant; the essential fact of the ritual is the transformation of the pack from lament to triumph. Canetti understands that fire is the symbol for the "suddenness" or "velocity" by which a crowd grows and is transformed. However, the tragic events recorded by Neophitos of Cyprus and Curzon, in Canetti's interpretation, arise from the contradiction inherent in the ritual. The danger of panic, he writes, is increased by two opposed groups: "the infidel Turks and the pilgrims who wanted to expel them."[79] Despite the fact that some scholars have found Canetti's description of the transformation of the "lamenting pack" into the "triumphant pack" to be a persuasive analysis, it does not fully explain the frenzy, chaos, disorder, or pandemonium that routinely characterizes the ritual.[80] If such tragedies were to happen yearly, it might explain the transformation. However, the disorder and chaos are programmatically a part of the Sabta Nur ritual, although usually far less extreme than what took place in 1834.

A more compelling interpretation might be located in the very nature of ritual itself. Victor Turner has argued that ritual creates alternative communities. In some cases these alternative communities are sustained for only a short time, the duration of the ritual; in other cases these communities endure for longer periods. But in each case they are the result of the power of ritual, which Turner described through the dynamics of communitas and liminality, of structure and antistructure.[81] Indeed, Turner's analysis of the power of ritual, what he often called the "ritual process," can be used to understand how ritual challenges the Status Quo. The normative social communities are maintained with great rigidity and fixedness by the Status Quo during the Sabta Nur. There is complete separation of the communities, who all occupy the same time frame but not the same spatial context. That is the power of the Status Quo, which is acknowledged by the communities participating in the ritual. They may test it or push it, and *sometimes* the exigencies and dynamics within each of the communities and their perception of their relationship to the others break the boundaries of the Status Quo. The descent of the Holy Fire marks the transformation of the diverse communities of the Church of the Holy Sepulcher, contrary to the Status Quo, into the one community which experiences the Resurrection. The ritual rupture of the Status Quo is then marked by the ritual experience of disorder and antistructure.

## CONCLUSION: AESTHETICS, POLITICS, AND BOUNDARIES

The Status Quo in the Church of the Holy Sepulcher during the Sabta Nur forces us to reconsider the meanings of time and space within religious traditions. The dominant scholarly tradition in the history of religions has argued that the categories of sacred time and space are substantive and consensual. By *substantive* I mean that the history of religions has treated them as if they exist in the phenomenal world, apart from human interpretation. By *consensual* I mean that the history of religions has assumed that a consensus of meaning for time and space exists and in this consensus there are no conflicts. If indeed there are conflicts of meaning, we have usually affirmed elite meanings over the popular or have simply catalogued them as if the different meanings have little or no consequence in the social world of religious traditions. The catalogues of meaning and the metaphors which have been used by historians of religions have produced an "aesthetics" of sacred time and space in which all the meanings, despite their differences, are understood to form a uniform complex of religious ideas. Conflictual meanings are marginalized, and space and time become thoroughly apolitical.

Recent studies of pilgrimage have challenged both the substantive and consensual models of sacred time and space. For example, John Eade and Michael Sallnow have suggested, against the interpretive paradigm of Victor Turner, that pilgrimage is made up of competing and often conflicting discourses of meaning and understanding brought to sacred shrines. These discourses are not somehow outside of the real meaning of the place but are constitutive of the cult itself.[82] Glenn Bowman, in his study of Christian pilgrimage to Jerusalem, argues that there is no meaning of sacred place apart from the sacred texts which make that place important. He concludes that pilgrimages "are journeys to the sacred, but the sacred is not something which stands beyond the domain of culture; it is imagined, defined, and articulated within cultural practice."[83] Bowman shows that among some forms of Christian pilgrimage to Jerusalem, the sacred center gains its sacrality, its centricity, from the sacred texts, the Gospel narratives of the New Testament, which are used to interpret space. There is no sacred space apart from text. Eade and Sallnow then describe this particular form of pilgrimage as "textual pilgrimage" in which the pilgrimage is really a "journey through a particular text, the authorized, biblical accounts of Christ's life and death. . . . Sacred geography is relevant only in so far as it illustrates an authoritative text." The great irony in the case of pilgrimage to Jerusalem, the place where Jesus' presence and absence are absolutely critical to what drives Christianity, is that "the power of person and the power of place recede against the far greater power of the word."[84] But we would add that the power of the word in this context is organized both spatially and temporally by the Status Quo.

Much of the most important work in the last two decades in the study of religion has demonstrated that the categories used by the scholars are contested within and between religious communities. Sacred space and time are more matters of interpretation, of setting boundaries and negotiating relationships, than they are fixed categories which have universal consent and agreement among the believers. In commenting on the work of Mary Douglas, Jonathan Z. Smith recalls an experience drawn from his youth working on a dairy farm in upstate New York. In the morning his boss would wash his hands, then go outside and rub them with dirt. When Smith asked about this curious series of actions, he was reminded by his host that folks from the city know little. Inside the house, he was told, it's "dirt"; outside, though, it's "earth." You wash it off to be with your family inside, and you put it on when you are with the animals outside. Smith uses this experience to argue against the substantive tradition of sacred and profane within the history of religions. "There is nothing," he writes, "that is inherently or essentially clean or unclean, sacred or profane. These are situational or relational categories, mobile boundaries which shift according to the map being employed."[85] At another point he reminds us of the similarity between attempts to fix canons and divinatory situations. He is struck by "the great variety of such canons and divinatory situations . . . by the differences in exegetical techniques and skills, by the variety of presuppositions. But the essential structure of limitation and closure along with exegetical ingenuity remains constant." The task of the history of religions, Smith argues, should be "an examination of the rules that govern the sharp debates between rival exegetes and exegetical systems in their efforts to manipulate the closed canon."[86] Sacred space and time must also be understood as structures of limitation and closure, like the canon or the process of divination with a fixed and limited number of objects to be interpreted and understood. Sacred space and time, then, are matters of context and relation, with specific grammars which make them meaningful. Human beings expend considerable energy in the construction and management of sacred time and space, in the fluidity of these structures and their relationships to the profane time and space around them. This exegetical activity should be our focus, and we should not overlook the fact that it often has profound implications for the political contexts of these "canons" of sacred time and space.

More recently Smith has persuasively argued that there is an intimate connection between ritual and place. He writes that "ritual is, first and foremost, a mode of paying attention. It is a process of marking interest." He indicates that our theological inheritance from the Protestant

Reformation has in many cases blinded us to this relationship, for all too often ritual is understood only to be blind and thoughtless habit. And, Smith argues, it is because ritual is a process of marking interest that place, or what I am calling *space* in this essay, plays such a fundamental role in ritual. He states that "place directs attention."[87] Smith's interpretation of ritual, then, adds two additional factors to our analysis of sacred time and space. In addition to uncovering the exegetical or constructed dimension of time and space, one must also come to terms with the precise mode of attention which regulates or manages time and space. Second, ritual's connection to place and time organizes, institutionalizes, and elaborates memory.

The operation of the Status Quo in the Sabta Nur ritual as I have described it here provides one of the strongest arguments against both the substantive and consensual interpretations of sacred space and time in the history of religions. There are no spaces or times which are inherently sacred or profane. Sacrality in time and space, as Smith has pointed out, is situational or relational; boundaries which separate sacred and profane are constantly in motion according to the intellectual system which perceives or maps them. But this is not simply a discovery made by historians of religions as they have gone back into the history of their discipline and revised some of its most important theoretical structures. Indeed, scholars in other fields, whose own research is seemingly far removed from the issues of sacred and profane, have reached similar conclusions. For example, we might cite David Harvey's study of the construction of Paris's Basilique du Sacré Coeur as only one example. The sacrality of Sacré Coeur can be understood only in relationship to another piece of symbolic geography, the Wall of the Communards in Père-Lachaise Cemetery. Both are charged religious and nationalist sacred spaces, but they cannot be understood apart from one another.[88] The Status Quo is, then, a relational and contextual map through which the sacred space and time of the Church of the Holy Sepulcher is constructed and managed. It is the specific grammar of sacred space and time in Christendom's most holy space. But there would be little need for the Status Quo if in fact only one grammar regulated the meanings of time and space. But time and space in the Church of the Holy Sepulcher are contested. There is no single meaning; rather, competing communities hold multiple, rival meanings.

When the Israeli police introduced barricades into the ritual of Sabta Nur in 1968 to separate the rival communities, the spatial construction of the Status Quo was made concrete. Ottoman, British, and Jordanian rulers of the city had used the bodies of the police guards and soldiers to separate the communities and thus mark the constructed space. Bishop Guregh Kapikian, the principal of St. Tarkmanchatz Secondary School and the chief supervisor for the restoration projects within the Armenian sections of the Church of the Holy Sepulcher, spends much of his time during Sabta Nur making certain that Armenian space as set forth by the Status Quo is not violated by others. He told me that under the Jordanians he would supervise a painstaking ritual of chalking the various communities' spaces on the floor of the church; only then did the soldiers or the police know where they were to stand in order to separate the groups.[89] The Israeli novelty was only one successive technique to solidify the structures of space and time during Sabta Nur.

But the Status Quo also articulates something which is most fundamental to all ritual. It marks a precise tapestry of interests, using Smith's terminology, which sets the sacred space and time of the Church of the Holy Sepulcher apart from other sacred spaces and other sacred times. It cannot be reduplicated in another locale. And at the same time, the Status Quo is that which activates or structures memory. There is no sacrality in the Church of the Holy Sepulcher apart from this elaborate system of explanation which guides the activities of the communities which must share the church.

## NOTES

1. Ulrich Seetzen, *Reisen durch Syrien, Palästina, etc.* (Berlin: G. Reimer, 1854–1859), cited in F. E. Peters, *Jerusalem: The Holy City in the Eyes of Chroniclers, Visitors, Pilgrims, and Prophets from the Days of Abraham to the Beginnings of Modern Times* (Princeton: Princeton University Press, 1985), 571–72.

2. Claude R. Conder, *Tent Work in Palestine*, 2 vols. (London: Richard Bentley and Son, 1879), 1:345.

3. For a discussion of the work of Seetzen and Conder, see Naomi Shepherd, *The Zealous Intruders: The Western Rediscovery of Palestine* (San Francisco: Harper and Row, 1987), esp. 46–48, 50–53, 211–15, and Yehoshua Ben-Arieh, *The Rediscovery of the Holy Land in the Nineteenth Century* (Jerusalem: Magnes Press of the Hebrew University of Jerusalem and the Israel Exploration Society, 1983), esp. 35–37, 39–43, 214–16, 224–25.

4. One of the best overviews of Jerusalem's Christian communities is Thomas A. Idinopulos, "Diversity and Conflict Amongst the Christian Communities," in A. L. Eckardt, ed., *Jerusalem: City of the Ages* (New York: University Press of America and the Academic Association for Peace in the Middle East, 1987), 253–67.

5. For the complete text and a discussion of Pope Benedict's outcry against the Balfour Declaration, see Sergio I. Minerbi, *The Vatican and Zionism: Conflict in the Holy Land—1895–1925*, trans. Arnold Schwarz (New York: Oxford University Press, 1990), 129–35.

6. See H. Eugene Bovis, *The Jerusalem Question 1917–1968* (Stanford: Hoover Institute Press, 1971), and Terrence Prittie, *Whose Jerusalem?* (London: Frederick Miller, 1981), esp. 41–44. See also Minerbi, *Vatican and Zionism*, 147–51, where he argues that this speech contained the foundations of the Vatican's

policy against Zionism for many years and included the charges (1) that Protestants were persuading the Arabs of Palestine to convert; (2) that the Jews were using the Mandate's regulations to oust the Christians of Palestine from their positions; (3) that the Jews were turning the Holy Places into pleasure spots; and (4) that the Great Powers must guarantee the rights of Catholics without impairing the rights of the Jews and without giving them any privileges.

7. Likewise, in France at the end of the war there was considerable debate and political agitation within Catholic circles to ensure that Palestine would not be "sold" to the Jews. For example, a French Catholic society called Les Amis de la Terre Sainte was formed to combat the Zionist movement. The society published four pamphlets in late 1918 and early 1919—Herbert Adams Gibbons, *Le Sionisme et la paix mondiale*, Jules Bernex, *La grande peine de la Palestine*, Sheik Youssef el-Khazen, *L'état Juif en Palestine*, and "Un ami de la Terre Sainte," *Dangers d'état Juif en Palestine*—which attracted considerable public attention. On the French Catholic reaction and the activity of Les Amis de la Terre Sainte, see Joseph Hajjar, *Le Christianisme en Orient: Etudes d'histoire contemporaine 1684–1968* (Beirut: Libraire du Liban, 1971), 198–204. Minerbi, *Vatican and Zionism*, cites extensive diplomatic records which indicate that the French Catholics' secondary position was that Catholic Belgium might be entrusted with the mandate over the Holy Land. While Minerbi's book treats the first half of the century, George E. Irani, *The Papacy and the Middle East: The Role of the Holy See in the Arab-Israeli Conflict, 1962–1984* (Notre Dame: University of Notre Dame Press, 1986), esp. 77–97, brings the issue to the most contemporary period.

8. In 1983 I was invited by the Armenian patriarchate to observe the ritual from the area reserved for their guests on the rotunda floor. In 1984 and 1985 I was allowed access to the Coptic and Greek Orthodox sections of the Church of the Holy Sepulcher. This access provided me with much greater movement in the church during the ritual. In 1986 I was invited by the Yehudah Litani, then Middle East editor of the *Jerusalem Post*, to help their correspondent, Dennis Silk, cover the ritual for the paper. Silk published his article, "The Holy Fire," in the *Jerusalem Post*, 27 May 1986, 5.

9. According to C. R. Ashbee's official record, *Jerusalem 1918–1920: Being the Records of the Pro-Jerusalem Council During the Period of the British Military Administration* (London: Council of the Pro-Jerusalem Society and John Murray, 1921), the members of the council during the period 1918–1920 were Sir Herbert Samuel, the honorary president of the council and high commissioner of Palestine; Ronald Storrs, president and governor of Jerusalem; the mayor of Jerusalem; the director of antiquities; the grand mufti of Jerusalem; the president of the Franciscan community and custodian of the Holy Land; the president of the Dominican community; the Greek Orthodox patriarch; the Armenian patriarch; the president of the Jewish community; the chairman of the Jewish Agency for Palestine; Rev. Père Abel of the École Biblique de Saint-Etienne; Captain Barluzzi; Eliezer Ben-Yehuda; Captain K. A. C. Creswell, inspector of monuments; M. D. Geddes; R. A. Harari; Musa Kazem Pasha El-Husseni, former mayor of Jerusalem; Commander H. C. Luke; Captain Mackay, inspector of monuments; Mr. Meyuhas; Captain Paribeni; Lazarus Paul, the acting representative of the Armenian patriarch; Lt.-Col. E. L. Popham; E. T. Richmond; D. G. Salameh, former vice-mayor of Jerusalem; Dr. Nahum Slouseh; Jacob Spafford; Lt.-Col.

Waters Taylor; Rev. Père Vincent of the Dominican Convent; Mr. John Whiting, honorary treasurer of the council; David Yellin, vice-mayor of Jerusalem; C. R. Ashbee, the honorary secretary of the council and civic adviser to the City of Jerusalem. The membership changed only slightly during the first years of the Mandate; see C. R. Ashbee, *Jerusalem 1920–1922: Being the Records of the Pro-Jerusalem Council During the First Two Years of the Civil Administration* (London: Council of the Pro-Jerusalem Society and John Murray, 1924).

10. H. C. Luke, "The Christian Communities in the Holy Sepulchre," in Ashbee, *Jerusalem 1920–1922*, 56. This essay included an elaborate architectural plan of the Church of the Holy Sepulcher, color coded to indicate custody by the various communities of areas within the church. In great part this division of space within the church is correct with some notable errors (e.g., he assigns custody of the Convent of Abraham on the southeastern side of the Parvis to the Greek Orthodox when it properly belongs to the Armenians, who in the late 1970s began a major renovation of this area).

11. In granting the Mandate of Palestine to the British, the League of Nations had agreed on two principles which appeared as articles 13 and 14 of the Mandatory charter. Article 13 gave the Mandatory power the responsibility of preserving existing rights in the Holy Places. Article 14 provided for the creation of a special commission to study, define, and determine rights and claims related to the Holy Places. This commission was never formed, and therefore the government of Palestine was under the obligation to maintain the Status Quo in every respect. The Mandate provided only that the British should maintain the Status Quo. Matters related to them (e.g., any change in custody) were under the exclusive power of the League of Nations. On 24 July 1924 the Court of Saint James and the King of England reconfirmed that all matters having to do with the Status Quo would not be subject to any court in Palestine but would be under the jurisdiction of the commission established by article 14, the high commissioner of Palestine, and the League of Nations.

12. Taysir Jbara, *Palestinian Leader Hajj Amin al-Husayni: Mufti of Jerusalem* (Princeton: Kingston Press, 1985), 103–17, argues that only after the 1929 riots did the British recognize al-Husayni as the most significant force against the Mandate. They determined to reduce his influence, encouraging internal dissension in the Palestinian nationalist community by exploiting the rivalry between the Jerusalem notable families, especially with regard to al-Husayni's World Islamic Congress held in Jerusalem in 1931. For a brilliant discussion of the complexities of the mufti's politics, see Philip Mattar, "The Mufti of Jerusalem and the Politics of Palestine," *Middle East Journal* 42 (1988): 227–40; and *The Mufti of Jerusalem: Al-Hajj Amin al-Husayni and the Palestinian National Movement* (New York: Columbia University Press, 1988).

13. Yehoshua Porath, *The Emergence of the Palestinian-Arab National Movement 1918–1929* (London: Frank Cass, 1974), 265–66. A weaker but nevertheless interesting account of the conflict is Mary Ellen Lundsten, "Wall Politics: Zionist and Palestinian Strategies in Jerusalem, 1928," *Journal of Palestine Studies* 7, no. 1 (Winter 1978): 3–27. She attempts to correct the portrayal of "fanatic" Arab leaders who initiated the struggle over Jewish control of the Western Wall from nothing by joining with the British to incite Muslim mobs into anti-Jewish vio-

lence. Her essay might have been substantially improved by considering Porath's analysis of the source material. Her argument consequently swings to the opposite extreme, marginalizing or negating the political achievements of Palestinian leaders. She write of al-Husayni that he "was trapped into a legalist position in which his best hope was to minimize the erosion of Muslim rights in the Wall area. This 'no-win' position resulted partly from his failure to include in the Muslim strategy the broader set of issues—including Arab rights to property and protection of livelihood—which the Wall dispute reflected. That these broader, socio-economic rather than strictly religious, aspects were a major cause of the August 1929 violence was evident not only in investigatory reports but in the nature of each violent incident leading up to the rioting of August 23" (23–24). Lundsten also seems unaware of how important the religious status quo was in the conflict. Indeed, as Porath underscores, Palestinian Muslims had a very long experience with struggles among the various Christian communities over their religious rights in the Church of the Holy Sepulcher, the Church of the Ascension, the Tomb of the Virgin, and the Church of the Nativity which had taught them that "any deviation from the customary habits created a new rule, and any change in the status quo inevitably became a new status quo" (261). This experience helps to explain the Palestinian fears of the gradual takeover of the Haram esh-Sharif by the Jews. While she faults those who have isolated this conflict from the history of the conflict between Jewish and Palestinian nationalisms, she commits the very same error. For example, she seems wholly unaware of Jewish efforts before World War I to purchase the area around the Western Wall, settled by the Maghribis, wholly consistent with the methods of exchange of *waqf* lands, Palestinian and Muslim approvals for the transaction (canceled only by the Turkish district governor), and later renewed efforts in 1919 to acquire property adjacent to the Western Wall which were thwarted by the high costs of the property and the fears of the district governor, Ronald Storrs, that the issue might inflame the community. Other important interpretations of the causes for the rioting are Philip Mattar, "The Role of the Mufti of Jerusalem in the Political Struggle for the Western Wall, 1928–29," *Middle Eastern Studies* 19 (1983): 104–18, and Naomi W. Cohen, *The Year after the Riots: American Responses to the Palestine Crisis of 1929–30* (Detroit: Wayne State University Press, 1988), esp. 16–49.

14. L. G. A. Cust, *The Status Quo in the Holy Places* (1930; rpt. Jerusalem: Ariel Publishing House, 1980), 9–10, 12.

15. Ibid.

16. Ibid.

17. Cust, *Status Quo in the Holy Places*, 9, notes that it was said to cost 2.5 million rubles to procure from the sultan the firman to repair the church and 1.5 million to rebuild the damaged areas.

18. Selim Sayegh, *Le statu quo des Lieux-Saints: Nature juridique et portée internationale* (Rome: Libreria Editrice della pontifica universita' Lateranense, 1971), app. 8, 254–55. While this agreement was signed by the relevant parties to the question, the cleaning of the wall has remained a disputed issue between the communities. In 1984 it provoked a club- and chair-swinging brawl which had to be broken up by Israeli troops. The wall was finally cleaned by Israeli police,

supervised by both Armenian and Greek Orthodox church officials and Bethlehem's Christian mayor, Elias Freij. This dispute was reported by Dan Fisher, "Eastern Rite Dispute over Cleaning of Nativity Church Worries Israel," *Los Angeles Times*, 26 December 1985.

19. The Katholikon's architectural style is the transitional style of Crusader art between Romanesque and Gothic styles. The Crusaders called this area of their church the Chorus Dominorum. It was situated over the Constantinian Triportico, which enclosed the hillock of Calvary in its southeast corner. See Virgilio C. Corbo, *Il Santo Sepolcro de Gerusalemme* (Jerusalem: Franciscan Printing Press, 1981), esp. vol. 2, diagrams 1, 3, and 6.

20. See Diane Herbert, "The Effect of the Status Quo of 1852 on the Christian Communities Inhabiting the Church of the Holy Sepulchre in Jerusalem," (M.A. thesis, University of California, Santa Barbara, 1985), which contains a great deal of interview material on the meaning of the Status Quo for the contemporary Christian communities.

21. Ibid., 21.

22. Nikos Kazantzakis, *Journeying: Travels in Italy, Egypt, Sinai, Jerusalem, and Cyprus*, trans. T. and T. Vasils (San Francisco: Donald S. Ellis, 1984), 153.

23. Cust, *Status Quo in the Holy Places*, 14–15.

24. Neophitos of Cyprus, *Extracts from Annals of Palestine, 1821–1841*, trans. S. N. Spyridon (1938; rpt. Jerusalem: Ariel Publishing House, 1981), 33.

25. The original foundation of this mosque is attributed to the Caliph Umar ibn al-Khattab after his army took the city in 638 c.e., although it perhaps dates from a period in the eighth or ninth centuries. In the popular mythology of Jerusalem, given by tour guides and even members of the Church of the Holy Sepulcher, it is usually said that either the caliph heard the call to prayer while visiting the church and, knowing that if he prayed there it would become a mosque, moved outside to pray or that he refused the Christian patriarch's invitation to pray at the Church of the Holy Sepulcher, saying, "If I had prayed in the church it would have been lost to you, for the Believers would have taken it saying: Umar prayed here." For one recent version of this, see Jerome Murphy-O'Connor, *The Holy Land: An Archaeological Guide from Earliest Times to 1700* (Oxford: Oxford University Press, 1986), 46. However, this attribution is not found in Muslim sources. The most expansive account of Umar's visit to the Church of the Holy Sepulcher is contained in the fourteenth-century *Muthr al-Ghirm*, written by the Jerusalemite Jamal ad-Din Ahmad and copied verbatim by later writers. According to this narrative, Umar visited the Church of the Holy Sepulcher, called the *kanîsah al-kumâmah*, "the Church of the Dungheap" (*kumâmah* being a play on the Arabic *kuyâmah*, which is the exact translation of the Greek *anastasis*, "resurrection") searching for the Sanctuary of David. The patriarch of the city attempted to identify the Church of the Holy Sepulcher with the Sanctuary of David, and the Caliph replied, "You are lying, for the Apostle described to me the Sanctuary of David and this is not it." See Guy Le Strange, *Palestine under the Moslems: A Description of Syria and the Holy Land from A.D. 650–1500* (1890; rpt. Beirut: Khayats, 1965), 141, and Peters, *Jerusalem*, 187–89. Also, Peters cites the text of Saladin's rededication inscription (*Jerusalem*, 356–57).

26. Cust, *Status Quo in the Holy Places*, 16.

27. Cust, *Status Quo in the Holy Places*, 23–26.

28. Cust, *Status Quo in the Holy Places*, 26. For a precise description of the Armenian claims to the Holy Places in the Church of the Holy Sepulcher, see Kevork Hintlian, *History of the Armenians in the Holy Land* (Jerusalem: St. James Press, 1976), esp. 40–42.

29. Daniel Rossing, personal interview, 25 January 1984.

30. Cust, *Status Quo in the Holy Places*, 30–33, describes how the British sought verification of trust-deeds for the Deir es-Sultan, which, according to the Ethiopians in Jerusalem, were on deposit in Addis Ababa. When the consul-general in Addis Ababa attempted to find them, he discovered that they were formerly in the possession of a Russian who was willing to sell them only at a very high price. Further, contradictory evidence was given to the British that the properties of the Deir es-Sultan had been sold to the Copts through the Orthodox Synod of Jerusalem. He concludes that "at all events, it is clear that the Regent Ras Taffari gave little credence to the fable of the deeds, and correspondingly small encouragement to the intrigues on their account" (33).

31. Meron Benvenisti, *Jerusalem: The Torn City* (Jerusalem: Isratypset, 1976), 275.

32. Daniel Rossing, personal interview, 25 January 1984.

33. Israel Lippel, personal interview, 15 May 1984. Naomi Teasdale, who represents the municipality of Jerusalem on the ministerial committee which was charged with the responsibility of resolving the case, articulated the issue somewhat differently. She said, "The conflict is of three hundred years' duration. Documents don't exist. No one knows to whom these two chapels actually belong. . . . Of course, it is a political matter because one cannot decide on the merits of the case. You give priority to whatever serves your interests. For a long time we had reasons to maintain the present situation. Although from time to time there is pressure from Egypt to give it to the Copts, especially from Boutros-Gali, who is a Copt himself. But the same reasons for not taking it from the Ethiopians are still maintained" (personal interview on 20 June 1984).

34. Archbishop Anba Basilios, personal interview, 13 June 1984.

35. "Egypt Asks Return of Coptic Section in Holy Sepulchre," *Jerusalem Post*, 10 June 1979, and "Government Seen Leaning Towards Copts in Jerusalem Church Dispute," *Jerusalem Post*, 22 November 1979.

36. Benny Morris, "Nothing Has Been Done to Solve Dispute over Holy Sepulchre," *Jerusalem Post*, 16 November 1986.

37. Haim Shapiro, "Ethiopian Jews Take Stand Against Copts in Holy Sepulchre Dispute," *Jerusalem Post*, 5 May 1986.

38. The major study of this ritual remains G. Klameth, *Das Karsamstagsfeuerwunder der heiligen Grabeskirche*, Studien und Mitteilungen aus dem kirchengeschichtlichen Seminar der theologischen Fakultät der k.k. Universität in Wien 13 (1915). Other important contributions are E. W. Hopkins, "The Cult of Fire in Christianity," in *Oriental Studies in Honour of Cursetji Erachji Pavry*, ed. J. D. C. Pavry (London: Oxford University Press, 1933), 142–50, and B. McGinn, "*Inter Sancti Sepulchri:* The Piety of the First Crusaders," in *The Walter Prescott Webb Memorial Lectures: Essays on Medieval Civilization*, ed. B. K. Lackner and K. R. Philp (Austin: University of Texas Press, 1978), 33–71.

39. Bartolph of Nangis, *Gesta Francorum*, in H. Hagenmeyer, ed., *Recueil des*

*historiens des croisades: Historiens occidentaux* (Paris: Publications Académie des Inscriptions et Belles Lettres, 1895) 3: 525.

40. Balderic of Dol, *Recueil des historiens des croisades* 4: 13.

41. Julian Morgenstern, *The Fire upon the Altar* (Leiden: E. J. Brill, 1963), 118.

42. John Wilkinson, ed and trans., *Egeria's Travels to the Holy Land* (Jerusalem and Warminister: Ariel Publishing House and Aris and Phillips, 1981), 123–26. See also Gabriel Bertoniere, *The Easter Vigil* (Rome: Pontifical Institute of Oriental Studies, 1972), 27–28.

43. John Wilkinson, *Jerusalem Pilgrims Before the Crusades* (Warminster: Aris and Phillips, 1977), 34, 119, 129.

44. For discussions of this process in pilgrimage, see Alphonse Dupront, "Pèlerinage et lieux sacré," in *Mélanges en l'honneur de Fernand Braudel*, vol. 2, *Méthodologie de l'histoire et des sciences humaines* (Toulouse: Edouard Privat, Éditeur, 1973), 189–206; May Vieillard-Troiekouroff, *Les monuments religieux de la Gaule d'après les oeuvres de Grégoire de Tours* (Paris: Librairie Honoré Champion, 1976), esp. 383–90; Peter Brown, *Society and the Holy in Late Antiquity* (Berkeley and Los Angeles: University of California Press, 1982), esp. 222–50, and Patrick J. Geary, *Furta Sacra: Thefts of Relics in the Central Middle Ages* (Princeton: Princeton University Press, 1978). For a general account of pilgrimage to the Holy Land before and after the Crusades, see Steven Runciman, "The Pilgrimages to Palestine Before 1095," in Kenneth M. Setton, ed., *A History of the Crusades*, vol. 1, *The First Hundred Years*, ed. Marshall W. Baldwin (Madison: University of Wisconsin Press, 1969), 68–80, and Henry L. Savage, "Pilgrimages and Pilgrim Shrines in the Palestine and Syria after 1095," in Kenneth M. Setton, ed., *A History of the Crusades*, vol. 4, *The Art and Architecture of the Crusader States*, ed. H. W. Hazard (Madison: University of Wisconsin Press, 1977), 36–68. See also Pierre Maraval, *Lieux saints et pèlerinages d'Orient: Histoire et géographie, des origines à la conquête arabe* (Paris: Éditions du Cerf, 1985), esp. 183–92. See also F. E. Peters, *Jerusalem and Mecca: The Typology of the Holy City in the Near East* (New York and London: New York University Press, 1986), esp. 27–59.

45. Peters, *Jerusalem*, 263.

46. Wiedemann, "Zum Wunder des heiligen Feuers," *Zeitschrift des deutschen Palästinavereins* 40 (1917): 249, cited in Morgenstern, *Fire Upon the Altar*, 117.

47. Peters, *Jerusalem*, 264–65.

48. Kevork Hintlian, personal interview, 22 April 1983.

49. Loring M. Danforth, *The Death Rituals of Rural Greece*, with photographs by Alexander Tsiaras (Princeton: Princeton University Press, 1982), suggests that the dead are buried with either a handwoven shroud or a shroud purchased on pilgrimage in Jerusalem, along with candles from the Holy Fire ritual and icons of the Resurrection of Christ. Stephen Graham, *With the Russian Pilgrims to Jerusalem* (London, Edinburgh, and New York: Thomas Nelson and Sons, 1916), 241–42, records a similar custom among Russian Orthodox pilgrims. He writes that "hundreds of pilgrims produced their black death-caps filled with sweet scented cotton-wool, and then extinguished the candles in them. These death-caps embroidered with bright silver crosses they proposed to keep to their death days and wear in the grave, cotton-wool and all. Other pilgrims carefully preserved their sacred fire, and getting out of the mob as quickly as they could carry

it to the hostelry, protecting it from the wind with their open palms. Others, more provident, lit the wicks in their double lanterns." See Gregory Schopen, "Burial 'Ad Sanctos' and the Physical Presence of the Buddha in Early Indian Buddhism: A Study in the Archeology of Religions," *Religion* 17 (July 1987): 193–226, for a comparative study of burial and the use of relics in Buddhism. An entirely different strategy is employed by the Copts. One of the first visits in Jerusalem of these pilgrims is to a Coptic family where they are tattooed. The tattoo design for the men is a very rudimentary tomb with Jesus ascending from it, while the women have geometric designs done on their forearms. The tattoos of the Copts is a way for the pilgrims to demonstrate through their own bodies that they have completed the pilgrimage and have participated in the drama at the center of the world. See Louis Keimer, *Remarques sur le tatouage dans l'Egypte ancienne* (Cairo: L'Institut Francais d'Archaeologie Orientale, 1948), esp. 107–13, and John Carswell, *Coptic Tattoo Designs* (Beirut: American University of Beirut, 1958).

50. Morgenstern, *Fire Upon the Altar,* 117.

51. Peters, *Jerusalem,* 523–24.

52. Ibid., 553.

53. Cunningham Geikie, *The Holy Land and the Bible: A Book of Scripture Illustrations Gathered in Palestine* (New York: John R. Anderson, 1890), 296. One very interesting pilgrimage account which runs counter to these descriptions of the gullible pilgrims and the deceitful clergy is presented in Stephen Graham's trip with a group of Russian Orthodox pilgrims to Jerusalem in 1916. Graham points out that from the time that the pilgrims arrived at the port of Jaffe until they reached Jerusalem they were warned by the clergy that they should not take the fire ritual too seriously. Graham also preserves the Russian Orthodox tradition of the origins of the fire. He writes that in the first century the patriarch Narcissus found "the lamps in the Sepulchre short of oil, [he] went to the brook of Siloam for water and filled the vessels of the church therewith. Fire came down from heaven and ignited the water so that it burned like oil, and the illumination lasted throughout the Easter service. Every Easter Saturday since then, fire has appeared from heaven at the Sepulchre. The miracle is not a new conception. In the Old Testament days fire came down from heaven and consumed the agreeable sacrifices. The Sacred Fire of Holy Saturday is sent by God as a sign that the sacrifice of His Son has been acceptable to Him. Perhaps in its origin the miracle was a way for the fire-worshippers to pass over into Christianity without shock. It is even to-day a great pagan festival, and there are as many Moslems as Christians eager to light their lamps and candles from it on Holy Saturday afternoon" (*With the Russian Pilgrims to Jerusalem,* 237–38). Nathan Schur, "Itineraries by Pilgrims and Travelers as Source Material for the History of Palestine in the Ottoman Period," in *Palestine in the Late Ottoman Period: Political, Social, and Economic Transformation,* ed. D. Kushner (Jerusalem and Leiden: Yad Izhak Ben-Zvi and E. J. Brill, 1986), 382–401, writes under the heading "Holy Places" that "no other topic is covered in such detail in every single travel description as this one. I have seen the Tomb of Rachel mentioned by over 400 pilgrims and travelers and the Church of the Holy Sepulchre by about double this number. Most of them are simple repetitions but there also exist interesting

descriptions which are especially thorough or which cover the subject from an unusual angle. Curzon, in 1834, for instance gives a detailed account of the panic and ensuing loss of hundreds of lives that year in the Greek ceremony of the Holy Fire; Warren explains the mechanics of exactly how this fire was lighted; Sieber and Wotruba and others give an interesting account of actual battles between Greek, Franciscan, and Armenian monks" (392).

54. Charles Warren, *The Temple or the Tomb? Giving Further Evidence in Favor of the Authenticity of the Present Site of the Holy Sepulchre* (London: Bentley, 1880), 9–10. For an interesting dialogue on the origin of the fire, see Thomas A. Idinopulos, "Holy Fire in Jerusalem," *Christian Century,* 7 April 1982, 407–9, where the author is pressed to explain how "they do it." Idinopulos admits that the patriarch probably uses a cigarette lighter. His interlocutor then says, "You think the people know this?" Idinopulos responds, "I doubt it. But if they did, it wouldn't matter to them." The interlocutor ends the brief dialogue by saying, "Then the miracle is not the fire but their faith."

55. Bernard McGinn, "*Iter Sancti Sepulchri:* The Piety of the First Crusaders," 58 n. 24, argues that the miracle of the fire had fallen into disrepute in the thirteenth century and its practice was forbidden by a bull of Gregory IX in 1238, probably because of "financial abuses that had grown up about it."

56. For a general description of the Holy Saturday liturgy in the Western Church, see Alan W. Watts, *Myth and Ritual in Christianity* (Boston: Beacon, 1968), 170–205.

57. Jean Gaillard and William Busch, *A Liturgical Commentary—Holy Week* (Collegeville, Penn.: Liturgical Press of the Order of St. Benedict, 1954), 107–10.

58. O. B. Hardison, *Christian Rite and Christian Drama in the Middle Ages: Essays in the Origin and Early History of Modern Drama* (Baltimore: Johns Hopkins University Press, 1965), 146.

59. Francis X. Weiser, *Handbook of Christian Feasts and Customs* (New York: Harcourt, Brace, 1958), 58.

60. The Crusader façade originally was a double door; the eastern doorway was closed as part of the renovations after the fire of 1808. William Harvey, *The Church of the Holy Sepulchre, Jerusalem: Structural Survey—Final Report* (London: Oxford University Press, 1935), 24, proposed that this eastern doorway be opened as part of a larger plan to restore and to conserve the Church of the Holy Sepulcher during the British Mandate. Harvey's *Structural Survey of the Church of the Nativity, Bethlehem* (London: Oxford University Press, 1935) has the best architectural plans showing the conflicting claims in the Greek Orthodox and Latin grottoes below the superstructure of the church.

61. Two examples of petitions collected at the column in 1986 are the following:

> For the health of
> Martha Vasiliki
> Evangelia Georgios and their children
> Panagiota Stavros and their children
> Asimina Theophanis and their children
> Maria Paraskos and their children

Galias [or possibly Gazias] Ioannis and their children
Rodokleia Soterios and their children
and relatives
Ippokratio [hospital]
surgery ear
for the health, enlightenment and long healthy life
Christos
Eleni Soteriou
child Ioannis
Evangelia
Aristidis

62. See, for example, the important discussions of rituals at the graves of Muslim saints in Emile Dermenghem, *Le Culte des Saints dans l'islam maghrébin* (Paris: Gallimard, 1954), 121–34; the *nadr* in Muslim pilgrimages to the tombs of saints in Nowal Messiri, "The Sheikh Cult of Dahmit," in *Nubian Ceremonial Life: Studies in Islamic Syncretism and Cultural Change,* ed. J. G. Kennedy (Berkeley, Los Angeles, and Cairo: University of California Press and American University in Cairo Press, 1978), 61–103; Rudolf Kriss and Hubert Kriss-Heinrich, *Volksglaube im Bereich des Islam,* esp. vol. 1, *Wallfahrtswesen und Heiligenverehrun* (Wiesbaden: Otto Harrossowitz, 1960); and Issachar Ben-Ami's discussion of visiting the graves of saints during *hillulot* in *Saint Veneration among the Jews in Morocco* (Jerusalem: Magnes Press of the Hebrew University of Jerusalem, 1984), esp. 85–98 (Hebrew). It is very common for Ashkenazic Jews to leave notes at sacred sites such as the Western Wall of the Temple Mount or at the graves of particularly powerful rabbis such as the Ari (Isaac Luria) or Moshe Cordovero in the Old Cemetery of Safed. However, Sephardic and Oriental Jews have adopted the Muslim practice of tying rags to the doors of the tombs of rabbis or to the iron enclosures surrounding their graves, as at the tomb of Rashbi (Shimon bar Yohai) and his son, Eliezer, at Meron. These rags play the same function as the notes left by the Greek Orthodox pilgrims at the Church of the Holy Sepulcher. See Tewfik Canaan, *Mohammedan Saints and Sanctuaries in Palestine* (1927; rpt. Jerusalem: Ariel, n.d.), esp. 103–6.

63. For example, Robert Curzon, *Visits to the Monasteries in the Levant* (1849; rpt. London: Arthur Barker, 1955), 193, estimated 17,000 pilgrims in 1834; James Finn, *Stirring Times or Records from Jerusalem Consular Chronicles of 1853 to 1856* (London: C. Kegan Paul, 1878) 2: 457, estimated eight thousand; Conder, *Tent Work in Palestine* 1: 341, estimated that two thousand people were crowded under the rotunda and ten thousand in all in 1873 and 1875; H. Rider Haggard, *A Winter Pilgrimage: Being an Account of Travels Through Palestine, Italy and the Island of Cyprus, Accomplished in the Year 1900* (London: Green and Company, 1901), 323, estimated six thousand.

64. Cust, *Status Quo in the Holy Places,* 67.

65. Ibid.

66. Ibid. Conder, *Tent Work in Palestine* 1: 339, described in 1873 the difficulties in maintaining the separation between the communities: "Nothing was more remarkable than the patience of the soldiery who had to keep order. The Greeks gave most trouble, and in 1873 the feeling evinced by them was very

bitter, because their favourite Patriarch had just been deposed. A very fat old colonel walked up and down, armed with a murderous *kurbaj,* or whip of hippopotamus hide; then he would sit on the floor and look at the crowd, sometimes putting an additional big soldier at a weak point in the line. . . . Sometimes the crowd became dangerous, and hissed. As fast as his legs could carry him, the Colonel rushed to the spot, and down came the whip; then where a moment before were angry faces and arms stretched out with clenched fists, there was suddenly nothing but a flat surface of backs, or a few arms raised to protect the heads. Yet on the whole it was a good-natured crowd, and the soldiers were wonderfully patient. Little incidents of a comic nature occurred, and an Arab chief, who tried to swagger down the lane, found his head-shawl off and far away in a moment, tossed from hand to hand amid shouts of laughter."

67. The difficulties of maintaining the separation between the communities is dramatically seen in Charles Harbutt's photograph of the Holy Fire ritual in Cornell Capa, ed., *Israel/The Reality: People, Places, Events in Memorable Photographs* (New York: Jewish Museum and World Publishing, 1969), n. p.

68. Meron Benvenisti, *Jerusalem: The Torn City* (Jerusalem: Isratypset, 1976), 273.

69. Curzon, *Visits to the Monasteries in the Levant,* 192–93.

70. Conder, *Tent Work in Palestine* 1: 338–39, recorded the following cheers: "This is the tomb of our Lord!" "God help the Sultan!" "O Jew, O Jews! Your feast is a feast of apes!" "The Christ is given us, with his blood he bought us. We celebrate the day and the Jews bewail!" and "The seventh is the fire and our feast, and this is the tomb of our Lord!"

71. *Jerusalem,* 273.

72. Reverend John Lundblad, pastor, Lutheran Church of the Redeemer, personal interview, 16 February 1984.

73. The so-called White Russian Orthodox church did not acknowledge the Moscow Patriarchate after the Russian Revolution in 1917 and has historically been composed of Russian Orthodox peoples outside of Russian and is anti-Soviet in its stance. The Red Russian Orthodox church, the Orthodox church within Russia and the former Soviet Union, acknowledges the Moscow Patriarchate. Immediately after the 1948 War of Independence, the Red Russian church established itself within the pre-1967 borders of Israel. The State of Israel recognized that church as the official Russian Orthodox church within Israel. The Red Russian church is recognized by the Christian world, is a member of the World Council of Churches, and has been recognized by the Greek Orthodox Community of Jerusalem since shortly after the Russian Revolution. However, the White Russian Orthodox church was given recognition by the Jordanians after 1948, and the vast land holdings of the Russian Orthodox church on the other side of the armistice line fell into their hands. After 1967 both groups found themselves within the jurisdiction of the State of Israel and particularly in Jerusalem.

74. Cust, *Status Quo in the Holy Places,* 69.

75. A. P. Stanley, *Sinai and Palestine in Connection with Their History* (London, 1856), cited in Elias Canetti, *Crowds and Power* (Middlesex: Penguin, 1973), 188. See the important discussions of Stanley in Yehoshua Ben-Arieh, *The Rediscovery*

*of the Holy Land in the Nineteenth Century* (Jerusalem: Magnes Press of the Hebrew University and the Israel Exploration Society, 1979), esp. 153–56, and Naomi Shepherd, *The Zealous Intruders: The Western Rediscovery of Palestine* (San Francisco: Harper and Row, 1987), esp. 94–96.

76. Neophitos of Cyprus, *Extracts from Annals of Palestine, 1821–1841*, trans. S. N. Spyridon (1938; rpt. Jerusalem: Ariel, 1981), 37–38.

77. Curzon, *Visits to the Monasteries of the Levant*, 197.

78. James Finn, *Stirring Times or Records from Jerusalem Consular Chronicles of 1853–1856* (London: C. Kegan Paul, 1878) 2: 458–60.

79. Elias Canetti, *Crowds and Power*, 191, 192.

80. For example, see Fouad Ajami, *The Vanished Imam: Musa al Sadr and the Shia of Lebanon* (Ithaca: Cornell University Press, 1986), esp. 151, where the author uses Canetti's "lamenting pack" to understand the nature of Shia Islam in general and the transformation of Lebanese Shi'ites around the figure of Musa al-Sadr.

81. See especially Victor Turner, *The Ritual Process: Structure and Anti-Structure* (Chicago: Aldine, 1969), and Turner, "The Metaphors of Anti-Structure," in his *Dramas, Fields, and Metaphors: Symbolic Action in Human Society* (Ithaca: Cornell University Press, 1974), 272–99.

82. John Eade and Michael J. Sallnow, eds., *Contesting the Sacred: The Anthropology of Christian Pilgrimage* (London and New York: Routledge, 1991), 5.

83. Glenn Bowman, "Christian Ideology and the Image of a Holy Land: The Place of Jerusalem Pilgrimage in Various Christianities," in Eade and Sallnow, *Contesting the Sacred*, 120.

84. Eade and Sallnow, *Contesting the Sacred*, 8–9.

85. Jonathan Z. Smith, *Map Is Not Territory: Studies in the History of Religions* (Leiden: E. J. Brill, 1978), 291.

86. Jonathan Z. Smith, *Imagining Religion: From Babylon to Jonestown* (Chicago: University of Chicago Press, 1982), 52.

87. Jonathan Z. Smith, *To Take Place: Toward Theory in Ritual* (Chicago: University of Chicago Press, 1987), 103.

88. David Harvey, "Monument and Myth: The Building of the Basilica of the Sacred Heart," in his *Consciousness and the Urban Experience: Studies in the History and Theory of Capitalist Urbanization* (Baltimore: Johns Hopkins University Press, 1985), 221–50.

89. Bishop Gureg Kapikian, Principal of St. Tarkmanchatz School, personal interview, 1 May 1984.

# SEVEN

# Redesigning Nature:
# John Constable and the Landscape
# of Enclosure

*Ann Bermingham*

Recent studies of British landscape painting attempt to understand it in terms of the cultural politics of the eighteenth and nineteenth centuries.[1] As this research has advanced beyond the rudimentary exercise of placing the work of art "in its social context," it has come to examine the power of form to generate meaning and has resulted in an interdisciplinary study of problems having to do with the relationship of representational practices to the social and psychological processes of signification. Rather than serving as mere examples or reflections of larger cultural ideologies, visual images are studied as one of the means through which these meanings are produced and transformed. Analyzing a work of art thus involves exposing its power to construct meaning and to proliferate the cultural values that it shapes and that traditional readings, even some of the social contextual kind, uncritically reiterate. This type of analysis abandons the traditional division of the work of art into discrete categories of style and content in favor of an analysis of it as a sign, text, or discourse which is inflected by class, gender, and ethnicity and entangled with cultural practices such as politics, science, religion, economy, and education.

This attention to the cultural meaning and signification of visual images has found one of its richest subjects in landscape painting. Since its establishment in the early seventeenth century as a distinct genre of painting, landscape has been seen to engage directly the problematics of realism. This view has led some art historians, such as Sir Ernst Gombrich, to propose that landscape painting is a mimetic operation whose purpose has been to mirror the real world and to develop and refine compositional schemata which enable this process of reflection.[2] Gombrich's theory was developed in opposition to an older argument which described landscape painting as the artist's heroic struggle to "see nature" free from any formal, artistic schemata so as to reproduce it with truth and objectivity. While opposed, the effect of both positions has been the same: that is, to isolate the process of landscape painting from anything that might impinge on the individual artist's act of manipulating form or perceiving nature, and ultimately (paradoxically) to make the image itself secondary to the artist's hermetic encounter with art and nature. Restoring landscape to its status as cultural sign has meant dismantling these accounts of landscape's realism by analyzing what is theoretically at stake in them.[3] In particular, it has meant attending to the way in which landscape painting naturalizes all its cultural signs, making the products of culture appear to be the work of nature and, in turn, seeing this "naturalization" as an ideological and semiotic process, one which is repeated and reaffirmed in traditional art historical accounts of landscape painting.[4]

My own work on landscape painting and its relationship to ideology is indebted to the work of Louis Althusser and Roland Barthes. Althusser defines ideology as "the imaginary relationship of individuals to their real conditions of existence."[5] As such, ideology is a series of signifying practices embedded in cultural institutions that constitute human beings as social subjects. These practices produce the lived relations that connect individuals to the society at large. Ideology is not specifically "false consciousness" but rather all the modalities and beliefs through which the consciousness of one's self as a subject come to be ordered. Unlike Althusser, I do not exempt science from ideology, nor do I think that ideology is finally determined by the economic. What I value in Althusser's notion is his insistence on the subject's imaginary relation to the lived world. This imaginary relationship appears to me to be historically and culturally constructed, while at the same time the experience of it is wholly personal, that is, subjective. Such an understanding of ideology allows one to examine pictorial art as the representational work of culture as it is experienced by individuals (both artists and viewers). As ideological operations, works of art can thus be seen to reference both culture and individual experience.

Naturalization, first identified by Marx as a key ideological maneuver of bourgeois capitalism and described by Barthes as a semiotic system of bourgeois realism, is a process whereby cultural institutions and representations are coded as "natural."[6] In this sense it is a representational mode common to both the social and the artistic symbolic order. In addition, naturalization allows us to explore the way in which concrete individuals are, to use Althusser's term, *interpellated* as subjects and the way subjects are interpellated as individuals.[7] For by coding society's institutional and representational practices as "natural," naturalization sets up a structure whereby individuals can recognize themselves as subjects only in relation to these practices and their naturalness. Thus, each individual's own subjectivity becomes conditioned on naturalization's symbolic construction of the social order. As an ideological and semiotic process, naturalization maps individual experience onto the broader social plane and establishes an illusory mutuality of essence and objective between them. In bourgeois democracies it attempts to erase the contradiction between individual desire and the common social good. In this essay I undertake to describe how naturalization might be seen to organize individual artistic practice and vision, and how this process in turn produces artistic representations that appear to be both highly individual while supporting a shared cultural ideal of the natural. In doing so, I will focus on the way in which pictorial naturalization constructs landscape as a particular experience of space and time.

As a semiotic mode of cultural representation, naturalization in the late eighteenth and early nineteenth centuries was tied to bourgeois society's need to legitimate its new economic power by coding it as "natural" and to extend that power by virtue of "natural right" to political power. In the early industrial period almost all change in Britain—social, political, economic—was accommodated under the rubrics of "nature" and "naturalness." This is particularly true of the transformation of the landscape through enclosure, a process which altered the face of the countryside. Throughout the eighteenth century, parliamentary bills of enclosure enabled landowners to acquire land which had once been held in common or waste land previously thought unsuitable for cultivation. Old commons and wastes were divided into fields that were fenced or hedged.[8] The purpose of enclosure was to augment agricultural production by putting more land under cultivation. Coupled with the new scientific and mechanical improvements in farming, enclosure vastly increased agricultural yield, making England the most agriculturally productive country in the world.

While enclosure was carried out by landowners—usually wealthy and sometimes aristocratic—the impetus for enclosure, the desire to improve the landscape and to increase its yield, reflects bourgeois market values.[9] The older aristocratic, paternalistic values of rural society were often both in cooperation and in conflict with those of enclosure, and the tensions of this situation generated a new kind of "landscape," an image of rural nature full of ambivalent meanings and ambiguities. As large portions of the countryside were altered by economy, the landscape of Britain was pictured in painting and gardening as an image of all that was stable and unchanging. Rather than expose or hide the results of enclosure, the "nature" embodied in British landscape painting and gardening neutralizes them by making them appear to be a part of nature itself.[10] In painting, naturalization coincided with a growing pictorial preoccupation with the way things "really look." The empirical approach to painting changed the way in which space and time were depicted in landscape. Problems of space were no longer formulated simply in terms of abstract generalities (the formulaic ordering of the composition into foregrounds, distances, and second distances) but also in terms of the individual appearances of a particular locale. The depiction of this place was, in turn, rendered instantaneously as an individual moment seen under a set of specific atmospheric conditions.

The paradox is that despite their increasing pictorial naturalism, landscape paintings' descriptions of space and time resulted in images that through their very claims to objective visual truth offered themselves as universal and universalizing, "natural" perceptions. Such images close off critical analysis through the power of their claim to a univocal discourse, the description of the way things "really are." Nowhere is the "universality" which naturalization imposes on culture and history and which the naturalistic style of landscape painting reproduces as optical truth more evident than in the landscape paintings of John Constable (1776–1837). Constable's landscapes both inscribe and obscure the naturalization of political economy and its power to reorder the experience of space and historical time.

Like his great contemporary J. M. W. Turner (1775–1851), Constable holds a central and indisputable place in the history of British landscape painting. While Turner is often celebrated as the preeminent painter of sublime, Continental scenery, Constable, who never left England, is loved as the "portraitist of England," the painter of English clouds and English weather—a John Bull in a painter's smock. The importance of Constable's reputation as the quintessential English painter was made clear to me when I visited his father's mill at Flatford, the scene of his most famous painting, the *Hay Wain* (figure 11). The actual site of the *Hay Wain* looks something like the photograph I took that day (figure 12). To take the picture, I positioned myself where I thought Constable must have stood in making his view, that is, a little to the left of the landing of the mill. Standing there and gazing across the inlet to what in Constable's day had been the farmer Willy Lott's cottage on the opposite bank, I became aware of the sound of a bus laboring down the hill that connected the Flatford area to the main highway. Grinding to a halt, it discharged what turned out to be the first of the day's innumerable waves of English tourists who, like me, had come to see "Constable Country."

I had noticed earlier a souvenir stand selling postcards and guide-

Figure 11. John Constable, *The Hay Wain*, 1821; oil on canvas, 51¼ × 73 inches (130.5 × 185.5 centimeters). London, The National Gallery.

Figure 12.  Willy Lott's cottage from Flatford Mill. Author's photograph.

books along with commemorative mugs and small ceramic models of Willy Lott's cottage. I had noted, too, that a cottage by the canal bridge, depicted by Constable in his *View on the Stour* of 1822, was now a National Trust tea room.[11] Jostled by tourists anxious to reproduce a version of the *Hay Wain* through the lenses of their cameras just as I had done only a moment before, I was stunned to see how powerfully Constable's own intimate biographical history and personal association with this particular landscape view had become a matter of public, even national, significance. I couldn't imagine such a thing happening in the United States; similar mass visits to the site of Thomas Cole's *Oxbow* or Frederick Church's *Niagara* in order to recover the artist's particular encounter with a specific landscape view seem unlikely, even inconceivable. Our sites of public pilgrimage are not formed or circumscribed by an individual artist's personal vision but by the obviously iconic and stylized expressions of national identity: the Lincoln Memorial, the Statue of Liberty, the Liberty Bell. In the case of the *Hay Wain*, the significance of the view painted by Constable had come to exceed its own history, as well as the private intentions of the artist or any art-historical discussions of his work. In representing a particular view from Constable's father's mill, the *Hay Wain* had come to connote all that is understood experientially and artistically by the term "English landscape"; moreover, at some deeper level it had come to stand for "Englishness" and perhaps even for England itself. At the scene of the *Hay Wain* I felt that I was in the presence of a "myth," a cultural representation that drew its strength from—and at the same time transcended—the specificity of the actual site.[12] Standing on the millbank surrounded by English tourists, I found myself participating in some powerful yet obscure ritual of national bonding.[13]

Constable was born the son of a prosperous miller in the Stour River valley. The river, which forms the county line between Suffolk and Essex, had been canalized in the eighteenth century to make it suitable for the transportation of agricultural produce to London. The rural landscape Constable painted in the early decades of the nineteenth century had, in the previous century, been economically transformed by the agrarian and industrial capitalism. About a year before John was born, the Constables moved from Flatford to a large Georgian brick house on the main street of the town of East Bergholt in Suffolk. His father, Golding, owned mills and warehouses at Flatford and Dedham and a windmill on the East Bergholt commons. On the evidence of the 1817 enclosure map for the region he appears to have been the fourth largest landholder in East Bergholt. The grain that Golding milled was shipped by barge down the Stour River to Mistly Harbor and was transported from there in one of his sailing ships to London, where it was traded on the corn exchange. In addition to trading wheat, Golding also traded coal, which he stored in a yard at Brantham. A fellow miller, John Croiser of Maldon Essex, noted in 1785 that "Mr. Constable, a man of fortune and a miller, has a very elegant house in the street and lives in the style of a country squire." [14] A similar observation was made by Francis Shoberl in his 1813 tour of England and Wales: "East Bergholt is a considerable village. . . . The residences of the rector, Dr. Rhudde, Peter Godfrey, Esq., Mrs. Roberts and Golding Constable, Esq., give this place an appearance far superior to that of most villages." [15] If today the region can be called "Constable Country," it is only because in some respects it has always been just that.

Constable's identification with the Stour Valley was already operational in his lifetime. Writing to his friend David Lucas in 1832, the artist told him of a conversation that had taken place with a fellow passenger in a coach ride from London to East Bergholt: "In passing through the valley about Dedham one of them remarked to me—on my saying it was beautiful—'Yes Sir—this is Constable's country!' I then told him who I was lest he should spoil it." [16] After Constable's death in 1837, his identification with the region continued and was assisted by publication of Charles Leslie's popular biography of the artist (1842). Leslie's biography was the first of many to propose that Constable's art originated in a deep, abiding reverence for the landscape of his youth. In 1893 Cooks added "A Visit to Constable's Country" to their list of tours, and the Great Eastern Railway Company arranged tours of the area from Colchester. [17] Throughout the nineteenth century, tour books of the region continually linked Constable to the Stour Valley. John Murray's *Handbook for Essex, Suffolk, Norfolk, and Cambridgeshire* is typical in this respect. In discussing the scenery of Suffolk, the author remarks that it "is not to be ranked with that of the bolder and more varied English counties. It has, nevertheless, its own distinctive charm and character. Its softer features are reflected very faithfully in many of Constable's best pictures." [18] When Murray's tourist enters Constable's country, he is greeted with the appropriate quotations from Constable's letters which Leslie had published in his biography. Thus, in the paragraph about the town and church of East Bergholt the famous passage from Constable's letter to his friend John Fisher is quoted: "I should paint my own places best; painting is but another word for feeling, and I associate 'my careless boyhood' with all that lies on the banks of the Stour; those scenes made me a painter, and I am grateful." [19] On Constable's own account (one which art historians have never ceased to retell) the Stour Valley called his art into being; preempting culture and society, it becomes the exclusive origin and object of Constable's art.

From the *Hay Wain* one would never suspect that the scene of Willy

Figure 13. Flatford Mill from Willy Lott's cottage. Author's photograph.

Lott's cottage, which looks so picturesquely secluded in the painting, was just a stone's throw away from a busy mill. The opposite view taken from the front door of the cottage is of Golding's mill at Flatford (figure 13). The spatial proximity between the father's economic intervention in the landscape and the son's naturalization of this process into a depiction of a rural harvest scene is striking. Situated in the center of a circular composition, the empty hay wain becomes a pivot around which the rest of the compositional elements are arranged—the curved riverbank to the left, the dog (whose back follows the line of the bank), Willy Lott's cottage, the isolated tree, the hay field, the clump of reeds with the fisherman and his boat, and finally the posts in the right foreground. The hay wain's presence in the composition is central but, in terms of the narrative events depicted in the painting, "unmotivated." It is difficult to explain why an empty hay cart would be making its way through what looks like a pond. Once, however, we know that our view is from the landing of Flatford Mill, the composition and its activity become clear. The "flat ford" behind the mill provided a passage through the river; here carts crossed the stream, making their way from the fields to the mill or to the barns behind it. One may presume that the hay wain has just delivered a load of hay and is returning to the distant field to be refilled by the mowers.[20]

The landscape is a closed, hermetic system of activity as surely as it is a visually closed and circular composition. Flatford Mill is both present in and absent from the *Hay Wain*. As the viewpoint from which the scene is surveyed, it is the organizing perspective of the painting, the one that literally forms and informs the composition. Nevertheless, Flatford Mill is a subject about which the painting falls silent. The painting simultaneously denies and asserts the presence of commerce in the landscape and the power of commerce to organize the landscape to its ends. It is a perspective that both evokes and obscures its literal and ideological point of view. In the face of the painting's "naturalness," it is difficult to realize that what we see from the landing at Flatford is not nature but the naturalized sphere of Golding's economic influence.

Every social order tends to produce in different ways and to different ends the naturalization of its own arbitrariness.[21] Naturalization is a representational process whereby nature is redefined so that it mirrors society and society is redefined in terms of this new nature. As the social order changes, so too does the image of nature that is its supposed mirror. We can track this social refashioning of nature in a comparison of two paintings of country estates: the anonymous *Bifrons Park, Kent* (1700–1765), done about 1745 (figure 14), and Constable's 1816 painting

Figure 14. British school, eighteenth century (formerly attributed to John Wooton and to Jan Siberechts), *Bifrons Park, Kent*, c. 1705–1710; oil on canvas, 61½ × 91½ inches (86.8 × 132.5 centimeters). New Haven, Yale Center for Brit-

Figure 15. John Constable, *Wivenhoe Park, Essex*, 1816; oil on canvas, 22¹/₈ × 39⁷/₈ inches (56.1 × 101.2 centimeters). Washington, D.C., National Gallery of Art, Widner Collection.

of *Wivenhoe Park* (figure 15). In the painting of Bifrons Park we see a country estate surrounded by walled formal gardens in the Dutch style popular at the end of the seventeenth century. The country outside the walls is divided into small hedged fields, and these are surrounded by a wild-looking landscape. Constable's landscape represents the country seat of General F. Slater Rebow near Colchester in Essex. In it we see a red brick Georgian house through a break in the trees at the crest of the hill. The house is totally subsumed into a bucolic agrarian landscape in which cows graze by the side of a river where fishermen haul their nets. Pressed as to which landscape looks the more "natural," we would be tempted to answer "Constable's," even though in reality it is as artificial as the other and the landscape that it depicts was as elaborately contrived as the Dutch garden in *Bifrons Park*.

Wivenhoe Park was designed to look natural, that is, to be an illusion of nature rather than nature itself. As a social construct it has a historical time and date. The kind of garden that we see in Constable's *Wivenhoe Park* was developed by Lancelot "Capability" Brown (1716–1783) in the 1760s. It replaced the smaller emblematic gardens of the first half of the century (such as Alexander Pope's garden at Twickenham), which had been characterized by circuit walks, pavilions, ruins, and grottos, with an expansive, naturally planted and designed landscape that was its own ornament. In the view of Bifrons Park the extent of the human agrarian intervention into nature is evident. The garden and the fields are sharply set off from the rest of the landscape, which still appears unimproved. In the second half of the century, as the real landscape became more regularized with its wastes and commons drained and hedged, the landscape garden became increasingly natural-looking. One of the results of extensive parliamentary enclosure was that by the time Constable was painting *Wivenhoe Park*, nature and the natural-looking landscape had taken refuge *inside* the garden.

The size of these gardens was a direct result of enclosure. Because of the vast amount of new land acquired through enclosure and given over to agriculture, a landowner such as General Rebow could afford to have an extensive garden, particularly when a portion of it was turned over to pasturage and the growing of timber. Whereas the formal garden such as we see in *Bifrons Park* was limited in its size and occupied a conspicuously ideal middle ground between the agricultural landscape and the unimproved landscape, natural-looking landscape gardens, such as Wivenhoe Park, were extensive and tended to collapse the distinction between nature and agriculture, becoming idealized, pastoral versions of both. With its livestock, fisheries, and woods, Wivenhoe Park presents both a timeless and modern image of agriculture. The modern improvements of pasturage and timber growing and the creation of ponds stocked with fish are subsumed into an image that suggests the classic Virgilian georgic. Such gardens created an ambiguous signification whereby the present became a version of the past and the past of the present. Similarly, in these gardens, with their naturalized plantings and earthworks, nature became the sign of property and property became the sign of nature. In short, what was new and artificial presented itself under the guise of the established and natural. Thus, the economic transformation of nature came to stand for nature itself, and this "nature" in turn was able to legitimate the new economic order.

As Gombrich points out in his discussion of *Wivenhoe Park* in *Art and Illusion*, Constable went against the grain of the earlier topographical tradition of depicting country houses, which had been characterized by a bird's-eye view of the estate—something more along the lines of the *Bifrons Park* composition—clearly showing its buildings, boundaries, and enclosures; instead, Constable focused more attention on the natural-looking landscape than on the house.[22] The formula Constable used was one that he had already employed (in 1809) when painting another country house, Malvern Hall.[23] This compositional solution is not unique to Constable; it can also be found in many of the country-house paintings of the second half of the eighteenth century, and ultimately it derives from seventeenth-century Italianate landscapes. The significance of this compositional approach to country-house painting goes beyond Gombrich's discussion of its local importance for Constable's developing naturalism. What is crucial is that it detached the genre from its origins in mapmaking and oriented it toward landscape painting proper. In doing so, it minimized the signs of property and ownership that had been the basic rational of the topographical tradition. It is not that *Wivenhoe Park* ceases to be a depiction of property but rather that these signs of ownership—the house and deer house, for instance—are so integrated into the landscape as to appear to be part of its natural order. Combined with Constable's naturalistic approach, this composition reconfirms at the level of pictorial style an aspect of the ideological meaning and function of the landscape garden itself.


Constable's scenes have empirical authenticity because they present a way of being in the world as a way of seeing the world; that is, they posit the point of view of a particular subject position as an objective optical truth. One of the most important critical tasks naturalism sets for the art historian is to reveal how it assumes certain cultural attitudes toward representation which are overdetermined—whether consciously or unconsciously, ambivalently or unambivalently—by questions of gender, ethnicity, and class. Dismantling the naturalness of naturalism involves a reassessment of the representational strategies that formulate and assist its claims to empirical objectivity: specifically it means analyzing the formal techniques of picture making which reinforce naturalism's universalizing vision. This approach can mean, for instance, coming to terms with the ideological uses and consequences of the change that came about in painting between the sixteenth and eighteenth centuries from a spatial system of linear perspective to an optical system of atmospheric and tactile naturalism. By the nineteenth century the space of the painting was no longer plotted on an ideal and even mathematically abstract grid; rather, it was designed according to the way it appeared to the eye or was reflected on the ground glass of a camera obscura. The optics of Newton and Locke eroded the study of linear perspective and replaced it with empiricism, with a system of optical relativity ever sensitive to the qualifications and contingencies of empirical vision. Thus, color and light, elements of painting which traditional academic discourse discredited because of their realistic effects and mutable character, preferring to them the ideal and stable principles of line, were eventually granted more attention precisely because of their power to influence and even change one's perception of a scene depending on the way they mutually interacted.[24] The great aesthetic debate in the early nineteenth century was over how responsive painting should be to the new science of empiricism—in other words, over how perceptual a painting should be.

A year before painting the *Hay Wain*, Constable had embarked on his famous series of cloud studies, the result of a growing preoccupation with light and atmosphere which, he felt, would give his work "a unity of effect." This unity of effect depends on showing a single moment in time, not as a classicist such as Gotthold Lessing would have it—that is, in terms of ideal abstraction of form from narrative—but in terms of a synthetic, illusionistic depiction of a specific time of day, light, and weather.[25] As Constable realized, the great difficulty with this naturalistic landscape style was that the individual details of the landscape (the descriptions of specific trees and shrubs, clouds, reflections, etc.) needed to be both individualized and subordinated. If they were ignored or generalized, the landscape would lose its empirical objectivity, and if they were asserted too forcefully and independently, they would rupture the perceptual unity of the scene. Constable's solution in the *Hay Wain* was to treat the landscape as the sum of its appearances, as a series of individual optical effects which exist in a state of contingency and interdependence. Their relatedness has to do with the fact that they are seen in a specific way, in a specific light, and under specific atmospheric conditions. The *Hay Wain*'s naturalism proposes that natural appearances are relative and mutable rather than absolute and unchanging, that their look depends on the conditions under which they are seen. The organizing principle of the painting's naturalism can be alternately described as either nature or human nature, that is, as either natural light or Constable's own perception of the scene.

The duality of this naturalism is largely the result of Constable's technique, that is, the sketchlike way in which he painted the *Hay Wain*. (I have discussed the importance of Constable's finish in conveying meaning in his art elsewhere and offer a summary of it here.)[26] In the 1820s Constable began to transpose the look of the preliminary oil sketch to the finished painting. Clearly this later finish differs from the smooth, almost transparent surfaces of earlier works such as *Wivenhoe Park*. The reasons for this change had to do with the associative properties of this finish, which Constable eventually wanted to incorporate into his larger, exhibition pieces. When we look at Constable's oil sketches, we are hard pressed to say whether what we are seeing is a record of emotion in the presence of the motif or a direct and rapid rendering alla prima of the transitory effects of light and atmosphere pervading the scene. The rough finish functions as evidence of both empirical observation and emotional response. The dual signification of his finish works to collapse the distinction between Constable and the landscape that he paints. In its most radical form it makes it impossible for us to decide which is being represented.[27] The visual and psychological effect conveyed by this encrusted finish is paradoxical: as the hypersensitive response to the fleeting appearances of light and atmosphere, it seems both immediate and tortuously labored. The surfaces of these paintings appear as poignant expressions of a passionate yearning for a natural transparency of style and the tangible evidence of its perpetual elusiveness.[28] In the end what one sees in the microcosmic instance of Constable's paint handling is not just a personal "style" but an ideological practice of conflating individual experience, desire, and power with the natural structure of the world. Within the larger context of history Constable's finish is a version of the same social order, manifest in places such as Wivenhoe Park, which attempted to see the results of the new, enclosed landscape as natural.

The *Hay Wain*'s insistence on the relativity of appearances is not an ideologically neutral position. Constable's naturalism contains assumptions about the order of the world that may be contextualized within the social practices and values of a certain class rather than within nature itself. We might begin by observing that the naturalism we find in the *Hay Wain* defines the act of perception as a mode of subordinating parts to a whole; in doing so, it privileges this form of visual synthesis by equating it with knowledge of the natural world. Constable himself wished to see his landscapes equated with natural philosophy. Addressing an audience at the Royal Society in 1836 he said, "Painting is a science, and should be pursued as an inquiry into the laws of nature. Why, then, may not landscape be considered as a branch of natural philosophy, of which pictures are but experiments?"[29] As a form of knowledge, the *Hay Wain*'s style makes our position as spectators superior to and disjunct from that of anyone represented in the painting—the field laborers, the hay wain's passengers, the washerwoman, or the fisherman in his boat. As outsiders we see in a way that those inside the painting cannot; moreover, this difference—and it was for Constable as well as his audience a class difference—is precisely the thing on which the realism of the painting relies. For the painting's spectators, our vision of the scene inscribes within it a vision of ourselves as not belonging to the world of the *Hay Wain*. Our exteriority is naturalized and hence legitimated as both objective nature and Constable's individual perception. The landscape and the rural society we see in it are composed of parts, parts which find their proper place only in a separate totalizing view—a view taken from Flatford mill, by the son of its owner.

   In this sense the *Hay Wain* is not about a rural harvest so much as it is about subjectivity and a specific subject position or class which is both represented and repressed in the *Hay Wain* as optical truth. However, insofar as class can be recovered in the painting, it is not a one-dimensional reality that the painting reflects but is always already a representation on which the painting reflects. It is class as Constable understood it, as he found it formulated in empiricist accounts of vision, as he reformulated it in the *Hay Wain,* and as we formulate it in looking at the painting. Throughout this essay I have been setting up parallels between naturalistic painting and semiotic and ideological processes of naturalization which I would now like to summarize. I have been attempting to equate the naturalistic style of landscape painting with the naturalization of bourgeois political economy. Both posit an originary "reality" or real nature which, in turn, the works of art or society reflect. Nevertheless, nature in and of itself is finally different from the works of art and society, and thus it can never be fully recovered or reconstituted by them. In Constable's art certain codes of representation—naturalistic light and brushwork, for instance—are intended to compensate for or overcome what is in fact the work's arbitrary relationship to the natural world. The example of Constable suggests that the development of naturalism in nineteenth-century landscape art is the first of many modernist strategies which anticipate and evade the potentially catastrophic social and cultural consequences of this arbitrariness.

   I wish to end by returning one last time to Constable, the *Hay Wain*, and Flatford Mill. Constable prided himself on never having left England, on being, as he called it, a "stay at home painter." If paintings like the *Hay Wain* are in some way quintessentially English, they are also, with their personal autographic finish and biographical overtones, quintessentially xenophobic. They say "home" in a way that resonates deeply for all of us, but perhaps especially so for a culture that secured its modern identity during the social upheavals of the Industrial Revolution in an attachment to a landscape that both denied and validated the new social order and to a "nature" that made what was alien seem familiar and what was unnatural seem natural. Paintings such as the *Hay Wain* and *Wivenhoe Park* continue to sustain their meanings by presenting aspects of a mythic past as fictionalized versions of the present. In doing so, they elude the concept and experience of historical time and transcend the sense of temporal and cultural difference. When this happens, Constable's country becomes "old England," which in turn becomes the "true England." The *Hay Wain* thrives on the myth of its own origin, an origin that the popular accounts of Constable's art seek in tours to Flatford, in Constable's correspondence, in photographs and postcards—in short, in all the critical and commercial enterprises that merely confirm the loss they are meant to recover. If the *Hay Wain* exists at all for us today it is as a sign, in the postmodernist sense, of all that perception and representation can neither measure nor contain.

## NOTES

1. This approach has developed from the work of Raymond Williams and E. P. Thompson. Recent examples would include John Barrell, *The Dark Side of the Landscape: The Rural Poor in English Painting, 1730–1840* (Cambridge: Cambridge University Press, 1980); Barrell, *The Political Theory of Painting from Reynolds to Hazlitt* (New Haven: Yale University Press, 1987); Michael Rosenthal, *Constable: The Painter and His Landscape* (New Haven: Yale University Press, 1983); David Solkin, *Richard Wilson: The Landscape of Reaction* (London: Tate Gallery Catalogue, 1982). I am grateful to Stephen Daniels, who read this essay and made helpful suggestions for its revision.

2. See Ernst Gombrich, *Art and Illusion: A Study in the Psychology of Pictorial Representation* (Princeton: Princeton University Press, 1956).

3. For a critique of Gombrich's position, see Norman Bryson, *Vision and Painting: The Logic of the Gaze* (New Haven: Yale University Press, 1983), 1–67.

4. For an account of how this new approach has affected studies of John Constable's landscapes, see my "Reading Constable," *Art History* 10 (March 1987): 38–58.

5. See my *Landscape and Ideology: The English Rustic Tradition, 1740–1860,* (Berkeley and Los Angeles: University of California Press, 1986). Specifically, Althusser's essay "Ideology and the State," in his *Essays on Ideology,* trans. Ben Brewster (London: Verso, 1976), is the basis for my own understanding of ideology.

6. Marx saw naturalization as an ideological and representational process whereby bourgeois society could express and ultimately universalize its relations and structures. In his critique of eighteenth-century political economy he exposed the popular Robinsonade, narratives of the isolated man who is posited as the product of nature and not history and whose relationship to the means of production is unmediated; such a figure is "as much of an absurdity as is the development of language without individuals living *together* and talking to each other" (*Grundrisse*, trans. Martin Nicolaus [New York: Vintage, 1973], 83–84). He substituted for it a notion of production as a social activity determined by concrete historical circumstances. Like the myths of political economy, modernist accounts of the history of art begin with the isolated figure of the artist and proceed to measure his or her genius in terms of ability to resist or oppose dominant culture. Barthes's analysis of naturalization in terms of the semiotics of realism is set forth in *S/Z: An Essay*, trans. Richard Miller (New York: Hill and Wang, 1974), and in *Mythologies*, trans. Annette Lavers (New York: Hill and Wang, 1957).

7. Althusser uses the term *interpellation* to describe the way in which individuals come to recognize themselves as subjects by identifying with a particular ideological representation of themselves. (See "Lenin and Philosophy," in his *Essays on Ideology*, 44–51.) Basically, he sees interpellation as a signifying process moving in one direction, from culture to the individual. I would propose that in the case of naturalization, not only individuals recognize themselves as subjects belonging to a particular kind of social order ordained by nature, but also in that they too partake of this same nature, they see the social order as an extension of their own individuality. It is this oscillating pattern that naturalization establishes that seems essential to bourgeois capitalist democracies if they are to reconcile individual desire and the will of the majority.

8. The expense of enclosure demanded a considerable outlay of capital. As a result, large landowners bought out smaller ones and farms of 20–30 acres disappeared, replaced by farms of 300–500 acres. Enclosure proceeded rapidly; a conservative estimate places the figures at 74,000 acres in the first half of the eighteenth century and 750,000 acres in the second half of the century. These figures do not include the most common form of enclosure, which was reached by private agreement among landowners. See W. E. Tate, *The English Village Community and the Enclosure Movements* (London: Gollancz, 1975), 365.

9. The question of "class" in the new agrarian economy of the eighteenth century is vexed by the fact that older patterns of wealth and landownership were destabilized by enclosure. Hence, the sorting out of the relative status and economic significance of the older class divisions which depended on landownership and the new social divisions which did not (tenant farmers, land agents, surveyors, commodities brokers and transporters, and so forth) is still debated by historians and sociologists. What is clear from the debates that enclosure provoked in the press and in Parliament is that it was perceived as a process allied to a developing urban, bourgeois market economy. For this reason enclosure was often initially opposed by old Tory landowners, for it threatened to replace the older paternalistic relationships between the rural landowning classes, tenant farmers, and laborers with what appeared to be new and purely economic ones. For extensive discussions of enclosure and its political, economic, and social di-

mensions, see J. D. Chambers and G. E. Mingay, *The Agricultural Revolution, 1750–1880* (London: Batsford, 1966); W. H. R. Cutler, *The Enclosure and Redistribution of Our Land* (Oxford: Oxford University Press, 1920); David Davis, *The Case of Labourers in Husbandry* (London, 1795); Frederick Morton Eden, *The State of the Poor* (London, 1795); J. L. Hammond and Barbara Hammond, *The Village Labourer, 1760–1830* (London: Longman, 1920); Gertrude Himmelfarb, *The Idea of Poverty: England in the Early Industrial Age* (New York: Knopf, 1984); G. E. Mingay, *English Landed Society in the Eighteenth Century* (London: Routledge and Kegan Paul, 1963); James Alfred Peacock, *Bread or Blood: A Study of the Agrarian Riots in East Anglia in 1816* (London: Gollancz, 1965); Thomas Ruggles, *A History of the Poor*, 2 vols. (London, 1795); Gilbert Slater, *The English Peasantry and the Enclosure of the Common Fields* (London: A. Constable, 1907); W. Smart, "Antecedents of the Corn Law of 1815," *English Historical Review* 24 (1909): 470–87; Tate, *English Village Community;* E. P. Thompson, *The Making of the English Working Class* (Harmondsworth: Penguin, 1977); F. M. L. Thompson, *English Landed Society in the Nineteenth Century* (London and Toronto: Routledge and Kegan Paul, 1963); Arthur Young, *Agriculture in Suffolk* (London, 1798); Arthur Young, ed., *The Annals of Agriculture*, 46 vols. (London, 1770–1813).

10. For an account of the naturalization of enclosure as it affected poetry, garden design, and landscape painting, see Raymond Williams, *The Country and the City* (London: Cambridge University Press, 1973); John Barrell, *Dark Side of the Landscape* and *The Idea of Landscape and the Sense of Place, 1730–1840: An Approach to the Poetry of John Clare* (Cambridge: Cambridge University Press, 1972); and my *Landscape and Ideology.*

11. The Flatford Mill area became the property of the National Trust in 1934. Willy Lott's cottage serves today as a field studies center.

12. In characterizing myth as a naturalized ideological representation, I am following Barthes formulation of myth as "depoliticized speech." See his *Mythologies,* 109–27.

13. The history of the painting is as follows: After being exhibited by Constable in 1821, the *Hay Wain* was bought by a Parisian art dealer, John Arrowsmith. It was taken to Paris and exhibited at the Salon of 1824, where it received the gold medal in landscape. It was subsequently sold to a private collector. In 1838, one year after Constable's death, it was acquired by Edmund Higginson and brought to England. In 1846 it was sold at Christie's for £378 to Thomas Rought. In 1866 it was bought for £1,365 by Henry Vaughan, who presented it to the National Gallery in 1886. The painting was engraved for the first time in 1884.

14. Quoted by Rosenthal, *Constable,* 8.

15. F. Shoberl, *The Beauties of England and Wales* (London, 1813) 14: 225.

16. Quoted in C. R. Leslie, *Memoirs of the Life of John Constable* (Ithaca: Cornell University Press, 1980), 213.

17. See Ian Fleming-Williams and Leslie Parris, *The Discovery of Constable* (London: Hamish Hamilton, 1984), 112.

18. John Murray, *Handbook for Essex, Suffolk, Norfolk, and Cambridgeshire,* 2d ed. (London, 1875), li–lii.

19. John Constable, *John Constable's Correspondence,* ed. R. B. Beckett (Ipswich, Suffolk: Suffolk Records Society, 1968), 12: 108. The publication of seven volumes of Constable's correspondence in which the artist repeatedly evokes the

Stour Valley as both his personal place of origin and the origin of his art has done nothing to retard the historical and critical tendency to conflate the artist with the landscape. Again see my "Reading Constable."

20. The hay would not be milled but would be stored in the barns attached to the mill.

21. Pierre Bourdieu, *An Outline of a Theory of Practice*, trans. Richard Nice (Cambridge: Harvard University Press, 1977), 164. Bourdieu calls the result of this naturalization the "doxa," a scheme of thought whereby the world of tradition is experienced as a "natural world" and thus taken for granted. See also Barthes, *S/Z*, and his discussion of the codes of bourgeois realism (18–20).

22. Gombrich, *Art and Illusion*, 387–88.

23. We know from Constable's letters that he did not have an entirely free hand in the composition. The Rebows wanted the painting to show the house as well as a rustic grotto which appears to the left of it and a deer house which appears to the right. The challenge Constable faced was to integrate these landmarks into a natural-looking landscape. After what appears to have been a number of false starts, Constable wrote to his fiancée on 30 August 1816 announcing with regard to the composition, "Today I have gotten over the difficulty, and begin to like it myself." See *John Constable's Correspondence* 6: 199.

24. This corresponds to their place within Locke's account of perception. In Locke the shape of an object is its primary characteristic while color and the object's reflective qualities are secondary. Nevertheless, because of their changeable nature color and light become the more problematic characteristics and hence more important to the whole experience of perception. See "On Perception," in his *Essay Concerning Human Understanding* (London: Everyman's Library, 1961), 67–69.

25. For a discussion of Lessing's ideas of time and space as they are formulated in his essay *Laocoon: An Essay upon the Limits of Poetry and Painting* (1766), see W. J. T. Mitchell, "Space and Time: Lessing's Laocoon and the Politics of Genre," *Iconology: Image, Text, Ideology* (Chicago: University of Chicago Press, 1986), 95–115.

26. See my "Reading Constable."

27. Constable, more so than Turner or any of his British contemporaries, was wholly preoccupied with the problem of finish. This is evident from his correspondence with family and friends and from his common practice of repainting works returned to him after exhibition. On the evidence of his letters and the appearance of the paintings today, almost all his large exhibition pieces of the 1820s and 1830s, including the *Hay Wain*, were repainted.

28. Constable described the white flecks of paint and the broken brushwork of his surfaces as his "dews," "breezes," and "lights." The enormous physical and psychological effort he put into them in order that they mimic the natural surfaces and appearances of the landscape is reported to his friend John Fisher. While less approving, the critics, echoing Constable's own naturalizing description of these marks, called them his "snow." See *John Constable's Correspondence*, 6: 78, 87, 124, 157, 167, 181–82, 185, 198, 200, 210–11, 216–17, 258.

29. John Constable, *John Constable's Discourses*, ed. R. B. Beckett (Ipswich, Suffolk: Suffolk Records Society, 1970), 69.

# EIGHT

# The Compulsion of Proximity

*Deirdre Boden and Harvey L. Molotch*

The new communication and information technologies so heighten global and temporal integration that many regard them as harbingers of a deeper transformation in social relations.[1] In the same way that previous commentators credited the steam engine and atomic bomb with ushering in new modes of civilization, so the "communications revolution" putatively brings a new form of social existence. These new technologies, ever growing in importance, render the "friction of distance" irrelevant as individuals, firms, and bureaucracies become "footloose." People can live where they want without loss of friendships or kin solidarity, and capitalism can progress beyond fixed production lines and trading centers into a contemporaneous, multilocational, nonstop world market.

Some have emphasized a dark side to this transformation. The physical problems of body fatigue and eyestrain induced by too much time in front of the computer are the least of the difficulties.[2] Continuing a line of theoretical development from the classic social theorists, the new technologies radically advance the "impersonality" of modern life, as the warm joys of intimate sociability are forever replaced by the cooler pleasures of technologically mediated communication. Although more people may be brought into touch with the whole world, many of these same individuals become mere appendages to their "smart" workstations, making them into the quiescent bodies of modern capitalism—Foucault's "corps dociles."[3] As surveillance instruments, the new technologies provide bosses not only with data on the results of the work process (e.g., overall sales or production figures) but also with feedback of precisely which workers are accomplishing which tasks at the moment of their accomplishment.[4] This brave new world of monitored social control brings a form of intrusion once possible only through direct and inefficient personal monitoring. The iron cage is replaced by the electronic trace.

In contrast to this range of views, we argue that the consequences for social life, whether benign or nefarious, have been exaggerated.[5] The robust nature and enduring necessity of traditional human communication procedures have been underappreciated. Modern systems, (including postmodern variants), inevitably rest on micro-orders;[6] modernity is achieved not just through computer circuit boards and devices such as voice mail, video conferencing, and fax reproduction but through the intensely social daily routines of humans thinking, cooperating, and talking face-to-face. Rather than being antithetical to advanced modernity, intimacy is the basis for it, just as surely as it was the bedrock of earlier tribal life. Copresent interaction remains, just as Georg Simmel long ago observed, *the* fundamental mode of human intercourse and socialization, a "primordial site for sociality," in Emanuel Schegloff's phrase.[7]

Modernity is made possible not by the substitution of new technologies for copresence but by *a tensely adjusted distribution of copresence and the more impersonal forms across individuals, tasks, places, and moments.* Although in some instances communication is best done by more impersonal means, modernity implies no dilution in the degree that face-to-face— or, more precisely, "copresent"—interaction is both preferred and necessary across a wide range of tasks. We hold it to be primary both because the most crucial tasks are handled with copresence and because copresence is biographically and historically prior to other forms of communication: infants first communicate through touch and copresent sights and sounds; writing and all other forms of media have been "essentially borrowed, adapted, specialized, and reduced from the resources first developed and acquired in co-presence."[8]

When people can't actually secure a needed state of copresence, they ordinarily strive to approximate it as best they can: the phone, for example, is better than a memo, a swift e-mail exchange better than a letter. This preference for "upgrade" toward the more personal forms of communication has consequences for how individuals structure their daily calendar and how human activity is organized geographically. Of real consequence, it is what we have termed the "compulsion of proximity."

By understanding the concrete features that make copresence so useful under particular circumstances, we will better understand what makes modern institutions possible. By distinguishing what is "lost" in the translation from copresent interaction to other modes, we can learn what people are trying to get back to when they say, as they often do, "We've gotta get together and talk soon," or what they appreciate when they exclaim, "It's good to hear the sound of your voice!" or "It's really great to see you again!" While acknowledging the role of new technologies in sustaining modernity—in allowing organizations to span spatial distance and endure over time (in Anthony Giddens's formulation)—this exercise will indicate some of the limits of the new media's capacity to act as a substitute for "simple" copresence. Such limits have implications for the future spatial and temporal patterning of organizations as well as for their internal structure. We will now unpack some of the ingredients of copresent interaction that make it so rich a form of communication.

## THE THICKNESS OF COPRESENT INTERACTION

Copresence is "thick" with information. Under any media condition, words derive their meanings only from contexts; copresence delivers far more context than any other form of human exchange. Context includes not just other words but facial gestures, body language, voice intonation, and a thousand other particulars. This information loading consists of details not only of the moment but also of past moments and future prospects that shape and reshape the flow of turns between parties. Interaction is a sequential affair, with the meaning of a particular utterance understood by reference to prior utterances in the same, previous, and anticipated conversational streams.[9] The words "I'll kill you" have completely different meanings when screamed by an adult in a dark alley, when yelled by a child aiming a cowboy pistol, or when squealed by a loving parent before tickling a four-year-old. The statuses of the individuals, their past history together, prior statements in the talk, the intonation of voices, and the physical body attitude—all are simultaneously "read" to constitute the very different, even opposite, senses of the same set of words.

The intensity of what Erving Goffman called the "focused attention" entailed by copresence means that communication can occur with no words whatever, as in a pregnant silence or the gleam in a romantic eye.[10] The meaning of any detail—including a word—derives from actors' work in using each particular to inform or "index" every other. In Harold Garfinkel's term, copresence best allows this "indexicality" (H. Paul Grice calls it "implicature") to manage the ambiguity inherent in any term or expression.[11] It is this richness of information that makes us feel we need copresence to know what is really going on, including the degree to which others are providing us with reliable, reasonable accounts. At the same time, copresence puts us "on the spot" by making our own dissembling, deviance, or other disfavored action easier to detect. The density of interactional detail of copresent encounters thus both engages and entraps us.

We encounter the liability of copresence when tasks are best accomplished by losing rather than gaining information, instances when copresence risks presenting *too much*. A fast-food employee taking an order communicates directly to the cook in the rear through the touch of a key on the cash register. Variants of this form of communication, stripped and simple, are obviously important to the modern world for moving data and messages across global space. Occasionally copresence is *"not enough"*—precisely because relying on its efficient thickness fails to display that enough trouble has been gone through. Thus, conventional etiquette places a premium on a written "thank you" for a nice dinner, rather than only the "too easy" face-to-face version delivered when taking one's leave.[12] There are thus numbers of reasons, some obvious and some not, why copresence is not the universal form of communication in modern society. But it does contain the kind of unique attributes that make it, in a bewildering world of technical innovation and communication bulk, the ordering device of all these other forms of communication as well as the basis of the larger social organization. We now inventory, in still finer detail, what copresence gives us.

### Body Talk

Body talk adds a visual vocabulary and social grammar that enables speakers to add nuance to language and even transform verbal meanings. The cues of physical movement, eye contact, facial expression, and body orientation relay substantive meaning in themselves—punctuating, elaborating, and orchestrating the meaning of spoken words as part of a "dance of life."[13] Body movements communicate status; high-status people have relaxed musculature compared to low-status people in mixed encounters.[14] Superordinates tend to lean if standing but remain stable (not rock) if sitting. Anyone, regardless of educational level, can read such signals. Similarly, individuals with poor language skills (either because of schooling deficit, personality disposition, or cultural strangeness) can invoke the body, including pantomime—and thus reach toward a more transcultural, transsituational basis of communication. They can also use body talk to challenge authority, even delivering rude insults, while perhaps avoiding official sanction by keeping their spoken words consistent with deferential expectations. As is generally the case when verbal and nonverbal cues are inconsistent, experimental evidence suggests that the nonverbal message overrides as the "real" information.[15] Copresence affords access to the body part that "never lies," the eyes—the "windows on the soul." Eye contact itself signals a degree of intimacy and trust; copresent interactants continuously monitor the subtle movements of this most subtle body part.[16] That Americans expect people to "look them in the eye" during a crucial conversation (as when, for example, they deny guilt or offer an apology) implies that they believe that the eyes are a truth detection mechanism.[17] This belief, regardless of its accuracy, translates into a felt need for copresence—at least by one of the interacting parties.

The very initiation of a turn at talk involves "sets of bodily movements" that bring speaker and hearer into deft alignment as interactants adjust to one another's vocal pitch and physical stance.[18] Readiness to receive an utterance is displayed through gaze, gesture, and body orientation—for example, tilting the head to one side.[19] In doctor-patient interaction, physician and patient alike engage in a detailed display of both vocal and nonvocal signals that pace and segment stages of the medical consultation as well as provide clinical information to one another.[20] Patients and physicians focus each other's attention from face to body (and back) as a means of directing interest first to the content of an utterance then to a body part or area of discomfort. Indeed, the very expression of pain and suffering may be seen as a fundamentally interactional issue, as patients mark feeling with sounds uttered at precise points in the examination.[21] However much physicians may privilege more mechanistic and remote sources of data (EKG, X ray), close interaction with patients (including physical observation and touch) is indispensable, ignored at risk of losing crucial information.[22] The medical examination not only offers an obvious site for copresence but provides a prototype of a minds-bodies interaction system that pervades social life.

In an extensive study of political speeches before live audiences, Maxwell Atkinson found that politicians, as part of the "language and body language of politics," make subtle use of physical gestures to cue audience applause—part of their arsenal of literally claptrap devices.[23] Charisma, rather than being the intrinsic property of a given speaker, comes through cueing skill, which can inform an audience when to remain breathless to allow a speaker to build toward a culminating point, precisely when to begin an applause, and just how long to "drown the speaker out."[24] Thus, so-called collective crowd behavior, as with the "trait" of charisma, is a fundamentally interactional exchange, and—important for our discussion—an interaction facilitated by the immediate feedback of multiple cues that copresence makes possible. Even if it takes place for no other reason than to be videocast or reported in the press (a "pseudo-event," in Daniel Boorstin's term), the live (copresent) political speech endures because it is the best basis for a good sound bite.[25]

Copresent people can physically touch. Touching is itself a *full vocabulary* of "deep significance" in which different meanings are provided by the degree of touch intensity, precise location of the body used (e.g., a physical brush with the shoulder versus the extended finger), and exact spot where the touch is placed.[26] At least for the U.S. context, the importance of touch has been experimentally demonstrated. Subjects receiving touch gestures in psychiatric interviews were more likely to engage in verbal interaction, rapport, and approach behaviors than those in control conditions.[27] Touch increases levels of self-disclosure from encounter group participants.[28] In one experiment investigators left a quarter in a public phone booth and then asked people leaving the booth if they had found a missing coin.[29] Subjects were more likely to say "yes" if the experimenter lightly touched them on the arm while asking. In another study a "librarian" who provided a half-second touch to subjects checking out books caused more reported satisfaction with library services, at least among women borrowers, than was reported by untouched control individuals.[30] Slide projectionists who casually rest a hand on a viewer's shoulder while adjusting the equipment raise viewers' reported evaluation of the slides being shown.[31]

Touch also implies rank: high-status people initiate touching more than low-status people, and there are also patterns having to do with sex, age, and location.[32] While video allows observers to witness touching, only copresence provides a means to experience it directly. Whatever crosscultural variations may exist in the precise meaning of the touch under different circumstances, touch itself seems universally a form of information.

Beyond sheer efficiency, use of the body in interaction feels good. We talk with our hands not because we are signing words, or even necessarily adding emphasis, but because the involvement of our full motor apparatus invigorates speaker as well as hearer. Our ability and insistence on coordinating our body actions with those of others lies at the heart of our sociability.[33] Human behavior that manages to fuse both mind and body in a single collaborated flow is intrinsically more satisfying than one in which just physical movement is involved (e.g., assembly-line monotony) or one in which only mental work takes place (e.g., writing chapters like this one). The coordinated use of mind, language, and body is a fulfilling mode of being in the world. So much is this the case that most of us use the "silent language" of the body even when there is no audience for it.[34] Chatting on the phone, we may nod, smile, grimace, even gesture for emphasis. At the word processor we may hit the keys with extra force to emphasize a point. Just as anyone who has made a serious effort in athletics realizes that physical accomplishment occurs only through coordination of the body *and* the mind (often accompanied by verbalization, e.g., grunts or "patter"), so it should be clear that conversation is a managed physical action as well as "brain work." Copresence makes use of this coordinated effort to the greatest degree.

### Self and Dignity

Interaction is intrinsic to the maturation process and to the very creation of a social self.[35] In many oral cultures people value both intense conversation and the silence between stories that marks the pleasure of simply being together. The survival rates of infants, whether human or of other primate species, are enhanced through interpersonal stimulation.[36] Without continuing and secure interaction with a primary care giver, infants protest, despair, and curtail exploratory behavior.[37] At least in the United States, babies barely three months old display a fascination with the human face that confirms it as "a central root of the human social bond"; in other cultures it may not be the face but some other aspect of copresence, such as physical contact, that is especially crucial.[38] The need to avoid "loneliness" and its pathological consequence apparently continues through adult life.[39] Indeed, daily interaction and the opportunity to flex verbal skills can delay the decline associated with extreme old age and perhaps forestall death. So important is copresent interaction that people will continue interacting even when the substance of the talk is unfavorable to their felt interests or when they must put up with "small insults" such as frequent interruptions of turns or being forced into topics not of their own choosing.[40]

Solitary confinement is a harsh punishment, and the precise conditions of prisoners' capacity to socialize with one another and visitors is a basis of dispute with authorities. If prisoners meet visitors on the opposite side of plate glass, with telephone sound links, the inability to touch is a substantial loss. Wire-mesh separations permit modified contact. It similarly matters to prisoners (and their attorneys) if communication with lawyers is limited to the phone or mesh settings or is otherwise impeded by physical barriers.[41]

### Commitment

Copresent interaction requires participants to set aside not only a specific time but also a shared space, as well as generally constraining other activities at the same moment or location. However intimate or innocuous the interaction, it must be precisely located in time and space, committing all concerned to rather singular dedication of body and mind. Anticipating Goffman's formulation several generations in advance, Gabriel Tarde remarked that conversation "marks the apogee of the *spontaneous attention* that men lend each other, by which they interpenetrate to a much greater depth than in any other social relationship" (emphasis in original).[42] When we are in copresence, we have some evidence that the other party has indeed made a commitment, if nothing else than by being there. Just getting together, either by making an appointment or stopping one's routine to stand and talk, provides evidence of commitment. The "civil disattention" produced by strangers in public settings stands in contrast to the sorts of interactional cues we both demand and display while together as workers, friends, or lovers.[43] Being kept waiting is an insult because it unilaterally delays the kind of "quality encounter" that one has mentally and physically organized one's life around.[44] We are irritated at those who take outside calls, gaze out the window, or read newspapers during *our* interaction with them. Such inattentiveness implies not just that the other person is "busy" but spills over and indicates something about the substance of the conversation: that it is not taken as very important or that the answer to a request will be no. Through variation in attentiveness, copresence maximizes the opportunity to display commitment and to detect a lack of it in others; hence, it adds substantive and nuanced information.

Being there for each other involves moment-to-moment irreplaceable opportunities to deal with "circumstantial contingencies."[45] Copresent interaction involves continuous production, with "no time out," in Garfinkel's loaded phrase.[46] Letters, memos, faxes, and e-mail are poor substitutes for gauging commitment; correspondents can do many things before answering one's pressing concerns or even *while* answering them. Neither prompt response nor level of involvement is guaranteed; they can even delegate the task of responding to a secretary or, in the modern case, a word processor with all but the opening salutation preprogrammed. The much-maligned postal service can be blamed for complete inattention ("must have been lost in the mail"), or the computer network can be described as "down."

Telephones are somewhat better. Small silences in a telephone exchange are read by both parties and may cause them to check both the talk and the technology ("Hello, are you there?"). Even putting someone on "hold" or providing the sounds that begin the closing of a conversation ("well, uh, I've got to . . .") requires split-second timing and collaborative effort.[47] Still, compared to copresence, it is easier to fake attentiveness by injecting "speech particle" utterances such as "uh-huh" and other "monitoring responses" at technically appropriate turn transition points than when face-to-face.[48] Nails can be filed and mail read with impunity; sudden exits can be explained away by pies in ovens and interlopers at the door.[49]

Nor has the development of electronic mail, which is indeed far more open and interactive than the traditional memo form, obviated the advantages of copresence.[50] E-mail has evolved into an interactional form of some intensity; users routinely "chat," exchange gossip, send computer jokes, circulate tips, advertise sexual preferences, and sometimes even argue.[51] But judging sincerity through e-mail (as with the phone) is made difficult by the fact it is easier to fake words than to disguise both words and the multiple gestures and stance that go with real-time–real-space interaction. The skill of great actors lies not in their diction and inflection but in their ability to synchronize words and body, the split-second timing and pacing of content with form, that makes for distinguished performance. In interaction—whether natural or simulated as such—timing is everything.

### Word Position as Information

Ordinary talk has strong enough organizational patterns that people can, especially when copresent, routinely detect departures from them. The field of conversation analysis has devoted twenty-five years to understanding how ordinary turn taking is indeed organized, documenting the ways that speakers repair "broken" or disrupted talk, maintain mutual orientation, and minimize disfluency.[52] One of the findings is that silence and interruption are both quite rare; the rhythm of verbal exchanges resembles the syncopation of jazz as participants pace each other's utterances on the beat and even half-beat to avoid awkwardness.[53] Listeners anticipate a speaker's talk trajectory with such precision that they generate replies that allow for no audible gap or disturbing overlap. Even when overlaps occur, they are brief and typically located either in the terminal syllable of a turn or at the earliest recognition point of the turn's ending. This means that even a brief silence is noticeable ("pregnant") as information.

Silences are only one type of substantive message from a larger number of talk-organizing cues. Scholars have discovered that speakers who turn down requests, invitations, and suggestions use a different sequencing format than those who accept. Acceptances tend to be delivered immediately; in fact, they often come before the end of the request turn (i.e., they are latched). Consider this fragment of real conversation between B and A transcribed to show precisely the instant (indicated with the symbol "[") when A begins responding to B's invitation:[54]

> B: Why don't you come and *see* me some ⌈times
> A:                                       ⌊I would like to

The immediacy of the response is the common timing format for acceptances to various types of invitations and requests.

But now notice the typical timing of a negative response in a conversation between a man named Heatherton ("H") and S (lapsed time between turns, in tenths of seconds, is in parentheses):[55]

> H:  I mean can we do any shopping for her or something like tha:t?
> →      (0.7)

*S:* Well that's *most* ki:nd Heather*ton* hhh At the moment *no:.* because
we've still got two bo:ys at home.

S opens the turn not with a direct refusal but with a preface (beginning with "Well") of the sort found routinely to signal a departure from
agreement.[56] Such terms as "well" (or "gee" or "gosh") are often mistak-
enly viewed as content-free and thus discouraged by high-school teachers of English and college speech professors. In fact, they actively mark
the initiation of some dispreferred action such as a refusal, rejection, or
declination. They usefully serve as interactional buffers, delaying and
cushioning the negative news while signaling its content as well as dis-
playing the speaker's concern to break the news gently.[57] The additional
uttered words hold back the refusal still longer. The seven-tenths of a
second "pure" silence (above, at arrow) performs a similar, and additive,
function. It is evidence of the more general finding that "speakers can
rely on the *positioning* of what they say to contribute to the *sense* of what
they say as an action."[58]

Among other things, by warning the proposer, inviter, or requester
that a negative is coming, silences allow the proposer to "pull back," perhaps qualifying or sweetening the deal with a better offer *before* the refusal can come.[59] Here is an example, also transcribed verbatim from
real life, with a telltale three-tenths of a second silence after the invitation to a meeting that allows such a scenario to unfold:[60]

*G:* W'd you like t'meet no::w,
→     (0.3)
*K:* [or late—] [Well,] not just now. (0.1) Maybe in 'bout ten minutes?

In this example the three-tenths of a second response delay permits
the inviter to amend the request (giving the responder a chance to meet
later instead); thus, a rejection has been eliminated. So frequent are such
response delays that should they not take place before a refusal, the
proposer notices that something is wrong. It is an offense, a denial of
what Garfinkel calls the "practical ethics" that are intrinsic to everyday
interaction. Fast denials wantonly rob the proposer of a chance to save
face with qualifying interjections or withdrawals; they imply a motivated
animosity. That is why they are rare.[61]

As John Heritage summarizes a range of findings on these matters,
the recurrent pattern of conversation timings "maximize the tendency
for socially solidary actions to take place."[62] The organization of talk,
in this regard, "itself is intrinsically 'biased' towards solidary actions."
Copresence provides the best circumstance for inserting delays before a
negative response and for such delays (or their absence) to be noticed
and exploited by the other party. Thus, the routine preference for soli-

darity can best operate as a noticeable feature of interaction under conditions of copresence.

This display of solidarity communicates trust. When people delay a negative response to allow withdrawal of a request, they have taken it on themselves to protect the other interactant—and they have done so without there being any explicit rule, norm, or law requiring them to do so. This consideration implies to the requester that subsequent interactions with the responder will likewise be benign, perhaps then coloring the *substance* of what goes on as the interactants make assumptions about one another's intentions in regard to honoring promises, pacts, and contracts. Thus, a certain form of trust can be displayed and appreciated between actors—a trust that derives from the observable timing and placement of talk and gesture. Such trust, we now know, is not just intrinsic to intimate relations within family units and other primary groups but is an essential mechanism of business and high-level negotiations among powerful state actors.[63] As Michael Storper and Allen Scott remark, "Communities of trust and the social construction of unwritten business norms are important foundations for the maintenance of an effective social division of labor. . . . Trust and personal experience are . . . important pre-conditions of much re-contracting behavior in modern business complexes."[64] *For actors to use time to achieve solidarity and trust, there must be a minimum amount of space between them.*

### Sequential Efficiency and Quick Turnaround

Copresence is efficient not just because so much information is present at any given moment (e.g., body talk, position of an utterance, speech particles) but also because it allows individuals to move rapidly through streams of turns, as each turn quickly leads, iteratively and implicatively, to the next. As interactants learn what is "really the substance of the matter," they can change topic without much delay, relatively unimpeded by, for example, topics as proclaimed in "in re" statements at the top of a memo. They can delicately shift topics, deftly avoid others, slide backward and forward across one level of a topic while exploring another.

In copresent interaction an apparently "simple question" may lead to a further question about its intended meaning, the range of its applicability, or the context to which it applies. Hearers may ask that a question be repeated, but in a somewhat different way, search for why it is being asked by asking still other questions, or provide a reason for not hearing or understanding before they finally do provide an answer. To use a clearly contrasting case, letter writers experience intervals of days (weeks and months, in some geographical combinations) between turns. Telephone users, while certainly caught up in an intense round of turn taking, have a less thick medium for mutual display of meaning. In copresence actors can see the slightest flick of an eyebrow to assess an appropriate point to jump into the flow of talk, to alter topic, and—even more critically—to qualify an offer or to withdraw a claim or retreat to safer conversational ground. Both consensus and conflict are more incisive and more immediate.[65] Friends and foes learn more from each turn, including what is demanded of the next turn and what to make of earlier stretches of interaction. The "Oh, I see what you're driving at" phenomenon is immediate, as the world is updated at each succeeding moment.

### Loose Talk: Efficient and Flexible

While precisely organized at one level, everyday talk is remarkable for its looseness in terms of topic, speaker participation, allocation of turns, and forms of speech. Unlike, say, courtroom proceedings or television news interviews, where one person asks questions and the other gives answers, in casual conversation turns are not preallocated in any specific way.[66] Similarly, speakers are not expected to use complete sentences (subject and predicate) or even real "dictionary" words. People can chuckle, exclaim, or emote. They can finish each other's sentences, collaborate in developing narratives, help jokes reach punch lines. They can collaboratively and simultaneously mold the ongoing interaction as they change the course and speed of conversational flow.

Other forms of communication—such as letters, memos, or computer messages—have more constrained formats. Some of this constraint may be cultural, some technologically intrinsic to the medium.[67] Memos, in particular, are "stripped-down" messages with formally prescribed opening and closing salutations ("To" and "From"). Memo etiquette discourages the kind of informal terms and phrases that can work their way into even the most formal copresent encounters. Memos are certainly no place for what Heritage calls "change-of-state" tokens such as "oh" or "ah" that can casually move interactants to another topic or "uh-huh" to indicate understandings of another's speech.[68] But in copresence these types of utterances are common, providing assurance of mutual intelligibility (among other functions) and thus enhancing communicative efficiency.

Some types of expression, such as laughter or displays of emotion, obviously lend themselves to copresence. We know that emotions are not simply "outbursts" driven by psychological or biological imperative but instead are strategic information displays linked to practical goals.[69] Copresence allows individuals to emote "properly" (indeed, it demands it), in sync with others' responses. Laughter is a systematically produced, socially organized activity, often occurring as a pulsed burst inserted into the stream of talk in a precise and orderly manner.[70] When emotional displays have an involuntary quality, as in blushing, the copresent display can serve as evidence of authenticity of a message (just as the same display can reveal an unintended truth).

Even if it were possible to convey emotions or other "human" modes of expression into such formats as memos, they tend to be excluded by office policy. We have examined a large number of business correspondence textbooks. They enjoin novices to make their memos "terse" and to focus directly on information, not on "the writer and background."[71] They warn against "unnecessary small talk, which has no place in business correspondence of any type."[72] We suspect that this advice is sometimes ignored and at other times is so slavishly obeyed that the office memo itself becomes a joke of noninformation. The orthodox memo form can, like the fast-food cashier's keypad, indeed work effectively, but only when backed by prior and subsequent face-to-face conversations that help turn it into good sense—a point made explicit in at least one of the business "how-to" books we consulted.[73] And this contexting copresence derives part of its effectiveness, even in business settings, from its incorporation of laughter and other affective material. To help "modernize" U.S. business at the turn of the century, there was enthusiasm for encouraging "young business men" to rely more on written communication: as one textbook expert averred, "A letter is but a talk on paper."[74] Letters were "oversold" in the same way that electronic media (including medical disagnostic devices) have more recently been misunderstood as simple (or superior) substitutes for copresent interaction.

The flexibility and multidirectionality of copresence allows seemingly irrelevant (but actually important) talk to occur on occasions otherwise dedicated to prescribed topics. Deirdre Boden has described how business meetings begin with "small talk" which contains and projects important substantive matters.[75] Participants update one another on both work and leisure, taking each other's measure in a way that will inform the meanings of later utterances. Premeeting talk typically weaves talk-at-work (personal) with talk-as-work (organizational) in ways that provide formative updates on colleagues' activities and moods, and the phases of talk are skillfully managed as practical matters. Items such as "Dja get the copy of the memo I sent you?" or (in an e-mail setting) "Just sent you a message about what we talked about yesterday" are interwoven with informal remarks on appearance ("Wow, all dressed up an' nowhere t' go"), weather, lunch plans, overwork, family news, and so forth. These strips of talk build interactional biographies as they provide organizationally relevant information. Such preliminary talk can, for example, indicate where the actors have been (e.g., "Just had a nice slow six-mile run"), what they have just done ("closed a deal"), or where they

are about to go ("I'm leaving for London in an hour"). The casual remarks provide details that, in substantive terms, inform the listener how
to take the unfolding business talk that will follow (e.g., I'm dealing with
a "relaxed athlete" or a "big operator" or a "corporate jet-setter"). Such
talk not only frames the succeeding interactions but also acts as the interactional "proving ground" in which participants display their communicative competence and, through appropriate displays of timing, utterance positioning, and body language, their interactional identities and
benign intentions.

*Special Circumstances Requiring Copresence*

Under certain circumstances the proclivity for copresence is especially
strong, including conditions considered sensitive, complex, or uncertain. Parents needing "real communication" with their children, professors and graduate students working out a dissertation topic, or neighbors trying to settle a long-running dispute are examples from mundane
settings. In a more formal context, criminal plea bargaining must be
face-to-face precisely because judicial *discretion* makes for a level of interactional complexity not found in other legal realms.[76]

In certain organizational instances proximity is negotiated as the need
arises. Boden has observed that organizational actors frequently discuss
opportunities for copresence on the phone, referring to past face-to-
face meetings and setting up future rendezvous.[77] Again, such discussion tends to happen particularly when matters appear to become sensitive, complex, or uncertain. In the context of e-mail, we have observed
numerous instances of such conditions leading to the need to "upgrade"
to copresence, as illustrated in this example:

> Well, maybe we could meet soon and discuss this face to face. :-)
> I'll be in Tennessee at the end of April/beginning of May visiting
>     David Lipton.

The reason for these compulsions toward proximity is not the amount
of detail to be handled in some technical or even simply cognitive sense.
Enormous quantities of detail are routinely transferred as data bases
across electronic networks. Instead, the key is that there is no set script
or standing recipe for arriving at an outcome. Unlike, say, ordering catalogue merchandise over the phone or sending inventory data through a
computer link, things must be worked out along the way.

Gail Jefferson notes that the telling of bad news may particularly entail getting off the phone to get together. Troubles, she reports, routinely bring pressure to upgrade interaction.[78] People who treat another's telephoned bad news with sympathy recurrently receive a

request to "come and see me." Indeed, as Jefferson goes on to note, the organization of telling "troubles" may, in some cases, be seen as interactionally designed actually to bring participants into copresence.

Especially needed if the news is tragic for the receiver, copresence can provide the full array of communicative resources to soften the blow, monitor the response, and further ameliorate distress. The recipient's next turn, even if it is only a split-second shriek or half-smile, can be caught to help prefigure a next response. For such reasons, enlightened clinics do not provide patients with diagnoses of life-threatening disease by mail or phone. To use any medium other than copresence is considered not merely discourteous but irresponsible.

Other forms of communication can be adapted to carry bad news. College "how-to" business books advise letter writers with disappointing news (e.g., job or contract rejections) to "buffer" their negative information with a preface that enables "sophisticated readers [to] know that bad news is coming, but still . . . be better prepared for it."[79] Even though letter writers can take such special measures to simulate the niceties of proximate talk, the strategy may not work if for no other reason than that the reader is free to skim, disattend to certain key phrases, or read information in a different order than displayed. Sequence design is at risk with paper (or even screen) communication, and misreadings are harder to detect and repair.

Sometimes those who give bad news want to avoid face-to-face contact precisely because they wish to hide from the other's reaction and avoid responsibility for interactional follow-up. We have all experienced the hard choice of painfully rejecting another face-to-face or "copping out" and using the mail or leaving a message on an answering machine. The "Dear John" letter is a legendary act of interactional cowardice.[80] More mundanely, bureaucrats who turn down hundreds of requests a day do so in writing because of the practical time constraints and also because they cannot become embroiled at the "human level" in so many cases.

But where the time and trouble are deemed worth it, even a fairly large group may try to work through copresence. The history of democratic thought includes a pondering of the best arrangements for political discourse, from Plato's search for the optimum number of citizens for the Agora to the ruminations on how many people should be in the houses of congress. Much of the extensive discussion in the *Federalist Papers* on the appropriate size of legislatures turns on the issue of just when the advantages of copresence are lost to the dynamics of an impersonal assembly. As it turns out, both the U.S. Senate and House of Representatives appear too large (and perhaps too public) for authentic communication. The result is not a retreat to new technologies (although they are no doubt used somewhat) but to committees, caucuses, staff meetings, and informal interchanges in which the "real business" of government is conducted.[81]

Business settings, including the marketplaces of capitalism, place a high premium on copresence because of the frequent need to develop complex understandings, arrange informal trade-offs, and deal with unanticipated tensions. What may be good news for one part of the firm (increased market share) may be bad news for another (tighter production schedule). Mitchel Abolafia reports that stock exchange traders have resisted substituting computer communication for their presence on the "floor," preferring the seeming chaos of the trading pit where they can watch one another's eyes and body movements to detect intentions to buy or sell.[82] Through close proximity, the general mood of the crowd can be used as a gauge of future market fluctuations. In a related phenomenon, brokerage houses on both sides of the Atlantic are said to have responded to the 1987 market crash by increasing client contact and reducing dependence on technology.[83]

Business leaders, despite the tons of hardware and shelves of software at their disposal, spend relatively little time themselves using them. DeLong estimates that only 10 percent of top executives use any kind of computer (although the number is growing).[84] Those executives who do use a computer spend little time (perhaps fifteen minutes) in front of it each day. The former president of the United States, George Bush, was not ashamed to reveal that he had no familiarity with a personal computer (or even a supermarket price scanner, the sight of which astonished him). But people who run large organizations spend a great deal of time talking: the higher their level in the organizational hierarchy, the greater their responsibility, and the more complex and far-reaching their decisions, the more they talk. Managers spend upwards of 75 percent of their workday engaged in meetings, telephone calls, and casual conversations, with about half of their total time in copresence.[85]

The indispensability of copresence among people in the highest circles is perhaps the underlying reason why they tend to flock together in the same clubs, neighborhoods, resorts, and central business districts around the world.[86] It drives diplomats to congregate in Geneva, academics to flock to national meetings, and executives to meet in airport VIP lounges. These are some of the reasons, we would argue, that explain why those at the very top of business structures are particularly active in complex interpersonal nets (including those linking their firms to other companies) and spend a good deal of their time nurturing such connections. Scholars who study corporate boards of directors consistently find that such boards draw their members from people in the same geographical region, with those who interlock different boards also drawn from the same region.[87] This finding implies that rather than having a footloose national corporate elite, business leaders associate heavily with those who are proximate. It also implies that corporations are directed and tied together by people who have prior face-to-face experience and who are capable of having further such contact as the need arises. Comembership on boards serves to structure the otherwise informal ties, providing for a regularity of copresence that elaborates patterns of face-to-face relations already in place.

Still another of the conveniences of copresent communication is that records of it (e.g., meeting minutes) can be retroactively designed to protect participants and their goals; indeed, there can be no trace left at all. This feature is important for talk that could do damage if received by the wrong party or taken in the wrong way, an obvious enough advantage when illegal acts are conspired. Ideally no records should exist, yet full understandings are imperative. Crime operates best through face-to-face meetings, including retreats at remote sites; use of the phone has resulted in a number of prosecutions of figures in organized crime (the CIA has analogous concerns). In the Iran-Contra scandals of the Reagan administration, crucial documents—including retrieved computer communications—were damaging to the conspirators.[88] In a less world-shaking scandal, American Airlines was prosecuted for rigging air fares when executive counterparts at Braniff tape-recorded the telephone conversation in which the conspiracy was proposed.[89] The safest place for such talk is probably the locker room, where naked people (men), liberated even from mikes disguised as tie pins, are truly free to get down to business. Nefarious or benign, some important events and high-powered careers are put in motion at gyms and their related facilities.[90]

Beyond outlaw acts and conspiracies, many types of bureaucrats, politicians, and business figures are sensitive to increasing scrutiny of their lives. Given that real-life actors are doing things which are potentially actionable in lawsuits, grievance procedures, labor complaints, affirmative action hearings, environmental review processes, and so forth, the best way to do business is in person. People can then communicate using the full array of copresent resources, without the need to judge how closely their words, especially as isolated utterances, conform to the expectations of those not present or to the types of speech thought proper for their office or exalted status. Perhaps the greatest damage done to Richard Nixon was release of the White House tapes (a needlessly self-inflicted surveillance)—not so much because they revealed illegal or immoral acts as because the texture of his everyday talk (replete with expletives and cavalier references to important global issues) was so offensive.[91] But all ordinary talk is inconsistent, at minimum, with the formal rules of grammar, and much of it is offensive to idealized social norms as well. In part this is because many people really do have unclean hearts, but it is also because they simply speak with common and vulgar idiom, jokes, and culturally prevalent conventions. They also rely on context provided by others' knowledge of biography and prior words to know an utterance is not "really" what it might seem. *In an increasingly regulated and formally adjudicated society, use of new technologies is thus checked by heightened danger in using them.*

### Geographic Implications

Different kinds of communication technologies are going to be favored for different sorts of uses and by different types of organizational actors. Consistent with the "footloose" school, there has been an obvious dispersion of low-skilled back-office jobs to locales remote from the headquarter control centers.[92] Places such as Omaha become the "800" phone-number centers for purchasers of products made by firms located at far distant points; readers of the *New Yorker* are asked to contact a Colorado address if they have a subscription problem.

But as the new technologies loosen locational bonds between some kinds of actors and producers, there is intensified attraction among others, a "decisive re-agglomeration."[93] The scattering made possible by the new technologies may indeed intensify the need for copresence among those who coordinate dispersed activities and interpret the information pouring in from far-flung settings. The more information produced by the new technologies, the higher the premium on copresence needed to design, interpret, and implement the knowledge gained. *In other words, the only way to deal effectively with the simple communication of high technology is with the medium of highest complexity—copresence.*

Although the exact reasons for urban reconcentration are seldom developed in the literature, we think the most crucial is the need for copresent interaction (rather than, for example, quick delivery of plans, materials, or access to maintenance personnel). Such copresence includes the "inadvertent" meetings that inevitably occur when people of the same ilk frequent the same spaces. As William Whyte opines, "The city is still the prime place . . . because of the great likelihood of *un*planned, informal encounters or the staging of them."[94] The type of economic function most affected is that of the corporate headquarters, but research and development seems also to require certain constellations of proximate actors,[95] as occurs in "innovation centers" such as California's Silicon Valley and Boston's Route 128 district. Even in the case of pure science, the information that makes possible experimental replication and advance does not rely only on the journals but also on interpersonal networks and at least periodic copresence among scientists.[96]

In those instances where geographic dispersion separates people who need to be in touch, business and organizational actors turn to copresence at conferences and retreats. The frequency of such meetings is said by one business writer to have "skyrocketed" because "specialists [need to] tell each other what they are doing."[97] A spatial consequence of this turn is the sustenance not only of major downtown and airport hotels but also of more remote conference centers where interaction can be intensified without competition from big-city lights.

## UNEVEN ACCESS TO ORDINARY TALK

However much copresent interaction remains the base of the social order, we have also acknowledged the importance of the new technologies working in tandem with them. Regardless of their subsidiary role, the number of people whose lives they encapsulate is massive. Modernity thus continues to develop its own division of labor, with the newest twist providing for innovative sets of social relations distinguished by the communications role their incumbents play in managing the worldwide integration of time and space.

Although people may prefer copresent interaction, access to such ordinary talk, at least in occupational settings, is being unequally distributed. The debate over the new technologies has often been one of who will have the *advantage* of access to them; job programs, for example, have been developed to fight poverty by bringing slum dwellers "up" to the exciting world of computers. Here we raise the contrasting issue of who will be able to have jobs that make use of the full resources of the mind and body in communicating with others.

The coming of new technologies has more dramatically affected the routines of low-wage office workers (most of whom are women) than any other group. While executives consult computers on an as-needed basis, and higher technicians gain job satisfaction from creative challenges of programming and diverse manipulations, lower-rung workers are more likely to be routinized. Rather than working in the home or in service jobs that are interpersonally based (food service, retail sales), they may now be facing a communication deskilling analogous to the mechanization of the human body accomplished by the assembly line.[98] At least for certain segments of the lower work force, people are separated from the routine use of thick communication in their work roles. It may be that we are in an awkward transition in which humans must enter data into machines which will one day be fed by real-time transactions themselves (as now occurs at automatic teller machines, for example). But the fact that U.S. job expansion has been most rapid in the lower reaches of the business service economy, in part because of the new technologies, implies that these low-grade but high-tech jobs will grow in number.

In the rush toward high tech it may well be that some organizations are unwisely designing jobs with a needlessly mechanistic view of how the new technologies best operate. Stripping away thick communication may inhibit workers' capacity to do their jobs well, even jobs that are centered on repetitive data entry tasks. Workplace research has made clear that organizational success does not rely on workers' unthinking rule following.[99] Instead, productivity occurs when workers mobilize their capacity for ad hoc solutions and their ability to structure their own tasks efficiently, sometimes in opposition to formal organizational strictures. There is always the danger, whatever the level of technology involved, of forcing knowledgeable people into the roles of "judgmental dopes," thus depriving the organization of people's common sense.[100] In a classic study of a Chicago machine shop, Donald Roy found that managers' insistence that they alone control information and the labor process served to lower productivity.[101] The steep hierarchies of American corporations inhibit communication and cooperation within and across industries.[102] Interactional isolation of workers, from both themselves and management, may turn out disastrous because workers often need both vertical and lateral communication if they are to do a proper job, and especially if they are to take advantage of the real potential of the new technologies for advancing their organization's goals.[103]

Whether to better meet organizational goals or to satisfy the deep human need for direct interaction, modern office employees, as with a previous generation of assembly-line workers,[104] try to gain social recesses in their work day, escapes from the technologies through which they do their jobs. They exploit face-to-face opportunities that occur when in the hallways or at the water cooler to exchange personal "pleasantries," which can in fact be a type of shoptalk. Face-to-face encounters can inform actors how to read computer messages they receive from one another, by inventing, in effect, a side discourse that provides meaning to the electronic cues. These interactions can lay the groundwork for beneficially bypassing official procedures or for making those very procedures function. When management treats talk "as an absence of work rather than as the very heart of work," both worker and firm can suffer.[105] This dispute strongly suggests a dialectic of struggle over the means of communication in which lower-level personnel, whether for their own benefit or that of the organization, strive to transcend the media forms to which they are relegated in the emerging time-space division of labor.[106]

## REPRISE

Modernity, according to classical social science, is antithetical to the personal, especially in the productive spheres. This is so because organization supposedly manifests itself through mechanistic transfers of material and energy as well as information. Bureaucratic rules, the "cash nexus," the scientific method, and, more recently, the information revolution putatively eliminate ambiguity. Thus, there is no need for subjective interpretations and the kind of face-to-face interaction which only "personal business" is thought to require.

We have instead insisted that features of copresent interaction make it fundamental to social order, both local and global. The immediacy and inherent indexicality of all human existence means that the fine, fleeting, yet essentially social moments of everyday life anchor and articulate the modern macro-order. Through the trust, commitment, and detailed understandings made possible in situations of copresence the essential space-time distantiation of modern society is achieved.

We have proposed that there is a hierarchy among forms of human intercourse:

1. People prefer copresence compared to other forms of communication, particularly in those activities which set the conditions under which more routine events occur.
2. Copresent interaction abounds under late modernity and, at least among some kinds of actors, is likely more frequent than ever.
3. Copresent interaction is dominant over other forms of communication in that other forms of communication take their shape through recall or anticipation of copresent talk, rather than the other way around.
4. Copresent interaction is crucial in that the most important communication among the most consequential actors is done with copresence, and this will continue to be the case.
5. This need for copresence limits the degree and kind of organizational, temporal, and spatial reshaping that the new technologies can induce.

The infusion of everyday life, including production and consumption as well as cultural forms, with temporally and spatially distant events marks the modern world. This world requires a delicate balance of copresence and absence. This balance can be achieved only through struggle, in part because it is often not apparent just which tasks require what kinds of media or the appropriate ratio of each for a given task, and in part because there may be opposition from those called on to play the least self-fulfilling roles in this production of modernity. Problems both of efficiency and social justice thus remain because even though the available technologies may change, the limits of expert knowledge as well as the interactive skills and social yearnings of human actors have not.

## NOTES

We acknowledge the helpful advice of Steven Clayman, Randall Collins, Carol Gardner, Anthony Giddens, Jack Katz, and Don Zimmerman. This chapter was the basis for an address given by Molotch at the Twenty-fifth Anniversary Conference of the Sociology Department, University of Essex.

1. Best known for this view are the "futurists" such as Alvin Toffler. See Toffler, *The Third Wave* (New York: William Morrow, 1980). See also Richard Louv, *America II* (New York: Penguin, 1983); John Naisbitt, *Megatrends* (New York: Warner, 1982). Those stressing the importance of the new technologies for important institutional activities such as business, government, and international relations include Marjorie Ferguson, ed., *New Communication Technologies and the Public Interest* (Beverly Hills: Sage, 1986); Donald MacKenzie and Judy Wajcman, eds., *The Social Shaping of Technology: How the Refrigerator Got Its Hum* (Milton Keynes, Eng.: Open University Press, 1985); J. Martin, *The Wired City* (Englewood Cliffs, N.J.: Prentice Hall, 1978); M. V. Porat, *The Information Economy: Definition and Measurement*, Office of Telecommunications Special Publications 77–12 (4) (Washington D.C.: U.S. Department of Commerce, Office of Telecommunications, 1977).

2. National Research Council, *Video Displays, Work, and Vision*, Report of the Panel on Impact of Video Viewing on Vision of Workers, Committee on Vision (Washington, D.C.: National Academy Press, 1983).

3. Michel Foucault, *Surveiller et punir* (Paris: Gallimard, 1975), 164–71. See also Stanley Cohen, *Visions of Social Control* (Cambridge: Polity, 1985), and Judith A. Perrolle, "Conversations and Trust in Computer Interaction," paper presented at the Annual Meeting of the Eastern Sociological Society, Boston 1987.

4. Rob Kling and Suzanne Iacono, "Computing as an Occasion of Social Control," *Journal of Social Issues* 40 (1984): 77–97; Constance Perin, "The Moral Fabric of the Office: Panopticon Discourse and Schedule Flexibilities," in Samuel Bacharach, Steven Barley, and Pamela Tolbert, eds., *Research in the Sociology of Organizations* (Greenwich, Conn.: JAI Press, 1990), 118–36; Shoshana Zuboff, *In the Age of the Smart Machine: The Future of Work and Power* (New York: Basic, 1988).

5. For complementary views at a theoretical level, see Anthony Giddens, *The Constitution of Society* (Cambridge: Polity, 1984); Giddens, *The Nation-State and Violence* (Cambridge: Polity, 1986). See also Lionel Nicol, "Communications Technology: Economic and Spatial Impacts," in Manuel Castells, ed., *High Technology, Space, and Society*, vol. 28 of *Urban Affairs Annual Reviews* (Beverly Hills: Sage Publications, 1985), 191–209.

6. We follow Giddens's use of "modernity" to encapsulate even the most re-

THE COMPULSION OF PROXIMITY

cent developments; postmodernism is, in Giddens's formulation, merely an extension of previous patterns of time-space instantiations. See his *The Consequences of Modernity* (Stanford: Stanford University Press, 1990). See also cf. Randall Collins, "The Microfoundations of Macrosociology," *American Journal of Sociology* 86 (1981): 984–1014.

7. Emanuel A. Schegloff, "The Routine as Achievement," *Human Studies* 9, nos. 2–3 (Special issue on interaction and language use, ed. Graham Button, Paul Drew, and John Heritage; 1986): 112.

8. Steve Clayman, personal communication, 15 September 1988. See also Jerome Bruner, *Child's Talk: Learning to Use Language* (New York: Oxford University Press, 1984); S. Ervin-Tripp and C. Mitchell-Kernan, eds., *Child Discourse* (New York: Academic Press, 1977); Charles Goodwin, *Conversational Organization: Interaction Between and Speaker and Hearer* (New York: Academic Press, 1981); S. C. Levinson, *Pragmatics* (Cambridge: Cambridge University Press, 1983).

9. The fundamental statement is Harold Garfinkel, *Studies in Ethnomethodology* (1967; rpt. Cambridge: Polity, 1984); see also Harvey Sacks, "Notes on Methodology," in J. Maxwell Atkinson and John Heritage, eds., *Structures of Social Action* (Cambridge: Cambridge University Press, 1984), 21–27.

10. Erving Goffman, *Encounters* (Indianapolis: Bobbs-Merrill, 1961).

11. This is, in effect, a sociologist's version of relativity theory in that everything in the interaction has the potential of changing *relative* to every other event in time and space. See Garfinkel, *Studies in Ethnomethodology;* H. Paul Grice, "Logic and Conversation," in Peter Cole and Jerry Morgan, eds., *Syntax and Semantics,* vol. 3, *Speech Acts* (New York: Academic Press, 1975), 41–58.

12. Carol Gardner provided us with this example (personal communication).

13. Interest in the body's orientation in space goes back to Hobbes in *De corpore* (1696). The concept of mental-physical synthesis is reflected in the early work of Mead and in Wittgenstein's later *Philosophical Investigations*. In *Phenomenologie de la perception* (Paris: Gallimard, 1945), Merleau-Ponty linked the body itself, through its physiology and expressive potential, to language as a condition for thought, producing "le present vivant" or living present of the mind. Examples of empirical studies include Michael Argyle, *Bodily Communication* (New York: Routledge, Chapman and Hall, 1988); Ray Birdwhistell, *Kinesics and Context: Essays in Body Motion Communication* (Philadelphia: University of Pennsylvania Press, 1970); Paul Ekman, *Telling Lies: Clues to Deceit in the Marketplace, Politics, and Marriage* (New York: Norton, 1985); Paul Ekman and Walter Friesen, "The Repertoire of Non-verbal Behavior: Categories, Origins, Usage, and Coding," *Semiotica* 1 (1969): 49–98; Paul Ekman and Walter V. Friesen, "Hand Movements," *Journal of Communication* 22 (1972): 353–74; Charles Goodwin, "The Interactive Construction of a Sentence in Natural Conversation," in George Psathas, ed., *Everyday Language: Studies in Ethnomethodology* (New York: Irvington, 1979), 97–123; Goodwin, "Restarts, Pauses, and the Achievement of Mutual Gaze at Turn Beginnings," *Sociological Inquiry* 50, nos. 3–4 (1980): 272–302; Edward T. Hall, *The Silent Language* (New York: Fawcett/Doubleday, 1959); Hall, *The Hidden Dimension* (New York: Doubleday, 1966); Adam Kendon, Richard Harris, and Mary Key Ritchie, *Organization of Behavior in Face-to-Face Interaction* (The Hague: Mouton, 1975).

14. Erving Goffman, *Relations in Public* (New York: Basic Books, 1971).
15. Albert Mehrabian, *Nonverbal Communication* (Chicago: Aldine-Atherton, 1972), 182.
16. See, for example: Ekman, *Telling Lies;* Goodwin, "Interactive Construction of a Sentence"; Goodwin, *Conversational Organization;* Goffman, *Encounters;* Goffman, *Behavior in Public Places: Notes of the Social Organization of Gatherings* (New York: Free Press, 1963); Birdwhistell, *Kinesics and Context.*
17. Suspicious parents and teachers have the power to demand that children "look at me when I talk to you."
18. John Local and John Kelly, "Projection and 'Silence': Notes on Phonetic and Conversational Structure," *Human Studies* 9 (1986): 185.
19. Charles Goodwin and Marjorie Goodwin, "Concurrent Operations on Talk: Notes on the Interactive Organizations of Assessments," paper presented at the Annual Meeting of the American Sociological Association, San Francisco, 1982.
20. Richard Frankel, "The Laying On of Hands: Aspects of the Organization of Gaze, Touch, and Talk in a Medical Encounter," in Sue Fisher and Alexandra Todd, eds., *The Social Organization of Doctor-Patient Communication* (Washington, D.C.: Center for Applied Linguistics, 1983), 19–55; Christian Heath, "The Display of Recipiency: An Instance of a Sequential Relationship in Speech and Body Movement" *Semiotica* 42, no. 2 (1982): 147–68.
21. Christian Heath, "Pain Talk: The Expression of Suffering in the Medical Consultation," *Social Psychology Quarterly* 52, no. 2 (1989): 113–25; see also Paul ten Have, "Talk and Institution: A Reconsideration of the 'Asymmetry' of Doctor-Patient Interaction," in Deirdre Boden and Don Zimmerman, eds., *Talk and Social Structure* (Berkeley and Los Angeles: University of California Press, 1992), 138–63.
22. Renee R. Anspach, *Deciding Who Lives: Fateful Choices in the Intensive-Care Nursery* (Berkeley and Los Angeles: University of California Press, 1993).
23. Maxwell J. Atkinson, *Our Masters' Voices: The Language and Body Language of Politics* (London: Metheun, 1984); Atkinson, "Understanding Formality: Notes on the Categorization and Production of 'Formal' Interaction," *British Journal of Sociology* 33 (1982): 86–117; John C. Heritage and David Greatbatch, "Generating Applause: A Study of Rhetoric and Response at Party Political Conferences," *American Journal of Sociology* 92 (1986): 110–57.
24. Heritage and Greatbatch, "Generating Applause," 118.
25. Daniel Boorstin, *The Image: A Guide to Pseudo Events in America* (New York: Harper, 1961).
26. Hall, *Hidden Dimension,* 57; for reviews of the touching literature, see Richard Heslin and Tari Alper, "Touch: A Bonding Gesture," in John Wiemann and Randall P. Harrison, eds., *Nonverbal Interaction* (Beverly Hills: Sage, 1983), 47–75; Robert G. Harper, Arthur Wiens, and Joseph D. Matarazzo, *Nonverbal Communication: The State of the Art* (New York: Wiley, 1978).
27. D. C. Aguilera, "Relationship Between Physical Contact and Verbal Interaction Between Nurses and Patients," *Journal of Psychiatric Nursing and Mental Health Services* 5 (1967): 5–21.
28. C. L. Cooper and D. Bowles, "Physical Encounter and Self-Disclosure," *Psychological Reports* 33 (1973): 451–54.

29. C. L. Kleinke, "Compliance to Requests Made by Gazing and Touching Experimenters in Field Settings," *Journal of Experimental Social Psychology* 13 (1977): 218–23; Kleinke, "Interaction Between Gaze and Legitimacy of Request on Compliance in a Field Setting," *Journal of Nonverbal Behavior* 5 (1989): 3–12.

30. J. D. Fisher, M. Rytting, and R. Heslin, "Hands Touching Hands: Affective and Evaluative Effects of Interpersonal Touch," *Sociometry* 39 (1975): 416–21.

31. C. J. Silverthorne, M. Micklewright, and R. Gibson, "Attribution of Personal Characteristics as a Function of Touch on Initial Contact," paper presented at the meeting of the Western Psychological Association, Sacramento, 1975.

32. Nancy Henley, *Body Politics: Power, Sex, and Nonverbal Communication* (Englewood Cliffs, N.J.: Prentice Hall, 1977).

33. Goffman, *Behavior in Public Places.*

34. Hall, *Silent Language.*

35. This is the foundational idea of social psychology, at least in the symbolic interactionist formulation. See Herbert Blumer, *Symbolic Interactionism: Perspective and Method* (1969; Berkeley and Los Angeles: University of California Press, 1986).

36. Harry F. Harlow and Margaret Harlow, "Social Deprivation in Monkeys," *Scientific American* 207, no. 5 (1962): 136–46; Rene A. Spitz, "Hospitalism: An Enquiry into the Genesis of Psychiatric Conditions in Early Childhood," in *The Psychoanalytic Study of the Child*, vol. 1 (New York: International University Press, 1958).

37. J. Bowlby, *Attachment and Loss*, 3 vols. (New York: Basic Books, 1969–1980).

38. Beatrice Beebe, "Micro-Timing in Mother and Infant," in Mary Key Ritchie, ed., *Nonverbal Communication Today: Current Research* (The Hague: Mouton, 1982), 170; Eleanor Ochs, *Culture and Language Development: Language Acquisition and Language Socialization in a Samoan Village.* (Cambridge: Cambridge University Press, 1988).

39. Phillip Shaver, "Being Lonely, Falling in Love: Perspectives from Attachment Theory," paper presented to the Ninety-fourth Annual Meeting of the American Psychological Association, Washington D.C., 26 August 1986.

40. Candace West and Don H. Zimmerman, "Women's Place in Everyday Talk: Reflections on Parent-Child Interaction," *Social Problems* 24 (1977): 521–29; Pamela Fishman, "The Interaction Work Women Do," *Social Problems* 25 (1978): 397–406; Harvey Molotch and Deirdre Boden, "Talking Social Structure: Discourse, Domination and the Watergate Hearings," *American Sociological Review* 50, no. 3 (1985): 273–88.

41. When discussing documents, lawyers and clients need to shift from one piece of paper to another and to point to segments of text as they become relevant in conversation. In jails where phone or mesh are ordinarily present, lawyers can request more ordinary room settings for conferences with clients on the grounds that documents must be mutually examined. (We are grateful to the prominent attorney Stephen L. Miles for pointing this phenomenon out to us.)

42. This quote is drawn from Gabriel Tarde, *Opinion and Conversation* (1898), as translated in Terry Clark, ed., *Gabriel Tarde: On Communication and Social In-*

*fluence* (Chicago: University of Chicago Press, 1969), 308. In the same paragraph, Tarde adds, "It is rightly said of a good conversationalist that he is a *charmer* in the magical sense of the word" (309; emphasis in the original).

43. Erving Goffman, *Strategic Interaction* (Philadelphia: University of Pennsylvania Press, 1969), 155–58.

44. Barry Schwartz, *Queuing and Waiting: Studies in the Social Organization of Access and Delay* (Chicago: University of Chicago Press, 1975); see also Eviator Zerubavel, *Hidden Rhythms: Schedules and Calendars in Social Life* (Chicago: University of Chicago Press, 1981); Hall, *Hidden Dimension*.

45. Michael Lynch, Eric Livingston, and Harold Garfinkel, "Temporal Order in Laboratory Work," in Karin Knorr-Cetina and Michael Mulkay, eds., *Science Observed: Perspectives on the Social Study of Science* (Beverly Hills: Sage, 1983), 219.

46. Harold Garfinkel, "A Reflection," *Discourse Analysis Research Group Newsletter* 3, no. 2 (1987): 5. This superficially banal statement has profound consequences not just for so-called micro-events like conversation but for all manner of social phenomena. The transsexual studied by Garfinkel (*Studies in Ethnomethodology*) accomplished her female gender only through extraordinary, ongoing attention to the tiniest details.

47. Robert Hopper, "Hold the Phone," in Boden and Zimmerman, *Talk and Social Structure*, 217–31; Harvey Sacks, "The Search for Help," Ph.D. diss., University of California, Berkeley, 1967; Emanuel A. Schlegoff and Harvey Sacks, "Opening Up Closings," *Semiotica* 7 (1973): 289–327; see also Graham Button and Neil Casey, "Generating the Topic: The Use of Topic Initial Elicitors," in J. Maxwell Atkinson and John C. Heritage, eds., *Structures of Social Action: Studies in Conversation Analysis* (Cambridge: Cambridge University Press, 1984), 167–90.

48. Emanuel A. Schegloff, "Discourse as an Interactional Achievement: Some Uses of 'Uh Huh' and Other Things That Come Between Sentences," in Deborah Tannen, ed., *Georgetown University Roundtable on Languages and Linguistics: Analyzing Discourse: Text and Talk* (Washington, D.C.: Georgetown University Press, 1981), 71–93. But see Fishman, "Interaction Work Women Do," for gender differences in these regards.

49. The limits of the phone were noted by Tarde in 1898 when, in comparing it with the manifold features of copresence, he exaggerated that "telephone conversations, which lack the majority of these interesting elements, tend to be boring unless they are purely utilitarian." See Clark, *Gabriel Tarde*, 309.

50. Lee Sproull and Sara Kiesler, "Reducing Social Context Cues: Electronic Mail in Organizational Settings," *Management Science* 32 (1986): 1492–1512.

51. Alessandro Duranti, "Framing Discourse in a New Medium: Openings in Electronic Mail," *Quarterly Newsletter of the Laboratory of Comparative Human Cognition* 8, no. 2 (1986): 64–71; Beryl L. Bellman, "Anonymity and Identity in Computer Conferencing Systems," paper presented at the Annual Meeting of the American Sociological Association, San Francisco, 1989.

52. The field of conversation analysis has established "bedrock" features of turn-taking interaction; see Douglas W. Maynard, "On the Interactional and Institutional Bases of Asymmetry in Clinical Discourse," *American Journal of Sociology* 92, no. 2 (1991): 448–95. For the foundational statement, see Harvey Sacks,

Emanuel A. Schegloff, and Gail Jefferson, "A Simplest Systematics for the Organization of Turn-taking in Conversation," *Language* 50 (1974): 696–735. Summary statements are also available in Don H. Zimmerman, "On Conversation: The Conversation Analytic Perspective," *Communication Yearbook* 11 (1988): 406–32; J. Maxwell Atkinson and John Heritage, eds., *Structures of Social Action* (Cambridge: Cambridge University Press, 1984); Deirdre Boden and Don H. Zimmerman, eds., *Talk and Social Structure* (Berkeley and Los Angeles: University of California Press, 1991); Paul Drew and John Heritage, eds., *Talk at Work* (Cambridge: Cambridge University Press, 1992).

53. David Sudnow, *Talk's Body: A Meditation Between Two Keyboards* (Harmondsworth: Penguin, 1979).

54. Quoted from Heritage, *Garfinkel and Ethnomethodology,* 273.

55. Ibid.

56. See, for example, Drew, "Speaker's Reportings"; Judy Davidson, "Subsequent Versions of Invitations, Offers, Requests, and Proposals Dealing with Potential or Actual Rejection," in Atkinson and Heritage, *Structures of Social Action,* 102–28. See also Schlegoff et al., "Preference for Self-Correction."

57. Harvey Sacks, "On the Preference for Agreement and Contiguity in Sequences in Conversation," in Graham Button and John Lee, eds., *Talk and Social Organization* (Clevedon, Eng.: Multilingual Matters, 1987), 54–58.

58. Heritage, *Garfinkel and Ethnomethodology,* 261; see also Button, "Moving out of Closings."

59. Davidson calls this phenomenon the "subsequent version" of an invitation or offer which seeks to achieve acceptance through alternative formulation; see Davidson, "Subsequent Versions," 104–5.

60. From data recorded by Boden.

61. Anita Pomerantz, "Agreeing and Disagreeing with Assessments: Some Features of Preferred/Dispreferred Turn Shapes," in Atkinson and Heritage, *Structures of Social Action,* 57–101.

62. Heritage, *Garfinkel and Ethnomethodology,* 276.

63. Mark Granovetter, "The Old and the New Economic Sociology: A History and Agenda," paper presented at the Conference on Economy and Society, University of California, Santa Barbara, 1988; Amitai Etzioni, *The Moral Dimension: Toward a New Economics* (New York: Macmillan, 1988), esp. 8; see also Giddens, *Consequences of Modernity.*

64. Michael Storper and Allen J. Scott, "The Geographical Foundations and Social Regulation of Flexible Production Complexes," in J. Wolch and M. Dear, eds., *The Power of Geography* (London and Boston: Allen and Unwin, 1989), 30. The formulation is from S. Brusco and Charles Sabel, "Artisanal Production and Economic Growth," in F. Wilkinson, ed., *The Dynamics of Labor Market Segmentation* (New York: Academic Press, 1981), 99–113. See also Stewart Macaulay, "Non-Contractual Relations in Business: A Preliminary Study," *American Sociological Review* 28 (1963): 55–67; Michael Storper and S. Christopherson, "Flexible Specialization and Regional Industrial Agglomerations," *Annals of the Association of American Geographers* 77, no. 1 (1987): 103–17.

65. See Douglas W. Maynard, "Social Conflict among Children," *American Sociological Review* 50 (1985): 207–23.

66. Atkinson and Drew, *Order in Court;* David Greatbatch, "A Turn-taking System for British News Interviews," *Language and Society* 17 (1988): 401–30.

67. Deborah Tannen, "Oral and Literate Strategies in Spoken and Written Narratives," *Language* 58 (1982): 1–21. In some island cultures, for instance, letter writing routinely involves great intimacy; even so, the writers express eagerness to be together. See Niko Besnier, "Literacy and Feelings: The Encoding of Affect in Nukulaelae Letters," *Text* 9, no. 1 (1989): 1–21.

68. John Heritage, "A Change-of-State Token and Aspects of Its Sequential Placement," in Atkinson and Heritage, *Structures of Social Action* (Cambridge: Cambridge University Press, 1984), 299–345. The "oh" marker in particular may be a general feature of talk across cultures, although research on the cross-cultural applications is incomplete.

69. Arlie Hochschild, *The Managed Heart* (Berkeley and Los Angeles: University of California Press, 1985); cf. Thomas Scheff, *Catharsis in Healing, Ritual, and Drama* (Berkeley and Los Angeles: University of California Press, 1979).

70. Gail Jefferson, "On Exposed and Embedded Correction in Conversation," in Button and Lee, *Talk and Social Organization,* 86–100.

71. Lassor Blumenthal, *Successful Business Writing* (New York: Putnam, 1976), 60; John Schell and John Stratton, *Writing on the Job: A Handbook for Business and Government* (New York: New American Library, 1984), 118.

72. Samuel Cypert, *Writing Effective Business Letters, Memos, Proposals and Reports* (Chicago: Contemporary Books, 1983), 239.

73. Charles T. Binsaw, Gerald J. Alred, and Walter Oliu, *The Business Writers' Handbook* (New York: St. Martin's, 1987).

74. Seymour Eaton, *How to Do Business as Business Is Done in Great Commercial Centers* (Philadelphia: P. W. Ziegler, 1896), 254–55, as cited in Zuboff, *In the Age of the Smart Machine,* 100.

75. Deirdre Boden, *The Business of Talk: Organizations in Action* (Cambridge: Polity, forthcoming).

76. Arthur Rosett and Donald R. Cressey, *Justice by Consent* (Philadelphia: Lippincott, 1976); Maynard, *Inside Plea Bargaining.*

77. Boden, *Business of Talk.*

78. Gail Jefferson, *Final Report to the (British) SSRC on the Analysis of Conversations in Which "Troubles" and "Anxieties" Are Expressed,* Report No. HR 4805/2, (1980), 12; see also Emanuel Schegloff, "On an Actual Virtual Servo-Mechanism for Guessing Bad News," *Social Problems* 35 (1988): 442–57; Douglas Maynard, "The Perspective-Display Sequence and the Delivery and Receipt of Diagnostic News," in Boden and Zimmerman, *Talk and Social Structure,* 164–94.

79. Schell and Stratton, *Writing on the Job,* 88–89. When advising students how to construct a business letter with good news, however, the authors instruct that "the good news—loud and clear—begins the letter" (75). See also Dianna Booher, *Send Me a Memo: A Handbook of Model Memos* (New York: Facts on File, 1984).

80. Mehrabian, *Nonverbal Communication,* 180.

81. Woodrow Wilson, *Congressional Government: A Study in American Politics* (Cleveland: Meridian, 1965); Roger Davidson and Walter Oleszek, *Congress and Its Members* (Washington, D.C.: Congressional Quarterly Press, 1990); Steven

Smith and Christopher Deering, *Committees in Congress* (Washington, D.C.: Congressional Quarterly Press, 1990).

82. Mitchel Abolafia's relevant writings include "Taming the Market: Self-Regulation in the Commodity Futures Industry," Ph.D. diss., State University of New York, Stony Brook, 1981; "Structured Anarchy: Formal Organization in the Commodity Futures Markets," in Patricia Adler and Peter Adler, eds., *The Social Dynamics of Financial Markets,* (Greenwich, Conn.: JAI Press, 1984); "Market Crisis and Organizational Intervention," paper presented at the annual meeting of the American Sociological Association, Washington, D.C., August 1985.

83. *The Economist,* May 1989.

84. As cited in William Bulkeley, "Special Systems Make Computing Less Traumatic for Top Executives," *Wall Street Journal,* 20 June 1988, sec. 2, p. 17.

85. Henry Mintzberg, *The Nature of Managerial Work* (New York: Harper and Row, 1973); Rosabeth Moss Kanter, *Men and Women of the Corporation* (New York: Basic, 1977). See also John Kotter, *The General Managers* (New York: Free Press, 1982), and Zuboff, *In the Age of the Smart Machine.* The intensity of talk, the breadth of contacts, and the types of people in interaction (e.g., colleagues versus underlings) varies, of course, by type of firm (see Calvin Morrill, "The Embeddedness of Executive Conflict Management," paper presented at the meeting of the American Sociological Association, Atlanta, 1988.

86. See G. William Domhoff, *The Higher Circles: The Governing Class in America* (New York: Random, 1971); Domhoff, *Who Rules America Now? A View from the 80's* (Englewood Cliffs, N.J.: Prentice Hall, 1983); Kanter, *Men and Women of the Corporation;* Thomas Koenig and Robert Gogel, "Interlocking Directorates as a Social Network," *American Journal of Economics and Sociology* 40, no. 2 (1981): 37–50; C. Wright Mills, *The Power Elite* (New York: Oxford University Press, 1956); Richard Ratcliff, Mary Gallagher, and K. S. Ratcliff, "The Civic Involvement of Bankers: An Analysis of the Influence of Economic Power and Social Prominence in the Command of Civic Policy Positions," *Social Problems* 26 (1979): 298–313.

87. Mintz and Schwartz, *Structure of American Business;* Roger Friedland and Don Palmer, "Space, Corporation, and Class: Toward a Grounded Theory," in this volume.

88. Alan A. Block, "The Khashoggi Papers," *Contemporary Crises* 12, no. 1 (March 1988): 25–63.

89. Bill Sing, "Airline Chief Barred from Fare Talks," *Los Angeles Times* 13 July 1985, sec. 4, p. 1.

90. For example, C. Shelby Coffey III, executive director of the *Los Angeles Times,* made his first contact with Otis Chandler (the paper's owner) "at a gym where they were pursuing their shared taste for weight lifting" (Alex S. Jones, "Los Angeles Times Names Heir Apparent to the Editor's Job," *New York Times,* 6 April 1988, sec. 1, p. 11).

91. cf. Michael Schudson, *Watergate in American Memory* (New York: Basic, 1992), 40.

92. Barbara Reskin and Heidi I. Hartmann, eds., *Women's Work, Men's Work: Sex Segregation on the Job* (Washington, D.C.: National Research Council, National Academy Press, 1986).

93. See Storper and Scott, "Geographical Foundations," 21–22. The roots of the argument go back to Jean Gottman; see his "Urban Centrality and the Interweaving of Quaternary Activities," *Ekistics* 29 (1970): 322–31.

94. William Whyte, *City: Rediscovering the Center* (New York: Doubleday, 1989), as cited in Marshall Berman, "Two Thousand Years of Street Smarts," *Village Voice: Literary Supplement*, November 1989, 9; emphasis in original.

95. Bruno Jobert, "Planning and Social Production of Needs," *Sociologie et sociétés* 6, no. 2 (1975): 35–51; E. J. Malecki, "Corporate Organization of R&D and the Location of Technological Activities," *Regional Studies* 14, no. 3 (1980): 219–34.

96. Bruno Latour, *Laboratory Life: The Construction of Scientific Facts* (Princeton: Princeton University Press, 1986).

97. George White, "Face to Face: Preference for Round Table Spawns Need for Conference Centers, Planners," *Los Angeles Times*, 28 March 1988, sec. 4, p. 5; see also Berman, "Two Thousand Years of Street Smarts." Some sense of the scale of this activity can be gleaned from the fact that the professional organization that arranges such events, the Meeting Planners International, now includes about eight thousand independent and corporate affiliated members.

98. We are not arguing that new technologies *equate* to deskilling; there is a division of labor within the new communications spheres as well as across firms and organizations that use them. For a review of the computer deskilling literature, see Kenneth Spenner, "The Upgrading and Downgrading of Occupations: Issues, Evidence, and Implications for Education," *Review of Educational Research* 5 (Summer 1985): 125–54. For an analysis of interpersonal satisfaction in even the most routine "interactive service" operations, such as Macdonald's, see Robin Leidner, *Fast Food/Fast Talk: The Everyday Life of Service Workers* (Berkeley and Los Angeles: University of California Press, forthcoming).

99. Don H. Zimmerman, "Tasks and Troubles: The Practical Bases of Work Activities in a Public Assistance Organization," in D. A. Hansen, ed., *Explorations in Sociology and Counselling* (Boston: Houghton Mifflin, 1969); see also Zuboff, *In the Age of the Smart Machine*.

100. Garfinkel, *Studies in Ethnomethodology*, 68.

101. Donald Roy. "Efficiency and 'The Fix,' " *American Journal of Sociology* 60 (1954): 155–66.

102. Suzanne Berger, Michael L. Dertouzos, Richard K. Lester, Robert M. Solow, and Lester C. Thurow, "Toward a New Industrial America," *Scientific American* 260, no. 6 (1989): 3947.

103. Zuboff, *In the Age of the Smart Machine*.

104. Charles Walker and Robert H. Guest, *The Man on the Assembly Line* (Cambridge: Harvard University Press, 1952).

105. Zuboff, *In the Age of the Smart Machine*, 201.

106. In his discussion of the "dialectic of control," Giddens stresses just such tension in the time-space management of organizations. See his *Constitution of Society* and *Consequences of Modernity*.

# NINE

# Space, Corporation, and Class: Toward a Grounded Theory

*Roger Friedland and Donald Palmer*

For almost a century social theorists marginalized the role of space in social structure. If space was considered at all, it was analyzed as a physical environment, a container, for social structure and action. While social theory has been criticized for its neglect of temporality, its ahistorical concept construction, it has rarely been criticized for aspatiality (see Soja's essay in this volume). Space was not analyzed as a constituent of social structure itself.

There has been a resurgence of interest in space as simultaneously a determinant, an outcome, and a medium of social action and social structure. Space, it is argued, is not just a natural stage for social action, nor does its organization merely reflect the imprint of social structure (see Friedland and Boden's essay in this volume). Rather, space, like time, is formed socially, and that formation is constitutive of society and constrains its reproduction.[1] This essay explores the relationship between space and the organizational and class structuring of the corporation.

This focus on space might seem unexpected, especially in relation to corporate behavior, given that technologies of transmitting persons, materials, and information increasingly overcome the friction of distance. As we enter a universal present, the spatiality of the economic structure might seem a particularly unfruitful avenue for theoretical and empirical investigation. But, as David Harvey has remarked, capital conquers space through space. As we argue, the geographic forms of capitalism—of firms, of production, of exchange, of social class formation—matter greatly not only to economic structure but to the changing ways in which people and places are connected to each other.

Sociologists have made major advances in showing the ways in which social structures precondition, undercut, or mediate the assumptions of rationality, competition, and efficiency made by neoclassical microeconomic analyses of firm behavior. But as in other areas of sociology, theorists of complex organizational structure and strategy have neglected the role of space.[2] When sociologists study the evolution of organizational populations, the structure of social networks in which firm exchanges are embedded, and the social organization of corporate power and capitalist class formation, space has been at most implicit, a unit of observation.

In essence, those social analysts who have demonstrated the consequentiality or "friction" produced by those social structures in which exchange is embedded have neglected the importance of space as a constituent of those social structures. Thereby, they must either posit disembodied social relationships which do not exist in space or implicitly accept a frictionless space economy. The spatial organization of the firm, the geographical structure of its environment, firm location as an economically relevant social resource and constraint, the geographical structure of the formal and informal networks in which firms are embedded—all have been neglected as explicit areas of analytic concern.

In this essay we lay out the implications of the aspatiality of diverse theories of organizational behavior—population ecology, resource dependency, class theory, and transaction costs. In particular we analyze the spatial distinctiveness of dominant corporations and the elites who control them. Not only do these organizations and the individuals and groups that comprise them socially structure space, but those constructions constrain their behavior and structure. As we seek to show, the spatial structure of social relations is an essential constitutent of those relations. Neglecting it, one is likely to misspecify theory in each of these theoretical domains.

## POPULATION ECOLOGY

Population ecology argues that organizational research should not study firms which adapt to their environments; rather, it should examine discrete, homogeneous populations of organizations which compete for variegated resources in the niches in which they find themselves. The primary mechanisms of organizational change are exogenous environmental selection pressures which produce differential birth and death rates of different organizational forms. The theory minimizes the possibility of adaptation, of change in strategy and structure, in response to environmental change.[3]

The definition of organizational populations and niches—and the tendency to make the definition of each depend on the other—has been problematic in the theory.[4] One attempted solution has been to define organizational populations as those with similar technologies, analogues to genetic codes in biotic population.[5] Another is to analyze niches as resource spaces independent of the organizations which exploit them.[6]

In practice, though, analysts define populations according to the industries in which firms produce and the niches they occupy as geographically delimited product and production markets. It is now recognized that firms can enter or leave such markets and can create, modify, and adapt to them through technological and product innovation.[7] However, the original human ecological insight that there was a spatiality to human systems has not been taken up. Niches and the population of organizations which occupy them have been studied in an aspatial way. Few have explored the spatial dimensions of niche selection, creation, and change and thus the spatial dimensions of organizational adaptation.

We argue that firms differ along three dimensions important for understanding the spatial character of such ecological processes: growth dependence, dominance, and mobility. Growth dependence refers to the extent to which the firm must rely on locally produced resources for survival. Dominance refers to the degree to which the firm controls the flow of important resources into the locale in which they are situated. Mobility refers to a firm's capacity to leave the locale.

Most population ecologists take the geographical scope of an organization's niche as given.[8] However, mobile firms can select their geographic niches—the territorial stage on which action is constructed. Large corporations have enormous capacities to reallocate their administrative and production activities in space. Of the 535 surviving firms which were listed among the largest 500 industrial public corporations by *Fortune* magazine in either 1960 and/or 1975, 28 percent relocated their headquarters between 1960 and 1975. Of the 437 surviving firms listed among the top 500 in either 1975 and/or 1985, 17 percent relocated between 1975 and 1985. Relocation of production is even more frequent. Between 1972 and 1978, for example, a random sample of 121 of America's largest industrial corporations opened 599 new plants.[9] In New York alone, 3,949 existing plants were relocated between 1961 and 1985.[10]

Firms producing in or maintaining linkages with organizations in multiple locales can shift resources from one place to another, often without creating new facilities or relocating old ones. Partly for this reason, they are less dependent on the growth of the locales in which they are situated. While John Freeman notes that organizational niches vary in geographic extensiveness, the relevant variation is across resources (markets or legitimacy, for example), not across organizations.[11] Multilocational corporations can redeploy resources more rapidly from lean to rich, unstable to stable, and turbulent to placid environments. The local subunits of multilocational manufacturing organizations may obtain information, product inputs, and capital from their parent organizations' other subunits operating in other locales, thereby reducing reliance on local agglomerative economies.[12] The headquarters of corporations whose leaders have extralocal social ties may be better able to contract with service organizations outside their headquarters' locales.[13]

Firm mobility and lack of dependence on the growth of a particular locale may reduce firm mortality. Economic geographers have shown that the production facilities of multilocational corporations are more insulated from the vagaries of the national business cycle and have lower closure rates than do those of locally controlled firms, even if (perhaps because) they do have higher rates of emigration.[14] Among the basic industries of the Midwest, survival rates have been greatest for those firms with the most complex, interlocal production and marketing structures. Complex, interlocal structures increase the range of cost and supply adaptation, as well as the ease of alternative geographic and product market penetration.

In fact, the work of some population ecologists is consistent with that of economic geographers. Canadian social service agencies which relocate their headquarters have lower mortality rates.[15] Semiconductor companies that are subsidiaries of larger national corporations generate stronger competition than independent firms.[16] Research on organizational mortality in the Pennsylvania telephone industry showed that multiexchange companies, which operated in several communities and thus were less growth dependent, had lower death rates than single exchange companies operating within smaller geographic areas.[17]

Further, just as firms can open and modify industrial niches,[18] so too with geographic niches. Ecologists take the geographic dimensions of an organizational niche as given. Restaurants feed on customers, the supply of which is indicated by local gross sales, and newspapers depend upon readership whose limits are given by local population size.[19] Neither sales totals nor population levels are considered to be a product of organizational behavior.

Nondominant, nonmobile firms must take a geographically delimited niche as given. For immobile organizations, there are no location decisions, only decisions about what to produce in the location in which their elites find themselves. Further, nondominant firms have little impact on the range and quantity of resources available in their environments. Thus, most entrepreneurs starting new firms, and particularly new forms, are local in origin. They don't decide to produce something and then choose a location. Rather, they find themselves in a location and decide to produce something appropriate to the local resource mix. Use of delimited geographical units to analyze birthrates of firms producing in industries early in the product cycle, such as new firms in plastics and electronics, is appropriate.[20]

Dominant, mobile firms, by contrast, are more likely to shape geographic niches through the economic multipliers they generate. In the nineteenth century towns and cities were often created as the result of the routing of railroad track and the siting of manufacturing facilities. Local growth depends on the location there of dominant firms.[21] The locational stability of "core" production facilities, those occupying privileged positions in the market structure of the economy, shapes the rate of divestment of linked industries from an area.[22]

Dominant, mobile firms also shape the development of the geographic niches they occupy through their political power over the local state.[23] Such organizations possess political power independently of their participation in local politics precisely because they generate its growth. There is a relationship between their presence and the adoption of policies which benefit them.[24] For these firms, significant aspects of a geographic niche are neither fixed nor exogenous.

Dominance, mobility, and the economic and political power they make possible may increase a firm's life chances. Of the 110 largest industrial corporations in 1919, only 8 had been liquidated by 1969.[25] More recently, one can observe that the largest corporations in the United States have suffered a continuous decline in their pretax rates of profitability over the last three decades. Because of their control over the most important flows of capital investment, and because they have become increasingly multinational and able to move their capital across state and national boundaries, they have been able to compensate for that decline with continuous reduction in their tax liability.[26] This power is attested to by the fact that by the 1970s their plant location decisions were not influenced by local tax rate variations, suggesting the intensity of interjurisdictional competition for their presence.[27]

Thus, we argue that firms which are not dependent on areal growth, which are dominant and mobile, are less likely to be subject to selection pressures.[28] Ironically, factors that generate these attributes are the same factors that population ecologists argue make organizations particularly sensitive to selection pressures. Michael Hannan and John Freeman maintain that old, large firms that are administratively and geographically complex are most subject to structural inertia and thus least able to adapt to environmental constraints.[29] Large, administratively and geographically complex firms are freighted with sunk costs; older firms with highly institutionalized norms and entrenched power structures. As a result, these kinds of firms are more difficult to change.

We diverge from Hannan and Freeman's claims for two reasons. First, their argument addresses only one source of organizational susceptibility to environmental constraints—the capacity to adapt. Another source is its ability to create and modify those very constraints. Economic and political power may substitute for adaptation.

Second, Hannan and Freeman essentially ignore the spatial dimension of adaptation. The factors which they claim generate structural inertia do not seem to undermine the mobility of large corporations—the principal vehicle of spatial adaptation.[30] We found that neither firm size nor age directly affected the capacity of large corporations to move their headquarters or to decentralize their production facilities in space in the 1970s and 1980s, although the size of a firm's headquarters complex may reduce the likelihood of headquarters mobility.[31] In fact, older firms were more diversified and, as a result, had more spatially dispersed production.[32] Further, administrative complexity (as indicated by the use of the multidivisional form) and geographic complexity (as indicated by the spatial dispersion of a firm's production) actually facilitated headquarter relocation and new plant decentralization.[33]

Population ecologists have not analyzed spatial behavior as a form of adaptation. As a result, they underestimate the flexibility of large, old, administratively and geographically complex organizations. And by focusing on the inability of such organizations to change themselves, they neglect their capacities to change their environments through selection, creation, or modification of the niches they occupy.

Finally, a firm's location in space also shapes its capacity to engage in spatial forms of adaptation. Places vary in their accessibility to resources of all kinds, information in particular. Central places (large metropolitan areas specializing in wholesale, retail, and banking activity and supporting extensive business services) are nodes in communication, product distribution, and capital market networks and have plentiful supplies of management and financial expertise. Thus, large corporations headquartered in such places are best able to disperse and decentralize the production in space.[34]

Corporations headquartered in central places are also better able to acquire other firms far from their headquarter's locale.[35] The greater supply of information in central places makes acquisitive expansion, especially into new industries, more feasible. Thus, firms headquartered in central places make a greater number of total acquisitions (and are in turn less likely to be acquired) than those headquartered in peripheral places.[36] The purchase of other firms in the same and linked industries is a strategy to manage interindustry uncertainty and the acquisition of unrelated businesses is a strategy to avoid such constraint.[37] In addition, we found that firms headquartered in central places were more diversified than those in peripheral locales.[38]

Interestingly, Hannan and Freeman speculate that IBM was slow to diversify into the mini- and microcomputer markets because it was large and old.[39] It is worth noting that IBM was headquartered in a relatively information-poor environment, the peripheral town of Armonk, New York, and that it chose that location at a time when it dominated the development of computer technology (and thus presumably had a low demand for external information). As the technology changed rapidly, however, it found itself at a competitive disadvantage and made major relocations of elite personnel into more information-rich locations, including Manhattan.

Thus, population ecology is most applicable to organizations that are growth dependent, immobile, and nondominant. It is not surprising that population ecologists concentrate their research on precisely these types of firms: restaurants, newspapers, labor unions, wineries, breweries, and firms early in the product life cycle. Even those who have begun to investigate the impact of spatial dominance on organizational death and growth rates study relatively growth-dependent and immobile organizations—independent telephone companies.[40] We would expect to find research on growth-independent, mobile, dominant organizations to provide weaker support for the basic ecological model.[41]

## CORPORATE AND CLASS POWER

Unlike analysts of population ecology, those who study resource dependency, power elite, and class focus on organizations which are both dominant and interlocal in structure. Their research has centered on the patterning of the interlock structure among the largest corporations and financial intermediaries in the United States, precisely those organizations that connect localities and increasingly determine any locality's prospects for growth. These approaches assume either that interlocks are devices by which corporations manage market uncertainty or constraint,[42] by which banks exercise hegemony,[43] or by which members of a capitalist class achieve cohesion.[44]

What they find, almost irrespective of the algorithm they use, are regionalized maps of interlocks.[45] This regionalization is particularly apparent when one analyzes directional interlocks where an inside director sits on the board of another company.[46] Using factor analysis, for example, Michael Allen studied the interlock structure among a sample of 250 large financial and nonfinancial corporations. The firms whose di-

TABLE 4.  Localization of Corporate Interlocks,
Direct Ties, 1965

|  | Industrial Interlocks | Financial Interlocks |
|---|---|---|
| Within city | .43 | .62 |
| Within SMSA | .51 | .70 |
| Within state | .60 | .75 |

SOURCE: Clifford Tadao Kono, "Weaving Spiders in Space: The Regionalization of Corporate Interlocks in the United States," M.A. thesis, University of California, Santa Barbara, 1990.

rectors comprised the cliques tended to be headquartered in the same geographical area, and if anything the basis of the clique structure had become increasingly geographical over the period.[47] When Mark Mizruchi analyzed the composition of "interest groups" between 1935 and 1974, he found a persistent but declining level of regionalization.[48] Just as in the case of population ecology, there is an observable but implicit geography. None of these theoretical approaches adequately explains the geographical patternings of the networks they discover.

Richard Scott and John Meyer have pointed out that most studies of organizational fields have focused on horizontal linkages within geographically delimited local areas.[49] They argue that the relevant organizational fields of most organizations are functionally differentiated sectors—industrial systems that are delocalized and institutionalized on a national and international basis. But from such a perspective it is difficult to explain the persistent regionalization of intercorporate structure. It is necessary to specify the role of space as it affects the nature of any organizational field and the process by which organizations adapt to, select, and thereby change that field. Network analysts have not yet developed an adequate theory to account for the geographical structures they continuously obtain.

At the firm level, regionalized interlocks are very important for most firms. This generalization is true for both direct industrial and financial interlocks, where an inside director sits on the board of another firm or financial intermediary (table 4). One possible explanation of the regionalized pattern of interlock network, consistent with resource dependency theory, is that organizations interlock with each other on a regional basis because of the regionalized nature of interindustrial dependencies. Resource-dependence theorists stress the ways in which organizations adapt, often through interorganizational cooperation, either to manage external uncertainty or to conform to institutionalized patterns of behavior. Interlocks are assumed to allow firms to exchange information, develop norms, and make commitments.

When a firm produces in an industry that depends heavily on another

industry either as a forward or backward market, that dependency is a potential source of uncertainty. Ronald Burt has argued that resource dependencies between industries are least uncertain when they are organized by competitive markets. However, many industries in the United ˢᵗᵃᵗᵉˢ are highly concentrated, with a few major firms able to set prices ˡˡᵘˢⁱᵛᵉ or at least corespective manner. Burt ar-
 nost uncertain when they
titive and has a high vol-
which is highly concen-
dustry with little capacity
lucing in an industry with
ace high levels of market
hich produce in industries
and tend to interlock with
h constrain them.[51]
, Burt included, have stud-
ms and the interlocks they
t analyze whether interlocks
icies are in fact regionalized.
dustries which constrain one
and/or plants and as a result
If this were the case, the re-
would be responsible for the

iat this may not provide the
nomy is constrained and man-
s do not perform that much
istraints with interlocks.[52] This
rlocks do not serve the function
terdependency very well or that
alternatıᵥᵉ tions which do not manage con-
straints through interlocking ᵗᵒ ... ᵇeing penalized for the omission.

There is evidence that most corporate interlocks are not used to manage a firm's most problematic resource constraints. In ethnographic work on American and British corporate elites, Michael Useem found that market norms prevented most directors he interviewed from using interlocks with firms with which they are interdependent in any kind of directly instrumental way. Useem argues that interlocks are used as a general "business scan," as a way to garner general information about corporate practices, regulatory and political changes, and macroeconomic expectations.[53] That interlocks are generally used by corporations to garner information about the economy would explain why they have so little impact on corporate profitability.

But why, then, are interlocks regionalized? The directors selected by a firm to provide such information were typically persons known and trusted by the firm's top officers. Interlocking is an intrusive form of interaction requiring high levels of trust. As Deirdre Boden and Harvey Molotch (in their essay in this volume) point out, copresence is necessary or advantageous to many forms of communication. Useem's ethnographic research indicates that invitations to join external boards follow "networks of ancient friendship and personal contacts," not "preexisting relations between firms."[54] In an analysis of the outside board members of the largest 100 industrials in the mid 1970s, Edward Herman found that 23 percent were chosen simply because the director was linked socially with the managing directors of the firm.[55]

Social interaction among corporate elites is regionalized. Executives headquartered in the same city, who live in the same neighborhoods and belong to the same metropolitan clubs, can see each other every day "naturally." We found that the probability that accidentally disrupted interlock ties would be reconstituted was a direct function of proximity of the two headquarters, after the level of resource interdependence had been statistically controlled. Similarly, Mizruchi found that headquarter location in the same state was the most important determinant of whether fifty-seven major corporations were interlocked directly or indirectly through financial intermediaries.[56]

Places vary as settings for elite social interaction. Many of the interlocking directors interviewed by Useem had met at exclusive clubs. In his study of American directors, those who sat on more than one board and thus were the carriers of the interlock network were four times more likely to be members of exclusive social clubs than those who sat on the board of a single company.[57] Participation in common social networks generates the contacts, the trust, and the capacity for social control which makes one a candidate for selection as a board member.[58] But places unevenly provide institutions for such social networks to form. We found that firms headquartered in a region which also hosted an exclusive upper-class club were much more likely to interlock within that region than those without such a club.[59] The higher level of local interlocking in regions with exclusive upper-class clubs was not the result of differences in the supply of local interlock partners; the result obtained even after controlling statistically for the number of corporations headquartered within the region. The magnitude of the effect declined as the level of scale increased. Trust may decay with distance because interactions are less frequent and involve less of the life space of the individuals involved.

It is possible that resource dependencies are regionalized, that the elites of firms producing in interdependent industries tend to interact with each other and thereby select each other as board members. Resource dependencies might therefore generate regionalized patterns of interlocks independently of their particular economic function for the firms. To argue thus, we need first to reexamine the relationship between resource dependence and corporate interlocking.

Studies at the industrial level show that resource dependencies shape corporate interlocks. However, studies at the firm level do not support this finding. Mizruchi's studies of *existent* interlocks among large American corporations in 1980 found that market constraints had no effect on the extent of direct or indirect interlocking among fifty-seven of the largest corporations.[60] We studied all accidentally disrupted interlock ties between firms and found that interindustrial resource constraints between them had no impact on the probability that they would reconstitute the ties.[61] Evaluated at the firm level, these results suggest that resource dependencies do not generate corporate interlocks.

Resource dependencies are not, however, spatially random. Preliminary evidence indicates that resource dependencies generate regionalized patterns of corporate headquarter location of firms producing in interdependent industries. In a reanalysis of our data on broken ties, Burt found that both industrial and financial constraints were associated with the colocation of constrained firms' headquarters.[62] Heads of corporations that buy and sell to each other are likely to know or know about one another because their centers of corporate decision making are more likely to be near one another; thus, their directors will be more likely to select each other to serve on their boards. The regionalized interlock network would be generated out of proximity and acquaintance, not out of instrumental concerns to manage resource dependencies. This situation would help explain why interlock ties between interdependent firms are not more likely to be reconstituted.

Perhaps, then, geographic proximity is a mechanism for coping with market uncertainties. The relationship between resource dependence and headquarter colocation suggests that corporations may colocate their headquarters as a way to manage presumably preexisting problematic resource interdependencies. Further, corporations facing serious market constraints are not headquartered just anywhere in the urban system. There is a relationship between a corporation's headquarter location in the urban system and its position in the market structure of the American economy. Corporations producing in industries which are highly autonomous—industries not heavily dependent on other concentrated industries—were likely to locate their headquarters in *less* central places with fewer other major corporations and financial intermediaries.[63] This finding suggests either that corporations may use headquarter location to manage the resource dependencies or that corporations headquartered in more peripheral places in the capitalist landscape are less likely to enter businesses with high levels of market constraint from distant corporate actors.[64] The colocation of plants of different firms may also be structured geographically to cope with market uncertainties.[65]

Headquarter colocation may be an *alternative* strategy to interlocking as a means to regulate market relationships with other firms. We found that when interlocked firms were more intrusively connected—through joint ventures or intercorporate stockholding—*and* they were located in the same place, when the interlock tie was disrupted, they were *less likely* to reconstitute it. This suggests that geographical proximity, and the social interaction it facilitates, functions as a substitute for more formal interlocks that would be used when forms of intercorporate coordination must be managed across large distances. This is also consistent with John Galeskiewicz et al.'s study of interorganizational interdependence in one city in which they found that interdependent firms were *not* likely to be highly interlocked.[66] Proximity may be a functional substitute for formal interorganizational ties.

Led by Cliff Kono, we have studied the propensity of firms to interlock within their headquarter region at three scales: city, SMSA, and state.[67] In our initial analyses we found that the local availability of corporate headquarters producing in industries that constrained one's profitability had little effect on the probability that one would interlock within the region. Further, the metric effect declined as the scale of the analyzed unit grew smaller. Resource dependencies approached a statistically significant effect on the probability of regionalized interlocking only at the state level. These results suggest that resource dependencies are more likely to lead to interlocks between firms when the interdependent firms are more geographically distant from each other. Resource dependencies may structure the interlock network only because the theory is assessed for aggregate industries and at the largest geographical scale—the national state.[68]

If corporations use proximity to locations where organizational sources of information about and control over problematic resources are concentrated as a strategy to adapt to resource uncertainty, then failing to specify the geographical structure will lead to a distorted picture. Resource dependence theory is likely to work best when resource dependencies are transacted across large distances. Studying the structure of interlock ties between firms without regard to the geography of those firms, one is likely to underestimate both the adoption of interlocking as a strategy to adapt to resource uncertainties and its success in doing so.

## FINANCIAL HEGEMONY

Bank centrality within these corporate interlock networks, both in the overarching national network and the regional networks, is the other constant in interlock research.[69] In 1973 more than three-quarters of the two hundred largest nonfinancial corporations in the United States had at least one commercial bank executive as an outside board member.[70] In the 1970s interlocks between financials and nonindustrial corporations constituted more than half of all interlocks in the system.[71] Mizruchi found that the relative centrality of commercial banks has remained stable in the interlock network between 1904 and 1974.

Power-structure theorists such as Beth Mintz and Michael Schwartz have argued that bank centrality in the interlock network reflects the hegemonic power of the banks.[72] In their formulation, because banks control access to capital, they establish the structural constraints within which most corporations must operate. The allocation of loan capital, a "universal" commodity, gives banks a general interest in the operation of all sectors. Mintz and Schwartz point to a number of structural features of America's financial institutions: the concentration of loan capital, the organization of lender unity through consortia, the banks' dominant role in institutional stockholding, and their discretionary use of their trust departments.[73] When combined with both general and specific tendencies toward capital shortage, these factors give banks the capacity to shape corporate policies, particularly at those junctures in any corporation's life when critical choices are made about recapitalization, restructuring, or merger.[74]

By international standards American firms raise a relatively large portion of their capital through retained earnings and equity offerings.[75] However, most firms endure periods when they must borrow large sums, particularly when share prices decline and investors demand high dividend payouts, thereby undercutting corporate capacities to expand through retained earnings or to raise capital on the equity markets. Banks shape the general intersectoral and interfirm allocation of capital and are the primary private agents by which capitalist "planning" occurs. They do not need to intervene in the operational decision making of corporations to which they make loans; rather, they need to garner information about all sectors of the economy, particularly those firms which are the heaviest users of capital. "For financial institutions, interlock centrality is an indicator of substantive preeminence in the process of decision making about capital flows," they note.[76]

If banks continue to be most central in the interlock network because they control the flow of capital, then those corporations which are most interested in influence over or information about that flow should be most interlocked with them.[77] Directional interlocks, in which an inside bank director sits on the corporation's board or vice versa, are assumed to allow bank information about and influence over corporate strategy, or to allow the corporation co-optation of an actual or potential source of capital and information about capital flows. It has long been known that corporations which experience high levels of financial dependence, as indicated by forms of indebtedness, interlock more with banks.[78] As corporations increase their debt levels, they appoint financial directors to sit on their boards.[79] Further, in our research we found that, in contrast to interindustrial interlocks, when an interlock tie between a corporation and a bank was accidentally disrupted, the tie was more likely to be reconstituted if the corporation was heavily indebted to its partner.[80]

These financial interlocks are consequential for actual firm access to and use of different forms of borrowing. Corporations with financial institutions represented on their boards are much more likely to turn to external financing than those without such representatives, net of market of micro- and macroeconomic conditions.[81] Indeed, the presence of a representative of a financial institution (commercial bankers, insurance executives, investment bankers) was positively associated with the amount of funds the corporation borrowed from that sector of the market (short-term debt, long-term debt, and bond issues, respectively).[82] The pattern of corporate dependence on borrowed capital is associated with the pattern of interlocking with financial intermediaries.

As we have seen, financial interlocks—the most common form—are even more regionalized than nonfinancial interlocks. This regionalization may reflect the fact that corporations tend to maintain commercial banking relationships with banks headquartered in the same region as they are. We have begun to analyze the geographical structure of corporate banking relations for a sample of the largest industrial corporations as of 1985.[83] Corporations usually select as their primary banker a regional banker, which has the most intimate knowledge about the corporation's financial position, which provides the corporation with financial expertise and information, and which probably takes the lead in organizing bank consortia which supply the corporation with loan capital (table 5). Clearly, corporations have a tendency to choose regional bankers as their primary bankers. But when they go outside their headquarter region when choosing a primary banker, they tend to go to New York bankers. Although there was less regionalization, the same patterns obtained when we analyzed all commercial bank relationships in which corporations were involved, as opposed to just their primary bankers.

From a financial hegemony perspective, one would expect the pattern

TABLE 5. The Geography of Primary Banking Relationships, 1985

| Corporate Headquarters | Same Region | | East | | Other | | Total | |
|---|---|---|---|---|---|---|---|---|
| | % | (n) | % | (n) | % | (n) | % | (n) |
| East | 99.0 | (98) | 0 | (3) | 1.0 | (1) | 100 | (102) |
| Midwest | 72.0 | (67) | 24.7 | (23) | 3.0 | (3) | 100 | (93) |
| West | 65.8 | (25) | 28.9 | (11) | 5.2 | (2) | 100 | (38) |
| South | 38.3 | (23) | 43.3 | (26) | 18.4 | (11) | 100 | (60) |
| U.S. sample | 72.6 | (213) | 21.5 | (63) | 5.8 | (17) | 100 | (293) |

of resource dependency—the extent to which corporations require large amounts of loan capital—to account for this geography of corporate bank contracting. The largest, most indebted firms should contract with nonlocal money center institutions. But, in fact, larger, more indebted corporations are no less likely to contract with local banks, nor are they more likely to contract with the most powerful New York money-center banks, than are smaller, less capital-hungry firms. This finding suggests that even those firms with huge demands for loan capital may contract locally.

What about financial interlocking? Similarly, larger corporations are also no less likely to *interlock* with regional banks. However, corporations with high levels of debt relative to the local supply of capital are more likely to interlock with banks outside the region, presumably to major money-market centers, than are those with lower loan demands relative to the local economy.

Corporations tend to contract with regional banks independently of their scale and demand for loan capital. In contrast, whether they interlock with regional banks depends on their demand for loan capital. On the surface these results are strange. One possibility is that regionalized banking contracts may not account for the regional financial interlock pattern. The bank-centered regionalized interlock network may function primarily as a mechanism not for the management of loan capital but—a matter we will explore below—for the regulation of regional growth.

Yet there is strong evidence that financial interlocks shape access to capital, and we know that financial interlocks are highly regionalized. The fact that corporations with high levels of debt are not more likely to contract but are more likely to interlock outside the region suggests that financial interlocks are motivated by financial dependence, but only when corporations are headquartered in a different region than the banks from which they borrow money. When corporations borrow from banks headquartered in the same region, interlocks may be less important than they are for borrowing relationships with more distant financial centers.[84]

If this is the case, corporations located in major financial centers will be better able to manage high levels of financial uncertainty and dependence on external capital than those located in cities which are not major banking centers. As in other studies, Donald Palmer and his colleagues found that corporations that were more dependent on loan capital were more likely to be heavily interlocked with banks.[85] But, net of these financial interlocks, they were also significantly more likely to be headquartered in major financial centers. This relationship held *not* because corporations were more likely to interlock with banks where a large number of major banks were close by. Financial interlocking was *not* a function of the number of banks in the headquarter city or suburbs. This suggests that the two mechanisms of securing information about or influence over capital flows—financial interlocks and location in a financial center—are independent strategies.

Because banks affect and have information about the interregional and interindustrial allocation of capital, they are major sources of strategic information. If corporate-bank interlocks are to function as the primary circuits of macroeconomic information flow (the social infrastructure of capitalist private planning), then those corporations—large, dispersed, diversified, facing high levels of market constraint—which have the greatest demand for such information and whose strategic decisions constitute that information should be most heavily interlocked with the banks. They are not. Those are precisely the kinds of corporations which tend to locate their headquarters in financial centers. Again, location appears to substitute for interlocking.

These results strongly suggest that headquarter location is a powerful determinant of a corporation's ability to manage uncertainty and to obtain the information financial intermediaries provide. They also suggest that failure to specify the regional distribution of banks and industrial corporations, as well as the regional organization of financial interlocks and contracts, will lead analysts both to underestimate the importance of financial intermediaries in the American economy and to overestimate the import of financial interlocks as the primary mechanism of bank influence.

## FRACTIONS OF CAPITAL OR REGIONAL GROWTH MACHINES? THE EVOLUTION OF THE AMERICAN INTERLOCK NETWORK

These dense interlock networks, with the largest banks and corporations at their center, are taken to indicate a class cohesion which undercuts the precondition of capitalist democracy—elite competition.[86] Class the-

orists typically take interlock structures to indicate the existence of a capitalist class whose individual members have interests above and beyond
the organizational entity with which they are primarily affiliated.[87]
Thus, those directors who are most central in the network, "the inner
circle," have both the capacity to pursue and interest in achieving the
condition necessary to sustain capital accumulation in the economy as a
whole.[88] Class theory is also typically unconcerned with the one constant
in their research—the regionalized pattern. Some have argued that the
regional clusters indicate interest group differentiation among the
American corporate elite.[89] Others suggest that the regionalized networks reflect patterns of social interaction among corporate elites.

The evolution of the American interlock structure in this century has
a number of characteristics. First, before the rise of the corporation and
the initial merger movement, which began in 1897, railroad corporations were at the center of a relatively sparse interlock network.[90] The
industrial corporations with which they were most intensely interlocked
were coal and telegraph. The interlock ties tended to indicate common
ownership and operational interdependence. Second, as the corporate
form spread and large holding companies were consolidated, the interlock network became more dense and the banking industry became increasingly central to the network. The pattern of interlocks gradually
emerged such that banks were at the center of both a single unitary
network and a series of regional networks.[91] Third, over time the network has become less centralized,[92] as interlocks have become less concentrated among firms and multiple cliques have formed.

There is perhaps a structure to this sequence. Those organizations
most central to the networks have low capacities to exit and are highly
dependent on the locations where they make their investments. As a
result, they have a vital interest in assuring that those locations grow.
Railroad corporations, historically bank-owned in the United States,
sank enormous capital in the laying of railroad lines and then depended
on the volume of business between the points those lines connected.
They, as well as the banks which owned them, thus not only played an
active role in sponsoring urban development but also participated in
various co-optive devices—including interlocks—to assure that growth.[93]
In the 1960s railroads and utilities were still the most heavily interlocked
and most central nonfinancial firms.[94] It is striking that those industries
that were highly interlocked with them were likewise similarly constrained in space—telegraph and coal. Publishing, shoes, liquor, lumber,
meat, and agricultural machinery were not heavily interlocked with the
railroads.[95]

If centrality in the economy were the source of centrality in the interlock network, we would expect that the displacement of rail by airlines

would lead these firms to equally high levels of interlock centrality. Given the relative ease with which airlines can shift capital in space, it has not. True, the centrality of transportation firms in the interlock network has declined over the century, but as of 1974 railroad firms were still more heavily interlocked than nonrailroad transportation firms.[96]

Similarly, banks, even the largest national banks headquartered in New York and Chicago, depend on regional growth. Banks hold the mortgages on major parcels of commercial and industrial land. As we have seen, a significant amount of commercial bank business is accounted for by locally headquartered firms who seek short-term and long-term financing from them and who deposit their funds with them. The provision of start-up capital is highly regionalized, based on trust between lender and borrower and on the possibility of observing the borrower's business practices. Regional banks grow in tandem with the corporations headquartered there.[97] Even the largest financial intermediaries tend to regionalize their investments. The most powerful determinant of the extent to which the largest financial intermediaries take major equity stakes in the same large industrial corporations is whether or not the corporations are headquartered in the same state.[98] Thus, regional banks will naturally recruit regionally headquartered corporations which generate the most important demand for their capital and the regional growth on which their own profitability and growth depend. National banks have been unable, by and large, to displace the regional banks because access to information about corporate behavior is regionalized. Indeed, during the 1980s regional banks in both the United States (and Germany) rose in importance relative to the big money-center banks.[99] In 1983 major corporations still did a majority of their commercial banking business with banks inside the metropolitan area in which they were located.[100] Thus, national banks must rely on regional banks as gatekeepers to national capital markets and on interlocks with important regional industrial firms for information about firms within the region.

Banks' dependence on their state, and even their city, of origin is in part a function of government policy. The United States is one of the few nations to have a competitive banking industry. It was not until the Federal Reserve was created in 1913 that the United States had a central bank. Savings and loans and commercial banks have, until recently, been constrained by law from interstate operations. This constraint was caused in part by populist fears in many states, fears shared by their business communities, that interstate banking would facilitate the takeover of their firms by out-of-state corporations.[101]

As a result of these forces, banks have not been able to exit and have remained, until recently, dependent on the growth of the region in which they are located. This is especially the case with regional, non-money-center banks. They have thus been central actors in what Harvey Molotch has referred to as the "local growth machine."[102] Therefore, they have been eager to co-opt the regionally dominant corporate actors who generate the most important flows of resources into those localities and states. Mintz and Schwartz argue that bank centrality in the interlock networks derives from their general interest in gathering information necessary to their role as allocators of capital. Because of the regionalized nature of information exchange, interlocks tend to be regionalized and banks tend to be at the center of the networks.

Corporations often depend on the growth of a locality or region. First, corporations have become increasingly powerful, with enormous market power, privileged access to capital markets, and the ability to control the most important flows of direct investment and commodities. They are thereby able to make strategic choices, to shape their environments, to choose between environments in which to operate. That very power makes information increasingly valuable to them. Information is generated randomly with respect to both source and time. Thus, potential sources of information must be continuously monitored.[103] Information of value cannot be easily validated; indeed, its very transmission may border on illegality. As a result, trust that derives from social interaction is vital. To achieve access to information and to be in a position to exchange it, regular social interaction with other elites is important. Such social interaction can be achieved only in a delimited region or locality. A corporate elite's social capital tends to be regionally "embedded."[104]

Second, to the extent that corporations have regionally concentrated production structures or locate their most innovative production in their headquarter locale, they depend on the cost of land, the availability of labor, and the potential competition for both. When, for example, major industrial corporations open new plants in younger industries, they tend to do so within their headquarter state.[105] As a result, large corporations are often highly sensitive to local public policies that might affect their profitability, whether pollution control, welfare policies, education, or taxation.

Thus, both kinds of firms—firms that depend on access to strategic information exchanged among regional elites and firms that depend on regional economic conditions for their profitability—are likely to be enormously concerned about the regional growth patterns in which banks are centrally involved. A region's major banks are private centers of both intercorporate communication and regional land-use planning, and they control access to nonlocal sources of capital. They are also likely to be prime movers in any infrastructural policies that will shape future growth—dams, roads, sewers, urban renewal, mass transit—not only because they are politically central but because they are typically the agents who approve and facilitate the issuance of the bonds used to finance them.[106] From the point of view of such corporations, it is perfectly reasonable for their officers to sit on the board of the bank, which has become more common than for bankers to sit on the industrial boards.[107] The latter pattern would be more consistent with a financial control relation, the former with an approach emphasizing the growth machine and regional capitalism. This interpretation makes sense of the fact that the largest corporations are *not* the most central industrial firms, particularly in the directional interlock network organized by inside members of the boards of directors.[108] One might expect such corporations to make the heaviest demands on national capital markets and thus be highly interlocked with national and regional banks. Such is not the case. These corporations are also most industrially diversified and regionally dispersed.[109] Their capacity to exit reduces their dependence on regional banks for capital and on regional economic conditions for profitability. We found that larger corporations with more geographically dispersed productive structures were less likely to have regionalized interlocks.[110] Because such corporations are not as central in the regional network, they are less central in the national network. The capacity to exit may be as important as external capital usage as a determinant of corporate centrality in the interlock network. It is not surprising that *regional* industrial corporations are most central in the directional interlock network.[111]

Now we come to the third generalization, that the corporate network has become less centralized, less unitary. The same kinds of factors can explain these changes. First, banks—particularly the large money-center banks—have been freed from their dependence on a given locality or state through the rise of international banking operations, regional banking consortia, and, most recently, interstate banking. Thus, their greater capacities for exit, along with their lesser growth dependence, has reduced their need for co-optation, for influence, for information. Reciprocally, corporations have increasingly been able to raise money by creating their own financial subsidiaries, by accessing Eurodollar markets, and by turning to other sources. Second, corporations have continuously increased their ability to move direct investment and liquid capital quickly over vast distances. Plant dispersion has steadily increased over time. Thus, corporate regional dependencies have steadily declined. This decline has reduced their interest in monitoring and controlling the regional economies. Third, and finally, corporate headquarters have relocated out of New York City and corporate regional complexes have risen elsewhere in the United States. To the extent that these interlock networks represent regionalized spatial as opposed to functional structures, the declining dominance of New York would lead to a fragmentation of the network. Such fragmentation has occurred despite the fact that concentration of capital, mergers across related and unrelated industries, and the general conglomeration of the economy has proceeded at a furious pace.

Thus, it is important to understand the nature of bank and corporate dependence on the growth and economic conditions of their region of operations, as well as their capacity to exit, in order to explain the regionalized interlock network. The density of the corporate interlock network and the centrality of corporations and financial institutions within it are likely to be shaped by their relationship to the regional economies in which they manage, produce, and market their goods.

### Transaction Costs

There have been various movements away from the organization as a unit of analysis. Population ecology took a population of organizations as the unit of analysis. Class theory took the capitalist class, for whose members organizations were mere instrumentalities. Transaction cost theory took the transaction as the unit of analysis and argued that the efficiency of conducting transactions determined whether or not transactions would be governed by the hierarchy within a firm or by the market between firms. Hierarchies, it was argued, arise to overcome the problematic nature of transactions between small numbers of actors, which are subject to opportunism.[112] Unlike the other theoretical traditions, transaction cost theory did take space into account. After all, it was the difficulties of surveillance and the high probabilities of opportunism as chains of command and production organization stretched across space that drove the emergence of hierarchy. Transaction cost theorists are well aware of distance as a source of opportunism and the implications of immobility for asset specificity.

But to a sociologist it should be evident that alternatives beside market and hierarchy can manage uncertain transactions, namely, social solidarity. In an important critique of the undersocialized theories of economists and their importation of oversocialized models of institutional structure, Mark Granovetter stressed that both market exchange and bureaucratic hierarchy are embedded in social relations which affect their operations.[113] Social networks may facilitate interfirm exchange under conditions where the new institutional economists would predict internalization through hierarchy. The fundamental problem for corporate elites is that their tasks cannot be routinized, performance is difficult to measure, and accountability is hard to achieve. The more uncertain the environment of a corporation, the more this is the case.

Rosabeth Moss Kanter has argued that the importance of trust becomes increasingly important as one ascends the bureaucratic hierarchy, and such trust is achieved through selection of elites based on social homogeneity.[114] Common social background and participation in a common, closed social network is essential to advancement in the upper reaches of the managerial hierarchy. Organizations thus depend on the existence of a capitalist class—as William Domhoff has described it, a "network of interacting and intermarrying families who perceive each other as equals and have distinctive lifestyles and values which differentiate them from other classes."[115] Clearly, a capitalist social class can be partially derived from its organizational functions.

Executives spend most of their time communicating with other elites outside the organization. Corporate elites must negotiate with strangers, strangers who make claims that cannot be easily validated. This condition dictates that corporations have incentives to internalize uncertainty through vertical and horizontal integration, and hence to create separate divisions to manage these complex structures. But it also suggests that corporate elites will attempt to construct political links, or interorganizational networks, with those with whom they interact and can trust.

Trust requires social interaction, and social interaction is regionalized in space. Advancement in a corporation requires that an ever larger percentage of the executive and his or her spouse's private life be organized around regional social interactions relevant to the corporation.[116] Executives are frequently recruited from particular neighborhoods, are expected to belong to certain clubs, and are often assigned to political participation in different organizations and policy groups. As we have seen, the existence of an exclusive upper-class social club in a city was a powerful determinant of a corporation's tendency to interlock with industrial and financial corporations within the region.[117] Corporate interlocks tend to be regionalized because of the familiarity and trust promoted by proximity and the social interaction it makes possible. Those regionalized interlock structures are not only a private control structure over the regional economy, regulating public policy initiatives and monitoring major land-use transformations, but important gateways to national and international corporations with which regional corporations interlock and do business.[118]

In the language of the transaction cost approach, social class is one mechanism to reduce the costs of transactions and the probability of opportunism. The building blocks of a capitalist class are thus the regionalized networks of social interaction between the families of corporate elites. We would expect these regionalized networks to be an important mechanism for political mobilization, for social control within the network, and for defense against external actors. Corporations whose managers are more central in the capitalist class—as indicated by board memberships, personal wealth, and listing in the Social Register—have been found to be less likely to be acquired and less likely to be acquired in a hostile manner.[119] Given the regionalization of interlocks and social class institutions, we might then expect the frequency and nature of mergers to differ depending on whether they occur within or between regions.

A case in point is the 1986 mobilization of the capitalist class within the San Francisco region to defend its central financial institution, locally headquartered Bank of America. When Bank of America was faced with serious financial loss caused in part by its Mexican investments, Los Angeles–based First Interstate made an initial takeover attempt. A decision was made to replace Bank of America's chief executive with a member of the local capitalist elite; moreover, at least two local financiers offered to raise the $1 billion or so it would take to save the bank—Richard Blum, the husband of Mayor Dianne Feinstein and the head of an investment firm, and Stanley Hiller of Hellman and Friedman, another local investment firm. Clearly, the maintenance of a powerful, locally headquartered financial complex was deemed critical by many San Francisco capitalists, and they used their regional networks to defend it against external takeover. In the words of the *New York Times* business reporter: "Civic and business leaders in San Francisco are also worried that San Francisco is losing out to Los Angeles as the financial center of the West. Many San Francisco corporations have been taken over by outside companies. If BankAmerica were to be swallowed by First Interstate Bancorp of Los Angeles, which has made a bid, it would be a crushing blow" (28 October 1986). Indeed, the very origin of the hostile takeover, which first began in the mid 1950s, derived from businessmen who were not only socially marginal—immigrants, foreigners, and Jews—but geographically marginal, coming from the Southwest.[120]

These regional networks of corporate cooperation are grounded in part in the federal structure of American politics, in which states have enormous authority over corporate governance, and in the many public policies that dramatically affect corporate profitability. During the 1980s, for example, there were movements in dozens of states to introduce legislation that would make takeover of firms headquartered in that state more difficult.[121] Similarly, regional banks created compacts to prevent takeovers by major New York banks.[122] Mizruchi analyzed the similarity of corporate political activity as measured by common congressional campaign contributions by corporate political action committees in 1980.[123] One of the most important determinants of this commonality was whether or not two corporations were headquartered in the same state.[124] Common plant locations did not matter. Whether the firms were directly interlocked or constrained each other in the market also had no effect on this commonality. Moreover, corporations in which the same large commercial banks and insurance companies had significant equity holdings or which were interlocked with the same financial intermediaries *were* more likely to contribute to the same candidates. Banks tend to interlock and own on a regionalized basis. The social structure of American capitalism is a regionalized network of corporate and financial elites.

## A COMPARATIVE GEOGRAPHY OF CLASS

We have argued that social class formation is contingent on the regional structure of corporate elites. Further, we have suggested that the formation of a capitalist social class reduces the uncertainty of intracorporate and intercorporate transactions. If this is so, we would expect that corporate structures designed to reduce or manage uncertainty might vary cross-nationally with the geographical structure of capital.

Table 6 lays out the number of the largest one thousand industrial corporations in Europe headquartered in a nation, as well as the number of those headquartered in the most central metropolitan region within that country. Capital is most geographically decentralized in the United States and Germany and most geographically centralized in France and England. These patterns of geographic centralization reflect differing urban structures that date back to the early nineteenth century. Paris and London have always enjoyed extraordinary primacy in terms of population relative to the French and British urban systems, compared to less hierarchical urban systems of Germany and Italy.[125] These divergent patterns of capitalist urbanization in fact built on geographic formations that date back to medieval times. As it collapsed, the Roman Empire left in its wake a string of cities that dotted the north-south trade route connecting the Mediterranean basin to the Rhine, Flanders, and the Baltic. In Europe geographically and politically centralized states such as England and France first emerged outside this trade belt. State formation came later and in a more decentralized fashion—as in the industrialized core of Germany and Italy—inside the belt.[126] (Significantly, Prussia—the Berlin-based, largely agrarian platform for German unification—was, just like the Ile de France—outside the trade belt.)

These contemporary patterns of geographical concentration of corporate and population are associated with historical state structures. Germany, the United States, and Italy were politically unified either late or incompletely (Germany, 1871; Italy, 1860) as compared to England and France, which were centralized completely and early on. Not incidentally, Germany and the United States experienced their industrialization at about the same time, much later than Britain and France. Both post–World War II Germany and the United States have federal structures in which the national capital does not coincide with the geographical center of corporate and financial power.[127] In Italy, which is now governmentally centralized, the state capital also does not coincide with the geographical center of capital.[128] In France and England, by contrast, the centralized state structure has its capital in the same location as do the most important corporations and banks.

Centralized states generated centralized urban systems in which their capital cities were preeminent. Not surprisingly, this pattern tended toward the geographic centralization of capital as well, given the importance of state issues—particularly ports, railroads, and other public construction—in the genesis of banking centers.[129] In America's fragmented financial system during the nineteenth century, for example, state banks were frequently required to hold state bond issues to back their notes.[130] In the United States and Germany, railroad finance was critical to the origins of the banks. The decentralized American and German governmental structures—which initially financed, promoted, and regulated railroad construction—produced a series of independent rail networks, each oriented to the major population centers within its borders.[131] The resultant rail network was more diffuse, more multiplex, thereby reinforcing the decentralized territorial distribution of economic activity and population. In contrast, the centralized British and French governmental structures generated rail networks centered on London and Paris. The railroads all led to and thereby reinforced the preeminent center of population and governmental authority. As a result, financial, population, and governmental structures of Germany and the United States were more decentralized in space, while those of Britain and France have been more centralized.

So, too, centralized states such as France and England also sponsored banks—the Bank of France (established by Napoleon in the early 1800s) and the Bank of England (established in 1694)—which acted as magnets to private competitors often originating elsewhere in the country. (In France the state actually eliminated provincial banks by decree in 1848.)[132]

These variations in geographical structure are associated with the historical adoption of bureaucratized, multilocational, diversified organizational structures. Like their American counterparts, German firms are among the most highly bureaucratized, on multidivisional lines, in Europe.[133] British and, presumably, French firms are much less diversified than German or American firms.[134]

The large capital requirements of vertical integration and diversification led to both the diffusion of stock ownership and the professionaliza-

TABLE 6. Corporate Headquarter Concentration in Several Western European Nations in 1975

| | Number of HQs | HQs in Metropole number (%) | State Structure | Family Ownership | Bank Loans Controlled from Center (%) |
|---|---|---|---|---|---|
| France | 112 | 98 (87) Paris | centralized Paris | high | 88 |
| England | 208 | 137 (65) London | centralized London | high | 86 |
| Italy | 48 | 22 (46) Milan | late-centralized Rome | high | 34 |
| Germany | 318 | 27 (8) Frankfurt | federal Bonn | low | 21 |
| United States | 500 | 90 (18) New York | federal Washington, D.C. | low | — |

SOURCES: Adapted from Michael Aiken, Kenneth Newton, Roger Friedland, and Guido Martinotti, "Urban Systems Theory and Urban Policy: A Four Nation Comparison," *British Journal of Political Science* 17 (1987): 341–58. Data for Europe and the United States refer to 1975. New York City has continued to lose its centrality; in 1985 only 61 corporations (or 12 percent) were headquartered there. The percentages of bank deposits and loans controlled from the dominant city are derived from L. Ahnstrom, *Styrande oche ledande verksamhet i Vasteuropa: En ekonomisk-geografist studie* (Stockholm: Almqvist and Wiksell, 1973), cited in Stein Rokkan and Derek W. Urwin, *Economy, Territory, Identity: Politics of West European Peripheries* (London: Sage, 1983), 41.

tion of management. As a result, family control of the major American corporations declined over the century. In 1932 Berle and Means reported that 56 percent of the 200 largest industrial firms were still owned or controlled by families or family groups.[135] Even using a less demanding criterion of stock ownership (4 percent versus 10 percent), by the late 1960s family control had dropped to 37 percent.[136] By the 1970s only 18 percent of the top management of the largest 200 nonfinancial firms represented a controlling ownership interest in the firm.[137] By 1980 the figure had dropped still further to 13 percent.[138]

In both England and France, multilevel, multi-industrial, multilocal bureaucratic hierarchies developed much later than in the United States or Germany. Significantly, family control of major corporations also remained more extensive in England and France well into the twentieth century than in the United States or Germany.[139] In France this control was achieved particularly through investment holding companies, which provided finance to compensate for an inadequately developed capital market and to avoid bank control.[140] In 1971 families held at least minority control in half of the largest 200 firms in France.[141] In Britain family firms actively resisted diversification in order to maintain their control.[142] As a result, in Britain, too, holding companies, as federations of family firms, remained dominant well into the post–World War II period.[143]

Thus, the geographical structure of capital—and the social interaction it facilitates—appears to affect the extent to which hierarchy replaces the market. Organizational concentration in space may minimize transaction costs and allow class to substitute for hierarchy.

In Britain and France the coincident spatial centralization of state authority and economic power made it much easier for the bourgeoisie to form into a self-conscious social class characterized by high levels of social interaction and a distinctive life-style. The existence of this class provided British and French corporate elites with channels of communication and social control outside the marketplace, as well as credentials that denote social connections and cultural competences—what Pierre Bourdieu has referred to as "social" and "cultural" capital—that shape recruitment because they select for executives who can use that social world to the benefit of the firms which employ them.[144]

In both Britain and France the major corporations and banks of both countries select their elite personnel disproportionately from a multigenerational, socially closed upper class. But the mechanisms differ. In Britain the corporate elite are drawn disproportionately from patrician families and children who attended upper-class "public schools."[145] In Britain the state has not intervened directly in the nation's industrial development. As a rule, careers in civil service and the corporate world have historically been separate. In France the state has been much more interventionist, indeed engineering from Paris the economic and spatial concentration of the corporate sector in Paris. French elite educational institutions—*les grandes écoles*—have supplied personnel for both state and corporate sectors. As a result, the French corporate elite tend to be drawn from children of old "owning" families and those who have attended the elite state-based *grandes écoles* which supply personnel to the Paris-based government.[146] In contrast to Britain, French state elites frequently migrate—the French call it *pantouflage*—to the corporate sector later in their careers. Spatial propinquity and common socialization in *les grandes écoles*—combine to provide continuous opportunities for social interaction between state and corporate elites. Not surprisingly, members of the *grands corps,* the most powerful and prestigious components of the public sector which draw their personnel overwhelmingly from *les grandes écoles,* are most central in the interlock network.[147]

British and French firms could rely on class solidarity, the social control and closure of the haute bourgeoisie. The geographical concentration of state authority and corporate power made bourgeois class formation easier. Not surprisingly, the corporate elites of both countries are noted for their social closure.[148] In neither country have business schools played an important role as an instrument for socialization and recruitment of the most important corporate elites.[149]

Given the difficulties of social control among more dispersed and competitive German and American capitalists, it is not surprising that corporations in these countries took the lead in funding management schools that would professionally socialize corporate elites.[150] In the United States and Germany education in elite private liberal arts universities and law and business schools is much more important to corporate recruitment than in Britain, where secondary schools matter, or in France, where elite state professional schools are critical.

Various authors have suggested that the adoption of bureaucratic structures, of accounting procedures, is a strategy to achieve legitimacy in the face of strangers who must make resource commitments to the organization.[151] That corporations have less complex, less formal structures where capitalists are geographically concentrated may be the result of highly inclusive networks of interactions among all corporate elites, hence of a national capitalist class. Class may substitute for institutionalization through hierarchy.[152] It is precisely in countries such as France and England where capital is nationally organized, where it exists as a self-conscious class rather than a highly disaggregated set of elites who share the same structural position, that the process of creating divisions and conglomerations came latest.

*A Comparative Look at the Interlock Structure*

But if the geography of capital matters to class formation, how does it affect the interlock structure? Given the centrality of financial institutions in the corporate interlock network, cross-national variations in the relationship between corporations and banks should significantly affect the structure of the network. In both Britain and the United States banks usually do not take major equity positions in single industrial corporations. In the United States, for example, of the 200 largest industrial corporations in 1966, only in 22 percent did any single bank or group of banks own 5 percent or more of the corporation's stock.[153] British and American firms have historically been more dependent on retained earnings to finance expansion and on the equity market to raise outside capital. When British and American firms must borrow large amounts from commercial and merchant banks, they borrow from a diverse set of financial institutions, as opposed to just one, so that unlike German firms, for example, they are—in the words of John Scott—dependent on a "constellation of interests."[154]

In France and Germany financial capital is less competitive, more concentrated, and has historically taken significant equity positions in the country's major industrial corporations. In both countries the equity markets are tiny and the shares of most corporations are not publicly traded. In France capital is largely controlled by both state banks and investment holding companies, while in Germany it is controlled by "universal banks." In contrast to American and British firms, German and French firms have been much more dependent on banks for their financial needs.[155] In 1980, for example, French nonfinancial corporations derived 71 percent of their external funds from the banks, while the German firms got well over 90 percent of their external financing from the banks.[156] In contrast, in 1979 U.S. nonfinancials derived only 48 percent of their external funds from short- and long-term debt, which marked a significant increase from earlier patterns.[157]

As a result, German and French financial institutions have much more direct influence over the strategic decision making of the countries' major firms. In France, as of 1980 state financial institutions controlled about 70 percent of all lending, which, when combined with the discretionary powers of the Bank of France to approve and subsidize major loans, added to French financial intermediaries' already considerable powers to intervene in the management of French firms.[158] In Germany shareholders deposit their shares with the banks, which are delegated to vote them as they see fit.[159] As a result, the large German banks vote 70 percent of the shares of the 425 largest firms. This degree of control has given the major financial intermediaries in both countries a

TABLE 7.    Corporate and Spatial Organization
in Comparative Perspective

|  | Spatial Centralization of the Corporate System | |
|---|---|---|
|  | Low | High |
| *Bank control of industry* | | |
| Low | United States<br>unitary network<br>.13 centralization<br>.04 density | Great Britain<br>segmented network<br>.12<br>.03 |
| High | Germany<br>unitary network<br>.27<br>.07 | France<br>segmented network<br>.13<br>.03 |

NOTE:  The figures refer to the centralization and density of the interlock network for the individual countries cross-classified by spatial centralization and bank control.

stake in and an instrument to assure the long-term profitability of the country's industrial corporations and to reorganize them when they see fit.[160] Associated with the high levels of bank ownership in France and Germany, restructurings are organized politically by financial intermediaries; in England and the United States, by contrast, they have tended to be accomplished through the equity market, including hostile takeovers (table 7).

Let us examine the interlock structure of these four nations. In all four countries banks are central to the interlock network, but the pattern varies cross-nationally. Even though they have divergent patterns of bank-corporate relations, the interlock network in Germany and the United States is a unitary network, while that of France and Britain is more segmented.[161] In France and England banks are at the center of specific multiple, functional, client-based interest groups, while in Germany and the United States they are at the center of a unitary national network, as well as the several regional networks.[162] The interlock structure among British and French firms is significantly less compact than that of the American and German firms, with a higher percentage of firms that are entirely isolated from the network and a lower density.[163]

In terms of density and centralization scores—the extent to which the interlock network contains a structural "center" made up of corporate elites who are central in the network and interlocked with each other—for the most recent cross-national interlock study, the British and French networks are both less centralized and less dense than the German network,[164] despite the fact that French bank-corporate relations resemble the German much more than they do the British. The lower densities of the British and French networks are probably partly due to the higher percentage of family-controlled firms in both countries, which avoid participation in the interlock network.[165]

However, the American interlock network is comparable to the British and the French. According to these measures, the United States appears as an aberrant case. The singularity of the American case reflects, we believe, the particularity of American financial intermediaries. German banks have long been able to lend nationally, to interlock with one another, and to take ownership positions in each other. German banks were "universal" banks combining commercial and investment functions. In Germany, Scott writes, "The banks . . . did not form specific combines or interest groups. The banks, the Allianz insurance, and the major industrials formed a dense core of 15 companies at the heart of a 34-member center which was particularly strong in heavy industry, mining, and utilities and which stretched across all German regions. . . . Primary financial interlocks tended to be associated with financial participations and other institutional links."[166]

American banks, in contrast, have been legally separated from the investment banks, constrained to operate in-state, and expressly forbidden from interlocking with each other for much of this century. As a result, the American interlock network is less dense, less centralized than it would otherwise be. If and as the constraints on interstate banking and bank-industrial ownership fall, it will be fascinating to watch these historic patterns change.

In the United States and Germany interlocking appears to have been a mechanism to achieve intercorporate social coordination and control, if not class cohesion, where spatial fragmentation makes that difficult. In France and England, where the spatial concentration of corporate elites facilitates social interaction and cohesion, interlocking is more likely to trace functional patterns of ownership and hegemony. Given the concentration of capitalists in Paris and London, the location there of exclusive institutions for social class interaction, and the pattern of frequent interaction with the state elites who control the most important parameters of economic policy, interlocking is superfluous to the formation of a national capitalist class. Indeed, in England outside or "nonexecutive" directors are a relatively recent and still poorly developed phenomenon encouraged by the Bank of England.[167]

In the United States some researchers assume that interlocking directorates are traces of class power. But the social interaction and cohesion that is provided by a geographical community may substitute for more organizationally bound forms of elite communication and social control. Thus, just as firms in the United States and Germany developed more complex, more bureaucratic, more multidivisonal structures earlier and more extensively than did firms in France or England, so, too, they also developed increasingly complex networks of interlocking directorates at the end of the nineteenth century.[168] In the United States and Germany interlocking was a mechanism to achieve limited coordination and social control where capital was geographically decentralized and highly competitive. In Germany in particular, regional cartels blossomed between 1875 and 1930.[169]

In the United States the merger movement that began in 1897 was in part an attempt by major firms such as U.S. Steel, ATT, and J. P. Morgan and Company to control increasing industrial competition from corporations headquartered and financed in multiple regional centers.[170] Economies of scale could be achieved at low production levels, financing could be accomplished internally, and technologies were rapidly changing. That merger movement failed to control the competition. As a result, businesses turned to interlocking and to government regulation to assure more control over their environments. One form that regulation took was the Federal Reserve Act of 1913, initiated by the New York–based banks, which faced increasing competition from regional banks in other states. In the United States the regionalized networks of corporations and banks became interest groups, based in part on their common interest in the regional economy in which their production and elite communities were situated and in part on their situation as interorganizational communities in competition with those located elsewhere in the country. Interstate banking regulation, which prevented interregional bank mobility and interregional bank stockholding, as well as restricting interbank interlocks (Clayton Act, 1914), assured that banks would have a central role and interest in assuring the internal coherence of the regional community. Similarly, antitrust legislation emerged in part as an institutional strategy by regional corporations to prevent integration into the consolidated structures being engineered by some of the largest corporate actors in America. And it was this very antitrust legislation that made it difficult for corporations to purchase others in the same or linked industries, thereby spurring diversification.[171]

As a result, American business leaders are distinctively lacking in class consciousness: they view themselves as competitive entrepreneurs and only rarely as members of a class with common interests.[172] Because of that regional decentralization, capital is not nationally organized as a class. A weak American state has reinforced that fragmentation through antitrust legislation and prohibition of cartels, something which has been legal for much of the twentieth century in many European nations. But as a result, the American government has also been prevented from decisively intervening into the organization or restructuring of capital.

Thus, the United States fought an interregional civil war over the state's right to make such an intervention. American businessmen distrust their state because they have been unable, given their geographical dispersion, from creating mechanisms of social control over their own members.[173] They do not trust the state because they cannot trust each other.

In France and England, by contrast, capital is geographically centralized and nationally organized as a self-conscious class. In both countries informal mechanisms based on community interaction and formal mechanisms of national organization exist by which to control their membership and achieve consensus. The organizational center of both the corporate and financial world is simultaneously the capital of a centralized state. Thus, the state is able to cooperate with businesspersons as a class.[174]

This essay has had one purpose—to demonstrate the relevance of space, both as a medium through which corporations adapt to changing environments and as a constituent of the corporate and class structures which constrains the strategies they adopt. We hope that we have at least begun the debate.

## NOTES

We are grateful for the comments and criticism of a number of friends and colleagues: Ron Aminzade, Bill Bielby, Michael Useem, Mark Mizruchi, Harvey Molotch, Charles Perrow, Sandy Robertson, Richard Scott, David Stark, and Magnus Stenbeck.

1. Pierre Bourdieu, *Outline of a Theory of Practice*, trans. Richard Nice (Cambridge: Cambridge University Press, 1977); David Harvey, *The Condition of Postmodernity* (Oxford: Basil Blackwell, 1989); Edward Soja, *Postmodern Geographies* (London: Verso, 1989); Anthony Giddens, *The Constitution of Society* (Berkeley and Los Angeles: University of California Press, 1984); and Giddens, *A Contemporary Critique of Historical Materialism* (London: Macmillan, 1981).

2. Conversely, scholars of territorial systems—cities, states, and nations—have neglected the organizational structures that compose and connect them. See Donald Palmer and Roger Friedland, "Corporation, Class, and City System," in Mark Mizruchi and Michael Schwartz, eds., *Intercorporate Relations: The Structural Analysis of Business* (Cambridge: Cambridge University Press, 1987), 145–84.

3. Michael T. Hannan and John H. Freeman, "Structural Inertia and Organizational Change," *American Sociological Review* 49 (1984): 149–64, and "The Population Ecology of Organizations," *American Journal of Sociology* 82 (1977): 929–64; Howard Aldrich and Jeffrey Pfeffer, "Environments of Organizations," in Alex Inkeles, ed., *Annual Review of Sociology* (Palo Alto, Calif.: Annual Reviews, 1976), 79–105.

4. Hannan and Freeman, "Population Ecology of Organizations," 934.

5. Bill McKelvey, *Organizational Systematics: Taxonomy, Evolution, Classification* (Berkeley and Los Angeles: University of California Press, 1982); Graham Astley, "The Two Ecologies: Population and Community Perspectives on Organizational Evolution," *Administrative Science Quarterly* 30, no. 2 (1985): 224–41.

6. J. Miller McPherson, "Evolution in Communities of Voluntary Organizations," in Jitendra V. Singh, ed., *Organizational Evolution: New Directions* (London: Sage, 1990), 53–77, and J. Miller McPherson and Lynn Smith-Lovin, "A Comparative Ecology of Five Nations: Testing a Model of Competition among Voluntary Organizations," in Glenn Carroll, ed., *Ecological Models of Organizations* (Cambridge, Mass.: Ballinger, 1988), 111–26.

Hannan and Freeman have proposed that populations might better be thought of as social constructions, the product of organizational self-definition, rather than objectively bounded and internally homogeneous collections of organizations. And from the very beginning these same authors suggested that environmental niches might best be considered heuristics formulated by researchers for analytic purposes rather than objectively definable resource spaces. See Michael T. Hannan and John H. Freeman, "Where Do Organizational Forms Come From?" *Sociological Forum* 1, no. 1 (1986): 50–72, and "Population Ecology of Organizations."

7. On the creation of new niches, see Astley, "Two Ecologies"; Jack Brittain and John Freeman, "Organizational Proliferation and Density-Dependent Selection: Organizational Evolution in the Semiconductor Industry," in John Kimberly, Robert Miles, and associates, eds., *The Organizational Life Cycle* (San Francisco: Jossey-Bass, 1980), 291–338; Jacques Delacroix and Michael Solt, "Niche Formation and Foundings in the California Wine Industry, 1941–84," in Carroll, *Ecological Models of Organizations,* 111–26. On corporate adaptation, see Jitendra Singh, David Tucker, and Robert House, "Organizational Change and Organizational Mortality," *Administrative Science Quarterly* 31, no. 2 (1986): 587–611; Howard Aldrich and Ellen Auster, "Even Dwarfs Started Small: Liabilities of Age and Size and Their Strategic Implications," *Research in Organizational Behavior* 8 (1986): 165–98.

8. Hannan and Freeman, "Structural Intertia"; Jacques Delacroix, Anand Swaminathan, and Michael Solt, "Density Dependence Versus Population Dynamics: An Ecological Study of Failings in the California Wine Industry," *American Sociological Review* 54, no. 2 (1989): 245–62.

9. Devereaux Jennings, Donald Palmer, and Roger Friedland, "Extending Dominance: Ecological, Economic, and Organizational Determinants of New Intraorganizational Ties from the Headquarter City," paper presented at the Pacific Sociological Association Meetings, April 1991.

10. Frank Romo and Michael Schwartz, "The Structural Embeddedness of Business Decisions," Russell Sage Foundation Working Paper no. 16, 1991.

11. John Freeman, "Ecological Analysis of Semiconductor Firm Mortality," in Singh, *Organizational Evolution,* 53–77.

12. Roger Hayter and H. D. Watts, "The Geography of Enterprise: A Reappraisal," *Progress in Human Geography* 7, no. 2 (1983): 157–81.

13. Donald Palmer, Roger Friedland, Amy Roussel, and Devereaux Jen-

nings, "Corporations and the Urban Business Service Sector," *Social Forces* 69, no. 1 (1990): 115–37.

14. R. A. Erickson, "Corporate Organization and Manufacturing Branch Plant Closures in Nonmetropolitan Areas," *Regional Studies* 14, no. 6 (1980): 491–502; Robert Stern and Howard Aldrich, "The Effect of Absentee Firm Control of Local Community Welfare: A Survey," in John J. Siegfried, ed., *The Economics of Firm Size, Market Structure, and Social Performance* (Washington, D.C.: U.S. Government Printing Office, 1980); David Barkley, "Plant Ownership Characteristics and the Locational Stability of Rural Iowa Manufacturing," *Land Economics* 54 (1978): 92–99; Barkley, "Plant Ownership"; R. A. Erickson, "Corporations, Branch Plants, and Employment Stability in Nonmetropolitan Areas," in John Rees, Geoffrey Hewings, and Howard Stafford, eds., *Industrial Location and Regional Systems* (Brooklyn: Bergin, 1981), 135–53.

15. Singh et al., "Organizational Change and Organizational Mortality."

16. Freeman, "Ecological Analysis of Semiconductor Firm Mortality."

17. William Barnett and Glenn Carroll, "Competition and Mutualism among Early Telephone Companies," *Administrative Science Quarterly* 32, no. 3 (1987): 400–421; Barnett and Carroll, "How Institutional Constraints Shaped and Changed Competition in the Early American Telephone Industry: An Ecological Analysis," Working Paper no. 4-89-6, School of Business, University of Wisconsin, Madison, 1990; William Barnett, "The Organizational Ecology of a Technological System," *Administrative Science Quarterly* 35, no. 1 (1990): 31–60.

18. Astley, "Two Ecologies"; Brittain and Freeman, "Organizational Proliferation."

19. John Freeman and Michael Hannan, "Niche Width and the Dynamics of Organizational Populations," *American Journal of Sociology* 88 (1983): 116–45; Glenn Caroll and Jacques Delacroix, "Organizational Mortality in the Newspaper Industries of Argentina and Ireland: An Ecological Approach," *Administrative Science Quarterly* 27 (1983): 169–98.

20. Johannes M. Pennings, "Organizational Birth Frequencies: An Empirical Investigation," *Administrative Science Quarterly* 27 (1982): 120–44.

21. Michael Aiken and Donald Strickland, "Corporate Control and Metropolitan Growth: A Four-Nation Comparison," typescript, 1983, Department of Sociology, University of Pennsylvania; Palmer, Friedland, Roussel, and Jennings, "Corporations and the Urban Business Service Sector."

22. Romo and Schwartz, "Structural Embeddedness of Business Decisions."

23. Roger Friedland and Donald Palmer, "Park Place and Main Street: Business and the Urban Power Structure," *Annual Review of Sociology* 10 (1984): 393–416.

24. Roger Friedland, *Power and Crisis in the City: Corporations, Unions, and Urban Policy* (London: Macmillan, 1983); Alexander Hicks, Roger Friedland, and Edwin Johnson, "Class Power and State Policy: The Case of Large Business Corporations, Labor Unions, and Governmental Redistribution in the American States," *American Sociological Review* 40 (1978): 302–15.

25. Herman, *Corporate Control.*

26. Benjamin Stein, for example, remarked that if not for the Reagan administration's corporate tax cuts, after-tax corporate profits of American firms

would have been substantially lower than those in the early 1970s (Stein, "Betrayer of Capitalism," *Barron's*, 3 April 1989, 7, 24–26).

27. Jennings, Palmer, and Friedland, "Extending Dominance."

28. Ecologists now recognize that larger organizations have superior survival chances, and they have shown that some forms of organizations, particularly those with considerable market power, can dominate others. We would argue that many of these effects are partially mediated by the fact that these firms are ecologically dominant and non-growth-dependent.

On the first point, see John Freeman, Glenn Carroll, and Michael Hannan, "The Liability of Newness: Age Dependence in Organizational Death Rates," *American Sociological Review* 48, no. 5 (1983): 692–710; Delacroix et al., "Density Dependence." On the second, see Astley, "Two Ecologies"; Barnett and Carroll, "Competition and Mutualism"; Barnett and Carroll, "How Institutional Constraints Shaped and Changed Competition"; Barnett and Amburgey, "Do Larger Organizations Generate Stronger Competition?" See also Michael T. Hannan and John H. Freeman, "The Ecology of Organizational Mortality: American Labor Unions, 1836–1985," *American Journal of Sociology* 94 (1988): 25–52.

29. Hannan and Freeman, "Structural Inertia and Organizational Change."

30. Population ecologists have documented that newer, smaller organizations, while they may be less structurally inert, are more liable to death. Young organizations are thought to suffer from a lack of formalized routines and external support, and small organizations are thought to lack resources of all kinds. See John Freeman, Glenn R. Carroll, and Michael T. Hannan, "The Liability of Newness: Age-Dependence in Organizational Death Rates," *American Sociological Review* 48 (1983): 692–710.

These liabilities outweigh the anticipated advantages that their relative malleability might afford. The liabilities of newness and smallness may be due as much to the relative geographic immobility of young and small firms. While neither age nor size directly affected corporate headquarter or plant location, both advanced age and large size were associated with diversification, which itself was associated with geographic dispersion and headquarter relocation. See Friedland, Palmer, and Stenbeck, "Geography of Corporate Production."

31. Roger Friedland, Sharon Reitman, and Donald Palmer, "The Dynamics of Corporate Headquarter Relocation in the United States, 1960–1975," typescript, 1989; Jennings, Palmer, and Friedland, "Extending Dominance"; Joseph H. Eisenberg and Roger Friedland, "Corporate Headquarters Relocation," *Real Estate Issues,* Fall/Winter 1990, 38–41.

32. Donald Palmer, Roger Friedland, and Magnus Stenbeck, "The Geographic Structure of Large Industrial Corporations," paper presented at the American Sociological Association Meeting, Detroit, Michigan, 1983.

33. Jennings, Palmer, and Friedland, "Extending Dominance"; Roger Friedland, Donald Palmer, and Joseph Eisenberg, "Headquarter Relocation, 1960–1985," typescript, 1992.

34. Roger Friedland, Donald Palmer, and Magnus Stenbeck, "The Geography of Corporate Production: Urban, Industrial, and Organizational Systems,"

*Sociological Forum* 5, no. 3 (1990): 335–59; Jennings, Palmer, and Friedland, "Extending Dominance."

35. Green and Cromley, "Merger and Acquisition Fields for Large United States Cities: 1955–1970," *Regional Studies* 184 (1984): 291–301.

36. Palmer and Friedland, "Corporation, Class, and City System."

37. Jeffrey Pfeffer and Gerald Salancik, *The External Control of Organizations: A Resource Dependence Perspective* (New York: Harper and Row, 1978); Ronald S. Burt, "Cooptive Corporate Actor Networks: A Reconsideration of Interlocking Directorates Involving American Manufacturing," *Administrative Science Quarterly* 25 (1980): 557–82.

38. Palmer, Friedland, and Stenbeck, "Geographic Structure."

39. Hannan and Freeman, "Structural Intertia and Organizational Change," 152.

40. Barnett, "Organizational Ecology of a Technological System"; Barnett and Carroll, "Competition and Mutualism"; Barnett and Carroll, "How Institutional Constraints."

41. For example, little support for the ecological view has been found in connection with the spread of the multidivisional form by large U.S. corporations. See Neil Fligstein, "The Spread of the Multidivisional Form," *American Sociological Review* 50 (1985): 377–91; Donald Palmer, Roger Friedland, Deveraux Jennings, and Melanie Powers, "The Economics and Politics of Structure: The Multidivisional Form and the Large U.S. Corporation," *Administrative Science Quarterly* 32, no. 1 (1987): 25–41; Donald Palmer, Deveraux Jennings, and Xueguang Zhou, "Late Adoption of the Multidivisional Form by Large U.S. Corporations: Institutional, Political, and Economic Accounts," *Administrative Science Quarterly* 38 (1993): 100–131.

42. Ronald S. Burt, *Corporate Profits and Cooptation* (New York: Academic Press, 1983); Pfeffer and Salancik, *External Control of Organizations.*

43. Beth Mintz and Michael Schwartz, *The Power Structure of American Business* (Chicago: University of Chicago Press, 1985).

44. Michael Useem, "The Social Organization of the American Business Elite and Participation of Corporation Directors in the Governance of American Institutions," *American Sociological Review* 44 (1979): 553–71; William G. Domhoff, *Who Rules America?* (Englewood Cliffs, N.J.: Prentice Hall, 1967); Domhoff, *The Higher Circles* (New York: Random, 1970); Domhoff, *Who Rules America Now?* (Englewood Cliffs, N.J.: Prentice Hall, 1983).

45. Michael Patrick Allen, "Economic Interest Groups and the Corporate Elite Structure," *Social Science Quarterly* 58, no. 4 (1978): 597–614; Allen, "The Structure of Inter-organizational Elite Cooptation: Interlocking Corporate Directorates," *American Sociological Review* 39 (1974): 393–406; James Bearden, William Atwood, Peter Freitag, Carol Hendricks, Beth Mintz, and Michael Schwartz, "The Nature and Extent of Bank Centrality in Corporate Networks," paper presented at the Annual Meeting of the American Sociological Association, San Francisco, August 1975; Beth Mintz and Michael Schwartz, "Interlocking Directorates and Interest Group Formation," *American Sociological Review* 46 (1981): 851–69; Mintz and Schwartz, "The Structure of Intercorporate Unity

in American Business," *Social Problems* 29 (1981): 87–103; Mintz and Schwartz, "Financial Interest Groups and Interlocking Directorates," *Social Science History* 7 (1983): 183–204; Mintz and Schwartz, *Power Structure of American Business;* Joel H. Levine, "The Sphere of Influence," *American Sociological Review* 37 (1972): 14–27; Peter Dooley, "The Interlocking Directorates," *American Economic Review* 59 (1965): 314–23; Sergei Menshikov, *Millionaires and Managers* (Moscow: Progress Publishers, 1969).

46. Mintz and Schwartz, *Power Structure.*

47. Allen, "Economic Interest Groups."

48. Over this period, despite an increase in the *number* of members located in the same locale, there had been a decline in the overall level of regionalization; Mark Mizruchi, *The American Corporate Network: 1904–1974* (Beverly Hills: Sage, 1982), 174.

49. Richard W. Scott and John W. Meyer, "The Organization of Societal Sectors," in J. W. Meyer and R. W. Scott, eds., *Organizational Environments: Ritual and Rationality* (Beverly Hills: Sage, 1983), 129–53.

50. Ronald S. Burt, "A Structural Theory of Interlocking Corporate Directorates," *Social Networks* 1 (1979): 415–35; Burt, "Cooptive Corporate Actor Networks: A Reconsideration of Interlocking Directorates Involving American Manufacturing," *Administrative Science Quarterly* 25, no. 3 (1980): 557–82; Burt, *Corporate Profits and Cooptations.*

51. Burt, "Cooptive Corporate Actor Networks."

52. Burt, *Corporate Profits and Cooptations,* 165–66.

53. Michael Useem, *The Inner Circle: Large Corporations and the Rise of Business Political Activity in the U.S. and U.K.* (New York: Oxford University Press, 1984), 50–52.

54. Ibid.

55. Edward S. Herman, *Corporate Control, Corporate Power* (New York: Cambridge University Press, 1981), 39. Herman argues that outside directors with personal links to management are chosen because they are more dependable allies in corporate politics.

56. Mark S. Mizruchi, "Market Relations, Interlocks, and Corporate Political Behavior," *Research in Political Sociology* 5 (1991): 167–208. This was also the case in a study of variation in common bank interlocks across twenty-five industrial sectors. See Mark S. Mizruchi and Thomas Koenig, "Economic Concentration and Corporate Political Behavior: A Cross-Industry Comparison," *Social Science Research* 17 (1988): 287–305.

57. Useem, *Inner Circle,* 64–66.

58. And participation in the interlock network only reinforces the trust and social interaction which makes further appointments likely.

59. Kono, Friedland, and Palmer, "Regionalization of Corporate Interlocks." Analyzing the personal network, Bearden and Mintz found that outsiders—directors from smaller firms and retired businesspersons from the sampled firms—provided the links within and between regional interlock nets. They also found that these outsiders were more likely to belong to elite social clubs than were insiders involved in direct interlocks. However, contrary to our analyses,

Bearden and Mintz find that members of the social upper class—as indicated by membership in an elite social club, for example—were no more likely to belong to the largely regional network components. Indeed, they found that directors drawn from the upper class were *less* likely to be major links in the regional networks. This suggests that elite social club membership may provide an *alternative* to interlocking. James Bearden and Beth Mintz, "The Structure of Class Cohesion: The Corporate Network and Its Dual," in Mizruchi and Schwartz, *Intercorporate Relations,* 187–207. See also Michael Soref, "Social Class and Division of Labor Within the Corporate Elite," *Sociological Quarterly* 17 (1976): 360–68.

60. Mizruchi, "Market Relations, Interlocks, and Corporate Political Behavior."

61. Donald Palmer, Roger Friedland, and Jitendra Singh, "The Ties That Bind: Organizational and Class Determinants of Stability in a Corporate Interlock Network," *American Sociological Review* 51 (1986): 781–96.

Burt, in a reanalysis of the data using different procedures, also found no direct effect of market constraint on the probability that a broken interlock would lead to withdrawal, continuation, or reconstitution. See Ronald S. Burt, "Broken Ties and Corporate Markets," typescript, Department of Sociology, Columbia University, 1986. It is, of course, possible that although the tie is not reconstituted with the same firm, it may be reconstituted with the same industry.

Stearns and Mizruchi have shown that industrial interlocks with financial corporations are likely to be reconstituted with the same financial institution when, among other things, there is a business relationship between the bank and the firm. However, many ties are reconstituted with the financial sector, as opposed to the same financial institution. The factors that predict reconstitution with the same firm have no impact on reconstitution with the same sector. See Linda Brewster Stearns and Mark S. Mizruchi, "Broken-Tie Reconstitution and the Functions of Interorganizational Interlocks: A Reexamination," *Administrative Science Quarterly* 31 (1986): 522–38.

62. Burt, "Broken Ties and Corporate Markets."

63. Roger Friedland, Donald Palmer, and Magnus Stenbeck, "Corporate Structure and the Urban Hierarchy," typescript, 1987.

64. We are indebted to Mark Mizruchi for this latter point.

65. Nondominant firms in more competitive industries tend to locate their plants proximate to dominant firms in less competitive industries as a way to manage the superior market power of the latter. This is the case, for instance, in the relationship between auto-parts producers, tire manufacturers, and some glass producers who are dependent on the auto industry. See Frank P. Romo, Hyman Korman, Peter Brantley, and Michael Schwartz, "The Rise and Fall of Regional Political Economies: A Theory of the Core," paper presented at the American Sociological Association Meeting, New York, August 1986.

66. Joseph Galaskiewicz, Stanley Wasserman, Barbara Rauschenbach, Wolfgang Bielefeld, and Patti Mullaney, "The Influence of Corporate Power, Social Status, and Market Position on Corporate Interlocks in a Regional Network," *Social Forces* 64, no. 2 (1985): 403–31.

326

67. Clifford Kono, Roger Friedland, and Donald Palmer, "The Regionalization of Corporate Interlocks," paper presented at the Pacific Sociological Association Meetings, San Diego, April 1991.

68. And Burt's analyses aggregated to the industrial, as opposed to firm, level.

69. Thus, among the large corporations listed in *Fortune* in the 1960s, banks had an average of twenty-five interlocks, while industrials averaged nine. See Mintz and Schwartz, *Power Structure*, 145. Pennings found that 43 percent of all directional interlocks, those thought to reflect organizational interests in influencing resource allocation as opposed to just information, involved financial firms; Johannes M. Pennings, *Interlocking Directorates* (San Francisco: Jossey-Bass, 1980).

70. Herman, *Corporate Control*.

71. Mizruchi, *American Corporate Network*, 137.

72. Mintz and Schwartz, *Power Structure*.

73. Seven money market banks control 20 percent of all bank assets. See Beth Mintz and Michael Schwartz, "Capital Flows and the Process of Financial Hegemony," in Sharon Zukin and Paul DiMaggio, eds., *Structures of Capital: The Social Organization of the Economy* (Cambridge: Cambridge University Press, 1990), 203–26. Half of all U.S. consortia are headed by four New York banks. See Mintz and Schwartz, *Power Structure*, 54.

74. But financial institutions also directly own a large percentage of all corporate equity. In measures of family ownership, 10 percent ownership has been assumed to be sufficient for a family to exercise control over a firm. In the mid 1970s, financial institutions—banks and insurance and investment companies—owned 10 percent or more of the stock of 77 percent of the largest 200 nonfinancials in the United States. See Herman, *Corporate Control*, 145. Mintz and Schwartz report that financial institutions control about 70 percent of the stock traded on the New York exchange. See Mintz and Schwartz, "Capital Flows," 209.

75. In 1956 nonfinancial corporations derived 65 percent of their capital resources from internal funds. By 1979 this figure had dropped to 49 percent. See Linda Brewster Stearns, "Capital Market Effects on External Control of Corporations," in Zukin and DiMaggio, *Structures of Capital*, 175–201. Over 30 percent of all corporate capital in the U.S. is borrowed from financial intermediaries. See Mintz and Schwartz, *Power Structure*, 45.

76. Mintz and Schwartz, *Power Structure*, 163.

77. Allen, "Structure of Interorganization Elite Cooptation"; Burt, "Cooptive Corporate Actor Networks."

78. Allen, "Structure of Interorganization Elite Cooptation"; Pfeffer and Salancik, *External Control of Organizations;* Burt, "Cooptive Corporate Actor Networks"; Linda Brewster Stearns and Mark S. Mizruchi, "Social and Economic Determinants of Corporate Financing," paper presented at the American Sociological Association Meeting, Chicago, August 1987. For the Canadian case, see Ornstein, "Interlocking Directorates in Canada."

79. Mark S. Mizruchi and Linda Brewster Stearns, "Organizational Responses to Capital Dependence: A Time-Series Analysis," paper presented at the

Annual Meeting of the American Sociological Association, New York, August 1986.

80. Palmer, Friedland, and Singh, "Ties That Bind."

81. *Net* here refers to covariation of an explanatory variable with the variable to be explained which is independent of its covariation with other independent variables which may also covary with the variable to be explained. Firms borrow when retained earnings are low, irrespective of the interest rate. Mark S. Mizruchi and Linda Brewster Stearns, "Governance Costs, Network Ties, and Institutional Processes: Why Do Corporations Borrow," paper presented at the Annual Meeting of the American Sociological Association, Cincinnati, August 1991.

82. Stearns and Mizruchi, "Social and Economic Determinants."

83. Joseph H. Eisenberg, Roger Friedland, and Frank G. Mittelbach, "Regional/Urban Location of Advanced Business Services Relative to Large Corporate Headquarters," paper presented at the Annual Meeting of the Western Regional Science Association, February 1990, Molokai, Hawaii; Joseph H. Eisenberg, Roger Friedland, Frank Mittelbach, and Donald Palmer, "How Big Is the Big Apple? The Territorial Organization of Corporate Contracting for Advanced Business Services," paper presented at the Annual Meeting of the American Sociological Association, Detroit, August 1990.

84. This may explain why interlocks with money-center bankers and insurance companies, which are more likely to be nonlocal, had such major effects on corporate lending behavior, while the presence of regional bankers on the corporate boards of director had little significant impact on the types of borrowing in which major corporations engage. It may also be a function of their relative powers over capital flows. See Stearns and Mizruchi, "Social and Economic Determinants." In this study, the presence of a regional, non-money-center banker on the corporate board had no impact on the level of short-term borrowing, the predominant form of lending in which they engage; but it did have a positive effect on the level of long-term public debt a firm incurred.

85. Donald Palmer, Jerald R. Herting, and P. Devereaux Jennings, "Two Potential Strategic Responses to Financial Dependence: Corporate Interlocking and Headquarter Location," paper presented at the Annual Meeting of the American Sociological Association, Atlanta, August 1988.

86. Mizruchi, *American Corporate Network;* J. Allen Whitt, *Urban Elites and Mass Transportation: The Dialectics of Power* (Princeton: Princeton University Press, 1982).

87. See Domhoff, *Who Rules?* Domhoff, *Who Rules Now?* Useem, *Inner Circle.*

88. Useem, *Inner Circle;* Useem, "Social Organization." Analyzing the "national" component of the person-based interlock network, Bearden and Mintz found that 50 percent of the component members belonged to elite policy-making groups, as opposed to the regional components, where only 17 percent belonged to such groups ("Structure of Class Cohesion," 201).

89. Paul Baran and Paul Sweezy, *Monopoly Capital* (New York: Monthly Review Press, 1966). Mizruchi suggests that this is not the case because of the high level of connectedness in the system as a whole (*American Corporate Network*).

90. William Roy, "The Unfolding of the Interlocking Directorate Structure in the United States," *American Sociological Review* 48 (1983): 248–57.

91. Michael Soref, "The Finance Capitalists," in Maurice Zeitlin, ed., *Classes, Class Conflict and the State*, (Cambridge, Mass.: Winthrop Publishers, 1980), 62–82; Mintz and Schwartz, *Power Structure;* Mizruchi, *American Corporate Network.* Since 1935, density has been relatively stable.

92. Mizruchi, *American Corporate Network.*

93. Those industries which were most fixed in space were also those most likely to have the most acerbic, violent labor confrontations, the result of their difficulty of redeploying their capital in space.

94. Mintz and Schwartz, *Power Structure*, 150.

95. Mintz and Schwartz argue that the oil industry never achieved high centrality in the interlock network because they did not make large demands on bank capital. We suspect alternatively that the oil industry was more mobile internationally and thus less dependent on national, let alone regional, growth.

96. Mizruchi, *American Corporate Network*, 117.

97. Mintz and Schwartz discuss the First National Bank of Chicago's attempting to provide investment to firms operating supermarkets in its region in response to the price-cutting behavior of the A&P chain, which dominated the Chicago market and was putting regional firms out of business; the example illustrates the regional interests of regional banks quite nicely (*Power Structure*, 111).

98. Mizruchi, "Market Relations, Interlocks, and Corporate Political Behavior."

99. Robert A. Bennett, "Regionals Rise in Bank Ranking," *New York Times*, 8 February 1988.

100. James O. Wheeler, "Corporate Spatial Links with Financial Institutions: The Role of the Metropolitan Hierarchy," *Annals of the Association of American Geographers* 76, no. 2 (1986): 262–74.

101. George Benston, "Federal Regulation of Banking: Historical Overview," in George G. Kaufman and Roger C. Kormendi, eds., *Deregulating Financial Services: Public Policy in Flux* (Cambridge, Mass.: Ballinger, 1986), 1–47.

102. Harvey Molotch, "The City as a Growth Machine: Toward a Political Economy of Place," *American Journal of Sociology* 82 (1976): 309–31; John Logan and Harvey Molotch, *Urban Fortunes* (Berkeley and Los Angeles: University of California Press, 1989).

103. Palmer, Friedland, and Roussell, "Corporations and the Urban Business Service Sector"; Friedland, *Power and Crisis*, 65–66.

104. Mark Granovetter, "Economic Action and Social Structure: The Problem of Embeddedness," *American Journal of Sociology* 91 (1985): 481–510.

105. Jennings, Palmer, and Friedland, "Extending Dominance."

106. Friedland, *Power and Crisis;* Friedland and Palmer, "Park Place and Main Street."

107. J. Fennema, *International Networks of Banks and Industry* (The Hague: Martin Nijhoff, 1982); Mizruchi, *American Corporate Network.*

108. Mintz and Schwartz, *Power Structure.* Bearden and Mintz found that executives of the smaller of the largest firms were very important to the multiple linkages that knit regions together; see "Structure of Class Cohesion."

109. Friedland, Palmer, and Stenbeck, "Geography of Corporate Production."

110. Kono, Friedland, and Palmer, "Regionalization of Corporate Interlocks."

111. Mintz and Schwartz explain this centrality of regional as opposed to national industrials based on the notion that they are more central within the regional network and thus better sources of information about the region (*Power Structure*, 190–97).

112. Oliver E. Williamson, "The Economics of Organization: The Transactions Costs Approach," *American Journal of Sociology* 87 (1981): 548–77; Williamson, "Transaction-Cost Economics: The Governance of Contractual Relations," *Journal of Law and Economics* 22 (1979): 223–61; Williamson, *Markets and Hierarchies* (New York: Free Press, 1975).

113. Granovetter, "Economic Action and Social Structure."

114. Rosabeth Moss Kanter, *Men and Women of the Corporation* (New York: Basic, 1977).

115. William G. Domhoff, *Who Really Rules? New Haven and Community Power Reexamined* (Santa Monica, Calif.: Goodyear Publishing, 1978), 12; E. Digby Baltzell, *Philadelphia Gentlemen: The Making of a National Upper Class* (New York: Macmillan, 1958).

116. Kanter, *Men and Women of the Corporation*.

117. Kono, Friedland, and Palmer, "Regionalization."

118. Friedland and Palmer, "Park Place and Main Street"; Friedland, *Power and Crisis;* Whitt, *Urban Elites and Mass Transportation;* Mintz and Schwartz, *Power Structure*.

119. Eric N. Berg, "Talking Deals: Social Stature's Role in Takeovers," *New York Times,* 11 January 1990, sec. C, p. 2; Donald Palmer, Xueguang Zhou and Yasemin Soysal, "The Other Contested Terrain: Mergers and Acquisitions Among Large US Corporations, 1963–1968," paper presented at the Society for Advancement of Socio-Economics, University of California, Irvine, 27 March 1992.

120. Paul M. Hirsch, "From Ambushes to Golden Parachutes: Corporate Takeovers as an Instance of Cultural Framing and Institutional Integration," *American Journal of Sociology* 91, no. 4 (1986): 800–836.

121. Lois Yoder, "The Corporate Takeover Regulatory Arena," in David L. McKee, ed., *Hostile Takeovers: Issues in Public and Corporate Policy* (New York: Praeger, 1989), 85–99.

122. Thomas H. Hammond and Jack H. Knott, "The Deregulatory Snowball: Explaining Deregulation in the Financial Industry," typescript, Michigan State University, East Lansing, 1987.

123. Mark S. Mizruchi, "Similarity of Political Behavior among Large American Corporations," *American Journal of Sociology* 95, no. 2 (1989): 401–24; Mizruchi, "Market Relations."

124. See also Val Burris, "The Political Partisanship of American Business: A Study of Corporate Political Action Committees," *American Sociological Review* 52 (1987): 732–44. But see Mark S. Mizruchi and Thomas Koenig, "Economic

Sources of Corporate Political Consensus: An Examination of Interindustry Relations," *American Sociological Review* 51 (1986): 482–91, as well as Mizruchi and Koenig, "Economic Concentration and Corporate Political Behavior."

Mizruchi's later study is based on 1,596 dyads among fifty-seven firms which were the three largest firms in the twenty major industries. (See "Market Relations.") These earlier studies with Thomas Koenig are organized around twenty-five industries (in which the four largest firms were aggregated). In these analyses, headquarter proximity had a negative effect on similarity of corporate political behavior. Mizruchi and Koenig suggest this result may be due to the large number of New York firms in the sample ("Economic Concentration and Corporate Political Behavior," 297–98).

125. Stein Rokkan and Derek W. Urwin, *Economy, Territory, Identity: Politics of West European Peripheries* (London: Sage, 1983), 41.

126. Ibid., 26–28. See also Stein Rokkan, "Dimensions of State Formation and Nation Building: A Possible Paradigm for Research in Variations Within Europe," in Charles Tilly, ed., *The Formation of National States in Western Europe* (Princeton: Princeton University Press, 1975), 562–600. Rokkan argues that distance from this trade belt was critical to the timing and success of state formation.

127. Between 1870 and post–World War II partition of Germany, both the state capital and financial capital were concentrated in the Prussian state capital of Berlin, where its central bank was also located.

128. Although the Bank of Italy is in Rome, financial intermediaries are concentrated in Milan.

129. For example, Crédit Mobilier and Société Générale both began in Paris in this way; see Charles P. Kindleberger, *Economic Response: Comparative Studies in Trade, Finance and Growth* (Cambridge: Harvard University Press, 1978).

130. Hugh Rockoff, "The Free Banking Era: A Reexamination," *Journal of Money, Credit, and Banking* 6 (1974): 141–67.

131. On the French and German comparison, which persisted for airports and highways, see Rokkan and Urwin, *Economy, Territory, Identity*, 11–13.

132. Kindleberger, *Economic Response*, 73.

133. Alfred D. Chandler and H. Daems, eds., *Managerial Hierarchies: Comparative Perspectives on the Rise of the Modern Industrial Enterprise* (Cambridge: Harvard University Press, 1980).

134. Jurgen Kocka, "The Rise of the Modern Industrial Enterprise in Germany," in Chandler and Daems, *Managerial Hierarchies*, 77–116.

135. Adolph Berle and Gardiner Means, *The Modern Corporation and Private Property* (New York: Harcourt, Brace, and World, 1932). Figures were based on a family or family group ownership of at least 10 percent of the corporation's stock. See also Alfred D. Chandler, *The Visible Hand: The Managerial Revolution in American Business* (Cambridge: Harvard University Press, 1977).

136. Philip Burch, *The Managerial Revolution Reassessed* (Lexington, Mass.: Heath, 1972).

137. Herman, *Corporate Control*. Data were for 1974.

138. John Scott, "Corporate Control and Corporate Rule: Britain in an International Perspective," *British Journal of Sociology* 41, no. 3 (1990): 351–73.

Scott reports that 32 of the largest 252 were "controlled by individuals or family groups" (368).

139. Maurice Levy-Leboyer, "The Large Corporation in France," in Chandler and Daems, *Managerial Hierarchies*, 117–60; John Scott, "Intercorporate Structure in Western Europe: A Comparative Historical Analysis," in Mizruchi and Schwartz, *Structural Analysis of Business*, 208–32. Family control is also more extensive in the Toronto-centered Canadian and Tokyo-centered Japanese economies.

140. On the French holding companies, see David Swartz, "French Interlocking Directorships: Financial and Industrial Groups," in F. Stokman, R. Ziegler, and J. P. Scott, eds., *Networks of Corporate Power: An Analysis of Ten Countries* (Cambridge: Polity, 1985), 184–98.

141. F. Morin, *La structure financière du capitalisme française* (Paris: Calmann-Levy, 1974); David Swartz, "French Corporate Leadership: A Class-Based Technocracy," *Research in Political Sociology* 2 (1986): 49–79. In the late 1970s, Swartz reports, families ran and controlled about 36 percent of France's largest 289 industrial and financial firms.

142. Derek F. Channon, *The Strategy and Structure of British Enterprise* (Boston: Harvard University Graduate School of Business Administration, 1973), 75–76.

143. In Britain family ownership remained significant until the 1960s. See Leslie Hannah, "Visible and Invisible Hands in Great Britain," in Chandler and Daems, *Managerial Hierarchies*, 41–76; Scott, "Intercorporate Structure," 221.

144. Pierre Bourdieu, *Distinction: A Social Critique of the Judgement of Taste*, trans. Richard Nice (Cambridge: Harvard University Press, 1984).

145. Michael Useem and Jerome Karabel, "Pathways to Top Corporate Management," *American Sociological Review* 51 (1986): 184–200; Michael Useem and Arlene McCormack, "The Dominant Segment of the British Business Elite," *Sociology* 15, no. 3 (1981): 381–406; Useem, *The Inner Circle*.

146. David Swartz reports that 81 percent of the French CEOs attended the *grandes écoles;* Swartz, "French, British and American Corporate Elite Recruitment: A Comparative Perspective," paper presented at the American Sociological Association Meeting, Chicago, August 1987. See also David Granick, *The European Executive* (New York: Doubleday, 1962).

147. On the relationship between *grandes écoles* and *grands corps*, see Ezra Suleiman, *Elites in French Society: The Politics of Survival* (Princeton: Princeton University Press, 1978). On the centrality of members of the *grands corps*, see Swartz, "French, British, and American," 16.

148. Swartz, "French, British, and American."

149. Capitalist class cohesion may, however, have its costs. Perhaps British and French firms, because of their capacities for coordination, were able to abrogate the market, to restrict output, to set prices and divide the market in a way that American and perhaps German firms were not. See Levy-Leboyer ("Large Corporation in France," 122) for the French case, and Hannah ("Visible and Invisible Hands," 67) for the British. It is striking that the composition and relative ranking of the largest firms in France remained relatively stable between the late nineteenth century and the 1960s ("Visible and Invisible Hands," 127).

Thus, it was the very minimization of transaction costs, the achievement of class in England and France, that may have slowed their technical and organizational development, thereby allowing American and German firms to outpace them. This may help solve the economic historian's puzzle why these differences developed as they did, which has variously been ascribed to slower market growth, which slowed diversification and the adoption of new organizational structures, or to the lack of legal cartel opportunities in the United States (Kocka, "Rise of the Modern Industrial Enteprise," 106). But Germany was also able to cartelize. Kocka gives centrality to the latecomer status of these two countries, forcing integration, and division of labor within rather than between firms, both to assure inputs and spread risk.

150. W. Lazonick, "Strategy, Structure, and Management Development in the U.S. and Britain," in K. Kobayashi, ed., *The Development of Managerial Enterprises* (Tokyo: Tokyo University Press, 1985). In the United States, attendance at elite business schools radically reduces the impact of social origins on one's managerial career; see Jeffrey Pfeffer, "Towards an Examination of Stratification in Organizations," *Administrative Science Quarterly* 22 (1977): 553–67.

151. Chandler, *Visible Hand;* John W. Meyer and Brian Rowan, "Institutionalized Organizations: Formal Structure as Myth and Ceremony," *American Journal of Sociology* 83 (1977): 340–63; Paul J. DiMaggio and Walter W. Powell, "The Iron Cage Revisited: Institutional Isomorphism and Collective Rationality in Organizational Fields," *American Sociological Review* 48 (1983): 147–60.

152. It is striking that corporations which adopt a multidivisional structure in the United States are more likely to be headquartered *outside* America's major financial centers. See Palmer, Friedland, Jennings, and Powers, "Economics and Politics of Structure."

153. Palmer, Herting, and Jennings, "Two Potential Strategic Responses."

154. John Scott, *Corporations, Classes, and Capitalism* (London: Hutchinson, 1979), 242. Because of federally regulated lending limits, American corporations seeking large loans have increasingly had to rely on syndicates of banks (Stearns, "Capital Market Effects"; Mintz and Schwartz, *Power Structure*). The British results are despite the fact that British banking is highly concentrated, with four London banks accounting for almost all retail banking: Barclays, Lloyds, Midland, and National Westminster (Scott, "Corporate Control and Corporate Rule").

155. When British firms do borrow, they are more likely to borrow on a short-term rather than long-term basis. In 1972, for example, 73 percent of the borrowing of nonfinancials was short-term in the United Kingdom, when compared to 49 percent in France and 30 percent in Germany; see G. Thompson, "The Relationship Between the Financial and Industrial Sectors in the United Kingdom Economy," *Economy and Society* 6, no. 3 (1977): 235–83. American firms, in contrast, are more like their French and German counterparts. In 1979, for example, 40 percent of American nonfinancial firms' borrowing was short-term; see Stearns, "Capital Market Effects," 194.

156. "A Survey of International Finance: The Ebb Tide," *Economist,* 27 April 1991, 42. As a result of France's nationalization of the banks in the 1980s and the explosion of the equity market, French firms in the 1980s moved decisively

away from debt toward equity, so that by 1988 bank borrowing accounted for only 53 percent of their external financing. The ratio of debt to assets dropped from 68 percent to 63 percent, which was still significantly higher than the average American ratio for 1965–1980, 43 percent (Stearns, "Capital Market Effects," 181). The comparable debt/asset ratio for Germany in 1988 was around 60 percent.

157. Stearns, "Capital Market Effects."

158. John Zysman, "The Interventionist Temptation: Financial Structure and Political Purpose," in W. Andrews and S. Hoffmann, eds., *The Fifth Republic at Twenty* (Albany: SUNY Press, 1980); Zysman, *Governments, Markets and Growth* (Ithaca: Cornell University Press, 1983); Peter Hall, *Governing the Economy: The Politics of State Intervention in Britain and France* (Cambridge: Polity, 1986).

159. Scott writes, "German industrialization was based around big banks and big joint stock companies organized into combines and cartels. Most of the larger German firms . . . were allies with the banks through capital and personal relations. The banks took shareholdings in the big firms, but the main base of the relationship was the voting rights which they held in their massive trust holdings—the so-called *Depotstimmrecht*" ("Corporate Control and Corporate Rule," 217). Regarding the percentage voting rights see Hall, *Governing the Economy*, 235.

160. Hall, *Governing the Economy;* Zysman, "Interventionist Temptation"; R. Ziegler, D. Bender, and H. Biehler, "Industry and Banking in the German Corporate Network," in F. Stokman, R. Ziegler, and J. P. Scott, eds., *Networks of Corporate Power: An Analysis of Ten Countries* (Cambridge: Polity, 1985), 91–111.

In the United States and Britain there has been a persistent rise in the level of instituional stockholding. In 1978 British financial institutions owned 50 percent of all common stock and 76 percent of all "preference" shares; Michael Useem, "Business and Politics in the United States and United Kingdom," in Zukin and DiMaggio, *Structure of Capital*, 269. In the United States in 1979, for example, institutional investors combined held 22 percent of the stock of large corporations; see Stearns, "Capital Market Effects," 190. However, the financial institutions which invest these shares tend to respond to declining share prices or dividends not by getting directly involved in management and corporate governance but rather by using disinvestment.

161. Scott, "Intercorporate Structure in Western Europe." The centralization and density measures are taken from Stokman, Ziegler, and Scott, *Networks of Corporate Power.*

162. Stokman, Ziegler, and Scott, *Networks of Corporate Power;* John P. Scott and C. Griff, *Directors of Industry* (Cambridge: Polity, 1984). In the British case, for example, Scott and Griff found "a number of loose bank-centred spheres of influence in which the executives of the major clients and customers of the leading banks were coopted to the various bank boards." See John Scott, "Networks of Corporate Power: A Comparative Assessment," typescript, University of Leicester, 1991. For the French case, see Swartz, "French Interlocking Directorships," 184–98.

163. Fennema, *International Networks.*

164. A structural "center" is the largest 2-clique of locally central enteprises

which are mutually reachable~at distance two or less (Scott, "Intercorporate Structure in Western Europe," 213).

165. Michael Patrick Allen, "Management Control of the Large Corporation: Comment on Zeitlin," *American Journal of Sociology* 8, no. 4 (1974): 885–93; Burt, "Cooptive Corporate Actor Networks."

166. "Intercorporate Structure in Western Europe." Here, as in the U.S. case, firms engaged in capital-intensive, relatively immobile forms of production were at the center of the interlock network.

167. "Outsiders Join the Board," *Economist,* 26 April 1986, 71.

168. Roy, "Unfolding of the Interlocking Directorate"; Fennema, *International Networks.*

169. Kocka, "Rise of the Modern Industrial Enterprise."

170. Gabriel Kolko, *The Triumph of Conservatism: The Reinterpretation of American History, 1900–1916* (Chicago: Quadrangle, 1967).

171. Hirsch, "From Ambushes to Golden Parachutes."

172. David Vogel, "Why Businessmen Distrust Their State: The Political Consciousness of American Corporate Executives," *British Journal of Political Science* 8 (1978): 45–78.

173. For the importance of trust as a condition of economic growth, see Lynne G. Zucker, "Production of Trust: Institutional Sources of Economic Structure, 1840–1920," in *Research in Organizational Behavior* (Greenwich, Conn.: JAI Press, 1986), 8: 53–111.

174. As David Vogel notes in his comparison of industrial regulation in the United States and England, in the United States regulations impose much greater costs on businesses, but there is a much lower level of voluntary compliance by businesses. In England, by contrast, regulations are comparatively weak, but compliance is almost total, resulting in a roughly equivalent outcome (Vogel, *National Styles of Regulation: Environmental Policy in Great Britain and the United States* [Ithaca: Cornell University Press, 1986]). Britain also has a voluntary code by which the business community regulates corporate takeovers.

# TEN

# Out of Place: Gender, Public Places, and Situational Disadvantage

*Carol Brooks Gardner*

*I spend most of my days in the bedroom of my house, thinking about how awful it would be if I went outside.*
—AGORAPHOBIC WOMAN

*Nowhere in this city is safe. The guys hoot and yell at you—at least they do at me. I spend more time than I'd care to deciding where I can go safely and what I should do to insure my own safety. It's enough to drive you crazy.*
—NONAGORAPHOBIC WOMAN

Sociologists have suggested how space becomes territory and how territories can be violated.[1] In addition, investigators have described how violators behave when they invade territories where other groups are understood to possess greater rights of presence and trespass. In this essay I want to consider public places as one territory to which men hold and display greater rights than do women, then to analyze the ways in which women modify their behavior when in public places. In order to understand the characteristics of violator responses in general, I have interviewed women about their strategies for presentation in public places. I have chosen to present the results of interviews with both agoraphobic and nonagoraphobic women since both groups report similar behavioral tactics. Moreover, presenting the similar conduct of individuals labeled "pathological" and "normal" indicates both the rationality of agoraphobics and the extreme behaviors that nonphobic women must enact.

Women sometimes feel public territories hold potential danger or at least afford them less welcome than men receive. In contrast, the home is a territory that liberated women, along with their traditional sisters, are encouraged to use as a refuge by a variety of belief systems, etiquette and crime prevention among them. Much work on the isolation of the housewife's activities supports this view, of course.[2] Indeed, the house has been a mythic symbol of safety, even life.[3] There is a long tradition of understanding the house as woman's sole domain. In early advice books women were told to make their homes symbolic cities, for actual cities were not their proper domain, or to make their homes symbolic fortresses, since these homes and the values they expressed were threatened by the outside.[4]

For Western culture, gender predicts characteristic behavior in both public and private territories. Certainly the canonical instance of public space is the urban street, and certainly the canonical instance of private space is the home. In this light we sometimes dichotomize territories as either public or private, in that we conduct ourselves in different ways and expect others to do so too in both types of space. Public and private territories have been identified with men and women respectively in studies of community, where public spaces have been analyzed as male preserves.[5] Notably, women's utopian or reform movements have radically redefined women's "domestic space."[6] Public territories are sometimes simplistically identified with the world of paid work and private territories with the world of unpaid housework; thus, the sociology of private territories such as the home is systematically devalued.[7] Ultimately, of course, the public/private dichotomy is itself subject to further refinement.[8]

In interactional terms women experience a *situational disadvantage* when in public places: that is, they experience a variety of unfavorable circumstances, handicappings, drawbacks, and abuses characteristic of this situation but not necessarily others. Some common components of situational disadvantage in public places are verbal catcalls, challenges, advice, and evaluation; a wide range of physical violence and the threat of violence; and being slighted in or barred from service situations. Experiencing all or many of these disadvantages on a regular basis can amount to what may be called *public harassment.* Other groups who can also be situationally disadvantaged in public places include people with some disabilities, those categorized as lesbian or gay, and racial and ethnic minorities. In return for venturing into public territory where they will feel less welcome than men, women necessarily develop strategies for ameliorating their territorial violation—methods that will both reduce their appearance in public places and ensure their ease and safety when they are there. It is with those strategies that I deal here.

I have drawn on data from eighteen months' participant observation of behavior in public places in Santa Fe, New Mexico, and coupled this work with a subsequent series of in-depth interviews done with agoraphobic and nonagoraphobic women in New Mexico.[9] I will argue that women and men are culturally predisposed to understand public territories in different ways and that there is ample warrant for women's distrust of public places. Therefore, it is not surprising that interactional patterns of agoraphobic and nonagoraphobic women are similar: nonagoraphobic woman have already absorbed the patterns that agoraphobia makes inescapable.

Fears of and preparations for presenting oneself in public can overwhelm the individual until being in public becomes virtually insupportable, as is the case with the sufferers from agoraphobia (literally, "fear of the marketplace"). All estimates of the percentage of agoraphobics agree that the majority are women, some estimates placing the number as high as 80 to 85 percent.[10] Agoraphobics—those who experience fear of being away from home and in public—often suffer spontaneous panic attacks in addition to the customary anticipatory anxiety of other phobics. An agoraphobic will experience not only fear of public places but also fear of any area that is at a distance from familiar and supportive surroundings like the home. Agoraphobia is known as "the housewife's disease" or as the "calamity syndrome," although it might equally well be termed the "milestone syndrome," since it frequently presents itself following an accident, illness, divorce, miscarriage, pregnancy, or childbirth.

Examining what is considered a neurotic response to public places on the part of women can illuminate the responses of nonphobic women, for both agoraphobics and nonagoraphobics share responses and tactics on a continuum. Agoraphobic women are in dire need of strategies to limit, defuse, or modify involvement with public life: besides the customary pressures of the nonphobic woman in public, the agoraphobic woman has the added weight of too great a feeling of involvement in public. One agoraphobic woman, for example, reports that she shakes whenever she goes out of the house alone or that she is forced to crawl along a pavement that seems to waver; she spends her days in the back bedroom of her home, since that is the farthest place from the street, passing her time in trepidation, thinking obsessively about the horrors that would await her if she dared to go out in public. She has further reduced her sphere by transforming her bedroom (and sometimes her bed) into the only safe zone of habitation, with occasional dashes to the kitchen or the bathroom; she even blacks out windows facing the street. Nonagoraphobic women erect strategies for dealing with public territories in the name of crime prevention, so that one nonagoraphobic has just as carefully planned out a series of safety and danger zones; another reports that she feels "less threatened" within the bedroom of her home, since it has limited access for prowlers. Thus, typical agoraphobic patterns of muting involvement in public places can highlight typical nonphobic ones. And both groups of women must be concerned with the possibility of public harassment, for these are territories where women are customarily situationally disadvantaged anyway.

## GENDER DIFFERENCES AND PUBLIC TERRITORIES

Presently, in public places the norm for behavior is that unacquainted persons will maintain a low level of explicit interaction with one another except in a few set situations. Verbal interaction, too, is minimized. Thus, the citizen has the right to request and the obligation to provide help to strangers, that is, to ask for and to receive small favors, services, and goods of narrowly specialized sorts. Common examples are opening a door for a stranger whose arms are full, helping with a flat tire, or offering the gift of a tissue or match. In some urban spaces and situations offering and responding to greetings will be optional, and in fewer spaces and situations greetings are felt to be obligatory. The individual can also engage in what she or he may feel are "time-filler" conversations—when, for instance, persons find themselves in some similar situation that is to be interpreted as the sharing of a trait or the sharing of a plight, as when strangers speak in doctors' offices or, still more transiently, at bus stops. Aside from these limited occasions for speech with strangers and from the often limited talk that occurs during business transactions, citizens in public places rarely speak to strangers.

Observant women, especially young women, will note that the treatment they receive from other citizens, especially men, contrasts with this norm. It is women as a category, not men, who receive speech in the form of street remarks,[11] that is, free evaluation of the figure they cut, their adjudicated mental and emotional state, and invitations to go a variety of places or commit a variety of acts. And there are unspoken functional equivalents to the harassment of street remarks that run along other communicative channels. Thus, women may find themselves receiving undue visual attention or being tweaked, fondled, pinched, jostled, poked, or even hit by men; or women may merely find that men invade the small envelope of private space the individual expects when in public.

Life-cycle events sometimes correspond to differential treatment in public places for women. Women typically report first noticing different treatment in the form of street remarks when they enter puberty—when a woman is, perhaps, beginning to change her physical appearance in ways that ensure that the public reaction to her will vary (in adolescence, the start of curves and differences in dress) and beginning to display a marked change in public appearance because of the accoutrements of marriage (a husband, children, and large grocery purchases, for example; pregnancy; or a changed, usually inferior style of clothing caused by keeping a family budget instead of a personal appearance budget). Interestingly, it is at just these times that agoraphobia appears. For all women, then, changes in appearance in public may well trigger different responses, which are actual events, not fancies of neurosis. Thus, agoraphobia often commences when women experience real changes in others' reactions to them in public places.

There is little escape for the woman either at adolescence or when married when in public: for the most part, she cannot *not* present a public appearance of adolescence or marriage or at least the proper age grade for these. Of course, a teen girl can adopt tomboyhood for a short period, thus deferring sexual evaluation by men; but this is a short-term solution at best and one dependent on a particular physiognomy. Similarly, although the married woman will find that there are times when she is unaccompanied by family and not belied by large grocery purchases, wearing a wedding ring will give her away at close range; and it is difficult for at least a few months not to look pregnant. Certain clothing changes vary with different points in the family cycle and have public repercussions.[12] Again, these are just those times when the woman's view of herself is undergoing changes and when the behavior of members of the public may mirror the changes they see in her or add their own commentary of reactions, thus transforming a private event into a public one.

Thus, verbal interaction can suggest that the woman is out of place in public territory, where she experiences a situational disadvantage, as do other groups who—in other circumstances—may enjoy considerable privilege. The public harassment they receive—verbal and nonverbal— is consonant with other differential treatment that women receive in public space, certainly not all of it ill, but certainly much of it so. Women in the past have been celebrated as etiquette's own darlings when in public places: the stereotype is of the man retrieving the woman's handkerchief, or ferrying her through the perils of curb or doorway, or ordering the meal that she will consume. But in fact these small attentions are generally the acts of men with whom the woman is acquainted and on whose social value she can be expected to count, since it is clear for the purposes of presentation in public that she herself is valued less. A woman alone is seen to be under the explicit control and protection of no one man; therefore, she is frequently controlled—less so protected— by any man who chooses.[13] When she encounters men to whom she is a stranger, much less than gallantry can easily result. There is also consid-

erable and unappreciated strain in traditional patterns of etiquette that
suggests that there is another reason for keeping to a home that comes
to seem like a bastion: if opportunities for criticism are so prevalent in
public places, the home can appear the only shelter from such criticism.
Young women of a time not so very distant received pointed advice in
regard to their conduct even at home:

> The pretty young woman living alone, must literally follow Cinderella's
> habits. To be out of the house late at night or sitting up, except to study,
> are imprudences she can not allow her self. If she is a widow her conduct
> must be above criticism, but if she is young and pretty and divorced, she
> must literally live the life of a Puritan spinster of Salem. The magpie never
> leaves her window sill and the jackal sits on the doormat, and the news of
> her every going out and coming in, of every one whom she receives, when
> they come, how long they stay and at what hour they go, is spread for
> broadcast.[14]

All women, moreover, are now advised to make their homes even
greater prisons by recommendations on crime prevention. For instance,
women are advised simply to stay home at night. Other recommendations exhort them to erect barricades. Sometimes the barricades involve
only certain prudent artifacts, such as locks, curtains that do not admit
light or allow shadow, window grilles, and other buffers and baffles to
entry and peeping. In other cases the barricades involve constant self-
monitoring and much preparation. All women are encouraged to think
of their homes as minor Maginot lines:

> With regard to windows, there is another important word on prevention:
> A woman should never be visible to persons on the outside, particularly if
> she is alone. Everyone from Peeping Toms to rapists and sadistic killers,
> let alone normal males, will be attracted if he spots a nude, semi-dressed,
> or even a fully but enticingly dressed woman through an uncurtained win-
> dow. Thin curtains will definitely not block anyone's view if there is a light
> on inside the room. Always draw the blinds (and keep your shadow off it)
> when dressing or undressing or walking around dressed in provocative
> clothing. The confessions of many of the rapists and sex deviates contain
> a statement to the effect "I first saw her through the window. . . ." . . . A
> pulled blind or drape may not be sufficient if there is a crack along the
> side or bottom through which the prowler could peek. Tonight, run a test
> of your privacy. Light the lights inside, draw all your drapes and blinds,
> then go outside and try to peek in. Better yet, get a tall man to do it for
> you, as he may be more the size of the prowler than you are, and he can
> spot peepholes that you would miss.[15]

With fortifications such as these, a woman may find herself no less preoccupied with crime at home than she is when she is outside.

It is not strange, then, that nonagoraphobic women, too, sometimes find only a tainted peace when at home. When even nonphobic women are encouraged to barricade themselves against the threats of the public, agoraphobic women take greater measures. Although the source of fear is different—the nonagoraphobic woman avoids criminal perpetrators; the agoraphobic woman also avoids the site as a known magnet for panic—women's descriptions of their actual practices often blur the boundaries between the nonphobic and phobic. An outgoing business-woman and mother of two said that when her husband was away on a trip, she took both children into her bedroom at dusk and pretended to herself that iron burglar gates caged the room. It is thus not so strongly contrastive when an agoraphobic reports that she envisions her house plated with steel walls and that this imaginary protection reduces her anxiety. Both crime prevention and etiquette, then, converge in their recommendations that there are certain reasons for keeping to one's house if one is a woman, and agoraphobia draws on and exacerbates these tendencies.

## SITUATIONAL DISADVANTAGE AND INTERACTION IN TERRITORIES

Etiquette and advice on crime prevention specifically counsel all women to limit their presence in public territory, at least when they are alone. Experiencing differential treatment in public places underscores this message, spurring women to evolve strategies for handling their dis-placement from public places. Cumulatively, these factors amount to a situational disadvantage for women in general in public places and per-haps fear of or distaste for public places themselves. Here I will concen-trate on three aspects of the disadvantage: self-selected absence from public places;[16] adopting a companion, either animate or inanimate, as guarantor of safety and ease when in public territory; and attempting to avoid disadvantage when in public places through extensive planning. Although all these tacks are characteristic of nonagoraphobic women, agoraphobic women use them too. An additional response, attempting to display a cover story or "gloss" for strategic behavior, is characteristic only of agoraphobic women, however.

### Absence

Nonagoraphobic women report avoiding public places or truncating their time there according to several algorithms: whether the place exists in what the woman considers a zone of safety; whether it is day or night; whether a woman is in a self-defined "good mood" or "feeling strong";

whether she has just experienced an unpleasant incident in public places. All nonagoraphobic women interviewed reported that they limited their presence in public to some degree, though men would report trepidation with regard to certain neighborhoods, too. Women have often chosen to be absent from public places as a solution to difficulties they might experience there, and such avoidance is often recommended to crime-conscious women. The virtues of absence in terms of effectiveness are especially appreciated by those most likely to appear ridiculous in public, as agoraphobics often rightly suspect they will.

In general, restriction to home and the perception of life outside the home or neighborhood as dangerous may be a phenomenon of lower-status groups in Anglo-American cultures. Members of the working classes, especially working-class women, often treasure home-centered privacy.[17] In the first place, living in dangerous neighborhoods can reasonably make the home seem a haven. And for people in these groups appearance in public can threaten self-image, for it will provide them with contrastive examples of behavior and appearance. So may it happen for women of all classes.

However, nonagoraphobic women, too, report calculated periods of absence from public places in order to preserve their self-image. Informants report that during periods of low self-esteem they will avoid public places. Or they sometimes avoid being in public when they believe their personal appearance to be less than it should be, such as when they are "a few pounds too heavy" or when they have "nothing [they] look really good in." Self-image is at the root of these withdrawals from the public eye, too. What is often feared is negative feedback from men rather than women. Some women specifically note that they have less objection to going to typically female haunts when they are in low spirits than to places where they believe they are more likely to encounter men.

### Companions

Companionship is a means of handling involvement difficulties for both agoraphobics and nonagoraphobics. In addition, women are routinely advised nowadays that a date or a husband can be secured by judiciously picking from the strangers that one observes in public places.[18] For nonagoraphobic women traditional etiquette, courtship practices, and crime prevention behaviors reinforce these patterns.[19] Nonagoraphobic women sometimes guiltily resort to companionship in order to make their time in public temporarily easier, as they are cautioned to do by crime-prevention advice; some agoraphobic women find that they are willing to get married with a similar ulterior motive of safety through companionship. Being accompanied provides a woman, either agoraphobic or nonagoraphobic, with an interactional buffer, a person who can reliably be expected to intercede for her with the public in general and to take over certain tasks that she is deemed unable to do or feels leery about doing; being absent even more reliably removes the possibility that she will experience difficulty—although, of course, there is little else she can expect to experience either.

Psychological theories about agoraphobia sometimes emphasize early separation anxiety as a cause.[20] If we can understand, for a moment, the psychological phenomenon of separation anxiety as occurring when we suspect we will be at a disadvantage in an unaccompanied future, then that description rightly applies to all women in public places. As children, agoraphobics are said to engage in constant self-monitoring. In this light agoraphobia might be seen as the transference of emotional self-monitoring into public behavioral monitoring through projection, where the public has replaced the authority figure of the parents. Agoraphobia most often becomes acute in women aged fifteen to thirty-five—just those years when women are considered most attractive and when the attention of the public, especially the male public, is most likely to be centered on them. Feminist interpretations hold that the typical points for the appearance of the agoraphobic woman's symptoms are at "two distinct points in a woman's life: in adolescence, when she is struggling to separate from her family and determine her own identity; and in the early years of marriage, particularly."[21]

Nonphobic women say they sometimes consider it wise to carry certain objects to provide themselves with an activity that will shield them from the intrusion of a male stranger (although they will often discover that these objects enable men to treat them as more involved than they would wish). If she carried a book, one woman said, she always had a ready refuge. In some cases, agoraphobics are able, once chaperoned, to venture out with less stress than usual. Some agoraphobics say they are dizzy in public unless they have someone along with them; once accompanied, some have a feeling representing the ultimate companionship, that of actually being transformed into someone else.[22]

Many agoraphobics arrange to have their children go with them for daily or weekly grocery shopping; one woman reported that her baby, ensconced in a stroller, accompanied her not only to the store but into her garden and garage. Others have constant companions even at home.[23] Those who use children as companions to reduce anxiety sometimes note that their use not only depersonalizes the child but also places both the child and the agoraphobic in jeopardy: the child cannot supply real aid, and the agoraphobic is often in no condition to note the needs of the child.[24] Yet nonagoraphobic women also report that they consciously manage to be accompanied by others because they are aware that most street remarks and other forms of harassment are aimed at

unaccompanied women, not at women shopping with their friends or
wheeling a baby carriage. When accompanied by a child, some women
note a transformation in men's remarks to them: although women get
catcalls when they are alone, when they have a child with them, men
may call out appreciative remarks about their mothering instincts or the
child's fine points.

Psychological observers usually mention the "secondary" or "hysteri-
cal" gains of agoraphobia for the agoraphobic who can command and
demand others to do her bidding. Frequently, too, friends and relatives
of the agoraphobic are accused of reinforcing her behavior by comply-
ing with her wishes for companionship, thus supplying her with a rich
life in the home to compensate for her inability to enjoy public places.
For example, friends may come to visit an agoraphobic woman; she
need not—indeed, they know she cannot—visit them. Some agoraphobics, in fact, rely on their parents to accompany them long into adulthood. One woman went to the movies only with an aged parent firmly
on each arm. There are adult agoraphobics who even sleep with their
parents in the safety of the parents' bed.[25]

One type of agoraphobia is encouraged by paranoid husbands in order to prevent their wives from being unfaithful—what Doris Lessing
referred to as a "wifely agoraphobia."[26] Here the wife obligingly develops a sort of functional agoraphobia that precludes the feared infidelity
by the most radical but simple method: since these husbands may inter-
rogate their wives if they go out alone or hire detectives to follow them
out of the house, the wives cease going out of the house at all.[27] Effectively, then, the companionship of men when in public places reduces
the agoraphobic woman's chances of meeting other men, much as nonphobic women understand that the companionship of one man represents romantic attachment to that man and thus precludes her making
other romantic contacts.

Some treatment programs for agoraphobia capitalize on the agoraphobic's need for a companion, substituting a psychiatric aide for the
companion of the agoraphobic's own choice. In these cases companionship is raised to a professional plane known only to nonagoraphobic
women—and their status is low—who hire paid escorts for the evening.
The nonphobic woman sometimes has her own personal "professional"
escort in the form of such regular companions as her sweetheart or husband; yet none of these is specifically trained to deal with the difficulties
of being in public, as is the agoraphobic woman's psychiatric companion.
This professional companion follows the phobic around, giving moral
support and providing a counterpoint of argument to attempt to convince her that, for example, she will not vomit if she goes to the grocery
store.

If an actual human companion is not available to the agoraphobic woman, a variety of substitute companions, sometimes inanimate ones, may be commandeered. This tendency occurs partly because escortage in public places is generally a feature of public life for women and partly because the agoraphobic woman has a tendency to "run through" or exhaust her complement of possible human companions. Friends of the agoraphobic not in the know can be used as companions only sporadically; if overused, they are likely to catch on. Children old enough to put two and two together can become wise even faster. Once a particular child begins to notice its mother's peculiarities, the mother may switch to another child, then another, and finally to a spouse or the still more taciturn and accepting family dog.

When animate companions fail, a woman sometimes turns to inanimate and talismanic ones. These amulets are in the way of immunological measures against fear: they suggest that an outside agency can help a woman. Some objects can have a double function, as can tranquilizers: an agoraphobic woman can carry these in case she needs to take them, but she can also see the fact of the bottle of tranquilizers as proof against panic. Some agoraphobics explicitly say that tranquilizers are substitute companions.[28]

Agoraphobics also carry other talismanic objects. One agoraphobic relied on a symbolically useful bottle of alcohol constantly carried in her purse; another fingered family photos to reassure herself. Nonagoraphobic women also report that a certain inanimate object will become in effect talismanic for them. For one woman, the talisman was a bestseller that she ritually toted but never actually read: she felt it represented an interactional resource should someone bother her.

Agoraphobics say they are helped by such inanimate companions as walking sticks or canes, crutches, umbrellas, suitcases, shopping carts, packages, baby carriages or strollers, bicycles (pushed or ridden), and hard candies held in the mouth. Shopping carts and baby carriages or strollers are traditional badges of office for women, testifying to a woman's achievement of gender, but many objects can suggest that the possessor is properly or prudently occupied. The carrier of an umbrella is seen to have an errand, to have considered the weather carefully and decided on a strategy that shows her or his good social sense. Yet when an agoraphobic tries to appear at ease and competent, her illness can transform the attempted achievement of mother or public citizen into a mockery of motherhood and good common sense. For instance, one woman agoraphobic carried a package to show that she was not walking on the street "for pleasure" but then became afraid to put it down at all; such behavior could cause those who have a chance to observe her about her errands to wonder at her propriety and goal orientation in public after all. Men will sometimes mock nonphobic women who are carrying everyday items on the streets; objects used by an agoraphobic woman can truly be arcane or be used in an occult manner. One phobic woman carefully and responsibly walked her bicycle on the sidewalks, making an impression of public spirit and courtesy for the traffic rights of others of her fellow citizens; when she found she could not leave her bicycle and must take it into a restaurant, however, that impression was shattered. Likewise, claims of being a happy and nonworking mother will be affected. One agoraphobic woman had a stroller with a baby, but she was afraid to let go of the stroller even when her baby was obviously anxious to be taken out.

The range of supplies that the agoraphobic uses are different from the secret stores of the nonagoraphobic. First, their object is different: the phobic hopes they will cap her fear and panic; the nonphobic hopes they will limit intrusion by strangers, usually men, and prevent her having to ask for aid from strangers, too.[29] Second, supplies differ in the degree to which they are felt to be crucial. Nonphobic women carry an armamentarium of possessions for intrusions that they fear will occur and for which they will otherwise be unprepared; agoraphobic women carry possessions for situations they are certain will occur.

Another difference between the agoraphobic and the nonagoraphobic woman is in the immediacy of the symbolism. It is one thing to carry a small portable hair dryer so that one's hair will look tidy, as one nonagoraphobic woman did; and it is another to carry an umbrella so that one will not faint, as more than one agoraphobic woman had done. For both agoraphobic and nonagoraphobic women, then, an umbrella can be an escort in much the same way that a man is: instead of pointing to the escorted person's worthiness as a companion for at least one person in the world, it points to her situational worthiness. She can claim another task when in public, a task that sidesteps for the moment the vulnerability of her status. These inanimate companions, then, are called as witnesses that some other thought than that of being in public is (or has been) in the woman's mind. At least she is, for example, a person reading a newspaper and keeping up on public events in the alert yet not intellectual way that paper-reading implies; at least she has looked out her window at the weather and determined to prepare for it by bringing an umbrella; at least, as her shopping cart shows the world, she is a person with a domestic task to do and possibly a family as well.

However, carrying inanimate objects is a solution that presents its own problems. Reading a newspaper or pulling a shopping cart can provide the occasion for passersby to comment on, say, current events or grocery prices to the woman. Thus, the newspaper and the shopping cart are topics as well as companions, and in this they are inferior to the shelter offered by a male companion or even sometimes a dog, either of which will often dispel intrusion. Another difference between inanimate companions and men (or large dogs) is that inanimate companions cannot guarantee a woman's personal safety in the same way that a man can. The exception here, of course, is the inanimate object that is in fact a weapon. However, the weapon has the disadvantage—one of many— that considerable upkeep, in the form of acquired skill and mental alertness, is required for its use, so the man companion still has his advantages.

Nonagoraphobic women make preparations for the future, but they do not usually reveal those preparations. Agoraphobic women are, of course, in the same boat, except that they have no choice but to display their safety supplies, which are all they have to stave off a panic attack and even greater public ridicule. The agoraphobic woman's talismans, being more consoling than functional, are even more likely than those of the nonphobic to provoke ridicule. Giving evidence in public that one considers artifacts—even public facilities—deeply important is not so rare, of course: part of the territorial model of interaction in public places is to consider one's chair, park bench, or space in a queue temporarily as personal property.[30] But the agoraphobic requires very different usage of inanimate objects. The agoraphobic's inanimate companions can provide the means that enable her to go out at all but can also ensure that she will appear ridiculous in just the ways she fears; in the same way, the nonphobic woman's accompaniment by a male escort— who, she feels, will add to the public ascription to her of the competence that comes with the achievement of male companionship—can also backfire by making her seem, for instance, less competent or independent than she would like.

For nonagoraphobic women, therefore, carrying inanimate companions visible to the public can elicit conversation or unwanted advances; concealing these objects leaves a woman situationally defined as "being in public" and nothing more; and failing to display them altogether leaves her without repair resources she may need to achieve a gender-appropriate appearance.

### Preparations

Forced into being minimally involved with the public realm in general and fearful of appearing too involved when they do venture into it, agoraphobic women will feel they still have a great deal of involvement with public places—if only because they must expend time and effort explaining why they must avoid the public. In this regard they share a concern with nonphobic women who take crime prevention so seriously that it is crime, not performance as public citizens, with which they are involved when they go into public; and phobic women also share with nonphobic women the same necessities to plan strategies that are the fate of nonphobic women when they must, for example, decide how to deal with street remarks.

Finding that there are certain times or places when the public is dangerous is common for all women in public. Nonphobic women use regional restrictions and mappings as tools to reduce their vulnerability while in public. When a woman decides to avoid any area but the well-lit center of town at night, she seeks to restrict the population of criminals—or those who might turn out to be criminals—with whom she comes into contact. In an exaggerated version of the mental mapping of the city that nonphobic women must accomplish, dividing the city into regions of safety and danger, the agoraphobic woman, too, has an elaborate division of the region outside her house into safety and danger zones. Unlike crime-conscious nonphobic women, the agoraphobic's mental map is designed not with an eye to reducing risk of rape, attack, or abuse on the streets. Instead, it is a tool to alleviate stress and dampen fear while in public, and the agoraphobic's signposts and zones are customarily rigidly drawn and may have features, such as medical way stations, that are foreign to nonphobics. The nonphobic woman will commonly plan her route in public to avoid construction sites where workers may hoot at her, regions where men will playfully or painfully solicit her favors, or areas with a high percentage of men where she will be scrutinized; the agoraphobic woman finds she must plan every step of even a simple or short walk—and then invest each step with fear. Therefore, agoraphobics will arrange forays to touch certain zones of relative safety or potential succor, if they cannot remain within such zones altogether.

For the agoraphobic, however, it is not, or is not merely, the places themselves that hold the danger; instead, the danger results from the agoraphobic's reactions in those particular places. Trips are planned beforehand with an eye to the proximity of doctors' offices, so that the agoraphobic can ask emergency aid in surroundings as sympathetic as may be hoped for; with an eye to phone booths, so that aid can be summoned if the agoraphobic finds it impossible to continue on her own; with an eye to police stations, in case more formal aid must be asked. Likewise, advice literature counsels crime-conscious women (nonphobic and phobic alike) to consider potential sources of aid when planning their routes.

For agoraphobics, dangerous regions can threaten to become universal, amounting to a sentence of absolute absence. But regions of danger may, on reflection, begin to bleed and blur for a nonphobic woman, too: she sometimes finds that no region seems reliably safe or that if it is unsafe to be out at 7:00 P.M., it is not much safer to be out at 6:00 P.M. Soon 5:00 P.M. will not seem so safe, and a woman may discover that she begins to be uneasy about the possibility of going out at 4:00 P.M. The typical pattern is that the agoraphobic reports acquiring progressively more, not fewer, danger zones; she may end by restricting herself to bed in her own home. Agoraphobic women who immure themselves in this way achieve a type of preventive detention that will not seem so foreign to nonphobic women, who must themselves employ anticipatory moves to avoid urban dangers and urban unpleasantries.

*Cover Stories*

Another aspect of an agoraphobic woman's prudent planning for appearance in public places is sometimes the explanation that she will use if she is challenged about her actions. Nonagoraphobic women, because their measures for being in public are consonant with a set of measures ratified by the culture or because their rationale is obvious, are seldom called on to explain them—to explain why, for example, they are walking with crutches or why they are carrying a heavy purse. Here the measures of agoraphobics differ, exposing them to questioning about the notable management measures they do take. Thus, the agoraphobic woman sometimes develops or attempts to develop a set of "glosses":[31] innocent or comprehensible explanations (or actions that suggest explanations) for her actions that do not reveal that she is what she is, a person afraid of public places. She may never actually use these cover stories, but they remain an uncomfortable presence in her mind, since she understands how unsatisfactory they would seem if trotted out.

The agoraphobic sometimes experiences a specific attack by watching the sky and surroundings grow darker and darker the farther she progresses from home. The pavement may wink and waver and buildings and walls close in on her, causing her to sink to the ground and proceed on her hands and knees. The elevator, department store floor, or entire building may seem about to tilt and topple. Tachycardia, jelly legs, nausea, diarrhea, and heavy sweating may aggravate her responses to the changes she perceives in her physical environment. She will therefore fear that her responses (crawling to cope with the wavering pavement, peering with a look of concentration to see through the rapidly darkening air, walking with one steadying hand on a wall or fence) will themselves cause ridicule, much as the nonphobic woman understands that she is under an obligation not to appear to be taking precautions for what she is told is the considerable danger of the city but to mount a personal manner that is calm and poised. The small, ineffective, and strangely touching methods that some agoraphobic women employ can also, on reflection, lead them to fear that they will appear ridiculous, as in the case of the woman who chose to wear jeans with reinforced knees as protection for those times when, she was sure, she would be called on to crawl home.

Both the phobic and nonphobic woman fear what they show by their fear. Often the fear of being ridiculed for the measures taken by the frightened agoraphobic woman is fully justified, as for the woman reduced to walking home through a hedge, slinking toward a destination by hiding in doorways, walking in the gutter, or crawling home down a highway. Other agoraphobic women say they have taken to entering doctors' offices to cadge tranquilizers or schedule immediate therapy sessions. Still others take especially small steps designed, they feel, the better to support them; and they bolt from sporting events, doctors', veterinarians', and dentists' offices, classrooms, department stores, restaurants, and elevators when their situation becomes too much for them.

All of these methods of coping with the fear of being in public places will likely require skillful and lengthy explanations by the agoraphobic who seeks to hide her affliction (and, considering that reactions to admitting that one has agoraphobia are often derisive, even a story that is not believed is felt to be better than admission of her phobia). In general, women agoraphobics and crime-conscious nonphobic women in public share deep concerns about how ridiculous they will look, the first group when they make what concessions they can to their phobia and the second when they attempt to stave off crime. If an explanation is given, however, the crime-conscious woman is in a better position than the agoraphobic, assuming both are truthful. The crime-conscious woman is more likely to be able to explain coherently, and it is still less morally reprehensible to be prudent than phobic.

With other tacks for coping, the agoraphobic sometimes attempts to manage impressions by way of nonverbal cover stories—to give a convincing performance of the citizen engaged in some pursuit that is not, whatever else it might be, a defense against agoraphobic panic. One agoraphobic stated that, when reduced to walking in the gutter, which she felt was a safer path than the sidewalk, she would busily look at the gutter contents as if she were seeking a lost object, collecting resalable refuse like aluminum cans, or conducting some arcane treasure hunt; once she babbled to passersby that she was looking for her child's lost ball. But this woman keeps good track of objects, does not recycle, seeks no treasure, and has no child.[32] Again, these tactics are successful if the panicked agoraphobic can summon enough confidence to perform them well, but they are likely to come under scrutiny by other members of the public sooner or later. For example, when an agoraphobic cowers before the shop window as if, she hopes, she is entranced by the wares, she may pass as an enthusiastic window shopper only so long as pas-sersby do not have the opportunity to note that she becomes equally enthusiastic at each and every window or that she remains quivering against the same window for ten minutes.

In addition to these special fears of and tactics for public presenta-tion, agoraphobics also experience the common fears of appearing ridic-ulous that all citizens do and the special fears of appearing ridiculous that the crime-conscious woman does when she performs actions that are unseen by others but that she feels privately are ridiculous. The "normal" fears of appearing ridiculous, however, may seem to fit right in with the agoraphobic's other fears of appearing ridiculous, and it will take a persuasive psychiatrist indeed to convince the agoraphobic that therapy will free her entirely from concern with public performance. In fact, initial psychiatric treatment may aggravate fears of looking ridicu-lous, for agoraphobia therapy, either incidentally or purposefully, some-times puts patients in embarrassing public situations in the name of de-sensitization therapy.

## DISCUSSION

There are several areas of disadvantage and discomfort to which women, in contrast to men, are subject when in public. Generally, appar-ent involvement needs to be modified more for women in public places than men: if deeply involved, women will be perceived as insufficiently caught up in the display of gender. Agoraphobic women may be argued to be, if only symbolically, the members of the society who most clearly demonstrate women's discomfort with public places. Although agora-phobic women are the clearest and most extreme class of women suffer-ers for whom public space is deeply problematic, even women not so classified may find that they avoid public space in favor of private. Inter-estingly, tacks taken by and advised for nonphobic women are also used by the phobic, demonstrating a sisterhood between the two classes of women and suggesting that they both respond to similar difficulties of presentation in public places.

Public territory in general is a different experiential entity for women and for men. Currently, for example, many middle-class Americans be-lieve that a number of satisfyingly diverse career paths are open to women, although further reflection might lead them to restrict the vi-sion of unimpeded opportunity to white women, to middle-class women, or to heterosexual women; feminist observers also speak of the gains American women have made over the last fifteen years or so. If these advances have indeed occurred, it is still true that they are—from the

perspective of spatial behavior—in some measure private gains, not public ones. It does not matter whether a woman in public spaces is on her
way to a board meeting or a PTA meeting: she can still be subjected to
public harassment from strange men.

For the most part I have been concerned with the symbolic differences that public and private territories hold for women, as those spaces
are represented and used both by agoraphobic and nonagoraphobic
women. Agoraphobic women certainly have different feelings about
public places than do women labeled "normal," but agoraphobic women
occupy a place on the same continuum as nonagoraphobic women: they,
too, have the same presentational concerns, use the same strategies, and
take, in some measure, the same risks. It is not so much, then, that there
is a set of women who are psychologically unbalanced with regard to
public places, but rather that there are sound reasons for all women to
feel vulnerable in public places and that agoraphobic women have an
added set of worries about presentation and experience.

A complete analysis of the public and the private should eventually
include a detailed discussion of any realm—public or private—into
which a group of individuals dare not venture or venture with trepidation, in addition to a realm designated or felt to be the individual's home
ground or keep. Forbidden realms, too, are accurate and important reflections of individual conduct and belief: the feared context functions
as a mirror that shows by contrast approved values and experiences.
Women, along with members of other groups who are situationally disadvantaged in public, sometimes feel that public places hold potential
danger or discomfort: public harassment engraves such a feeling into
the sensibilities of many women. In contrast, private places such as the
home are sites that liberated women, along with their traditional sisters,
are encouraged to use as a refuge.

The high prevalence of agoraphobia for Anglo-American women is a
functional equivalent of public harassment, closing off public places for
women too neurotically frightened to enter them. Agoraphobia shows
us the different ways in which women and men are disposed to understand public places—and it emphasizes that women's distrust of public
places is both something for which there is ample warrant and something which the culture sustains by supplying a psychologically stigmatiz-
ing label for those who have an extreme version of this fear. The sisterhood of agoraphobic and nonagoraphobic women is shown by their
shared strategies for handling fear and public harassment. Agoraphobia
erects for a woman a steadfast psychic barrier against the threats posed
by streets and places of business, parallel to the barriers that the public
harassment of others present to her.

## NOTES

1. Specifically, see Erving Goffman, *Relations in Public* (New York: Basic, 1971), and Stanford Lyman and Marvin B. Scott, "Territoriality: A Neglected Dimension," in *Social Problems* 15 (Fall 1967): 243–44.

2. See, e.g., Hannah Gavron, *The Captive Wife* (Harmondsworth, Eng.: Penguin, 1966); Herbert Gans, *The Levittowners* (New York: Pantheon, 1967), 225–34; and Ann Oakley, *The Sociology of Housework* (New York: Pantheon, 1974), 88ff.

3. For a general view of this symbolism, see Gaston Bachelard, *The Poetics of Space* (Boston: Beacon, 1964), 3–37, 211–31; for an example of one particular culture, see Elizabeth G. Traube, *Cosmology and Social Life: Ritual Exchange among the Mambai of East Timor* (Chicago: University of Chicago Press, 1987), 66–80.

4. One such book is that of Christine de Pizan, *The Book of the City of Ladies* (1405; London: Pan, 1983); see esp. 8–11.

5. Two examples among many are Rayna Reiter, "Men and Women in the South of France: Public and Private Domains," in Rayna Reiter, ed., *Toward an Anthropology of Women* (New York: Monthly Review Press, 1975), and Laurence Wylie, *Village in the Vaucluse* (Cambridge: Harvard University Press, 1974).

6. Dolores Hayden, *The Grand Domestic Revolution* (Cambridge: MIT Press, 1981), 135ff.

7. Karen V. Hansen, "Transcending the Public/Private Divide: Feminist Theory and 'The Social,' " paper presented at the Annual Meeting of the American Sociological Association, San Francisco, August 1989. See also her "Feminist Conceptions of Public and Private: A Critical Analysis," *Berkeley Journal of Sociology* 32 (1987): 105–28.

8. See the typologies of Lyman and Scott, "Territoriality," and of Goffman, *Relations in Public*.

9. All examples used without other specific citations are derived from interviews conducted with fifteen agoraphobic and thirteen nonagoraphobic women, residents of Santa Fe, New Mexico (population 52,000). The agoraphobic informants were gathered by snowball sampling and had all been clinically labeled. All either had undergone or were undergoing one of a variety of therapies for agoraphobia. Both agoraphobic and nonagoraphobic informants participated in in-depth, free-form interviews ranging from forty-five minutes to three hours. Interviews dealt with attitudes toward and participation in public places. For the agoraphobic women, four of the interviews took place on the telephone; all other interviews were in person. Interviews took place in 1986–87. I had previously completed a lengthy participant observation of public places in Santa Fe during the period 1979–1981.

10. I. M. Marks and E. R. Herst, "A Survey of 1,200 Agoraphobics in Britain," *Social Psychiatry* 5, no. 1 (1970): 16–24; R. O. Snaith, "A Clinical Investigation of Phobias," *British Journal of Psychiatry* 114 (1968): 673–98.

11. Carol Brooks Gardner, "Passing By: Street Remarks, Address Rights, and the Urban Female," *Sociological Inquiry* 50 (1980): 328–56.

12. Mildred Tate and Oris Glisson, "Family Cycle," in Mary Ellen Roach and

Joanne Bubolz Eicher, eds., *Dress, Adornment, and the Social Order* (New York: Wiley, 1965), 87–88. With regard to public presentation, single women of an earlier age were disadvantaged in a way unknown to single women of the present day (Nancy L. Peterson, *Our Lives for Ourselves: Women Who Have Never Married* [New York: Putnam, 1981]). Earlier, single women were often poor relations with minuscule clothing allowances; now, they often have the resources to show themselves off to better advantage than their married sisters.

13. In this light, agoraphobic women's withdrawal from public places can be seen as the replacement of external, common, and male controls with a plethora of internal, privatized controls created by the female self.

14. Emily Post, *Etiquette* (New York: Funk and Wagnalls, 1924), 294.

15. Robert G. Barthol, *Protect Yourself* (Englewood Cliffs, N.J.: Prentice-Hall, 1979), 42–43.

16. In contrast to the barring through physical inaccessibility that some people with disabilities, for example, still experience.

17. Information on gender and working-class conceptions of home are given in Madeline Kerr, *The People of Ship Street* (London: Routledge and Kegan Paul, 1958), 99–103; John Osborne, *A Better Class of Person* (New York: Dutton, 1981), 45; Lee Rainwater, "Fear and the House-as-Haven in the Lower Class," *Journal of the American Institute of Planners* 32, no. 1 (1966): 23–37; and Betty Spinley, *The Deprived and the Privileged* (London: Routledge and Kegan Paul, 1953), 56.

18. Advice directed toward heterosexuals is found in manuals such as those of Dr. Martin Gallatin, *How to Be Married One Year from Today: Lover Shopping for Men and Women* (New York: Shapolsky, 1987); Dr. Margaret O'Connor and Dr. Jane Silverman, *Finding Love: Creative Strategies for Finding Your Ideal Mate* (New York: Crown, 1989); and Dr. Diana Sommerfield, *Single, Straight Men: 106 Guaranteed Places to Find Them* (New York: St. Martin's, 1986).

19. Carol Brooks Gardner, "Safe Conduct: Women, Crime, and Self in Public Places," *Social Problems* 37, no. 3 (August 1990): 311–28.

20. John Bowlby, *Attachment and Loss*, vol. 2, *Separation* (New York: Basic, 1973).

21. Carolyn Cott Washburne and Diane L. Chambless, "Afraid to Leave the House? You May Have Agoraphobia," *Ms.*, September 1978, 46. See also Joy B. Reeves, "Toward a Sociology of Agoraphobia," *Free Inquiry in Creative Sociology* 14, no. 2 (November 1986): 153–58, and A. de Swaan, "The Politics of Agoraphobia," *Theory and Society* 10 (1981): 359–85.

22. Edouardo Weiss, "Federn's Ego Psychology and Its Application to Agoraphobia," *Journal of the American Psychoanalytic Association* 1 (1953): 614–28; see esp. 623–24.

23. And see, with regard to this point, the reminiscences of agoraphobics: Julie Baumgold, "Agoraphobia: Life Ruled by Panic," *New York Times Magazine*, 4 December 1977, 44–48, 52–53, 129–35, esp. 48, and William Ellery Leonard, *The Locomotive God* (London: Chapman and Hall, 1928), 256–57, 282, 352, 343–44.

24. See the anecdote in J. Christopher Clarke and Wayne Wardman, *Agoraphobia: A Clinical and Personal Account* (New York: Pergamon, 1985), 3.

25. Joshua M. Perman, "Phobia as a Determinant of Single-Room Occupancy," *American Journal of Psychiatry* 123 (1966): 609–12; see 611.

26. R. Julian Hafner, "Agoraphobic Women Married to Abnormally Jealous Men," *British Journal of Medical Psychology* 52 (1979): 99–104; Tom Kraft, "Sexual Factors in the Development of the Housebound Housewife Syndrome," *Journal of Sex Research* 6, no. 1 (February 1970): 59–63.

27. The fine points of the paranoid husbands' understanding of agoraphobia neatly dovetail with what many psychologists feel lies in the woman's own mind: anxiety in the street represents the unconscious temptation to engage in sexual adventures, or the opportunity to be judged and found guilty, and hence punished. In the latter case, for phobic women the street is a place to be seen and to be caught, whereas for nonphobic women who receive street remarks it is a place to be observed and rated.

28. And see the anecdotes in Barbara Gordon, *I'm Dancing as Fast as I Can* (New York: Harper and Row, 1979), 39, 115.

29. One nonagoraphobic woman interviewed carried in her purse, in addition to less notable items, a spare pair of pantyhose, lest hers ripped; a backup book to read, in case she finished her primary reading material; candy, cigarettes, matches, and spares of all these; a small flashlight; a freon horn for self-defense; and a complete set of make-up supplies, in case any substantial portion of her make-up came to harm.

30. See Goffman, *Relations in Public,* and Philip D. Roos, "Jurisdiction: An Ecological Concept," *Human Relations* 21 (1968): 75–84, for general territorial typologies of public places; and, for one case in particular, see Alan Lipman, "Chairs as Territory," *New Society* 9 (April 1967): 564–66.

31. The term is Goffman's (*Relations in Public*).

32. See also the examples given in Joy Melville, *Phobias and Obsessions* (New York: Coward, McCann, and Geoghegan, 1977), 23.

# ELEVEN

# The Israeli Memory of the Shoah: On Symbols, Rituals, and Ideological Polarization

*Saul Friedlander and Adam B. Seligman*

The Shoah, referring to the Nazi destruction of European Jewry, has become an integral part of the Israeli collective memory.[1] The lasting impact of this past on the hundreds of thousands of survivors who reached Israel,[2] and often on their children as well, the establishment of national rituals of commemoration, the development of specific school curricula, a fast growing historiography, the ongoing use of media renditions, as well as artistic and literary reelaborations of the events—all of these have created a vast domain of public reference to this past. Its effects can be diversely evaluated, but in no way dismissed.

"The trauma of the Holocaust," wrote Amos Elon in 1971, "leaves an indelible mark on the national psychology, the tenor and content of public life, the conduct of public affairs, on politics, education, literature and the arts." All over the country countless private and public monuments to the grimmest phase of European history perpetuate a memory which lies in all its morbidity at the center of Israel's historic self-image. If, in Israeli eyes, the world at large has tended to forget too soon, Israelis hardly give themselves a chance. The traumatic memory is part of the "rhythm and ritual of public life."[3] If anything, this impact has grown in the 1970s and 1980s, sometimes in paradoxical ways.

Here we consider a very limited aspect of this representation: its congruence with religious tradition, some of its symbolic expressions in Israeli public life,[4] and, incidentally, the growing ideological instrumentalization of this ritualized memory.

## SOME REMARKS ON THE MOLD OF TRADITION

The short period of time that elapsed between the catastrophe of European Jewry and the creation of the Jewish state presented the official discourse with a framework both natural and deeply embedded in Jewish tradition, that of "catastrophe and redemption." The basic elements of this framework are an essential background for the contemporary discourse.

Jewish tradition is often characterized by its attempts to define collective identity in time through the elaboration of a meaningful history. Collective existence within historical time was understood in terms of a theodicy of history. Consequently, there developed within Judaism a continual and salient tension between historical existence and redemption.[5]

On the one hand, redemption, as conceived in the Bible and by the apocalyptic writers, bore no relation to historical processes. Redemption broke with ordinary history. In Gershom Scholem's terms, redemption would be "transcendence breaking in on history."[6] Indeed, during the centuries of Jewish dispersion, exile had no meaning in its relation to redemption and was mostly considered as a cathartic preparation for it. As the exile was a divine punishment, only God could terminate it, and so for the majority of Jews messianism had to be passive.[7] The very dichotomy of historical delay and anticipated redemption resulted in strict warnings against any attempt to "hasten the End."

On the other hand, the very constitution of the Jewish people was posited in history.[8] Both the archetypical images of society's emergence into history and redemption from history were this-worldly and were played out in the arena of history. The covenant of Abraham and the Laws of Moses, both historical events marking the birth of the nation, were perceived as taking place within the course of historical time. Similarly, the images of redemption, the resurgence of the rule of the house of David, the building of the Temple, and the gathering of the exiles were treated as events taking place within the orders of the world, and so within history proper.[9] Consequently, and in marked contradiction to the above tradition, there emerged the conception of an "active messianism" which entailed the Jews' active participation in furthering the process of salvation.[10]

The conflation of these traditions—the devalorization of the exile, on the one hand, and the historical nature of collective identity on the other—was of great consequence for the patterning of Jewish memory over the ages. In a condition where "the biblical past was known, the messianic future assured, [and] the in-between-time obscure," historical events were interpreted according to a particular mythic and biblical pattern.[11]

Traditional memory, which was organized religiously by the *Halacha*, or Jewish law, could not, however, by definition include a realized time of redemption, except in its ritualized form in Passover and Yom Kippur—the two holy days which celebrate the collective and individual moments of redemption respectively. With the restructuring of Jewish history in the twentieth century, however, the ritual definition of redemption was transformed, as was the perception of current events.

For the ultra-Orthodox Jews, the *haredim,* who rejected any idea of redemption as a process actively fostered within historical time, the very essence of Zionism was unacceptable and could lead only to punishment and catastrophe. For other Orthodox Jews who accommodated Zionism to Judaism, as well as for secular Jews, with the creation of the State of Israel historical events leading to national rebirth were part of a process of redemption. As we shall see, however, this view was itself variable and complex, running from an allegorical interpretation favored by most Jews to a literal interpretation offered by proponents of an "active messianism" which emerged in Israel in the 1970s and 1980s. In both cases, however, the lacuna of past models of structuring historical memory—built around exile and exodus—was consummated not in religious rituals but in a vision of national-religious or secular redemption. Within these frameworks, the Shoah seemed to find its deeply significant place.

## COMMEMORATIVE DATES, RITUALS, SITES

For some ultra-Orthodox Jews, such as the Satmar Rebbe Yoel Taitlbaum, the extermination of the Jews of Europe was, according to the interpretation just mentioned, divine punishment for attempting to hasten the End, that is, for Zionism.[12] Usually, however, such extreme positions were not expressed even in the ultra-Orthodox community. The commemoration of the Shoah was linked to the framework of catastrophe and redemption, although redemption still remained outside of the process of historical time.

When, in June 1984, the cornerstone was laid for the World Center of the Belzer Chassidim in Jerusalem, the Belzer Rebbe (*rebbe,* as opposed to *rabbi,* is a ritual and political leader of a Chassidic community) declared: "When redemption comes, God will collect the stones and timber from which the synagogues and *yeshivot* [religious schools] were built, show them to the Children of Israel and tell them: All you have now comes from the sacred work and Torah and prayer of those who lived in the Diaspora."[13] The symbolic salvaging of the destroyed synagogues establishes the link between the world of yesterday, the synagogues of the *Gola,* or exile, and the ultimate redemption in the days of the Messiah.[14]

More significant within Israeli society is the interpretation of the Shoah adopted by religious Zionism. In December 1949 the ashes of Jews exterminated in the Flossenburg camp were transferred to Israel.

The director of a department in the Ministry of Religious Affairs, Rabbi
S. Z. Kahana, took the decision that these ashes would be buried in Jerusalem on Mount Zion, on the tenth of Tevet, the day in Jewish tradition
for reciting the prayer for all the departed. He suggested that this
should become the fixed date for the commemoration of the Shoah.[15]
The chief rabbinate accepted Kahana's proposal and a symbolic pattern
emerged, firmly structuring commemoration of the Shoah among religious Zionists.

The tenth of Tevet is the date on which the first siege of Jerusalem
by the Assyrian King Nebuchadnezzar began, the beginning of the traditional Jewish sequence of catastrophes structured by repeated destruction and exile. However, Mount Zion is, according to religious tradition,
the burial place of King David. Since the Messiah is related to King David (Ben David), Mount Zion is fundamentally a site and symbol of redemption. The decision taken by the rabbinate reflects a recurrent symbolic pattern, a link between destruction and redemption: "At the
Holocaust memorial site on Mount Zion," said Rabbi Pinchas from Kar-
titz, "we mourn and grieve, bow and sit in ashes, and at the same time
we are resurrected and lift our heads."[16] By uniting both temporal and
spatial metaphors, a unitary symbol congruent with tradition was being
established. Implicitly, the catastrophe of European Jews was likened to
the redemption of Israel and the beginning of the messianic process.

In *Civil Religion in Israel* Charles Liebman and Eliezer Don-Yehiya
distinguished between two main periods in the process of symbol formation of the new Jewish state. During the first period, up until the late
1950s, which they call "statism," they perceive mixed strategies of "con-
frontation" with the traditional symbolic world of Judaism and of "dissolution," aiming at a limited instrumental selection and reappropriation
of some traditional symbolic elements. The second period witnesses the
stage-by-stage creation of a civil religion, with its myths and rituals increasingly dominated by the strategy of reinterpretation.[17] According to
this analysis, the Shoah is of minor significance during the statist period,
as the values of the *Yishuv*, or settlement, and the new state seem mas-
sively dissonant with the so-called passivity of European Jewry which led
to their extermination "like sheep to slaughter." During the early statist
period a commemoration day and commemoration sites were established; but it was only during the later phase that the Shoah became a
central myth of the civil religion of Israel.[18]

That the evolution took place according to these general lines of development is unquestionable, but it would possibly be more correct to
describe it as a continuous process in which the Shoah took on increasing
centrality in public life from the Eichmann trial onward.[19] Moreover,
from the onset, whatever the "strategy" leading from religious tradition

to civil religion, it nonetheless seems to have maintained the traditional mythic patterns of historical memory.

On 12 April 1951 a law was passed establishing a formal Holocaust commemoration day: *Yom HaShoah,* or Holocaust Day.[20] The Warsaw ghetto revolt had started on Passover night, 14 Nissan (19 April) 1943. The commemoration day was set on 27 Nissan, as close to 14 Nissan as religious laws prohibiting mourning during the days of Passover would allow.[21] In his official interpretation of the Knesset's choice of 27 Nissan, Rabbi Mordechai Nurock, who headed the Knesset committee in charge of this matter, declared: "We had to choose a date that also fits most massacres of European Jewry and the ghetto revolt that took place in Nissan. That is why the Knesset committee chose the end of Nissan when many sacred communities were killed by the Crusaders, forefathers of the Nazis."[22]

During the Knesset debate Rabbi Nurock clearly linked the destruction of European Jewry to the creation of the state: "Honorable members of the Knesset," he declared, "we have seen a graveyard in front of us, a graveyard for six million of our brothers and sisters, and maybe because of their blood, shed like water, have we been privileged to have our state."[23] Thus the link between destruction and heroism was consecrated. Moreover, within the same global framework of interpretation, the date chosen starts a series of three closely related commemorations: Yom HaShoah is soon followed by the commemoration day for the soldiers fallen during Israel's wars, and at sunset on that day, Independence Day celebrations begin.

The choice of the date, supported by the evidence of Nurock's statements, immediately suggests the following:

—the reinsertion of the Holocaust within the historical series of Jewish catastrophes;

—the establishment of a causal link, possibly a necessary one, between the destruction of European Jewry and the birth of Israel, which is an indirect attempt to give a new dignity to the Jews of the Diaspora, whether victims or survivors;

—the combination of both events in a new symbolic unity in which the creation of the state itself is inserted into the mythic pattern of catastrophe and redemption.

These elements clearly repeat the fundamental sequence of catastrophe and redemption which we already identified in the religious commemoration. Redemption here loses its explicit religious connotation and becomes rebirth in secular but no less mythic and metahistorical terms. The traditional patterns are implicitly maintained.

The shifting emphasis from the catastrophe and destruction to the centrality of armed revolt, which seemed to have been the main reason for the choice of the date of commemoration in Nissan, has in itself a redemptive aspect: from passive catastrophe to redemptive struggle, linking the fighting Zionist Youth of the ghettos to the armed struggle for the state. In a sense, *Shoah Vegvura* (catastrophe and heroism) is another formula for *Shoah Vetekuma* (catastrophe and rebirth)—that is, possibly, for *Shoah Vegeulah* (catastrophe and redemption).

The shift from "catastrophe" to "catastrophe and heroism" became the focal point of the representation of the destruction of European Jewry in Israel's official memory.[24] It aimed not only at commemorative affirmation but at "saving the honor" of Diaspora Jewry by countering the prevalent contempt for the so-called passivity of the victims.[25]

The simplistic symmetry of catastrophe and heroism was criticized both by some nonreligious survivors,[26] for whom armed revolt was not the only form of heroism, and by religious circles, which considered martyrdom itself, not heroism or armed revolt, as the supreme value. This basic structure nonetheless remained at center stage of the official memory, at least until the mid or late 1960s. The mobilizing and integrative function of this symbolic structure was too essential during the early years of the new state to be easily discarded. Its consonance with the dominant values of the state has already been pointed to. Moreover, one should remember in this regard the substantial influence of the various organizations of ghetto fighters and partisans.[27] The "shame" of the mere survivor was being mythically erased.[28]

The official attempts to mold and remold this mythic pattern continued well into the 1970s. In 1977, when the Likud came to power, Prime Minister Menachem Begin suggested that the Shoah as such be commemorated on 9 Av, the day of the destruction of the Temple. He referred to all the historical catastrophes of the Jewish people commemorated on that day, including, for instance, the massacres of Magenza and Vermeiza as well as the expulsion from Spain, using thereby all the patterns of traditional Jewish memory. But the commemoration of the fighting was supposed to be moved to another day and set together with the Remembrance Day for the soldiers fallen in the wars of Israel, on the eve of Independence Day.[29]

We do not know why Begin tried to separate the commemoration of the "catastrophe" from that of "heroism." In any event his rhetoric of commemoration as far as the Shoah itself was concerned was consonant with the religious pathos which suffused his political rhetoric and vision. By linking the Shoah to the main religious commemoration of destruction in Jewish tradition, he made of the Shoah itself a symbol of the *Galut*, of exile, itself resonant with all its historical and theological meanings. In so doing, however, he divorced it from its redemptive context (of *Gevurah,* or "heroism," and by implication the establishment of the state), unless he remembered the old folk tradition which placed the birth of the Messiah on the very day the Temple was destroyed. He thus reinserted the Shoah into the traditional pattern of Jewish history, dissociating it from the vision of historical "fulfillment" embodied in the state. It is perhaps for this very reason that Begin's proposal was rejected by the Knesset.

### SITES OF MEMORY

One of the most explicit arenas wherein the mythic pattern of cosmic evil and redemption, of death and rebirth, is enacted is the construction of sites dedicated to the memory of the Shoah.

At ritual sites the organization of space is often used as a metaphor for the ordering of human existence and as a symbolic referent for the ultimate values of a culture.[30] Judaism's sacred space has, moreover, a specific geopolitical locus—the land of Israel and, more specifically, Jerusalem. "God's shrine [in Jerusalem] is a confirmation of social and religious order, it is an *imago mundi* giving the land cosmic significance."[31]

In modern Israeli society the ethical valorization of sacred time and space and the social order so confirmed resides no longer in strictly religious terms but in the secular idiom of modern Jewish national identity. It is therefore not surprising that the very archetypal structure of the locations commemorating the Shoah link together the catastrophe of the Shoah and the redemptive aspects of the state of Israel. In this reenactment the sacred center, the *axis mundi* of Zion as the "foundation stone of origins, the center point from which the cosmic spring swells," is secularized in terms of the state of Israel. In the return to Zion, "to the sacred center" where "time and space are redeemed," the chaos of the exile is refuted. The Jerusalem of Solomon has been characterized by Michael Fishbane as "the new Sinai, a cosmic mountain and . . . source of order." As such it partakes in the duality of all sacred sites and times, carrying within it not only the regeneration of a rebirth but the symbolization of death as well. As Fishbane notes, in the biblical idiom Jerusalem is not only "a mountain of God" but an "entrance to the netherworld as well."[32]

A similar structuring of sacred space can be observed in the manner in which the Shoah, as epitome of evil and chaos, is located in respect to the modern symbol of order and integrated existence, the state of Israel. At the Yad Mordechai commemoration site, for instance, visitors move a few steps up from the dimly lit basement of the Shoah to the better lit space commemorating the ghetto fighters and up again to the clear light of *Tekuma* (rebirth) in the main hall. This movement is expressed in much starker terms in the internal layout and particularly in the function of the official Remembrance Authority, established on 19 August 1953: "Yad Vashem. Heroes and Martyrs Memorial Authority."

At Yad Vashem the first section describes the preextermination persecutions which took place between 1933 and 1939. The second section seems to stand by itself: it is devoted to the annihilation process between 1941 and 1945. This annihilation cannot be linked to the traditional sequences of persecution, known throughout Jewish history and repeated during the first phase of the Nazi era. In the third section liberation comes. But this is not the end of the narrative; it leads of necessity to the shores of *Eretz Israel,* the ultimate redemption.[33]

The coherence of the symbolic expression of this memory of the Shoah seems unquestionable. However, both the message and the functions of the symbolic expressions of this memory show fundamental paradoxes and ultimately a disturbing undertone.

Let us consider the site of *Yad Vashem,* that is, the area on which it was built. A considerable number of possible places were suggested by various organizations when the law for the establishment of a commemoration authority was passed in 1953. In August 1953 the minister of education and culture, Ben-Zion Dinur, decided that Yad Vashem would be built on the Mount of Remembrance in the outskirts of Jerusalem. Theodor Herzl had been buried there in August 1949, and a military cemetery had been established on the same site soon after the end of the fighting around the city.

The Mount of Remembrance was, in a sense, divided into two very distinct areas: the part of the hill facing Jerusalem is the military cemetery and the burial place for the founder of Zionism and some of its main leaders. The part facing the hills, with its back to the city, became the commemoration center for the destruction of European Jewry. This setting seems to establish a hierarchy within the symbolic reference points of the new society. On a manifest level the symbols of the new state take precedence over those of destruction.

However, this last point is more ambiguous than it seems. In Israel there is no equivalent of the Tomb of the Unknown Soldier. In some countries such a tomb is replaced as a central symbol of national identity by the tomb of the founder of the state (the "Tomb of the Liberator" in Latin American countries—that of San Martin, for instance, in Argentina). Whatever the mode of commemoration, such tombs or monuments are the hallowed places where foreign dignitaries express their identification with the country they visit and where ritually the group confirms its own identity. But in Israel foreign dignitaries visit neither the military cemetery on the Mount of Remembrance nor the tomb of Herzl. It is Yad Vashem which fulfills this symbolic function.

One could argue that there is an element of psychological conditioning in this choice. We believe, however, that this ritual has a latent significance of much wider importance. In a strangely contradictory way the Remembrance Authority, which does not face the city of Jerusalem but the hills—which at first glance is not the dominant symbol in the hierarchy of symbols—has become nonetheless the central hallowed place presented to the attention of the world, a place where the visitor identifies with what appears as the raison d'être of the Jewish state. The message could be that Yad Vashem, the central commemorating place of the Shoah, is the very basis of the legitimacy of the State of Israel. The hierarchic unity of the symbol—the Mount of Remembrance—thus betrays a continual tension. Not only is the metahistorical meaning of the Shoah realized in the redemptive moment of the state, but the state itself is valorized in terms of the Shoah.

This implicit mode of legitimation of the state entails, in fact, a link between the religious view of the uniqueness of Israel and its secular version constantly present in Zionism—and constantly in contradiction with its manifest aim of normalizing Jewish fate.[34]

## THE IDEOLOGICAL POLARIZATION

The Six-Day War opened a new phase in the perception of the Shoah, as it opened a new phase in the evolution of Israeli society.[35] The Shoah at first had a national significance, one formalized and ritualized, with an unperceived message and function; over time, though, it became increasingly part and parcel of the new ideological confrontations within Israeli society. It became instrumentalized at the partisan level as political polarization grew.[36]

In the national-messianic context the activation of one of the traditional readings of the meaning of redemption can be perceived. This camp fulfills three main criteria of this particular interpretation of catastrophe and redemption:

—a tendency to equate the hostility of the Arabs with Nazi attitudes
    toward the Jews;
—the willingness to use symbols of the Shoah for self-identification
    and self-justification in the context of the internal political fight;
—the emphasis on the isolation of Israel, the rhetoric of destruction,
    and the uniqueness of the Jewish fate, all leading to a vision
    of redemption.

These elements are well known. Menachem Begin's rhetoric during the Lebanon War is a good illustration of the first point.[37] The use of the yellow star by the settlers at Yamit—who forcibly resisted Israeli efforts to move them from their coastal community as part of the Camp David settlement with Egypt—is an example of the second aspect. The whole rhetoric of catastrophe and redemption practically identifies the third aspect with the mythical structure of the memory of the Shoah. The last point indicates that, as in several other central domains of Zionist ideology, the new messianic nationalism has taken over symbols elaborated within the framework of traditional Zionism and, by pushing them to the extreme, has appropriated their core content.

The significance of this appropriation is obvious. The mythic memory of the Shoah, which emerged so clearly during the 1950s and 1960s, became an integral part of the mythology of the messianic Zionism of the 1970s and 1980s, owing in part to the inherent logic of its message. The uniqueness of Jewish fate and the link between catastrophe and redemption have together become the essential belief of an extremely vocal, if limited, sector of Israeli society. What had been an essential symbolic pattern of commemoration of the past for a society achieving independence became a potent guiding myth for one of the extreme segments of this same society. The latent content of the message became the explicit program of a political faith.

This move from latent message to manifest faith was, however, inherent in the very symbolic logic which identified the Israeli state with the redemptive moment in history. The legitimation of current historical processes in mythic terms carried with it the potential for a messianic nationalism, the more effective for being linked, in many ways, to that "active messianism" deeply ingrained in a specific tradition of Judaism.[38]

In contrast to these interpretations stands the discourse of the more liberal and left-wing elements of the population. Although much more diverse and less "coherent," these interpretations integrate the memory of the *Shoah* with a more universalist and rational discourse. Its major points can be summed up as follows:

—a tendency to compare some Jewish behavior in the occupied territories or in relation to the Palestinians in general with some aspects of Nazi behavior toward the Jews or with fascism in more general terms;
—the rejection of any form of mythical structuration of the memory of the Shoah and the emphasis on its overall human and banal aspects;
—the belief in the comparability and universalization of the phenomenon, stemming almost of necessity from the two previous postulates.

The identification of some Jewish behavior with that of the Nazis found its expression in a new form of subversive literary use of symbols, in a kind of reversal of the accepted vision, in some sort of literary defiance and breaking of taboos, which became particularly clear during the Lebanon War. In the words of one interpreter, "The images themselves, the emblems of Nazism, now seem to have been released from social taboo by acts of literary defiance against the very rhetoric which proclaims, officially, that Jews are constitutionally *incapable* of oppressive behavior and attitudes."[39]

The subversive use of symbols is but one expression among others of ideological defiance. The comparability and univerzalisation of the Shoah led to a number of contradictions. In the opening article of a 1986 issue of the left-wing periodical *Politika* devoted to the *Shoah*, its author stressed the need for comparability and universalization, an imperative for which the ideological reasons were obvious. However, in presenting his own position, the author stated the following, which in a way canceled his own premises: "In no case do I wish to say," he wrote, "that the Shoah was less than absolute evil [*ro 'a muchlat*]."[40] "Absolute evil" makes comparison and universalization difficult.

In a sense the political heirs of the left-wing organizations which thirty years before had more or less created the myth of catastrophe and rebirth were now those who, because of the evolution of Israeli society, were attempting to do away with this mythical memory of the past, whereas the political opposition of the 1950s and 1960s was appropriating for its own cause the core of that mythical memory, turning its latent content into a manifest message.

In other words, with the establishment of the State of Israel, both the destruction of European Jewry and the very creation of the state were formulated in collective memory in traditional religious patterns of catastrophe and redemption. However, once the redemptive moment in history became identified with the state, its particular articulation became the province of competing political visions pursuing their own, mutually exclusive interpretations of the state and of the fulfillment of redemption.

It can perhaps be added that the conflicting "ideologies" of the present represent two poles of a dichotomy which has always existed within Jewish historical consciousness. For the redemptive vision in Judaism contained both particularistic elements focused on the national, ethnic, and ascriptive definitions of the messianic community as well as a more universalistic vision of the end of days and freedom from the thralldom of history.

In *Zakhor* Yosef Yerushalmi states that the image of the Shoah "is being shaped, not at the historian's anvil, but in the novelist's crucible" and that the Jews are awaiting the creation of some new metahistorical myth which, like the mystical world of the Kabbalah after the expulsion from Spain, will give a new meaning to the cataclysmic past.[41]

In fact, the evolution seems far more complex. In Israel, beyond the trends we alluded to, a new sensitivity, possibly a new authenticity regarding the Shoah, seems to be appearing, particularly on the literary scene. "The individual sensibilities," writes Sidra Ezrahi, "which had been rendered historically insignificant when juxtaposed with the socially ritualized codes, are now harnessed to an equally public enterprise of denationalizing memory and challenging exclusive claims to the inheritance."[42] By contrast, the hard-core mythification of the Shoah still elicits a significant echo within a given sector of Israeli society.

Another dichotomy appears in recent approaches to the Diaspora. A growing search for authenticity—illustrated, for instance, by Claude Lanzmann's "Shoah"—is countered, particularly on the American scene, by massive trends of vulgarization reinforced by the media industry and specific kinds of ongoing commemorative endeavors.[43] Thus, conflicting tendencies in the representation and interpretation of the extermination of the Jews of Europe appear, and not only in international debates concerning the place and significance of these events in history. Within the Jewish world as well we will probably be faced for a long time to come with an ongoing and conflicting process of shaping and reshaping, writing and rewriting the story of what appears to be an indelible but essentially opaque past.

## NOTES

Some of the issues dealt with in this paper were first presented by Saul Friedlander in the Hannukah Lecture, delivered at the Jerusalem Van Leer Foundation on 31 December 1986 and published as "Die Shoah als Element in der Konstruktion Israelischer Erinnerung," *Babylon, Beitraege zur iuedischen Gegenwart* 2 (1987): 3–27.

1. The use of the term *Shoah* to designate the catastrophe of European Jewry under the Nazis appears, according to Uriel Tal, from 1940. Between 1940 and 1942, the term *Hurban*, with its Jewish historical and Yiddish connotations, was one of the first, spontaneous choices (similar to the term *catastrophe*). According to Tal, "all Biblical meanings of the term *Shoah* clearly imply divine judgement and retribution." In modern Hebrew use, the term underwent "a structural transformation. . . . Existential and historical thought develops non-Biblical and non-theological forms of interpretation. . . . The existential and historical meaning of *Shoah* implies metaphysical doubt, reconsideration of the validity of man's rational faculties, sometimes even personal indulgence in despair" (Uriel Tal, "Excursus on the Term *Shoah*," *Shoah: A Review of Holocaust Studies and Commemorations* 1, no. 4 (1979): 10–11).

2. Approximately 250,000 survivors reached Israel during the immediate postwar years. The number of these immigrants ultimately grew to around 400,000.

3. Amos Elon, *The Israelis: Founders and Sons* (New York: Holt, Rinehart, and Winston, 1971), 199.

4. For very insightful references to this issue, see Charles S. Liebman and Eliezer Don-Yehiya, *Civil Religion in Israel: Traditional Judaism and Political Culture in the Jewish State* (Berkeley and Los Angeles: University of California Press, 1985).

5. R. J. Werblovsky, "Messianism in Jewish History," in H. H. Ben-Sasson and S. Ettinger, *Jewish Society Through the Ages* (New York: Schocken Books, 1971), 32; Sigmund Mowinckel, *He That Cometh* (Oxford: Oxford University Press, 1959), 261–345.

6. Gershom Scholem, "Towards An Understanding of the Messianic Idea in Judaism," in his *The Messianic Idea in Judaism* (New York: Schocken Books, 1971), 10.

7. Amos Funkenstein, "Le Messianisme passif," in *Maimonide: Nature, histoire et messianisme* (Paris, 1988), 97.

8. Yehezkel Kaufman, *The Religion of Israel: From Its Beginnings to the Babylonian Exile* (Chicago: University of Chicago Press, 1960), 132, 151; Mowinckel, *He That Cometh*, 82, 151.

9. Mowinckel, *He That Cometh*, 155–86.

10. Funkenstein, "Le Messianisme actif," in *Maimonide*, 103.

11. Yosef Hayim Yerushalmi, *Zakhor: Jewish History and Jewish Memory* (Seattle: University of Washington Press, 1982), 24.

12. Rabbi Yoel Taitlbau, *Va Yoel Moshe*, quoted in Amos Funkenstein, *L'Allegmagne nazie et le génocide juif* (Paris: Gallimard, 1985), 446.

13. Sermon of the Belzer Rebbe, *Hamachane HaHaredi*, no. 188 (June 1984).

14. The necessary link between *Hurban* (a term used more commonly among Orthodox Jews than *Shoah*) and messianic redemption is strongly emphasized in the immediate postwar rabbinic literature. Drawing on a considerable number of such sources, Gershon Greenberg sums up: "In the ontological battle, God's Presence is evident. In Germany [among rabbis residing on German soil after the war], *Hurban* is described as the pain preceding the redemption in which history under God culminates. In New York, the *Hurban* is aligned with previous catastrophes, but in addition precludes redemption. The Nazis serve God, as does Hitler himself. Elberg speaks of the *Hurban* as an outpouring of divine wrath, as a holy sacrifice before God. The martyrs are filled with a special strength to endure God. Hitler is God's ultimate definition of what exile is for the Jews. Our rabbis do not speak of God's hiddenness, of his departure from the world. To the contrary, the *Hurban* is God's aggressive manifestation in history" (Greenberg, "Orthodox Jewish Theology, 1945–1948: Responses to the Holocaust," in *Remembering for the Future*, ed. Y. Bauer et al. [Oxford: Oxford University Press, 1988], 1024).

15. Letter from Dr. S. Z. Kahana to the Chief Rabbinate, Jerusalem, 25 December 1949, Archive of the Chief Rabbinate, Jerusalem.

16. S. Z. Kahana, "Hamashmaut Haleumit Simlit shel Martef Hashoah be Har Zion," *Hatzofeh*, 16 December 1956.

17. Liebman and Don-Yehiya, *Civil Religion in Israel*, 23.

18. Ibid., 21. In 1980 Jacob Neusner pointed to the same "status" of the "Holocaust" among American Jewry: "What we have done is to make the murder of the Jews of Europe into one of the principle components of the civil religion of American Jews" (Neusner, "Beyond Catastrophe and Before Redemption," *Reconstructionist* 44 [April 1980]).

19. One tends to forget that two major debates of the early and mid 1950s dealt indirectly or directly with the Shoah: the German reparations debate and the Kastner trial. One may argue, however, that in both cases the immediate internal political issues linked to the debates draw most of the attention. Thus, the importance of the Eichmann trial in this process remains central: "The trial," in Alan Mintz's words "had the force of an electrifying discovery. . . . The trial resembled nothing so much as, *mutatis mutandis*, a massive Passion play, in which the members of an entire community play parts" (Mintz, *Hurban: Responses to Catastrophe in Hebrew Literature* [New York: Columbia University Press, 1984], 239–40).

20. The first appellation was "The Holocaust and Ghetto Uprising Memorial Day—A Day of Perpetual Remembrance for the House of Israel." It became, from 1953 on, the "Holocaust and Heroism Remembrance Day." Only in 1959 did another law impose public observance; an amendment to the law, passed in 1961, required places of entertainment to be closed on the eve of that day. See Nathan Eck, "Holocaust Remembrance Day," *Encyclopedia Judaica* (Jerusalem: Keter, 1971) 8: 916–17.

21. In the Diaspora, 19 April remains the usual commemoration day.

22. *Knesset Record*, 1st Knesset, 3d sess., 12 April 1951, 1656.

23. Ibid., 1657.

24. In his comment on the law, Rabbi Nurock expanded on this issue: "We are proud of our brothers and sisters who saved the honour of the nation; who performed miraculous deeds of bravery and showed the wild beasts that the People of Israel is not sheep led to slaughter; who found a way to die worthy of upright people and heroes, so that all generations to come may know how to cherish and respect the memory of the nation's victims: this is our comfort in our distress" (ibid., 1656).

25. For a particularly crass expression of this kind of contempt within Zionist-Socialist lore, see, for instance, the following Kibbutz Haggada (Passover saga) excerpt: "Hitler alone is not responsible for the death of six million—but all of us, and above all, the six million. If they had known that the Jew has power, they would not have all been butchered. . . . The lack of faith, the ghettoish-exilic self-denigration . . . contributed its share to this great butchery" (quoted in Liebman and Don-Yehiya, *Civil Religion in Israel*, 102).

26. Chana Zemer, *Dvar Hapoelet*, April 1963.

27. Incidentally, the protohistoriography of the Shoah was mainly produced by former partisans and ghetto fighters; and the early historiography, approximately until the mid 1960s, tended to reinforce the pattern of official memory.

On these issues in Israeli historiography, see, among others, Yisrael Gutman, "Jewish Resistance—Questions and Assessments," typescript, revised English version of "Hahitnagdut hajehudit leturotena—Kavim lesikum," in his *Bealata ubema'avak* (Tel Aviv, 1985).

28. Another function of this emphasis put on the heroism of the Jews in the Gola may well have been that of assuaging an underlying sense of guilt. An ongoing debate about the role of the Yishuv in potential efforts to save some of the European Jews from the Shoah has brought forth contending positions about what was done or could have been done. The facts are open to interpretation. What is certain, however, is that on the symbolic level, at least, the Yishuv did not offer a convincing proof of its total commitment to help. As Antek Zuckerman, one of the leaders of the Warsaw ghetto revolt, expressed it in a conversation with the writer Haim Guri, "Why did not one come? Not a single one!" (see Dina Porath, *Hanhaga Bemilkud: Hayishuv Nochach Hashoah 1942–1945* [Tel Aviv: 1986], 405).

29. *Knesset Record,* 9th Knesset, 1st sess., 2 August 1977, 567.

30. See Mircea Eliade, *The Sacred and the Profane* (New York: Harper and Row, 1956), 17, 20–67; Jonathan Smith, *Map Is Not Territory* (Leiden: Brill, 1978), 88–146.

31. Michael Fishbane, "The Sacred Center: The Symbolic Structure of the Bible," in M. Fishbane and P. Flohr, *Texts and Responses* (Leiden: Brill, 1975), 21.

32. Ibid.

33. James E. Young, "Memory and Monument," in Geoffrey Hartman, ed., *Bitburg in Moral and Political Perspective* (Bloomington: Indiana University Press, 1986), 103–13.

34. The reference to the Shoah as demonstrating, in secular terms, the uniqueness of the history of the Jewish people among the nations can already be found in speeches made in 1943 by Ben Zion Dinur (then Dinaburg). Cf. Uriel Tal, "Excursus on the Term *Shoah,*" 10.

35. For Israeli society, this change is obviously linked to the effects of the occupation of the West Bank and Gaza and the political evolution that ensued. It may well be, moreover, that the perception of the possible destruction, during the weeks preceding the Six-Day War, reinforced the identification with the fate of European Jews within wide strata of the population. The 1973 Yom Kippur War was another stage in this process, as was the Lebanon War of 1983. The impact of the 1967 and 1973 wars in terms of awareness of the Shoah have been measured in various polls as well as in terms of increased attention to the Shoah in school curricula and educational material. Cf. Simon N. Herman, "In the Shadow of the Holocaust," *Jerusalem Quarterly,* no. 3 (Spring 1977): 85–97; Haim Schatzker, "The Holocaust in Israeli Education," *International Journal of Political Education,* no. 5 (1982): 77. As for the Lebanon War, it was accompanied and followed by a considerable growth of literary renditions of the Shoah, both "subversive," and of more general portent. Among the authors, suffice it to mention, at random, the names of Yossi Hadar, Yehoshua Sobel, Hanoch Levin, Motti Lerner, Shmuel Hastari, David Grossman, and Ori Orlev. Cf. Shaul Friedlander, "Die Shoah als Element."

Regarding the American Jewish scene, it is commonly accepted that the May

1967 period represents a decisive turning point in the awareness of the Holocaust. See, for instance, Jacob Neusner, "A 'Holocaust' Primer," *National Review,* 3 August 1979, 977, and, in particular, Loen A. Jick, "The Holocaust: Its Use and Abuse within the American Public," *Yad Vashem Studies* 14 (1981): 313.

36. For illustrations of some aspects of this instrumentalization, see Gerald Cromer, "Negotiating the Meaning of the Holocaust: An Observation on the Debate about Kahanism in Israeli Society," *Holocaust and Genocide Studies* 2, no. 2 (1987): 289–90.

37. For instance, Begin wrote to President Reagan in the midst of the war: "May I tell you, dear Mr. President, how I feel these days when I turn to the Creator of my soul in deep gratitude: I feel as a prime minister empowered to instruct a valiant army facing 'Berlin,' where amongst innocent civilians, Hitler and his henchmen hide in a bunker deep beneath the surface" (*Jerusalem Post,* 3 August 1982).

38. Funkenstein, "Interprétations théologiques," in *Maimonide,* 467.

39. Sidra Dekoven Ezrahi, "Revisioning the Past: The Changing Legacy of the Holocaust in Hebrew Literature," *Salmagundi,* nos. 68–69 (Fall 1985): 270.

40. Adi Ophir, "Al Chidush Hashem," *Politika,* no. 8 (June–July 1986).

41. Yerushalmi, *Zakhor,* 98.

42. Ezrahi, "Revisioning the Past," 270. The allusion here is probably to the work of such writers as Ahron Appelfeld and Dan Pagis.

43. The tendency toward an excessive simplification and vulgarization of the representations and commemorations of the Holocaust on the American Jewish scene has been insufficiently analyzed. Apart from Jacob Neusner's and Leon Jick's articles, see in particular the most incisive comments in Robert Alter, "Deformations of the Holocaust," *Commentary* 71, no. 2 (February 1981), 48–54. A full-length study of this phenomenon remains necessary.

## TWELVE

# Geosophia, Geognosis, and Geopiety: Orders of Significance in Japanese Representations of Space

*Allan G. Grapard*

*There is more work in interpreting interpretations than in interpreting things.*
—MONTAIGNE, *ESSAIS*

In this chapter I present preliminary investigations of meanings that have been attributed to some forms of social space in premodern Japan and am concerned with the relations between power and knowledge which undergirded that historical significance. I focus on some spatial practices which, while appearing to be religious, exhibit a political character that is related to the discourses of power through which various conceptualizations of the Japanese territory came to be associated with the specificity of cultural identity. I will also suggest that sometimes spatial practices consolidated political power, whereas at other times they seemed to protest against it. In other words, the following discussion is concerned not so much with examining logico-mathematical categories resulting in the mental creation of "ideal" space as it is with suggesting that all spatial practices are social products, tools for thought and action, and hence, a means of domination. My thinking on the topic is informed in part by the work of Henri Lefebvre on the production of space, in which he suggests that "social space will be revealed in its particularity to the extent that it ceases to be indistinguishable from mental space (as defined by philosophers and mathematicians) on the one hand, and physical space (as defined by practico-sensory activity and the perception of 'nature') on the other."[1]

Recently Robert Sack wrote that "spatial analysis [is the study of] the interrelationships between activities in the landscape and their spatial properties." Suggesting that the history of meanings of space might be pursued through interdisciplinary and cross-cultural studies, he went on to suggest that "territoriality's changing functions help to understand the historical relationships between society, space, and time."[2] However, Sack seems to reduce every territory-related practice to "spatial forms taken by power" and to assume that all power is a matter of human relations or their reified forms. For him, territoriality is a geographic strategy to control people and things by controlling area.

While I agree with the ideological premises of Sack's position, I would argue that his analysis fails to offer a complete representation of the way in which social groups produce space and give meaning to it. One need not have a territory in order to give meaning to space, and territoriality is only one of several possible ways in which people produce a space to which they relate in emotional as well as other manners. Among the cultural factors that shape the way in which people construct such spaces are shared understandings about how knowledge is gained. The implication of Michel Foucault's analysis, for example, of the intimate and historically specific relation between power and knowledge is that histories of spatial organization and of the meaning of space must be connected and conjointly related to power and epistemology. It is fallacious to assume that the concept of power which sustained territorial practices in the pre-Renaissance eras is the same as that operative today; that people have always shared the same conditions that made knowledge possible; or that the relation between power and knowledge was always equivalent.

In contradistinction to Sack's and Lefebvre's more recent views on human territoriality, scholars of religious history have studied the forms of space they term "sacred" as though they were devoid of historical conflict in their origins as well as in their maintenance. Following the work of Mircea Eliade in this respect, they treat the power of sacred spaces as though it were intrinsic to those places and "always already there," with little regard for sociological or political factors, and as if power were a numinous entity that has never changed and whose origins and status are relegated *in illo tempore*. Scholars who follow Eliade's analysis of sacred space rarely discuss epistemological issues except in the most general terms, and they tend to obfuscate the social and political components of its formulation and maintenance. In this essay I will try to posit a perspective that is different from Sack's and from the traditional treatment of sacred space by historians of religions.

In the course of past attempts to initiate a comprehensive historical analysis of Japanese religious geography, I was left with the conclusion that the study of space in Japan was inseparable from the study of its politico-religious culture, a conclusion I was not then willing to state because I thought that much more research was required on nonpolitical aspects of the spatial experience of the body.[3] However, further research showed that such experience was rarely divorced from attempts to politicize it or at least to inscribe it within social relations of power. In the following discussion of a few distinct but recurrent representations of place at different points in Japanese history, I will suggest that these representations hide certain existential concerns and reification processes that are typical of a politico-religious intention and that might be analyzed collectively under the name of "representational spaces." Such analysis yields the basic spectrum of values held by a society which tended to project power relations in spatial terms and offers insights into the ways in which some Japanese groups have gone about constructing, representing, and reproducing a distinct experience of the social space. These representations evidence the existence of codes that may have been at work in the production of certains forms of social space, and the discussion that evolves below is meant to answer, in part, Lefebvre's call for theoretical analysis: "If indeed spatial codes have existed, each characterizing a particular spatial/social practice, and if these codifications have been *produced* along with the space corresponding to them, then the job of theory is to elucidate their rise, their role, and their demise."[4]

## GEOSOPHIA, GEOGNOSIS, GEOPIETY

Over a long period the Japanese people have developed intense relationships to specific places that are manifest in ritual practices and spatial modes of behavior as well as in a vast number of texts where they take on an emotional and philosophical character. This cultural phenomenon deserves a special lexicon. I have opted for three terms which express different behavioral modes that can be associated with particular speculative moods in regard to space and time. These terms have been constructed on the basis of the term *philosophy*, "love of wisdom."

*Geosophia* (from the Greek *gaia*, "earth," and *sophia*, "wisdom") refers, in the following, to particular forms of knowledge of the spatial environment and to specific relations of society to the natural world. Studies of geosophia might be conducted on practices such as geomancy, on preferred conditions of living space at the level of the house or village, or on other types of spatial arrangement.

I would like to define the term *geognosis* (from *gaia*, "earth," and *gnosis*, "knowledge") as something akin to a type of soteriological knowledge (i.e., leading to salvation) that is gained through specific spatial practices of a predominantly ritual or mystical character. Here the term *gnosis* is used with an emphasis on what could be said to correspond, in character, to the high theology of the Gnostics; I use this term, therefore, with the understanding that it differs from the cognate term *geognosy*, which some geographers have used to refer to the scientific analysis of geology.

Both geosophia and geognosis are connected with systems of symbolic representation, but their epistemological frameworks and intentionality differ in each case. Whereas *geosophia* might be characterized as the establishment of a wise use of the earth by humans and to a certain instrumentality, *geognosis* refers to a specific knowledge that is claimed to have been extracted from the earth itself, to correspond in mysterious ways to sacred scriptures and to divine rule, and to lead either to mystical achievement or to religious salvation.

*Geopiety* usually refers to a primarily religious mood of relation to sacred places. I see it as a set of beliefs and practices subsumed under geognosis as if it were its protosecular form, i.e., a distinct set of conceptualizations and practices that stand halfway between the mystical aspects of geognosis and the secular, modern forms of relationship to place. This attitude is evident in a number of texts and is related to the premodern practices of pilgrimage, which are themselves related to a certain form of government. In geopiety the emphasis is on the attitude of pious reverence to what has been called 'sacred space' by historians of religions.

Of these terms, only *geopiety* has been widely used by geographers and historians of religions. One could add to these categories that of geopolitics, but with the understanding that on the level of nationalism the practices of geopolitics are not self-critical and are, in fact, informed by geosophia, geognosis, and geopiety.[5] Geopolitics is related to the consolidation of modern nation-states, which always evidences particular techniques for occupying space and for establishing ever more precisely defined social spaces. The four categories named above are not intended to be all-inclusive; rather, they refer to systems of representation and to modes of spatial behavior that provide a privileged entry into the spatial aspects of cultural identity and their related power structures.

In the case of the analysis of temporal aspects one might use, on the basis of the Greek term *chronos,* "time," related terms such as *chronosophia, chronognosis,* and *chronopiety,* provided one keeps in mind that time and space share structural intimacies in their conceptualization and production.[6] These categories will be presented sequentially, which might lead the reader to assume that they historically follow each other. However, the case for a diachronic analysis would have to be made by demonstrating what caused epistemological shifts from one category to the other and by showing in some detail how certain forms of power made possible, or rendered obsolete, certain types of knowledge. That is impossible within the limits of this chapter, which focuses on a few premodern practices and ideas within the Japanese context alone. It is now obvious, however, that the study of "chronotypes" is essential and must be sytematically related to studies of spatial practice. Indeed, in the

introduction to *Chronotypes: The Construction of Time* John Bender and
David Wellbery write that "chronotypes are models or patterns through
which time assumes practical or conceptual significance. Time is not
given but . . . fabricated in an ongoing process. Chronotypes are themselves temporal and plural, constantly being made and remade at multiple individual, social, and cultural levels. They interact with one another, sometimes cooperatively, sometimes conflictually. They change
over time and therefore have a history or histories, the construal of
which is itself an act of temporal construction. . . . Chronotypes are not
produced *ex nihilo;* they are improvised from an already existing repertoire of cultural forms and natural phenomena."[7]

## THE GEOSOPHIC STRUCTURATION OF SPATIAL EXPERIENCE

Under the term *geosophia* I subsume a certain balance of fears and desires, and specific uses of space, whose analysis indicates that human
spatial choices were determined in part by sheer environmental necessity and in part by a set of "assumed connivances" between mankind and
its natural milieu. These choices were expressed in a number of texts
that describe techniques of ritual construction, modes of selection of residences, and choices concerning travel, agricultural work, and the like.
Being the sum total of the knowledge and techniques that pertain to
those choices, *geosophia* captures what will be termed the "classical hermeneutics of natural forms," that is, modes of interpretation of the perceived relations of oppositions and interactions that were thought to obtain between the natural world and human culture.

Comparative considerations aside, the information on ritual constructions gathered by Swiss architectural anthropologists working in Japan
demonstrates that archaic ritual binding and hut structures can be interpreted as systems of signs and symbols.[8] To state that all such ritual
activities and structures were fundamentally related to territory would
be exaggerated because, although they were certainly related to the human tendency to invest space with particular sociopolitical meanings,
they were also related to ritual tendencies to construct space on the basis
of formal oppositions whose meaning (a term in which aesthetic satisfaction can be included) resides in their structure alone.[9] The same type of
work ought to be done in the case of the more complex architectural
structures of Shinto shrines and Buddhist temples, which were organized to represent cosmographic notions and to overturn or reinforce
(and re-enforce) social rules at the time of ritual performance.[10] The
question under consideration, however, concerns not so much those architectural constructions in which specific views might have been encoded as the act of investing particular elements of nature or entire geo-

graphic areas with a meaning that made certain actions possible, or through actions that made the imposition of particular meanings appear natural. This investment of meaning might be termed *semiotic reduction*—that is, the act of claiming that natural forms are morphemes or "semiographs" that are semantically charged and can be decoded with the help of techniques of interpretation.[11] Mountains are the most obvious Japanese example, although other natural phenomena have also been the object of such reduction.[12]

As stated earlier, the sacredness of certain places has generally been regarded by scholars of religions as a static and consensual phenomenon. In these studies there is, in contradistinction with Sack, no power and hence no history. However, it must be emphasized that the sacredness of mountains in the classical periods of Japan's history was related to a very precise sense of orientation that was itself related to conquest and land possession and therefore to violence and conflict. Scanning ancient documents such as *Kojiki (Record of Ancient Matters,* compiled in 712 C.E.) and *Fudoki (Record of Local Surveys,* compiled in the second half of the eighth century) for religious and political aspects of the perception and organization of place by people of the Nara period (710–784), we find numerous instances of highly structured spatial zones whose construction can be interpreted in terms of the following five principles.[13] First, the mountains that permitted a bird's-eye view of land to be conquered or protected came to be treated as emblems of sovereignty over that land. Second, these mountains were climbed by rulers and their sacerdotal representatives at specific times for the purpose of performing rituals aimed at enhancing their legitimacy and at bonding the territorially related social groups they aspired to bring under their governance.[14] Third, a worship of natural cosmic phenomena—such as stars and planets, the sun and the moon, water and fire—took place on those mountains. Originally that worship was probably not related to the power of rulers, but natural phenomena came rather early to be associated with, and to symbolize, imperial rule and thus were appropriated.[15] Fourth, the worship of mountains seems to have been related to cults of the dead almost everywhere in Japan. Consequently, mountains and other natural emblems of legitimacy came to be the object of rituals that retain traces of both fertility and ancestor cults. What might be the earliest examples of such rituals in the archipelago can be seen today in Tsushima and Iki, where they are subsumed under the name of *himachi,* "waiting for the sun."[16] Fifth and last, similarly perceived land configurations tended to be looked for in different places, and sacred mountains were often chosen on the basis of their perceived resemblance to definite morphological types. One sees duplications of these basic structures of places that were chosen as cult sites throughout Japan during the Nara period. Although it is necessary to offer a complete study of these phenomena as they appear in the earliest texts, the discussion will be limited to two eighth-century examples drawn from *Fudoki*, a record of land, products, and legendary history:

> District of Kishima. To the south of the district office is a mountain that stands alone, composed of three peaks that follow a southwest-northeast axis. Its name is Kishima. The southwestern peak is called Hikogami (male deity), the central peak is called Himegami (female deity), and the north-eastern peak is called Mikogami (august child deity). Another name for Mikogami is Ikusagami (army deity): when the mountain shakes, it is said that an army is in movement. Every year in spring and in autumn men and women of the region take *sake* [rice wine] and *koto* [a kind of zither] and, holding hands, climb the mountain in order to contemplate the land-scape. There they drink, sing, and dance. When the festivities end, they return to the plain below. Here are the words of their song:
>
> > Mount Kishima,
> > Steep slopes struck by hail!
> > Losing hold of the grass,
> > I take my beloved's hand.
>
> This is called song in the manner of Kishima.[17]

This case is interesting in several respects. The structure of sacred geography of Kishima in the western island of Kyushu was "duplicated" in Yamato in central Japan and in Kashima in eastern Japan, to the point that even the song in the manner of Kishima is offered by *Fudoki* for Mount Tsukuba.[18] By *duplication* I mean that the orientation of villages vis-à-vis mountains of similar appearance was copied, that ritual forms were duplicated, and that similar types of *kami*, or divine entities, were worshiped.[19] One is thus left with the impression that the provinces of Hizen and Hitachi, while separated by a thousand kilometers, were colo-nized by the same people, who reestablished in unfamiliar surroundings familiar principles for the organization of life, and that these modes of organization entailed ritual practices based on the agricultural timetable. It is of some interest to note that particular ritual forms and spatial modes of organization in the case of Mount Tsukuba were kept for cen-turies and still exist today, as is evidenced by recent studies of the area's confraternities.[20] Confraternities of belief have always developed spe-cific ties between given regions and sacred mountains and have fostered distinct cultural identities and particular environmental practices. These confraternities were in fact so distinct, and therefore so potentially un-controllable, that the only way the government found to manage them was to co-opt their worship of certain places by assimilating the local deities to the national pantheon and granting them a high status and by attempting to put the government's own ritual specialists in charge of the cults. This was true of all sacred mountain confraternities for much of Japanese history until in 1872 the Japanese government prohibited those cults and abolished all mountain cult confraternities.

In a totally different mode of interpretation, the case of Ikusagami Peak is fascinating because it evidences a phenomenon that can be explained in terms of a dialectic between nature and culture, which belongs to a specific epistemological realm that consisted of views on systematic relations between language and natural forms and between human behavior and the world of nature. One such view, which circulated widely in Nara and Heian Japan (from roughly the eighth to the twelfth centuries), held that natural phenomena of a cataclysmic character were signs of impending disaster in society or—as was more often the case—of a cosmic reaction to improper human behavior. This phenomenon is not Japanese in origin; it can be observed much earlier in China, where it was readily interpreted by the first-century skeptic philosopher Wang-ch'ung:

> Originally there were no calamities or omens, or if there were, they were not considered as reprimands from Heaven. Why? Because at that time people were simple and unsophisticated, and did not restrain or reproach one another. Later ages have gradually declined—superiors and inferiors contradict one another, and calamities and omens constantly occur. Hence the hypothesis of reprimands from Heaven has been invented. Yet the Heaven of today is the same Heaven as of old—it is not that Heaven anciently was kind, and now is harsh. The hypothesis of Heaven reprimands has been put forward in modern times, as a surmise made by men from their own subjective feelings.[21]

That philosopher was attacking a political movement he called "phenomenalism," which emphasized the belief that human behavior affected natural phenomena. If natural calamities were caused by an inadequate harmonization of politics with the natural course of things, it was argued, a ruler who staked his legitimacy in the claim that his rule was grounded in a "natural way," such as a "mandate of Heaven," could be criticized: natural disasters were indications of discontent on the part of that Heaven. However, the views of the "phenomenalists" cannot be reduced to mere political maneuver, for they would not have been accepted if the conditions for knowledge that made such beliefs acceptable had not been present. These conditions entailed the notion that the structure of the world was similar to the structure of the human body and that both were endowed with the capacity of speech. Ritualized speech and physical activities were thus perfect vehicles for the harmonization of the microcosm with the macrocosm.[22] Ritualized speech and behavior, thought to be "the natural way of things," acted on natural phenomena and reinstated human society in its original sociocosmic harmony, while the signs found in nature were seen as hiding from common perception—but revealing to the trained eye—messages of cosmic proportions. In this type of episteme, divination and astrology played a central role, for they were a set of practices based on the notion that messages could be read from marks in nature; they were techniques to pass from marks in nature to signs in culture. Here a distinction must be posited between the technician of the art of divination and the figure who takes the power to interpret the signs hidden in nature. As Wang-ch'ung also wrote: "Someone asked whether a sage could make divination. Yang Hiung replied that a sage could certainly make divination about Heaven and Earth. If that is so, continued the questioner, what is the difference between the sage and the astrologer? He replied, 'The astrologer foretells what the effects of heavenly phenomena will be on man; the sage foretells what the effects of man's actions will be on the heavens.'"[23]

The idea of a similarity between the microcosm and the macrocosm belonged to the type of conditions for knowledge which sustained the *Book of Changes* (*I-ching*) and the entire world of divination, be it through deer bones (scapulimancy) or tortoise shells (plastromancy). Geomancy (*feng-shui*), which partook of the same realm, was also used in Japan.[24] Certain perceived morphological identities were interpreted as subtle indications to the effect that the world was to be read like a text, that this world hid in its natural forms and movements secret springs of wisdom which, properly tapped, ensured a harmonious integration of humans within the larger cosmos. Believing in an ideal harmony between the structure of the world and themselves, humans were on the lookout for such signs in nature. The world was then conceived of as a text to be decoded, and geosophia was the classical hermeneutics of natural forms. A corollary of these views was that humans might see themselves as the agents of cosmic change, so that whenever disastrous events occurred in the natural world, they embarked on protracted rites of penitence to pacify the moral reactivity of nature, and whenever auspicious events occurred, they performed rituals of gratitude. Since disease was seen as a calamitous event in the microbody of the cosmos, it was treated in the same way: by penitence and ritual actions.

What counted for people of the time was that there could not be a single natural phenomenon without its corresponding cultural "echo." Michel Foucault made sense of this type of phenomena, in the case of pre-Renaissance Europe, by stating that the dominant episteme of resemblance affected all modes of knowledge and reduced aspects of the natural world to resembling aspects in the cultural world, and vice

versa.[25] I believe that the same type of episteme governed Nara and
Heian Japan. The hypothesis of such an episteme explains in part the
system of sacred geography in which cultural patterns were duplicated
in certain resembling natural configurations and in which rituals concerning the relationship of humans to the environment were predominant. These rituals were intricately connected to the legitimacy of rulers,
but in such manner that most people believed that certain locales were
to be treated as supernatural protectors of human affairs. A good example is found in *Fudoki:*

> On the tenth day of the fourth month of each year a ritual feast is held
> and rice wine is served. Members of the Urabe sacerdotal lineage assemble
> men and women, and day after day, night after night, people deport them-
> selves in drinks, songs, and dances. These Urabe dwell in the immediate
> surroundings of the shrine. The configuration of the land is ideal: high
> and flat, sea to the east and to the west, regular arrangement of hills, val-
> leys, and villages. Trees on the mountain and grasses on the plain form
> natural hedges, and water is plentiful, running in the streams and from
> springs in the cliffs. Houses are built on elevations, with hedges of pine
> trees and bamboo to protect them. Passing through these villages in
> spring, one is met by fragrances emanating from a hundred plants; pass-
> ing through in autumn, one can view the natural brocade offered by the
> leaves of the trees. One must admit that this region is the natural darkling
> residence of the deities, the natural site of their miraculous workings. It
> is impossible to describe in detail the bountiful and delicate character of
> this land.[26]

The rulers then came to be regarded as simple mediators of such
transcendent powers, and sacred geography became a kind of political
geography, since specific deities worshiped in shrines were considered
to own and protect discrete geographical areas. A good proof that this
was indeed the case is provided by the fact that, when the government
ruled the country as a unified territory, it brought many of the Shinto
shrines and Buddhist temples that had been erected privately in various
parts of the land under its control and requested that rituals of protection of the state (and the emperor's body) be performed therein.[27] Once
unified, the pantheon, which was made up of all deities said to govern
these specific areas, provided the people spiritual and economic protection and was organized as a hierarchy that mirrored the ordering of
society or stood as its ideal model. One might suspect that the areas under control of the deities that formed such a pantheon corresponded
exactly to the territorial limits of the government. However, this does
not seem to have been the case. A comparison with Sri Lanka shows that
religious and political geographies do not necessarily correspond to each
other; in Japan they even led to military conflict. Therefore, extreme

caution should be taken not to reduce every spatial practice related to religious geography to territory building by rulers.[28] However, it is possible—if not most probable—that various social forces competed in designing territories, and this fact might account for the discrepancies.

*Chronosophia* might be defined as a set of ritual practices inscribed within concepts of cyclical time, that is, of time thought of in spatial terms, because time was directly related to the apparent movement of the sun and the moon. Furthermore, each month of the year, each day of the month, and each hour of the day were thought to correspond to various points of the compass: winter corresponded to the north, summer to the south, and so on. In such a scheme each spatial arrangement was related to a temporal aspect, which in turn determined ritual cycles. In China some of those emblems corresponded directly to the mandate of heaven, so that a dynasty, for example, was symbolized by a color which itself corresponded to an orientation and to a season. Concepts of time as they are manifest in mythology corresponded to speculations concerning the origins of the world and to the determination of certain places as supernatural bearers of a potential for cosmic renewal. That is why rulers found it necessary to control not only space but also time through the ritual manipulation of symbols. Naturally, this manipulation served as a model for controlling the spatial activities of humans, and tools for the measurement of time, such as drums, bells, and clepsydras, were political instruments of control and the prerogative of government offices and of Shinto shrines and Buddhist temples. Furthermore, the ways in which "origins" were conceptualized became potent political tools for the grounding of claims to legitimacy. In this respect it is instructive to study competing philosophies of time as they arose in correspondence with specific political philosophies and legitimacy claims.

## THE GEOGNOSTIC INVESTMENT OF MEANING IN SPACE

In contradistinction to *geosophia*, the word *geognosis* has the advantage of suggesting that the nature of the relationship between humans and place was structured by a slightly different epistemological realm that will be presented shortly. It also suggests that the environment in general, and certain places in particular, were seen as natural repositories of a potential knowledge infused with soteric characteristics, that is, a knowledge that offers the path to salvation. Therefore, prescribed spatial practices in certain geographical areas were efforts to decode or decipher a vast body of signs partly hidden and partly revealed in the world of natural forms, as in the case of geosophia. In the case of geognosis, however, this body of signs, once decoded, revealed more than the possibility of physical and economic integration into the world: it formed a scripture that expounded the nature of salvation as well as the techniques leading to it; furthermore, it was directly related to the political power of the ruling elite, either by submission or opposition to it. There was no notion of salvation in geosophia, for the simple reason that salvation is not part of the native (Shinto) religious system; that notion was introduced by Buddhism.

The introduction of Shingon Esoteric Buddhism (a form of Buddhism related to Tantrism and emphasizing ritual activities) in the Heian period (794–1185) provided the philosophical and ritual rationales for the creation of a nationwide network of religious geography that embodied cosmological and cosmographic notions. In 814 Kūkai (774–835), the founder of that branch of Esoteric Buddhism, produced the first account of the ascent of a mountain for spiritual purposes.[29] This text can still be seen as a stone inscription in the Chūzenji Temple on the side of the lake bearing the same name in Nikko and may have influenced not only the entire development of mountain asceticism (*Shugendō*) in Nikko during the Heian and Kamakura periods (794–1185; 1185–1333) but also visits to that sacred place in the Edo period (1615–1868). Two remarks can be made concerning this site. First, Kūkai's text intimates structural similarity between the natural landscape and descriptions of Pure Lands (the dwellings of buddhas) that are found in Buddhist scriptures. The result was that people thought of the site as a transcendental abode on earth of a buddha or a *bodhisattva*, a semimetaphysical being almost at the level of Buddhahood. Second, for Kūkai there is no doubt that the landscape not only stood in a mirror relation to the mind of the Buddha but was that mind itself. Therefore, the landscape exhibited characteristics usually associated with the mind of the Buddha. It also did what that mind does: it spoke in a natural language what people conceived of as a supernatural discourse. Thus, waves, pebbles, winds, and birds were the elementary and unconscious performers of the cosmic speech of buddhas and bodhisattvas; and mountains, springs, lakes, trees, flowers, stars, and vistas were morphological manifestations of the body of those divine entities that revealed to the trained eye the very essence which was thought to pervade the realm of natural forms. This view was made possible by the classical tenet of Buddhist philosophy, "Form is emptiness, and emptiness is form," which unleashed a plethora of statements of immanence because it was thought that the ultimate character of the Buddha, namely, emptiness, was no longer separate from this lower world of forms. In other words, certain places and rituals performed there were inserted, at least during the

Heian period, in a mode of thinking based on the notion that mind/body and cosmos, words and world, and buddhas and world shared profound and demanding structural intimacies.

Another main philosophical proposition of Esoteric Buddhism was that one could realize Buddhahood in this body and in this life by virtue of the notion that the cosmos was the discourse of a Buddha in its "Body of Essence" and that the human body, normally conceived of as inferior and impure, could be ritually transmuted into such a transcendent body, mainly through the agency of ritual practice and spatially encoded behavior.[30] The differences between Esoteric and Exoteric Buddhism could be expressed in the following terms: whereas exotericism held that Buddhahood cannot be achieved in this body and that the Buddha's Body of Essence does not preach, esotericism maintained that one can achieve Buddhahood and that the Body of Essence does preach. The question then was: what exactly is that discourse of the Body of Essence of the Buddha, and how can it be perceived?[31]

One answer to this question was given in terms of a Shingon praxis with which native creeds and practices could readily be combined. Mind and body were trained through initiations and rituals in whose culmination rested the ultimate vision of esotericism: the nondual character of absolute essence and relative phenomena. In this culmination an ascetic practitioner of esotericism performed rituals on spatially oriented diagrams, called mandalas, that were purported to represent the inner structure of the cosmos and the Buddha. These rituals aimed at letting the practitioners identify with the Buddha by penetrating the triple mystery of the body, speech, and mind of the Buddha and by gaining access to an ecstasy where distinctions between relative and absolute, Buddha and the world, and all other oppositions dissolved. Esoteric Buddhism, however, came to be closely associated with the native (Shinto) religious system for various reasons that are both religious and political. Although space prevents me from discussing this complex and locale-specific system of associations in detail, it must be pointed out that combinations between Esoteric Buddhism and the indigenous discourse (of Shinto) were facilitated by the early Japanese notion that the natural world was a divine creation of the sexual body, whereas the cultural world was the result of purification of the body in a natural environment; this notion meshed well with the Esoteric Buddhist notion that this world was the real body of the Buddha, and rites of purification meshed well with esoteric Buddhist practices. Japanese mythology, as compiled in 712 in *Kojiki* and in 720 in *Nihongi*, had encoded those oppositions between nature and culture, and ritual practices ensured their survival; it should be underlined that those practices of purification were closely associated with social hierarchy.[32] Yet a third area of systematic combination between esotericism and the indigenous discourse concerns the sacred character of political rule, which was expressed in the following manner: the emperor's body was regarded as a microcosmic emblem of the world; as such, it was a symbolic construct that was then subjected to rituals that would ensure the survival of its macrocosmic dimension, the world.[33] The structure of enthronement rituals thus exhibits indigenous cosmology and cosmography.[34] In the native imperial religion, Amaterasu, the entity that was regarded as the ancestral spirit of the imperial line, was a sociocosmic emblem "born" from a purification of the head of the primal cosmic man. While Amaterasu represented the sacred character of imperial rule, the light of heaven (and later the sun) was only its emblem: it was a metaphor for the representation of the power reigning over society. And so it could easily be associated with the universal Buddha of light in Esoteric Buddhism that is represented at the center of the mandalas, especially since the rituals of initiation into Esoteric Buddhism were based on enthronement rituals in India. In such conditions the quasi-theocratic political discourse became an element in the evolution and phenomenology of sacred geography, under the auspices of combinations between esotericism and the native tradition.[35]

Finally, the claim that the cosmos was the very discourse of the Buddha was also, though perhaps only in part, grounded in the episteme of resemblance mentioned by Foucault. A fundamental difference with *geosophia*, however, was that the recognition of the ultimate nondifferentiation (*nifuni*) of the Buddha and the world was experienced *geognostically* as a state of grace and as a liberating knowledge. Mystical practices by mountain ascetics in the Kunisaki Peninsula reveal these modes of thought and their epistemological basis.

Kunisaki is an almost circular peninsula jutting forth into the Inland Sea from the northeastern part of Kyushu, one among hundreds of preferred sites for geognosis. It was conceived over the course of the Heian period as being the natural embodiment of the Lotus Sutra, a major scripture of Buddhism, through a complex process which might be termed *intertextualization* and in which stones, trees, and water sources were seen as propounding a natural teaching to which was ascribed a relation of nonduality to the teachings of the Lotus Sutra.[36]

In order to indicate this nonduality, the mountain ascetics of Kunisaki established symbolic correlations between a tripartite distinction in the contents of the scripture on the one hand and the natural configurations of the peninsula on the other. They then erected cultural artifacts on the mountain to make this principle visible: in the peninsula's major valleys, which they identified with the eight scrolls of the scripture, they built twenty-eight temples that corresponded to the twenty-eight chapters of the text, and it is said that they carved as many stone statues as there are words in the text of the scripture, more than sixty-nine thousand.[37] The result of this system of symbolic correspondences was that walking in the mountains while listening to their natural sounds was equivalent to reading the scripture—assimilating it, letting it become one's body, one's mind. In this sense the distinction between scripture and the natural world disappeared, culture became nature, and vice versa. In the European context, Foucault writes, "There is no difference between the visible marks that God has stamped upon the surface of the earth, so that we may know its inner secrets, and the legible words that the Scriptures, or the Sages of Antiquity, have set down in the books preserved for us by tradition."[38]

Through their practices the mountain ascetics hoped to decipher signs hidden in natural forms. To their eyes a stone had, for example, a status of significance that was assessed both because it had been the site of a divine intervention and because it was mediated by a mystical experience. That stone was then perceived as something that hid and at the same time revealed an essence which was none other than a sign and which, when combined with all such signs hidden in caverns, springs, and cliffs, formed a "natural text" that required an interpretation from which an ultimate meaning leading to liberation from suffering was derived. This liberation was accomplished by claiming that that natural text, the texture of nature, stood in a relation of intertextuality with the scripture of the Lotus. The text that was thought to be hidden in nature was now given the status of a scripture, and nature came to be seen as the unedited manuscript of primal demiurges. In that edited version nature was the true teaching of buddhas and bodhisattvas, whose original manifestations had been the native *kami*. Decoding that natural manuscript offered knowledge of the kind that a sacred scripture might instill. On the level of the "unedited version," one obtained a "natural knowledge" (geosophia) and, on the level of the newly edited version, one gained a "soteric wisdom" (geognosis). However, because the manuscript was thought to be the actual world, the body was important (since the body is both natural and cultural). Thus, the ascetics' "reading" of the natural text of mountains and rivers involved physical austerities and ascetic practices whereby their bodies and minds established structural and semantic correlations between the scripture and the natural text. Their praxis rendered the world transparent so that it might reveal the ultimate meaning of life and death, and so that the distinctions between mind, body, and world disappeared.[39]

Thus rendered, the speech of nature was soteric because it was the very discourse of the Buddha, whose function was to dispel ignorance and lead to salvation. On the political level it must be emphasized that the original native cult that developed in Kunisaki was dedicated to a group of deities that were believed to protect Japan against foreign invasions. The phenomenon described above evolved, therefore, as part and parcel of the processes of state formation in which the Japanese territory was formulated as an entity that is imbued with a sacred character.

Certain landscapes were thought of as the natural forms of the teachings of buddhas and kami, as repositories of convincing arguments concerning ultimate freedom. This "natural rhetoric"—if one may call it that—was initiated by practices among which rituals of penitence had a special position. This comment needs some elaboration because it qualifies what has been called, too simplistically, the Japanese love of nature.

Many scriptures of Mahāyāna Buddhism open and close on cosmic visions, and many meditational techniques are meant to induce visionary experiences. In the process of contemplating manifold universes, rhythms of the heart and of breathing stop punctuating the vertigo of time and open up onto an ecstasy of timelessness. The tongue of the Buddha reaches out to the farthest galaxies, while rays of light shoot forth from the tuft between his eyebrows and reveal countless worlds in which an infinite number of buddhas preach the same sermon. Devotees numerous as the grains of sand of the Ganges sit in adoration, while *stupas* (pagodalike buildings) spontaneously emerge from the earth, stones fly, and springs miraculously appear. In such a spectacular cosmoscape, the words of those buddhas fall like rain, penetrate all nooks and crannies like thin mists, and settle onto myriad leaves. Even a single drop of dew reflects these worlds and contains all of them without exploding, and these worlds all enter that drop of dew without ever becoming wet. Huge nets streak through galaxies, jewels strung at each knot, each facet of the jewels mirroring all the other worlds that are reflected in all other facets on the nets, while six-tusked elephants dance on lotus blossoms.

These "pleasurable visions" (*rakken*) are the result of rites of penitence, particularly of those rites dedicated to the Bodhisattva Samantabhadra and to the Buddha of Medicine, in connection with the Lotus Sutra. The central part of those rites of penitence consists in ritual purification of the sense organs, in the course of which the ego stops being a screen that prevents an adequate and unspoiled perception of phenomena and instead becomes transparent. The purification of sense organs is achieved by penitence and results in an unadulterated perception of reality, what we call visionary experiences. These experiences occur, however, only after the illusory character of the ego has been recognized; the transcendental aspect of the natural world manifests itself only when the boundaries of the person have dissolved. Then and only then can the natural world permeate the mind and the body and lead to salvation. On the political level, many of the rituals of penitence mentioned above were performed in the context of guilt associated with the deaths that had been caused by the territory builders: rituals of release of animal life were directly related, in Kunisaki and other sites of cult, to the expiation of the mass murders of indigenous Kumaso tribes that had taken place in early Japanese history, to the forced relocation of entire villages at the time, or to later civil wars that decimated the population of various areas.

Another example of mountain asceticism which gives us access to the principles of representation of place in Japanese culture is the mountainous area related to the neighboring Kunisaki Peninsula, Mount Hiko.[40] Three shrines are located on the triple peak of Mount Hiko: the northern peak was the residence of a deity worshiped in the form of a male monk, the southern peak was the residence of a male deity worshiped in its secular attire, and the central peak was worshiped in the form of a female deity. The three deities were combined with members of the Buddhist pantheon. However, the Hiko complex or system involved much more than just Mount Hiko itself; it included two major ranges of mountains, one spreading north to Nakama through Kubote and Fukuchi, and another west to Dazaifu through Mount Hōman. Specific rites and practices that developed on these vast mountain ranges were described toward the end of the Muromachi period (1433–1585) by a certain Akyū-bō Sokuden, originally from Mount Futara in Nikko. These texts—named *Shugendō shūyō hiketsu-shū* (A compendium of secret transmissions of the essentials of mountain asceticism) and *Sampō sōshō hōsoku mikki* (The secret record of practice and ritual at the three summits)—became popular during the Edo period (1615–1868) and were widely circulated. In earlier times the *Hiko-san ruki* (A historical record of Mount Hiko, dated 1213) had stated the following about Mount Hiko: "The three peaks [of Mount Hiko] are beyond the grasp of thought processes, because they symbolically manifest the triple truth of the global verity and express the nonhorizontality and nonverticality of things in the manner of the syllable [i]."[41]

There were, at the time, two major branches of Esoteric Buddhism in Japan: the Shingon branch (Tōmitsu), and the Tendai branch (Taimitsu). While both branches developed specific philosophies of language, the Tendai branch tended to play on graphic representations in order to subvert language by suggesting that reality is beyond the binary oppositions that sustain linguistic expression.[42] In those word games, language played the double role of being at once a concealer and a revealer: when a document says that the relation between three peaks is like a relation of nonverticality and nonhorizontality within a single graph that is pronounced [i], it is asserting a large number of interpretive principles. One is the denial of the categories of horizontality and verticality, which were widely used in esoteric circles, coupled with the assertion that the essence of things is neither within nor beyond form. Another is evident in the term "in the manner of," a part of the term *shinnyo*, "suchness" or "truth." It is the principle of what Foucault called the "semantic web of resemblance" that was linked to the syntax of the world. Furthermore, the text states that a given geographic area is the natural embodiment of truth. Since "place" was conceived of "in the manner of" a scripture, space was traversed, as Foucault says, as if it were a process of acquisition of truth. The aforementioned *Sampō sōshō hōsoku mikki* incorporated esoteric doctrine, as in the following proposition:

> The western range of summits corresponds to the Diamond mandala; from the effect one turns to the cause; it is the "tails" course which takes place in autumn and corresponds doctrinally to the conversion of all living things.
> The central summit corresponds to the perfect union of the Diamond and Womb mandalas; it is beyond cause and effect; it is the summer course which is neither "heads" nor "tails," and in which no distinction is made between self and other.
> The eastern range of summits corresponds to the Womb mandala; starting from the cause one turns toward the effect; it is the "heads" course of spring, in which one looks up in quest of the Mind of Awakening.[43]

This device entailed applying a praxis of esotericism to govern movements of the body and other ritual practices in the mountains: spring and autumn represented a binary opposition as "heads" (*jun*) and "tails" (*gyaku*), which were alternate directional courses of walk in the mountains, and were separated by summer, which stands beyond that opposition.[44] In typical Buddhist fashion the first course was associated with a personal quest for awakening, the second with a quest for the salvation of others, and the last with the lack of distinction between oneself and others and between awakening and illusion. On the level of native (Shinto) interpretation, the spring course corresponded to the germination of grains, while the fall corresponded to harvest, and the mountain ascetics participated in fertility rites to which they brought the mountains' regenerative powers.

On a more sophisticated level this device entailed a complex and literal projection of the two basic mandalas of Esoteric Buddhism over vast geographical areas: the Womb mandala, which represents the world of relative phenomena, and the Diamond mandala, which represents the world of absolute principle. It is as if each mandala were spread over the earth as a transparency, and the sun—like a projector—sent the image onto the surface of the earth. Each divinity represented in the mandala transparency then found itself as if seated on a mountain peak, on a rock near a waterfall, or in a cavern along the various ranges of summits. That geographical area was thereby "invested" with the same character-istics as a mandala, which became the mental map that the mountain ascetics used to enter the mountains and to perform the same rituals in front of a stone or a tree as they would be performing in front of deities represented in a painted mandala in a temple. In consequence, these ritually defined areas became through practice the body, speech, and mind of the Buddha, of which mandalas were graphic representations. The ascetics, through special exercises of mystical identification, merged with the Buddha's "natural" substance, speech, and consciousness. Many of these areas were territories of major shrines and temples, but the practices that evolved there point to the existence of notions of territory that differ from the common meaning of the term because of ecologi-cally sound practices on the part of the ascetics. Today the majority of those ancient "territories" are "nature parks" protected by the govern-ment. In his works Kūkai was careful to emphasize that mandalas were graphic representations of the structure of the Buddha, which itself was none other than the deep structure of the mind. Since from the perspec-tive of esotericism no distinction was made between the mind and the body, or between this mind/body and the natural world in which people live, it may be advanced with some degree of confidence that mandalas were maps of the mind and that those landscapes onto which mandalas had been projected were gigantic mindscapes. The *Kubote-san engi* (Ori-gins of the Kubote [sacred] mountain) put it quite well:

> The convoluted structure of cliffs and caverns are as many marvelous places in nature that manifest the Diamond and the Womb mandalas. . . . These peaks are the superior areas in which the king of awakening, Mahā-vairocana, resides in permanence through present, past, and future; they are the supernatural massifs in which the world-honored One resides per-manently and preaches the *dharma*. Mountains and rivers, plants and trees, all manifest the profound principle of the Middle Path, while stones, cliffs, peaks, and caverns all intimately reveal the inner structure of the four types of mandalas. . . . Indeed, such is the Buddha Land of the Unique Vehicle and of the Triple Mystery.[45]

Furthermore, Mount Hiko itself was conceived of as consisting of four horizontal layers, the lowest one being the shared site of residence for lay people and mountain ascetics, the second one being the location of villages in which only mountain ascetics could reside while observing minute taboos on their behavior, the third one being a zone rich in caves in which the ascetics engaged in their austerities in total seclusion, and the highest layer consisting of the summits of the mountain where no-body was allowed to dwell, but where brief visits on the part of ascetic leaders were allowed, provided no bodily fluid was produced or scattered there. Based on the vertical opposition between purity and pollution, the mountain thus became a social space, reserved for men, in which behavior was highly codified. Mount Hiko and its associated ranges of summits were thus experienced as physical "cosmograms" of the Diamond and Womb mandalas, as a social space governed by specific rules and laws, and were regarded as "semiographs" in whose interplay ultimate meanings could be deciphered through ritual spatial practices. Ageless litholatry (stone worship) and the high Buddhist philosophy of immanence thus fused to produce a culture composed of popular and elite elements, in which the belief that the world should be experienced as a multifaceted dialogue reigned supreme. Because they were conceived of as "natural texts," these areas had two unequal "depths" that could be reached depending on the level of analytical acumen and grammatical knowledge one brought to bear on them. On the superficial level each stone, tree, cavern, peak, shrine, and temple was surrounded by a historical discourse recorded in the texts which relate the mythical origins of the sites, their legends, the hagiographies of ascetics, and other historical details. This discourse was available to noninitiates. However, there was also a deeper current, reserved to the initiates, which required a hermeneutics of depth interpretation and used complex word games in order to jump beyond casual meanings and other normal experiential frameworks and thus to reach a zone free from oppositions. That discourse did not speak of historical time and human events, connected though these were felt to be to supernatural forces. Instead, it conjured a world of meaning that transcended history and rested on visions in which traditional conceptualizations of time disappeared. In *chronognosis,* time was no longer cyclical; it was more akin to an eternal present, because time was not felt to be susceptible to devolutionary processes such as are found in nature. This new conceptualization of time had political overtones, in the sense that the power of rulers was legitimized by rituals whose structure was similar to those performed on the spatial diagrams of the mandalas; the rulers' power was thus thought to be stabilized over time as well. Furthermore, the political power of rulers was reinforced by the use of prophecies issued from the major cult centers they supported, and some rulers were regarded as manifestations on earth of the divinities worshiped in those cultic sites. On a more mystical level chronognosis was linked to a psychological orientation in which it was expected that "normal" time would be thoroughly transcended. The ultimate liberation from suffering was equivalent to a liberation from a time and a space that were conceived of as limitations to absolute being, and was realized through the reinsertion of man into ritually transmuted time and space that were conceived as absolute.

GEOPIOUS APPROACHES

Geognosis remained, however, a privileged experience for highly educated anchorites; their less educated followers had to be content with
*geopiety.* Whereas geognosis belonged to the epistemological framework
used by the mountain anchorites and their aristocratic patrons, geopiety
was its secularized version, which reflected the epistemological shifts and
other religious and political changes that occurred in the Edo period
(1615–1868) and which found expression in various genres of the travel
literature of the time. There was a fundamental difference between the
exercises of mountain ascetics and the travels of townsmen and poets of
the period, a difference that involved much more than the distinction
between the mystical insights of anchorites and the ordinary viewing of
tourists and that might be approached through the bias of the analysis
of time. In mountain asceticism, time was to be transcended, thus opening onto a liberation from the bonds of cause and effect which determined one among ten possible levels of rebirth. This liberation was a
release from history and from the train of transmigration, and the geognostic spatial moves were believed to have the power to eradicate time,
that is, causal relationships. However, in the case of townsmen and poets
such as Bashō (1644–1694), travels to famous places (*meisho meguri*)—
which had originated in pilgrimages—entailed an investigation of the
*history* of those places, an attention to what might be termed secular time
and to the past. In the pilgrimage process, people got close to a sacred
space and thereby metaphorically returned in time to the origins of the
sacredness of that place. The closer to the sacred spot, the closer to the
time of the origins—and the farther away, the more distant from those
events that had radically changed their character.

Few people, though, could experience the pilgrim's process in that
way; the majority simply learned about the past and enjoyed the beauty
of certain landscapes, but only as a secular reflection of the aesthetics of
cosmic visions that once had been projected onto, or were claimed to
have been extracted from, certain configurations of the land. The poet
Bashō engaged in travels and ensured that he would see such famous
places as Matsushima at the full moon and that his haiku on Mount Gas-
san ("Moon Peak") would include mention of the moon. His poetry
verged on vision and timelessness, as when he wondered whether the
Mogami River had taken the sun with it into the ocean. He also made
sure that his visits to specific places of cult would take place at the occasion of ritual performances (*ennichi*) or even better, as in the case of Ise,
that he would be there at the time of the *sengū* rituals performed once
every twenty years, at which time the shrines were built anew.[46] However, his travel diary, the *Oku no hosomichi,* can be seen as no more than

a protosecular, this-worldly formulation of the cosmic wanderings of mountain ascetics. And so when Bashō visited Nikko in 1689 (discussed above in the section "Geognosis"; "Nikko" means "solar radiance"), he mused over its character and wondered whether Kūkai had had a revelation of what the place would be like some 850 years later, for according to Bashō, that "Solar Radiance" pervaded his world. However, Bashō was not making a subtle remark on the character of visionary light as much as he was commenting on the rule of the Tokugawa shogunate, which was symbolized by its ancestor Ieyasu, who had been deified as the "Great Avatar Illuminating the East" and was worshiped in the Nikko mausoleum. Bashō wrote: "In the present day this sacred light [of the deified ancestor of the Tokugawa shoguns] is resplendent in Heaven. Its beneficent influence pervades the eight directions, and the four classes of people spend peaceful days in the security of their homes."[47]

During the Edo period again, sacred sites were related to the legitimacy of a rule whose sacred character was subtly reinforced or questioned by mass pilgrimage. The configurations of those sites were mental or cognitive maps from which people extracted information concerning the sociopolitical construction of their world. By that time Japan was experienced predominantly as a domain of sacred political character symbolized and protected by the cult dedicated to the dead leaders of the military government. In stark contrast, the mass pilgrimages to Ise (the ancestral shrine of the imperial lineage), which took place at roughly the same time, represent a competitive political view, which ultimately prevailed in 1868, when the military government fell and the emperor came back to power. Edo travel literature manifests a level of sophistication and a relationship to place that are neither secular nor exactly sacred, grounded neither in time nor in timelessness, and for which adequate categories remain yet to be found. I suspect that geognosis and geopiety are fundamentally related elements, particularly in the political realm. Indeed, a vast body of literature to which little attention has been paid might provide insights into the nature of that relationship; that is the genre of *kaikoku shūyōki* (records of practice through travel) and of *annaiki* (spiritual guides through the land). These works were written during the Edo period by ascetics who went from mountain to sacred mountain throughout the country and who popularized the notion that Japan was a sacred land (*shinkoku*). The first version of the genre seems to be the *Notes on Peregrinations around the Country (Kaikoku zōki)*, which is the diary of Dōkō, who was the abbot of the Shōgo-in temple and a son of the Regent Konoe no Fusatsugu and who set out twice on long travels to mountain centers of the Kantō and Kansai regions at the beginning of the second part of the fifteenth century.[48] Much research needs to be conducted on those texts, whose tone and style exhibit the infrastructure of geopiety as it was refined during the Edo period. Geopiety, however, also appears differently in other texts and practices whose structure is closely related to those guides, one of which is presented below.

## THE UNDERGROUND TEXTUALITY OF COSMIC RENEWAL

The practice of burying Buddhist scriptures (*maikyō*) is an old and complex phenomenon. Suffice it to say it was believed that copying scriptures and burying them in sacred spots would enable one to build vast amounts of merit. It was also said that when the Buddha of the Future would appear in this world, these buried texts and their pagodalike containers would spontaneously rise from the earth and appear in the light of cosmic renewal. Thus, the words of the Buddha were interred in expectancy of the ultimate apotheosis of the Buddha, his sermon, and his devotees. Vast amounts of scriptures were interred in Japan between the Heian and late Edo periods; some places were thought to be more numinous than others; some temples made their reputation (and amassed considerable wealth) as burial centers of those textual "time capsules."

The example that is provided below entailed traveling to thirty-six sacred sites in western Japan and burying a scripture in each place; this feat was accomplished by an ascetic (*gyōja*) sponsored by a nun who was unable to travel and her family. It is of interest because that travel began in 1653, thirty-six years before Bashō embarked on his travel which became the basis for his famous poetical diary, the *Oku no hosomichi*.

A few years ago archaeologists excavated in Nara a metal pagodalike urn which contained, among other things, thirty-six "receipts" (*nōkyō uketorisho*) from shrines and temples of the western part of Japan. Each receipt was handwritten, named the place and the date, briefly recorded the history of each temple and shrine and the events related to buddhas and kami that were worshipped there, and added a few words whose purpose was to enhance the supernatural character of the cultic sites. According to those receipts, on 16 October 1653 a certain Ganshū-bō, of Shimotsuke province, set out on his trip as a proxy for a nun called Myōkō-ni and some 210 signatories of a petition. The petition beseeches the buddhas and the kami that reside in those sites to grant the signatories fulfillment of their desires, longevity, and escape from disasters.[49] Ganshū-bō first went to the Kasuga-Kōfukuji shrine-temple multiplex, where he buried the first scripture; he then left Nara, to which he returned some fourteen and a half months later, on 27 February 1655.[50] The signatories then convened, collected the "receipts," and put them into the urn that was recently excavated in Nara.

The practice of traveling to various sacred sites in order to bury scriptures for votive purposes is documented as early as the eleventh century; its origin is unclear, although it seems to be related to the legend according to which Saichō (767–822) interred a pagoda in eight parts of the country to protect it. The sixteenth century seems to have been the time at which that practice peaked. As many as 168 urns deposited between 1513 and 1571, a time of major military conflicts and political uncertainty, have been excavated in the Hachimangū Shrine of Shimane, for instance. The example described above is the last known case.

A few remarks can be made about this spatial practice, which remains to be studied in detail. With regard to the travels of poets and townsmen, there is a striking difference that is related to the distinction between surface and depth interpretations. Travels that involved burying scriptures were of a religious nature, were structured in terms of particular doctrines of merit, and were set within an institutional framework, whereas those undertaken by Bashō and other townsmen either were not so set or were set in competing frameworks. This distinction is evident in the differing attitudes toward "text" manifested in the two instances. The ascetics set scriptures into the earth, returning to chthonian darkness scriptures that had been associated with nature itself by geognosis. Since the sponsors of such practices expected a better life in the future as the outcome of their activities, this was an investment in future or delayed gratification. In contradistinction, Bashō tagged his poems onto the pillars of huts or scattered them with studied nonchalance along his path, in clear view of all. This practice seems to be related to a dominant aspect of Edo culture: instant gratification. One text was hidden in darkness with hopes that one day it might be brought into the light of cosmic renewal; other texts were left in view of all so that they might be immediately enjoyed under the auspices of what was claimed to be an enlightened rule. The former practice, standing midway between geognosis and geopiety, might be interpreted as having a political dimension of protest if only because it is obvious that those who went around burying messianic texts were not satisfied with their living conditions: theirs was an underground protest, if I may be forgiven the pun, because they could never express it in clear view of all. In contradistinction, for all his poetical genius Bashō stood on the side of the government, and the question of whether he would have entertained a fruitful conversation with someone like Ganshū-bō or Akyū-bō Sokuden is of no little interest.

The "sense of place" that is evident in Bashō's geopious work was informed by history, but it lacked the soteriological components visible in earlier practices. It was linked to new dimensions of society, to a market economy, to "pleasure" travel, and to poetical expression on the part of lay people who donned religious clothes toward the end of their life and who experienced space and time according to aesthetic principles whose geognostic origins they could only vaguely intuit—if they had not forgotten them altogether. Tourism was born.

## CONCLUSION

The representation of place depended on epistemological categories which sustained the world of representation in Japanese culture and were associated with certain ruling classes. There were three major forms of representation: geosophy, geognosis, and geopiety, each connected with different "chronotypes" and each corresponding to structurally different modes of spatial behavior.

On one of several levels, the episteme of resemblance, which seems to have governed modes of knowledge for the better part of Japanese history, posited the centrality of language in order to establish strategic relations of similitude between the mind and the natural world. Geosophically, the experience of the world was governed by an analysis of oppositions in time and space to which specific emblematic meanings were attributed. Geognostically, a few landscapes were experienced as texts that were said to be natural representations of the mind of the Buddha or of his manifestations as native divinities from which the aristocrats who governed classical Japan claimed to be descended. Geopiously, the same landscapes were experienced as repositories of past history but were manipulated so that they could be conceived of as emblems of warrior sovereignty. In such a scheme "the order of things" was manifested as a semantics and was expressed in the logic of erudition and magic that either supported or opposed various discourses of political power. Conversely, political power encouraged certain types of knowledge and censored others. The economic dimensions of these phenomena remain to be studied, although Japanese premodern pilgrimages to sacred sites have been the object of historical inquiry from this perspective by Shinjō Tsunezō.[51]

On another level, there were oppositions between high and low, between mountains and plains or cities, between sacred and profane. The passage of time was overcome at the top, while it was measured at the bottom. At the bottom, things were still deciphered and decoded, but as legends which, like the legends on a map, did not manifest a transcendental discourse but simply a historical one. They were, as Foucault put it, *legenda*, "things to be read."[52] At the top, travel had a metaphysical character; at the bottom, travel was physical. Traversing space was, at the top, equal to the acquisition of truth; at the bottom, it was equal to an acquisition of historical and social information. The manuscript had been edited again, but this time it expressed even more clearly categories of power and social order.

These orders of significance involved space and time and were determined by the different epistemological realms that governed the oppositions between nature and culture. Indeed, the Edo period saw a shift to a new episteme in which language played a totally different role and in which the position of nature was radically different, as is made evident by the scholars of Nativist Studies (*Kokugaku*) and by a "modern" Buddhist linguist such as Jiun Sonja (1718–1804). Neo-Confucianism and "Dutch studies" (*Rangaku*) had much to do with this shift, as appears most pointedly in the work of Miura Baien (1723–1789), who lived on the slopes of Kunisaki Peninsula and labored to change the interpretation of natural phenomena and of language itself.[53] The world of nature was subjected to a new interpretation which in turn caused a shift in the position of humans, who were no longer the locus of a dialogue with a world defined in such manner that they could repudiate an anthropocentric position while affirming the centrality of meaning.[54] Different forms of knowledge made possible fundamentally different modes of experience and production of social space. In the Edo period literature took on other tones, and knowledge moved from textual exegesis and hermeneutics to knowledge of language. The introduction of Western perspective caused shifts in the drawn representations of space: a world of interpretation separates Maruyama Okyo's tradition-oriented carp paintings from his use of perspective in paintings of Kyoto.[55] Furthermore, other political and economic spatial practices, now subsumed under radically different modes of knowledge and their accompanying discourses of power, arose and came to dominate and determine complex relationships of humans to their environment, as well as their representations thereof.

## NOTES

This chapter is a revised version of a paper presented at the University of California, Berkeley, in May 1986 at a symposium on places, maps, and travel in premodern Japan, "Putting Place on Paper."

1. Henri Lefebvre, *The Production of Space*, trans. Donald Nicholson-Smith (Oxford: Basil Blackwell, 1991), 27.

2. Robert David Sack, *Human Territoriality* (Cambridge: Cambridge University Press, 1986), 5, 26. It is interesting to note that Anne Buttimer wrote in a review of Sack's *Conceptions of Space in Social Thought* (London: Macmillan, 1980) that "Sack is obviously opening the doors for humanists, assuring them that within that broad canvas provided by his orthographic projection there is room to sketch the drama of diachronic as well as synchronic patterns and processes of space conceptions" but that "he might in fact have come to regard magic,

myth, ritual and language as bearing conceptions of space which were anything but 'fused' or 'unsophisticated,' rather they might be regarded as fluid, theory-laden, recipes for action and thought" (*Progress in Human Geography* 7, no. 2 [1983]: 298–99).

3. See Allan Grapard, "Flying Mountains and Walkers of Emptiness: Toward a Definition of Sacred Space in Japanese Religions," *History of Religions* 21, no. 3 (1982): 195–221.

4. Lefebvre, *Production of Space*, 17.

5. That is particularly the case in Japan, where religion and politics were little separated in the past.

6. An interesting treatment of time and power is offered in Jacques Attali, *Histoires du temps* (Paris: Fayard, 1982).

7. John Bender and David Wellbery, eds., *Chronotypes: The Construction of Time* (Stanford: Stanford University Press, 1991), 4.

8. See Nold Egenter, *Bauform als Zeichen und Symbol* (Zurich: ETH, 1980); Gaudens Domenig, "Der Weg als parastatische Ergänzung des Ortes," in F. Oswald, ed., *Urphänomene der Architektur* (Zurich: ETH, 1977).

9. Some places (sacred trees, stones, etc.) were treated ritually only for their qualities of a religious character or because of "supernatural" characteristics, such as thermal springs or ponds inhabited by salamanders.

10. There is no systematic study of the relations between doctrine and architectural form in the case of Buddhist temples, even though it is clear that cosmographic notions determined the form of constructed space and the performance of ritual in ways that differed for each Buddhist lineage. For a comprehensive treatment of ritual and architecture in one Indian case, see Frits Staal, *Agni* (Berkeley: Asian Humanities Press, 1982).

11. It is clear from mythology that elements such as water and fire were treated as symbols, i.e., interpreted as meaningful. Written in the eighth century C.E., Japanese mythology is highly encoded by complex systems of representation and exhibits a remarkable knowledge of space. See Donald Philippi, trans., *Kojiki* (Tokyo: Tokyo University Press, 1968).

12. Mountain worship is an ancient phenomenon in Japan; after the introduction of Taoism and Buddhism from China and Korea around the fourth century, various mountain cults were systematized and unified, mostly under the influence of Shingon and Tendai Esoteric Buddhism, and a well-organized mountain religion called *Shugendō* developed in several hundred cult sites. Although the government banned the religion in 1872, there are sporadic signs of renewal in contemporary Japan. See, among others, Byron Earhart, *A Religious Study of the Haguro Sect of Shugendo* (Tokyo: Sophia University Press, 1970).

13. For *Kojiki*, see above, note 9. *Izumo fudoki* was translated by Aoki Michiko (Tokyo: Sophia University, 1974). *Hitachi fudoki* was translated by Akashi Mariko et al., in *Traditions* 1, no. 2 (1976): 23. The reader can also refer to W. Aston, trans., *Nihongi* (Tokyo: Tuttle, 1978).

14. For a comparison with similar practices in China, see Michel Soymié, *Le Lo-feou chan: Etude de géographie religieuse, Bulletin de L'Ecole Française d'Extrême-Orient* 48, no. 1 (Hanoi, 1942).

15. The association between symbols and the rulers may have originated in

the fact that astronomers and diviners were closely related to rulers, who ordered from them projections on the outcome of travel, warfare, crops, etc. See Kenneth DeWoskin, *Doctors, Diviners, and Magicians of Ancient China: Biographies of Fang-shih* (New York: Columbia University Press, 1983).

16. See Nagatomi Hisae, "Urabe no seiritsu ni tsuite," in *Shintō-shi ronsō* (Tokyo: Kokusho Kankōkai, 1985); see also Nakano Hatayoshi, "Tsushima ni okeru sangaku shūkyō," in Gorai Shigeru, ed., *Sangaku shūkyō-shi kenkyū sōsho* (Tokyo: Meicho Shuppan, 1978).

17. Akimoto Yoshirō, ed., *Fudoki* (Tokyo: Iwanami Shoten, 1956), 515.

18. Ibid., 35–61.

19. See the study of these duplications in Inoue Tatsuo, *Kodai ōken to shūkyō-teki bemin* (Tokyo: Kashiwa Shobō, 1980), 190–255.

20. See Maki Masako, "Tsukuba-yama shinkō no shinkō-kan," *Gendai shūkyō* (Tokyo) 2 (1979). See also Anne-Marie Bouchy, "The Cult of Mount Atago and the Atago Confraternities," *Journal of Asian Studies* 46, no. 2 (May 1987): 255–78.

21. Joseph Needham, *Science and Civilisation in China* (Cambridge: Cambridge University Press, 1959) 3:368–75.

22. On concepts of the body and the Chinese versions of microcosm and macrocosm, see Kristofer Schipper, "The Taoist Body," *History of Religions* 17, nos. 3–4 (1978): 355–86. On the topic of ritual language and its power over natural phenomena, see Maurice Godelier, *Horizons: Trajets marxistes en anthropologie* (Paris: Maspéro, 1977) 2: 258–70.

23. Needham, *Science and Civilisation in China.*

24. See Stephen Feuchtwang, *An Anthropological Analysis of Chinese Geomancy* (Vientiane: Vithagna, 1974).

25. Michel Foucault, *The Order of Things* (New York: Random, Vintage, 1970); see esp. ch. 2, "The Prose of the World."

26. Yoshiro, *Fudoki*, 69–71.

27. See Allan Grapard, "Institution, Ritual, and Ideology: The Twenty-Two Shrine-Temple Multiplexes of Heian Japan," *History of Religions* 27, no. 3 (1988): 246–69, and Grapard, "Religious Practices in the Heian Period," in *The Cambridge History of Japan*, vol. 2 (Cambridge: Cambridge University Press, forthcoming).

28. See Deborah Winslow, "A Political Geography of Deities: Space and the Pantheon in Sinhalese Buddhism," *Journal of Asian Studies* 43, no. 2 (1984): 273–91. Winslow writes that "there are parallels between the political bureaucracy and the pantheon"; however, "differences in pantheon rank are not manifested in a hierarchy of territory size and stacking," and "people *think* of the pantheon as functioning territorially, like the administrative system, even though it does not" (288).

29. See Allan Grapard, trans., "Stone Inscription for the Monk Shōdō, Who Crossed Mountains and Streams in His Search for Awakening," in Michael Tobias and Harold Drasdo, eds., *The Mountain Spirit* (New York: Overlook Press, 1978), 51–59.

30. See Yoshito Hakeda, trans., *Kūkai: Major Works* (New York: Columbia University Press, 1972).

31. This important question in the history of Buddhist philosophy had a par-

ticularly distinguished career in the Japanese cultural context. See William
LaFleur, "Saigyō and the Buddhist Value of Nature," *History of Religions* 13, nos.
2–3 (1973).

32. See Donald Philippi, trans., *Kojiki.* On the relationship between purification practices and social order, see Allan Grapard, "Excesses of Vision and Visions of Excess: Women and Transgression in Japanese Mythology," *Japanese
Journal of Religious Studies* 18, no. 1 (1990): 3–22.

33. On the symbolic body of a political figure thought of as the supernatural
protector of geographical and political areas, see Allan Grapard, "Japan's Ignored Cultural Revolution: The Separation of Shinto and Buddhist Divinities in
Meiji (*shimbutsu bunri*) and a Case Study: Tōnomine," *History of Religions* 23, no.
3 (1984): 240–65.

34. See Robert Ellwood, *The Feast of Kingship: Accession Ceremonies in Ancient
Japan* (Tokyo: Sophia University Press, 1973).

35. The legitimacy of Japanese emperors always rested on premises that had
a Shinto aspect issued from shrines that governed specific territories and a Buddhist aspect issued from those temples that attempted to develop the same spatial, territorial framework. Combinations between Shinto and Buddhist deities
remained politically relevant until 1868.

36. See Allan Grapard, "Lotus in the Mountain, Mountain in the Lotus: The
*Rokugō Kaizan Nimmon Daibosatsu Hongi,*" *Monumenta Nipponica* 42, no. 1 (Tokyo,
1986): 21–50, and Grapard, "The Textualized Mountain—Enmountained Text:
The Lotus Sutra in Kunisaki," in George and Willa Tanabe, eds., *The Lotus Sutra
in Japanese Culture* (Honolulu: University of Hawaii Press, 1989), 159–89.

37. It should be understood that the carvings were undertaken as ritual practices whereby each stone was transformed and became the embodiment of a
specific divine entity and meaning, so that there was much more at work in this
phenomenon than a relation of similarity or a metaphor. When the text of the
scripture was copied by brush, copyists were to use animal hair, bamboo sticks,
stone ink containers, water from sacred springs, paper from natural bark: only
natural elements could be used for the transcription of a scripture.

38. Foucault, *Order of Things,* 33.

39. This vision could not have evolved without the integration of concepts of
the body within a larger framework of reference; this integration suggests that
a history of these concepts in relation to spatial and other practices is an imperative academic topic.

40. The island of Kyushu alone counts more than 115 major sacred mountains onto which complex systems of practice and interpretation were projected.

41. In Gorai Shigeru, ed., *Shugendō shiryō-shū* (Tokyo: Meicho Shuppan,
1984), 463.

42. See Allan Grapard, "Linguistic Cubism: A Singularity of Pluralism in the
Sannō Cult," *Japanese Journal of Religious Studies* 14, nos. 2–3 (Nagoya, 1987):
211–34.

43. In Nakano Hatayoshi, ed., *Hiko-san to Kyūshū no Shugendō* (Tokyo: Meicho Shuppan, 1977), 45.

44. In other words, the activities of Mount Hiko's anchorites were also deter-

mined by considerations of time and climate: spring was associated with personal quests, autumn with helping others, and summer with both.

45. In Gorai, *Shugendō shiryō-shū*, 519.

46. Following concepts of cyclical time and renewal, the government sponsored, for at least twelve hundred years and at great expense, exact rebuilding of the major Shinto shrines it used for legitimacy purposes. The last reconstruction of Ise took place in 1973.

47. My translation.

48. There are several manuscript versions of the *Kaikoku zōki*. Some excerpts appear in Sakamoto Tarō et al., eds., *Shintō Taikei* (Tokyo: Seikosha, 1984) 31:119–22.

49. Okumura Hideo, "Kyōzuka ihō," in Sasaki Gōzō and Okumura Hideo, eds., *Shintō no bijutsu* (Tokyo: Gakken, 1979), 158–59.

50. On the importance of the Kasuga-Kōfukuji multiplex and its sacred spaces, see Allan Grapard, *The Protocol of the Gods: A Study of the Kasuga Cult in Japanese History* (Berkeley and Los Angeles: University of California Press, 1992). Ganshū-bō visited Anodera Sairyū-in in Tamba, Reiōzan Kompon-jingūji in Wakasa, Iwashimizu Hachimangū in Yamashiro, Kichōzan Eifukuji in Kawachi, Matsuodera in Izumi, Shitennōji in Settsu, Shashinzan Dairyūji in Awa, Gotaizan Konjiki-in in Tosa, Sugaozan Daihōji in Iyo, Senzan Senkōji in Awaji, Shoshazan in Harima, Shōkyōzan Hattōji in Bizen, Chūsen Daijingū in Mimasaka, Kibitsumiya Honganji in Bicchū, Kibitsu no miya in Bingo, Ikutsushimasha in Aki, Shinjizan Miidera in Suō, Ninomiyakōgō-sobyō in Nagato, Anrakuji Temmangū in Chikuzen, Takaratama Tamatare no miya in Chikugo, Chigurizan Hachimangū in Hizen, Aso jinja in Higo, Mukahagizan Dainichidera in Hyūga, Shōhachimangū in Osumi, Ichinomiya Hachimangū in Satsuma, Subaru Hachimangū in Bungo, Usa Hachimangū in Buzen, Shōhachimangū in Iwami, Kokubunji in Oki, Izumo jinja in Izumo, Daisenji in Hōki, Ichinomiya in Inaba, Yōfu jinja in Tajima, and, finally, Jōshōji in Tango.

51. Shinjō Tsunezō, *Shaji sankei no shakai keizai shi-tenki kenkyū* (Tokyo: Hanawa Shobō, 1964).

52. Foucault, *Order of Things*.

53. Miura Baien was one of Japan's first positivists. A few excerpts of his writings and a brief analysis are found in Theodore deBary, ed., *Sources of Japanese Tradition* (New York: Columbia University Press, 1958) 2:480–88.

54. It is interesting to see how the U.S. Supreme Court has attempted to restitute nature's right to speech and standing in court. See Roderick Nash, *The American Environment* (New York: Knopf, 1976), which quotes Justice William O. Douglas's following opinion: "Environmental issues should be tended by the inanimate object itself. . . . Those inarticulate members of the ecological group cannot speak. But those people who have so frequented the place as to know its values and wonders will be able to speak for the entire ecological community."

55. See reproductions of those paintings in Suzuki Susumu, ed., *Okyo to Gōshun* (Tokyo: Shibundō, 1969).

# THIRTEEN

# On the Archaeology of Late Modernity

*Paul Rabinow*

Planning has at least two archaeological moments, one of which I call *techno-cosmopolitanism* and the other *middling modernism.* They are both modern in that they proceed under the imperatives of social modernity—industrialization, bureaucracy, and welfare. Techno-cosmopolitanism shares with other modern projects an understanding that society must be constructed, planned, and organized through art and science. It seeks this end through the use of already existing cultural, social, and aesthetic institutions and spaces seen to embody a healthy sediment of historical practices which need reorganization. Techno-cosmopolitanism is the operationalization of history, society, and culture. It is technological in that the operations are scientifically arrived at and can be specified; it is cosmopolitan in that these technological operations themselves are applied to specific customs, cultures, countries. Thus, while the principles of urban planning in Morocco or Brazil are the same, the well-planned city in Morocco will by necessity differ from one in Brazil in accordance with the specificities of the histories, topographies, cultures, and politics of these places. The art of urban planning and of a healthy modern society lies precisely in the orchestration of the general and the particular.[1]

Middling modernism shares the norms of industrialization, health, and sociality as well as the technological processes aimed at operationalizing social practices. However, the material it operates on is no longer the sedimented historical and cultural practices of a particular society which it seeks to bring into modernity; rather, the "human material," to use a telling phrase of Maurice Halbwachs, on which it works is a universal subject whose needs, potentialities, and norms can be discovered by science. Techno-cosmopolitanism was less audacious in claiming that health, productivity, and efficiency (an orderly modern society) could be achieved only through a reordering and reactivation of essentially healthy sedimented practices; society depended on history. Middling modernism's project was more audacious, seeking to create New Men freed, purified, and liberated to pursue new forms of sociality which would inevitably arise from healthy spaces and forms. Science, particularly social science, would define humanity's needs, and technical planners would meet them.

## TECHNO-COSMOPOLITANISM

Let me illustrate these processes. In 1899 Tony Garnier won the coveted Prix de Rome at the Ecole des Beaux Arts competition with a neoclassical drawing of a large bank. In 1902 Garnier sent back to the guardians of the tradition at the Institut de France an unprecedented plan, *Une Cité Industrielle*. This plan has been taken by Le Corbusier among others as one of the central forerunners of modern planning. It embodies— although no manifesto accompanied it—the elements of the emergent modern, welfare society in one paradigmatic representational "work of art."

Garnier's plan is intended as a socialist *cité* in the sense of a polis, not merely a town plan. Garnier incorporates the whole region, in keeping with the school of French historical regional geographers. The plan is not utopian, based on technically precise considerations; it was designed to be built, and in fact it was partially implemented in Lyons, where Garnier spent his working life. Garnier's plan is admittedly ambiguous. Various strains of modern planning and modern society can be found in it. Le Corbusier saw it as a precursor of high modernism. It also was taken up by socialist reformers and by "enlightened" colonialists, such as Hubert Lyautey in Morocco. This ambiguity reveals its representational and normative power.

Garnier's plan emphasized zoning; interestingly, the city's zones embody the modern ambition of spatially and representationally distributing the functions of social life: modern, welfare social life. The planned city featured the following components: *Work:* among the planned industries were futurist cement plants before the futurists. *Leisure and sports:* the planned city would have establishments for the improvement of the body and for recuperation after work. *Domestic life:* the residents would live in a housing zone artfully equipped with scientifically mandated schools, creches and medical facilities as well as pedestrian areas. *Health:* a sanatorium would be built on the choicest land, nestled against the hills and exposed to the most sun, and a generous number of the most advanced hospitals would care for general health and for the statistically inevitable accidents which industry would produce. *Administration:* the center of the city (Garnier's city had no churches and no police stations) was given over to assembly and concert halls for public discussion, socialist culture. And *history:* located in the central administrative complex was an empty building, the archives. As Halbwachs, who belonged to the same reformist wing of French socialism as Garnier, was to theorize later, without collective memory there would be only the alienation of capitalism. Finally, an old town is sketchily added upriver from the industrial city, a reminder and symbol of the sedimentation of history in a socialized nature.

### Morocco

One possible development of the principles of Garnier's plan was most fully carried out in Morocco, the last French colonial adventure. It was in Morocco that techno-cosmopolitanism was most fully enacted. Governor-General Hubert Lyautey and his team sought to operationalize every aspect of human life from artisan crafts to hydraulics. Lyautey's technicians undertook extensive study of all dimensions of Moroccan life. This period of inquiry into North African society has been characterized as the least "Orientalist" period because of the high quality of the ethnographic and historical work produced/ Then Lyautey's team sought to orchestrate—following the newly articulated principles and schemata of planning—these historical, cultural, and social practices and institutions into an artificial, organic whole. Lyautey was not seeking to create these elements ex nihilio; he believed strongly that only the historically sedimented social practices had the potential to be modernized and remain healthy. He was not a high modernist or a utopian. It is in this sense that his project can be called cosmopolitan. Although the technical principles were universal, they had to be applied in each specific case with a detailed attention to local circumstances—topography, history, power. Only then would they yield an orderly, efficient, productive, and healthy society.

Just as Garnier produced palpable representations of his *Cité*, so, too, Lyautey was convinced (although he was much more explicit and sophisticated about it) that representation was a crucial factor in making the order-inducing norms a reality. The investment in representation (and consequent belief that it was possible) can be seen in the plans of Lyautey and his architect Prost (a friend and colleague of Garnier's at the Villa Medici in Rome) for the central plaza of Casablanca, where, as in Garnier's *Cité*, Morocco's administrative headquarters would be located. The buildings were to be constructed with the most modern of technical means in terms of construction techniques and were to serve modern aims of government. Their architectural style was neo-Moorish, an authentic pastiche style if you will, in which elements of former Moroccan styles and decorative motifs, catalogued and systematized by Lyautey's scholars, were joined together into a neo-Moorish form. The style and the technique served the new protectorate's goal of dominating Morocco while modernizing it. During World War I, when French troops were substantially withdrawn from Morocco, Lyautey and Prost rushed ahead with the façades of these public buildings as a means of defining this new space and staking out a future politics. Representation, norms, and power went hand in hand.

Today Lyautey's project might be seen as a kind of archaeology of postmodernism, but I think this would be an error. Certainly his intent was different: these planner-conquerors thought it mattered a great deal that the representations were the right ones; it was precisely because they were seen as historically and culturally sedimented that they had normative power. After World War II high modernists scornfully saw Lyautey's project as kitsch; postmodernists might find it more pleasing to interpret it as a self-styled pastiche. Both interpretations miss the historical point of an ongoing attempt to embody and marry norms and rooted representations into an effective social force capable of shaping environment and action. Lyautey hoped that it would be through this new spatial-social environment that he could establish a field of power relations through which he could direct Morocco's destinies.

## THE AGGLOMERATION: TOWARD THE SOCIOTECHNICAL ENVIRONMENT

Lyautey had invested heavily in the power of forms to reinvigorate sedimented social relations and shape new ones. The leading urban reformer of the interwar period, Henri Sellier, solidly anchored in French socialist conceptions of justice and faced with many more practical constraints, came to pose the problem of the ordering of space and population in a different fashion. The object on which Sellier operated was the *agglomeration*. The agglomeration was no longer a territorial unit in the sense of a space defined by long-term historico-natural processes. It was no longer primarily a historico-natural milieu. Nor was it a public social-political space, which the French refer to as *la cité*. Rather, it was becoming, at least discursively, a more abstract space—a sociotechnical environment—in which operational transformations were regulated by specialists. The norms guiding Sellier's emerging socialist modernism were the welfare of the population, the maximization of individual potential, and their linkage through efficient administration, directed by committed specialists dedicated to the public good.

After World War I Sellier cast the problem in terms of how to mobilize political support for a flexible new administrative structure, one based on statistical projections and abstract social unities, while retaining more traditional political accountability and social linkages. For Sellier and his allies, the Parisian agglomeration formed a single socioeconomic unit. The older administrative grid, composed of the city and its surrounding communes, was not simply outmoded but positively detrimental to healthy development. For housing, for transportation, for social life in general, there was a total lack of coherent policy. The absence of any effective land policy meant that the suburbs of Paris offered inexpensive locations for industry to exploit in a socially and hygienically irresponsible manner. Such development was occurring at the expense of what Sellier called "social cost." The task was to develop techniques to combat the social plagues accompanying unregulated capitalist expansion.

Halbwachs identified the increasingly feeble fabric of social relations among workers as the chief danger facing French society. He reasoned that since modern work conditions were producing increasingly desocialized individuals, the answer to social health lay in creating the richest possible social milieu away from work. Following this logic, Sellier called on architects and urbanists as well as social scientists to produce and regulate an optimum social environment as the means to rehumanize modern life. He proposed a ring of garden cities around Paris, composed through architectural compositional methods still drawn largely from the Beaux Arts–derived urbanism, employing regional styles, and oriented toward a new type of citizen, the employee.[2]

By the mid 1930s Sellier was frustrated by lack of success, and his conceptions evolved, or better, involuted. He reluctantly placed less emphasis on local political participation and more on social scientific administration and the exigencies of cost analysis. In important ways Sellier was a transitional figure. While clinging to an older socialist symbolism (politically, historically, socially), during the course of the interwar period he gradually adopted a more modernist sociological and administrative language of self-referential form unmoored from these older referents. One can see Sellier as embodying the tensions inherent in keeping some relationship between a socialist conception of *la cité*, that public space of politics, and the agglomeration, that anonymous space of regulation and rationalization.

### Planning

In the interwar period proposals abounded on the need for experts to exercise more power to overcome crippling political blockages and bring France into what was increasingly referred to as the modern world. During the 1930s there was a good deal of discussion about planning in

France as in other industrial countries, and after 1935 a certain number of proplanning technicians even held government positions. However, as the technical tools, statistical data, and the like required for modern planning were largely unavailable, most of the self-proclaimed plans which flourished during the interwar period were little more than manifestos. Still, they are important for creating a discursive space which would be filled during and after Vichy in a much more substantial and enduring manner.[3]

American and German models of industrial modernization fascinated a sector of the French business community and intelligentsia as early as the Universal Exposition of 1900 but attained a sustained vigor only during and after World War I. The social and political implications of Taylorism were particularly captivating to groups such as the Musée Social, an early advocate of its introduction into diverse realms of French life. On the Left, Edouard Herriot proposed a technologically inspired Fourth Republic as a means of overcoming the continuing parliamentary blockages of what he perceived to be France's national interest. Henri Fayol and the movement for management reform (combining Taylorism and Fordism) advocated molding the state in the image of a new, efficient industrial apparatus. Fayol's dramatic proposals—to transfer state bureaucracies to private hands—were not followed, but new management methods were instituted to some extent in both French business and government. The main institutional enthusiasts for planning ideas during the interwar period were the unions, particularly the leftist CGT, convinced that experiments during the war had demonstrated the compatibility of industrial productivity, higher wages, and improved negotiating power for workers.[4]

Before World War I the French public sector, largely inherited from the ancien régime except for the railroads, consisted mainly of artistic workshops. The state, consistent with liberal doctrine, had no program for economic management and lacked the data and analytic tools to invent one. This situation changed dramatically during World War I. The role of the state expanded at unprecedented rates: military expenditures exploded such that service on the debt exceeded the entire prewar budget. Disparate conceptions of how to orchestrate and make the relations of state and industry more efficient and productive competed within the government during the war. Organizational methods, the information necessary to carry them out, and political strategies to implement them took a leap forward in complexity. However, in France many of these "modernized" institutional arrangements were dismantled immediately after the war. The key players—cartelized industrialists, politicians, and a small group of bureaucrats who had become specialists in navigating between the conflicting institutional forces of French society,

and believers in the new techniques of understanding and regulation—
remained on the scene in an uneasy relationship during the interwar
years.[5]

## Description

Urban description in the interwar years vacillated between an organic
and a mechanical set of metaphors. The term *function,* taken over from
the biologists and geographers, shakily bridged the metaphoric field. On
the mechanist side Leon Jaussely argued that the economic organization
of the city should be considered as the "Taylorization of a vast workshop, where for the most precise reasons, each thing had a precise reason for being in one and only one place."[6] He provided a kind of manifesto in the first issue of *La vie urbaine.* Urbanism grew out of geography.
Geographers provided two essential tools: first, the detailed and comprehensive analysis of *genre de vie;* second, the technical means of representing these givens in a standard form. Jaussely claimed that the life of
a city in its entirety could be reproduced through graphic means, and
almost entirely on a series of exact plans drawn to the same scale. Jaussely produced maps of climatic conditions, topography, demography,
historical influence, social and professional locations, ethnic groups,
population movement, economic activity, circulation patterns, public
and private spaces, construction, overcrowded housing, death and morbidity rates, and traffic accidents. Combining this swirl of variables into
a single plan required a complexity of presentation that Jaussely barely
intuited.[7]

On the organicist side Louis Bonnier compared the city with a living
organism evolving in space and time. Bonnier proposed to study Paris as
a spatial distribution of a population, one which ignored older arbitrary
administrative distinctions drawn up for historical reasons relating to
political or military considerations, not ones of population per se.[8] Bonnier presented a series of remarkable maps showing the spatial growth
of the Parisian agglomeration as well as the changing densities of specific
areas. Population, Bonnier argued, occupied a different space than politics; Jaussely would have added that economics did as well. Uniting all
the variables into a common field required new conceptions of space and
society and a new understanding of how to bring them into a common
frame.

## Garden Cities and Human Material

Sellier and his allies fought for a planned, socially hygienic, and aestheti-
cally coordinated series of garden cities coordinated with public housing
development in Paris itself. Sellier's strategy for the Parisian agglomeration turned on land acquisition by the communes and coordination ef-

forts in all domains by his office at the departmental level. This strategy implied two important innovations: state intervention in the definition of change, and identification of the need to invent and then plan for the placement of new social unities. The lead article of the 1923 issue of *La vie urbaine* was a report by Sellier on the International Conference on Garden Cities and Urban Planning, held in Paris in October 1922.[9] Sellier urged the creation of a series of satellite garden-city settlements. He admired the English accomplishments but was opposed to literal imitations, especially of the ideal of self-contained satellite cities. Ebenezer Howard's vision could not serve directly as a model for France because it planned for cities separate from large agglomerations. One might say that for Sellier, the English put too much emphasis on the garden and not enough on the city. For Sellier, the suburb was urban.

Despite the sociological inconvenience, Sellier favored retaining the commune as a baseline unit because of its historical significance as well as the social and political anchorage it provided for *la cité*. For political reasons Sellier opposed the creation of a single unified commune, which he feared would drown out the voices of elected officials and give a totally free hand to administration. Democracy required a local, socially grounded countervoice to governmental bureaucracy. When such a counterweight was weak, it needed to be strengthened; when it was absent entirely, it needed to be invented.

Although the importance of industry was primary, Sellier paid very little explicit attention to it.[10] What images there were of work were largely negative: work and its sites were tiring, polluted, noisy, ugly, unhealthy. Just as there was no valorization of working-class sociality per se or revolutionary politics, so, too, there was no reform project for industry. Sellier's counterimage was peace and calm after work. This humanism was meant literally: a refusal of working-class isolation and brutalization as well as an affirmation of a modern, socialist republican citizenry. To explain this compensatory, rehabilatory stance toward modern work, we turn to Maurice Halbwachs.

Halbwachs, in his "Matière et société," presented one of the first French theories of alienation, basing his argument in good Durkheimian fashion on social rather than economic alienation. Halbwachs defined industrial workers as that group of men who, "in order to carry out their jobs, must orient themselves toward matter and leave society behind."[11] He proceeded through an ingenious demonstration showing how industrial workers' representations of themselves and others were mediated by matter and how this mediation deformed the workers' representations of both nature and society. The natural tendency to value the picturesque in nature grasped as a whole and the inherent value of social relations in a social whole was reduced to "sensations mechanically associated in a closed series."[12] The opposite of this situation, the norm of social health, as it were, was social life at its most intense—urban life—where both nature and culture were appreciated fully for their social worth.

The supposed advances in industrial relations were accelerating this negative process, not improving it. The introduction of Taylorism refined the decomposition of social relations. On the one hand, it enforced the standardization of all individuality among workers; on the other hand, the introduction of management specialists who did not share skills or social life with the workers marked an important loss of autonomy for the industrial worker. The result was to increase desocialization. The industrial worker in modern society increasingly formed representations of himself along an axis of inanimate matter, one which led him away from society. The situation of salaried employees was only marginally better. Halbwachs showed how their status was determined by their general lack of independence, initiative, and responsibility. As was the case with the rest of the emerging middle classes, their work was characterized by an ambiguous technicity. These people applied predefined rules to specified situations, but little more was demanded or permitted of them. This "materialized humanity" only followed the great tides of social change in a dominated fashion. Their situation was an ambiguous one, neither fully dominated nor dominant. Halbwachs approvingly quotes Tocqueville on the spirit of the middle classes as one which mixes that of the people and the aristocracy; such a spirit can produce miracles, but by itself it would never produce a government or civilization of virtue and grandeur. Clearly Halbwachs felt that a vision of social justice and techniques to implement it were needed to save the new employees from mediocrity or worse.

### Socialist Social Space

Sellier's concern for creating new forms of social bonds—in many ways parallel to Lyautey's conceptions of pacification except that the groups to be pacified were not yet in existence—was explicitly developed in a 1922 article in *La vie urbaine*, "Les centres sociaux dans les régions rurales aux Etats-Unis." Sellier pointed to American small-town or rural innovations which he believed could be applied in France to *urban agglomerations*.[13] Sellier was enthusiastic about the American experience of rural civic centers. They were excellent devices for the development of social life, promising to preserve and revitalize both rural habitation and population. Sellier valorized the sheer intensification of social activity per se. Once a combination of economic activity and civic administration was set in place, and once a space was created, new and healthy social unities would emerge, and older ones would be stabilized and regenerated. Although the functioning and financing of these civic centers varied a great deal, they all shared a number of common features. At a minimum they all contained an auditorium (with folding chairs) available for multiple purposes from banquets to speeches and a kitchen; in larger towns they might boast a café, billiards room, library, and visiting room for the county health officer and agricultural agent as well as the chamber of commerce.

Sellier knew that parallel spaces existed in French cities. The *Maison Commune* or *Maison pour Tous* was a transformation of the earlier socialist *Bourse du Travail* or Social Catholic Foyer social spaces. It became a characteristic form of the new French interwar cities, especially (if not uniquely) in the socialist municipalities. It has been called the major socialist "equipmental" contribution. A simply constructed but large building, in small towns placed next to sports facilities, should house a library, a sewing room for women, child-care facilities and *une buvette de tempérance*.[14] Often placed at the city's symbolic center, it embodied hopes for new modern civilization, the best of politics, education, and culture. The idea of an autonomous social space, neither directly a governmental building nor a private mercantile amusement space, had a complex history throughout the nineteenth century. Jean-Louis Cohen (in the spirit of Halbwachs) argues that it would be naive to reduce the production of these spaces entirely to reformers' projects; they corresponded to social demands as well. The changing position of fortresses of union activity to a broader and more diffuse place of sociability (and of education) occurred slowly but surely as the Left assimilated the existence of the Third Republic and vice versa.[15]

Sellier's aim was to provide the cadre for a renewed modern sociality. Sellier's consistent goal (one he never achieved) was to make garden cities complete social cells, composed of inhabitants from a wide range of social categories, thus avoiding an unhealthy isolation stemming from the irrational development of cities and their consequent class hostility. He fully accepted the principle of different classes of housing for different social categories. Part of the division of classes in the garden cities was linked to the ground rent idea: fancier houses, higher taxes, more housing and services. Sellier was not alone in this acceptance of the spatial separation of classes. The only two French projects in the first half of the century which do not program explicit social class differences were Tony Garnier's *Cité Industrielle* and Le Corbusier's *Cité Radieuse*. Neither really addressed the problem: Garnier was planning to accommodate only one class, while Le Corbusier's standards were universalist, the *L'homme-type*.

Sellier, following Halbwachs, was guided by a norm of social life in which the mixing of classes intensified the representations of society. He thought the working class, the salaried employees, and the lower middle classes were precisely those social groups most in need of a rich, independent social setting, one in which the picturesque had an important function to play. He envisioned garden cities as a quarter or neighborhood, a part capable of serving specific needs in the best possible manner but not cut off from the city. This principle was important: neither Sellier nor the Conseil General de la Seine sought to destroy Paris; they meant instead to preserve it by relieving the conditions of congestion, by creating urban suburbs as part of a new agglomeration. The garden city was to be neither a complete city nor a suburban scattering of individual houses, but a social unity, attached to an urban center, improved according to the latest principles, assembling diverse social categories, devoted to strengthening the social exchanges and solidarity and moral bonds.

### Suresnes

As Sellier was mayor of Suresnes, it was an obvious candidate for the implementation of his plans. For well over a thousand years the village of Suresnes, on the western outskirts of Paris, had lived from its vineyards. During the seventeenth century it became a fashionable site of aristocratic houses; the Rothschilds built a mansion there in the nineteenth. By the end of the nineteenth century, as with other suburbs around Paris, a railroad linked Suresnes to Paris; the village was transforming itself into an industrial site. The Rothschilds built a steel tube factory; a bicycle factory set up shop; then the first automaker (Darracq in 1905). Others followed: aviation motors; an electricity plant (Westinghouse); Hewitt, a biscuitry; an important perfume factory. By the end of the nineteenth century Suresnes's population had grown to eleven thousand. Although some vineyards were still active, its future lay elsewhere.[16]

Following Sellier's ideas, the plan for Suresnes sought to orient a preexisting evolutionary development. The garden city of Suresnes was to be built on thirty hectares acquired by the Department of the Seine adjacent to the existing town. The study of the site was followed by a general design of the whole. Within this whole, elements (streets, squares, edifices, houses, trees, sports fields, schools, shops, communal buildings) were distributed according to the urbanist's art. Services were literally embodied in functionally specific buildings deployed as morphological elements. Symbolically, social services were given a central localization. They formed the focus of the city's circulation system and in large part took the place of monuments. Sellier's team paid particular attention to educational and hygienic services as well as new spaces for modern social life. For Suresnes three main zones were delimited: an industrial zone in which housing was discouraged; a residential zone reserved for individual houses and small businesses; and a model garden city guided by strict modern health considerations of maximum light and building controls. The plan called for 1,300 lodgings distributed in 550 individual houses grouped around gardens and 750 lodgings in collective houses of three to four stories grouped along the main thoroughfares. The plan allowed for three to five rooms for each family, with running water, electricity, gas, a garage, and even central heating for some. In Suresnes, Sellier introduced cooperatives of consumption and production, mutualist restaurants and pharmacies. Community centers were included in the plans for almost all the garden cities.

It was no accident that most of the proposed garden city sites were located adjacent to older towns. Whenever Sellier spoke of the "cities of tomorrow," he almost always evoked an older preserved core and a periphery organized along modern planning principles but maintaining strong ties with the older city. In the first issue of the *Bulletin de la Société Historique de Suresnes* (1920) Sellier argued for the importance of preserving some of the old quarters of Suresnes to conserve a sense of its identity. The old city played a historical, touristic role and kept alive the city's character, the specificity of its culture. Sellier and his friend Marcel Poëte had together established a course on urbanism and the history of Paris at the Ecole Pratique des Hautes Etudes, which stressed the importance of local historical determinants in the definition, growth, and future of cities. Sellier took its scientific importance quite literally. Before establishing the plan for Suresnes, Sellier undertook a detailed study of the commune's evolution. He wrote an article for the first issue of the historical society's annual bulletin entitled "The Future of Suresnes Tied to Its Past," which chronicled the town's growth, its periods of health and decline. Sellier presented his program of reform as the logical end of the commune's historical development, in conformity with the town's particularities. An enlightened municipal administration understood that in urban evolution as in biology there was always a high price to be paid for a brutal rupture between the past and the present. It followed that the scientific understanding of history was the key to constructing a healthy future. In this belief Sellier remained firmly rooted in what we have been calling techno-cosmopolitanism.

Historical discourse also had additional roles to play. The Historical Society of Suresnes was used by Sellier as a means for building consensus or at least communicating with potentially hostile social groups and local notables in Suresnes. It also served to establish him as a historical figure in his own right. During a period of intense change the discourse of history became a privileged medium of communication. In 1926 Sellier met and enthusiastically supported local initiatives for an artistic and historical society. He welcomed the idea of a *fête municipale,* and the municipality financially supported these efforts to build a consensus on Suresnes's past and present. Although former comrades in the Communist party criticized his participation with church leaders and industrialists, Sellier was conscious of the need to broaden his political and social base. Historical discourse, as a promoter of both unity and division, has played an extremely central role in French life.[17] Sellier had learned, and learned to practice, a "heroic" history of the exemplary figures of the Left. He transformed this mode of historical moralizing into a legitimizing discourse for his own social policies; he often cited Saint Vincent de Paul's charitable works in Suresnes, and frequently cited his "namesake" Henri IV. Sellier appeared in the pages of the association's bulletin as the patron of Suresnes, without mention of political party. The society contributed to making him a legend, hoping to form a consensus around his person if not his ideas.

### THE SOCIAL-TECHNICAL ENVIRONMENT: MIDDLING MODERNISM

In 1938 Louis Boulonnois, one of Sellier's chief counselors in Suresnes, published *L'oeuvre municipale de M. Henri Sellier à Suresnes,* which can be considered an official presentation of Sellier's program in its final form.[18] Boulonnois, who referred to Sellier as "Maître," had been a schoolteacher in Suresnes before joining Sellier's administration. Married to one of Suresnes's new corps of social workers, he might be characterized as a fully integrated member and apostle of the new reformist socialist administration. Although by 1938 Sellier himself was increasingly bitter, Boulonnois remained optimistic. The goal was no longer limited to meeting housing needs or even to the systematic distribution of welfare institutions throughout the city, although, as Sellier was keenly aware, these objectives were far from having been attained. By the mid 1930s a complementary task (sketchily present in Sellier's earlier projects) had been brought to center stage: to reach out from public buildings to institute a comprehensive program of physical and moral preventive care to cure social ills. The priority was no longer the isolation and rectification of islands of pathology; rather, the new program amounted to a blueprint for the scientific administration of modern life as a whole.

The new objectives of municipal organization were to predict and prepare for accidents and to specify needs—put most broadly, to prepare the instruments of social defense. Although programs served the public good, Boulonnois saw his role as technical rather than political. Care of the collectivity fell to administration, these technicians argued with a beguiling understatement, because the ordinary citizen, preoccupied with the details of day-to-day life, all too frequently neglected to plan ahead. Administration's role as arbiter and planner might not always be appreciated by the average citizen, but that ingratitude was the price to be paid for the larger public good, whose self-appointed guardian Boulonnois and associates had become. *Prévoyance* had moved from being the individual moral virtue par excellence to be inculcated by discipline and surveillance, to being a normalizing administrative function guided by science and operating on a population. The transition to technocratic modernism would be completed when the population's norms of health became functions of the instruments of measurement themselves.

Boulonnois argued that the role of administration was the scientific arbitration of social conflict. Successful management entailed more comprehensive and sophisticated knowledge of the population (particularly its range of differences and its future development) as well as more flexible, more continuous, more farsighted means of administering its needs. The ideal target population for scientific administration, he argued, was one still in a molten social state, that is, not fixed in its historical, geographical, or social milieu. It was public service which, in the last instance, was charged with analyzing, producing, and directing a new social solidarity among these new men. The symbol "plan" provided Boulonnois with the metaphoric bridge to connect social organization with the individual. His penchant for slogans served him well in this instance; he presented the task as "To bestow on the allotments a city plan [*un plan de ville*], and symmetrically on the assisted families a life plan [*un plan de vie*]."[19] We can see presented here, baldly and bluntly to the point of caricature, a project of middling modernist totalization and individualization. This was no longer a project of regulating and ameliorating a locale and its inhabitants but of treating both as matter to be formed and normed literally at will—or, more accurately, through a thoroughly voluntarist program.

In this discourse society, the state, and the individual were potentially transparent to one another. To achieve the articulation between these institutions and the population, social facts had to be brought into a standardized grid. This process entailed an objective and objectifying vocabulary for individual and social needs as well as a functionalist understanding of institutions. To this technician's vision of social reality was attached a conception of the state as a set of bureaus whose job was to deliver functionally specific public services—roads, water, agriculture, hygiene, housing—and to provide, as Jürgen Habermas is fond of saying, "steering mechanisms" for the whole society. Although Boulonnois's proposals were formed as part of a socialist humanist project, Vichy and subsequent French regimes carried out a parallel project for the state, albeit with different aims.

The central locus for the intersection of the macro- and micro-knowledges and powers was probably housing, although it is important to emphasize that social housing was in the process of being redefined as an abstract question of technical spaces and scientifically established needs rather than as a specifically disciplinary concern. In 1934, for example, an international effort was set in motion to establish a homogeneous typology of housing. These standards were adopted for the census to permit a standardized analysis of needs, a more substantial base for prevision. Concurrent with the establishment of these technical standards (and organizing them) was a set of normalizing criteria for their usage. Norms and means were now joined. These norms of sociability were based on *la famille normale moyenne:* a stable and rational household. The norms not only classified families but also served as the basis of intervention to hasten their creation and stabilization. However, the criteria for identifying normality were not static; the scientific definitions of needs was constantly being reevaluated. Further, families who failed to qualify for housing were not definitively eliminated from the pool but, rather, were offered the possibility of consulting with social workers and reapplying. Once they aligned their practices with those of the scientifically defined and selected normal community, they might qualify for housing.

Boulonnois urged his colleagues to replace the older humiliating investigations with a more precise understanding of community needs as well as a feeling of solidarity with those who failed to meet the standards. The links between the administration, its technical experts, and the population whose welfare it protected operated as a new social division of work, the norm and means of a new social solidarity. The scientifically cautioned conditions of habitation established the means for the extension of the normalization process. The administration defined the normal use of a house, making it the condition for occupation. For example, the functions of rooms were specified; the size of apartments was determined by family size (with specified upper limits); and modern conveniences like gas and electricity were required. As a consequence, the plan called for regular payment not only of rent but also of gas bills; gave social workers the right to enter houses to check hygiene; and established an obligatory system of insurance. All these improvements and regulations implied a regular salary and reinforced regular habits. Many of these criteria were not new, but given the new administrative structure, they led gradually to state measures (in relation to a normal family) used to establish rent, state subventions, and so on. Various systems of control were put in place in accord with these normalized and scientific standards: obligatory visits to the public baths, weekly visits from social workers who established typical household budgets, and the like.

Universalizing norms and a system of stratification gradually displaced the class-based disciplinary tactics of hygiene as well as environmentalist localisms in defining and enforcing a new social reality. The bacteriological and class phase was passing to a functionalist and normalizing sociological one. Once the normalized *mode de vie* became a category defined in terms of *niveau de vie*, the surpluses added to it became the basis of a differential status. The older class and "type" understanding was giving way to a stratification and "distinction" grid.[20] During the course of the 1920s and 1930s the object of intervention slowly shifted from city planning to the management of *la matière sociale*. Instead of a functionally harmonized urbanity, Sellier and his team were constrained by their political weakness and worsening economic conditions to limit, grudgingly and gradually, the scope of their interventions to perfecting specific social spaces and social sciences.

The loss involved, the diminished social and socialist vision, was clearer to Sellier than to his followers. Sellier's assistants became almost evangelistic spokespersons for the creation of modernized tools of sociological analysis of needs and norms of life as well as enthusiastic participants in the invention of social actors to implement these new techniques. While Sellier clung to history and locale as sources of legitimacy and solidarity, his younger assistants and successors were perhaps more consistent, gradually stripping away such architectural, historical, and social references in the name of efficiency science, progress, and welfare. This transition has been nicely characterized as a move from a *plan de ville* to a *plan de vie*. Georges Canguilhem, analyzing a parallel change in psychology, characterizes it as a shift from utilitarianism—utility for man—to instrumentalism, that is, man as a means of utility. The sea change in techniques, objects, and goals can be seen as a shift to seeking laws of adaptation to a sociotechnical milieu, no longer to a historico-natural one.[21] The change constitutes an important element in the transition to middling modernism.

NOTES

1. For a full elaboration of this position, see Paul Rabinow, *French Modern: Norms and Forms of the Social Environment* (Cambridge: MIT Press, 1989).

2. Georges Teyssot, "Civilisation du salarie et culture de l'employé: Variations sur Siegfried Kracauer, Ernst Bloch et Walter Benjamin," *Les cahiers de la recherche architecturale* 15–17 (1985): 36–41.

3. For a detailed discussion of neosocialist alternatives, see Zeev Sternhell, *Ni droite ni gauche: L'idéologie fasciste en France* (Paris: 1983).

4. Charles S. Maier, "Between Taylorism and Technocracy: European Ideologies and the Vision of Industrial Productivity in the 1920s," *Journal of Contemporary History* 5, no. 2 (1970); Henri Le Chatelier, *Le Taylorisme,* 2d ed. (Paris: Dunod, 1934). For workers' resistance, see Albert Thomas, preface to *Scientific Management in Europe,* by Paul Devinat (Geneva: Internation Labor Office, 1927). Thanks to Professor Mary McLeod for her thesis and articles cited below and her helpful comments and discussions.

5. Richard F. Kuisel, *Capitalism and the State in Modern France: Renovation and Economic Management in the Twentieth Century* (Cambridge: Cambridge University Press, 1981); Martin Fine, "Toward Corporatism: The Movement for Capital-Labor Collaboration in France, 1914–1936," Ph.D. diss., University of Wisconsin, Madison, 1971. John F. Godfrey, *Capitalism at War: Industrial Policy and Bureaucracy in France, 1914–1918* (Leamington Spa, Eng.: Berg, 1987).

6. Leon Jaussely, preface to *L'étude pratique des plans de ville,* by Raymond Unwin (Paris: Librairie Centrale des Beaux-arts, 1922), vii.

7. Leon Jaussely, "Chronique de l'urbanisme," *La vie urbaine,* nos. 1–2 (March–June 1919): 184–85.

8. Louis Bonnier, "La population de Paris en mouvement, 1800–1861," *La vie urbaine,* nos. 1–2 (March–June 1919), 8.

9. Henri Sellier, "Conference internationale des cités-jardins et de l'amenagement des villes," *La vie urbaine,* no. 18 (15 February 1923): 11–21.

10. On the history of this theme, see Jean-Pierre Epron, ed. "L'usine et la ville 1836–1986: 150 ans d'urbanisme," *Culture Technique* (Spring 1986): special issue.

11. Maurice Halbwachs, "Matière et société," in *Classes sociales et morphologie,* ed. V. Karady (Paris: Minuit, 1972), 60.

12. Ibid., 68.

13. Henri Sellier, "Les centres sociaux dans les régions rurales aux Etats-Unis," *La vie urbaine,* no. 4 (1922): 1.

14. Donat-Alfred Agache, J. M. Auburtin, and E. Redont, *Comment reconstruire nos cités détruites: Notions d'urbanisme s'appliquant aux villes, bourgs et villages* (Paris: Colin, 1915), 33.

15. Jean-Louis Cohen, "Des bourses du travail au temps des loisirs les avatars de la sociabilité ouvrière," in his *Architectures pour le peuple: Maisons du peuple— Belgique, Allemagne, Autriche, France, Grande-Bretagne, Italie, Pays-Bas, Suisse* (Brussels: Archives de l'Architecture Moderne, 1984), 159.

16. René Sordes, *Histoire de Suresnes: Des origines a 1945* (Suresnes: Société Historique de Suresnes, 1965), 460–75.

17. For an extensive literature, see Pierre Nora, ed., *Les lieux de mémoire,* vol. 1, *La République* (Paris: Gallimard, 1984).

18. Louis Boulonnois, *L'oeuvre municipale de M. Henri Sellier à Suresnes* (Paris: Berger-Lerrault, 1938).

19. Ibid., 80.

20. Pierre Bourdieu, *La distinction, critique sociale du jugement* (Paris: Minuit, 1979).

21. Georges Canguilhem, "Qu'est-ce que la psychologie," in his *Etudes d'histoire et de philosophie des sciences* (Paris: Vrin, 1983), 378–79.

# CONTRIBUTORS

*Ann Bermingham* is a Professor of Art History at the University of California, Santa Barbara. She is the author of *Landscape and Ideology: The English Rustic Tradition, 1740–1860,* and co-editor with John Brewer of *The Consumption of Culture: Image, Object, Text* (forthcoming). She is currently writing a book on drawing as a social practice in eighteenth- and nineteenth-century Britain.

*Richard Biernacki* is Assistant Professor of Sociology, University of California, San Diego. He is completing a book about the cultural origins and consequences of national differences in concepts of labor as a commodity in Western Europe, to be published by the University of California Press.

*Deirdre Boden,* formerly Jean Monnet Fellow at the European University Institute in Florence, now teaches sociology at Lancaster University. Her current interests include language, organizations, and globalization, and she is writing a book on telecommunications and the Gulf War. Recent publications are *The Business of Talk: Organizations in Action* (1994) and *Talk and Social Structure* (1991).

*Roger Friedland* is writing about the spatial structure of corporations, the deterritorialization of the body of Christ, and the cultural politics of space and time in Jerusalem. This latter, written with Richard D. Hecht, will eventuate in two volumes, both published by Cambridge University Press—*To Rule Jerusalem,* on the contemporary struggles over the organization and meaning of Jerusalem's space and time, and *Jerusalem: The Profane Politics of a Sacred Place,* on the relationship between sacrality and sovereignty. Friedland is located in the Department of Sociology, University of California, Santa Barbara.

*Saul Friedlander* is Professor of Modern European History at Tel Aviv University and Professor of History at the University of California, Los Angeles. He has written several books on the Nazi period and on the history of the Holocaust. His latest publication is the volume he edited in 1992 for Harvard University Press, *Probing the Limits of Representation: Nazism and the "Final Solution."*

*Carol Brooks Gardner* is Associate Professor of Sociology and Women's Studies at Indiana University, Indianapolis. Her main interests are the study of gender and social interaction. She is completing a book on gender and public harassment.

*Anthony Giddens* is Professor of Sociology at Cambridge University. He is the author of numerous books on social theory, the most recent of which is *The Transformation of Intimacy: Sexuality, Love and Eroticism in Modern Societies* (1992).

*Allan G. Grapard,* Associate Professor of Religious Studies at the University of California, Santa Barbara, specializes in Japanese intellectual history. Born in France and trained in Paris and Kyoto, he is the author of two books, *Kukai: La vérité finale des trois enseignements* (Poeisis, 1985) and *The Protocol of the Gods: A Study of the Kasuga Cult in Japanese History* (University of California Press, 1992). He is now completing a third book, *Usa, Hiko, and Kunisaki: Essays in Geohistorical Synthesis.*

*Richard D. Hecht* is Professor of Religious Studies at the University of California, Santa Barbara. He has published a series of articles on the politics of Philo of Alexandria's interpretation of scripture and is coauthor, with Ninian Smart, of *The Sacred Texts of The World: A Universal Anthology* (Macmillan and Crossroad, 1982). Hecht is working on the politics of Jewish, Christian, and Muslim pilgrimage. The essay in this volume is part of his research with Friedland on the politics of sacred space in Jerusalem. Other essays include "The Politics of Holy Place: Jerusalem Temple Mount/*haram esh-sharif*," in Scott and Simpson-Housley, eds., *Sacred Places and Profane Spaces* (Greenwood Press, 1991), and "Divisions at the Center: The Organization of Political Violence at Jerusalem's Temple Mount/al-Haram al-Sharif—1929 and 1990," to be published in a volume edited by Paul R. Brass. An article on the Palestinian Muslim pilgrimage to Nebi Musa will appear in *Religion.*

*David Hockney* is an artist and set designer living in Los Angeles. Beyond his paintings and lithographic work, many of which experiment with perspective and time, Hockney is known for his photocollages, multipage faxes, and still video portraits. He has also produced many set designs for operas, including *The Rake's Progress, The Magic Flute, Tur-*

*andot,* and, most recently, *Die Frau ohne Schatten.* His latest book is *That's the Way I See It* (1993).

*Stephen Kern* is the author of *Anatomy and Destiny: A Cultural History of the Human Body* (1975) and *The Culture of Time and Space: 1880–1918* (1983). His latest book is *The Culture of Love: Victorians to Moderns* (Harvard University Press, 1992). Kern is Distinguished Professor of History at Northern Illinois University.

*Harvey L. Molotch,* Professor of Sociology at the University of California, Santa Barbara, writes about domination and control as implemented through both mass media and interpersonal communication. He is also an urban scholar whose book *Urban Fortunes* (with John Logan) won the Robert Park Award and was named the 1990 Distinguished Contribution by the American Sociological Association.

*Donald Palmer* is Associate Professor of Organizational Behavior in the Graduate School of Management at the University of California, Davis. His research focuses on the network of intraclass relationships in which leaders of large U.S. corporations are embedded (e.g., interlocking directorates), the influence these relationships have on corporate behavior (e.g., headquarter and plant locations, organizational strategy and structure, mergers and acquisitions), and the impact of this behavior on the communities in which corporate units are situated. His most recent article, coauthored with Roger Friedland, Amy Roussel, and P. Devereaux Jennings, was "Corporations and the Advanced Business Service Sector," published in *Social Forces* (1990).

*Paul Rabinow* is Professor of Anthropology at the University of California, Berkeley. He published *French Modern: Norms and Form of the Social Environment* (MIT Press, 1989). His current work concerns biotechnology and the modernization of life.

*A. F. (Sandy) Robertson* taught development studies and directed the African Studies Centre at Cambridge University before joining the Anthropology Department at the University of California, Santa Barbara. Recent books include a study of sharecropping in Africa (*The Dynamics of Productive Relationships,* Cambridge University Press, 1987) and *Beyond the Family: The Social Organization of Human Reproduction* (Polity and the University of California Press, 1991). His current research is on intergenerational transfers and the welfare of the elderly in Catalonia.

*Adam B. Seligman* has lectured in sociology at the Hebrew University of Jerusalem and at the University of California at Los Angeles. For the past two years he has been Fulbright Fellow at Eotvos Lorand University, Budapest. He has published widely in the fields of social theory, religious history, seventeenth-century history, and political sociology. His books include *Order and Transcendence: The Role of Utopias and the Dynamics of Civilizations* (Brill, 1989), with S. N. Eisenstadt and L. Roniger, *Centre Formation, Protest Movements, and Class Structure in Europe and the United States* (Pinter Press, 1987), and, most recently, *The Idea of Civil Society* (Free Press, 1992).

*Edward W. Soja* is Professor and Associate Dean in the Graduate School of Architecture and Urban Planning at UCLA. His interests in theories of space and in the exemplariness of Los Angeles as an urban text are combined in his collection of critical essays, *Postmodern Geographies: The Reassertion of Space in Critical Social Theory* (Verso, 1989). He is currently working, with Barbara Hooper, on "The Spaces That Difference Makes," an exploration of the spatiality of identity politics and the formation of polycentered communities of resistance.

# INDEX

Compositor: Maple-Vail Manufacturing Group
Text: 10/12 Baskerville
Display: Baskerville
Printer and binder: Maple-Vail Manufacturing Group